Feminisms

Sandra Kemp is Quintin Hogg Research Fellow in English at the University of Westminister. She writes on fiction, feminist literary theory, art, and dance. Her publications include *Kipling's Hidden Narratives* (1987), *Italian Feminist Thought* (1989), and *Edwardian Fiction: An Oxford Anthology* (co-edited with Charlotte Mitchell and David Trotter, 1996).

Judith Squires is a lecturer in political theory at the University of Bristol. She writes on politics, philosophy, and cultural studies. Her publications include *Gender and Political Theory* (1998), *Cultural Readings of Imperialism* (with Benita Parry and Keith Ansell-Pearson, 1997), *Cultural Remix* (with Erica Carter and James Donald, 1993), *Space and Place* (with Erica Carter and James Donald, 1993), and *Principled Positions* (1993). She was editor of the journal *New Formations* from 1990 to 1997.

'a very impressive collection...The editors have come up with a remarkably thorough cross-section of texts from an intellectual stand-point, and have also managed to choose essays that are readable and exciting. The section on Technologies is especially original, provocative, and forward looking. Even a jaded old 70s "femocrat" like myself would enjoy teaching the book in a wide variety of courses on feminist theory and contemporary thought.'

Elaine Showalter, Princeton University

'a comprehensive, ambitious and brilliantly thought-out collec-tion.... The conceptual framework is innovative and subtle: it intro-duces the material without falling prey to easy categorizations or ready-made labels. Respectful of the diversity of positions that co-exist within feminism, the Reader also reflects the feminist commitment to the politics of experience and to the empowerment of women. This Reader is the ideal companion for anyone who is engaged in research or reflection on contemporary feminism.'

Rosi Braidotti, Utrecht University

'an anthology which will no doubt influence scholarship for years to come'

Gayatri Chakravorty Spivak, Columbia University

'This rich and comprehensive collection of diverse and challenging essays introduces its readers to all the shifting topics, controversies and conflicts at the cutting edge of feminist scholarship since 1980—insights enough to inspire even the most sceptical of feminists.'

Lynne Segal, Middlesex University

'Rather than trying to hide behind old categories or forcing us into new paradigms that feel contrived, the editors have given us a wonderfully diverse sampling of the richness that is feminisms. They celebrate the diversity, map its interconnections, suggest the possibilities of continuing to think, to talk, and to act together. Readers will recognize old friends among the selections as well as be introduced to pieces that they always meant to read.... It will be a valuable text for classes and an equally valuable reference tool.'

Jean F. O'Barr, Duke University

'Squires and Kemp's classification into subject areas aptly resists assump-tions about "types" of feminists. They have assembled eighty-six pieces which testify to a new diversity in feminist writing, and their introduc-tions to the materials convey the excitement that this diversity brings.'

Jennifer Hornsby, Birkbeck College, London

'Judith Squires' and Sandra Kemp's *Feminisms* is that ideal text and reference book—a compendium of the range of feminist criticism since the late 1970s. Whether used in courses or as a handy reference, this Oxford Reader will more than repay its cost. Where else, in one volume, can we read and re-read the most interesting critical work from British, French, and United States theorists?

'Paced with substantive (and in some cases highly original) introductions throughout.... While it might be less than academic to label *Feminisms* "a great read", it is.'

Linda Wagner-Martin, University of North Carolina

'This Reader brings together a valuable collection of essays... bracketed by exceptionally clear and useful thematic introductions that highlight debates and diversity. The diverse voices represented in the eighty-six esays, dating from 1980 through the mid-1990s, will necessarily prompt critical thinking and dissuade any reader that feminist theory is either monolithic or dull.'

Barbara D. Miller, George Washington University

A provocative reader, for what it includes and what it leaves behind. ... Innovative, inclusive, interesting.'

Shulamit Reinharz, Brandeis University

OXFORD **READERS**

The Oxford Readers series represents a unique interdisciplinary resource, offering authoritative collections of primary and secondary sources on the core issues which have shaped history and continue to affect current events.

OXFORD READERS

Feminisms

Edited by Sandra Kemp *and* Judith Squires

Oxford · New York

OXFORD UNIVERSITY PRESS

1997

OXFORD
UNIVERSITY PRESS

Great Clarendon Street, Oxford OX2 6DP
Oxford University Press is a department of the University of Oxford.
It furthers the University's objective of excellence in research, scholarship,
and education by publishing worldwide in
Oxford New York
Auckland Cape Town Dar es Salaam Hong Kong Karachi
Kuala Lumpur Madrid Melbourne Mexico City Nairobi
New Delhi Shanghai Taipei Toronto
With offices in
Argentina Austria Brazil Chile Czech Republic France Greece
Guatemala Hungary Italy Japan South Korea Poland Portugal
Singapore Switzerland Thailand Turkey Ukraine Vietnam

Oxford is a registered trade mark of Oxford University Press
in the UK and in certain other countries

Published in the United States
by Oxford University Press Inc., New York

Introduction, selection, and editorial material
© Sandra Kemp and Judith Squires 1997

The moral rights of the author have been asserted

Database right Oxford University Press (maker)

Reprinted 2009

All rights reserved. No part of this publication may be reproduced,
stored in a retrieval system, or transmitted, in any form or by any means,
without the prior permission in writing of Oxford University Press,
or as expressly permitted by law, or under terms agreed with the appropriate
reprographics rights organization. Enquiries concerning reproduction
outside the scope of the above should be sent to the Rights Department,
Oxford University Press, at the address above

You must not circulate this book in any other binding or cover
And you must impose this same condition on any acquirer

ISBN 978-0-19-289270-6

Printed in the United Kingdom by
Lightning Source UK Ltd., Milton Keynes

For Jack, Josh, and Abigail

Contents

2. Epistemologies

3. Subjectivities

4. Sexualities

5. Visualities

6. Technologies

Feminisms

Introduction

There they go, our brothers who have been educated at public schools and universities, mounting those steps, passing in and out of those doors, ascending those pulpits, preaching, teaching, administering justice, practising medicine, transacting business, making money. It is a solemn sight always—a procession . . . For we have to ask ourselves, here and now, do we wish to join that procession, or don't we? On what terms shall we join that procession? Above all, where is it leading us, the procession of educated men?

Virginia Woolf

The diversity within feminism is now well established. The plural of our title (feminisms) reflects both the contemporary diversity of motivation, method, and experience among feminist academics, and feminism's political commitment to diversity—its validation of a multiplicity of approaches, positions, and strategies.

Current forms of feminism grew out of the women's movements and consciousness-raising groups of the 1960s, and were initially based occupationally in publishing and journalism, and politically in civil rights campaigns and Marxism. Other earlier contributors include suffrage and trades union movements. It is conventional to distinguish two waves of feminism, the first wave spanning the period 1830–1920 and the second wave from 1960 to the present. According to this schema first-wave feminism is characterized by its grounding in a classical liberal rights perspective and its focus on campaigns for women's enfranchisement and the extension of civil rights to women. The period from 1920 (following the achievement of the vote for women) is usually assumed to be one of relative inactivity for feminism. However, by the 1960s the widespread growth in educational opportunities for women, coupled with their entry into various previously all-male professions, the establishment of legislation on abortion and equal pay, and the introduction of widely available birth control, created conditions in which feminist activism could resurface. Second-wave feminism, frequently dated as emerging with the publication of Betty Friedan's *The Feminine Mystique* in America in 1963, was characterized throughout the 1960s and 1970s by extensive and active networks of informal women's groups. It is only recently in France, Britain, and America (the countries from which the feminist discourses explored in this collection have emerged) that the universities and the institutions of psychoanalysis have become the favoured arenas of debate—generating an extensive body of feminist literature, but also straining the earlier second-wave commitment to both informal organizational structures and accessible political debates.

The single most distinguishing feature of feminist scholarly work has been its overtly political nature, and feminism's commitment to material and social change has played a significant role in undermining traditional academic boundaries between the personal and the political. Feminist theory is also traditionally characterized by its interdisciplinarity—its transgression of the usual subject divides (e.g. literary, historical, philosophical, psychological, anthropological, and sociological). However, there has always been a contradiction in feminisms between feminism's theoretical refusal to countenance 'master narratives' and the political ascendancy of certain canonical texts: the growth of feminist theory was marked by the appearance of what rapidly became classic feminist texts (for example in the early 1970s writings by Germaine Greer, Juliet Mitchell, Mary Daly, and Kate Millett). In the 1960s, 1970s, and early 1980s feminist theory was also predominantly Western and motivated by white and/or heterosexual interests. More recent feminist writing has tended to be overtly critical of this exclusivity of focus. Some also argue that the urgent attempt to define a feminist aesthetic and to radically rethink existing systems of thought, resulted in empty jargon, new clichés, and stock phrases.

At a time when the current trend is most definitely to denounce totalizing theories, to celebrate difference, recognize 'otherness', and acknowledge the multiplicity of feminisms, any attempt to define or represent 'feminism' will inevitably prove problematic. What is more, in a period popularly characterized as 'post-feminist' we find both that feminists have gained legitimacy and respect within academia (whilst problematizing the category 'woman' and moving towards analyses of 'gender') and that women outside the academy continue to engage in political struggle (whilst rejecting any definition of themselves as 'feminist'). In this context it is simply not clear, if ever it was, what being a feminist might mean or involve. The development of multiple feminist theoretical perspectives and the painful splintering of the women's movement occurred almost simultaneously with the growth of second-wave feminism, despite its oft-presumed unity. Today such fragmentation is largely viewed as symptomatic of, rather than problematic for, feminist endeavours. In this context, it is our intention that the reader should gain a sense of the dynamic nature of feminist debates, the genuine diversity within current feminist theory and the issues at stake in the differing approaches towards feminist activism.

Those who most frequently and assuredly lay claim to the title 'feminist' now tend to be those who have defined their career in no small part through this identity. As a result, it is not marginalization but institutionalization, not silencing but selling-out, which appears to preoccupy current feminist self-reflections. Whilst this development is positive to the extent that it represents an institutional recognition of feminists, there is concern that the emergence of 'femocrats'—a new breed who have used feminism as a tool to engineer professional success—generates a language of feminist theory and criticism which can be exclusive and alienating to those who are not a part of such professions. Countering this trend, one strategy is to turn to a 'popular feminism', which interestingly does not name itself feminist, which is to be found in the everyday—in the plots of TV soaps, in the narratives of popular fiction, in the battles over employment legislation and maternity rights, etc.: 'while Feminism was worrying about concepts like "fragmentation" and "identity"', remarks Andrea Stuart, 'Elle . . . was playing with them.'[1] Whilst accepting this approach as helpful, in compiling this collection we—the editors—have worked on the assumption that the theoretical feminism which emerges from academia *is* valuable, notwithstanding its (apparent) exclusivity. In making this claim we are not insensitive to the political origins of feminism or its firm commitment to grounding all theory in practice; nor do we seek to silence the voice of non-academic forms of feminism. Talk of diversity should assure that, if nothing else, one should cease to seek single agendas, prescriptive modes of discourse, and unified audiences. Valuing the theoretical does not deny other discourses, rather feminist theory might best be viewed as one legitimate element of a wider feminist endeavour. Indeed, in cultures so resistent to 'intellectuals' and in which the antimony between thought and the feminine is so deeply rooted, it should be a matter of some pride and of much import to take up this role.

However, some have seen such a focus on the theoretical as inevitably diverting energy and attention away from feminist activism. As is noted in this collection: 'it sometimes seems as though feminism's recent arrival within the academy has coincided with the demise of that once powerful network of grass-roots organizations which, certainly in the seventies and early eighties, constituted the heart of the women's movement' (Susannah Radstone, p. 105). Yet this coincidence should not be interpreted as causal: nor should the institutionalization of feminism be viewed as synonymous with its engagement with the theoretical. There are possibilities for critical, explorative, and revolutionary thought which exist only if one is willing to move beyond the everyday, the institutional, and its constraints. Primitive subjectivism is, Mary Evans warns, 'characteristic of some of the most reactionary social organizations in existence' (p. 20). There are radical, transformative, and highly exciting possibilities offered in theoretical, aesthetic, and performative exploration. It is not 'theory' itself which feminists should be wary of, but particular forms of theorizing which operate to reinforce the status quo rather than challenge its operation. To assume that work which is 'difficult' is élitist is to confuse the form with the context. For whilst this may be contingently so—given existing cultural expectations and opportunities—it is certainly not inherently the case. In fact, the theoretical, the exploratory, the unexpected, are potentially more challenging of any norms which inscribe élites, than are practices which are immediately read and assimilated.

What then are the aims of feminist theory? Jane Flax states in this collection: 'A fundamental goal of feminist theory is (and ought to be) to analyze gender relations: how gender relations are constituted and experienced and how we think or, equally important, do not think about them. The study of gender relations includes but is not limited to what are often considered the distinctively feminist issues: the situation of women and the analysis of male domination' (p. 171). Accordingly, it is clear that the strength of such theoretical work lies in the 'critical distance' gained in considering existing gender relations—a critical distance which provides an opportunity for renegotiating these relations afresh. Feminist theory might then be best characterized as critical analyses of the dynamics of gender and sexuality.

Notable shifts in feminist theorizing from the early years of second-wave feminism to the present day include the extent to which many theorists now insist on broadening their scope beyond the exclusive focus on male dominance, and assert their commitment to plural and inevitably partial theoretical perspectives: monocausal and totalizing theories of patriarchy have largely been replaced by multifaceted explorations of the contingencies of gendered identity. One striking continuity within second-wave feminisms, however, lies in the feminist commitment to political change, to politically motivated research, and politically engaged theory.

The pieces in this collection are then unapologetically theoretical, but much more ambivalently academic. For though academia does provide many (though by no means all) of the places in which such creativity can emerge, it also hedges these spaces around with the barriers of intellectual convention and disciplinary canons. Meaghan Morris valiantly asserts that: 'institutionalization is not another name for doom, that fate worse than death. It's an opportunity, and in many instances a necessary condition for serious politics.'[2] But much more common is the ambivalence articulated by Jane Gallop: 'I do not want to celebrate our being in [academia]. Being in something that is a transmitter of elitist values. Being in a discourse that is constituted, at this point in time, as marginal to the larger culture and society. But I do not want to bemoan it either' (p. 110). For many, it would seem that the two battles fought—to assert one's agenda as a feminist within academia, and then as an academic within feminism—have created ambivalence about claiming a status as both feminist and academic. Manifestations of ambivalence about the professionalization of feminism, experienced not only as theoretical or political tension, but also as deep personal uncertainty, abound—despite (in part because of) the phenomenal proliferation of academic feminist conferences and publications. For ourselves, it was the process of convening a conference of feminist theory at Glasgow University in 1991 that first forced us to confront this issue directly. As Susannah Radstone indicates in her reflections on this conference (pp. 104–8), the need to contemplate the shifting position of feminism *vis-à-vis* political and professional engagement is now intense.[3]

The acceptance of feminist research within academia has been painfully denied for far too long. Once (largely) adopted, the floodgates have been burst asunder with an absolute deluge of writings. Since the early 1980s the pace of debate has been intense, the range of research immense. We have attempted to capture a sense of this rapid movement within feminist theory and criticism, along with the attendant fluctuations and turmoil, by presenting a large number of abridged extracts chronologically, dating from 1980 to the present day. In so doing we hope that the reader will gain a sense of how debates within feminist theory have developed: how theorists have built on one another's work and argued with one another; how certain issues have emerged or faded whilst other concerns have continually recurred in changing form.

The ontological insecurity of 1980s feminists within academia, coupled with the changing political climate during this period, seems to have ousted certain debates previously thought central to the women's movement from the feminist theoretical agenda. It is not then only the *presence* of the theoretical, but also the *nature* of the theories, which is distinctive in recent feminist work. The early feminist stress on the sociological and material is not represented here. This is not simple oversight, it is indicative of the field. To focus on those material matters which generated so much feminist debate in the 1970s would actually produce a less than representative indication of debates that truly spark current feminist controversy and engage theoretical reflection. We want to draw attention to this development and invite reflection upon the shift.

Feminist theoretical endeavour has increasingly challenged the dominance of materialist theoretical perspectives, focusing in their place on processes of symbolization and representation. The search for depictions of women that escape the straitjacket of already-existing symbolic forms has led to analyses of the relation between images and social representation, identity and the upholding of social orders. Questions of vision, power, and knowledge are also evident in redefinitions of women's relation to the camera and 'the gaze' more generally. Feminist inquiry in the visual field has led to a new matching of female subjectivity with the agency of the look. The strength of female spectator theory lies precisely in its stress on feminisms as a heterogeneous cultural and political activity and not as a discrete methodological strategy. As Michèle Barrett notes in this collection: 'In the past ten years we have seen an extensive "turn to culture" in feminism. Academically, the social sciences have lost their purchase within feminism and the rising star lies with the arts, humanities, and philosophy' (p. 112). That this is undeniably the case offers the reader an insight into our selection criteria, giving priority as we do to issues concerning visual representation and reception.

We chose Susan Derges's image for our cover as it seems to us that this work manifests precisely the attention to female subjectivity, to self-reflexivity, and aesthetic contemplation of multiplicity and difference which have so preoccupied feminist theorists since the early 1980s. The visual, epistemological, and ontological questions being worked through here have generated an enormous feminist and multimedia literature during the past two decades.

It is significant that the focus of such questioning is not primarily the central question of early second-wave feminism—'what is to be done?', but rather the more reflexive, 'what is the basis of my claim to knowledge' and 'who is the "I" that makes such a claim?' This shift from the overtly collectivist and political to the more individualist and philosophical might be viewed negatively as a shift from insurrection to introspection, or positively as the coming to age of feminism as an intellectual endeavour, or perhaps more neutrally as simply symptomatic of the 1990s. However one views the development, it is clear that epistemological, ontological, and representational questions currently serve as a key locus of feminist concern and the significant grounds for dispute between feminists.

The shift from 'things' to 'words' is evident across the spectrum of feminist theorizing—whatever the academic discipline of the writer. Indeed, the mobility of theory—taking the theoretical tools of one discipline to engage with issues in another—is perhaps nowhere more evident than within feminist writings of the past twenty years, disciplinary divisions crumbling in the light of the appeal to ideas from elsewhere. Derridian deconstructive reading, Lacanian psychoanalysis, and Foucauldian discourses of power and corporeality, for instance, have proved invaluable tools to feminist theorists across the disciplines. It is this theoretical restlessness which means that any productive engagement with contemporary feminism requires a non-disciplinary approach. For this reason, we have traversed academic disciplines in formulating the sections in this collection, such that the reader will be able to engage with the most frequently asked (though rarely conclusively answered) questions preoccupying contemporary feminist theorists. These questions include: what are the appropriate methods and locations for theorizing as a feminist; what are the goals of feminist theory; how does feminism relate to the female and to the feminine; why and in what ways is sexuality central to feminism and to what extent does sexuality shape our subjectivity; how central are images in constructing or expressing our identities as women and what might feminist strategies of representation entail; and finally, what constitutes the relations between women, nature, and technology and how might we use technologies to resist, negotiate, or transform dominant perceptions of femininity?

Reference to the mobility of theory between disciplines should not however blind us to the relative immobility of theory across more geographical boundaries. The academic dominance of 'Anglo-American' feminist theory has been modified by the engagement of American and British feminists with 'French feminism' since the early 1980s, but an open engagement with voices from elsewhere is still far from a reality. The cultural and economic forces which promote certain national and ethnic perspectives over others are played out within feminist theory as elsewhere.

Accordingly, the pieces in this collection originate overwhelmingly from Britain and America, with key interventions from France (notably Wittig, Kristeva, Cixous, and Irigaray), for these are the voices that have dominated recent debates within Western academic feminism.

In addition to jettisoning disciplinary constraints, we have also opted not to categorize feminisms according to constituent types—liberal, Marxist, socialist, radical, or psychoanalytic. In adopting and modifying existing theoretical divisions from within the Western canon as the basis for such taxonomies, the implication—that we hope to avoid—is that feminist theory understands itself as simple modification of the pre-existing canon. Further, whilst clearly not generating fragmentation itself, the rigid classification of feminist theories has at times worked to polarize perspectives and rigidify conflicts. Avoiding such reductive taxonomies, we have therefore chosen to structure our approach to debates within contemporary feminist theory according to issues rather than perspectives. Structured in this way, the reader will hopefully be given an insight into the context in which feminist interventions have been made, but spared the overly constricting frameworks of evaluation that reductive taxonomies construct. Within this general schema we have arranged the material in six sections which each take as their focus a key debate within current feminist discourse: Academies, Epistemologies, Subjectivities, Sexualities, Visualities, and Technologies. The selections therefore stand alone, but also form part of a larger argument which will emerge when read in their chronological context.

We open with 'Academies', a section which poses a particularly pertinent question for many feminist theorists: is the institutionalization of feminist criticism and theory a sell-out to academic respectability, or an opportunity for serious politics? The pieces in this section consider the implications (positive and negative) of the acceptance of feminist theory by the academy, and the ways in which educational and cultural institutions affect the work of feminist scholars. To open with this debate may strike some as being overly introspective, placing feminism too narrowly within the university and failing to appreciate its wider social engagement. However, academia *is* now the context in which a significant body of feminist debate takes place and the long-standing feminist preoccupation with speaking from one's own experience demands that those within the universities work through the issues pertaining to this fact. As the following five sections comprise material which is largely a product of academic feminism, reflection of the implications of this focus is apposite.

Sections 2 and 3—'Epistemologies' and 'Subjectivities'—focus on the epistemological and ontological issues which have proved to be so central to feminist debate in the 1980s and 1990s. Epistemological allegiances (empiricist, standpoint, and postmodern) have become a useful way of marking divisions in feminist theory. That these epistemological categories have largely come to replace the radical, liberal, and Marxists divisions, which were primarily political divisions, is an interesting shift in its own right. Noteworthy too is the extent to which feminist theory since 1980 has been characterized by debate between standpoint perspectives (often drawing upon object-relations psychoanalysis) and postmodern perspectives (many of which draw upon Lacanian psychoanalysis). The pieces in this section introduce many of the key issues which underpin all feminist theorizing, and the reader may wish to start here if a general introduction to current feminisms is wanted. The 'Subjectivities' section focuses on debates between social constructivist and essentialist theorists, highlighting the issues at stake in the invocation of the category of 'woman'. At the heart of this debate stands a dispute regarding the significance of sexual difference: is 'woman' an essence or a social construct? Those voices deemed essentialist (proposing an ahistorical and immutable 'womanness' outside the field of political intervention) have been subject to increasing critique from postmodern and deconstructive perspectives during the period under consideration, such that 'essentialism' has largely come to signify reactionary and problematic politics within academic feminisms. The dominance of various forms of social constructivist theories is now modified mainly by those who advocate the need for a kind of 'strategic essentialism'.

The range of perspectives found in the debate over subjectivities is also to be found within feminist debates about sexualities, visualities, and technologies, where analyses range from critiques of dominant patriarchal structures (be they sexual, visual, or technological) to explorations of multiple feminist strategies for subversion and creativity. In the context of feminist approaches to sexuality, debate has been played out in particularly bitter form, with those feminists who problematize heterosexuality and advocate specific forms of feminist sexuality clashing with those who pursue more diverse and mutable explorations of sexual pleasure. In relation to 'Visualities' the debate encompasses critiques of stereotyped images of women (in film, television, and advertising) to considerations of the constitution of feminist cinema, photography, fine art. In 'Technologies' the debate is between those who argue that all technology is encoded in masculine terms and should be rejected in the name of the 'natural', and those who are keen to explore the productive possibilities for technological development, perceiving even our understanding of 'nature' to be socially constructed.

One of the most striking developments within academic feminisms not explicitly addressed here is the shift from 'working on women' to 'theorizing gender'. The proliferation of feminist theoretical writing over the past two decades and the academic status attained by feminist criticism has resulted in numerous paradoxes: not least the extent to which feminist theory and criticism become valued tools concurrent with their gradual distancing from the category 'woman'. When, for example, Tania Modleski quotes Peter Brooks saying: 'Anyone worth his salt in literary criticism today has to become something of a feminist',[4] she highlights both the dominance of feminist criticism within some areas of academia and also its tendency to be appropriated for male exploration once it has gained this privileged status. The acceptance of feminist theory within the academy and the shift towards theorizing not 'woman' but 'gender' adds another layer to the reflection that the feminist move into the academy coincides with the demise of an active women's movement. As Rosi Braidotti asks, 'why is it that as soon as feminists began thinking out loud for themselves, male thinkers took up the "feminine" as their own cause? What made them want to embark on this sudden "feminization" of their own modes of thinking?'[5] Whilst the cynical response is to point to the attendant status gained by men who make this move, the more optimistic and more significant response is to acknowledge the vital political achievement that theorizing gender represents.

This transition from working on women to theorizing gender is ubiquitous in current publication lists and teaching curricula. It is a manifestation of the realization that any change in the status of women will involve some change in that of men. Echoing developments in feminist theory, the 1980s witnessed a growing concern about—and literature on—the shifting nature of men's lives. As Lynne Segal notes, 'books researching fatherhood, men's violence against women and children, male identities and male mythologies now interrogate men, as a sex, in a way until recently reserved for women—as a problem.'[6] Following feminist theory a stage further it has now become *de rigueur* to speak of 'masculinities' in the plural and to explore the fluctuating constitution of hegemonic and subordinate forms of masculinity.[7] Far from assuming the polarized analyses of some forms of early second-wave feminism in which 'all men' oppressed 'all women', modish sexual politics currently takes as its focus the transgression of all existing gender boundaries. In this context, any insistence on the presence of 'women'—whether it be in the classroom or on a reading list—seems to some as simply a retreat to a rather old-fashioned essentialist politics of numbers.

In the light of this development, our decision to focus exclusively on women, as both the authors and subjects of our selections, may appear to some as wilfully backward-looking. We do so not only for the pragmatic reason that a collection on Gender is to follow in this series of Readers, but also for the more principled, if contingent, reason that the categories of 'man' and 'woman' (in all their complexity and multiplicity) currently remain constitutive of our identities, and in hierarchically inscribed ways. If current trends are followed, it would seem unlikely that any disciplinary division between 'feminism' (which excludes men) and 'gender' (which does not) will be sustainable. At this point, however, we have made it our task to document developments within feminisms up to the point at which this shift to a more inclusive gender politics appears both a desirable option and a real possibility.

Whether the fragmentation, institutionalization, and culturization of feminism are perceived as the sorry demise and de-radicalization of feminism, or as the maturation of increasingly flexible, self-reflexive, and multiple feminisms, one thing is evident: there is no unchanging feminist orthodoxy, no settled feminist conventions, no static feminist analyses. Feminism is diverse and it is dynamic. The changes within feminisms in the last sixteen years alone are testament to this.

Section 1

Academies

INTRODUCTION

> We don't seem very able to theorize how we speak as feminists wanting
> social change from within our positions in the academy.
>
> Jane Gallop

In 1984 bell hooks reflects on the 'growing disinterest in feminism as a radical
political movement' and the increasing inability to arrive at a unified definition of feminism itself. A decade later Anna Yeatman writes of the ways in
which academic feminism, or 'femocracy', has been characterized by various
attempts to respond to challenges of 'otherness'. In these pieces, and in all
those within this section, we find the two issues which have most preoccupied
and characterized feminist theorizing in the 1980s and 1990s: the fragmentation and institutionalization of feminism itself. The intersection of these
two concerns leads to an attentiveness to representation and method: who
speaks, in the name of whom and in what voice? The academic location of
feminist reflections on fragmentation, coupled with sensitivity to questions of
authenticity, has created a desire to examine both the location and the form of
one's own voice as feminist/theorist, and to grapple with the tensions (both
productive and counter-productive) between the theoretical and the autobiographical, the institutional and the political, the general and the particular.

bell hooks's confident assertion that feminism 'is the struggle to end sexist
oppression' reflects feminism's roots in the political aspirations of the
women's movement, but is also, already, tempered by a concern to avoid
assimilation to particular norms of dominant feminisms. The process by
which feminists became distanced from the assumed sisterhood of a unified
women's movement is discussed by Anne Phillips in her reflections on the
political practices of the women's movement in the 1970s. These practices
emphasized participation and friendship, but at the cost of accountability and
diversity. There were significant political and ontological lessons to be
learned: the price of assumed commonality was ultimately painful fragmentation.

Yet if feminism was losing its sense of identity as a political movement, it
was finding a new identity in the universities. By the early 1980s the academic
discipline of Women's Studies was firmly established, despite hostility from
those who viewed this as an inevitable de-radicalization of feminism. Mary

Evans, one of the foremost founders of Women's Studies within British universities, reflecting upon both the charges made from within feminism of abstraction, élitism, and co-option, and the marginal status of the discipline within the academy, highlights the tensions of this move towards institutionalization. By 1994 Anna Yeatman is able to reflect more positively on the incorporation of feminism within the academy. Feminist theory, she claims, has 'matured to the point where it is able to subject its own premises to an ironical, skeptical and critical mode of analysis'. As such it is entirely within the critical, reflective, and sceptical spirit of the contemporary university, but a long way from the early political ethos of the women's movement.

The question as to whether theoretical language is a help or a hindrance to the pursuit of political objectives found fairly uniform resolution in favour of the theoretical during the early 1980s. Feminist theory proliferated and feminist criticism became notoriously 'difficult'. If some of the pieces in this collection appear surprisingly complex or overly theoretical to the reader expecting feminist writing to be more direct and polemical, this is indicative of a debate played out within feminist thought itself throughout the past two decades. But debate it still is, for there are many who are more sceptical than is Yeatman about the realization of the voice of the organic intellectual. Theory, Barbara Christian states, 'has become a commodity because it helps determine whether we are hired or promoted in academic institutions'. In the context of 'the race for theory' many may have (wilfully) overlooked the inappropriateness of theory for certain contexts and the extent to which dominant theoretical paradigms privilege certain ways of being. Whether instructive or insidious, the race for theory has unquestionably shaped feminist writing during recent years. Yet the concern to espouse a theoretical perspective sensitive to Christian's critique has led many, rather than giving up on the theoretical, to turn to that form of theorizing which is non-totalizing, to take the postmodern turn and to directly address the issue of 'otherness'.

Part of the process of working through what it means to occupy a position as a feminist within the academy has involved engaging with the question of the 'other woman'. Chandra Mohanty puts it thus: 'feminist scholarship . . . is not the mere production of knowledge about a certain subject. It is a directly political and discursive practice in that it is purposeful and ideological. . . . There can, of course, be no apolitical scholarship.' In attempting to speak of 'Woman' feminist theorists inevitably construct discursive categories which represent the complexity of women in a relation which is not one of direct identity. Mohanty's concern is that Western feminist self-presentations and their re-presentation of women in the Third World are mutually constitutive along power-laden axes. Adopting the deconstructive/postmodern theoretical frame popularized by 'the French feminists' many sought to avoid the totalizing strategies of the modernist grand-narratives of previous social-scientific discourses, and thereby be politically sensitive to 'otherness'. But being attentive to otherness has itself operated to construct categories of the 'other' in a socially divisive manner.

Feminism's turn to theory and its institutionalization occur simultaneously during the early 1980s. The sense of anxiety that this insider status might have been achieved at the cost of a relative inattentiveness to difference (racial, sexual, national, etc.) fuels current debates about the place of 'otherness' in feminist discourse. No matter how sincere the attempt to adopt a theoretical stance sensitive to otherness, feminist theorists seem destined to court criticism for their assimilatory tendencies. Note, for example, Helena Michie's reflection that feminist explorations of otherness end up absorbing otherness 'into an increasingly capacious notion of the self'. The question of whom one speaks for when one speaks as a feminist from within the academy negotiates all that has most preoccupied feminist theorizing in recent years: the tensions between self-presentation and the re-presentation of others, between the political and the academic, between the personal and the theoretical.

Concern that the theorization and institutionalization of feminism might be internally connected, has led to what Nancy Miller calls 'symptoms of literary theory's mid-life crisis', and has moved many academic feminists to reflect upon their own use of the theoretical. 'Now I write for women, rather than as in my early work, constructing a polemic directed against men,' notes Cora Kaplan. Ambivalence about the theoretical has led many to adopt an autobiographical voice (or personal criticism) as they turn their attention from the theoretical debates of psychoanalysis and deconstruction to reflect on the very institutions in which these debates took place. For Jane Tompkins the renegotiation of theoretical and political issues requires the recognition of the conflict between 'two voices inside me ... one writes for professional journals, the other in diaries, late at night'. Such a strategy does of course issue its own challenge to the academy: questioning the epistemological privileging of rationality over emotion and the general over the particular. But, it also invokes the assertion—as made by Barbara Smith—that drawing upon individual experience is not enough.

Reading theory through experience is rarely easy. As Elspeth Probyn reflects: 'how could it be that raising the theoretical necessity of recognizing, of putting into words, the ways in which we read theory through experience should produce a feeling of isolation?' Concern about whether the enunciation of experience should be interpreted as emotional touches upon a second-generation academic feminist concern to distinguish their methodological strategies from earlier non-academic feminisms. The self, in current appeals to experience, is seen as 'a theoretical manoeuvring, not as a unifying principle'. The upshot of this location of the self is, for Probyn, a strategy of 'an emotional foregrounding of the self as a way of critically acknowledging the ontological and epistemological bases of knowledge formation'. Such a foregrounding is, of course, further complicated by the instability of identity, as Cora Kaplan notes when she speaks of 'foregrounding the inherently unstable and split character of all human subjectivity'. Not even the self offers a stable location from which to speak. In this light, foregrounding should perhaps be understood as a process of self-definition, or envisaging oneself as a subject. For, as Teresa de Lauretis notes, identification—whereby the human subject is constituted—is 'all the more important, theoretically and politically, for women who have never before represented ourselves as subjects, and whose images and subjectivities—until very recently, if at all—have not been ours to shape, to portray, or to create'.

1 In Praise of Theory: The Case for Women's Studies

One of the most obvious results of contemporary feminism has been the establishment of a new academic subject: that of Women's Studies.[1] None of the courses can be said to have been welcomed with wild enthusiasm by the male academic establishment: at best a benign tolerance has allowed academics to teach courses about that half of the population which has been generally invisible in much of traditional scholarship. Yet at the same time as those of us teaching Women's Studies have been arguing with the more articulate battalions of male chauvinism, we have also been faced with a more problematic form of opposition, in the shape of criticism from other feminists who have voiced either misgivings or outright hostility to the mere idea of Women's Studies, and have condemned Women's Studies as incompatible with feminism. These criticisms have often been far more difficult to deal with than those of the academic arrière-garde since they are often better arguments and are capable of including those acute fits of sisterly soul-searching which can paralyse all further activity. Disagreeing with Professor D. E. D. Wood is one thing, disagreeing with a woman who prefaces all her remarks with an invocation of sisterhood is another, and far more fearful, experience.

The argument put forward by some feminists suggests that Women's Studies represent either the exploitation or the de-radicalization (or both) of feminism and the women's movement. By becoming part of what is an elitist, and essentially male system of higher education, it is argued that those who teach (and presumably also those who study) Women's Studies only serve their own professional interests and those of patriarchy and the male ruling class. The energies that should be directed towards the transformation of social and sexual relationships are, it is suggested, dissipated in narrow scholastic battles which serve only to perpetuate those hierarchies of control and authority to which the women's movement is opposed.

Inevitably this argument poses the crucial question of whether or not Women's Studies—as a distinct area of study within the academy—is feminist in any meaningful sense. Many feminists would agree that a distinction must be made between Women's Studies and feminist studies, and that only the latter is a viable and defensible form of feminist activity. As I shall argue in this paper I do not think this is the case.

Women's Studies is Feminist Studies

My major reason for supposing that no distinction exists between Women's Studies and feminist studies is two-fold: first, because Women's Studies and feminist studies both challenge male intellectual hegemony. In asserting, describing and documenting the existence of women, both women's studies and feminist studies propose a radical change in the theoretical organization of the universe. [...]

Women's Studies is [...] a self-conscious determination to show that both the content and form of existing knowledge is related to the unequal distribution of social power between men and women. The second reason that I would propose for there being no distinction between feminist and Women's Studies is that the distinction often rests upon a falsely homogeneous view of feminism. Women's Studies is seen as the reactionary, incorporative, pro-status quo activity whilst feminism is always radical, always antithetical to existing society. Yet feminism—as everyone in the women's movement knows—comes in a variety of forms, some of which are far from incompatible with industrial capitalism as we know it. To suppose, therefore, that feminism and feminist studies, has an inevitable theoretical coherence and radicalism which Women's Studies lacks is to run the risk of reifying a quite mythical unity. [...]

Theory versus Experience

A further argument, derived in part from a hostility to theoretical speculation that is a well-documented feature of British life, deserves less detailed attention. Nevertheless, it does demand mention. It is the contention—argued most passionately by some feminists—that there is no necessary difference between reported, subjective experience and theoretical and analytical work. This position would therefore assign the same importance, both practical and theoretical, to the work of a feminist theorist (by which I mean someone who has attempted a coherent analysis of her situation and that of other women) and any statement about her situation by any woman. This is emphatically not to say that a woman expressing horror or dislike at her situation does not have the same right to express that dislike or the same claim to be taken seriously as the theorist with a range of five-volume arguments at her disposal, but that a distinction has to be made between the analysis of subordination of all women and the subjective and personal reaction to that subordination by one woman.

Yet analysis of the situation of women is in some ways deeply problematic for the women's movement, since the first phenomenon that meets us when we attempt to analyse the situation of women is that it is many and varied. Thus we confront a fundamental issue within the women's movement: exactly what constitutes the oppression of women and who decides if it exists? It is clear from the reaction of many women (both in this country and in the Third World) that Western feminism has often made too many, too ethnocentric judgements about the nature of oppression.

In our attempt to achieve objective analytical accounts of the situations of women we are, therefore, stuck with theory. If this can be tolerated—and clearly some feminists do not tolerate it, seeing theory as a masculinization of that apparently exclusively female virtue of feeling—the existence of theory still poses problems for feminists. Three difficulties about the existence and elaboration of feminist theory and analysis come to mind. The first is the issue of the accessibility of theoretical discussion about women to all women, with the implication that it is possible that feminist theory may become the preserve of a small élite, which occasionally issues statements on what to think and how to think it, to the rest of the women's movement. The second issue is the problem of how feminist energy should be directed, and whether or not the intellectual and indeed practical resources that are directed into the development of feminist theory and Women's Studies would not be better employed in other ways, such as participation in grass-roots organizing. The third problem concerning feminist theory is the criticism that the develop-ment of feminist theory serves the career and professional interests of those involved in its development, makes experts of a small group and—this is related to the first point—denies the rank and file of the movement access to decision making and control of the formulation of policy.

Whilst these issues are common to the Left as Western Europe has known it, they are also a large part of feminism's dissatisfaction with traditional Left wing parties and organisations. Indeed, as Sheila Rowbotham, Lynn Segal and Hilary Wainwright have argued, it is essential to feminism that it should organize in a much more democratic and less authoritarian way than the traditional male Left. The contribution of feminism to the Left has been, they argue, the demonstration that political power does not have to ossify in the hands of a small élite and that it is possible for radical, left-wing organizations to be both effective and democratic. It is arguable that Rowbotham and her co-authors place too much emphasis on disillusionment with the authoritar-ian male Left in explaining the commitment to democracy within the women's movement since that very Left which is castigated in *Beyond the Fragments* has not been without its own democratic impulses recently. Never-theless, whatever the origin of its democratic ideals, the British women's movement is deeply hostile to, and suspicious of, institutionalized power in any shape or form, be it intellectual or organizational. Yet despite this suspicion, British feminism does have an indigenously produced theoretical tradition of some sophistication, within and related to a women's movement which is deeply suspicious of all forms of élitism. [...]

But there is no necessary reason within the practice of producing theory why a precise theoretical language, or theory itself, should become the preserve of a small élite. Theory is much more likely to become élitist for reasons outside itself; that is, the social conditions in which intellectual life takes place produce the possibility of élitist theory, rather than the theory itself to condemn theory because of the possibility, however small, that it will remain the preserve of an élite, suggests a quite uncritical, and indeed reactionary, acceptance of a society in which access to higher education and critical thought is denied to many people. The implication of a claim that all analysis must be understood by all, is that those committed to change must accept the given divisions within any society and not attempt to do anything to change those divisions except in terms of those existing divisions. Thus we would have theory for graduates, the school-leavers with O levels, the almost illiterate and so on. The production of all these different theories would satisfy those who want to make feminism accessible to everyone, yet they would do nothing to challenge existing inequalities or hierarchies.

The Risks of Anti-Theoreticism

Perhaps the crucial problem of feminist theory is not, however, its accessibility but about the resources that its production commands. The second issue about feminist theory is, therefore, the criticism that producing theory drains the women's movement of energy and talent that might be better spent elsewhere. Feminism (like socialism), it is argued, faces the appalling spectre of being so pre-occupied with interpreting events in the light of theory that it is rapidly overtaken by events and becomes the victim, rather than the vanguard, of history.

Yet an equally awful prospect is that feminism, in refusing to develop a coherent theory, remains at that stage of primitive subjectivism that is characteristic of some of the most reactionary social organizations in existence. That is not to say that all theories are necessarily right, but that the exercise of the construction of a rational case is the first step towards a real understanding of the social world. [...]

Feminist theory can, hopefully, lead us away from the blind alley of subjective feeling and subjective action. Yet the case against theory makes a great deal of the distinction between the production of theory and action which seems to suggest a theory of knowledge in which thought and action have no effect on each other. This view invokes a picture of human beings as headless chickens: the head, full of theory, lies inert and ineffective, while the headless body, empty of direction, rushes around in mindless circles. This dichotomy between theory and practice leads to some bizarre conclusions about the social world: that 'action' or practice is in some way separable from thought and that theory is always the soft option and action always the role of the true believer. It is seldom allowed that human beings have not only achieved a practical mastery of nature, but have also created most elaborate systems of thought, belief and ideology, which have critical effects on the material conditions of life of millions of people. The production of counter-ideologies may, therefore, be as much part of a struggle of the oppressed as any other.

Profiteering Feminists?

The final criticism of feminism theory which has been named here is that the production of theory by feminists is motivated exclusively by the desire for self-aggrandisement of some kind. Protagonists of this argument go on to suggest that the production of feminist theory is in itself often suspect, in that it increases the discrepancy between highly educated women—able to write, and presumably understand, theory—and those women with little or no higher education.

The first part of this criticism of feminist theory—that it enhances the status, and the wealth, of those women producing it—is difficult to accept as a measured or rational criticism. It is undeniable that a few—a very few— women have grown rich by writing feminist, or quasi-feminist books, but in comparison to these quite exceptional cases there are literally hundreds of women in schools, universities and various other institutions who have battled, and are battling, to suggest that women do have special interests, and that the discussion and consideration of these interests merits attention. [. . .]

But many other feminists do not, of course, write best-sellers. We toil away in more prosaic and limited ways: proposing courses on Women's Studies, attempting to do feminist research or to encourage women students to set their sights above the given limits of female achievement. We must ask if these activities prolong élitism, or serve our professional interests. Suppressing, at this stage a desire to launch into biographical anecdote, I would argue that this is emphatically not the case: in most cases our professional interests would be best served by keeping well away from Women's Studies, let alone feminism.

But the reasons for saying that this is the case are more complex than might be supposed. The simple answer—and indeed an important part of the answer—is that Women's Studies is seen by many male academics as both a personal and an intellectual threat. It is very difficult to demonstrate this in academic terms: that is, I cannot say that you should turn to journal X or Y to see an example of this blatant prejudice. Academics are generally loathe to put on paper something which might correspond to an unsubstantiated opinion, or prejudice. The bias against women is much more subtle therefore than blatant, clear sexism, and frequently takes the form of the exclusion of women rather than bias against them.

So many male academics simply didn't see women as part of the social world, rather than taking a conscious decision to exclude them from it. To be asked, therefore, to make a conscious decision about *including* women, is something of a problem for individuals who have previously refused to recognize that the issue exists. It takes an effort of will to appreciate that the boundaries of a particular subject are neither as accurate nor as inclusive as has been hitherto supposed. Feminism poses, therefore, a genuine instance of a paradigm shift—a shift which like many other shifts is inevitably resisted by those committed to the modes and practices of thought and existing knowledge.

Sex-Blind Disciplines?

In resisting the discussion of women in the curriculum, academics (of both sexes) generally fall back on two arguments. First, that the existing literature on women is inadequate and second, that although it is conceded that it may be necessary for women to occupy a more central place in the disciplines than previously, the central issues of all subjects are sex-blind, and will remain untouched by the discussion of women.

The denial of the relevance of the study of women, and the specificity of the female case, to the central issues of a subject has important practical and intellectual consequences within the academy, one of which is the possibility of the pejorative labelling of women who produce work on women as narrow specialists in esoteric fields, whilst more conventional studies become important works of scholarship.

The history of theoretical feminism in Britain and the United States has yet to be written. However, when it is documented it would seem likely on the evidence so far available that women engaged in feminist research do not profit by that exercise in any orthodox sense, either inside or outside the academy. There are few indications at present that British or North American universities see Women's Studies as anything other than a peripheral or temporary phenomenon. Whatever the indications that the subject might be popular or lively it remains—as do its practitioners—in an outer courtyard, far removed from the real centres of academic power and authority. Given these factors it is unlikely that those who decide to accept feminism, and work for it, will be able to ignore the consistent marginality and academic deviance of their position.

['In Praise of Theory: The Case for Women's Studies', in Gloria Bowles and Renate Duelli Klein (eds.), *Theories of Women's Studies* (London: Routledge, 1982), 219–28.]

BELL HOOKS

2 Feminism: A Movement to End Sexist Oppression

A central problem within feminist discourse has been our inability to either arrive at a consensus of opinion about what feminism is or accept definition(s) that could serve as points of unification. Without agreed upon definition(s), we lack a sound foundation on which to construct theory or engage in overall meaningful praxis. Expressing her frustrations with the absence of clear definitions in a recent essay, 'Towards A Revolutionary Ethics', Carmen Vasquez comments:

We can't even agree on what a 'Feminist' is, never mind what she would believe in and how she defines the principles that constitute honor among us. In key with the American capitalist obsession for individualism and anything goes so long as it gets you what you want. Feminism in American has come to mean anything you like, honey. There are as many definitions of Feminism as there are feminists, some of my sisters say, with a chuckle. I don't think it's funny.

It is not funny. It indicates a growing disinterest in feminism as a radical political movement. It is a despairing gesture expressive of the belief that solidarity between women is not possible. It is a sign that the political naïveté which has traditionally characterized woman's lot in male-dominated culture abounds.

Most people in the United States think of feminism or the more commonly used term 'women's lib' as a movement that aims to make women the social equals of men. This broad definition, popularized by the media and main-stream segments of the movement, raises problematic questions. Since men are not equals in white supremacist, capitalist, patriarchal class structure, which men do women want to be equal to? Do women share a common vision of what equality means? Implicit in this simplistic definition of women's liberation is a dismissal of race and class as factors that, in conjunction with sexism, determine the extent to which an individual will be discriminated against, exploited, or oppressed. Bourgeois white women interested in women's rights issues have been satisfied with simple definitions for obvious reasons. Rhetorically placing themselves in the same social category as oppressed women, they were not anxious to call attention to race and class privilege.

Women in lower class and poor groups, particularly those who are non-white, would not have defined women's liberation as women gaining social equality with men since they are continually reminded in their everyday lives that all women do not share a common social status. Concurrently, they know that many males in their social groups are exploited and oppressed. Knowing that men in their groups do not have social, political, and economic power, they would not deem it liberatory to share their social status. While they are aware that sexism enables men in their respective groups to have privileges denied them, they are more likely to see exaggerated expressions of male chauvinism among their peers as stemming from the male's sense of himself as powerless and ineffectual in relation to ruling male groups, rather than an expression of an overall privileged social status. From the very onset of the women's liberation movement, these women were suspicious of feminism precisely because they recognized the limitations inherent in its definition. They recognized the possibility that feminism defined as social equality with men might easily become a movement that would primarily affect the social standing of white women in middle and upper class groups while affecting only in a very marginal way the social status of working class and poor women. [. . .]

Many women are reluctant to advocate feminism because they are uncertain about the meaning of the term. Other women from exploited and oppressed ethnic groups dismiss the term because they do not wish to be perceived as supporting a racist movement; feminism is often equated with white women's rights effort. Large numbers of women see feminism as synonymous with lesbianism; their homophobia leads them to reject association with any group identified as pro-lesbian. Some women fear the word 'feminism' because they shun identification with any political movement, especially one perceived as radical. Of course there are women who do not wish to be associated with women's rights movement in any form so they reject and oppose feminist movement. Most women are more familiar with negative perspectives on 'women's lib' than the positive significations of feminism. It is this term's positive political significance and power that we must now struggle to recover and maintain.

Currently feminism seems to be a term without any clear significance. The 'anything goes' approach to the definition of the word has rendered it practically meaningless. What is meant by 'anything goes' is usually that any woman who wants social equality with men regardless of her political perspective (she can be a conservative right-winger or a nationalist communist) can label herself feminist. Most attempts at defining feminism reflect the class nature of the movement. Definitions are usually liberal in origin and focus on the individual woman's right to freedom and self-determination. In Barbara Berg's *The Remembered Gate: Origins of American Feminism*, she defines feminism as a 'broad movement embracing numerous phases of woman's emancipation'. However, her emphasis is on women gaining greater individual freedom. Expanding on the above definition, Berg adds:

It is the freedom to decide her own destiny; freedom from sex-determined role; freedom from society's oppressive restrictions; freedom to express her thoughts fully and to convert them freely into action. Feminism demands the acceptance of woman's right to individual conscience and judgment. It postulates that woman's essential worth stems from her common humanity and does not depend on the other relationships of her life.

This definition of feminism is almost apolitical in tone; yet it is the type of definition many liberal women find appealing. It evokes a very romantic notion of personal freedom which is more acceptable than a definition that emphasizes radical political action.

Many feminist radicals now know that neither a feminism that focuses on woman as an autonomous human being worthy of personal freedom nor one that focuses on the attainment of equality of opportunity with men can rid society of sexism and male domination. Feminism is a struggle to end sexist oppression. Therefore, it is necessarily a struggle to eradicate the ideology of domination that permeates Western culture on various levels as well as a commitment to reorganizing society so that the self-development of people can take precedence over imperialism, economic expansion, and material desires. Defined in this way, it is unlikely that women would join feminist movement simply because we are biologically the same. A commitment to feminism so defined would demand that each individual participant acquire a critical political consciousness based on ideas and beliefs.

All too often the slogan 'the personal is political' (which was first used to stress that woman's everyday reality is informed and shaped by politics and is necessarily political) became a means of encouraging women to think that the experience of discrimination, exploitation, or oppression automatically corresponded with an understanding of the ideological and institutional apparatus shaping one's social status. As a consequence, many women who had not fully examined their situation never developed a sophisticated understanding of their political reality and its relationship to that of women as a collective group. They were encouraged to focus on giving voice to personal experience. Like revolutionaries working to change the lot of colonized people globally, it is necessary for feminist activists to stress that the ability to see and describe one's own reality is a significant step in the long process of self-recovery; but it is only a beginning. When women internalized the idea that describing their own woe was synonymous with developing a critical political consciousness, the progress of feminist movement was stalled. Starting from such incomplete perspectives, it is not surprising that theories and strategies were developed that were collectively inadequate and misguided. To correct this inadequacy in past analysis, we must now encourage women to develop a keen, comprehensive understanding of women's political reality. Broader perspectives can only emerge as we examine both the personal that is political, the politics of society as a whole, and global revolutionary politics. [. . .]

When feminism is defined in such a way that it calls attention to the diversity of women's social and political reality, it centralizes the experiences of all women, especially the women whose social conditions have been least written about, studied, or changed by political movements. When we cease to focus on the simplistic stance 'men are the enemy', we are compelled to examine systems of domination and our role in their maintenance and perpetuation. Lack of adequate definition made it easy for bourgeois women, whether liberal or radical in perspective, to maintain their dominance over the leadership of the movement and its direction. This hegemony continues to exist in most feminist organizations. Exploited and oppressed groups of women are usually encouraged by those in power to feel that their situation is hopeless, that they can do nothing to break the pattern of domination. Given such socialization, these women have often felt that our only response to white, bourgeois, hegemonic dominance of feminist movement is to trash, reject, or dismiss feminism. This reaction is in no way threatening to the women who wish to maintain control over the direction of feminist theory and praxis. They prefer us to be silent, passively accepting their ideas. They prefer us speaking against 'them' rather than developing our own ideas about feminist movement.

Feminism is the struggle to end sexist oppression. Its aim is not to benefit solely any specific group of women, any particular race or class of women. It does not privilege women over men. It has the power to transform in a meaningful way all our lives. Most importantly, feminism is neither a lifestyle nor a ready-made identity or role one can step into. Diverting energy from feminist movement that aims to change society, many women concentrate on the development of a counter-culture, a woman-centered world wherein participants have little contact with men. Such attempts do not indicate a respect or concern for the vast majority of women who are unable to integrate their cultural expressions with the visions offered by alternative woman-centered communities. [. . .]

The willingness to see feminism as a lifestyle choice rather than a political commitment reflects the class nature of the movement. It is not surprising that the vast majority of women who equate feminism with alternative lifestyle are from middle class backgrounds, unmarried, college-educated, often students who are without many of the social and economic respon-sibilities that working class and poor women who are laborers, parents, homemakers, and wives confront daily. [. . .]

To emphasize that engagement with feminist struggle as political commit-ment we could avoid using the phrase 'I am a feminist' (a linguistic structure designed to refer to some personal aspect of identity and self-definition) and could state 'I advocate feminism.' Because there has been undue emphasis placed on feminism as an identity or lifestyle, people usually resort to stereotyped perspectives on feminism. Deflecting attention away from stereo-types is necessary if we are to revise our strategy and direction. I have found that saying 'I am a feminist' usually means I am plugged into preconceived notions of identity, role, or behaviour. When I say 'I advocate feminism' the response is usually 'what is feminism?' A phrase like 'I advocate' does not imply the kind of absolutism that is suggested by 'I am'. It does not engage us in the either/or dualistic thinking that is the central ideological component of all systems of domination in Western society. It implies that a choice has been made, that commitment to feminism is an act of will. It does not suggest that by committing oneself to feminism, the possibility of supporting other political movements is negated. [. . .]

The shift in expression from 'I am a feminist' to 'I advocate feminism' could serve as a useful strategy for eliminating the focus on identity and lifestyle. It could serve as a way women who are concerned about feminism as well as other political movements could express their support while avoiding linguistic structures that give primacy to one particular group. It would also encourage greater exploration in feminist theory.

The shift in definition away from notions of social equality towards an emphasis on ending sexist oppression leads to a shift in attitudes in regard to the development of theory. Given the class nature of feminist movement so far, as well as racial hierarchies, developing theory (the guiding set of beliefs and principles that become the basis for action) has been a task particularly subject to the hegemonic dominance of white academic women. This has led many women outside the privileged race/class group to see the focus on developing theory, even the very use of the term, as a concern that functions only to reinforce the power of the elite group. Such reactions reinforce the sexist/racist/classist notion that developing theory is the domain of the white intellectual. Privileged white women active in feminist movement, whether liberal or radical in perspective, encourage black women to contribute 'experiential' work, personal life stories. Personal experiences are important to feminist movement but they cannot take the place of theory. [. . .]

Defining feminism as a movement to end sexist oppression is crucial for the development of theory because it is a starting point indicating the direction of exploration and analysis.

The foundation of future feminist struggle must be solidly based on a recognition of the need to eradicate the underlying cultural basis and causes of sexism and other forms of group oppression. Without challenging and changing these philosophical structures, no feminist reforms will have a long range impact.

[*Feminist Theory: From Margin to Centre* (Boston: South End Press, 1984), 17–31.]

TERESA DE LAURETIS

3   Aesthetic and Feminist Theory: Rethinking Women's Cinema

When Silvia Bovenschen in 1976 posed the question 'Is there a feminine aesthetic?', the only answer she could give was, yes and no: 'Certainly there is, if one is talking about aesthetic awareness and modes of sensory perception. Certainly not, if one is talking about an unusual variant of artistic production or about a painstakingly constructed theory of art.'[1] If this contradiction seems familiar to anyone even vaguely acquainted with the development of feminist thought over the past fifteen years, it is because it echoes a contradiction specific to, and perhaps even constitutive of, the women's movement itself: a twofold pressure, a simultaneous pull in opposite directions, a tension toward the positivity of politics, of affirmative action on behalf of women as social subjects, on one front, and the negativity inherent in the radical critique of patriarchal, bourgeois culture on the other. It is also the contradiction of women in language, as we attempt to speak as subjects of discourses which negate or objectify us through their representations. As Bovenschen put it, 'we are in a terrible bind. How do we speak? In what categories do we think? Is even logic a bit of virile trickery? . . . Are our desires and notions of happiness so far removed from cultural traditions and models?' (p. 119).

Not surprisingly, therefore, a similar contradiction was also central to the debate on women's cinema, its politics and its language, as it was articulated within Anglo-American film theory in the early 1970s in relation to feminist politics and the women's movement on the one hand and to artistic avant-garde practices and women's film-making on the other. There, too, the accounts of feminist film culture produced in the mid to late 1970s tended to emphasize a dichotomy between two concerns of the women's movement and two types of film work that seemed to be at odds with each other: one called for immediate documentation for purposes of political activism, consciousness-raising, self-expression or the search for 'positive images' of women; the other insisted on rigorous, formal work on the medium—or better, the cinematic apparatus, understood as a social technology—in order to analyse and disengage the ideological codes embedded in representation.

Thus, as Bovenschen deplores the 'opposition between feminist demands and artistic production' (p. 131), the tug of war in which women artists were caught between the movement's demands that women's art portray women's activities, document demonstrations, etc., and the formal demands of 'artistic activity and its concrete work with material and media', so does Laura Mulvey set out two successive moments of feminist film culture. First, she states, there was a period marked by the effort to change the *content* of cinematic representation (to present realistic images of women, to record women talking about their real-life experiences), a period 'characterized by a mixture of consciousness-raising and propaganda'.[2] This was followed by a second moment in which the concern with the language of representation as such became predominant, and the 'fascination with the cinematic process' led film-makers and critics to the 'use of and interest in the aesthetic principles and terms of reference provided by the avant-garde tradition' (p. 7).

In this latter period, the common interest of both avant-garde cinema and feminism in the politics of images, or the political dimension of aesthetic expression, made them turn to the theoretical debates on language and imaging that were going on outside of cinema, in semiotics, psychoanalysis, critical theory and the theory of ideology. Thus it was argued that, in order to counter the aesthetic of realism, which was hopelessly compromised with bourgeois ideology, as well as Hollywood cinema, avant-garde and feminist film-makers must take an oppositional stance against narrative 'illusionism' and in favour of formalism. The assumption was that 'foregrounding the process itself, privileging the signifier, necessarily disrupts aesthetic unity and forces the spectator's attention on the means of production of meaning' (p. 7).

While Bovenschen and Mulvey would not relinquish the political commitment of the movement and the need to construct other representations of woman, the way in which they posed the question of expression (a 'feminine aesthetic', a 'new language of desire') was couched in the terms of a traditional notion of art, specifically the one propounded by modernist aesthetics. Bovenschen's insight that what is being expressed in the decoration of the household and the body or in letters and other private forms of writing is in fact women's aesthetic needs and impulses, is a crucial one. But the importance of that insight is undercut by the very terms that define it: the 'pre-aesthetic realm'.

After quoting a passage from Sylvia Plath's The Bell Jar, Bovenschen comments (pp. 132–3):

Here the ambivalence once again: on the one hand we see aesthetic activity deformed, atrophied, but on the other we find, even within this restricted scope, socially creative impulses which, however, have no outlet for aesthetic development, no opportunities for growth. . . . [These activities] remained bound to everyday life, feeble attempts to make this sphere more aesthetically pleasing. But the price for this was narrow-mindedness. The object could never leave the realm in which it came into being, it remained tied to the household, it could never break loose and initiate communication.

Just as Plath laments that Mrs Willard's beautiful home-braided rug is not hung on the wall but put to the use for which it was made, and thus quickly spoiled of its beauty, so would Bovenschen have 'the object' of artistic creation leave its context of production and use-value in order to enter the 'artistic realm' and so to 'initiate communication'; that is to say, to enter the museum, the art gallery, the market. In other words, art is what is enjoyed publicly rather than privately, has an exchange value rather than a use-value, and that value is conferred by socially established aesthetic canons.

Mulvey, too, in proposing the destruction of narrative and visual pleasure as the foremost objective of women's cinema, hails an established tradition, albeit a radical one: the historic left avant-garde tradition that goes back to Eisenstein and Vertov (if not Méliès) and through Brecht reaches its peak of influence in Godard and, on the other side of the Atlantic, the tradition of American avant-garde cinema. 'The first blow against the monolithic accumulation of traditional film conventions (already undertaken by radical film-makers) is to free the look of the camera into its materiality in time and space and the look of the audience into dialectics, passionate detachment.'[3] But much as Mulvey and other avant-garde film-makers insisted that women's cinema ought to avoid a politics of emotions and seek to problematize the female spectator's identification with the on-screen image of woman, the response to Mulvey's theoretical writings, like the reception of her films (co-directed with Peter Wollen), showed no consensus. Feminist critics, spectators and film-makers remained doubtful. For example, Ruby Rich:

According to Mulvey, the woman is not visible in the audience which is perceived as male; according to Johnston, the woman is not visible on the screen.... How does one formulate an understanding of a structure that insists on our absence even in the face of our presence? What is there in a film with which a woman viewer identifies? How can the contradictions be used as a critique? And how do all these factors influence what one makes as a woman filmmaker, or specifically as a feminist filmmaker?[4]

The questions of identification, self-definition, the modes or the very possibility of envisaging oneself as subject—which the male avant-garde artists and theorists have also been asking, on their part, for almost one hundred years, even as they work to subvert the dominant representations or to challenge their hegemony—are fundamental questions for feminism. If identification is 'not simply one psychical mechanism among others, but the operation itself whereby the human subject is constituted', as Laplanche and Pontalis describe it, then it must be all the more important, theoretically and politically, for women who have never before represented ourselves as subjects, and whose images and subjectivities—until very recently, if at all—have not been ours to shape, to portray, or to create.[5]

There is indeed reason to question the theoretical paradigm of a subject–object dialectic, whether Hegelian or Lacanian, that subtends both the aesthetic and the scientific discourses of Western culture; for what that paradigm contains, what those discourses rest on, is the unacknowledged assumption of sexual difference: that the human subject, Man, is male. As in the originary distinction of classical myth reaching us through the Platonic tradition, human creation and all that is human—mind, spirit, history, language, art, or symbolic capacity—is defined in contradistinction to formless chaos, *phusis* or nature, to something that is female, matrix and matter; and on this primary binary opposition, all the others are modelled. As Lea Melandri states,

Idealism, the oppositions of mind to body, of rationality to matter, originate in a twofold concealment: of the woman's body and of labor power. Chronologically, however, even prior to the commodity and the labor power that has produced it, the matter which was negated in its concreteness and particularity, in its 'relative plural form,' is the woman's body. Woman enters history having already lost concreteness and singularity: she is the economic machine that reproduces the human species, and she is the Mother, an equivalent more universal than money, the most abstract measure ever invented by patriarchal ideology.[6]

That this proposition remains true when tested on the aesthetic of modernism or the major trends in avant-garde cinema from visionary to structural-materialist film, on the films of Stan Brakhage, Michael Snow or Jean-Luc Godard, but is not true of the films of Yvonne Rainer, Valie Export, Chantal Akerman or Marguerite Duras, for example; that it remains valid for the films of Fassbinder but not those of Ottinger, the films of Pasolini and Bertolucci but not Cavani's, and so on, suggests to me that it is perhaps time to shift the terms of the question altogether.

To ask of these women's films: what formal, stylistic or thematic markers point to a female presence behind the camera?, and hence to generalize and universalize, to say: this is the look and sound of women's cinema, this is its language—finally only means complying, accepting a certain definition of art, cinema and culture, and obligingly showing how women can and do 'contribute', pay their tribute, to 'society'. Put another way, to ask whether there is a feminine or female aesthetic, or a specific language of women's cinema, is to remain caught in the master's house and there, as Audre Lorde's suggestive metaphor warns us, to legitimate the hidden agendas of a culture we badly need to change. 'The master's tools will never dismantle the master's house'; cosmetic changes, she is telling us, will not be enough for the majority of women—women of colour, Black women, and white women as well; or in her own words, 'assimilation within a solely western-european her-story is not acceptable'.[7] It is time we listened. Which is not to say that we should dispense with rigorous analysis and experimentation on the formal processes of meaning production, including the production of narrative, visual pleasure and subject positions, but rather that feminist theory should now engage precisely in the redefinition of aesthetic and formal knowledge, much as women's cinema has been engaged in the transformation of vision.

Take Akerman's *Jeanne Dielman* (1975), a film about the routine, daily activities of a Belgian middle-class and middle-aged housewife, and a film where the pre-aesthetic is already fully aesthetic. This is not so, however, because of the beauty of its images, the balanced composition of its frames, the absence of the reverse shot, or the perfectly calculated editing of its still-camera shots into a continuous, logical and obsessive narrative space; but because it is a woman's actions, gestures, body, and look that define the space of our vision, the temporality and rhythms of perception, the horizon of meaning available to the spectator. So that narrative suspense is not built on the expectation of a 'significant event', a socially momentous act (which actually occurs, though unexpectedly and almost incidentally, one feels, toward the end of the film), but is produced by the tiny slips in Jeanne's routine, the small forgettings, the hesitations between real-time gestures as common and 'insignificant' as peeling potatoes, washing dishes or making coffee—and then not drinking it. What the film constructs—formally and artfully, to be sure—is a picture of female experience, of duration, perception, events, relationships and silences, which feels immediately and unquestionably true. And in this sense the 'pre-aesthetic' is *aesthetic* rather than *aestheticized*, as it is in films like Godard's *Two or Three Things I know about Her*, Polanski's *Repulsion*, or Antonioni's *Eclipse*. To say the same thing in another way, Akerman's film addresses the spectator as female.

The effort, on the part of the film-maker, to render a presence in the feeling of a gesture, to convey the sense of an experience that is subjective yet socially coded (and therefore recognizable), and to do so formally, working through her conceptual (one could say, theoretical) knowledge of film form, is averred by Chantal Akerman in an interview on the making of *Jeanne Dielman*:

I *do* think it's a feminist film because I give space to things which were never, almost never, shown in that way, like the daily gestures of a woman. They are the lowest in the hierarchy of film images. . . . But more than the content, it's because of the style. If you choose to show a woman's gestures so precisely, it's because you love them. In some way you recognize those gestures that have always been denied and ignored. I think that the real problem with women's films usually has nothing to do with the content. It's that hardly any women really have confidence enough to carry through on their feelings. Instead the content is the most simple and obvious thing. They deal with that and forget to look for formal ways to express what they are and what they want, their own rhythms, their own way of looking at things. A lot of women have unconscious contempt for their feelings. But I don't think I do. I have enough confidence in myself. So that's the other reason why I think it's a feminist film—not just what it says but *what* is shown and *how* it's shown.[8]

This lucid statement of poetics resonates with my own response as a viewer and gives me something of an explanation as to why I recognize in those unusual film images, in those movements, those silences and those looks, the ways of an experience all but unrepresented, previously unseen in film, though lucidly and unmistakably apprehended here. And so the statement cannot be dismissed with commonplaces such as authorial intention or intentional fallacy. As another critic and spectator points out, there are 'two logics' at work in this film, 'two modes of the feminine': character and director, image and camera, remain distinct yet interacting and mutually interdependent positions. Call them femininity and feminism, the one is made representable by the critical work of the other; the one is kept at a distance, constructed, 'framed', to be sure, and yet 'respected', 'loved', 'given space' by the other.[9] The two 'logics' remain separate: 'the camera look cannot be construed as the view of any character. Its interest extends beyond the fiction. The camera presents itself, in its evenness and predictability, as equal to Jeanne's precision. Yet the camera continues its logic throughout;

Jeanne's order is disrupted, and with the murder the text comes to its logical end since Jeanne then stops altogether. If Jeanne has, symbolically, destroyed the phallus, its order still remains visible all around her.'[10] Finally, then, the space constructed by the film is not only a textual or filmic space of vision, in frame and off—for an off-screen space is still inscribed in the images, although not sutured narratively by the reverse shot but effectively reaching toward the historical and social determinants which define Jeanne's life and place her in her frame. But beyond that, the film's space is also a critical space of analysis, an horizon of possible meanings which includes or extends to the spectator ('extends beyond the fiction') in so far as the spectator is led to occupy at once the two positions, to follow the two 'logics', and to perceive them as equally and concurrently true.

In saying that a film whose visual and symbolic space is organized in this manner *addresses its spectator as a woman*, regardless of the gender of the viewers, I mean that the film defines all points of identification (with character, image, camera) as female, feminine, or feminist. However, this is not as simple or self-evident a notion as the established film-theoretical view of cinematic identification, namely, that identification with the look is masculine and identification with the image is feminine. It is not self-evident precisely because such a view—which indeed correctly explains the working of dominant cinema—is now accepted: that the camera (technology), the look (voyeurism), and the scopic drive itself partake of the phallic and thus somehow are entities or figures of a masculine nature. [. . .]

The project of women's cinema, therefore, is no longer that of destroying or disrupting man-centred vision by representing its blind spots, its gaps or its repressed. The effort and challenge now are how to effect another vision: to construct other objects and subjects of vision, and to formulate the conditions of representability of another social subject. For the time being, then, feminist work in film seems necessarily focused on those subjective limits and discursive boundaries that mark women's division as gender-specific, a division more elusive, complex and contradictory than can be conveyed in the notion of sexual difference as it is currently used.

The idea that *a film may address the spectator as female*, rather than portray women positively or negatively, seems very important to me in the critical endeavour to characterize women's cinema as a cinema for, not only by, women. It is an idea not found in the critical writings I mentioned earlier, which are focused on the film, the object, the text. But rereading those essays today, one can see, and it is important to stress it, that the question of a filmic language or a feminine aesthetic has been articulated from the beginning in relation to the women's movement: 'the new grows only out of the work of confrontation' (Mulvey, p. 4); women's 'imagination constitutes the movement itself' (Bovenschen, p. 136); and in Claire Johnston's non-formalist view of women's cinema as counter-cinema, a feminist political strategy should reclaim, rather than shun, the use of film as a form of mass culture: 'In order to counter our objectification in the cinema, our collective fantasies must be released: women's cinema must embody the working through of desire: such an objective demands the use of the entertainment film'.[11]

Since the first women's film festivals in 1972 (New York, Edinburgh) and the first journal of feminist film criticism (*Women and Film*, published in Berkeley from 1972 to 1975), the question of women's expression has been one of both self-expression and communication with other women, a question at once of the creation/invention of new images and of the creation/imagining of new forms of community. If we re-think the problem of a specificity of women's cinema and aesthetic forms in this manner, in terms of address—who is making films for whom, who is looking and speaking, how, where—and to whom—then what has been seen as a rift, a division, an ideological split within feminist film culture between theory and practice, or between formalism and activism, may appear to be the very strength, the drive and productive heterogeneity of feminism. In their introduction to the recent collection, *Re-Vision: Essays in Feminist Film Criticism*, Mary Ann Doane, Patricia Mellencamp and Linda Williams point out:

If feminist work on film has grown increasingly theoretical, less oriented towards political action, this does not necessarily mean that theory itself is counter-productive to the cause of feminism, nor that the institutional form of the debates within feminism have simply reproduced a male model of academic competition. . . . Feminists sharing similar concerns collaborate in joint authorship and editorships, co-operative filmmaking and distribution arrangements. Thus, many of the political aspirations of the women's movement form an integral part of the very structure of feminist work in and on film.[12]

The 're-vision' of their title, borrowed from Adrienne Rich ('Re-vision— the act of looking back, of seeing with fresh eyes', writes Rich, is for women 'an act of survival'), refers to the project of reclaiming vision, of 'seeing difference differently', of displacing the critical emphasis from 'images of' women 'to the axis of vision itself—to the modes of organizing vision and hearing which result in the production of that "image"'.[13] I agree with the *Re-Vision* editors when they say that over the past decade feminist theory has moved 'from an analysis of difference as oppressive to a delineation and specification of difference as liberating, as offering the only possibility of radical change' (p. 12). But I believe that radical change requires that such specification not be limited to 'sexual difference', that is to say, a difference of women from men, female from male, or Woman from Man. Radical change requires a delineation and a better understanding of the difference of women from Woman, and that is to say as well, *the differences among women*. For there are, after all, different histories of women. There are women who masquerade and women who wear the veil; women invisible to men, in their society, but also women who are invisible to other women, in our society.[14]

The invisibility of Black women in white women's films, for instance, or of lesbianism in mainstream feminist criticism, is what Lizzie Borden's *Born in Flames* (1983) most forcefully represents, while at the same time constructing the terms of their visibility as subjects and objects of vision. Set in a hypothetical near-future time and in a place very much like lower Manhattan, with the look of a documentary (after Chris Marker) and the feel of contemporary science fiction writing (the post-new-wave science fiction of Samuel Delany, Joanna Russ, Alice Sheldon or Thomas Disch), *Born in Flames* shows how a 'successful' social democratic cultural revolution, now into its tenth year, slowly but surely reverts to the old patterns of male dominance, politics as usual, and the traditional left disregard for 'women's issues'. It is around this specific gender oppression, in its various forms, that several groups of women (Black women, Latinas, lesbians, single mothers, intellectuals, political activists, spiritual and punk performers and a Women's Army) succeed in mobilizing and joining together: not by ignoring but, paradoxically, by acknowledging their differences.

Like *Redupers* and *Jeanne Dielman*, Borden's film addresses the spectator as female, but it does not do so by portraying an experience which immediately feels one's own. On the contrary, its barely coherent narrative, its quick-paced shots and sound montage, the counterpoint of image and word, the diversity of voices and languages, and the self-conscious science-fictional frame of the story hold the spectator across a distance, projecting toward her its fiction like a bridge of difference. In short, what *Born in Flames* does for me, woman spectator, is exactly to allow me 'to see difference differently', to look at women with eyes I've never had before and yet my own; for, as it remarks the emphasis (the words are Audre Lorde's) on the 'interdependency of different strengths' in feminism, the film also inscribes the differences among women as *differences within women*.

Born in Flames addresses me as a woman and a feminist living in a particular moment of women's history, the United States today. The film's events and images take place in what science fiction calls a parallel universe, a time and a place elsewhere that look and feel like here and now, yet are not, just as I (and all women) live in a culture that is and is not our own. In that unlikely, but not impossible universe of the film's fiction, the women come together in the very struggle that divides and differentiates them. Thus what it portrays for me, what elicits my identification with the film and gives me, spectator, a place in it, is the contradiction of my own history and the personal/political difference within myself.

'The relationship between history and so-called subjective processes', says Helen Fehervary in a recent discussion of women's film in Germany, 'is not a matter of grasping the truth in history as some objective entity, but in finding the truth of the experience. Evidently, this kind of experiential immediacy has to do with women's own history and self-consciousness.'[15] That, how, and why our histories and our consciousness are different, divided, even conflicting, is what women's cinema can analyse, articulate, reformulate. And, in so doing, it can help us create something else to be, as Toni Morrison says of her two heroines: 'Because each had discovered years before that they were neither white nor male, and that all freedom and triumph was forbidden to them, they had set about creating something else to be.'[...]

The gender-specific division of women in language, the distance from official culture, the urge to imagine new forms of community as well as to create new images ('creating something else to be'), and the consciousness of a 'subjective factor' at the core of all kinds of work—domestic, industrial, artistic, critical or political work—are some of the themes articulating the particular relations of subjectivity, meaning and experience which en-gender the social subject as female. These themes, encapsulated in the phrase 'the personal is political', have been formally explored in women's cinema in several ways: through the disjunction of image and voice, the reworking of narrative space, the elaboration of strategies of address that alter the forms and balances of traditional representation. From the inscription of subjective space and duration inside the frame (a space of repetitions, silences and discontinuities in *Jeanne Dielman*) to the construction of other discursive social spaces (the heterogeneous but intersecting spaces of the women's 'networks' in *Born in Flames*), women's cinema has undertaken a redefinition of both private and public space that may well answer the call for 'a new language of desire' and may actually have met the demand for the 'destruction of visual pleasure', if by that one alludes to the traditional, classical and modernist canons of aesthetic representation.

So, once again, the contradiction of women in language and culture is manifested in a paradox: most of the terms by which we speak of the construction of the female social subject in cinematic representation bear in their visual form the prefix 'de-' to signal the deconstruction or the destructuring, if not destruction, of the very thing to be represented. We speak of the de-aestheticization of the female body, the desexualization of violence, the de-Oedipalization of narrative, and so forth. Rethinking women's cinema in this way, I may provisionally answer Bovenschen's question thus: there is a certain configuration of issues and formal problems that have been consistently articulated in what we call women's cinema. The way in which they have been expressed and developed, both artistically and critically, seems to point less to a 'feminine aesthetic' than to a feminist *de-aesthetic*. And if the word sounds awkward or inelegant to you . . .

['Aesthetic and Feminist Theory: Rethinking Women's Cinema', *New German Critique*, 84 (1985); repr. in E. Dierdre Pribram, *Female Spectators: Looking at Film and Television* (London and New York: Verso, 1988), 174–87.]

4 Speaking/Writing/Feminism

My mother describes me at eleven months, a particularly small baby, bundled, propped and harnessed in my pram outside our New York apartment house, addressing startled passers-by with the adult precision of newly learnt speech: 'Hellow, pretty lady!' Speaking came early, came easy, eliciting surprise, approval and even tangible reward. This first gratifying experience of public speaking (I cannot remember it) seemed to set a pattern which allowed me the courage forever after to break through the patriarchal convention that enjoined women to deferential silence. I have always enjoyed the sound of my own voice, even when it has irritated and offended others. As a young political woman my lack of inhibition about public speaking frequently got me into trouble with the male-dominated left. It also, occasionally, got me where I not so secretly wanted to be—on a soapbox, addressing a crowd. In school, at university, but most of all as an academic, this 'unnatural' articulacy has helped to mark me out as a rebel. In professional gatherings where women are in a very small minority, it is normal for them to accept their marginality by staying relatively quiet. My frequent interventions ensure that my social behaviour as well as my opinions are displeasing to my colleagues. In the last fourteen years a very large part of my political and intellectual life has taken place inside the Women's Movement. Of all the changes that feminism has made in my private and public behaviour none has been so hard to learn or to keep to as shutting up so that others may speak.

All forms of public performance seemed to come from a desire that I could neither rationalize or suppress and that overrode self-consciousness. By the time I was nine I had found a relatively acceptable outlet in acting. From then until my early twenties I had no other ambition, and while acting in no way contained my appetite for oral expression, it helped to explain it in terms of an artistic aspiration which could only spring from an eccentric expressive temperament. Nevertheless speaking up, at home, at school, on the stage, always seemed to involve a sense of danger and challenge which I fed on. Writing, on the other hand, was to begin with an act of conformity with family and school. Writing in my Jewish, middle-class intellectual family was the most approved activity. Books and the written word were so highly valued (I was allowed to throw almost anything in a tantrum *except* a book) that my own written efforts were usually accompanied by a kind of terror that they would be derivative, cliché, inauthentic. From my first attempt at fiction, a garbled pastiche of *Lamb's Tales from Shakespeare* called 'The Lovers', to this piece in process, all my narrative or reflexive writing, including letters and diaries, has felt haunted by the language of others. Every fragment of imaginative prose or verse from the age of six onwards has given me that stale ghosted feeling *as I wrote it*, as well as when I read it back afterwards. It took me a long time to find a voice and a genre of writing that gave me the sense that I was cutting across the 'givenness' of social relations.

The difference in my experience of oral and written expression seems worth pursuing for a bit longer, since the causes and effects of the social sanction against women's speech and writing has, for some years now, been the central feminist issue that shapes all my research. Inside my family, as I have said, all the unspoken pressures and desires on and for me, as a precociously clever child, were towards channelling my talents into some sort of writing. To write was to do what my father did and what my mother valued. Talking, or more accurately, talking back, got me into endless trouble. My childhood and adolescence was one long struggle with a paternal authority which had imagined a gentler, more docile daughter. Neither of my parents thought much of my dramatic ambitions or talents though they did nothing to discourage me; on the contrary they made considerable sacrifices of time and money to help me along. Yet I could not fail to understand their disappointment. A sort of political puritanism made the exploitation of one's own voice and body too bound up with egotism and personal desires. In writing, the family morality seemed to say, the suspect personal gratifications of self-expression were reduced to an acceptable, ethical level through the displacement of words from mouth to printed page. This implicit critique of theatrical self-presentation became linked for me with the whole range of frivolous, sensual, self-indulgent activities from dressing up—an elaborate event in the 1950s—to secret masturbation. All these were practices my parents disapproved of, or would have done, I was sure, if they had known about them. Acting, speaking, showing off my adolescent body, worst of all touching it, were, I was convinced, tainted in my parents' eyes with egotism in general and female narcissism in particular. Dressing up and showing off were complicit in their minds with the worst aspects of femininity as the dominant culture decreed it. How much of this was projected guilt is hard to tell. I couldn't have put all these impressions into words in my teens. Still, if anyone had asked me what their model of a good socialist woman was I would have been able to describe her. She was the woman who had ignored her emergent sexuality in adolescence, sublimated desire, dressed and spoke soberly and used the last leisured years of childhood to learn that she might teach. I was a child of the 1950s and Rosa Luxemburg was a remote and scary figure. My heroine, in so far as I had one, was Sarah Bernhardt. As Hamlet.

The 1950s for left-wing Americans were a frightening, demoralizing decade. Our family clung together. I kept secrets that I had never been told. I shared my parents' politics—(how could I not?—I still do in great part) and found it difficult to criticize the social inflections of their views. In some upside-down way writing became saturated with a set of ethical prescriptions that I could neither refuse nor wholly accept. It became what others desired of me, and only sometimes what I wanted for and of myself. It became the other of an illicit, politically incorrect femininity in which I desperately wanted to be inscribed, the other too, of my formidable and undervalued ambitions as an actress. Although I gave voice to the words of the playwright on the local stage it was there, above all, that I felt I uttered myself. For a very long time, longer than I care to think, even *now*, writing is too often the act of a dutiful daughter. It was at my desk and my typewriter that I felt spoken, not by the culture that disapproved of women writing only a little less than it disliked women speaking in public, but by that powerful alternative culture in which I was raised.

In my personal history, then, the psychic contradiction between woman's speech and her femininity was given an eccentric twist. If the construction of femininity roughly follows the dominant psychic structures of a given society, any particular instance will have its own inflection. While I understand, as an abstraction, that my wilfully raised voice usurps 'the place and tone of a man', for me speaking out is also deeply entwined with femininity, with, for example, a conventional desire to be looked at. That extended angry verbal struggle with my father—what did I have but words to get his attention, to intervene between him and my mother, and what did he give me back but words? For many women sexuality is spoken through their social silence. For me, language did what my meagre child's body (I could pass easily for ten or eleven at seventeen) could never do. In recent years I have been giving more and more public lectures, often to audiences of women only, but invariably on feminist subjects. My talks are never given from a written text; I rarely refer to notes. These occasions bring the ethical and political imperatives through which I was raised together with my irrepressible and unregenerate desire to speak out, to have a direct, unmediated contact with an audience. Very often the subject of these talks mirrors the meaning of the event for me—an historical and theoretical account of the related suppression of women's speech, writing and sexuality.

There still remains the difficult subject of this essay—my own writing. I have deferred it as long as I could, deferred the actual writing of this section for months because I thought that I could not bear to see what I would say. As I get older—I am forty-two as I write this—the possibility of writing has largely replaced the possibility of new emotional and sexual adventures as a subject for fantasy. It is the activity in which I would now prefer to recognize myself. 'Writer' ranks way above 'mother', 'teacher', 'speaker', as a vocational identity. As a young woman, writing seemed to threaten femininity—to leave me stranded on the dry shores of the incest taboo, my father's daughter and no one's lover. Now, when I feel sure that no one will love me in the body who does not first love me for my words, writing promises too much in the way of fantasized libidinal reward instead of too little. There seems often to be too much invested in its success: political effectiveness, professional status, recognition within feminism, the self-respect that comes with completing a self-imposed task, and sometimes pleasure in the process itself. How did this puritanical work, so often in my teens and twenties an escape from the insistent desire of and for a man, become, in my thirties, the process and polemic of desire? What follows is a narrative that has been only partly worked through. I do not see it as typical or representative. I offer it with some diffidence as a history that might contribute something to the understanding of the relationship of women to writing.

In 1973 I was separated from my husband with a five-year-old child to support, a university job that I needed to hold on to and an ugly battle to acquire academic tenure ahead. I was thirty-three years old and had been working on an unfinished DPhil thesis for some seven years. The subject—Tom Paine and the radical press in the late eighteenth century—was partly inherited from my father who as a young man had adopted Paine as one of his radical heroes. I too was drawn to Paine for his marvellous popular rhetoric, his democratic politics, his personal eccentricities and his vision of self-determination based on a dream of universal literacy. Paine was a figure easily appropriated by the new left politics in which I had been involved in America. Perhaps he was a bit too like the young male left who wanted the women in the movement as tea-makers, typists, envelope lickers, and, in the memorable words of Stokely Carmichael—'prone'. Certainly the subject was top-heavy with associations that made me nervous of it as well as fascinated by it. In any case I was working on this thesis at some disadvantage, 3,000 miles away from not one but three supervisors, a benign but internally divided trinity of male historians. By 1973 the subject had gone a bit stale on me and I had outgrown the liberal paradigm in which the original project was couched without having acquired the theoretical tools to reformulate it. I had made myself politically extremely unpopular at my workplace by taking an active and vocal part in a bitter row about free speech and the Vietnam War, which split my department and made my subject chairman into an enemy. Even so, he thought well of the thesis, and it seemed crucial that I complete it in order to be given tenure.

At this point, with everything pressing me towards doing what was asked of me by my institution, I abandoned the dissertation, not formally but quite definitively, and began an entirely different project—the construction of a critical anthology of women's poetry. I found a publisher, negotiated a fee and finished the book in about eighteen months. It, and not my uncompleted work on Paine, was assessed finally as the research that secured my job. I have never touched the thesis again, nor have I ever written to my supervisors to explain why. I knew that it was impossible for me to write anything more for the judgement of those fair-minded, affectionate men, nor could I find a language adequate to explain my defection as something other than disability.

Perhaps I should have sent them a copy of the anthology, for in the introductory essay I described women's embattled relationship to poetry, the most highly valued discourse in western culture. There, too, I spoke of the ways in which writing poetry involved women in complex moments that were simultaneously resistant and submissive to the dominant patriarchal culture. There were analogies to my own history, but I did not try to think about them. I never sent my supervisors either the book or a letter of explanation; my boorish silence must have satisfied some need in me for a violent and irrevocable break with a project too intimately tied up with my family. For when I abandoned the dissertation I also seem to have stopped writing simply through and for my father's desire. My thesis especially, but much of the writing I had done as undergraduate and post-graduate were, I now think, intended above all to win my father's approval. Metaphorically these pieces had use value only; I made them for domestic consumption. In so far as they served to further my career as an academic that career too became bound to my father's will, in ways that made me, in the first years as a teacher, dislike this 'second choice' profession as if it were a forced marriage.

At that particular moment in my life, the marketplace offered and supported a kind of freedom, capitalist in its terms, that I could not find in the academy. Because of my personal history, writing for the university system became writing for patriarchy par excellence. It was extraordinarily important to me that my anthology was paid for, circulated and sold, for at that time feminism had almost no purchase or currency within English universities, and especially not within literary studies. In evading some of the conditions of production imposed by the institution and in redefining my subject I had, at last, found a place from which I could write, as I could speak, to a wider audience than one man.

The 'self' that occupies the place-from-which-I-can-write exists as a necessary fiction for writing, a sometimes fantasy of autonomy and authority that persists, if I am exceptionally lucky, until the end of the writing project. There is a temptation, which has found its way into much recent feminist criticism, to celebrate this writing identity both as a temporary escape from femininity, and as a model for a post-feminist female identity that will endure through the history of an individual. It is perhaps a common-sense indulgence to see woman in this supposed moment of defiance and rupture as woman as she must become outside and beyond patriarchal inscription. While I think that defiance is a component of the act of writing for women, I would now prefer to emphasize the fluctuant nature of subjectivity that the contrast between the writing and non-writing identity highlights.

In the early stages of thinking about women and writing I had, in common with other feminists, talked mostly about the ways in which women were denied access to something I have called 'full' subjectivity. While any term so abstract evokes more meaning than it can possibly contain in a given context, what I was working towards was a description of a position within culture where women could, without impediment, exist as speaking subjects. I now think that this way of posing the question of writing/speaking and subjectivity is misleading. It assumes, for instance, that *men* write from a realized and realizable autonomy in which they are, in fact, not fantasy, the conscious, constant and triumphant sources of the meanings they produce. This assumption is part of an unreconstructed romantic definition of the poet as it was most eloquently expressed in Wordsworth's 1800 introduction to *Lyrical Ballads*. Here the poet has a universalized access to experience of all kinds, feels things more deeply, and expresses those feelings 'recollected in tranquillity' for all men. It did not take much thought to point out how difficult it was for women to appropriate this romantic definition of genius and transcendence, given the contemporary restraints on their experience and the contempt in which their gender-specific feelings were held. A more interesting question was about the status of the definition itself, which even today has enormous currency within traditional literary criticism. How far was it an ideological fiction? In what sense could any writing or writer or indeed any *actor* in history *be* that romantic subject? For if one were to accept a modern re-working of the romantic definition of the creative process, then as a feminist 'full subjectivity' would become a political goal for feminism, as well as a precondition for all acts of struggle and intervention, writing included.

In the last few years I have come round to a very different perspective on the problem, drawn from Marxist and feminist appropriations of psychoanalytic and structuralist theories, but confirmed, I think, by my own and other women's fragmented experience of writing and identity. Rather than approach women's difficulty in positioning themselves as writers as a question of barred access to some durable psychic state to which all humans should and can aspire, we might instead see their experience as foregrounding the inherently unstable and split character of all human subjectivity. Within contemporary western culture the act of writing and the romantic ideologies of individual agency and power are tightly bound together, although that which is written frequently resists and exposes this unity of the self as ideology. At both the psychic and social level, always intertwined, women's subordinate place within culture makes them less able to embrace or be held by romantic individualism with all its pleasures and dangers. The instability of 'femininity' as female identity is a specific instability, an eccentric relation to the construction of sexual difference, but it also points to the fractured and fluctuant condition of all consciously held identity, the impossibility of a willfull, unified and cohered subject.

Romantic ideologies of the subject suppress this crucial and potentially hopeful incoherence, or make its absence a sign of weakness and thus an occasion for mourning or reparation. Feminism has been caught up far too often in this elegiac mood, even when on other fronts it has mounted an impressive critique of Western rationalism as a phallocratic discourse of power. One option within feminism to combat the seeming weakness which inheres in women's split subjectivity has been to reassert an economy of control, to deny the constant effect of unconscious processes in utterance and practice, and to pose an unproblematic rationalism for women themselves, a feminist pysche in control of femininity. For myself, this avenue is closed, if only because it makes me feel so demoralized, a not-good-enough feminist as I was a not-good-enough daughter. I would rather see subjectivity as always in process and contradiction, even female subjectivity, structured, divided and denigrated through the matrices of sexual difference. I see this understanding as part of a more optimistic political scenario than the ones I have been part of, one that can and ought to lead to a politics that will no longer overvalue control, rationality and individual power, and which, instead, tries to understand human desire, struggle and agency as they are mobilized through a more complicated, less finished and less heroic psychic schema.

This perspective makes better sense of my own experience as writer and speaker, both as a dutiful daughter and now as a feminist, and gives me some clues as to what enabled the passage between these two moments. Neither activity or position has given me a security of identity nor do I any longer see that as a meaningful objective. However, the stakes and contradictions involved in writing and speaking as a feminist have shifted, although not always in easily apparent ways. The way I write has hardly changed since I was an undergraduate. I always favoured a rich, fruity prose, leavened and larded with word play and jokes that fleshed out the didactic skeleton of my arguments and broke up the high seriousness of academic discourse. Puns and risqué metaphors are a way of making the hard puritanical business of writing more fun, more libidinal, and therefore, more mine. I never need to tell jokes when I am giving a talk, nor do they seem to be necessary to hold an audience to a serious theme. Speaking involves a bodily presence, is itself a pleasure. However, in the teaching situation, in the solemn, tense occasion of tutorial or seminar, vulgar wisecracks spring to my lips unbidden. I understand better now, why I make these formal rhetorical choices. That knowledge in itself has changed the condition of utterance.

Tillie Olsen, the American writer and critic, has explored the multiple ways in which women's silences as writers have been overdetermined in western culture. Her overview is always both Marxist and feminist, but she always emphasizes the importance of the individual situation. In my own family history the dominant prejudices against female utterance were only ever mobilized against my speaking voice. It is that voice from a position of opposition that has emerged confident, playful and fluent. My pleasure and confidence in writing has been as hard to achieve, as unreliable, though at certain rare moments as thrilling, as sexual pleasure. Familial disavowal and/

or support always has complex and mediated effects in relation to dominant ideologies. All my published writing has been within and for feminism. These days, however, the conditions of production have shifted. Now I write into a constituted discipline of recognized intellectual importance. I write for women, rather than as in my early work, constructing a polemic directed against men. And I have noticed a change in the content and direction of my work that is a bit worrying. The critical sections of the poetry anthology were almost always positive appraisals, a revision and revaluation of lost or dismissed writing. These days I have moved away from mildly eulogistic projects, and instead have engaged in a series of fairly heavy debates with other feminists and other feminisms, historical and contemporary. This internal polemic suggests that the habit of writing in opposition is deeply ingrained, in fact the only tolerable mode of writing for me. Even within the women's movement that has given purpose and meaning to my life and my words, I remain something of an ungrateful child.

[*Sea Changes: Culture and Feminism* (London: Verso, 1986), 219–28.]

JANE TOMPKINS

5 Me and My Shadow

I wrote this essay in answer to Ellen Messer-Davidow's 'The philosophical bases of feminist literary criticisms', which appeared in the Fall 1987 issue of *New Literary History.* [. . .]

There are two voices inside me answering, answering to, Ellen's essay. One is the voice of a critic who wants to correct a mistake in the essay's view of epistemology. The other is the voice of a person who wants to write about her feelings (I have wanted to do this for a long time but have felt too embarrassed). This person feels it is wrong to criticize the essay philosophically, and even beside the point: because a critique of the kind the critic has in mind only insulates academic discourse further from the issues that make feminism matter. That make *her* matter. The critic, meanwhile, believes such feelings, and the attitudes that inform them, are soft-minded, self-indulgent, and unprofessional.

These beings exist separately but not apart. One writes for professional journals, the other in diaries, late at night. One uses words like 'context' and 'intelligibility', likes to win arguments, see her name in print, and give graduate students hardheaded advice. The other has hardly ever been heard from. She had a short story published once in a university literary magazine, but her works exist chiefly in notebooks and manila folders labelled 'Journal' and 'Private'. This person talks on the telephone a lot to her friends, has seen psychiatrists, likes cappuccino, worries about the state of her soul. Her father is ill right now, and one of her friends recently committed suicide.

The dichotomy drawn here is false—and not false. I mean in reality there's no split. It's the same person who feels and who discourses about epistemology. The problem is that you can't talk about your private life in the course of doing your professional work. You have to pretend that epistemology, or whatever you're writing about, has nothing to do with your life, that it's more exalted, more important, because it (supposedly) *transcends* the merely personal. Well, I'm tired of the conventions that keep discussions of epistemology, or James Joyce, segregated from meditations on what is happening outside my window or inside my heart. The public–private dichotomy, which is to say, the public–private *hierarchy*, is a founding condition of female oppression. I say to hell with it. The reason I feel embarrassed at my own attempts to speak personally in a professional context is that I have been conditioned to feel that way. That's all there is to it.

I think people are scared to talk about themselves, that they haven't got the guts to do it. I think readers want to know about each other. Sometimes, when a writer introduces some personal bit of story into an essay, I can hardly contain my pleasure. I love writers who write about their own experience. I feel I'm being nourished by them, that I'm being allowed to enter into a personal relationship with them. That I can match my own experience up with theirs, feel cousin to them, and say, yes, that's how it is.

When he casts his leaves forth upon the wind [said Hawthorne], the author addresses, not the many who will fling aside his volume, or never take it up, but the few who will understand him.... As if the printed book, thrown at large on the wide world, were certain to find out the divided segment of the writer's own nature, and complete his circle of existence by bringing him into communion with it.... And so as thoughts are frozen and utterance, benumbed unless the speaker stand in some true relation with this audience—it may be pardonable to imagine that a friend, a kind and apprehensive, though not the closest friend, is listening to our talk.   (Nathaniel Hawthorne, 'The Custom-House', *The Scarlet Letter and Other Tales of the Puritans*, ed. with introd. and notes by Harry Levin (Boston: Houghton Mifflin, 1960–1), 5–6.)

Hawthorne's sensitivity to the relationship that writing implies is rare in academic prose, even when the subject would seem to make awareness of the reader inevitable. Alison Jaggar gave a lecture recently that crystallized the problem. Western epistemology, she argued, is shaped by the belief that emotion should be excluded from the process of attaining knowledge. Because women in our culture are not simply encouraged but *required* to be the bearers of emotion, which men are culturally conditioned to repress, an epistemology which excludes emotions from the process of attaining knowledge radically undercuts women's epistemic authority. The idea that the conventions defining legitimate sources of knowledge overlapped with the conventions defining appropriate gender behavior (male) came to me as a blinding insight. I saw that I had been socialized from birth to feel and act in ways that automatically excluded me from participating in the culture's most valued activities. No wonder I felt so uncomfortable in the postures academic prose forced me to assume; it was like wearing men's jeans.

Ellen Messer-Davidow's essay participates—as Jaggar's lecture and my précis of it did—in the conventions of Western rationalism. It adopts the impersonal, technical vocabulary of the epistemic ideology it seeks to dislocate. The political problem posed by my need to reply to the essay is this: to adhere to the conventions is to uphold a male standard of rationality that militates against women's being recognized as culturally legitimate sources of knowledge. To break with the convention is to risk not being heard at all.

This is how I would reply to Ellen's essay if I were to do it in the professionally sanctioned way. [. . .]

Messer-Davidow assumes that if we change our epistemology, our practice as critics will change, too. Specifically, she wants us to give up the subject–object theory, in which 'knowledge is an abstract representation of objective existence', for a theory which says that what counts as knowledge is a function of situation and perspective. So far, so good. The trouble is she believes that it follows from this latter theory that knowledge will become more equitable, more self-aware, and more humane.

I disagree. Knowing that my knowledge is perspectival, language-based, culturally constructed, or what have you, does not change in the slightest the things I believe to be true. All that it changes is what I think about how we get knowledge. The insight that my ideas are all products of the situation I occupy in the world applies to all of my ideas equally (including the idea that knowledge is culturally based); and to all of everybody else's ideas as well. So where does this get us? Right back to where we were before, mainly. I still believe what I believe and, if you differ with me, think that you are wrong. If I want to change your mind I still have to persuade you that I am right by using evidence, reasons, chains of inference, citations of authority, analogies, illustrations, and so on. Believing that what I believe comes from my being in a particular cultural framework does not change my relation to my beliefs. I still believe them just as much as if I thought they came from God, or the laws of nature, or my autonomous self.

Here endeth the epistle.

But while I think Ellen is wrong in thinking that a change of epistemology can mean a change in the kinds of things we think, I am in sympathy with the ends she has in view. This sympathy prompts me to say that my professionally correct reply is not on target. Because the target, the goal, rather, is not to be fighting over these questions, trying to beat the other person down. (What the goal is, it is harder to say.) Intellectual debate, if it were in the right spirit, would be wonderful. But I don't know how to be in the right spirit, exactly, can't make points without sounding rather superior and smug. Most of all, I don't know how to enter the debate without leaving everything else behind—the birds outside my window, my grief over Janice, just myself as a person sitting here in stockinged feet, a little bit chilly because the windows are open, and thinking about going to the bathroom. But not going yet.

I find that when I try to write in my 'other' voice, I am immediately critical of it. It wobbles, vacillates back and forth, is neither this nor that. The voice in which I write about epistemology is familiar, I know how it ought to sound. This voice, though, I hardly know. I don't even know if it has anything to say. But if I never write in it, it never will. So I have to try. (That is why, you see, this doesn't sound too good. It isn't a practiced performance, it hasn't got a surface. I'm asking you to bear with me while I try, hoping that this, what I write, will express something you yourself have felt or will help you find a part of yourself that you would like to express.)

The thing I want to say is that I've been hiding a part of myself for a long time. I've known it was there but I couldn't listen because there was no place for this person in literary criticism. The criticism I would like to write would always take off from personal experience. Would always be in some way a chronicle of my hours and days. Would speak in a voice which can talk about everything, would reach out to a reader like me and touch me where I want to be touched. [. . .]

The father tongue is spoken from above. It goes one way. No answer is expected, or heard.

. . . The mother tongue, spoken or written, expects an answer. It is conversation, a word the root of which means 'turning together.' The mother tongue is language not as mere communication, but as relation, relationship. It connects. . . . Its power is not in dividing but in binding. . . . We all know it by heart. John have you got your umbrella I think it's going to rain. Can you come play with me? If I told you once I told you a hundred times. . . . O what am I going to do? . . . Pass the soy sauce please. Oh, shit . . . You look like what the cat dragged in. (pp. 3–4)

Much of what I'm saying elaborates or circles around these quotes from LeGuin. I find that having released myself from the duty to say things I'm not interested in, in a language I resist, I feel free to entertain other people's voices. Quoting them becomes a pleasure of appreciation rather than the obligatory giving of credit, because when I write in a voice that is not struggling to be heard through the screen of a forced language, I no longer feel that it is not I who am speaking, and so, there is more room for what others have said.

One sentence in Ellen's essay stuck out for me the first time I read it and the second and the third: 'In time we can build a synchronous account of our subject matters as we glissade among them and turn upon ourselves' (p. 79).

What attracted me to the sentence was the 'glissade'. Fluidity, flexibility, versatility, mobility. Moving from one thing to another without embarrassment. It is a tenet of feminist rhetoric that the personal is political, but who in the academy acts on this where language is concerned? We all speak the father tongue, which is impersonal, while decrying the fathers' ideas. All of what I have written so far is in a kind of watered-down expository prose. Not much imagery. No description of concrete things. Only that one word, 'glissade'.

> Like black swallows swooping and gliding
> in a flurry of entangled loops and curves...

Two lines of a poem I memorized in high school are what the word 'glissade' called to mind. Turning upon ourselves. Turning, weaving, bending, unbending, moving in loops and curves.

I don't believe we can ever turn upon ourselves in the sense Ellen intends. You can't get behind the thing that casts the shadow. *You* cast the shadow. As soon as you turn, the shadow falls in another place. Is still your shadow. You have not got 'behind' yourself. That is why self-consciousness is not the way to make ourselves better than we are.

Just me and my shadow, walkin' down the avenue.

It is a beautiful day here in North Carolina. The first day that is both cool and sunny all summer. After a terrible summer, first drought, then heat-wave, then torrential rain, trees down, flooding. Now, finally, beautiful weather. A tree outside my window just brushed by red, with one fully red leaf. (This is what I want you to see. A person sitting in stockinged feet looking out of her window—a floor to ceiling rectangle filled with green, with one red leaf. The season poised, sunny and chill, ready to rush down the incline into autumn. But perfect, and still. Not going yet.)

How can we speak personally to one another and yet not be self-centered? How can we be part of the great world and yet remain loyal to ourselves?

It seems to me that I am trying to write out of my experience without acknowledging any discontinuity between this and the subject matter of the profession I work in. And at the same time find that I no longer want to write about that subject matter, as it appears in Ellen's essay. I am, on the one hand, demanding a connection between literary theory and my own life, and asserting, on the other, that there is no connection.

But here is a connection. I learned what epistemology I know from my husband. I think of it as more his game than mine. It's a game I enjoy playing but which I no longer need or want to play. I want to declare my independence of it, of him. (Part of what is going on here has to do with a need I have to make sure I'm not being absorbed in someone else's personality.) What I am breaking away from is both my conformity to the conventions of a male professional practice and my intellectual dependence on my husband. How can I talk about such things in public? How can I *not*.

Last night I saw a movie called *Gunfight at the OK Corral*, starring Burt Lancaster and Kirk Douglas. The movie is patently about the love-relationship between the characters these men play—Wyatt Earp and Doc Holliday. The women in the movie are merely pawns that serve in various ways to reflect the characters of the men, and to advance the story of their relationship to one another. There is a particularly humiliating part, played by Jo Van Fleet, the part of Doc Holliday's mistress—Kate Fisher—whom he treats abominably (everybody in the movie acknowledges this, it's not just me saying so). This woman is degraded over and over again. She is a whore, she is a drunkard, she is a clinging woman, she betrays the life of Wyatt Earp in order to get Doc Holliday back, she is *no longer young* (perhaps this is her chief sin). And her words are always in vain, they are chaff, less than nothing, another sign of her degradation.

Now Doc Holliday is a similarly degraded character. He used to be a dentist and is now a gambler, who lives to get other people's money away from them; he is a drunk, and he abuses the woman who loves him. But his weaknesses, in the perspective of the movie, are glamorous. He is irresistible, charming, seductive, handsome, witty, commanding; it's no wonder Wyatt Earp falls for him, who wouldn't? The degradation doesn't stick to Kirk Douglas; it is all absorbed by his female counterpart, the 'slut,' Jo Van Fleet. We are embarrassed every time she appears on the screen, because every time, she is humiliated further.

What enrages me is the way women are used as extensions of men, mirrors of men, devices for showing men off, devices for helping men get what they want. They are never there in their own right, or rarely. The world of the Western contains no women.

Sometimes I think *the world* contains no women.

Why am I so angry?

My anger is partly the result of having been an only child who caved in to authority very early on. As a result I've built up a huge storehouse of hatred and resentment against people in authority over me (mostly male). Hatred and resentment and attraction.

Why should poor men be made the object of this old pent-up anger? (Old anger is the best anger, the meanest, the truest, the most intense. Old anger is pure because it's been dislocated from its source for so long, has had the chance to ferment, to feed on itself for so many years, so that it is nothing but anger. All cause, all relation to the outside world, long since sloughed off, withered away. The rage I feel inside me now is the distillation of forty-six years. It has had a long time to simmer, to harden, to become adamantine, a black slab that glows in the dark.)

Are all feminists fueled by such rage? Is the molten lava of millenia of hatred boiling below the surface of every essay, every book, every syllabus, every newsletter, every little magazine? I imagine that I can open the front of my stomach like a door, reach in, and pluck from memory the rooted sorrow, pull it out, root and branch. But where, or rather, who, would I be then? I am attached to this rage. It is a source of identity for me. It is a motivator, an explainer, a justifier, a no-need-to-say-more greeter at the door. If I were to eradicate this anger somehow, what would I do? Volunteer work all day long?

A therapist once suggested to me that I blamed on sexism a lot of stuff that really had to do with my own childhood. Her view was basically the one articulated in Alice Miller's *The Drama of the Gifted Child*, in which the good child has been made to develop a false self by parents who cathect the child narcissistically. My therapist meant that if I worked out some of my problems—as she understood them, on a psychological level—my feminist rage would subside.

Maybe it would, but that wouldn't touch the issue of female oppression. Here is what Miller says about this:

Political action can be fed by the unconscious anger of children who have been . . . misused, imprisoned, exploited, cramped, and drilled. . . . If, however, disillusionment and the resultant mourning can be lived through . . ., then social and political disengagement do not usually follow, but the patient's actions are freed from the compulsion to repeat. (p. 101)

According to Miller's theory, the critical voice inside me, the voice I noticed butting in, belittling, doubting, being wise, is 'the contemptuous introject.' The introjection of authorities who manipulated me, without necessarily meaning to. I think that if you can come to terms with your 'contemptuous introject ', learn to forgive and understand them, your anger will go away. But if you're not angry, can you still act? Will you still care enough to write the letters, make the phone calls, attend the meetings? You need to find another center within yourself from which to act. A center of outgoing, outflowing, giving feelings. Love instead of anger. I'm embarrassed to say words like this because I've been taught they are mushy and sentimental and smack of cheap popular psychology. I've been taught to look down on people who read M. Scott Peck and Leo Buscaglia and Harold Kushner, because they're people who haven't very much education, and because they're mostly women. Or if not women, then people who take responsibility for learning how to deal with their feelings, who take responsibility for marriages that are going bad, for children who are in trouble, for friends who need help, for themselves. The disdain for popular psychology and for words like 'love' and 'giving' is part of the police action that academic intellectuals wage ceaselessly against feeling, against women, against what is personal. The ridiculing of the 'touchy-feely,' of the 'Mickey Mouse,' of the sentimental (often associated with teaching that takes students' concerns into account), belongs to the tradition Alison Jaggar rightly characterized as founding knowledge in the denial of emotion. It is looking down on women, with whom feelings are associated, and on the activities with which women are identified: mother, nurse, teacher, social worker, volunteer.

So for a while I can't talk about epistemology. I can't deal with the philosophical bases of feminist literary criticisms. I can't strap myself psychically into an apparatus that will produce the right gestures when I begin to move. I have to deal with the trashing of emotion, and with my anger against it.

This one time I've taken off the straitjacket, and it feels so good.

['Me and My Shadow', in Linda Kauffmann (ed.), *Gender and Theory* (Oxford: Blackwell, 1989); parts originally appeared in *New Literary History*, 19 (Autumn 1987), 121–39.]

GAYATRI CHAKRAVORTY SPIVAK

6 French Feminism in an International Frame

A young Sudanese woman in the Faculty of Sociology at a Saudi Arabian University said to me, surprisingly: 'I have written a structural functionalist dissertation on female circumcision in the Sudan.' I was ready to forgive the sexist term 'female circumcision'. We have learned to say 'clitoridectomy' because others more acute than we have pointed out our mistake.

But Structural Functionalism? Where 'integration' is 'social control [which] defines and *enforces . . . a degree of solidarity*'? Where 'interaction, seen from the side of the economy,' is defined as 'consist[ing] of the supply of income and wealth applied to purposes strengthening the persistence of cultural patterns?'[1] Structural functionalism takes a 'disinterested' stance on society as functioning structure. Its implicit interest is to applaud a system—in this case sexual—because it functions. A description such as the one below makes it difficult to credit that this young Sudanese woman had taken such an approach to clitoridectomy:

In Egypt it is only the clitoris which is amputated, and usually not completely. But in the Sudan, the operation consists in the complete removal of all the external genital organs. They cut off the clitoris, the two major outer lips (*labia majora*) and the two minor inner lips (*labia minora*). Then the wound is repaired. The outer opening of the vagina is the only portion left intact, not however without having ensured that, during the process of repairing, some narrowing of the opening is carried out with a few extra stitches. The result is that on the marriage night it is necessary to widen the external opening by slitting one or both ends with a sharp scalpel or razor so that the male organ can be introduced.[2]

In my Sudanese colleague's research I found an allegory of my own ideological victimage:

The 'choice' of English Honors by an upper-class young woman in the Calcutta of the fifties was itself highly overdetermined. Becoming a professor of English in the U.S. fitted in with the 'brain drain'. In due course, a commitment to feminism was the best of a collection of accessible scenarios. The morphology of a feminist theoretical practice came clear through Jacques Derrida's critique of phallocentrism and Luce Irigaray's reading of Freud. (The stumbling 'choice' of French avant-garde criticism by an undistinguished Ivy League Ph.D. working in the Midwest is itself not without ideology-critical interest.) Predictably, I began by identifying the 'female academic' and feminism as such. Gradually I found that there was indeed an area of feminist scholarship in the U.S. that was called 'International Feminism': the arena usually defined as feminism in England, France, West Germany, Italy, and that part of the Third World most easily accessible to American interests: Latin America. When one attempted to think of so-called Third World women in a broader scope, one found oneself caught, as my Sudanese colleague was caught and held by Structural Functionalism, in a web of information retrieval inspired at best by: 'what can I do *for* them?'

I sensed obscurely that this articulation was part of the problem. I re-articulated the question: What is the constituency of an international feminism? The following fragmentary and anecdotal pages approach the question. The complicity of a few French texts in that attempt could be part both of the problem—the 'West' out to 'know' the 'East' determining a 'westernized Easterner's' symptomatic attempt to 'know her own world'; or of something like a solution—reversing and displacing (if only by juxtaposing 'some French texts' and a 'certain Calcutta') the ironclad opposition of West and East. As soon as I write this, it seems a hopelessly idealistic restatement of the problem. I am not in a position of choice in this dilemma.

To begin with, an obstinate childhood memory.

I am walking alone in my grandfather's estate on the Bihar–Bengal border one winter afternoon in 1949. Two ancient washerwomen are washing clothes in the river, beating the clothes on the stones. One accuses the other of poaching on her part of the river. I can still hear the cracked derisive voice of the one accused: 'You fool! Is this your river? The river belongs to the Company!'—the East India Company, from whom India passed to England by the Act for the Better Government of India (1858); England had transferred its charge to an Indian Governor-General in 1947. India would become an independent republic in 1950. For these withered women, the land as soil and water to be used rather than a map to be learned still belonged, as it did one hundred and nineteen years before that date, to the East India Company.

I was precocious enough to know that the remark was incorrect. It has taken me thirty-one years and the experience of confronting a nearly inarticulable question to apprehend that their facts were wrong but the fact was right. The Company does still own the land.

I should not consequently patronize and romanticize these women, nor yet entertain a nostalgia for being as they are. The academic feminist must learn to learn from them, to speak to them, to suspect that their access to the political and sexual scene is not merely to be *corrected* by our superior theory and enlightened compassion. Is our insistence upon the especial beauty of the old necessarily to be preferred to a careless acknowledgment of the mutability of sexuality? What of the fact that my distance from those two was, however micrologically you defined class, class-determined and determining?

How, then, can one learn from and speak to the millions of illiterate rural and urban Indian women who live 'in the pores of' capitalism, inaccessible to the capitalist dynamics that allow us our shared channels of communication, the definition of common enemies? The pioneering books that bring First World feminists news from the Third World are written by privileged inform-ants and can only be deciphered by a trained readership. The distance between 'the informant's world', her 'own sense of the world she writes about', and that of the non-specialist feminist is so great that, paradoxically, *pace* the subtleties of reader-response theories, here the distinctions might easily be missed.

This is not the tried nationalist claim that only a native can know the scene. The point that I am trying to make is that, in order to learn enough about Third World women and to develop a different readership, the immense heterogeneity of the field must be appreciated, and the First World feminist must learn to stop feeling privileged *as a woman*. [. . .]

I am suggesting, then, that a *deliberate* application of the doctrines of French High 'Feminism' to a different situation of political specificity might misfire. If, however, International Feminism is defined within a Western European context, the heterogeneity becomes manageable. In our own situation as academic feminists, we can begin thinking of planning a class. What one does not know can be worked up. There are experts in the field. We can work by the practical assumption that there is no serious communication barrier between them and us. No anguish over uncharted continents, no superstitious dread of making false starts, no questions to which answers may not at least be entertained.

Within such a context, after initial weeks attempting to define and name an 'American' and an 'English' feminism, one would get down to the question of what is specific about French feminism. We shall consider the fact that the most accessible strand of French feminism is governed by a philosophy that argues the impossibility of answering such a question.

We now have the indispensable textbook for this segment of the course: *New French Feminisms: An Anthology*, edited by Elaine Marks and Isabelle de Courtivron.[3] In the United States, French feminism or, more specifically, French feminist theory, has so far been of interest to a 'radical' fringe in French and Comparative Literature departments rather than to the feminists in the field. A book such as this has an interdisciplinary accessibility. This is somewhat unlike the case in England, where Marxist feminism has used mainstream (or masculist) French 'theory'—at least Althusser and Lacan—to explain the constitution of the subject (of ideology or sexuality)—to produce a more specifically 'feminist' critique of Marx's theories of ideology and reproduction.

Because of a predominantly 'literary' interest, the question in French feminist texts that seems most relevant and urgent is that of a specifically feminine discourse. At the crossroads of sexuality and ideology, woman stands constituted (if that is the word) as object. As subject, woman must learn to 'speak "otherwise"', or *make audible* [what]...suffers silently in *the holes of* discourse' (Xavière Gauthier, p. 163). [...]

As soon as one steps out of the classroom, if indeed a 'teacher' ever fully can, the dangers rather than the benefits of academic feminism, French or otherwise, become more insistent. Institutional changes against sexism here or in France may mean nothing or, indirectly, further harm for women in the Third World. This discontinuity ought to be recognized and worked at. Otherwise, the focus remains defined by the investigator as subject. To bring us back to my initial concerns, let me insist that here, the difference between 'French' and 'Anglo-American' feminism is superficial. However unfeasible and inefficient it may sound, I see no way to avoid insisting that there has to be a simultaneous other focus: not merely who am I? but who is the other woman? How am I naming her? How does she name me? Is this part of the problematic I discuss? Indeed, it is the absence of such unfeasible but crucial questions that makes the 'colonized woman' as 'subject' see the investigators as sweet and sympathetic creatures from another planet who are free to come and go; or, depending on her own socialization in the colonizing cultures, see 'feminism' as having a vanguardist class fix, the liberties it fights for as luxuries, finally identifiable with 'free sex' of one kind or another. Wrong, of course. My point has been that there is something equally wrong in our most sophisticated research, our most benevolent impulses. [...]

I emphasize discontinuity, heterogeneity, and typology as I speak of such a sex-analysis, because this work cannot by itself obliterate the problems of race and class. It will not necessarily escape the inbuilt colonialism of First World feminism toward the Third. It might, one hopes, promote a sense of our common yet history-specific lot. It ties together the terrified child held down by her grandmother as the blood runs down her groin and the 'liberated' heterosexual woman who, in spite of Mary Jane Sherfey and the famous page 53 of *Our Bodies, Ourselves*,[4] in bed with a casual lover—engaged, in other words, in the 'freest' of 'free' activities—confronts, at worst, the 'shame' of admitting to the 'abnormality' of her orgasm: at best, the acceptance of such a 'special' need; and the radical feminist who, setting herself apart from the circle of reproduction, systematically discloses the beauty of the lesbian body; the dowried bride—a body for burning—and the female wage-slave—a body for maximum exploitation. There can be other lists; and each one will straddle and undo the ideological–material opposition. For me it is the best gift of French feminism, that it cannot itself fully acknowledge, and that we must work at; here is a theme that can liberate my colleague from Sudan, and a theme the old washerwomen by the river would understand.

['French Feminism in an International Frame', *Yale French Studies*, 62 (1981), 192–220; repr. in Gayatri Chakravorty Spivak, *In Other Worlds: Essays in Cultural Politics* (London: Routledge, 1987), 134–53.]

HELENA MICHIE

7 Not One of the Family: The Repression of the Other Woman in Feminist Theory

Feminism has come to occupy a contradictory place with regard to the family and to the familial drama at the heart of all psychoanlytic and some socio-logical accounts of gender. Accused by their critics of being antifamily, femin-ists have become, in the idiom that will be explored here, home-wreckers. Certainly the dominant metaphors of feminist critiques of society are familial in origin; the world 'patriarchy' itself, familiarly ensconced at the center of the feminist lexicon, locates power in literal and metaphorical fatherhood and defines the family as the scene, if not the source, of women's oppression.

There is within feminism, however, a mirror tendency to reclaim the family and to reproduce it in altered form. The figural response to patriarchy is the 'sisterhood' invoked as its challenge. The attack, then, comes from within the family, and from within the structuring metaphor that makes intimacy the place of conflict. It is by displacing that conflict generationally, by circumvent-ing the mother and projecting aggression onto a historical, diachronic pro-cess, that feminists appropriate for themselves and their sisters the power of teleology and of progress. The struggle of *many* sisters with a *single* father is no simple reenactment of the Oedipal triangle, as it is almost inevitably construed. Criticized repeatedly for its ahistoricism, its synchronicity, and its isolationist insistence on the single child, the Oedipal conflict is disrupted although not dismembered by the introduction of politics and community as they enter onto the familial stage embodied severally as 'sisters'.

Sisterhood projects a series of daughters who usurp the function and privilege of the father by reproducing themselves. In choosing sisterhood over daughterhood, feminists have turned their gaze horizontally and have chosen—or tried to choose—to mirror each other and not the father. The axis of symmetry, the mirror of likeness upon which the Oedipal triangle is based, moves, then, from the space between father and daughter to the space(s) between sisters. Perhaps more important, feminist disruption of the symmetry to which the traditional Oedipal triangle accedes mixes the dominant metaphor, renders ungrammatical the word of the father, and exposes the faulty syntax of what Jacques Lacan calls his Law. It is important, however, that syntax, word, and language remain familial matters; the new grammar is still the grammar of the family.

If the clash between sister and father produces the rhetorical energy that fuels feminist practice, it is the relation between the mother and the daughter that has become the locus of the reproduction of feminist psychoanalytic discourse. For American object-relation theorists like Nancy Chodorow as well as neo-Lacanians like Hélène Cixous and Luce Irigaray, it is the problematic bond between mother and daughter that produces language, identity, and a provisional notion of 'self' in the little girl. Feminists have, largely, turned their gaze from the Oedipal triangle to the pre-Oedipal period in which the girl struggles with her likeness and unlikeness to her mother before her entrance into and her inscription within the law of the father.

For a variety of historical and political reasons which I will not go into here, feminist literary theorists have followed psychoanalysis in recentering their inquiry around the mother.[1] While very early feminist theorists like Kate Millett struggled with the words of literary and academic fathers, more recent critics and theorists on both sides of the Atlantic have begun to turn their attention to maternal figures, maternal discourse. This discourse has taken many forms and has both figured in and figured almost all major feminist projects. Canonical revision has, for example, frequently been articulated as a search for foremothers; feminist poststructuralists have looked for the place of the mother in producing the *jouissance* that for critics from Roland Barthes to Jacques Derrida in turn produces and disseminates meaning, desire, and language; linguistic theorists have scanned literature and language for marks of *écriture féminine*, the mother tongue, what Cixous so famously refers to as 'white ink...good mother's milk'. Perhaps more fundamentally, motherhood and the maternal body have been seen as the location of language and self, the place where the female subject and the female narrative 'I' are produced and reproduced.

As feminist discourse converges on the mother and the sister, it begins to problematize its own central metaphors. Most feminist theorists now acknowledge on some level at least the ambivalence of the mother—daughter relation, the painful tension in the female subject between love and matrophobia, likeness and unlikeness, the need for nurture and the need for separation.[2] Jane Gallop has explored the often-bitter rivalry between sisters for the love of the father, and increasingly, for self-love.[3]

Although theorists locate the causes of tension and rivalry differently— Chodorow, for example, sees matrophobia as a production of patriarchal familial relations, while Gallop seems to see it as an inevitable component of the growth of both mother and daughter—the mother—daughter relation is invoked as much to dramatize and problematize notions of the female self as it is to produce an integrated and integrative notion of female selfhood. No matter how problematized, metaphors of sisterhood and motherhood remain central to the feminist project. 'Sister' and 'mother' become the vessels that contain, shape, and delimit feminist discourse just as the family as it is now construed contains and shapes the roles and bodies of 'real' mothers and sisters.

What about the woman who is not one of this family, the 'other woman' who comes from outside to disrupt the home? It is this Other woman who concerns me here; it is she in her many guises for whom this paper attempts to make room. In popular parlance the Other woman is the mistress, the rival, the sexual threat. She is, however, Other in other senses: she is the third-world woman, the lesbian, the antifeminist, the one who is excluded from or resists the embrace of Oedipal sisterhood. While this paper cannot hope to deal effectively with all Other women, cannot even hope to name them since it is the nature of otherness to resist incorporation even by the act of naming, it is the beginning of an exploration of what lies outside what Gallop has called 'the pitfall of familial thinking'.[4]

The 'Other Woman' is a phrase, a name, a non-name, that is beginning to surface in feminist writing and thinking. It finds a place in a veritable litany of popular and academic book titles. To name a few: the best-selling novel, *Other Women*, by Lisa Alther, about the relationship between a female psychologist and a lesbian patient; *The Other Woman: Stories of Two Women and a Man*, an anthology of short stories edited by Susan Koppelman; *The New Other Woman*, by Laurel Richardson, a sociological study of single women who have affairs with married men, and of course, Luce Irigaray's critique of the phallogocentrism of Western metaphysics, *Speculum of the Other Woman*. The very similarity of the titles hints at a problem central to feminist perceptions of otherness; these titles, hardly Other to each other, at once name the Other woman and insert her into familiar sexual tropes. [. . .]

Gallop ends this essay, which explores sexual difference as a space between women, with a fragment of the quotation from Spivak with which she ended 'Monster' and which she has already placed so securely in the body of this essay. She ends with the 'necessarily double and no less urgent questions of feminism: "not merely who am I? But who is the other woman?" ' By repeating Spivak's questions at the end of the essay, Gallop obviously underscores their centrality. By making them central, by placing them in, as it were, her mosaic, she is denying that they are Other. By ending two essays with the words of the same Other woman, she is rendering Spivak's words familiar and welcoming her into the family. The mirror that so frighteningly replicates women in 'Monster' is held up to Spivak's face. In looking over Spivak's shoulder, Gallop sees Jane Gallop. The question, 'who is the Other woman' transforms itself on the surface of the mirror into the questionable statement 'The Other Woman is myself.' Gallop's essay, like many rhetorical and political gestures that begin as explorations of Otherness, ends by absorbing Otherness into an increasingly capacious notion of self. It is this capacious and hungry self—most benignly embodied in the metaphor of sisterhood—that feminists must learn to recognize so that they can ultimately recognize the face outside the mirror: the face of the Other woman.

['Not One of the Family: The Repression of the Other Woman in Feminist Theory', in Marleen S. Barr and Richard Feldstein (eds.), *Discontented Discourses: Feminism/Textual Intervention/Psychoanalysis* (Champaign: University of Illinois Press, 1989), 15–28.]

ELAINE SHOWALTER

8 A Criticism of Our Own: Autonomy and Assimilation in Afro-American and Feminist Literary Theory

In the summer of 1985, I was one of the speakers at the annual conference on literary theory at Georgetown University. On the first morning, a distinguished Marxist theorist was introduced, and as he began to read his paper, there appeared from the other side of the stage a slender young woman in a leotard and long skirt who looked like a ballet dancer. Positioning herself a few feet from the speaker, she whirled into motion, waving her fingers and hands, wordlessly moving her lips, alternating smiles and frowns. There were murmurs in the audience; what could this mean? Was it a protest against academic conferences? A Feifferesque prayer to the muse of criticism? A celebratory performance of the Althusserian two-step? Of course, as we soon realized, it was nothing so dramatic or strange. Georgetown had hired this young woman from an organization called Deaf Pride to translate all the papers into sign language for the hearing-impaired.

Yet from the perspective of the audience, this performance soon began to look like a guerrilla theatre of sexual difference which had been staged especially for our benefit. After the first ten minutes, it became impossible simply to *listen* to the famous man, immobilized behind the podium. Our eyes were drawn instead to the nameless woman, and to the eloquent body language into which she mutely translated his words. In this context, her signs seemed uncannily feminine and Other, as if we were watching a Kristevan ambassador from the semiotic, or the ghost of a Freudian hysteric back from the beyond. Anna O. is alive and well in Georgetown!

The feminist implications of this arrangement were increasingly emphasized, moreover, throughout the first day of the conference, because, although the young woman reached ever more dazzling heights of ingenuity, mobility, and grace, not one of the three white male theorists who addressed us took any notice of her presence. No one introduced her; no one alluded to her. It was as if they could not see her. She had become transparent, like the female medium of the symbolists who, according to Mary Ann Caws, 'served up the sign, conveying it with fidelity, patience, and absolute personal silence. She herself was patiently ruled out.'[1]

Sitting in the audience that first morning, I wondered what would happen when *I* was introduced as the fourth speaker. I had wild fantasies that Georgetown would provide a bearded male interpreter who would translate my paper into the rhetoric of deconstruction. (It turned out that there were two young women who alternated the task of interpretation. This does not seem to be a man's job.) I wondered too how I should speak from the position of power as the 'theorist' when I also identified with the silent, transparent woman? The presence of the other woman was a return of the repressed paradox of female authority, the paradox Jane Gallop describes as fraudulence: 'A woman theoretician is already an exile; expatriated from her *langue maternelle*, she speaks a paternal language; she presumes to a fraudulent power.'[2] The translator seemed to represent not only the *langue maternelle*, the feminine other side of discourse, but also the Other Woman of feminist discourse, the woman outside of academia in the 'real world', or the Third World, to whom a Feminist critic is responsible, just as she is responsible to the standards and conventions of criticism.[3] Gayatri Chakravorty Spivak has reminded us that she must always be acknowledged in our work: 'Who is the other woman? How am I naming her? How does she name me?'[4]

At the Georgetown conference, my awareness of the Other Woman was shared by the other women on the program; all of us, in our presentations, introduced the interpreter, and changed our lectures in order to work with her presence. Yet the only male speaker who took notice of the interpreter was Houston Baker. By the time he spoke on the second day, Baker had learned enough sign language to produce a virtuoso translation of the beginning of his own talk, and to work with the translator in a playful duet.

The Georgetown conference was not the first time that Afro-American and feminist critics have found ourselves on the same side of otherness, but it was certainly one of the most dramatic. For those of us who work within 'oppositional' or cultural criticisms—black, socialist, feminist, or gay—questions of the critic's double consciousness, double audience, and double role come with the territory and arise every day. They are not just the sort of global questions Terry Eagleton poses in *Literary Theory*, as to whether an analysis of the Lacanian imaginary can help welfare mothers, but more mundane problems of ethnicity and ethics: how we will answer the mail, how we will conduct ourselves in the classroom or on the podium, and how we will act not only in symbolic relationships but also in real encounters with constituencies inside and outside of academia.

In this essay, I briefly sketch out the parallel histories of Afro-American and feminist literary criticism and theory over the past twenty-five years, in order to learn from our mutual experience in relation to the dominant culture. This may seem like a strange moment for such a project. In both feminist and

Afro-American criticism, the Other Woman, the silenced partner, has been the black woman, and the role played by black feminist critics in bridging the two schools is controversial. While black and white feminists have objected to the sexism of black literary history, black women have also challenged the racism of feminist literary history. Black male writers have protested against the representation of black men in the fiction of Afro-American women novelists, and Ishmael Reed's latest novel, *Reckless Eyeballing* (1986), imagines a violent vengeance on feminists in general and black feminist writers in particular.

Yet this record of misunderstanding obscures what I think are the strong and important connections between the two kinds of cultural criticism; we have much to gain by a dialogue.[5] Both feminist and Afro-American criticism have brought together personal, intellectual, and political issues in our confrontations with the Western literary tradition. We have both followed traditional patterns in the institutionalization of critical movements, from our beginnings in a separatist cultural aesthetics, born out of participation in a protest movement; to a middle stage of professionalized focus on a specific text-milieu in an alliance with academic literary theory; to an expanded and pluralistic critical field of expertise on sexual or racial difference. Along with gay and post-Colonial critics, we share many critical metaphors, theories, and dilemmas, such as the notion of a double-voiced discourse, the imagery of the veil, the mask, or the closet; and the problem of autonomy versus mimicry and civil disobedience.

In abandoning marginal territories of our own for places in the poststructuralist critical wilderness, do black and feminist critics also risk exchanging authenticity for imitation, and self-generated critical models for what Lisa Jardine calls Designer Theory? If we oppose the idea that women should have the exclusive franchise on 'gender' or blacks the franchise on 'race', what can be the distinguishing idiom or role of the black or feminist critic, and how do we identify the place from which we speak? Can we make the compromises necessary for acceptance by the mainstream, and still work for a criticism of our own? Or is the dream of an alternative criticism which is 'simultaneously subversive and self-authenticating' the most utopian of all sub-cultural fantasies?[6] [. . .]

Before the Women's Liberation Movement, criticism of women's writing took the form of an *androgynist poetics*, denying the uniqueness of a female literary consciousness, and advocating a single or universal standard of critical judgment which women writers had to meet. The women's movement of the late 1960s initiated both a *feminist critique* of male culture and a *Female Aesthetic* celebrating women's culture. By the mid-1970s, academic feminist criticism, in league with interdisciplinary work in women's studies, entered a new phase of *gynocritics*, or the study of women's writing. With the impact of European literary and feminist theory in the late 1970s, *gynesic* or poststructuralist feminist criticism, dealing with 'the feminine' in philosophy, language, and psychoanalysis, became an important influence on the field as a whole. And in the late 1980s, we are seeing the rise of *gender theory*, the comparative study of sexual difference.

In contrast to black criticism, where integrationist poetics is at least currently unacceptable, androgynist poetics continues to have many partisans among women writers, creating an apparent conflict between writers and critics that the media have relished. It disturbed many feminist critics, including myself, when Gail Godwin and Cynthia Ozick attacked the *Norton Anthology of Literature by Women* on the grounds that the creative imagination is sexless and that the concept of a female literary tradition was insulting to women who (like Godwin) regard themselves as disciples of Joseph Conrad. I think it unlikely that black writers will raise similar objections to the forthcoming *Norton Anthology of Black Literature*, edited by the indefatigable and phenomenal Skip Gates.

Nevertheless, androgynist poetics, which can be an unexamined misogyny that demands a spurious 'universality' from women's writing, as integrationist poetics did from black writers, as well as a form of feminine self-hatred, also speaks for genuinely serious and permanent concerns within feminist criticism. The androgynist position was articulated early on by Mary Ellmann in *Thinking About Women* (1969), which wittily deconstructed the pernicious effects of thinking by sexual analogy; and by Carolyn Heilbrun in *Toward a Recognition of Androgyny* (1973), which argued that 'our future salvation lies in a movement away from sexual polarization and the prison of gender'.[7] Among contemporary American writers, Joyce Carol Oates is probably the most persuasive representative of this position. In an essay entitled '(Woman) Writer: Theory and Practice' (1986), Oates protests the category of 'woman' or 'gender' in art: 'Subject-matter is culture-determined, not gender-determined. And the imagination, in itself genderless, allows us all things.'

Since the 1970s, however, while acknowledging the writer's need to feel free of labels, most feminist critics have rejected the concept of the genderless 'imagination', and have argued from a variety of perspectives that the imagination cannot escape from the unconscious structures and strictures of gender identity. These arguments may emphasize the impossibility of separating the imagination from a socially, sexually, and historically positioned self, as in Sandra Gilbert's sensible insistence that 'what is finally written is, whether consciously or not, written by the whole person. . . . If the writer is a woman who has been raised as a woman—and I daresay only a very few biologically anomalous human females have *not* been raised as women—how can her sexual identity be split off from her literary energy? Even a denial of her femininity. . would surely be significant to an understanding of the dynamics of her aesthetic creativity.'[8] A more systematic feminist critique of the woman writer's unified and sexless 'imagination' comes from Lacanian psychoanalysis, which describes the split in the female subject within language. In a psycholinguistic world structured by father-son resemblance and by the primacy of male logic, woman is a gap or a silence, the invisible and unheard sex. In contrast to the 'writer only' problems of androgynist poetics, therefore, most feminist critics insist that the way to contend with patriarchal bias against women is not to deny sexual difference but to dismantle gender hierarchies. Not sexual difference itself, but rather its meaning within patriarchal ideology—'division, oppression, inequality, inter-iorized inferiority for women'—must be attacked.[9]

The first break with androgynist poetics was the affirmation of woman-hood as a positive factor in literary experience. As in the development of a Black Aesthetic, the Female Aesthetic evolved during the early years of the women's liberation movement as a radical response to a past in which the assumed goal for women's literature had been a smooth passage into a neuter and 'universal' aesthetic realm. Instead the Female Aesthetic maintained that women's writing expressed a distinct female consciousness, that it constituted a unique and coherent literary tradition, and that the woman writer who denied her female identity restricted or even crippled her art. At the same time, a feminist critique of androcentric literature and criticism examined the 'misogyny of literary practice: the stereotyped images of women in literature as angels or monsters, the...textual harassment of women in classic and popular male literature, and the exclusion of women from literary history'.[10]

Virtually all of the romantic and invigorating images of independence that characterized the Black Aesthetic have their counterpart in the Female Aes-thetic as well. In contrast to the hegemony of what it characterized as the arid and elitist 'methodolatry' of patriarchal criticism, the Female Aesthetic pro-posed the empowerment of the common woman reader (indeed we could also see here a conjunction of Women's Liberation with what Terry Eagleton has called the Reader's Liberation Movement), and the celebration of an intuitive female critical consciousness in the interpretation of women's texts. In striking parallels to the Black Aesthetic, the Female Aesthetic also spoke of a vanished nation, a lost motherland; of the female vernacular or Mother Tongue; and of a powerful but neglected women's culture. In her introduc-tion to an anthology of international women's poetry, for example, Adrienne Rich put forth the compelling hypothesis of a female diaspora:

The idea of a common female culture—splintered and diasporized among the male cultures under and within which women have survived—has been a haunting though tentative theme of feminist thought over the past few years. Divided from each other through our dependencies on men—domestically, tribally, and in the world of patron-age and institutions—our first need has been to recognize and reject these divisions, the second to begin exploring all that we share in common as women on this planet.[11]

This phase of intellectual rebellion, gynocentrism, and critical separatism was a crucial period in the experience of women who had always played subordinate roles as dutiful academic daughters, research assistants, second readers, and faculty wives. Via the Female Aesthetic, women experimented with efforts to inscribe a female idiom in critical discourse and to define a feminist critical stylistics based on women's experience. In 'Toward a Feminist Aesthetic' (1978), Julia Penelope Stanley and Susan J. Wolfe (Robbins) proposed that 'the unique perceptions and interpretations of women require a literary style that reflects, captures, and embodies the quality of our thought', a 'discursive, conjunctive style instead of the complex, subordinating, linear style of classification and distinction'.[12]

French feminist writing of the same period, although it came out of radically different intellectual sources, also produced the concept of *écriture féminine*, analyzing women's style as a writing-effect of rupture and subversion in avant-garde literature, available to both men and women, but connected or analogous to female sexual morphology. The French feminist project of 'writing the body' is a particularly strong and revolutionary effort to provide women's writing with an authority based in women's genital and libidinal difference from men. While the French critique of phallocentrism takes very different paths in the work of Hélène Cixous, Luce Irigaray, and Julia Kristeva, all explore the possibility of a concentric feminine discourse. Whether clitoral, vulval, vaginal, or uterine; whether centered on semiotic pulsions, childbearing, or jouissance, the feminist theorization of female sexuality/textuality, and its funky audacity in violating patriarchal taboos by unveiling the Medusa, is an exhilarating challenge to phallic discourse.

Yet the Female Aesthetic also had serious weaknesses. As many feminist critics sharply noted, its emphasis on the importance of female biological experience came dangerously close to sexist essentialism. Its efforts to establish a specificity of female writing through the hypothesis of a women's language, a lost motherland, or a cultural enclave, could not be supported by scholarship. The initial identification with the Amazon as a figure of female autonomy and creativity (in the work of Monique Wittig and Ti-Grace Atkinson, among others), and with lesbian separatism as the correct political form for feminist commitment, was both too radical and too narrow for a broadly based critical movement. The concepts of female style or *écriture féminine* described only one avant-garde mode of women's writing, and many feminists felt excluded by a prescriptive stylistics that seemed to privilege the non-linear, experimental, and surreal. Insofar as the Female Aesthetic suggested that only women were qualified to read women's texts, feminist criticism ran the risk of ghettoization. Finally, the essentialism of the universal female subject and the female imagination was open to charges of racism, especially since black women's texts were rarely cited as examples. As black women and others within the women's movement protested against the inattention to racial and class differences between women, the idea of a common women's culture had to be re-examined.

Gynocritics, which developed alongside the Female Aesthetic in the 1970s, has been an effort to resolve some of these problems. It identified women's writing as a central subject of feminist criticism, but rejected the concept of an essential female identity and style. In an essay called 'Feminist Criticism in the Wilderness' (1981), a response to Geoffrey Hartman whose title now seems feeble compared to the brilliant riposte of Skip Gates, I argued against feminist fantasies of a wild zone of female consciousness or culture outside of patriarchy, declaring instead that 'there can be no writing or criticism outside of the dominant culture'. Thus both women's writing and feminist criticism were of necessity 'a double-voiced discourse embodying both the muted and the dominant, speaking inside of both feminism and criticism'.[13]

Instead gynocriticism has focused on the multiple signifying systems of female literary traditions and intertextualities. In studying women's writing, feminist critics have challenged and revised the prevailing styles of critical discourse, and asked whether theories of female creativity could be developed instead from within the female literary tradition itself. Influenced by the interdisciplinary field of women's studies, they have brought to their reading of women's texts theories and terms generated by the work of such feminist scholars as the historian Carroll Smith-Rosenberg, the psychologist Carol Gilligan, and the sociologist Nancy Chodorow, whose enormously influential study *The Reproduction of Mothering* (1978), revised Freudian psychoanalysis and British object-relations psychology to emphasize the pre-Oedipal phase as the key factor in the construction of gender identity.

The work of Smith-Rosenberg, Chodorow, and Gilligan has led to a wide range of studies in philosophy, social history, and religion endorsing what are called 'matriarchal values' of nurturance, caring, nonviolence, and connectedness, and urging their adoption by society as a whole. Feminist critics have used metaphors of this idealized maternity both in the quest for a strong literary matrilineage, and in the rejection of the adversary method in critical discourse. In a famous and moving essay, Alice Walker has described black women writers' 'search for our mother's gardens', tracing the suppressed creativity of black women under slavery and poverty to non-verbal art forms.[14] In sharp contrast to the Oedipal poetics of aggression, competition, and defense put forth by Harold Bloom, some American feminist critics have postulated a pre-Oedipal 'female poetics of affiliation', dependent on the daughter's bond with the mother, in which intergenerational conflict is replaced by female literary intimacy, generosity, and continuity. Joan Lidoff, Judith Kegan Gardiner, and Elizabeth Abel are among the feminist critics who see women's fluid ego boundaries affecting plot and genre conventions, blurring the lines between lyric and narrative, between realism and romance. Here the Female Aesthetic and postmodernism join in a celebration of heterogeneity, dissolving boundaries, and *différence*.

Although I can hardly claim to be an innocent bystander on the subject of gynocriticism, I would argue that over the past decade it has been sufficiently large, undogmatic, and flexible to have accommodated many theoretical revisions and criticisms, and it has been enormously productive. In a relatively short period of time, gynocritics has generated a vast critical literature on individual women writers, persuasive studies of the female literary tradition from the Middle Ages to the present in virtually every national literature, and important books on what is called 'gender and genre': the significance of gender in shaping generic conventions in forms ranging from the hymn to the Bildungsroman. Nevertheless, many of the original gynocritical theories of women's writing were based primarily on nineteenth-century English women's texts, so that a black feminist critic such as Hortense Spillers sees 'the gynocritical themes of recent feminist inquiry' as separate from a 'black women's writing community'.[15] Only in recent years has attention to black women's writing begun to address and redress this issue.

A pivotal text of gynocritics is Sandra Gilbert and Susan Gubar's monumental study *The Madwoman in the Attic* (1979). Gilbert and Gubar offer a detailed revisionist reading of Harold Bloom's theory of the anxiety of influence, transforming his Freudian paradigm of Oedipal struggle between literary fathers and sons into a feminist theory of influence which describes the nineteenth-century woman writer's anxieties within a patriarchal literary culture. Strongly influenced by the work of Gilbert and Gubar, the theoretical program of gynocritics by the 1980s has been marked by increasing attention to 'the analysis of female talent grappling with a male tradition', both in literature and criticism, a project that defined both the female literary text and the feminist critical text as the sum of its 'acts of revision, appropriation, and subversion', and its differences of 'genre, structure, voice, and plot'.[16] Gynocritics had derived much of its strength from its self-reflexive properties as a double-voiced mode of women's writing; the anxieties of the nineteenth-century woman writer were much like those of the modern Feminist critic attempting to penetrate literary theory, the most defended bastion of patriarchal prose. Now, as Feminist critics began to profit from their labors and to enjoy some prestige and authority within the profession of literary studies, questions of the complicity between the feminist critical talent and the male critical tradition became acute, and the acts of theoretical revision, appropriation, and subversion in gynocritics itself became the source of a troubling, sometimes obsessive and guilty, self-consciousness.

About this time, too, as reports on the French feminists began to appear in women's studies journals, and as their work became available to American readers through translation, a new group of feminist critics entered the field, primarily through departments of French and Comparative Literature. They saw post-Saussurean linguistics, psychoanalysis, semiotics, and deconstruction as the most powerful means to understanding the production of sexual difference in language, reading, and writing, and they wrote in a language accessible chiefly to other literary critics, rather than to a wider audience. Following the work of Jacques Derrida, Jacques Lacan, Hélène Cixous, Luce Irigaray, and Julia Kristeva, Franco-American feminist critics focused on what Alice Jardine calls 'gynesis': the exploration of the textual consequences and representations of 'the feminine' in Western thought. Deconstruction has paid little attention to women writers individually or as a group; 'for Derrida and his disciples', Jardine notes, 'the question of how women might accede to subjecthood, write texts or acquire their own signatures, are *phallogocentric* questions'.[17] Some poststructuralist feminist critics thus maintain that 'feminist criticism should avoid "the women's literature ghetto" . . . and return to confrontation with "the" canon'.[18] While gynocritics looks at the patrilineage and matrilineage of the female literary *work*, poststructuralist feminist criticism views the literary *text* as fatherless and motherless; its feminist subjectivity is a product of the reading process. From a gynesic perspective, moreover, disruptions in discourse constitute disruptions of the patriarchal system.

Gynesic criticism has been a major intellectual force within feminist discourse, but the gynesic project has also raised a number of problems. First of all, as black poststructuralism has questioned the transcendent black self, however, so poststructuralist feminist criticism has had to wrestle with the paradox of fundamental theoretical affiliations that undermine the very notion of female subjectivity. Other modes of feminist criticism have had the empowerment of the female subject as a specific goal. Within the Female Aesthetic, female consciousness was celebrated as an interpretive guide; within gynocritics, the woman critic could use her own confrontation with the male critical tradition and her own experience of writing as a guide to understanding the situation of the woman writer. But if women are the silenced and repressed Other of Western discourse, how can a Feminist theorist speak *as* a woman about women or anything else? As Shoshana Felman asks, 'If "the woman" is precisely the Other of any conceivable Western theoretical focus of speech, how can the woman as such be speaking in this book? Who is speaking here, and who is asserting the otherness of the woman?'[19] Kaja Silverman also admits that 'the relationship of the female subject to semiotic theory is . . . necessarily an ambivalent one. The theory offers her a sophisticated understanding of her present cultural condition, but it also seems to confine her forever to the status of one who is to be seen, spoken, and analyzed.'[20] The rhetorical problems of expressing a black male self to which Gates briefly alludes in 'Criticism in the Jungle' are much less disabling than the burden, inherent in a gynesic feminist criticism heavily and necessarily dependent on psychoanalytic theory, of speaking from the feminine position of absence, silence, and lack.

Furthermore, while poststructuralist feminists have played a significant role within poststructuralism as translators and advocates, as well as critics, of the European male theorists, the male feminists who have participated in gynesis, with some outstanding exceptions (such as Neil Hertz, Stephen Heath, and Andrew Ross) have tended to present themselves as metacritical masters of the feminine rather than as students of women's writing, or critics of masculinity. When the Australian critic Ken Ruthven (sometimes called the Crocodile Dundee of male feminism) observes in his book *Feminist Literary Studies: An Introduction*, that 'the female "problematic" is too important to be left in the hands of anti-intellectual feminists', and could be subjected to much more rigorous metacritical inspection by impartial men like himself, it's difficult not to be suspicious. Since, when you come right down to it, Ruthven argues, feminist criticism is 'just another way of talking about books', and he is a guy who 'makes a living talking about books', it would be churlish (or girlish) to try to keep him out of the conversation.[21] In other cases, as I have learned from sad experience, 'male feminists' do not even bother to read the feminist critical texts they are allegedly responding to, since they always already know what women think. Poststructuralism and feminism are a familiar and almost obligatory critical couple in the 1980s, but they are still having to work at their relationship.

Finally, some recent discussions of what they call 'Anglo-American' feminist criticism by poststructuralist feminists have been startlingly *ad feminam* and harsh, introducing a tone of acrimony into what we had hoped was a mutual, if pluralistic, enterprise, and eliciting equally intemperate attacks on 'theory' in defensive response. Certainly there are real issues at stake in the theoretical debates, as well as struggles for what Evelyn Fox Keller has called epistemic power in the feminist critical arena. But the polarization of feminist discourse along dualistic lines seems particularly unfortunate at a moment when there is such a lively exchange of ideas. While *The Madwoman in the Attic* has yet to be translated into French, gynesic criticism has been widely read by American feminist critics; it has modified American work in gynocritics, and vice-versa. It's not exceptional that Sandra Gilbert, for example, should have edited the first English translation of Cixous and Catherine Clément's *La Jeune Née*, or on the other hand, that Barbara Johnson is currently working on black women writers. The complex heterogeneities of contemporary feminist discourse cannot be reduced to hierarchical oppositions.

The latest and most rapidly growing mode of feminist criticism is gender theory, corresponding to the Third-World critic's focus on 'race'. Within American feminist scholarship, the term 'gender' is used to mean the social, cultural, and psychological constructs imposed upon biological sexual differ-ence. Like 'race' or 'class', 'gender' is a fundamental or organic social variable in all human experience. Within gender theory, the object of feminist criti-cism undergoes another transformation; unlike the emphasis on women's writing that informs gynocritics, or on the signification of 'the feminine' within gynesis, gender theory explores ideological inscription and the literary effects of the sex/gender system: 'that set of arrangements by which the biological raw material of human sex and procreation is shaped by human social intervention'.[22]

The interest in gender theory is not confined to feminist criticism, but has also appeared in feminist thought in the fields of history, anthropology, philosophy, psychology, and science. In 'Anthropology and the Study of Gender', Judith Shapiro argues that the goal of feminist research is not to focus on 'women', and thus to reify female marginalization, but rather 'to integrate the study of gender differences into the central pursuits of the social sciences'.[23] In the natural sciences, the path-breaking work of Evelyn Fox Keller, Ruth Bleier, and Donna Haraway has analyzed 'the critical role of gender ideology in mediating between science and social forms'.[24] The most searching analysis of gender as a historical concept has been carried out by Joan W. Scott; in an essay called 'Gender. A Useful Category of Historical Analysis', Scott outlines three goals of gender theory: to substitute the analysis of social constructs for biological determinism is the discussion of sexual difference; to introduce comparative studies of women and men into the specific disciplinary field; and to transform disciplinary paradigms by adding gender as an analytic category.[25] [. . .]

Where do we go from here? The parallels between Afro-American and feminist criticism show how problematic the idea of a unified 'black' or 'female' self has become. Whether it is the linguistic skepticism of poststruc-turalism, or our acknowledgment of the differences between women that stops us, Feminist critics today can no longer speak as and about women with the unselfconscious authority of the past. The female subject, we are told, is dead, a position instead of a person. Our dilemma has even reached the pages of the New Yorker; in Tama Janowitz's short story 'Engagements', a graduate student in feminist criticism at Yale takes notes as her distraught professor tells of being severely attacked for trying to talk about 'women' and 'female identity' at a Poetics of Gender conference.[26] Without a claim to subjectivity or group identity, how can we have a feminist criticism of our own?

Black and Third-World critics haunted by the messages of poststructural-ism are now facing the same dilemma. Is there a critic-position as well as a subject-position? Gates asks whether 'the critic of black literature acquires his or her identity parodically, as it were, in the manner of the parrot', but hopefully concludes that 'we are able to achieve difference through repetition' by looking at a different critical object.[27] Homi Bhabha addresses the issue in the contexts of colonialist discourse, citing 'mimicry' as a form of 'civil disobedience within the discipline of civility: signs of spectacular resistance'.[28] In Ce Sexe qui n'en est pas un, Luce Irigaray too locates the subversive force of Feminist discourse in a playful mimesis, a mimicry both of phallocentric discourse which exceeds its logic, and of the feminine position within that system. Yet playing with mimesis cannot offer us authority except in individual star turns, especially if the dominant culture wants to play with your mesis too. And in mimicking the language of the dominant, how can we guarantee that mimicry is *understood* as ironic—as civil disobedience, camp, or feminist difference rather than as merely derivative?

Feminist criticism can't afford to settle for mimicry, or to give up the idea of female subjectivity, even if we accept it as a constructed or metaphysical one. To paraphrase Baker, men's clubs hardly ever think of metaphysics before they keep women out; we need what Gayatri Spivak calls a 'strategic essentialism' to combat patriarchy.[29] Neither can we abandon our investigation of women's literary history, or give up the belief that through careful reading of women's texts we will develop a criticism of our own that is both theoretical and feminist. This is a task worth pursuing for its intellectual challenge and for its contribution to a truly inclusive theory of literature, rather than for its 'defense' of women's creative gifts. The goal Virginia Woolf envisioned for feminist writers and critics in 1928, to labor in poverty and obscurity for the coming of Shakespeare's sister, no longer seems meaningful or necessary. Our enterprise does not stand or fall by proving some kind of parity with male literary or critical 'genius'; even assuming that a female Shakespeare or a female Derrida would be recognized, to question the very idea of 'genius' is part of Woolf's legacy to us.

Despite our awareness of diversity and deconstruction, feminist critics cannot depend on gynesic ruptures in discourse to bring about social change. During a period when many of the meager gains of the civil rights and women's movements are being threatened or undone by Reaganism and the New Right, when, indeed, there is a backlash against what the Bennetts and Blooms see as too *much* black and female power in the university, there is an urgent necessity to affirm the importance of black and female thinkers, speakers, readers, and writers. The Other Woman may be transparent or invisible to some; but she is still very vivid, important, and necessary to us.

['A Criticism of Our Own', in Ralph Cohen (ed.), *The Future of Literary Theory* (New York and London: Routledge, 1989), 168–88.]

BARBARA CHRISTIAN

9   The Race for Theory

I have seized this occasion to break the silence among those of us, critics, as we are now called, who have been intimidated, devalued by what I call the race for theory. I have become convinced that there has been a take-over in the literary world by Western philosophers from the old literary elite, the neutral humanists. Philosophers have been able to effect such a take-over because so much of the literature of the West has become pallid, laden with despair, self-indulgent, and disconnected. The New Philosophers, eager to understand a world that is today fast escaping their political control, have redefined literature so that the distinctions implied by that term, that is, the distinctions between everything written and those things written to evoke feeling as well as to express thought, have been blurred. They have changed literary critical language to suit their own purposes as philosophers, and they have re-invented the meaning of theory.

My first response to this realization was to ignore it. Perhaps, in spite of the egocentrism of this trend, some good might come of it. I had, I felt more pressing and interesting things to do, such as reading and studying the history and literature of black women, a history that had been totally ignored, a contemporary literature bursting with originality, passion, insight, and beauty. But unfortunately it is difficult to ignore this new take-over, theory has become a commodity because that helps determine whether we are hired or promoted in academic institutions—worse, whether we are heard at all. Due to this new orientation, works (a word which evokes labor) have become texts. Critics are no longer concerned with literature, but with other critics' texts, for the critic yearning for attention has displaced the writer and has conceived of himself as the center. Interestingly in the first part of this century, at least in England and America, the critic was usually also a writer of poetry, plays, or novels. But today, as a new generation of professionals develops, he or she is increasingly an academic. Activities such as teaching or writing one's response to specific works of literature have, among this group, become subordinated to one primary thrust, that moment when one creates a theory, thus fixing a constellation of ideas for a time at least, a fixing which no doubt will be replaced in another month or so by somebody else's competing theory as the race accelerates. Perhaps because those who have effected the take-over have the power (although they deny it) first of all to be published, and thereby to determine the ideas which are deemed valuable, some of our most daring and potentially radical critics (and by *our* I mean black, women, Third World) have been influenced, even co-opted, into speaking a language and defining their discussion in terms alien to and opposed to our needs and orientation. At least so far, the creative writers I study have resisted this language.[1]

For people of color have always theorized—but in forms quite different from the Western form of abstract logic. And I am inclined to say that our theorizing (and I intentionally use the verb rather than the noun) is often in narrative forms, in the stories we create, in riddles and proverbs, in the play with language, since dynamic rather than fixed ideas seem more to our liking. How else have we managed to survive with such spiritedness the assault on our bodies, social institutions, countries, our very humanity? And women, at least the women I grew up around, continuously speculated about the nature of life through pithy language that unmasked the power relations of their world. It is this language, and the grace and pleasure with which they played with it, that I find celebrated, refined, critiqued in the works of writers like Toni Morrison and Alice Walker. My folk, in other words, have always been a race of theory—though more in the form of the hieroglyph, a written figure which is both sensual and abstract, both beautiful and communicative. In my own work I try to illuminate and explain these hieroglyphs, which is, I think, an activity quite different from the creating of the hieroglyphs themselves. As the Buddhists would say, the finger pointing at the moon is not the moon.

In this discussion, however, I am more concerned with the issue raised by my first use of the term, *the race for theory*, in relation to its academic hegemony, and possibly of its inappropriateness to the energetic emerging literatures in the world today. The pervasiveness of this academic hegemony is an issue continually spoken about—but usually in hidden groups, lest we, who are disturbed by it, appear ignorant to the reigning academic elite. Among the folk who speak in muted tones are people of color, feminists, radical critics, creative writers, who have struggled for much longer than a decade to make their voices, their various voices, heard, and for whom literature is not an occasion for discourse among critics but is necessary nourishment for their people and one way by which they come to understand their lives better. Clichéd though this may be, it bears, I think, repeating here.

The race for theory, with its linguistic jargon, its emphasis on quoting its prophets, its tendency towards 'Biblical' exegesis, its refusal even to mention specific works of creative writers, far less contemporary ones, its preoccupations with mechanical analyses of language, graphs, algebraic equations, its gross generalizations about culture, has silenced many of us to the extent that some of us feel we can no longer discuss our own literature, while others have developed intense writing blocks and are puzzled by the incomprehensibility of the language set adrift in literary circles. There have been, in the last year, any number of occasions on which I had to convince literary critics who have pioneered entire new areas of critical inquiry that they did have something to say. Some of us are continually harassed to invent wholesale theories regardless of the complexity of the literature we study. I, for one, am tired of being asked to produce a black feminist literary theory as if I were a mechanical man. For I believe such theory is prescriptive—it ought to have some relationship to practice. Since I can count on one hand the number of people attempting to be black feminist literary critics in the world today, I consider it presumptuous of me to invent a theory of how we *ought* to read. Instead, I think we need to read the works of our writers in our various ways and remain open to the intricacies of the intersection of language, class, race, and gender in the literature. And it would help if we share our process, that is, our practice, as much as possible since, finally, our work *is* a collective endeavor.

The insidious quality of this race for theory is symbolized for me by a term like 'Minority Discourse'[2]—a label that is borrowed from the reigning theory of the day but which is untrue to the literatures being produced by our writers, for many of our literatures (certainly Afro-American literature) are central, not minor. I have used the passive voice in my last sentence construction, contrary to the rules of Black English, which like all languages has a particular value system, since I have not placed responsibility on any particular person or group. But that is precisely because this new ideology has become so prevalent among us that it behaves like so many of the other ideologies with which we have had to contend. It appears to have neither head nor center. At the least, though, we can say that the terms 'minority' and 'discourse' are located firmly in a Western dualistic or 'binary' frame which sees the rest of the world as minor, and tries to convince the rest of the world that it *is* major, usually through force and then through language, even as it claims many of the ideas that we, its 'historical' other, have known and spoken about for so long. For many of us have never conceived of ourselves only as somebody's *other*.

Let me not give the impression that by objecting to the race for theory I ally myself with or agree with the neutral humanists who see literature as pure expression and will not admit to the obvious control of its production, value, and distribution by those who have power, who deny, in other words, that literature is, of necessity, political. I am studying an entire body of literature that has been denigrated for centuries by such terms as *political*. For an entire century Afro-American writers, from Charles Chestnutt in the nineteenth century through Richard Wright in the 1930s, Imamu Baraka in the 1960s, Alice Walker in the 1970s, have protested the literary hierarchy of dominance which declares when literature is literature, when literature is great, depending on what it thinks is to its advantage. The Black Arts Movement of the 1960s, out of which Black Studies, the Feminist Literary Movement of the 1970s, and Women's Studies grew, articulated precisely those issues, which came *not* from the declarations of the New Western Philosophers but from these groups' reflections on their own lives. That Western scholars have long believed their ideas to be universal has been strongly opposed by many such groups. Some of my colleagues do not see black critical writers of previous decades as eloquent enough. Clearly they have not read Wright's 'A blueprint for Negro Writing', Ellison's *Shadow and Act*, Chesnutt's resignation from being a writer, or Alice Walker's 'In search of Zora Neale Hurston'.[3] There are two reasons for this general ignorance of what our writer-critics have said. One is that black writing has been generally ignored in the USA. Since we, as Toni Morrison has put it, are seen as a discredited people, it is no surprise, then, that our creations are also discredited. But this is also due to the fact that until recently, dominant critics in the Western world have also been creative writers who have had access to the upper-middle-class institutions of education and, until recently, our writers have decidedly been excluded from these institutions and in fact have often been opposed to them. Because of the academic world's general ignorance about the literature of black people, and of women, whose work too has been discredited, it is not surprising that so many of our critics think that the position arguing that literature is political begins with these New Philosophers. Unfortunately, many of our young critics do not investigate the reasons *why* that statement—literature is political—is now acceptable when before it was not; nor do we look to our own antecedents for the sophisticated arguments upon which we can build in order to change the tendency of any established Western idea to become hegemonic.

For I feel that the new emphasis on literary critical theory is as hegemonic as the world which it attacks. I see the language it creates as one which mystifies rather than clarifies our condition, making it possible for a few people who know that particular language to control the critical scene—that language surfaced, interestingly enough, just when the literature of peoples of color, of black women, of Latin Americans, of Africans, began to move to 'the center'. Such words as *center* and *periphery* are themselves instructive. *Discourse, canon, texts*, words as Latinate as the tradition from which they come, are quite familiar to me. Because I went to a Catholic Mission school in the West Indies I must confess that I cannot hear the word 'canon' without smelling incense, that the word 'text' immediately brings back agonizing memories of Biblical exegesis, that 'discourse' reeks for me of metaphysics forced down my throat in those courses that traced *world* philosophy from Aristotle through Thomas Aquinas to Heidegger. 'Periphery' too is a word I heard throughout my childhood, for if anything was seen as being at the periphery, it was those small Caribbean islands which had neither land mass nor military power. Still I noted how intensely important this periphery was, for US troups were continually invading one island or another if any change in political control even seemed to be occurring. As I lived among folk for whom language was an absolutely necessary way of validating our existence, I was told that the minds of the world lived only in the small continent of Europe. The metaphysical language of the New Philosophy, then, I must admit, is repulsive to me and is one reason why I raced from philosophy to literature, since the latter seemed to me to have the possibilities of rendering the world as large and as complicated as I experienced it, as sensual as I knew it was. In literature I sensed the possibility of the integration of feeling/knowledge, rather than the split between the abstract and the emotional in which Western philosophy inevitably indulged.

Now I am being told that philosophers are the ones who write literature, that authors are dead, irrelevant, mere vessels through which their narratives ooze, that they do not work nor have they the faintest idea what they are doing; rather, they produce texts as disembodied as the angels. I am frankly astonished that scholars who call themselves marxists or post-marxists could seriously use such metaphysical language even as they attempt to deconstruct the philosophical tradition from which their language comes. And as a student of literature, I am appalled by the sheer ugliness of the language, its lack of clarity, its unnecessarily complicated sentence constructions, its lack of pleasurableness, its alienating quality. It is the kind of writing for which composition teachers would give a freshman a resounding F.

Because I am a curious person, however, I postponed readings of black women writers I was working on and read some of the prophets of this new literary orientation. These writers did announce their dissatisfaction with some of the cornerstone ideas of their own tradition, a dissatisfaction with which I was born. But in their attempt to change the orientation of Western scholarship, they, as usual, concentrated on themselves and were not in the slightest interested in the worlds they had ignored or controlled. Again I was supposed to know *them*, while they were not at all interested in knowing *me*. Instead they sought to 'deconstruct' the tradition to which they belonged even as they used the same forms, style, language of that tradition, forms that necessarily embody its values. And increasingly as I read them and saw their substitution of their philosophical writings for literary ones, I began to have the uneasy feeling that their folk were not producing any literature worth mentioning. For they always harkened back to the masterpieces of the past, again reifying the very texts they said they were deconstructing. Increasingly, as *their* way, *their* terms, *their* approaches remained central and became the means by which one defined literary critics, many of my own peers who had previously been concentrating on dealing with the other side of the equation, the reclamation and discussion of past and *present* Third World literatures, were diverted into continually discussing the new literary theory.

From my point of view as a critic of contemporary Afro-American women's writing, this orientation is extremely problematic. In attempting to find the deep structures in the literary tradition, a major preoccupation of the new New Criticism, many of us have become obsessed with the nature of reading itself to the extent that we have stopped writing about literature being written today. Since I am slightly paranoid, it has begun to occur to me that the literature being produced *is* precisely one of the reasons why this new philosophical-literary-critical theory of relativity is so prominent. In other words, the literature of blacks, women of South America and Africa, etc., as overtly 'political' literature, was being pre-empted by a new Western concept which proclaimed that reality does not exist, that everything is relative, and that every text is silent about something—which indeed it must necessarily be.

There is, of course, much to be learned from exploring how we know what we know, how we read what we read, an exploration which, of necessity, can have no end. But there also has to be a 'what', and that 'what', when it is even mentioned by the New Philosophers, are texts of the past, primarily Western male texts, whose norms are again being transferred onto Third World, female texts as theories of reading proliferate. Inevitably a hierarchy has now developed between what is called theoretical criticism and practical criticism, as mind is deemed superior to matter. I have no quarrel with those who wish to philosophize about how we know what we know. But I do resent the fact that this particular orientation is so privileged and has diverted so many of us from doing the first readings of the literature being written today as well as of past works about which nothing has been written. I note, for example, that there is little work done on Gloria Naylor, that most of Alice Walker's works have not been commented on—despite the rage around *The Color Purple*[4]— that there has yet to be an in-depth study of Frances Harper, the nineteenth-century abolitionist poet and novelist. If our emphasis on theoretical criticism continues, critics of the future may have to reclaim the writers we are now ignoring, that is, if they are even aware these artists exist.

I am particularly perturbed by the movement to exalt theory, as well, because of my own adult history. I was an active member of the Black Arts Movement of the 1960s and know how dangerous theory can become. Many today may not be aware of this, but the Black Arts Movement tried to create Black Literary Theory and in doing so became prescriptive. My fear is that when Theory is not rooted in practice, it becomes prescriptive, exclusive, elitist.

An example of this prescriptiveness is the approach the Black Arts Movement took towards language. For it, blackness resided in the use of black talk which they defined as hip urban language. So that when Nikki Giovanni reviewed Paule Marshall's *Chosen Place, Timeless People*, she criticized the novel on the grounds that it was not black, for the language was too elegant, too white.[5] Blacks, she said, did not speak that way. Having come from the West Indies where we do, some of the time, speak that way, I was amazed by the narrowness of her vision. The emphasis on *one way* to be black resulted in the works of Southern writers being seen as non-black since the black talk of Georgia does not sound like the black talk of Philadelphia. Because the ideologues, like Baraka, came from the urban centers, they tended to privilege their way of speaking, thinking, writing, and to condemn other kinds of writing as not being black enough. Whole areas of the canon were assessed according to the dictum of the Black Arts Nationalist point of view, as in Addison Gayle's *The Way of the New World*, while other works were ignored because they did not fit the scheme of cultural nationalism.[6] Older writers like Ralph Ellison and James Baldwin were condemned because they saw that the intersection of Western and African influences resulted in a new Afro-American culture, a position with which many of the Black Nationalist ideologues disagreed. Writers were told that writing love poems was not being black. Further examples abound.

It is true that the Black Arts Movement resulted in a necessary and important critique both of previous Afro-American literature and of the white-established literary world. But in attempting to take over power, it, as Ishmael Reed satirizes so well in *Mumbo Jumbo*, became much like its opponent, monolithic and downright repressive.[7]

It is this tendency towards the monolithic, monotheistic, and so on, that worries me about the race for theory. Constructs like the *center* and the *periphery* reveal that tendency to want to make the world less complex by organizing it according to one principle, to fix it through an idea which is really an ideal. Many of us are particularly sensitive to monolithism because one major element of ideologies of dominance, such as sexism and racism, is to dehumanize people by stereotyping them, by denying them their various-ness and complexity. Inevitably, monolithism becomes a metasystem, in which there is a controlling ideal, especially in relation to pleasure. Language as one form of pleasure is immediately restricted, and becomes heavy, abstract, prescriptive, monotonous.

Variety, multiplicity, eroticism are difficult to control. And it may very well be that these are the reasons why writers are often seen as *persona non grata* by political states, whatever form they take, since writers/artists have a tendency to refuse to give up their way of seeing the world and of playing with possibilities; in fact, their very expression relies on that insistence. Perhaps that is why creative literature, even when written by politically reactionary people, can be so freeing, for in having to embody ideas and recreate the world, writers cannot merely produce 'one way'.

The characteristics of the Black Arts Movement are, I am afraid, being repeated again today, certainly in the other area to which I am especially tuned. In the race for theory, feminists, eager to enter the halls of power, have attempted their own prescriptions. [...]

That tendency towards monolithism is precisely how I see the French feminist theorists. They concentrate on the female body as the means to creating a female language, since language, they say, is male and necessarily conceives of woman as other.[8] Clearly many of them have been irritated by the theories of Lacan for whom language is phallic. But suppose there are peoples in the world whose language was invented primarily in relation to women, who after all are the ones who relate to children and teach language. Some Native American languages, for example, use female pronouns when speaking about non-gender-specific activity. Who knows who, according to gender, created languages. Further, by positing the body as the source of everything French feminists return to the old myth that biology determines everything and ignore the fact that gender is a social rather than a biological construct.

I could go on critiquing the positions of French feminists who are them-selves more various in their points of view than the label which is used to describe them, but that is not my point. What I am concerned about is the authority this school now has in feminist scholarship—the way it has become *authoritative discourse*, monologic, which occurs precisely because it does have access to the means of promulgating its ideas. The Black Arts Movement was able to do this for a time because of the political movements of the 1960s—so too with the French feminists who could not be inventing 'theory' if a space had not been created by the women's movement. In both cases, both groups posited a theory that excluded many of the people who made that space possible. Hence one of the reasons for the surge of Afro-American women's writing during the 1970s and its emphasis on sexism in the black community is precisely that when the ideologues of the 1960s said *black*, they meant *black male*.[9] [...]

My major objection to the race for theory, as some readers have probably guessed by now, really hinges on the question, 'For whom are we doing what we are doing when we do literary criticism?' It is, I think, the central question today, especially for the few of us who have infiltrated academia enough to be wooed by it. The answer to that question determines what orientation we take in our work, the language we use, the purposes for which it is intended.

I can only speak for myself. But what I write and how I write is done in order to save my own life.[10] And I mean that literally. For me literature is a way of knowing that I am not hallucinating, that whatever I feel/know *is*. It is an affirmation that sensuality is intelligence, that sensual language is language that makes sense. My response, then, is directed to those who write what I read and to those who read what I read—put concretely—to Toni Morrison and to people who read Toni Morrison (among whom I would count few academics). That number is increasing, as is the readership of Walker and Marshall. But in no way is the literature Morrison, Marshall, or Walker create supported by the academic world. Nor given the political context of our society, do I expect that to change soon. For there is no reason, given who controls these institutions, for them to be anything other than threatened by these writers.

My readings do presuppose a need, a desire among folk who like me also want to save their own lives. My concern, then, is a passionate one, for the literature of people who are not in power has always been in danger of extinction or of cooptation, not because we do not theorize, but because what we can even imagine, far less who we can reach, is constantly limited by societal structures. For me, literary criticism is promotion as well as under-standing, a response to the writer to whom there is often no response, to folk who need the writing as much as they need anything. I know, from literary history, that writing disappears unless there is a response to it. Because I write about writers who are now writing, I hope to help ensure that their tradition has continuity and survives.

So my 'method', to use a new 'lit. crit.' word, is not fixed but relates to what I read and to the historical context of the writers I read *and* to the many critical activities in which I am engaged, which may or may not involve writing. It is a learning from the language of creative writers, which is one of surprise, so that I might discover what language I might use. For my language is very much based on what I read and how it affects me, that is, on the surprise that comes from reading something that compels you to read differently, as I believe literature does. I, therefore, have no set method, another prerequisite of the new theory, since for me every work suggests a new approach. As risky as that might seem, it is, I believe, what intelligence means—a tuned sensitivity to that which is alive and therefore cannot be known until it is known. Audre Lorde puts it in a far more succinct and sensual way in her essay 'Poetry is not a luxury':

As they become known to and accepted by us, our feelings and the honest exploration of them become sanctuaries and spawning grounds for the most radical and daring of ideas. They become a safe-house for that difference so necessary to change and the conceptualization of any meaningful action. Right now, I could name at least ten ideas I would have found intolerable or incomprehensible and frightening, except as they came after dreams and poems. This is not idle fantasy, but a disciplined attention to the true meaning of 'it feels right to me.' We can train ourselves to respect our feelings and to transpose them into a language so they can be shared. And where that language does not yet exist, it is our poetry which helps to fashion it. Poetry is not only dream and vision; it is the skeleton architecture of our lives. It lays the foundations for a future of change, a bridge across our fears of what has never been before.[11]

['The Race for Theory', in Linda Kauffmann (ed.), *Gender and Theory* (Oxford: Blackwell, 1989), 225–36; repr. (with changes) from *Cultural Critique*, 6 (Spring 1987), 51–63.]

ALICE JARDINE

10 Notes for an Analysis

If we bring two spaces—academia *and* psychoanalysis—together as psycho-analysis *in* the university, we arrive at a place where something is happening that deserves our notice. And/In—no simple opposition or analogy. I hope you will grant me the benefit of the doubt, even if not demonstrated now, that I am conscious of the fact that there are no simple inside/outside dichotomies here: on this note, we could perhaps re-member and be guided by the ins and outs of transference between 'Literature' and 'Psychoanalysis' orchestrated so beautifully and influentially for us by Shoshana Felman over ten years ago.[1]

Also, we will not demonstrate here—even if we must never and can never leave behind—the macropolitics *organizing* the ins and outs, interior and exterior frontiers of these two mental institutions (psychoanalysis and the university): first, *money* of course; and second, an organization, conception of *the mental*, of the mental apparatus which psychoanalysis and the university mirror constantly in each other: a particular figuration of the highest faculties, constructed at the beginning of the nineteenth century in Berlin. And, of course, both psychoanalysis and the university are institutions *with schools*, and as David Carroll has pointed out recently and succinctly, 'Institutions and schools exist to occupy positions of power, to neutralize dissent, and to domesticate all oppositional forces and foreign bodies; their authority depends on it.'[2] How can we possibly forget that both of these institutions finally report to the state? Note Nietzsche on the professor's speaking mouth with many ears, the university culture machine, and so-called academic freedom—as in *On The Future of Our Educational Institutions;*[3] or, more visibly, let us not forget the collaboration of institutions of psychoanalysis with certain Latin American or Soviet states as noted, for example, in Derrida's 'Géopsychanalyse—"and all the rest of the world" '.[4]

For now, all of these difficult questions will simply have to underwrite what I want to voice here—haltingly, tentatively—about two *particular* political problems currently preoccupying me—and a few others I think.

The first problem is sometimes referred to in working shorthand as the dilemma of short-term vs. long-term political effects, of working *fast* vs. working *slow.* This debate, in literary critical circles, is most often articulated in traditional binary fashion as: (1) construction vs. deconstruction; (2) the drive to name vs. disarticulation; (3) unity vs. heterogeneity; (4) the Cartesian 'I' vs. complex subjectivity; (5) Anglo-American vs. French; and, increasingly, as (6) a return to literary history vs. literary theory—there is even the question of 'politically correct texts of pleasure' vs. 'politically wrong texts of jouissance'. The dis-ease associated with these ultimately epistemological battles currently continues to spread on the international scene in several different forms: for example, critical legal studies people are attacked because of anxieties about how endless deconstruction of the legal text leaves no room for legal definition; activists argue that the 'undecidable'—as the very definition of the political—evoked by Barbara Johnson's stunning essay on 'Apostrophe, animation, and abortion' probably did not, after all, get very many people out to vote no (which meant yes) in the Massachusetts Abortion Referendum in November 1986.[5] In a different scene, and in Richard Rorty's words, we see such twisted battles as where 'the French critics of Habermas [are] ready to abandon liberal politics in order to avoid a universalist philosophy, and . . . Habermas [is] trying to cling to a universalist philosophy, with all the problems that involves, in order to prop up a liberal politics'.[6] Or, for example, we hear debates over whether in the United States we must take the time to think through the paleonomic and tropological implications of

'Apartheid' and 'Solidarity' or rather, go out and do/write/say whatever is necessary to provoke immediate US divestment from South Africa.[7] That is, there seems to be growing political impatience with the debate over how politically patient one should be. And the solution of 'one always does both anyway'—i.e. act conservatively and radically at the same time—seems to be wearing thin, when it's not wrapped up in pluralist giftwrap and handed over to the powers that be. I am particularly concerned in this context by what I have analysed elsewhere as a kind of territorializing of more specific- ally feminist versions of these questions by *paranoia* and *fetishism*.[8] While both participate in what I call 'a demand for doubling', paranoia is about deciding, defining, making strong cases; fetishism about the both, neither/nor, refusal to decide, define, or go to court. I am referring here, for example, to the difference between asserting that 'women are different from men' (implying we *know* what women are) and saying (in the same breath) 'Women are different. No they are not'—implying we *do not* know what they are. I have suggested that the current period of tense coexistence of these two states is about living and thinking in a mode of *impossibility* sometimes referred to in other contexts as 'postmodernism', a state within which women are caught like everyone else ... But we will return to the impossible in a moment.

The second immediate political problem with which I am concerned as a feminist teaching in the university is with the problems and questions arising now that there are at least two generations of explicitly and politically feminist women professors in the academy: let us say those who received their Ph.D. between 1968 and 1978 and those who received it after 1978. Now I want to emphasize '*at least two* generations' and '*explicitly* and *politically* feminist' here for two reasons. First because, of course, there are technically three (soon to be four) generations of women professors in the United States today. Most significantly, there is an important generation of women who received their Ph.D. (often long) before 1968. Secondly, however, what is more important here than the question of 'generation' is the question of one's discursive, political positioning *vis-à-vis* the women's liberation movement. Before 1968 it was difficult, if not impossible, to be an explicitly political feminist scholar in the institution. And I think it is safe to say that the majority of those women who were allowed access, before the late 1960s, to full status as professors were not explicitly political feminists. Many were, in fact, resistent when not hostile to feminism even as they were fighting feminist battles every day of their lives. Those extraordinary few women full profes- sors who were explicitly and politically feminist before 1968 were most extraordinary indeed and I would include them within the first post-1968 generation. (It is perhaps important to remember that these women often did not receive recognition for their (feminist) work until relatively late in their careers—that is to say, until *after* 1968.) Let us just say that it is the two generations of explicitly and politically feminist women who have come to intellectual/academic age since 1968 that will be of primary interest to me here.[9]

Now, first of all, there is the question of what the institution has done/is doing to all of these generations of women: that is a long story. What happens to women 'constrained to transport the discourse of men and the body of women',[10] has, of course, been analysed for a long while. Alternatives include: be alone, isolated, and asexual; get sick; at least act, look, and speak neuter; or leave. I am talking about the power of the desire of the homosocially patriarchal academy to force women to relinquish 'the feminine'—in the strong Irigarayan force of the term, what Juliet Mitchell describes as 'the Other' for both sexes[11]—so as to make them, first, 'undesirables' within dominant heterosexual ideology and, then, eventually, *ne-euter* (neither one nor the other) in the terms of male representations. This desire creates either (as Mary Ann Doane puts it) 'an asexual . . . perfect and unthreatening mate for the "good old Americano" '[12]—or else has you kicked out. This situation has raised a lot of questions—especially on the part of an upcoming generation, the young women Ph.D. students I know—about what price they are willing to pay, how much they are willing to give up, for a place in the academy. That is, a lot of them—those who are politicized at least—do not want to live like the first generations of academic women have had to live.

But there is also the perhaps even more difficult question of the relationships *between* the two post-1968 generations of feminist women in the academy. I would like to avoid the mother/daughter paradigm here (so as not to succumb simply to miming the traditional father/son, master/disciple model), but it is difficult to avoid at this point being positioned by the institution as mothers and daughters.[13] Structures of debt/gift (mothers and increasingly daughters control a lot of money and prestige in the university), structures of our new institutional power over each other, desires and demands for recognition and love—all of these are falling into place in rather familiar ways. Accusations fly about on both sides as to who is really feminist or not; who has been recuperated or not; who is just miming the masters (is it the often more history-minded mothers or more theory-minded daughters?); whose fault is it that there is a general perception that feminism has become facile, tamed while, precisely, the humanities are being feminized? People are asking—or should be—how did we get to the intellectual and political point where one of the reigning topics of discussion among supposedly politicized women is often quite exclusively hiring/firing and chances for tenure? It sometimes sounds, as Patricia Baudoin has put it, as if the *political* has become the *personal*—as if our professional status has even become our personal status.[14] And throughout all of this, no one, neither mother nor daughter, can ever seem to accomplish enough . . .

At this point, I would like to suggest that, with a slight change of optic, it is in fact *feminist women*, of both of these post-1968 generations in the academy, who are in a special, strategic position as new kinds of subjects to think through and act upon these problems, together, in potentially new and radical ways. I think this potential exists because feminism, psychoanalysis, and the institution are, today, triply implicated in a major historical, archaeological, epistemological mutation: a mutation of the public and private spheres, a new kind of interference between the *polis* and *ta oikeia*.[15] *At the same time*, there is a massive *oedipalization* as privatization of the public sphere and a massive *publification* (in Latin, democritization) of the private sphere. More specifically (and narrowly given the contexts and texts which interest us here), there is a reconfiguration of public and private spaces throughout our institutions; in the university, for example, (a particular scene of representation), *concurrent with the entry of women into that scene*. Further, *both* women and psychoanalysis are entering that scene *together*, disrupting it—which is logical since women are psychoanalysis's reason for existence, its history and stories: we are its cases (as Mary Ann Doane reminds us: the text of the unconscious *is* the female hysteric).[16] In fact, many of the same women who are disrupting the institution work in psychoanalysis, a lot of them are even *in* analysis (usually with women). Even more specifically, this mutation of the public and private, the contamination of the classic scene of representation with and through 'the other scene' (scene of the other), has a lot to do (as you might guess) with writing and the voice: this is a dichotomy perhaps intellectually problematized years ago but which has continued to structure our energies and affects in specific ways. We have learned how writing and the voice weave together, overlap, are exchanged—through the voice's writing and writing's voice—always, but differently. At the same time, we have thought less perhaps about what this new kind of knowledge is doing to the patriarchal institution and its systems of representation: public writing (scientific, academic, and literary publishing) and the public voice (lecturing and teaching) have traditionally been gendered as male; private writing (diaries and letters) and private voice (intimacy; the analytic space) have been gendered as female. That has begun to change with women's history-making move from the private to the public (their massive publification) and the creation of certain chiasmatic and paradoxical situations such as writing being gendered as feminine in the male public sphere; or, as Juliet Mitchell has pointed out, the fact that feminism and psychoanalysis share a central paradox which is shaking up the pedagogue in all of us: they are both *humanist* (concerned with how the 'I' is constructed) and, at the same time, and often through the same moves, dramatically *counter-humanist* (decentering the Man in each of us).[17]

What I am trying to get to here is a new and different scene, at a new intersection of psychoanalysis, feminism, and the institution, where a radical deconstruction of the academic subject is taking place; where a radically new kind of knowledge is being produced; and where women are becoming radical agents of that new knowledge and of political change *if* and *when* they actualize freely the mutations and paradoxes I have been referring to. In order to think just a bit more about all of this—especially about the two specific problems I raised concerning (1) short-term and long-term political effects and (2) generations of women—I would like to suggest returning to this intersection briefly from two other, different directions: first, more 'abstractly', in terms of the radical differences between the 'analytic' and 'pedagogic' scenes (to which women have had special access) and secondly, more 'concretely', by thinking about two other generations of women— those at the beginning of this century and those at its end who have some- how, in some form, for some reason, *written* about their own psychoanaly- sis—a very odd thing to do.

Jane Gallop has come close to defining the institution as massive group transference.[18] I would add: if that institution is the university, it is the very site of the 'being-up-front' mentioned earlier on. The *traditional* institutional scene at least is anywhere the scene of representation is based on the mirror and where women's discourse is carefully controlled, sometimes by her own narration. It is a 'life-trap' (in Rilke's phrase), where there are 'practical demonstrations' of pre-packaged knowledge, the 'object of university dip- lomas'.[19] Again, without wanting to forget that there are no easy oppositions here, no pure spaces, I do think there is *another* scene, a scene of psychic logic tentatively evoked in my opening notes: an analytic scene between two, increasingly between two women. An entire issue of a feminist journal in Europe, *BIEF*, has recently been devoted to the twentieth-century analytic space as a *female* space to which women have increasingly turned in much larger numbers than men (especially with a certain democritization of analy- sis under the influence of feminism). Women have done this not *just* as (or not only just as) victims in search of an other private space because access to a public voice and public writing is still, historically, very difficult for women;[20] but they have turned to this other space also as *artists* and *agents of change* who can there let go of the all-powerful fantasmatic other holding them back.

The institutional scene is to the analytic scene as assurance is to the lack thereof; as self-mastery is to the relinquishing of control; as fast is to slow; as product is to process; certainty to doubt; as emphasis on success is to failure; gaining time to losing and wasting it; as project is to projection; reason to unreason; *la gestion* (bureaucracy) to gestation (nurturing); as solutions are to dissolutions; progressions to regressions; required good humor and social smiles to tantrums and tears; as consolidate is to *ana-lyein* (to break up or to loosen); as memorizing is to anamnesis; the voluntary to the involuntary; gain to loss; as that which has already been said is to that which language does not yet know how to say. In the institutional scene, what is important is the best possible performance. In the analytic scene, what is important is to dream. In the pedagogical scene, one must make known an object, make it universally knowable; whereas, of course, the dream is not reproducible, can never be made universally accessible.[21] In short, the bodies of teaching and bodies of the unconscious were never supposed to meet. But they have and it is women who know about that. [. . .]

So now what scene are we left in? Is the only answer to these public and private, generational, short- and long-term dilemmas, to be an activist, analyst, professor, writer of both generations all at once!? Impossible for most of us. And that is the note upon which I would end: these notes were taken because it seems to me that feminism has not yet thought through what we shall call here the function of the *radical feminist intellectual, teacher, and writer* in the way other radical movements have at least tried to do. It seems to me that if we could do that by looking carefully at (instead of avoiding) the new and strong tensions between and within psychic and representational spaces—as well as between and within generations of women—then the radical political potentials located at the intersections we have been criss-crossing here could begin to be orchestrated in new ways. Feminist women could then assume together a renewed and privileged political position as the *agents* of radical change evoked earlier on.

I would just add a few measures to that note. First, I think that this new kind of feminist intellectual must fully inscribe herself within an ethics of impossibility. Second, she might do so through an acute attention to something other than past, present, or future: the *future anterior*, the privileged modality, as we know, of the psychic, the poetic, the feminist, and the postmodern. Lacan:

What is realized in my history [my story] is not the past definite of what was, since it is no more, or even the present perfect of what has been in what I am, but the future anterior of what I shall have been for what I am in the process of becoming.[22]

Moving from an individual to a collective analytic perspective, the future anterior incorporates the possibility of understanding the history/story we are, through and from the perspective of the generation before us, in so far as that perspective becomes or is now our own—and is realized in the future. Further, to the extent that each generation is necessarily in a transferential relation to the other, what one generation criticizes in the other may (and probably must) echo the difficulties within itself. In other words, to place ourselves within a generation of women, while paying attention to the multiple projections inherent to the scene of psychoanalysis, might help us to identify our own blindspots. So that, finally, to place ourselves, *as feminist women*—across the generations—together, at the very place of the most chiasmatic, most paradoxical intersections of the future (*post*) anterior (*modo*) can allow us to do away with paranoia (and its publics); fetishism (and its privates); and the concept of 'generation' altogether.

But then perhaps you should just consider what I have been writing here as but some notes upon a mystic writing pad . . .'

['Notes for an Analysis', in Teresa Brennan (ed.), *Between Feminism and Psychoanalysis* (London: Routledge, 1989), 73–85.]

BARBARA SMITH

11   The Truth that Never Hurts, Black Lesbians in Fiction in the 1980s

Just as surely as a Black woman writer's relationship to feminism affects the themes she might choose to write about, a Black woman critic's relationship to feminism determines the kind of criticism she is willing and able to do. The fact that critics are usually also academics, however, has often affected Black women critics' approach to feminist issues. If a Black woman scholar's only connection to women's issues is via women's studies, as presented by white women academics, most of whom are not activists, her access to movement analyses and practice will be limited or nonexistent. I believe that the most accurate and developed theory, including literary theory, comes from practice, from the experience of activism. This relationship between theory and practice is crucial when inherently political subject matter, such as the condition of women as depicted in a writer's work, is being discussed. I do not believe it is possible to arrive at fully developed and useful Black feminist criticism by merely reading about feminism. Of course every Black woman has her own experiences of sexual political dynamics and oppression to draw upon, and referring to these experiences should be an important resource in shaping her analyses of a literary work. However, studying feminist texts and drawing only upon one's *individual* experiences of sexism are insufficient.

I remember the point in my own experience when I no longer was involved on a regular basis in organizations such as the Boston Committee to End Sterilization Abuse and the Abortion Action Coalition. I was very aware that my lack of involvement affected my thinking and writing *overall*. Certain perceptions were simply unavailable to me because I no longer was doing that particular kind of ongoing work. And I am referring to missing something much deeper than access to specific information about sterilization and reproductive rights. Activism has spurred me to write the kinds of theory and criticism I have written and has provided the experiences and insights that have shaped the perceptions in my work. Many examples of this vital relationship between activism and theory exist in the work of thinkers such as Ida

B. Wells-Barnett, W.E.B. Du Bois, Lillian Smith, Lorraine Hansberry, Frantz Fanon, Barbara Deming, Paolo Freire, and Angela Davis.

A critic's involvement or lack of involvement in activism, specifically in the context of the feminist movement, is often signally revealed by the approach she takes to Lesbianism. If a woman has worked in organizations where Lesbian issues have been raised, where homophobia was unacceptable and struggled with, and where she had the opportunity to meet and work with a variety of Lesbians, her relationship to Lesbians and to her own homophobia would undoubtedly be affected. The types of political organizations in which such dialogue occurs are not, of course, exclusively Lesbian and may focus upon a range of issues, such as women in prison, sterilization abuse, reproductive freedom, health care, domestic violence, and sexual assault.

Black feminist critics who are Lesbians can usually be counted upon to approach Black women's and Black Lesbian writing nonhomophobically. Non-Lesbian Black feminist critics are not as dependable in this regard. I even question at times designating Black women—critics and noncritics alike—as feminists who are actively homophobic in what they write, say, or do, or who are passively homophobic because they ignore Lesbian existence entirely. Yet such critics are obviously capable of analyzing other sexual and political implications of the literature they scrutinize. Political definitions, particularly of feminism, can be difficult to pin down. The one upon which I generally rely states: 'Feminism is the political theory and practice that struggles to free *all* women: women of color, working-class women, poor women, disabled women, lesbians, old women—as well as white, economically privileged, heterosexual women. Anything less than this vision of total freedom is not feminism, but merely female self-aggrandizement.'

A Black gay college student recently recounted an incident to me that illustrates the kind of consciousness that is grievously lacking among non-feminist Black women scholars about Black Lesbian existence. His story indicates why a Black feminist approach to literature, criticism, and research in a variety of disciplines is crucial if one is to recognize and understand Black Lesbian experience. While researching a history project, he contacted the archives at a Black institution that has significant holdings on Black women. He spoke to a Black woman archivist and explained that he was looking for materials on Black Lesbians in the 1940s. Her immediate response was to laugh uproariously and then to say that the collection contained very little on women during that period and nothing at all on Lesbians in any of the periods covered by its holdings.

Not only was her reaction appallingly homophobic, not to mention impolite, but it was also inaccurate. One of the major repositories of archival material on Black women in the country of course contains material by and about Black Lesbians. The material, however, is not identified and defined as such and thus remains invisible. This is a classic case of 'invisibility [becoming] an unnatural disaster', as feminist poet Mitsuye Yamada observes.[2]

I suggested a number of possible resources to the student and in the course of our conversation I told him I could not help but think of Cheryl Clarke's classic poem, 'Of Althea and Flaxie'. It begins:

> In 1943 Althea was a welder
> very dark
> very butch
> and very proud
> loved to cook, sew, and drive a car
> and did not care who knew she kept company with a woman.[3]

The poem depicts a realistic and positive Black Lesbian relationship which survives Flaxie's pregnancy in 1955; Althea's going to jail for writing numbers in 1958, poverty, racism, and, of course, homophobia. If the archivist's vision had not been so blocked by homophobia, she would have been able to direct this student to documents that corroborate the history embodied in Clarke's poem.

Being divorced from the experience of feminist organizing not only makes it more likely that a woman has not been directly challenged to examine her homophobia, but it can also result in erroneous approaches to Black Lesbian literature, if she does decide to talk or write about it. For example, some critics, instead of simply accepting that Black Lesbians and Black Lesbian writers exist, view the depiction of Lesbianism as a dangerous and unacceptable 'theme' or 'trend' in Black women's writing. Negative discussions of 'themes' and 'trends', which may in time fade, do not acknowledge that for survival, Black Lesbians, like any oppressed group, need to see our faces reflected in myriad cultural forms, including literature. Some critics go so far as to see the few Black Lesbian books in existence as a kind of conspiracy and bemoan that there is 'so much' of this kind of writing available in print; they put forth the supreme untruth that it is actually an advantage to be a Black Lesbian writer.

For each Lesbian of color in print there are undoubtedly five dozen whose work has never been published and may never be. The publication of Lesbians of color is a 'new' literary development, made possible by alternative, primarily Lesbian/feminist presses. The political and aesthetic strength of this writing is indicated by its impact having been far greater than its actual availability. At times its content has had revolutionary implications. But the impact of Black Lesbian feminist writing, to which Calvin Hernton refers, should not be confused with easy access to print, to readers, or to the material perks that help a writer survive economically.

Terms like 'heterophobia', used to validate the specious notion that 'so many' Black women writers are now depicting loving and sexual relationships between women, to the exclusion of focusing on relationships with men, arise in an academic vacuum, uninfluenced by political reality. 'Heterophobia' resembles the concept of 'reverse racism'. Both are thoroughly reactionary and have nothing to do with the actual dominance of a heterosexual white power structure.

Equating Lesbianism with separatism is another error in terminology, which will probably take a number of years to correct. The title of a workshop at a major Black women writers' conference, for example, was 'Separatist Voices in the New Canon'. The workshop examined the work of Audre Lorde and Alice Walker, neither of whom defines herself as a separatist, either sexually or racially. In his introduction to *Confirmation: An Anthology of African American Women*, co-editor Imamu Baraka is critical of feminists who are separatists, but he does not mention that any such thing as a Lesbian exists. In his ambiguous yet inherently homophobic usage, the term 'separatist' is made to seem like a mistaken political tendency, which correct thinking could alter. If 'separatist' equals Lesbian, Baraka is suggesting that we should change our minds and eradicate ourselves. In both these instances the fact that Lesbians do not have sexual relationships with men is thought to be the same as ideological Lesbian 'separatism'. Such an equation does not take into account that the majority of Lesbians of color have interactions with men and that those who are activists are quite likely to be politically committed to coalition work as well.

Inaccuracy and distortion seem to be particularly frequent pitfalls when non-Lesbians address Black Lesbian experience because of generalized homophobia and because the very nature of our oppression may cause us to be hidden or 'closeted', voluntarily or involuntarily isolated from other communities, and as a result unseen and unknown. In her essay, 'A Cultural Legacy Denied and Discovered: Black Lesbians in Fiction by Women', Jewelle Gomez asserts the necessity for realistic portrayals of Black Lesbians:

These Black Lesbian writers . . . have seen into the shadows that hide the existence of Black Lesbians and understand they have to create a universe/home that rings true on all levels. . . . The Black Lesbian writer must throw herself into the arms of her culture by acting as student/teacher/participant/observer, absorbing and synthesizing the meanings of our existence as a people. She must do this despite the fact that both our culture and our sexuality have been severely truncated and distorted.

Nature abhors a vacuum and there is a distinct gap in the picture where the Black Lesbian should be. The Black Lesbian writer must recreate our home, unadulterated, unsanitized, specific and not isolated from the generations that have nurtured us.[4]

This is an excellent statement of what usually has been missing from portrayals of Black Lesbians in fiction. The degree of truthfulness and self-revelation that Gomez calls for encompasses the essential qualities of verisimilitude and authenticity that I look for in depictions of Black Lesbians. By verisimilitude I mean how true to life and realistic a work of literature is. By authenticity I mean something even deeper—a characterization which reflects a relationship to self that is genuine, integrated, and whole. For a Lesbian or a gay man, this kind of emotional and psychological authenticity virtually requires the degree of self-acceptance inherent in being out. This is not a dictum, but an observation. It is not a coincidence, however, that the most vital and useful Black Lesbian feminist writing is being written by Black Lesbians who are not caught in the impossible bind of simultaneously hiding identity yet revealing self through their writing.

Positive and realistic portrayals of Black Lesbians are sorely needed, portraits that are, as Gomez states, 'unadulterated, unsanitized, specific'. By positive I do not mean characters without problems, contradictions, or flaws, mere uplift literature for Lesbians, but instead, writing that is sufficiently sensitive and complex, which places Black Lesbian experience and struggles squarely within the realm of recognizable human experience and concerns.

As African-Americans, our desire for authentic literary images of Black Lesbians has particular cultural and historical resonance, since a desire for authentic images of ourselves as Black people preceded it long ago. After an initial period of racial uplift literature in the nineteenth and early twentieth centuries, Black artists during the Harlem Renaissance of the 1920s began to assert the validity of fully Black portrayals in all art forms including literature. In his pivotal essay of 1926, 'The Negro Artist and the Racial Mountain', Langston Hughes asserted:

We younger Negro artists who create now intend to express our individual dark-skinned selves without fear or shame. If white people are pleased we are glad. If they are not, it doesn't matter. We know we are beautiful. And ugly too. The tom-tom cries and the tom-tom laughs. If colored people are pleased we are glad. If they are not, their displeasure doesn't matter either. We build our temples for tomorrow, strong as we know how, and we stand on top of the mountain, free within ourselves.[5]

Clearly, it was not always popular or safe with either Black or white audiences to depict Black people as we actually are. It still is not. Too many contemporary Blacks seem to have forgotten the universally debased social–political position Black people have occupied during all the centuries we have been here, up until perhaps the Civil Rights Movement of the 1960s. The most racist definition of Black people has been that we were not human.

Undoubtedly every epithet now hurled at Lesbians and gay men—'sinful', 'sexually depraved', 'criminal', 'emotionally maladjusted', 'deviant'—has also been applied to Black People. When W. E. B. Du Bois described life 'behind the veil', and Paul Laurence Dunbar wrote,

> We wear the mask that grins and lies,
> It hides our cheeks and shades our eyes,—
> This debt we pay to human guile;
> With torn and bleeding hearts we smile,
> And mouth with myriad subtleties.
>
> Why should the world be overwise,
> In counting all our tears and sighs?
> Nay, let them only see us, while
>   We wear the mask.[6]

what were they describing but racial closeting? For those who refuse to see the parallels because they view Blackness as irreproachably normal, but persist in defining same-sex love relationships as unnatural, Black Lesbian feminist poet, Audre Lorde, reminds us: " 'Oh,'' says a voice from the Black community, "but being Black is N O R M A L !" Well, I and many Black people of my age can remember grimly the days when it didn't used to be!'[7] Lorde is not implying that she believes that there was ever anything wrong with being Black, but points out how distorted 'majority' consciousness can cruelly affect an oppressed community's actual treatment and sense of self. The history of slavery, segregation, and racism was based upon the assumption by the powers-that-be that Blackness was decidedly neither acceptable nor normal. Unfortunately, despite legal and social change, large numbers of racist whites still believe the same thing to this day.

The existence of Lesbianism and male homosexuality is normal, too, traceable throughout history and across cultures. It is a society's *response* to the ongoing historical fact of homosexuality that determines whether it goes unremarked as nothing out of the ordinary, as it is in some cultures, or if it is instead greeted with violent repression, as it is in ours. At a time when Acquired Immune Deficiency Syndrome (AIDS), a disease associated with an already despised sexual minority, is occasioning mass hysteria among the heterosexual majority (including calls or firings, evictions, quarantining, imprisonment, and even execution), the way in which sexual orientation is viewed is not of mere academic concern. It is mass political organizing that has wrought the most significant changes in the status of Blacks and other people of color and that has altered society's perceptions about us and our images of ourselves. The Black Lesbian feminist movement simply continues that principled tradition of struggle.

['The Truth that Never Hurts: Black Lesbians in Fiction in the 1980s', in Joanne Braxton and Andree Nicola McLaughlin (eds.), *Wild Women in the Whirlwind: Afro–American Culture and the Contemporary Literary Renaissance* (New Brunswick, NJ: Rutgers University Press, 1990), 693–8.]

12 Under Western Eyes: Feminist Scholarship and Colonial Discourses

Any discussion of the intellectual and political construction of 'third world feminisms' must address itself to two simultaneous projects: the internal critique of hegemonic 'Western' feminisms, and the formulation of autonomous, geographically, historically, and culturally grounded feminist concerns and strategies. The first project is one of deconstructing and dismantling; the second, one of building and constructing. While these projects appear to be contradictory, the one working negatively and the other positively, unless these two tasks are addressed simultaneously, 'third world' feminisms run the risk of marginalization or ghettoization from both mainstream (right and left) and Western feminist discourses.

It is to the first project that I address myself. What I wish to analyze is specifically the production of the 'third world woman' as a singular monolithic subject in some recent (Western) feminist texts. The definition of colonization I wish to invoke here is a predominantly *discursive* one, focusing on a certain mode of appropriation and codification of 'scholarship' and 'knowledge' about women in the third world by particular analytic categories employed in specific writings on the subject which take as their referent feminist interests as they have been articulated in the U.S. and Western Europe. If one of the tasks of formulating and understanding the locus of 'third world feminisms' is delineating the way in which it resists and *works against* what I am referring to as 'Western feminist discourse', an analysis of the discursive construction of 'third world women' in Western feminism is an important first step.

Clearly Western feminist discourse and political practice is neither singular nor homogeneous in its goals, interests, or analyses. However, it is possible to trace a coherence of *effects* resulting from the implicit assumption of 'the West' (in all its complexities and contradictions) as the primary referent in theory and praxis. My reference to 'Western feminism' is by no means intended to imply that it is a monolith. Rather, I am attempting to draw attention to the similar effects of various textual strategies used by writers which codify Others as non-Western and hence themselves as (implicitly) Western. It is in this sense that I use the term *Western feminist*. Similar arguments can be made in terms of middle-class urban African or Asian scholars producing scholarship on or about their rural or working-class sisters which assumes their own middle-class cultures as the norm, and codifies working-class histories and cultures as Other. Thus, while this essay focuses specifically on what I refer to as 'Western feminist' discourse on women in the third world, the critiques I offer also pertain to third world scholars writing about their own cultures, which employ identical analytic strategies.

It ought to be of some political significance, at least, that the term *coloniza-tion* has come to denote a variety of phenomena in recent feminist and left writings in general. From its analytic value as a category of exploitative economic exchange in both traditional and contemporary Marxisms (cf. particularly contemporary theorists such as Baran 1962, Amin 1977, and Gunder-Frank 1967) to its use by feminist women of color in the U.S. to describe the appropriation of their experiences and struggles by hegemonic white women's movements (cf. especially Moraga and Anzaldúa 1983, Smith 1983, Joseph and Lewis 1981, and Moraga 1984),[1] colonization has been used to characterize everything from the most evident economic and political hier-archies to the production of a particular cultural discourse about what is called the 'third world'.[2] However sophisticated or problematical its use as an explanatory construct, colonization almost invariably implies a relation of structural domination, and a suppression—often violent—of the heterogen-eity of the subject(s) in question.

My concern about such writings derives from my own implication and investment in contemporary debates in feminist theory, and the urgent political necessity (especially in the age of Reagan/Bush) of forming strategic coalitions across class, race, and national boundaries. The analytic principles discussed below serve to distort Western feminist political practices, and limit the possibility of coalitions among (usually white) Western feminists and working-class feminists and feminists of color around the world. These limitations are evident in the construction of the (implicitly consensual) priority of issues around which apparently *all* women are expected to organ-ize. The necessary and integral connection between feminist scholarship and feminist political practice and organizing determines the significance and status of Western feminist writings on women in the third world, for feminist scholarship, like most other kinds of scholarship, is not the mere production of knowledge about a certain subject. It is a directly political and discursive *practice* in that it is purposeful and ideological. It is best seen as a mode of intervention into particular hegemonic discourses (for example, traditional anthropology, sociology, literary criticism, etc.); it is a political praxis which counters and resists the totalizing imperative of age-old 'legitimate' and 'scientific' bodies of knowledge. Thus, feminist scholarly practices (whether reading, writing, critical, or textual) are inscribed in relations of power— relations which they counter, resist, or even perhaps implicitly support. There can, of course, be no apolitical scholarship.

The relationship between 'Woman'—a cultural and ideological composite Other constructed through diverse representational discourses (scientific, literary, juridical, linguistic, cinematic, etc.)—and 'women'—real, material subjects of their collective histories—is one of the central questions the practice of feminist scholarship seeks to address. This connection between women as historical subjects and the re-presentation of Woman produced by hegemonic discourses is not a relation of direct identity, or a relation of correspondence or simple implication.[3] It is an arbitrary relation set up by particular cultures. I would like to suggest that the feminist writings I analyze here discursively colonize the material and historical heterogeneities of the lives of women in the third world, thereby producing/re-presenting a composite, singular 'third world woman'—an image which appears arbitrarily constructed, but nevertheless carries with it the authorizing signature of Western humanist discourse.

I argue that assumptions of privilege and ethnocentric universality, on the one hand, and inadequate self-consciousness about the effect of Western scholarship on the 'third world' in the context of a world system dominated by the West, on the other, characterize a sizable extent of Western feminist work on women in the third world. An analysis of 'sexual difference' in the form of a cross-culturally singular, monolithic notion of patriarchy or male dominance leads to the construction of a similarly reductive and homogeneous notion of what I call the 'third world difference'—that stable, ahistorical something that apparently oppresses most if not all the women in these countries. And it is in the production of this 'third world difference' that Western feminisms appropriate and 'colonize' the constitutive complexities which characterize the lives of women in these countries. It is in this process of discursive homogenization and systematization of the oppression of women in the third world that power is exercised in much of recent Western feminist discourse, and this power needs to be defined and named.

In the context of the West's hegemonic position today, of what Anouar Abdel-Malek (1981)[4] calls a struggle for 'control over the orientation, regulation and decision of the process of world development on the basis of the advanced sector's monopoly of scientific knowledge and ideal creativity', Western feminist scholarship on the third world must be seen and examined precisely in terms of its inscription in these particular relations of power and struggle. There is, it should be evident, no universal patriarchal framework which this scholarship attempts to counter and resist—unless one posits an international male conspiracy or a monolithic, ahistorical power structure. There is, however, a particular world balance of power within which any analysis of culture, ideology, and socioeconomic conditions necessarily has to be situated. Abdel-Malek is useful here, again, in reminding us about the inherence of politics in the discourses of 'culture':

Contemporary imperialism is, in a real sense, a hegemonic imperialism, exercising to a maximum degree a rationalized violence taken to a higher level than ever before—through fire and sword, but also through the attempt to control hearts and minds. For its content is defined by the combined action of the military-industrial complex and the hegemonic cultural centers of the West, all of them founded on the advanced levels of development attained by monopoly and finance capital, and supported by the benefits of both the scientific and technological revolution and the second industrial revolution itself. (145–6)

Western feminist scholarship cannot avoid the challenge of situating itself and examining its role in such a global economic and political framework. To do any less would be to ignore the complex interconnections between first and third world economies and the profound effect of this on the lives of women in all countries. I do not question the descriptive and informative value of most Western feminist writings on women in the third world. I also do not question the existence of excellent work which does not fall into the analytic traps with which I am concerned. In fact I deal with an example of such work later on. In the context of an overwhelming silence about the experiences of women in these countries, as well as the need to forge international links between women's political struggles, such work is both pathbreaking and absolutely essential. However, it is both to the *explanatory potential* of particular analytic strategies employed by such writing, and to their *political effect* in the context of the hegemony of Western scholarship that I want to draw attention here. While feminist writing in the U.S. is still marginalized (except from the point of view of women of color addressing privileged white women), Western feminist writing on women in the third world must be considered in the context of the global hegemony of Western scholarship—i.e. the production, publication, distribution, and consumption of information and ideas. Marginal or not, this writing has political effects and implications beyond the immediate feminist or disciplinary audience. One such significant effect of the dominant 'representations' of Western feminism is its conflation with imperialism in the eyes of particular third world women.[5] Hence the urgent need to examine the *political* implications of our *analytic* strategies and principles.

My critique is directed at three basic analytic principles which are present in (Western) feminist discourse on women in the third world. [. . .]

The first analytic presupposition I focus on is involved in the strategic location of the category 'women' vis-à-vis the context of analysis. The assumption of women as an already constituted, coherent group with identical interests and desires, regardless of class, ethnic or racial location, or contradictions, implies a notion of gender or sexual difference or even patriarchy which can be applied universally and cross-culturally. (The context of analysis can be anything from kinship structures and the organization of labor to media representations.) The second analytical presupposition is evident on the methodological level, in the uncritical way 'proof' of universality and cross-cultural validity are provided. The third is a more specifically political presupposition underlying the methodologies and the analytic strategies, i.e. the model of power and struggle they imply and suggest. I argue that as a result of the two modes—or, rather, frames—of analysis described above, a homogeneous notion of the oppression of women as a group is assumed, which, in turn, produces the image of an 'average third world woman'. This average third world woman leads an essentially truncated life based on her feminine gender (read: sexually constrained) and her being 'third world' (read: ignorant, poor, uneducated, tradition-bound, domestic, family-oriented, victimized, etc.). This, I suggest, is in contrast to the (implicit) self-representation of Western women as educated, as modern, as having control over their own bodies and sexualities, and the freedom to make their own decisions.

The distinction between Western feminist re-presentation of women in the third world and Western feminist self-presentation is a distinction of the same order as that made by some Marxists between the 'maintenance' function of the housewife and the real 'productive' role of wage labor, or the character-ization by developmentalists of the third world as being engaged in the lesser production of 'raw materials' in contrast to the 'real' productive activity of the first world. These distinctions are made on the basis of the privileging of a particular group as the norm or referent. Men involved in wage labor, first world producers, and, I suggest, Western feminists who sometimes cast third world women in terms of 'ourselves undressed' (Michelle Rosaldo's [1980] term), all construct themselves as the normative referent in such a binary analytic.[6] [...]

[...] [A] comparison between Western feminist self-presentation and Western feminist re-presentation of women in the third world yields sig-nificant results. Universal images of 'the third world woman' (the veiled woman, chaste virgin, etc.), images constructed from adding the 'third world difference' to 'sexual difference', are predicated upon (and hence obviously bring into sharper focus) assumptions about Western women as secular, liberated, and having control over their own lives. This is not to suggest that Western women *are* secular, liberated, and in control of their own lives. I am referring to a *discursive* self-presentation, not necessarily to material reality. If this were a material reality, there would be no need for political movements in the West. Similarly, only from the vantage point of the West is it possible to define the 'third world' as underdeveloped and economically dependent. Without the overdetermined discourse that creates the *third* world, there would be no (singular and privileged) first world. Without the 'third world woman', the particular self-presentation of Western women mentioned above would be problematical. I am suggesting, then, that the one enables and sustains the other. This is not to say that the signature of Western feminist writings on the third world has the same authority as the project of Western humanism. However, in the context of the hegemony of the Western scholarly establishment in the production and dissemination of texts, and in the context of the legitimating imperative of humanistic and scientific discourse, the definition of 'the third world woman' as a monolith might well tie into the larger economic and ideological praxis of 'disinterested' scientific inquiry and pluralism which are the surface manifestations of a latent economic and cultural colonization of the 'non-Western' world. It is time to move beyond the Marx who found it possible to say: They cannot represent themselves; they must be represented.

> 'Under Western Eyes: Feminist Scholarship and colonial Discourses', in Chandra Mohanty, Ann Russo, Louris Torres (eds.), *Third World Women and the Politics of Feminism* (Bloomington: Indiana University Press, 1991), 51–6, 74–5; this is an updated and modified version of an essay published in *Boundary,* 2 12, No. 3/13, No. 1 (Spring/Fall 1984), and repr. in *Feminist Review,* 30 (Autumn 1988).]

ANNE PHILLIPS

13 Paradoxes of Participation

The contemporary women's movement emerged in the 1960s in the context of a generalized radicalism in the liberal democracies, in which ' "participatory democracies" . . . appeared everywhere like fragile bubbles'.[1] [. . .]

In most of the newly formed women's groups, any kind of hierarchy was automatically suspect. Meetings were informal and only loosely structured; in a comparison that was to be frequently invoked in the early years, they were patterned on a gathering of friends. Women came together to share their experiences—the consciousness-raising that was such an important part of early involvement—and to work out actions and campaigns. In these meetings no one voice should ever claim to be more definitive than another. By the same token, no one woman should be able to assume responsibility for the more interesting or influential tasks. Expertise and authority should be divided and shared: democracy was conceived not as a matter of representation or accountability but as a genuine equalization of power.

In her introduction to the first anthology of writings from the US women's liberation movement, Robin Morgan illustrates some of this early vision with her account of the lot system and the disc system, both devised by women's groups in the United States. The first was a way of pre-empting the inequalities that come from the division of labour. All the tasks associated with the group were divided up according to whether they were creative or routine, and each member then drew lots for one of each kind. The second system tackled the inequalities that arise in group discussion. Every woman began the meeting with an identical number of discs. Each time she spoke she 'spent' one of these, and once she had run through her entire supply she was expected to keep herself quiet.

The first time this system was tried, the apocryphal story goes, no one in the room had any discs left after fifteen minutes. The second meeting was slow almost to silence because everyone was hoarding her discs. Gradually, the device worked its way into everyone's consciousness as a symbol for the need to listen to each other, and not interrupt or monopolize the conversation.[2]

Overly mechanistic as these examples now sound, the ideals they reflect were widely shared. That each woman should be equally respected was almost a founding principle, and equal respect is hard to sustain where there are clearly leaders and led.

Most of the radicals of the period had an idea of sharing things around—tasks, expertise, influence, the length of time each member could speak—but this radical equality of participation assumed a particular significance for women. Every organization has its division of labour between 'mental' and 'manual', creative and routine tasks, but the long association of women with office work has usually guaranteed that they are the ones who type the leaflets, take the minutes and bring the tea. Every organization has its complement of good talkers and silent listeners, but the construction of male and female identities has usually meant that women are disproportionately represented in the listening camp. What could appear as a general problem to other radical movements became for women a matter of the power between women and men. The women's movement was thus acutely sensitive to the relations of dominance and subordination that emerge in the course of discussions or get reflected in the distribution of work. An unequal distribution of skills was thought to be inevitably correlated with an unequal distribution of power.

Especially in the first years of the movement, there was, then, an emphasis on either sharing or rotating responsibilities. The first national newsletter in the USA—*Voice of the Women's Liberation Movement*—was edited by different women for each issue; the national newsletter of the UK movement—*WIRES*—was produced by different groups that volunteered for the job. Papers that circulated at conferences were commonly written by groups rather than individuals. The conferences themselves would be organized not by an elected co-ordinating committee, but simply by collectives that had proposed themselves for the task. The occasional disarray that went along with this was thought well worth it, for a range of skills and responsibilities was in principle being made accessible to every woman, and no one could use her superior knowledge to claim for herself superior power.

In the 1970s at least, this anti-authoritarianism infected even the more 'professional' women's organizations. In *The Politics of Women's Liberation*, Jo Freeman reports that by 1973–4 the 'younger wing' of the US movement had successfully carried its ideals of participatory democracy into the more orthodox arrangements of the National Organization of Women (NOW), and that the organization was under increasing pressure to change its overly hierarchical practices.[3] The texture of their meetings then became an important political issue. As in the smaller, more overtly radical, groups, there was a stress on informality, on blending the logic of argument with the passion of personal experience and on avoiding a confrontational or domineering style. Unlike the 'younger wing', NOW continued to proceed by way of motions, debates and majority votes. But Freeman notes that it had begun to reject 'the assumption that "one side must win" for the assumption that, with sufficient effort invested, a compromise acceptable to all can be found'.[4]

Whether it was the older or younger wing, there had to be a way of taking decisions. Women's groups had to work out their plan of action in any campaigns, while national conferences had to formulate priorities and demands. In the case of Britain, for example, the initial demands were extended and revised in plenary sessions at later annual conferences; the very sharp disagreements over wording and emphasis that surfaced in the 1978 meeting heralded the end of the national conference. Decisions were made, and the outcome was felt to matter, and yet the conference was not conceived as a representative institution. Like the citizens' assemblies of ancient Greece, the national conferences were open to all: all that is, except men, and with a frequent question mark over women journalists who were reporting for the national press. The size of each conference depended only on how many women chose to attend, and while the choice about where the next conference should be held was frequently debated in terms of equalizing access from all over the country, there was no formal mechanism for ensuring regional balance. Each woman spoke for herself, not as a delegate from an affiliated group, and where there was a vote each woman counted just as one.

In many political organizations—trade union, political party, pressure group—meetings and conferences are primarily about making decisions. In the women's liberation movement, this was a subsidiary feature, and the emphasis was much more on meeting, talking, acting, sharing experiences and ideas. Politics and friendship were often elided, perhaps most strikingly in this quote from Robin Morgan:

This is not a movement one 'joins'. There are no rigid structures or membership cards. The Women's Liberation Movement exists where three or four friends or neighbours decide to meet regularly over coffee and talk about their personal lives. It also exists in the cells of women's jails, in the welfare lines, in the supermarket, the factory, the convent, the farm, the maternity ward, the streetcorner, the old ladies' home, the kitchen, the steno pool, the bed. It exists in your mind, and in the political and personal insights that you can contribute to change and shape and help its growth.[5]

In similar vein, though without so completely dissolving the distinction between political action and meeting your friends, one London group noted in 1971 the benefits they derived from organizing on a small, local basis. They were always bumping into one another outside as well as inside meetings, thus 'cutting down the schizophrenia of most political action'.[6] Instead of seeing politics as something 'out there' or regarding meetings as a duty and a task, women could experience their involvement as an extension of their everyday life.

[. . .] The association between politics and friendship, and the way this can increase the excitement and interest in meetings, was certainly a feature of the women's liberation movement—though perhaps particularly so for those who had no children, or who had not yet exhausted themselves in years of political life. For many women, the movement became their life, the women's group their closest friends. In such a context, the extra time it takes to do things collectively rather than on your own is not necessarily seen as a cost, and while it can be unbearable to attend yet another over-long meeting with people you dislike, the experience is very different when the others at the meeting are friends.

It was not long, of course, before people noted the limits of friendship,[7] the two most serious being that it is impossible to include everyone in the circle of your friends, and that it is hard to disagree without more fundamentally falling out. Despite the rapid growth of the women's movement, with new groups springing up all over the place and ideas spreading fast from one country to another, it was apparent to most of those involved that they were a pretty unrepresentative bunch. Mostly in their twenties or thirties; overwhelmingly white; very often college-educated and holding a degree. There seemed to be a trade-off between the intensity with which those who *were* involved committed themselves, and the capacity of the movement to extend its appeal. This in turn seemed to be related to precisely those aspects that had brought politics and friendship together. For those already involved, the absence of formal structures, the informality, the shared jokes and references, were a part of what the movement was about. These very same phenomena could seem mysterious and exclusionary to those not yet accepted as friends.

This makes a neat entry point for the unsympathetic critic, who can draw on the usual range of complaints against participatory democracy to note that this is unequal and unfair. Had Giovanni Sartori, for example, deigned to notice the women's movement, he would have had a wonderful time. Here we have precisely that equation of more democracy with more participation—and precisely the anticipated problems, that only a few women will attend. Membership becomes self-selecting and exclusive, while the time constraints that Michael Walzer noted work even more acutely where women are involved. How many can reorganize their lives to include the evening meetings, daytime actions, weekend conferences that the women's movement usually entailed? Yet activity and involvement were being presented as the only way to belong, leaving no room for the 'half-virtuous' woman who had neither time nor inclination for this.

It is a considerable tribute to contemporary feminism that these problems were all aired internally, and attention extended to include many more. The recent experience of the women's liberation movement thus provides us with one of the fullest explorations of the strengths and weaknesses of participatory democracy, and though the issues that arose have precursors in theoretical literature, they are in this context more nuanced and detailed. The movement that is sometimes hailed from outside as a model of participatory democracy is also one of the richer sources for thinking about participation and its problems. Among the problems that feminists began to raise, five stand out as particularly pertinent:

1. By refusing to distinguish political from other aspects of equality and insisting on a thoroughgoing equalization of involvement and skills, the movement was forcing many women to deny their talents and abilities and was wasting their energy and time. Democracy was becoming inefficient.

2. By relying so heavily on face-to-face meetings, women's groups were sending conflict underground and producing what was a false consensus. Women were being pressured to pretend to agree.

3. By refusing to formalize the structures of decision-making, women's groups and conferences were also refusing to develop procedures for accountability. No leaders or elites were acknowledged, but this meant that *de facto* leaders and elites went unchecked.

4. By the same token, the absence of formal procedures for membership, delegation or representation meant that the movement could never say for whom or for how many it spoke. It could not then engage with authority in influencing politics outside; it could not claim the legitimacy of a representative body.

5. By making the meeting such a central part of involvement, the movement inevitably limited its membership, ending up as an unrepresentative few.

These issues were raised and discussed from early in the history of the women's liberation movement, so early indeed that they predate the moment at which most women would say that they 'joined'. A number of them surface, for example, in Jo Freeman's *The Tyranny of Structurelessness*, a highly influential essay which circulated inside the US movement in 1970, was reprinted that same year in the *Berkeley Journal of Sociology* and was subsequently copied and distributed in a variety of pamphlet forms. The problems of participation were voiced almost in unison with the ideals.

[*Engendering Democracy* (Cambridge: Polity Press, 1991), 121–45.]

14 Feminist Confessions: The Last Degrees are the Hardest

In a reading group I belonged to in the mid-eighties, we talked on and off about the liabilities that attached to the transfer of the adjective 'feminist' from a political movement to a critical label. One of the women in the group objected hotly to receiving professional invitations to speak 'as a feminist' at conferences and campuses. She wanted, she said, to be invited for herself, as 'a critic'—minus any label or constituency; and mimed the dismay of the generic departmental host, who finding himself saddled with the feminist speaker imported to his campus for the occasion, attempts to naturalize the event and banish discomfort in his role by being humorous: 'Why don't we go have some feminist ice cream,' he chortles, 'ho, ho, ho.' I understood perfectly what she meant, but at the same time, I found myself stuck on the very point. Who would I be on those occasions, if not the 'feminist' speaker?

In the last couple of years, I have begun to ponder the implications of that critic's revolt against the feminist label. Not because I resent the label's application to my work, or feel intellectually reduced by feminism's engagements, but because the resistance she expresses to a *position of representativity* bears a certain kinship, I think, to two distinct phenomena that have emerged together on the critical horizon over the decade of the eighties—albeit on separate tracks. The first (although it is not practiced uniquely by feminists or women) can be seen to develop out of feminist theory's original emphasis on the analysis of the personal: I'm referring to the current proliferation in literary studies of autobiographical or personal criticism. [. . .] This outbreak of self-writing, which may be interpreted, no doubt, as one of the many symptoms of literary theory's mid-life crisis, also intersects with a certain overloading in cultural criticism of the rhetorics of representativity (including feminism's)—the incantatory recital of the 'speaking as a's and the imperialisms of 'speaking for's. I read this work as a renewed attention to the unidentified voices of a writing self outside or to the side of labels, or at least at a critical distance from them, and at the same time as part of a wider effort to remap the theoretical. The spectacle of a significant number of critics getting personal in their writing, while not, to be sure, on the order of a paradigm shift, is at least the sign of a turning point in the history of critical practices.

The other development is a visible trend (important enough for the MLA Commission on the Status of Women to take it up as an issue) of attacks on academic feminism—a kind of critical misogyny practiced by women as well as men—that has been cropping up (along with gay bashing) in a variety of institutional contexts and guises.[1] What should we make of this published violence against feminist ideology in general and individual critics in particular (ad feminam)? One could of course take the fatalistic view that every critical movement has its allotted life span in academia and is meant to be superseded: the new criticism is now old, structuralism is post, why not also feminism? Or the Old Testament line that since feminism as a mode of critique began by attacking other positions, why shouldn't it get attacked back (a version of childhood cries of injustice: she started it)? Or maybe it's simply the case that feminism is now seen to be powerful enough to inspire the kinds of resentments that any configuration perceived to be 'overrepresented' is thought to deserve?[2]

One might also take the longer and more productive view that feminism needs to be self-critical in order to evolve, and that these volleys offer an occasion to reexamine the assumptions of its operations. The dislocations within feminism, moreover—the refusal of a hegemonic and unitary feminism—have already instituted this process. In this sense, I would argue, representativity is a problem *within* feminism itself. [. . .]

In 1980, a few days before he died, Roland Barthes gave an interview that was published in *Le Nouvel Observateur* under the title 'The Crisis of Desire'. Invited to comment on the new conformity and the failure of all protest movements in France, Barthes remarks that 'the only effective marginalism is individualism'.[3] He then goes on to make the claim, not fully worked out, that this individualism—refashioned—could be understood as radical and not a return to a petit-bourgeois liberalism. Barthes writes: 'The mere fact, for instance, of thinking my body until I reach the point at which I know that I can think *only* my body is an attitude that comes up against science, fashion, morality, all collectivities' (85). The language of his thinking here intersects unexpectedly with Adrienne Rich's body prose in 'Notes for a Politics of Location'.[4] Rich writes: 'Perhaps we need a moratorium on saying "the body". For it's also possible to abstract "the" body. When I write "the body", I see nothing in particular. To write "my body" plunges me into lived experience, particularity. . . . To say "the body" lifts me away from what has given me a primary perspective. To say "my body" reduces the temptation to grandiose assertions' (215). Rich's commitment to the political, to militancy, to the collective; Barthes's complete resistance to all of the above: 'I've never been a militant and it would be impossible for me to be one for personal reasons I have about language: I don't like militant language' (86): despite the gulf separating their views of the intellectual's role in cultural criticism, what joins them, I think, is the sense they share of the ways in which one's own body can constitute an internal limit on discursive irresponsibility, a brake on rhetorical spinning. The autobiographical act—however self-fictional, can like the detail of one's (aging) body, produce this sense of limit as well: the resistance particularity offers to the grandiosity of abstraction that inhabits what I've been calling the crisis of representativity.[5] (Perhaps we also need a moratorium on *reciting the litany* of RaceClassGender and instead a rush into *doing* positive things with those words.)[6]

Both Barthes's last words about individualism and the inward focus of autobiographical writing present obvious problems for a social, affirmative activism in which—'as a feminist'—I still believe. In the face of the visible extremes of racism or misogyny, or the equally violent silences of theoretical discourses from which all traces of embodiment have been carefully abstracted, the autobiographical project might seem a frivolous response. How can I propose a reflection about an ethics in criticism (an ethics requires a community) from these individualistic grounds? But the risk of a limited personalism, I think, is a risk worth running—at least the movement of a few more degrees in self-consciousness—in order to maintain an edge of surprise in the predictable margins of organized resistances.[7]

If we further entertain the notion that the recognition of zones and boundaries is not necessarily the gesture of a personal territorialism—a nationalism of the 'I'—but rather the very condition of exchange with another limited other, the contract of this writing and reading then can be seen as the chance for a vividly renegotiated sociality.

This is easier said than done. On the occasions I record here, I have been scheduled explicitly or implicitly as the 'feminist' speaker. There is nothing surprising in this (after all, I am a feminist critic and grateful to be invited altogether) or wrong. I think it's a good thing that feminists get asked to speak (even if they are meant only to be the gender-token in the round up of the usual theory suspects). But what chance does any 'I' have of undercutting its customary self-representation in the face of the expectations accompanying an 'as a': the burden of 'speaking for'? When I first gave 'Philoctetes' Sister: Feminist Literary Criticism and the New Misogyny', I explained that it was part of this book then called 'The Occasional Feminist' (my hope for some time off from my 'as a' performances). In the question period, an assistant professor speaking 'as a feminist' critic, prefaced her remarks—about the fate of feminist critics in departmental demographics: isn't one enough?—by saying that I wasn't an occasional feminist but an established feminist (one of the ones, presumably, who are enough). For her, there was no way I could make the very distinction I needed to answer her question—from her side: that her department had to be led to see that there were important differences among feminists and that therefore one couldn't possibly be enough (is one Shakespearean enough?). To be sure, she wasn't entirely wrong to refuse my claims for particularities within feminism: hadn't I just given a paper in which I myself say that I am standing in feminism's place and receive, as a 'convenient metonymy', the attacks directed at it? Can I have it both ways? That is the project of this book: to make room for both the identification and the difference. Can this be done?

There's a danger in being born with a decade, or almost. One tends to conflate (solipsistically) things that might not have anything to do with each other. The 1970s were my thirties; the 1980s my forties. I've become middle-aged along with the coming of age (the so-called institutionalization) of feminist criticism. Having gotten through the eighties (and Reagan) in feminism, *with* feminism, however, I confess to feeling a good deal more sanguine about feminism than about me: after all, this wave of the movement—as well, of course, as the new generations moving within it—is a lot younger than I am and better prepared to work for change.

[*Getting Personal: Feminist Occasions and Other Autobiographical Acts* (London and New York: Routledge, 1991), pp. ix–xv.]

SUSANNAH RADSTONE

15 Postcard from the Edge: Thoughts on the 'Feminist Theory: An International Debate' Conference held at Glasgow University, Scotland, 12–15 July 1991

For if Ariadne has fled from the labyrinth of old, the only guiding thread for all of us now is a tightrope stretched above the void.

(Rosi Braidotti[1])

At the 'Feminist Theory' conference I met a woman who had arrived in Britain with an Australian touring circus, and she told me a little of her story. She said that she'd abandoned the world of the academy some years ago for a life of physical adventure, but now, considering a return to more intellectual pursuits, here she was at Glasgow, taking a look around. Locked into conference mode, I faltered—what to talk about, if not our institutions and the ups and downs of academic life? 'So, do you walk the tightrope, or ride the trapeze?' I hazarded, eventually. 'No, *never*, because it *hurts!*', was her emphatic and down-to-earth response. Memories are notoriously slippery; partial, fractured, idiosyncratic and screening, perhaps, as much as they reveal, but as I think back over Glasgow, it's this fragment of a conversation—this glimpse of the circus with its pains and its pleasures, that I recall.

'Feminist Theory: An International Debate' was a large event although, with three hundred participants, sixty of them speakers, attendance nevertheless fell two hundred short of the five hundred women and sixty men who, so I've read, arrived in Oxford twenty-one years ago for the first national gathering of the Women's Liberation movement at Ruskin College.[2] Twenty-one years is a long time, and it's tempting to draw comparisons between the two events—more tempting still, perhaps, to construe the passing of those twenty-one years as feminist theory's 'coming of age'. But that's a temptation best avoided, for feminism's history stretches back a good deal further than a mere twenty-one years. To speak of feminism's coming of age would also place the many feminisms of Glasgow within one history and, by analogy, a normative one at that—the history of the individual's accession to 'equal rights'. More seriously still, perhaps, a 'coming of age' story implies, too, a degree of closure, whereas it's my hope that twenty-one years on, we're still only just beginning.

Ruskin and Glasgow were certainly very different events. To begin with, what Glasgow appeared to put on display was the extent of feminism's recent professionalization. Indeed, it sometimes seems as though feminism's arrival within the academy has coincided with the demise of that once powerful network of grass-roots organizations which, certainly in the seventies and early eighties, constituted the heart of the women's movement. The 1991 annual conference of the Women's Studies Network (UK) took place on the weekend prior to the Glasgow conference.[3] Here, representatives from women's pressure groups did speak alongside a truly international group of feminist academics, but so often, now, these groups appear to represent the interests of women *within* the academy, and to risk losing a more broad-based constituency outside educational establishments. At Glasgow, the conference participants—mainly white and middle class—were drawn, in the main, from those of us whose feminism is inextricably bound up with our professional lives within the academy. Unlike the Ruskin meeting, which was arguably an event *of* the women's movement, it is therefore as a predominantly academic-institutional event, at which feminist academics 'did theory', that Glasgow might most appropriately be remembered.

But how far did this difference of address and constituency shape the different agendas of Ruskin and Glasgow? Compared with Glasgow's super-abundance of plenaries and panels—with strands on 'psychoanalysis and the spectator' vying with those on 'gay identities' or 'representation and memory' in the first time-slot alone, the Ruskin College agenda appears stark in the extreme: 'the social role of women', 'women and the economy', 'women and revolution' and a final plenary which asked, simply, 'where are we going?' Yet when I read about the Ruskin event, what's striking are the feelings of excitement, optimism and *shared* hope that it engendered, and when I remember Glasgow, it's with ambivalence. For me, it seems, Glasgow brought home the losses, as well as, or perhaps more than, the gains of the last twenty-one years. In my own paper for Glasgow, I discussed women's 'fictions of remembering' and argued, following Mary Jacobus,[4] that although the suffusion of much feminist theory by nostalgia warrants careful critique, nostalgia nevertheless symptomatically evidences a wish—a wish that things could be different. Why, though, did Glasgow seem to me to evidence the loss of that previous moment's collective energy and hope? And how might we most productively learn from Glasgow's version of the current state of feminist theory?

The Glasgow event was neither divisive nor unhappy. From the 'wining and finger buffeting' of the opening Friday night reception, through the Sunday night social at the Glasgow Winter Gardens—with its vaulted glass roof, earthen floor, lights and music putting me in mind, once again, of the circus, to the closing plenary's pre-selected cross section of speakers, the show rolled smoothly. Twenty-one years on, feminist theory's relations with the newspapers, TV and radio appeared solid, if not entirely unproblematic, as a veritable media circus documented our activities from morning until night. An early morning radio encounter between one of the conference's organizers, Sandra Kemp, and the Conservative MP Edwina Currie, was followed by the arrival of the *Daily Telegraph*'s photographers, who were, strangely, and much to the dismay of the majority of women participants, ejected from the main conference hall due to the loud objections of one male participant, and who were later to be seen taking snapshots of the conference organizers on the steps of the main venue. By any of the 'performance indicators' of academic enterprise, then, Glasgow was undoubtedly a success. Uncoincidentally, perhaps, it is around this concept of performance that many of the questions prompted for me by Glasgow have come to settle.

My first, and perhaps keenest intimation of unease came on Friday night, when, at the opening reception, held in the awesome marbled halls of the Kelvingrove Art Gallery, Glasgow's Lord Provost—a woman—delivered a heart-rending speech of welcome. She felt, she told us all, an abiding sense of gratitude for and commitment to the struggles which had enshrined women's—and especially working-class women's—rights to education, since, as a child of the Glasgow tenements, it was via education that she had accomplished her undoubtedly tough journey from the Gorbals to the civic hall. This was a story that moved me, a story told bravely, and a story told from the heart—a story, though, which appeared destined to fall into the void. For, unlike at Ruskin, at Glasgow there remained no place, apparently, for the questions implicitly raised by the Lord Provost's welcoming address—questions about women and class, women and education, and women and the welfare state, to name but a few. In the all-too-brief closing question-time, one participant argued that this absence should be seen as the absence of the sociologists from Glasgow. But although there were, indeed, few sociologists at the conference, my own view is that we are all, in each of our disciplines, equally responsible for the difficulties in which feminist theory—from its inception, always an interdisciplinary area—now finds itself. It would therefore be inappropriate to demand of the sociologists alone a reconstructed theory that can resituate these questions on feminism's agenda.

Glasgow [. . .] was clearly shaped, more than anything, by those insecurities and doubts which currently shake feminist theory to its core, producing a range of questions concerning the status of the category 'woman': is a politics grounded in women's *collective* experience still desirable, given poststructuralism's deconstruction of binary oppositions? Should we not acknowledge more fully differences between women, as well as differences which cut across the man/woman opposition? Can 'woman' be thought outside of biological essentialism, and if so, how? Given this agenda, the question I want to ask—and it's a vexing one—is this: can the 'ontological insecurity' at the heart of feminist theory's engagements with poststructuralism and postmodernism be negotiated without consigning the voice of that woman from the Gorbals to the void? Or are such endeavours doomed to break up on the rocks of the essentialism/anti-essentialism debate? And did Glasgow—or, more properly, the conference route that I as one participant took—seek or offer answers to these questions?

My second moment of unease came during the Saturday morning opening session of the 'conference proper', a performance by the V-girls—five women who tour a ninety-minute skit of a feminist literary conference, this time a conference about *Heidi*. The show had us in stitches. They lampooned Lacan and parodied the feminist literary theorist's love of repetition and alliteration. Keen evocations of the paradoxical imbrication of academic sisterhood with competitive institutional politics followed on the heels of a sharp attack on those tightrope walkers who embrace poststructuralism whilst insisting on the authority of their textual analyses—an attack to which several later speakers self-mockingly (and defensively) returned. The V-girls performed feminists performing feminist theory and we laughed. But their act, and the world it represented was so very bleak and cold. And at the heart of this performance there lay a desire—a (nostalgic?) desire for less ambivalent modes of female bonding. [. . .]

Across the midnight blue cover of *Patterns of Dissonance*[5] stretches a tightrope, and on this tightrope, arms outstretched, is poised a tiptoed figure whose status as embodied being or mechanical figure remains ambiguous: a fitting image indeed with which to represent feminist theory's current precariousness. I'll choose to end this report by celebrating one Glasgow performance which walked this tightrope and had me, for one, holding my breath. Ailbhe Smyth's paper, 'A reading from the book of beginnings' was performed twice: first, in the panel entitled 'postmodernism', and then, fittingly—given the term's critical status within theories of femininity—as an *encore* with which to close the final plenary. Smyth's 'a reading . . .' tiptoed across more than one tightrope: part poetry, part theory, she told her own story, her own life, by means of quotation, and by means of Irish folktale and riddle, thereby posing a series of questions about narrative, about autobiography, about performance and about the status of theories such as those of postmodernism within our lives and work. In a recent issue of *Differences*, Wendy Brown comments that feminist theory's recently acquired skills in 'politicising the "I"' may be 'at odds with the requisites for developing a political conversation among a complex and diverse "we"'.[6] Perhaps one strategy for negotiating this tightrope was offered by one participant— Maureen McNeil's—response to Smyth's presentation, for as she put it, what we risk, in our autobiographical work is a fall into narcissism, but what we gain, when it works, is a discourse that 'pushes out'. For me, Smyth's paper did precisely that, it 'pushed out', engaging and moving me by enacting what Gayatri Chakravorty Spivak has described recently as 'a sort of deconstructive homeopathy, a deconstructing *of* identities *by* identities...by thinking of oneself as an example of certain kinds of...narratives. A...claiming of an identity from a text that comes from somewhere else.'[7] Perhaps here, at least, we find the beginnings of a practice that can rescue the voice from the Gorbals from the void. A tightrope walked, then, to end the conference: a conference at which the woman from the circus may have felt more at home than she expected?

['Postcard from the Edge', *Feminist Review*, 40 (1992), 85–93.]

JANE GALLOP

16 Around 1981: Academic Feminist Literary Theory

Around 1981, a good number of feminist literary academics in this country were focused on the 'difference between French and American feminism', on the question of psychoanalysis or deconstruction and their usefulness or danger. 'We' were not only American feminists like me who thought French psychoanalytic, deconstructive theory a great thing but also those who expended a good deal of energy attacking it. Around 1981, this conflict, this debate seemed central, and to many more academic critics than me, to feminist literary studies.

Whereas in the early eighties the project focused on the theoretical debate, by the late eighties it was organized around the institutionalization of feminist literary criticism. By which I mean its acceptance as a legitimate part of literary studies. I locate that 'event' around 1981 and am interested in what led up to it and the subsequent effect it had on feminist criticism.

Although the readings that follow are undeniably textual, the framework would link text to extratextual event, institutional context, and power distribution. By power, I mean specifically the changing power of feminist criticism in relation to the institution, and of various feminist critics in relation to each other and to the institution. The institution here is the literary academy, which is at once a discursive field, a pedagogical apparatus, a place of employment, a site of cultural reproduction, an agency of cultural regulation, and an institution generally marginal to power and values in American society.

My change of focus from theoretical debate to institutional history corresponds to a shift of focus in the American literary academy between the early and the late eighties. Whereas around 1981 literary critics and English Departments were intensely concerned with the question of poststructuralism, by 1987 the theoretical action had moved to 'institutions' and 'history'.

Not only do I as a writer undergo these small historical translocations, not only does feminist criticism's relation to the literary academy shift, but that institution itself is going through increasingly fast changes. The image of deconstruction, for example, goes from dangerous outsider to established rearguard in less than a decade. The increased attention to history in both feminist and non-feminist literary theory must certainly be related to this acceleration in critical fashions which forces upon us an awareness of living in history.

We might also map these moments onto the two major books on feminist criticism to date: Toril Moi's in 1985 and Janet Todd's in 1988.[1] Reflecting currents of the early eighties, Moi subtitles her volume *Feminist Literary Theory* and focuses on the debate about poststructuralism, siding with 'theoretical' feminism, by which she means poststructuralist. Typifying later trends, Todd entitles her contribution *Feminist Literary History*, complains of ahistoricism and calls for a historical and historicized feminist criticism. First conceived simultaneously with Moi's project, and then reconceived at the moment Todd writes, the present book could be said to move from Moi to Todd. Yet I would also hope to make explicit the relation between my perspective and its inevitable historical limitations, so as to suggest some way of understanding feminist criticism that is explicitly historical and thus not simply relativistic or reactional.

I want to stress the pain of history for those of us trying to produce knowledge. Even if we have no illusions or beliefs in the enduring, we want our understandings to last at least until they can be written, published, and read. This book, which took too long to write, not only passes through two different theoretical formations but around 1989 begins to feel the pressure of a third and grows increasingly anxious as I push to get it done and out before its power of strategic intervention is lost, before it enters a configuration different than the one for/in which it was written.

My focus is the institutionalization of feminist criticism; what, it might be asked, do I think about that? I think it is a fact. And I notice it is a fact rarely spoken of objectively. The word 'institutionalization' sounds like some form of incarceration. The academicization of feminist criticism is generally discussed as if it had happened against our will.

The word 'academic' itself is more often than not pejorative rather than descriptive. I notice that academic feminists accuse other academic feminists of being 'academic'. This sort of aggressive dissociation clouds our under-standing of how we got here. None of us just woke up one day to discover that she had a Ph.D., a full-time academic job, much less tenure. This disavowal of the academic also deflects us from the question of what we ought to and could do now that we have a voice within this institution. We don't seem very able to theorize about how we speak, as feminists wanting social change, from within our positions in the academy.

My insistence that we recognize that we are, or that feminist criticism is, in the academy has sometimes been taken for a celebration of that fact. I worry that my statements will be sucked into a machine which demands that one either condemn 'academic feminism' or stand accused as an 'academic feminist'. If I'm not bemoaning the selling-out of feminist criticism to aca-demic respectability, then I must be one of those bourgeois feminists whose only goal is such respectability. Maybe I am; one shouldn't be too quick to deny any accusation voiced by more than the odd individual. But I continue to feel the necessity for an analysis which includes the academic location of the accusers.

I do not want to celebrate our being in. Being in something that is a transmitter of elitist values. Being in a discourse that is constituted, at this point in time, as marginal to the larger culture and society. But I do not want to bemoan it either. I want to understand why we are located here, how we got here, what we sacrificed to get here, what we gained: all as preliminaries to the question of how do we do the most good, as feminists, as social and cultural critics, speaking from this location.

Much talk about institutionalization implicitly construes institutions as monolithic, unchanging, or even inherently evil. Institutions have histories, are in history. When we conceive of them as unchanging, we have less chance of wittingly affecting their direction.

Around 1987, Meaghan Morris wrote: 'Institutionalization is not another name for doom, that fate always worse than death. It's an opportunity, and in many instances a necessary condition, for serious politics.'[2] Heartened by this statement, I also note that Morris writes at quite a remove from the American academic context. An Australian, although she has done various temporary teaching stints in universities, she is not 'an academic' but supports herself by her writing.

I note also that her statement occurs in an anthology which debates the relation of men to feminism. That debate which drew quite a bit of energy in the mid-eighties must, I think, also be understood in relation to the academ-icization of feminism. A phenomenon such as men protesting their exclusion from feminist theory could only occur in the wake of some sort of institu-tionalization.

In 1984 a male academic begins his book on feminist criticism protesting for some two dozen pages his right to enter the field. He bases his claim on 'the intervention of feminism in English studies' which makes it very much his business. Whereas Moi's book is subtitled *Feminist Literary Theory* and Todd's book is called *Feminist Literary History*, this book by K.K. Ruthven is entitled *Feminist Literary Studies*, emphasizing the academic location of the enterprise.[3] The *Men in Feminism* debate itself must also be understood as a debate about the institutional status of feminist (literary) theory.

[...] I think the debate about 'French feminism' or poststructuralist theory, the argument about whether feminist criticism should be defined as the study of women writers, and the acrimony and guilt around the question of race for and by white feminists must all also be understood in relation to the possibility or the fact of institutionalization.

Both the implicit definition of feminist criticism as the study of women writers and the appearance of French-style poststructuralist feminism in this country took place in the late 1970s. Both, I believe, contributed enormously to the acceptance of feminist criticism by the literary academy. The first helped define feminist criticism as a subfield, thus giving it a place within the literary academy without necessarily calling the whole into question, as well as making it seem like every department should have one. The second rode in on the coattails of the quick rise of deconstruction in American English Studies. 'Theory' included a 'feminist' component, although it also dismissed feminist criticism that was not properly 'theoretical'. These two trends have usually been opposed in feminist critical histories, but I would contend that they not only were strikingly contemporaneous but that, as separate and distinct strategies for feminist inclusion, they worked, if unwittingly, together. By the mid-eighties work on women writers based in poststructuralist theory is very widespread and constitutes the center of academic feminist criticism.

A decade later, conflict over race has taken the place of these two debates as the point of densest energy in academic feminism. This one is not a theoretical debate: no white critic claims we should ignore race or stick to writing about white women. But between feminist critics there is the same intensity, anxiety, and anger sparked by the earlier debates. Race was by and large not a question, for white literary academics, in the seventies. I would contend that one reason it is such a heated topic now is that it is also a debate about the institutional status of feminist criticism, an anxious non-encounter with the fact of our specific location as insiders.

[*Around 1981: Academic Feminist Literary Theory* (London and New York: Routledge, 1992), 1–6.]

17 Words and Things: Materialism and Method in Contemporary Feminist Analysis

> What, in short, we wish to do is to dispense with 'things' ... To substitute for the enigmatic treasure of 'things' anterior to discourse, the regular formation of objects that emerge only in discourse.
>
> Michel Foucault

The ambition to dispense with 'things'—and to value 'words' more—has caused some general perplexity and irritation. Many feminists, in particular, have traditionally tended to see 'things'—be they low pay, rape, or female foeticide—as more significant than, for example, the discursive construction of marginality in a text or document. In this essay I want to explore how the issue of the relative status of things and words has become a central one in contemporary social theory and philosophy, and why feminists have a particularly strong investment in this question. [. . .]

In the past ten years we have seen an extensive 'turn to culture' in feminism.[1] Academically, the social sciences have lost their purchase within feminism and the rising star lies with the arts, humanities, and philosophy. Within this general shift we can see a marked interest in analysing processes of symbolization and representation—the field of 'culture'— and attempts to develop a better understanding of subjectivity, the psyche, and the self. The type of feminist sociology that has a wider audience, for example, has shifted away from a determinist model of 'social structure' (be it capitalism, or patriarchy, or a gender-segmented labour market or whatever) and deals with questions of culture, sexuality, or political agency—obvious counterbalances to an emphasis on social structure.

Such academic developments are part of a much more general shift within feminism, at least in Britain and in Europe generally. In publishing, for instance, the sales of fiction have rocketed and non-fiction plummeted. Feminism sells best as fiction, and attempts to write and market modern versions of the classic feminist non-fiction blockbusters have been notably unsuccessful. Interestingly, too, feminist cultural commentary and discussion has often tended to draw on the pleasures of fiction: the things we want to write and read about are romance, crime, melodrama, and so on.

These developments raise some complex questions, not least that of the disillusionment and critique that presaged this new direction. In this chapter I shall not explore the political why or the historical when of these changes, although these are highly significant questions. I want to focus instead on the implications, and on the issues at stake, in this move from one cluster of disciplines to another. At the outset, I would suggest that it will not be adequate simply to shift attention in one direction rather than another, or even to apply the critical tools of one discipline to another's traditional subject matter. The issues of what weight to attach to these various subject matters (the economic or the aesthetic, for example) will eventually have to be rethought. Meanwhile, we can certainly say that the words/things balance has been shifted away from the social sciences' preoccupation with things and towards a more cultural sensibility of the salience of words.

Finally, we might ask what it signifies that the post-modern term 'meta-narrative' has become so appealing. Many who do not really agree with the arguments of Jean-François Lyotard are none the less happy to describe large-scale political and intellectual projects as the 'meta-narratives' of feminism, democratism, and so on. The interest here lies in our willingness to fictional-ize these entities and to regard them as stories (narrative: to tell a tale, give an account). To say this is not to pose a crude antithesis between 'politics' and 'fiction', but it is to remark on how helpful many have found it to use a metaphorical fictionalizing as a critical tool for unlocking the objectivist pretensions of things like rationality, the Enlightenment, or even feminism. [. . .]

1. First, we can see a general critique of *theoretical universalism*. It is not necessary to reiterate here the major political impact of the recognition that western feminism of the 1970s spoke in a falsely universalized voice. The need to register and engage with the implications of differences among women has been the subject of considerable debate. Elizabeth Spelman has quoted the poet Gwendolyn Brooks in this context: 'The juice from tomatoes is not called merely *juice*. It is always called TOMATO juice.' Spelman observes that 'Even the most literal reading of Brooks ought to make us ask whether we're more careful about what we order in a restaurant than we are in thinking of women as the particular women they are.'[2] I'm not sure how far one can push this metaphor for the problem of difference in feminism. Aren't there situ-ations in which one might opt for 'juice' generically, if offered that or alcohol? (Isn't there even something *very* particular about tomato juice that illustrates the commonality of other fruit juices?)

These debates within feminism form part of a much broader current of contemporary thought in which universalistic theoretical discourses have been subjected to sustained and profound critique. The two clearest cases to take are Marxism and psychoanalysis, both of which can be shown to operate in a strongly universalistic mode in terms of their explanatory claims.[3]

2. Secondly, there has been an extensive critique of two central aspects of what is usually referred to as 'Enlightenment' thought, or philosophical 'liberalism': the doctrine of *rationalism* and the '*Cartesian*' concept of a human subject. Feminist political theorists and philosophers have built up a

considerable body of work on the masculine character of 'rationalism', and these debates are represented elsewhere.[4] The so-called 'Cartesian subject' is a topic of complex debate, and much of what is written within post-structuralist and post-modern thought touches on this question. At the heart of the issue is the model of the rational, centred, purposive (and in practice modern European and male) subject for whom Descartes deduced 'cogito ergo sum'. There are so many things wrong with this model of subjectivity, one scarcely knows where to begin. It displaces and marginalizes other subjects and other forms of subjectivity. It also denies what many would now accept as a central contribution of psychoanalysis—that the self is built on conflict and tension rather than being an essential or given. Yet the critique of this model of subjectivity has brought in its train a whole set of new problems, nearly captured in the title of Kate Soper's article 'Constructa Ergo Sum?' If we replace the given self with a constructed, fragmented self, this poses not only the obvious political question of who is the I that acts and on what basis, but the more teasing conundrum of who is the I that is so certain of its fragmented and discursively constructed nature.[5] Hence the critique of the Cartesian subject has posed a new set of questions about identity and experience, developed in the arguments of, for example, Chandra Talpade Mohanty and Biddy Martin.[6]

3. Thirdly, we can speak of *the gendering of modernity* as a new critical enterprise. One can increasingly identify a debate on the implications, for feminism, of the various critiques of modernism and modernity. Griselda Pollock's discussion of the artist, iconic for the modernist project, has illuminated in great detail the cultural meaning of the masculinity inscribed within that figure.[7] The problem remains, however, that feminism is itself too indebted to 'modernist values' and an emancipatory, liberal project to be able to cut loose from the culture and discourse within which it was formed. Susan Hekman points out that one cannot 'simply' suggest that 'the feminist critique extends the post-modern critique of rationalism by revealing its gendered character'.[8] This is because one cannot readily separate out the constituent elements of an integrated theoretical and political 'package'. Hence one may object to Enlightenment dualisms in which the feminine, or women, are always cast as inferior to the masculine, or men, but a thorough-going post-modern abandonment (in so far as this is possible) of these binary structures would be rejected by many feminists.

4. Fourthly, we can see a new *critique of materialism* in these debates. [. . .]

Arguments about materialism have a very different purchase in different academic subjects. Materialist assumptions, whether Marxist or not, are common in the social sciences, and flourish particularly in the notion of a determining 'social structure' on which culture and beliefs, as well as subjectivity and agency, rest. Nevertheless, there has long been what one might regard as an alternative tradition within social theory, emphasizing experience and attempting to understand society without the aid of a social structural model. Phenomenology is an obvious case here, as is the work of Simmel. Recent years have seen a rise of interest in various traditions of social theory—phenomenology, hermeneutics, subjectivist sociology and so on— previously somewhat neglected. The materialist model with the greatest epistemological power is the paradigm of classical Marxism, a formative influence within European social theory.

On the other side of the social sciences/arts divide, the problem of materialism has not had an undue impact on disciplines that have taken the text as by definition constituting the object of study. In history, however, the ramifications of a critique of materialist premises have proved extensive. History's ambiguous position has rested on the fact that what was tradition-ally sought was a reconstitution or reconstruction of 'social reality', but one necessarily based methodologically on a reading of textual evidence. Thus the question of how historiography adjusts to a rethinking of the balance between text and reality is a particularly acute one. [. . .]

Debates in philosophy and social theory, and the parallel discussions in the humanities, take place in an institutional context. I want next to focus on some of the disciplinary aspects of these debates. In the first place, one can note that feminist scholarship has always had the ambition to transcend disciplinary boundaries. Like Marxism, it has tended to regard them as constructions of an unenlightened system that are better ignored. The philosophy of 'women's studies' is very clearly based on this recognition. In practice, however, there are two widely recognized limitations of working under the rubric of 'women's studies': that it leaves the mainstream definition of the academic subjects unchallenged and even denuded of feminist scholars (an aspect of 'ghettoization') and that it militates against developing an understanding of men, masculinity and the interaction of the sexes (the subject matter of the alternative rubric of 'gender'). I am not interested here in these issues, important though they are. I want to focus instead on some of the problems that arise in relation to feminist concerns and the academic disciplines—outside women's studies—in more general terms.

It is not too banal to observe that most feminist scholars have been trained within the conventions of one or the other of the academic disciplines in the arts and social sciences. The marks of these specific trainings are often indelible. They are particularly visible in feminist work, in that one discipline after the next has historically gained a certain 'influence' within contemporary feminism. This often comes up in the context of accusations of using 'jargon', which usually means using another discipline's accepted terminology: I tend not to perceive my own disciplinary vocabulary as jargon.

Disciplines do not simply generate jargon, though; they rest on distinctive assumptions and conventions as to what their objects of study are and what methods are appropriate to study them. Academic debate can reduce itself, on occasion, to a simple trading of assumptions across disciplinary divides. Foucault developed ideas of disciplinary apparatus and discursive policing to describe the practices that regulate what can be said within a discipline, and has shown how Canguilheim's idea of knowledge being 'in the true' can be applied. 'Within its own limits, each discipline recognises true and false propositions; but it pushes back a whole teratology of knowledge beyond its margins.' So unless a proposition is 'within the true' of these requirements at the time, it cannot be accepted as true. Foucault gives the example of Mendel, whose theories were rejected in the nineteenth century, because he spoke of objects and used methods that were alien to the biology of his time. Foucault concludes (surprisingly to those who insist on regarding him as a complete relativist) that 'Mendel spoke the truth, but he was not "within the true" of the biological discourse of his time.'[9]

To speak 'within the true' of a particular discipline is to speak within a complex web of inclusions and exclusions. Differences of time and space are crucial in understanding these requirements in specific contexts. In contemporary western feminist theory there are clearly different conventions of reference as between, say, Australian, European, and US feminists—the sense of what you need to know about to be up with your field is very different.[10] Similarly, for instance, there are significant differences between the different disciplines as to how far interdisciplinarity is desirable or necessary, and significant differences between national and regional disciplinary development of subjects in various parts of the world. To understand these patterns in their complexity would require extensive knowledge and—not least—would require an insight into the educational aspects of colonization in the past and the effects of these on the present distribution of academic power.

Another way of thinking about Foucault's notion of the boundaries of particular disciplines might be to consider a licence to ignore. There is, if you like, an informal division of labour in which certain questions are assigned to one subject and can thus legitimately be ignored by another. In particular, I think one can see this process in the informal division of labour between the arts/humanities critical disciplines and the social sciences. One effect of what I have called here a shift from 'things' to 'words' is a destabilization of this informal disciplinary division of labour. However, it seems to me that the form this has taken has been to open up new substantive areas, or topics, of study to scholars from disciplines that had previously regarded them as beyond the range of what could be studied. The more ambitious task of rethinking the appropriate *methods* of study, and developing ways of genuinely working across disciplines, has lagged behind. The kinds of example that one might give here are obviously contentious, and I will try to present them in a constructive spirit.

The 'post-colonial subject', for example, is better known as a phenomenon of the archive or psyche than as an agent in labour migration or a victim of globalizing managerial strategies.[11] The reasons for this are complex. Feminist economists and sociologists have taken up these issues but the lines of communication between them and literary readers and scholars are institutionally poor.[12] There has also been an evident vacuum within feminist social science on these issues, in my view because the social structural model has proved particularly unwieldy in the face of a triple interaction of disadvantage. Ideally, we would be able to complement knowledge of post-coloniality drawn from textual and archival sources and often focusing on subjective and symbolic questions with a richer social, economic, and political treatment of this historical theme. These various aspects of the subject are not in competition with each other, and nor should any aspect be given, in the abstract, greater epistemological significance. But they call for a variety of competences, training, and knowledges.

In practice, the recent shifting of disciplinary definitions of appropriate subject matter has often meant an export of methods and techniques. The redefinition of 'literary criticism' is a very important case in point. Certainly one can say that the traditional 'canon fodder' approach has been destabilized, although with complex consequences. Barbara Christian, for example, clearly struck a nerve in pointing to the pursuit of theory for its own sake in literary study and the consequent neglect of reading texts of feeling as well as thought.[13] I want to focus here on a different aspect of this destabilization— the relation between critical reading method and the text or object of study.

One development in the intellectual 'crisis' of literary criticism has been to turn critical attention to texts way outside the previously accepted 'literary' range. The school of thought known as 'new historicism' took a lead in reading social, medical, legal, and political documents alongside literary texts; Derridian techniques of reading have played an important part in this development. More generally, one can hear at any up-to-date literary critical meeting (the MLA being the ideal type) many a paper in which the most mundanely social of sources are decoded, deconstructed and 'read' using the critical armoury of modern textual interpretation. The question to be asked, however, is whether these exercises are more than a method bored by its usual stamping ground. How, in particular, does the knowledge gained by such readings interact with what we know from social history, or sociology, about Victorian drains or 1950s cross-dressing practices?

If all this is to say that one trend has been the application of literary critical techniques to social historical documents and archives, read as 'texts', another important trend has been to retain the canon of classical literary texts but to 'read' them through a completely different interpretative grid. The most influential example of this at present is the application of psychoanalytic concepts as a method of literary criticism. This, too, raises some complex questions. Given that psychoanalysis has a history of being one of the most 'reductive' of perspectives, in that its strong explanatory claims, exclusion of other factors and incipient theoretical universalism are legendary, it is perhaps ironic that (from the point of view of its practitioners) in this process its epistemological status is dramatically altered. It is increasingly apparent that the working assumptions of those who use psychoanalytic concepts as a method of reading texts are strongly at variance with the assumptions of those who practise psychoanalysis in a therapeutic context. Although there is a certain amount of movement from one to the other, there is none the less a distance and sometimes outright conflict between free-floating cultural analysis and the clinical institution. One might pose this as a breach between 'psychoanalysis', where certain assumptions hold true across the schools of Freudians, Kleinians, Lacanians, and others, and a *post-psychoanalysis* whose object is exclusively symbolic.[14]

Psychoanalysis is poised at a complex conjunction of 'words and things', some variants facing exclusively towards the symbolic realm of language and representation while others (though stopping short of the 'real event' mentality) would endorse claims that psychic experience carries some sort of causal power in a subjective history.

To refer to these differences of method and epistemology is to raise the question of how objects of study are constituted within the various disciplines. To ignore this question is to work within very narrow confines. There may be some apprehension that to pose the question is itself to endorse or imply a search for a 'general theory' or 'integrated perspective', but I do not think that this is the likely outcome. On the contrary, to address the specific 'truths' of the different disciplines is to discover not the controlling modernism of a fully integrated general theory of knowledge, but precisely the reverse—an incommensurability of knowledges that provokes interesting reflection.

It would, I believe, be useful to consider further the implications of what in Foucauldian vein one might regard as 'disciplinary truth apparatuses'. In the examples I have raised here I have tended to focus on the questions of which I have some experience (sociology and literary studies), and this is inevitable since one cannot speak outside these conventions altogether. It is worth noting, however, that these disciplinary apparatuses are not simply relics of the bad old disciplines, but are powerful and living developments within the good new ones too. 'Women's studies', 'cultural studies', 'lesbian and gay studies' have quickly lost their initial openness of perspective and developed highly distinctive assumptions and conventions (disciplinary paradigms) within which each operates. In feminist studies ambivalence about academic privilege may have marginalized these problems. Yet we might perhaps be in a better position politically if the institutional context of particular knowledges, and the varying powers that go with them, were more openly addressed.

As far as the issue of materialism is concerned, it seems likely that it will take a long time before the far-reaching influence and effects of the structure–culture and base–superstructure dichotomies have been registered, still more worked through. Certainly this is true for feminists working within the disciplinary bases of the social sciences and history. In the arts and humanities the impact of post-structuralism, albeit still highly contentious, has been much greater. Feminist theory has been able to take up a number of issues outside that classically 'materialist' perspective: in particular the analysis of corporeality and of the psyche. 'Post-structuralist' theories, notably Derridian deconstructive reading, Lacanian psychoanalysis, and Foucault's emphasis on the material body and the discourses of power, have proved very important in this. Feminists have appropriated these theories rather than others for good reasons: these theorists address the issues of sexuality, subjectivity, and textuality that feminists have put at the top of the agenda. In considering the debates that now ramify around feminism and post-structuralism, it is clear that the classic materialist presuppositions are increasingly harder to apply usefully.

To say that is not, however, to endorse a wholesale conversion to 'post-structuralism'. The many post-structuralist and post-modernist critiques of liberal and Marxist thought have decisively exposed the fundamental flaws of those earlier theories. Whether, however, they can promise a more useful alternative is a much more vexed question. In the meantime, there are losses attached to a wholesale abandonment of the areas of study traditionally denoted by the academic disciplines of sociology, political economy, economics and politics.

There is another, paradoxical, aspect of modern feminist deployment of the status historically attributed to materiality in an economic sense. While social class is definitely *non grata* as a topic, one may creditably speak of 'proletarianization' and 'exploitation' in the context of global capitalism and racially driven disadvantage (rather like the legal class discrimination that continues in Britain, in education and housing, for example, where analogous cases of sex and race discrimination would be at risk of prosecution). This is surely something of an anomaly, if a politically explicable one.

Finally, I want to conclude with a point about the issue of materialism and the theoretical 'grounding' of political practice. In the debates around feminism and post-modernism some have argued for a 'modernist' conception of rationalism, egalitarianism and autonomy as the basis of an emancipatory practice, in feminism as elsewhere. On this model, the work of Habermas and critical theory, for example, could be seen to rescue feminism from the irrationalism and political limitations of post-modern perspectives. Clearly this discussion is part of a broader debate as to whether feminism is 'essentially' a modernist or a post-modernist enterprise. There are some good reasons for holding either position on this and, indeed, for the third position that feminism straddles and thus destabilizes the modern–post-modern binary divide.[15] It seems to me, however, that we do not necessarily need more and better theories legitimating or justifying feminist political practice. Such a need is based on an assumption that political values are produced by scientific analysis (the type case being the classical 'scientific' as opposed to utopian definition of Marxism). This 'scientism', taken to its extreme, strips values from politics, and this has also been the effect of the blanket anti-humanism that has characterized post-structuralism and certain schools of feminist thought. Debates about ideology and subjectivity have shown that we need a better conception of agency and identity than has been available in either (anti-humanist) post-structuralist thought or its (humanist) modernist predecessors. It may well be that to develop a better account of subjective political motivation we shall have to reopen in new and imaginative ways the issue of humanism. Meanwhile, perhaps, it will be important to assert that political objectives are in an important sense constituted on the basis of values and principles—that they cannot be grounded in a scientific social analysis but spring from aspiration rather than proof.

['Words and Things: Materialism and Method in Contemporary Feminist Analysis', in Michèle Barrett and Anne Phillips (eds.), *Destabilizing Theory: Contemporary Feminist Debates* (Cambridge: Polity Press, 1992), 201–19.]

NAOMI SCHEMAN

18 Changing the Subject

My colleagues, especially those who teach the introductory course, frequently lament their students' inability to write. The fault is variously placed—on the public schools, on television, on our own composition program—and various solutions are suggested, ranging from trying to have smaller recitation sections so TAs can spend more time working with students on their writing, to doing away with paper writing altogether in favor of examinations.

Recently one colleague remarked on the startling improvement in the quality of the papers he is now receiving from students in his introductory class. Using Mill's method, it is unreasonable to attribute the improvement to the public schools, to television, to the composition program, or to our talented but still overworked TAs [*teaching assistants*]. Rather, the one thing that has changed and that seems the obvious and, I think, correct, explanation for the improvement is the change in the nature of his paper assignments.

Briefly put, he is now asking his students to communicate with him, with each other, and with the texts they are reading, and he has made it clear to them that he believes they have interesting things to say.

It seems a trivial commonplace to say that writing is a form of communication between author and reader. But many who would never go along with the trendy deconstructions of that idea seem to ignore it in their teaching, or to reduce the communication in question to the students' communicating to the teacher whether or not they can accurately and with apparent understanding reproduce what the teacher already knows. It's as though we regarded as the paradigm examples of small children's communicating with us their parroting back their best attempts at pronouncing the words we sound for them. One sign that we treated student writing, or speaking, as a mode of communication, would be our observance, and our expectation of their observance, of some of the basic norms of respectful communication: on our part, don't ask questions you know the answers to; and, on theirs, don't tell someone what you have reason to believe they already know.

Another commonplace (interestingly enough, also one for which analytic philosophers have been castigated) is that philosophy is a continuous conversation. We stage encounters between Aristotle and Descartes, and we join in. Our expectation for our students is that they, too, will participate in the conversation, but according to the usual ways of teaching, there's very little room for them to do so in an original or distinctive fashion unless they are well on the way to becoming one of us. Having something new to say, something that will be recognized as a contribution to the conversation, is hardly what we usually expect of our undergraduates. If they say something we hadn't expected, that will usually be reason to think that they hadn't quite gotten the point or understood the assignment or grasped the argument.

These assumptions on our part—that genuine contributions to the conversation that is philosophy are made by philosophers (that is, by people who think in ways similar to those who have been participants so far) and that what others say may be interesting in some way but isn't really germane—are hardly opaque to our students, who figure out that if what they are trying to do is to learn philosophy and to demonstrate that learning, they are better advised to sound as much like their teachers as they can and to say what they figure we would say rather than what they would say if they took our questions to be real ones, that is, if they took us really to care about their answers as something other than diagnoses of their abilities and achievements in coming to sound just like us.

Such considerations apply, in varying degrees, to all our students, of whatever gender, race, or cultural or economic background. And some of them will in fact respond eagerly to the terms we set: they will take on the apprenticeship, producing competently crafted work, acquiring the skills, by practicing on the arguments of others, that will allow them someday to produce original arguments of their own. There is no telling in advance who these students will be, and we need to be as ready to see the seeds of philosophical talent in a Black woman as in a white man. We need to be open to the possibility that any of our students will fall in love with the subject as it is, however traditionally it is taught, and that they will be good at it.

But they will be few. And, increasingly, the attention paid to race and gender inside and outside the university means that fewer and fewer of our students who are not white males will fail to notice or to care that nearly all of us, and nearly all the authors we teach, are. We may think they are wrong to care, that the attention is a bad and divisive thing, keeping students from claiming what could otherwise belong as much to them as to their white male fellow students. I don't think the attention is a bad thing; I think it reveals divisions that were always there though usually invisible from the side of privilege. (It's like the attention to sexual harassment, which leads many men to wax nostalgic for the harmless fun of a more comfortable, less self-conscious time. The cost of their comfort was the silence of the women who were victimized by that 'harmless fun'. The problem with raising awareness about race and gender is that those who had the privilege not to think about racism and sexism now have to. At least a little. Those on the other side have rarely had that luxury, and the few who have, if only in the precincts of philosophy, have had to deal with the estrangement that comes with being 'the exception'.)

But even if we think the attention is a bad thing, it isn't going to go away. Very few of our women students, for example, are likely to enter our class-rooms as oblivious as I was in 1965 to the near absence of women from the tradition we study. Not only are they more likely than I was to notice it, more important, they are more likely to think that it matters, that it's not a dismissible consequence of the fact that before very recently women were rarely encouraged or even allowed to do philosophy. And students of color are less likely now not to notice or to care that what we name philosophy is a set of distinctively European responses to distinctively European takes on questions asked, variously, all over the world. One might well study those responses as culturally specific, but such an attempt is usually defeated by the solipsistic imperialism of high European culture, which takes the forms of its own subjectivity to be universal. And it has gotten hard not to notice how many people were never meant to count as examples of the allegedly generic man.

One way we can respond, if we take these concerns seriously, is to expand the range of voices we engage in conversation. That is, we can add to our reading lists people who speak from perspectives that are not among the privileged. We can find ways to generalize the questions to which the philosophers we have been trained to read are giving answers in ways that show those questions to have been asked and answered by others. This is not a wholly new skill for a professionally trained philosopher: on the face of it Aristotle and Descartes weren't asking the same questions, and though Descartes surely had Aristotle in mind when he framed his questions, it didn't work the other way around. It takes an imaginative leap, of the sort we are trained to make, to figure out what Aristotle might say back to Descartes, to continue the conversation.

By bringing noncanonical voices into the conversation, we can set the stage for our students' participation in it. The people we are trained to read were not talking to people like our students—in most cases not solely because people like our students weren't born yet. We need to allow our students to notice this exclusion, to get angered by it, to ask themselves whether they want to become more like the people the philosophers are addressing (who will, of course, differ, depending on the philosopher), or whether they want to change the terms of the conversation. We can encourage them to believe that they have something to say, something we do not know, something the philosopher (or those, like us, who are committed to keeping the philosopher's words alive) needs to hear. Other voices can both model this sort of engaged talking back and serve as mediators, people with whom students may well feel readier to converse, by whom they may better expect to be understood.

We need to resist the temptation to present noncanonical voices as representative, as introducing diversity by giving the Black or women's or whatever perspective. Such voices need to be diverse and to disagree among themselves. One of the sillier arguments against taking diversity as a reason for affirmative action has it that doing so presupposes that there is a distinctive perspective a member of the group in question will bring. The reality, of course, is exactly the reverse: it is when members of marginalized groups are scarce that those who are present are put in the role of representatives of their race, gender, disability, sexual identity, or whatever. One of the goals of affirmative action is to have enough members of such groups around that the diversity among them is always apparent (meaning both that there are enough people for the diversity to be represented and that they are sufficiently at home not to need to hide their diversity behind a united front).

We will, most of us, need to reach a bit to include voices from beyond the philosophical pale, and I appreciate the worry that many have about treating such work disrespectfully, out of an all-too-familiar omnivorous arrogance that picks up bits and pieces of exotica to add a little spice. It isn't enough to point out that we feel fully competent to teach, say, Plato, so how can our contemporary, the Black lesbian poet and theorist, Audre Lorde, be too great a reach: we needn't worry about arrogantly appropriating Plato. Assuaging my fears of lacking mastery is one thing; assuaging my worries about the political meaning of claiming it is quite another.

But why do I need to master the voices I invite into my classroom? I certainly need to have something to say about them, enough to introduce them to those who are unfamiliar with them, and something to say to them, some way of starting a conversation I hope the students will continue. But we worry that our treatment of a text will be superficial, that we will miss, perhaps because of cultural differences, its subtleties and depths. It would be salutary just to acknowledge this fear, to accept the likelihood that we will, in fact, miss a lot, that we are not expert guides to these texts. We can locate ourselves and the world of academic philosophy we inhabit in the broader world by drawing connections both with parts of that broader world we know very well indeed and with parts of it that are strange to us.

The connections to what we know well can involve bringing the actual, historically specific, nongeneric people we are into our classrooms, using our own experiences as touchstones for philosophical reflection. This can be hard for us to do: we, after all, are the ones who succeeded in an educational system that rewarded the disciplining of the personal, idiosyncratic voice. It is no wonder that so many academic feminist theorists reproduced the spurious universalizing for which we rightly castigated privileged men: we had learned to trust our own voices precisely to the degree that we had learned to sound like them. Having served a long and successful apprenticeship in silencing the unrulier voices in our own heads, we were not apt to be very good at hearing those coming from others'. If we are inviting into the conversation a wider range of real people, we will need to join in as real people, not as disinterested anthologizers and critics. No one really is generic, however much privilege may encourage some to believe they are; no one has only ruly voices in her or his head.

Until we have gotten to the point where, despite long years of having been taught otherwise, students see us as real people, it will be hard for them to believe that, when they write papers for us to read, they are writing to a real person. We cannot expect that philosophy will come alive for them, will connect to the people they are, if they do not see it doing so for us, or if the enthusiasm they see us as having for our work seems so unconnected from anything they can see themselves as caring about that we might as well be another species. Especially until we are real enough to them for them to write intelligibly for our eyes it helps to have them write to and for each other, to trade papers and write responses. And taking each other seriously that way, as readers and critics, can help to break the hold of the idea that authority flows unidirectionally from text to teacher to student. We shouldn't underestimate our power in the classroom, in particular the power to say, 'this is to be taken seriously; this is worth your attention; this is the real stuff'.

Thus, the inclusion of other voices, authorized by their placement on the syllabus as contributors to philosophical conversation, can convey the message that what counts as philosophy is not fixed and that contributing to it does not require sounding like any of the previous participants. It may seem to us that students who bring up experiences of poverty or racism or abuse (or, for that matter, experiences of cooking or canoeing or dancing) in a discussion of Kant are changing the subject; they are no longer talking about what Kant was talking about, hence aren't contributing to the conversation we were having with Kant. But there are other senses of 'changing the subject': changing the subject matter of philosophy and changing the nature of the subject who philosophizes. In both these senses the student may well be changing the subject—if those of us charged with its preservation and canonical development have the courage and the humility to listen.

['Changing the Subject', in *Engendering the Subject* (New York and London: Routledge, 1993), 177–81; originally published in *American Philosophical Association (APA) Newsletter on Feminism and Philosophy,* 92/2 (Fall 1993).]

ELSPETH PROBYN

19 Materializing Locations Images and Selves

A few days ago I had the experience of lecturing about experience. To be more precise about it, I gave a talk about the category of experience within feminist cultural studies to a multidisciplinary seminar which carries the rather intriguing title of 'Les femmes devant les systèmes normatifs'. It was a puzzling experience: speaking of how my experience had informed the way in which I interpreted the theories of others made me feel like I was out on a limb with nothing beneath me. This was strange because the seminar is normally both a stimulating and comfortable place; composed of seven women professors from a range of disciplines and interested students, rigorous and even-handed intellectual give-and-take is the norm. However, the discussion following my talk *seemed* (this is, after all, my reconstruction) to revolve around the emotionality of my remarks. In my private post-mortem of the seminar, it felt as if I had gone where no woman had gone before. Before this is chalked up to delusions of grandeur, simple fatigue, or merely catchy images from *Star Trek*, I want to emphasize the irony of the situation: how could it be that raising the theoretical necessity of recognizing, of putting into words, the ways in which we read theory through experience should produce a feeling of isolation? Why should speaking something that is so common make me feel like an alien?

Coming down to earth I realized that the particularities of where we speak are as important to the signification as the content of what we are saying. The place where I was speaking hovered between the private and the public; for all its 'homey' feeling, in the final instance it was a classroom in a francophone university, an institution still touched by discursive traditions quite different from my own. Still, this does not explain why my enunciation of experience was taken as emotional, nor why that articulation bothers me.

The fact that it bothered me is perhaps, in part, due to the way in which some feminists of my generation at least are haunted by the 'touchy-feely' approach of feminism. In reaction to this, I have been guilty of the kind of over-jargonizing (and I am not alone in this) which strives to render feminism somehow more 'scientific'. While we are quite literally based in emotions, current feminism, as a body of theories, flees emotionality. There are, of course, reasons for this as well, some of them internal to feminism. But some of them have to do with how feminism is sometimes viewed by others. As Raymond Williams puts it:

It is understandable that people still trapped in the old consciousness really do see the new movements of our time—peace, ecology, feminism—as primarily 'emotional'. Those who have the most to lose exaggerate this to 'hysterical', but even 'emotional' is intended to make its point.[1]

While feminism is hardly a 'new' movement (new to Williams perhaps), being 'emotional' and the subsequent slide to 'hysterical' is a charge all too familiar to feminists. Being written off as 'emotional' is, as it is supposed to be, often humiliating; the idea is to attack at the level of the self. However, etymologically, being humiliated is not far from humility, that state of being humble, lowly and modest. And as Williams points out, emotions and 'emotional' movements can be characterized by their attachment to the lowliness of the everyday:

it is in what it dismisses as 'emotional'—a direct and intransigent concern with actual people—that the old consciousness most clearly shows its bankruptcy. Emotions, it is true, do not produce commodities. Emotions don't make the accounts add up differently. Emotions don't alter the hard relations of power. But where people actually live, what is specialised as 'emotional' has an absolute and primary significance.[2]

Thus, emotions point to where feminist criticism has to go; more to the point, they are also where feminism has always and already been. As Joanne Braxton says of reading black women's autobiographies, 'I read every text through my own experience, as well as the experiences of my mother and my grandmothers'.[3] While experience is not necessarily emotions and emotions cannot take the place of theory, what I want to argue is that emotions can point us in certain critical directions. In this chapter I want to examine an emotional foregrounding of the self as a way of critically acknowledging the ontological and epistemological bases of knowledge formation. My interest here is in feminist uses of the autobiographical as a tactic within the production of theory, or more precisely within the process of speaking theoretically. This is to consider uses of the self that can capture 'characteristic elements of impulse, restraint and tone; specifically affective elements of consciousness and relations: not feelings against thought, but thought as felt and feeling as thought'.[4] As Joseph Bristow states, 'to try to think and feel in this way can engage emotions which may be processed in order to redefine how stories may be historically understood'.[5] Using some examples of recent feminist criticism of autobiographies I want to think through a series of questions regarding the possible construction of a specifically feminist speaking position within cultural theory. Can a feminist insistence on the autobiographical sustain a critical and political speaking position without privileging an onto-logical category of 'femaleness'? Is there a way of using the self that does not condense into a privileged moment of 'me'? Can stories be told through selves and through emotions without being at the expense of other stories and selves? How can we respect the local conditions that give rise to those stories and understand them without extrapolating to generalities about women's selves? [. . .]

To investigate the possibilities of the self as an active articulation of the discursive and the lived, I'll turn now to some exemplars of feminist discourse on the self and the autobiographical, and then to an instance of a feminist folding of the image of the self within a theoretical text. Much feminist literary criticism has, understandably enough, been concerned with con-structing a distinctly feminist discourse of the female reader. Faced with the legacy of New Criticism's privileging of the text, or with the assumption of a universal (and male) 'reader', feminist critics have sought to reveal the gendered specificity of women's reading and writing. Often this works to reveal the embodied nature of texts; to disturb the neutrality of the text. [. . .] [A] textual selfhood is central in feminist criticism. But however important it may be, the material operations of the self tend to be overlooked as the text gets read.

Judith Gardiner starts her investigation 'On Female Identity and Writing by Women' with the statement, '[a] central question of feminist literary criticism is, Who is there when a woman says "I am"?'[6] She goes on to define 'female selves' based on her reading of Nancy Chodorow:

Thus I picture female identity as typically less fixed, less unitary and more flexible than male individuality, both in its primary core and in the entire maturational complex developed from this core. These traits have far-reaching consequences for the dis-tinctive nature of writing by women.[7]

Hence, for Gardiner, 'female identity is a process' which then partly explains women's approaches to writing: 'One reflection of this fluidity is that women's writing often does not conform to the generic prescriptions of the male canon'.[8] Thus the roving female identity cannot be captured within one genre:

Women's novels are often called autobiographical, women's autobiographies, novel-istic . . . Because of the continual crossing of self and other, women's writing may blur public and private and defy completion.[9]

While Gardiner's assumption of a strict equivalence between a psychological model of feminine identity and women's forms of writing is especially blatant here, it is a fairly common trait among some feminist literary critics. The move is to identify women's psychological being and then to apply it to a general process of reading or writing. However, when social conditions are collapsed within a psychological rendition of 'woman', some rather large generalizations are bound to occur. Thus, Judith Fetterley posits a universal and transhistorical condition for women which then agrees with how women read: women suffer,

not simply the powerlessness which derives from not seeing one's experience articu-lated, clarified, and legitimated in art, but more significantly, the powerlessness which results from the endless division of self against self, the consequence of the invocation to identify as male while being reminded that to be male—to be universal . . . is to be *not* female.[10]

Conceived in a pervasive 'powerlessness', in the face of the male women's selves come to be united. The absence of women's experiences in the text then leaves the woman reader nowhere. While this is a salient point, I'm not sure if it leads to what Patrocinio Schweickart posits as the efficacy of androcentric literature: 'it does not allow the woman to seek refuge in her difference. Instead, it draws her into a process that uses her against herself'.[11] Powerlessness becomes a key image within this particular system, yet its work is not explored; it is merely assumed. Indeed, the image of power-lessness becomes cut off from where it lodges in the real, and as such it loses the capacity to provide a point of view into the complexity of women not having power. It operates at the level of the text but does not open up into its involvement in the real.

Some recent perspectives on women's autobiography within literary criti-cism expand upon the correlation of woman within the text and woman as writer of the text. For Sidonie Smith the genre of autobiography is especially interesting because of its 'maleness': 'Autobiography is itself one of the forms of selfhood constituting the idea of man and in turn promoting that idea'. Smith describes women's struggles against the dictates of the autobiograph-ical canon.[12] 'I am' becomes, for Smith, an impossible statement for women writers. As she argues:

Since the ideology of gender makes of woman's life script a nonstory, a silent space, a gap in patriarchal culture, the ideal woman is self-effacing rather than self-promoting, and her 'natural' story shapes itself not around the public, heroic life but around the fluid, circumstantial, contingent responsiveness to others that, according to patriarchal ideology, characterizes the life of woman but not of autobiography.[13]

Thus women's stories of their lives are cancelled out by the larger narrative of gender. 'Self-effacing' and 'self-promoting' become the two poles around which gender is articulated. There is, however, little movement here as women's lives are described as a state of being and not the stuff of art. Hence for Smith, patriarchy pre-empts any self-representation on the part of women; their 'meaning' is already assigned. This description functions as an onto-logical sentencing of women, based in the primacy of their posited being. The image of powerlessness is again fundamental here and Smith goes on to characterize women's writing as 'impossible':

[If] she conforms totally to that ideal script, she remains bound (her book, her 'self') always in her relationship to men (and their progeny) and defined always in relationship to a life cycle tied to biological phenomena and the social uses to which those phenomena are put: birth, menarche, marriage, childbirth, menopause, widow-hood.[14]

While Smith clearly puts the blame for women's condition on 'patriarchal ideology', she also holds onto a psycho-sexual model strongly influenced by Chodorow. She has no problem assigning certain qualities to women ('fluid-ity', 'contingent responsiveness to others'); the trouble is that patriarchy doesn't appreciate these virtues. The life cycle is what allows for these feminine attributes but, 'her life story is like every other female life story'. This then is the only story women can write and one that no one (no man) wants to hear. Women (as historical subjects) therefore disappear into an ontological argument about their being. The very pervasiveness of the image of powerlessness flattens out any possible epistemological or ontological distinctions. Smith's landscape of equivalences ('book', 'self', 'life cycle') makes it difficult to conceive of any position from which a woman might speak. The problem with Smith's argument is that there is no 'point of view' other than the silence of the flip side of patriarchy. Rather than making the image of oppression work for women by locating its 'faire', its work within the social, Smith paints woman into a corner leaving her no place to speak from. The pall of powerlessness is all we have as Smith brings forth a final silencing figure of the castrated mother:

the authority to speak as 'representative' man and 'representative' woman derives from the erasure of female sexuality; for the male-identified fiction commands the repression of the mother, and the 'good woman' fiction commands the repression of female eroticism.[15]

For Smith then, women can only speak as a woman masquerading as a man (and repressing the mother) or into the silence of a patriarchal script (repres-sing the female). Thus the only speaking position for women is when 'phallogocentric discourse has permitted women powerful life scripts'. And these scripts depend upon the writer having 'successfully escaped the drag of the body, the contaminations of female sexuality'. To state the obvious, this doesn't leave one a great deal of room. In a move reminiscent of early psychoanalytic film theory, woman cannot initiate the 'gaze', she *is* the image. In Smith's argument, woman is her 'life script/cycle'; there can be no distance between her self and her representation as women's existence is written by her historical and biological fate.

Her characterization of autobiography is understandably grounded in an ontological split

privileging the autonomous or metaphysical self as the agent of its own achievement and in frequently situating that self in an adversarial stance toward the world, 'auto-biography' promotes a conception of the human being that valorizes individual integrity and separateness and devalues personal and communal interdependency.[16]

Smith here performs a double articulation of genre and gender: autobiography necessitates a unique self; the masculine self is grounded in 'separateness'; women's gender is constituted in 'interdependency'; a woman's self is excluded on the grounds of gender from this genre. Woman's very 'femaleness', her ontological state of being, excludes her from speaking. The problem is not that women's writing may be historically more 'personal' and involved in a community; it is rather that this situation is described under the sign of powerlessness instead of epistemological circumstance. In other words, Smith's argument is ultimately uninterested in the grounds that allow for some women to speak in certain circumscribed ways. She has insisted on the lack of women's enunciative endeavours as an adjunct of their state of powerlessness. This psycho-sexual model of women is therefore seen both as evidence of and the basis for women's inability to speak. This mode of analysis closes down any avenue of investigation; various 'facts' may be inserted into this reasoning, but as a line of inquiry it cannot itself raise new questions. The effects of women's uses of the self are known in advance.

In contrast to this approach which confines itself to analysing the system in which the self is caught, there are other possibilities of the self, understood as 'a point of view', which open up questions about the formation of knowledges and their relation to the lived nature of the image. Again, as Le Doeuff characterizes this approach:

The 'point of view' is not concerned with creating that which it is trained on; of course, it allows for the construction of questions and modes for analyzing the scrap of reality that is under its consideration, it does so in such a way as to allow these questions to meet up with the facts: one can only say, therefore, that it produces things.[17]

Thus the 'point of view' doesn't create that which it describes; it has to construct questions from the level of the reality that it is trained upon. It produces or provokes connections; this is to realize the self's doubled locations.

In her article, ' "Not Just a Personal Story": Women's *Testimonios* and the Plural Self' (1988), Doris Sommer 'shifts the focus from the portrait produced to the productive trope of self-reference'. Here the self is to be used to provoke connections and produce new articulations. Sommer is particularly concerned with the operations of Latin American women's *testimonios* (accounts of the self). She describes the use of the self in these accounts: 'the singular represents the plural not because it replaces or subsumes the group but because the speaker is a distinguishable part of the whole'.[18] Sommer identifies two different spheres of the self's operations:

In rhetorical terms, whose political consequences should be evident in what follows, there is a fundamental difference here between the *metaphor* of autobiography and heroic narrative in general . . . and *metonymy*, a lateral identification through relationship, which acknowledges the possible differences among 'us' as components of the whole.[19]

This analytic perspective on the uses of the self is obviously very different from Smith's, for whom the self is 'indistinguishable and always replaceable'.[20] In contrast to the latter's construction of a biologically based self-same story, Sommer's emphasis on metonymy allows the self lateral movement. Remembering Jakobson's (1972) distinction between metaphor as paradigmatic and metonymy as syntagmatic, we can see that certain uses of the self may move away from a logic of substitution. However, while this may be an improvement on Smith's closing down of the self, Sommer's concentration on the metonymical ultimately undermines her insights about the *testimonios*. In this particular case, the self has more to do with the materiality of the reality that it is describing than with any metonymic movement to create an 'us'. Sommer is after all talking about texts that speak of actual suffering and that are often written in dangerous circumstances. These circumstances bring forth particular styles of writing; as Sommer says, 'these intensely lived testimonial narratives are strikingly impersonal'.[21]

The 'strikingly impersonal' nature of these uses of the self may in fact have more to do with the concrete situations in which they are written than with linguistic notions of metonymy. Sommer's depiction of the testimonies of these Latin American women readily recalls de Certeau's sense of 'tactics'. The self cannot operate from a position of stability or strength. As Sommer tells us, these stories speak of immediate and terrifying situations: 'raped countless times by Somoza's National Guardsmen . . . her mother's torture at the hands of the Guatemalan army . . . the baby kicked out of her during torture in a Bolivian prison . . .'[22]; as Sommer says, these accounts of the self question the 'academic pause we take in considering how delayed or artificial . . . reality is'. Given the danger of where they speak from, these voices constitute calculated actions determined by the absence of a proper locus. The abstraction of one's experiences into writing is a practical and a political necessity. These women need to tell of themselves (to help others) as they need to avoid making that self into a locus (thus inviting retaliations against themselves). The self here, because of specific historical reasons, takes on the tactical logic of guerrilla warfare. As Sommer says of the movements required:

As working-class or peasant women involved in political, often armed, struggle, the subjects of these narratives move about in a largely unmapped space. Or it is a space on which competing maps are superimposed, where no single code of behavior can be authoritative?[23]

These women then cannot afford the luxury of a stable and singular self. Working in this complex situation, they are simultaneously 'a mother, a worker, a Catholic, a Communist, an indigenist, and a nationalist'.[24] While one could say that their location demands several contradictory 'subject positions', I think that it goes deeper than this. When Domitilia, a woman tortured in a Bolivian prison, is given the 'choice' of naming fellow revolutionaries or losing her children, her cell-mate tells her: 'You shouldn't think only as a mother, you've got to think as a leader'. It is not that Domitilia is positioned both as mother and leader, but that she must (for her mental and physical survival) 'think her self' as mother *and* leader. These two points of view are not allowed to be exclusionary; they must be used together in order to provoke ways of thinking through the situation, a way of producing knowledge about what to do.

I do not want to extrapolate from this particular situation to render some universal model of the self and its relation to textuality. To do so would be the height of intellectual insensitivity. We can nonetheless take from these instances ways of looking at the self that emphasize the levels at which the self actively works in given situations. The very situated responses of these women must deny a reduction of their selves into a psychological model of 'woman'. These *testimonios* cannot be seen as just another replaying of woman's 'life script' or as merely a reconstruction of the self within an endlessly repeated psycho-biological story. Against such abstractions, we need to see that the projections of various selves are ways of 'expressing ourselves' for individual women in specific situations; as a Guatemalan woman states, there is no one 'immutable way'. These very local uses of the self situate their locations at a conjuncture. In writing they produce a document that places both the writers' selves and the situation in relief. Such use of the self is an act (and entails others) which arises from the situation as it comments upon it. It is in this sense that we can understand the self as image:

it produces things, in the sense that it is quite an art, and an act, to make something apparent, to produce an object that will be considered as a document, to bring out of the shadows and to put forward 'facts' that, in the final instance, are never given.[25]

So the image of the self in the case of these Latin American women's testimonies produces something, makes something appear, which can be considered a conjunctural document of the self and of the times. The self comes out of 'the shadows' to put forward 'the facts', facts which are never officially given. This movement brings to mind an image of the Argentine 'mothers of the disappeared' who, in the face of official disavowal, used their bodies and selves in an effort to bring the facts of torture and murder out into the open. Their pictures of their 'lost' daughters and sons were documents of facts that were not given. These examples could be said to demonstrate a sense of the self which moves metonymically to articulate experience, location and history without reifying an ontology of being. [. . .]

[...] The testimonies of individual women tortured and raped deeply challenge any notion of extrapolation to a global women's community. As Gloria Anzaldua writes of 'illegal' Mexican women, 'la mujer indocumentada . . . leaves the familiar and safe homeground to venture into unknown and possibly dangerous terrain. This is her home | this thin edge of | barbwire'.[26] Anzaldua's image reminds us forcefully of the material reality of living at, and perhaps speaking from, that thin line—a line which cannot be moved metonymically beyond the concrete locality of its construction. Thus, while the selves in those writings may indeed reach other women, and touch us, they remain committed to their social and historical locations. As Biddy Martin says of the specificity of lesbian autobiographies:

the feminist dream of a new world of women simply reproduces the demand that women of color (and women more generally) abandon their histories, the histories of their communities, their complex locations and selves, in the name of a unity that barely masks its white, middle-class cultural reference/referent.[27]

Instead of the image of powerlessness that circulates in Smith's model of autobiography, or even Sommer's image of a generalized community, Martin emphasizes the conjunctural moment in constructing local selves: 'The invocation of the sights, smells, sounds and meanings of "the street" works to locate the author concretely in geographic, demographic, architectural spaces'.[28] It is then in the 'sights and smells' of 'complex locations' that the images for speaking the self emerge. These images, taken from an everyday reality, can be refracted as a point of view into the lived, bent back into the smell and the sounds from which it is taken. This point of view works against what Martin calls 'the assumptions that there are no differences within the "lesbian self" and that lesbian authors, autobiographical subjects, readers, and critics can be conflated'.[29] In order to be analytically useful the self cannot be conflated with ontological notions based in a primacy of 'femaleness'. Moreover, as Martin points out, women marginalized through sexual preference or colour must seek out their difference and refuse to be generalized in the name of a globalizing image. [. . .]

Responding to the problematic of a feminist speaking position, we can say that certain uses of the self work to figure the local sites and conjunctural moments necessary to the development of a feminist enunciative practice. This project involves transforming discursive material to allow women 'a place from which to speak and something to say'. Neither of these requisites can be taken lightly. [. . .] Thinking of certain feminist practices of globalizing the local should remind us that this too can take away the place from which other women speak. Formulating women's selves as monolithic and impossible structures obviously leaves one little room and not much to say. What I have argued here is that we need an 'operative reasoning', an operative speaking, which both figures a place and enables a point of view into the social construction of that place. The operation of images taken from that place can be seen as points of view that may disable and transform discursive practices that silence women.

At the beginning of this chapter I spoke of the difficulty of speaking, of an image of being stranded out on a limb with nowhere to go and nothing below, as the spectre of emotionality haunted and taunted me. Both the feeling of speaking into a void—that no one can hear you—and the feeling that what one is saying is merely emotional drivel—that you are saying nothing (new)—are obvious impediments to speaking as a woman. No one wants to consciously fall into a personal abyss. However, what I am suggesting is that there are rhetorical tactics that can rework how the personal is put into discourse. Rather than throwing us into a discursive darkness, certain images of the self may rearrange where we speak from as well as the spaces in which 'we' are spoken.

In positing the self as an analytic level in the construction of a conjunctural site, I do not want to reify local sites. It is important to remember de Certeau's use of the tactic. If the self as a way of figuring different relations in the social formation is to be analytically useful, it cannot be condensed into a 'proper locus'. As I have argued, the self cannot be seen as an entity that binds women together in the face of racial, sexual, national, and other differences. The self must therefore be seen as a theoretical manoeuvring, not as a unifying principle. The self can be made to work to articulate an epistemological critique of the discursive ordering of the social and to affirm an ontological recognition of the affectivity of emotions and things. Instead of speaking the self as an endless repetition of women's ontological being as a script, the self as an image and images of the self can comment on the conjuncture of discourses and everyday commonplaces. Speaking the self does not necessarily imply any triumphant move; rather as a theoretical level, the self may simply and quietly enable yet more questions, yet more theoretical work. As Morris states: '[f]or the lovers of high-speed iconoclasm, the lowly labour of listening carefully to a text connotes the fussiness of housewives' psychosis'.[30] This is not to say that a feminist speaking position is comparable to housework; it is to say that the work of formulating enunciative practices that can speak certain unasked questions may be equally never-ending.

[*Sexing the Self: Gendered Positions in Cultural Studies* (London and New York: Routledge, 1993), 82–107.]

20 The Place of Women's Studies in the Contemporary University

Women's Studies came into being with the development of the second wave of the feminist movement toward the end of the 1960s, at a time in which a higher education system, a university system, was well established in advanced capitalist countries. [...]

The social movements of the sixties drew much of their base from university students and it was inevitable that the kinds of claims they were making, both in terms of values and in terms of claims about the nature of reality, would find reflection in academic curriculum. So the second wave of the feminist movement was taken up within the university and expressed as Women's Studies. This means that Women's Studies is necessarily bound up with the projects of professionalization that the contemporary university represents. The first wave of feminism, the wave that we associate with the second half of the nineteenth century and the first two decades of this century, was conterminous with the professionalization of knowledge. Not only was there an especial attraction for nineteenth century feminists of the professional ideals of career open to talent and of trained service, but many of these feminist reformers were profoundly engaged with projects that laid the groundwork for social work and the other human services as professions.[1] The confluence of the first wave of feminism with that of professionalization did not mean that feminist values were allowed to contaminate the culture of scientific objectivity and value-neutrality which characterized the ethos of the professions. That now there is an open politics of contesting and contestable knowledge claims within the contemporary university is an important change which may owe more to the subjection of the university to 'outside' political influence than to the self-regulation of the collegial community of the autonomous university.[2] Such political influence represents a demand that the public universities democratize themselves, in the sense of being more accountable to the community of tax-paying citizens which funds them. Such democratization has been understood to mean that universities should adapt their entry and other credentialling procedures so as to permit access and entry to groups traditionally poorly represented in higher education. It has been also understood to mean that the values of movements placed in a contestatory relationship to modern Western, patriarchal rationalism should enter the intellectual debates of the university.

This politicization of the university has been understood by many of the custodians of Western, masculinist reason to constitute a threat to the very foundations of the university. There is an uneasy and often highly conflictual relationship between the older principle of rational enquiry and that of multiple, contestable and openly politicized claims on 'truth'. Where this relationship works as a binary opposition between two camps in the contemporary university, there is a dreadful game played out between a scientistic representation of rational enquiry, on the one hand, and 'politically correct' forms of moral certitude on the other. Necessarily, the first wins hands down since the latter abandons all pretense to rational enquiry and commits itself to moral terror as its practice. The promise for the future lies in refusing this binarism and in an open, reflective embrace of the tensions which arise as to the question of what rational enquiry means in a universe of multiple, politicized truth claims where there can be no monorational mode of closure for debate. The politics of Women's Studies within the contemporary university is thoroughly subject to the tensions between rational enquiry and political correctness. However, it is arguable that it has been assisted in making this a productive and creative intellectual enterprise by a further development, the challenge to Western (white and middle class) feminism by non-Western women and women of color. This challenge has unsettled the moral certainties of this movement-oriented intellectual discipline and propelled it into its own distinctive sociology of knowledge.

The feminist movement has been increasingly challenged, from about the end of the 1970s onward, by non-Western women and by women of color. These challenges have brought out the neglect of class, racist, and ethnic oppression by the feminist movement, with its tendency to concentrate on gender issues. Those making these challenges have said over and over again that the feminist movement's tendency to oppose women to men overlooks the critical fact that, for black women, depending on the context, racist oppression may be often more primary than gender oppression, and that in opposing racism their allies are black men, not white women. This kind of politics is expressed by the Afro-American feminist theorist bell hooks.[3] [...]

It is logical that the only women who are positioned to make gender inequality their primary concern are those of dominant race, ethnic and class status. However, this is not an insight achieved by these women on their own: it has depended on challenges from women positioned in ways which exclude them from this privilege. The effect of these challenges has been to make evident the interested quality of feminist politics and ideology, an interestedness that expresses the tendency of its leaders and followers to be white, western and middle-class. Thus Nancy Cott a feminist historiographer of US feminism, makes this quite clear in the introduction to *The Grounding of Modern Feminism*: 'The woman's rights tradition was historically initiated by, and remains prejudiced toward, those who perceive themselves first and foremost as "woman", who can gloss over their class, racial, and other status identifications because those are culturally dominant and therefore relatively invisible.'[4]

If this is generally true of feminism, it is especially true of its professional domains: femocracy.[5] The degree to which academic practitioners of

Women's Studies have been willing to respond to these challenges has been mixed. It is fair to say that the theoretical work with which Women's Studies is currently associated is a genuine and positive response to those challenges. There are several aspects of this response. First, there is a deconstructive response, which demonstrates that feminism as critique necessarily confirms the very ground it seeks to challenge. Thus feminism as critique tends to reproduce and confirm the binarisms of a patriarchal gender division of labor, and, paradoxically, becomes complicit with that order.[6] This deconstructive response conduces to an examination of the history of how Women's Studies and feminism have participated in western, white and masculinist modes of knowledge. For example, there is work on how white women in colonial settings were and are complicit in a gendered way with white, western, masculinist colonization, and on how this colonization has inscribed the policing binarism of 'good' and 'bad' women within the racialized hierarchies of colonizer and colonized.[7]

A second response to these challenges has been a theory of the intersections between different bases of oppression, that is, working with the idea that there are multiple bases of oppression, that there is class, gender, ethnicity, race, sexuality, and that not any one of these bases of oppression can be viewed as a master key to the rest, that they have to be treated analytically separately and then examined in their historically specific intersections. This is making for some mature and exciting work.[8]

A third response which is clearly indicated by the second is the opening up in theoretical and practical terms of a politics of voice and representation within Women's Studies. Specifically, in theoretical terms, Women's Studies is beginning to debate the proposition that white western women cannot speak for all women. It is now accepted that for all women to be a part of Women's Studies a dialogical process has to be opened up which is open to differently positioned women, that is, women who regard themselves as differently positioned in terms of ethnicity, race, class and sexuality. This is a politics of difference and it is arguable that it is predicated on abandoning a radical feminist insistence on the unity of women. This is a highly contentious proposition at the current time, especially as it calls into question ideas of immediate and transparent personal experience and face-to-face community. Iris Young argues against the totalizing tendency of these ideas and the way in which they work to suppress or to deny difference, and she is one of the more significant feminist theorists of a democratic politics of difference.[9]

These theoretical responses are emergent, they have a kind of maturity, but they have a long way to go. They are participating in a more general theoretical renaissance. Women's Studies, or, more adequately, the feminist theory that I have indicated, is contributing to a significant new wave of theorizing in the humanities and the social sciences, a wave just as significant as the intellectual revolution which psychoanalysis, sociology, and anthropology brought about at the turn of the nineteenth century into the twentieth century. This new body of theory is both supremely skeptical and democratic in relation to the values which are always embedded in knowledge. It refuses to authorize any knowledge claim that makes that claim appear as though it is grounded in the nature of things, as though it is a mirror image of something out there that is simply true. This is a radical skepticism which accepts Nietzsche's proposition that truths are metaphors. This is because truths are a function of the politics of representation, it being representations rather than reflections of reality that are at issue. My point is that such skepticism is in the traditions of the modern university. It is democratic because it is able to use methods of analysis which show how any positive representation of humanity tends to 'other' that which it is not. This kind of analysis creates a space for those who have been 'othered' in discourse.

Feminist representations construct their own representational economies of inclusions and exclusions. An example of this is the commonly held feminist view that women are more cooperative than men. The new critical theorizing problematizes all aspects of that statement. It questions for whom and in what contexts it is meaningful to speak of all women. Secondly, it suggests that, if some insist on speaking for all women, this is because they are naturalizing the condition of being a woman, a rhetorical gambit that contradicts precisely where feminist interventions tend to operate, namely to denaturalize, to refuse to essentialize this business of being a woman. It also brings out the way in which the proposition that women are more cooperative than men necessarily conforms to a binary politics of inversion which 'others' men, and conflates who men might become with a patriarchal, masculinist *status quo*. This particular representation also 'others' women who are not cooperative or who refuse to conform to what cooperative means within the rhetorical context at hand.

If the new critical theorizing problematizes this kind of binary categorical claim for women it does so in a spirit of self-critical irony. It accepts not only as a condition of feminism that such binary categorizing is necessary. It makes it clear that the very necessity of feminism arises from the material existence of a patriarchal ideological binary and hierarchical ordering of the terms male (masculine, men) and female (feminine, women). In short, this theorizing adopts a deconstructive relationship to its own discursive practice.[10]

This example underlines the point that feminist theory has matured to the point where it is able to subject its own premises to an ironical, skeptical and critical mode of analysis. Here I join and celebrate with Teresa de Lauretis in her statement that:

A feminist theory begins when the feminist critique of ideologies becomes conscious of itself, and turns to question its own body of writing and critical interpretations, its basic assumptions and terms and the practices which they enable and from which they emerge. This is not merely an expansion or a reconfiguration of boundaries, but a qualitative shift in political and historical consciousness. This shift implies, in my opinion, a dis-placement and a self-displacement: leaving or giving up a place that is safe, that is 'home,' (physically, emotionally, linguistically and epistemologically) for another place that is unknown and risky, that is not only emotionally but conceptually other, a place of discourse from which speaking and thinking are at best tentative, uncertain and unguaranteed. But the leaving is not a choice: one could not live there in the first place.'[11]

De Lauretis goes on to say: 'Both dis-placements, the personal and the conceptual, are painful—either the cause or the result of the pain, risk and a real stake.' This thematic of how an open politics of representation tied as it is into a contemporary politics of difference, requires us to relinquish that great icon of the cult of domesticity—'home' as refuge and sanctuary in relation to the fray of the public marketplace—is importantly developed by Minnie Bruce Pratt in her 'Identity: Skin Blood Heart'. There Pratt, a white, middle class, Protestant, Southern US woman, shows how the home of her childhood was predicated on strictly and violently policed exclusion of all that is (who are) not white, middle class, Protestant, 'normal', thus prescribing her own exclusion as the lesbian she becomes later.

I offer this quick sketch, and that is all it is, of how contemporary, critical, feminist theorizing operates, to indicate how far it is from ideological self-congratulation and dogma, and how much it participates in the critical, reflective and skeptical spirit of a university. My argument is also that it is this spirit which is as central now as it ever was to a democratic and non-totalizing politics. It is undoubtedly true that such critical theorizing depends on the legitimacy a university affords not only to critical reflection but to the erudition and scholarship on which such reflection depends. In short, the professionalism of modern university-based knowledge is required for this critical theorizing to be possible.

If, then, we acknowledge the merit of the by-now established lines of critique of professional domination, it cannot be because those of us who are critical feminist theorists are willing to abandon our professionalism. It is arguable that all professions make a bid for power through their monopoly on particular kinds of knowledge claim. It is this which is at issue in the critiques of professional domination, as with the women's health movement in relation to the medical profession. It is no less at issue in respect of critical feminist theorists. The fact that this is so, however, does not warrant the abolition of the authority which resides in scholarly erudition and expertise. The answer lies not in attempting to preempt the differentiation of expert and non-expert feminist theorizing by making all conform to the homogenizing dictates of feminist community and its inevitable, totalizing moral strictures. Instead, it lies in maintaining this differentiation while requiring both dialogue and accountability across it. [. . .]

The fundamental obligation of a university-based Women's Studies practitioner is to be an expert in terms of the conventions of scholarly expertise which characterize the contemporary university. In this regard, her service delivery roles concern her university-based constituencies: primarily her students, both undergraduate and graduate, whom she is inducting into this scholarly discipline, but also her academic peers, and the academic management of the institution to whom she is responsible for her university practice. For her *expertise*, accountability to these constituencies overrides accountability to extra-university constituencies.

Academies in the politically marked university disciplines—such as Women's Studies and Maori Studies—are accountable also to extra-university constituencies of those who make claims on them through shared political and movement affiliation. For her politics, accountability to these constituencies overrides accountability to these university-based constituencies. However, as will be clear, this is not a simple issue.

If the Women's Studies academic has an obligation of accountability for her value orientation and her politics to these constituencies, [. . .] this obligation cannot be understood as one which requires her to deny the ways in which her scholarly expertise informs her values and politics. These ways make her a critical and reflective participant in politically-oriented dialogue, and she may often substitute reflection for policy action to the justifiable frustration of those oriented to action. In this context, she has a dual obligation: (1) to be an effective communicator in relation to these non-academic constituencies; (2) to appreciate and respect their expressed needs for how she realizes her role in relation to them, which, among other things, may require that she become more familiar with the world of policy action.

The requirement of effective communication requires her to become bi– if not multi-lingual in the sense of being able to operate across different contextually bound dialects and modes of rhetoric. Anyone who aspires to be a public intellectual must develop these lingual competences. Her own academic language must appear as so much arcane jargon to non-initiates. Lingual difference of this kind is one of the clear hallmarks of the line dividing expert from non-expert knowledge. Her academic language is appropriate for the university classroom and for communication to her academic peers. It is not appropriate for communication to non-academic audiences, but, again, her 'plain' language competences will be always colored by the byzantine intricacies and esoterica of her academic tongue. What her 'mother' tongue is, is a moot point since like all intellectuals her self(ves) has(ve) become re created through the rhetorical artifice of the modern intellectual disciplines.

It cannot be denied that those who claim expertise have a tendency to construe their relationship to the non-expert along hierarchical lines so that the former believe they know *in general* more than the latter, that their esoteric language makes them *in general* cleverer and more insightful than the latter. These beliefs are clearly undemocratic. If, ultimately, knowledge is oriented by some reference to need, it is clear that no amount of expert attention to need can substitute for what I have called above 'expressed' need, or need as constructed by those who have the need. The non-expert knowledge of needy persons is just as much crafted by experience and learning as is expert knowledge. They remain, however, different kinds of knowledge.

Much of my argument here concerns this difference and its importance. If it is important to require Women's Studies academics to be politically accountable to the expressed needs of women's movement constituencies, it is equally important to accept that their expert knowledge has a place in relation to these expressed needs. This kind of knowledge permits these needs to be historically situated, critically and reflectively analyzed. Among other things, this ensures that the interested quality of feminism, its inflection by the privileged race, ethnic and class positioning of its follower, is subject to critical challenge and reflection. This, in turn, conduces to a democratic politics of difference within feminism, one in which it is accepted that the needs of differently positioned women are different. The values of reflective critique, empirically oriented enquiry and logically coherent analysis remain as crucial to the health of an emancipatory social movement such as the women's movement as they are in general to a society oriented within democratic, dialogical and civil process.

[*Postmodern Revisionings of the Political* (New York: Routledge, 1994), 42–53.]

Section 2

Epistemologies

INTRODUCTION

A feminist is a woman who does not allow anyone to think in her place.

Michèle Le Doeuff

The pieces in this section question whether feminist critiques of traditional epistemologies imply the existence of a specifically 'female' knowledge. Questions concerning the nature of knowledge and the validity of knowledge claims have been central to feminist writings. Much early writing was taken up with establishing and exploring the extent to which traditional epistemologies worked to systematically exclude the possibility that women could be the agents of knowledge. The development of such critiques of traditional epistemologies as specifically 'male' has generated debate concerning the existence and/or nature of a specifically 'female' knowledge. Hence, in addition to the critical project, an assertive project outlining possible feminist epistemologies has also developed. Though diverse in form, these feminist epistemological frameworks tend to share a critical stance in relation to rationality, objectivity, and universality, asserting the significance and legitimacy of emotional, politically engaged, and particularistic ways of knowing.

Alison Jaggar claims, in a manner characteristic of much feminist epistemology, that: 'it is necessary to rethink the relationship between knowledge and emotion and construct conceptual models that demonstrate the mutually constitutive rather than oppositional relationship between reason and emotion'. What makes this suggestion feminist is the attendant claim that emotion has historically been culturally associated with subordinate groups—particularly women—and that this presumption has served to legitimate the silencing of those deemed irrational. The politically sensitive issues here, assuming one accepts the analysis thus far, are twofold: whether one should reject the epistemological value of the emotional or claim it as invaluable; and whether one should then respond by asserting the value of women's special relation to the emotional, or by debunking it as myth, or indeed—productively engaging with the paradoxes which inhabit the heart of feminist theorizing—by doing both.

One of the most significant strands of thought on this issue draws upon the insights of historical materialism to generate an account of experiences common to all women which provides a foundation for a women's 'standpoint' which has privileged epistemological status. We find this approach in the work of both Jaggar and Hartsock. It is Jaggar's claim that the 'outlaw emotions' of subordinate groups, though apparently unreasonable, actually serve to highlight lived contradictions which dominant forms of reason mask. As such they provide a basis for a fuller, more adequate epistemology. This line of argument is developed by Nancy Hartsock: 'As an engaged vision,' she argues, 'the understanding of the oppressed, the adoption of a standpoint, exposes the real relations among human beings as inhuman, points beyond the present, and carries a historically liberatory role.' Note that this perspective adopts an explicitly emancipatory position, that it assumes a notion of the 'real', that certain social groups have better access to this reality, and finally that the shared understanding generated within subordinate groups are not given but must be generated through struggle. These claims are married to another set of claims about the social status of women in order to provide the basis for a distinctly feminist standpoint. At heart, the claim is that the sexual division of labour provides the basis for two distinct epistemological perspectives.

Whilst aspects of Hartsock's argument have been subject to feminist critique (notably the presumed commonality of women's experience and hence the unity of the standpoint generated; and the exclusive focus on work as determining experience, overlooking the fields of family, motherhood, and sexuality), the basic notion of standpoint epistemology has been highly influential. Patricia Hill Collins, for example, explores the subjugated knowledge of Black African-American women as the basis for constructing an Afrocentric feminist epistemology. In this, her approach echoes that of Hartsock. Where she differs is in the explicit focus on one particular group of women—signifying the fracturing of the claimed common feminist standpoint into a plethora of epistemological groupings, and in her synthesis of both the Afrocentric and feminist standpoints—challenging the suggestion that discrete oppressions can be quantified and ranked.

In addition to standpoint theory, many feminist epistemological explorations also draw on the psychological theories of both Nancy Chodorow and Carol Gilligan as the basis for an explanation of the deficiencies of dominant conceptions of rationality (note that Collins draws upon both in her portrayal of an Afrocentric feminist epistemology). Many have developed this analysis to argue that Cartesian dualism is rooted in the psychosexual development of men and represents a denial of the feminine. Chodorow's early writing offered an important framework from which to develop such a perspective, developing as it did a psychological account of the ways in which the experience of mothering shapes male and female psyches differently. The asymmetrical organization of parenting, with the mother as primary parent, is argued by Chodorow to account for gender-differentiated modes of orientation. Girls, she argues, 'emerge from this period with a basis for "empathy" built into their primary definition of self in a way that boys do not.' The epistemological implications of adopting this 'object-relations' theory are that such an analysis may provide an account of why the impersonal, objectifying, universalizing stance of rationality is so deeply associated with masculinity. It might also help to clarify what a more characteristically female epistemology comprises.

Gilligan's claim that women's experience of interconnection shapes their moral domain and gives rise to a different moral voice complements Chodorow's account of psychic development and has been widely used as a basis for feminist epistemological writing. Gilligan's distinction between an 'ethic of justice' and an 'ethic of care' has been put to extensive use by subsequent feminist theorists in a wide range of disciplines. Seyla Benhabib, to take one prominent example, uses Gilligan's distinction to develop a typology of the generalized and the concrete other as a basis for developing a critique of Kantian rights-based moral and political philosophy. This critique, one should note, does not involve the rejection of the general in favour of the concrete, but rather proposes that we 'recognize the dignity of the generalized other through an acknowledgement of the moral identity of the concrete other'. In other words, Benhabib is sceptical that simply advocating the empathetic stance of the ethic of care will suffice for a critical feminist epistemology. For the ability to take the standpoint of others into account requires more than empathy, it requires institutions and procedures which will allow the voices of others to be articulated. Here we find a re-emergence of the theme of 'otherness', introduced in the first section, again serving to question the adequacy of the presumed feminist orthodoxy. The concern is that an epistemological position premised on interconnectedness and caring may be more likely to produce commonality and assimilation than openness to radical alterity.

This concern with difference is increasingly central in feminist theory, and requires a commitment to radical political engagement if it is to be recognized. As Iris Young argues: 'if we give up the ideal of impartiality... we require real participatory structures in which actual people, with their geographical, ethnic, gender and occupational differences, assert their perspectives on social issues within institutions that encourage the representation of their distinct voices'. It is significant here that whilst Young articulates a critique of universality akin to that of earlier standpoint theorists, she also speaks of the need to recognize not a singular different voice of women, but difference itself—in all its multiplicity. This shift is indicative of the wider move within feminist theory from standpoint to postmodern feminisms, not to mention, as Elizabeth Wright notes: 'postmodernism's transgression of the boundaries between art, criticism and theory'.

Postmodern writings problematize the notion of a uniform women's experience found in some feminist epistemological writings and emphasize the importance of difference. For those who adopt a postmodern feminist stance, the early standpoint perspective is rendered problematic. Sensitivity to partiality of all standpoints, to the complexity of perception, to the fragility of the psyche, and the ubiquity of power renders the more basic assertions of standpoint feminism woefully inadequate. Having accepted the notion that different standpoints provide groundings for different epistemologies, one is obliged, it is argued, to address the political issue of what constitutes a group unified enough to share a single standpoint. This issue has led to severe criticism of the notion that there might be a single 'women's perspective' and increasing interest in various forms of postmodern feminism. The extent to which feminist theories, of many different types, have subjected enlightenment rationality to critique, and the searching way in which feminists have questioned the attempts within their own ranks to develop a different epistemological voice, leads some to suggest that feminism might, in these senses at least, be an intrinsically postmodern discourse.

Perhaps the central paradox running through the above debates has been that any attempt to define a feminist epistemology requires an acknowledgement that we seek recognition of a gendered identity that has itself, in Patricia Waugh's words, 'been constructed through the very culture and ideological formations which feminism seeks to challenge and dismantle'. The degree of self-reflexivity that this acknowledgement requires is more commonly associated with postmodernism than with feminism, but is increasingly common to both. By way of an example, note Jane Flax's comment that: 'in this paper, I will be moving back and forth between thinking about gender relations and thinking about how I am thinking—or could think—about them'. But note too, that Flax's self-reflexivity is not bought at the cost of political engagement: 'without feminist political actions,' she says, 'theories remain inadequate and ineffectual'.

This returns us to our opening theme: to the tension between the political and the theoretical. If feminism is to retain any form of cohesive identity it must hold onto its commitment to an emancipatory project. As such, feminist theoretical scepticism of Enlightenment discourses cannot, as some other forms of postmodernism have, lead to an absolute rejection of all the epistemological claims of modernity. Once again—as in the previous section—we find that in current feminist writing it is the privileging of women's subjective experience (however that might be framed) and the commitment to political change that recur (in admittedly divergent forms) as the distinctive and fundamental aspects of a potential self-reflexive, feminist epistemology.

21 In a Different Voice

Over the past ten years, I have been listening to people talking about morality and about themselves. Halfway through that time, I began to hear a distinction in these voices, two ways of speaking about moral problems, two modes of describing the relationship between other and self. Differences represented in the psychological literature as steps in a developmental progression suddenly appeared instead as a contrapuntal theme, woven into the cycle of life and recurring in varying forms in people's judgments, fantasies, and thoughts. The occasion for this observation was the selection of a sample of women for a study of the relation between judgment and action in a situation of moral conflict and choice. Against the background of the psychological descriptions of identity and moral development which I had read and taught for a number of years, the women's voices sounded distinct. It was then that I began to notice the recurrent problems in interpreting women's development and to connect these problems to the repeated exclusion of women from the critical theory-building studies of psychological research.

[...] The disparity between women's experience and the representation of human development, noted throughout the psychological literature, has generally been seen to signify a problem in women's development. Instead, the failure of women to fit existing models of human growth may point to a problem in the representation, a limitation in the conception of human condition, an omission of certain truths about life.

The different voice I describe is characterized not by gender but theme. Its association with women is an empirical observation, and it is primarily through women's voices that I trace its development. But this association is not absolute, and the contrasts between male and female voices are presented here to highlight a distinction between two modes of thought and to focus a problem of interpretation rather than to represent a generalization about either sex. In tracing development, I point to the interplay of these voices within each sex and suggest that their convergence marks times of crisis and change. No claims are made about the origins of the differences described or their distribution in a wider population, across cultures, or through time. Clearly, these differences arise in a social context where factors of social status and power combine with reproductive biology to shape the experience of males and females and the relations between the sexes. My interest lies in the interaction of experience and thought, in different voices and the dialogues to which they give rise, in the way we listen to ourselves and to others, in the stories we tell about our lives. [...]

The criticism that Freud makes of women's sense of justice, seeing it as compromised in its refusal of blind impartiality, reappears not only in the work of Piaget but also in that of Kohlberg. While in Piaget's account[1] of the moral judgment of the child, girls are an aside, a curiosity to whom he devotes four brief entries in an index that omits 'boys' altogether because 'the child' is assumed to be male, in the research from which Kohlberg derives his theory, females simply do not exist. Kohlberg's six stages that describe the development of moral judgment from childhood to adulthood are based empirically on a study of eighty-four boys whose development Kohlberg has followed for a period of over twenty years.[2] Although Kohlberg claims universality for his stage sequence, those groups not included in his original sample rarely reach his higher stages.[3] Prominent among those who thus appear to be deficient in moral development when measured by Kohlberg's scale are women, whose judgments seem to exemplify the third stage of his six-stage sequence. At this stage morality is conceived in interpersonal terms and goodness is equated with helping and pleasing others. This conception of goodness is considered by Kohlberg and Kramer[4] to be functional in the lives of mature women insofar as their lives take place in the home. Kohlberg and Kramer imply that only if women enter the traditional arena of male activity will they recognize the inadequacy of this moral perspective and progress like men toward higher stages where relationships are subordinated to rules (stage four) and rules to universal principles of justice (stages five and six).

Yet herein lies a paradox, for the very traits that traditionally have defined the 'goodness' of women, their care for and sensitivity to the needs of others, are those that mark them as deficient in moral development. In this version of moral development, however, the conception of maturity is derived from the study of men's lives and reflects the importance of individuation in their development. Piaget,[5] challenging the common impression that a developmental theory is built like a pyramid from its base in infancy, points out that a conception of development instead hangs from its vertex of maturity, the point toward which progress is traced. Thus, a change in the definition of maturity does not simply alter the description of the highest stage but recasts the understanding of development, changing the entire account.

When one begins with the study of women and derives developmental constructs from their lives, the outline of a moral conception different from that described by Freud, Piaget, or Kohlberg begins to emerge and informs a different description of development. In this conception, the moral problem arises from conflicting responsibilities rather than from competing rights and requires for its resolution a mode of thinking that is contextual and narrative rather than formal and abstract. This conception of morality as concerned with the activity of care centers moral development around the understanding of responsibility and relationships, just as the conception of morality as fairness ties moral development to the understanding of rights and rules.

This different construction of the moral problem by women may be seen as the critical reason for their failure to develop within the constraints of

Kohlberg's system. Regarding all constructions of responsibility as evidence of a conventional moral understanding, Kohlberg defines the highest stages of moral development as deriving from a reflective understanding of human rights. That the morality of rights differs from the morality of responsibility in its emphasis on separation rather than connection, in its consideration of the individual rather than the relationship as primary, is illustrated by two responses to interview questions about the nature of morality. The first comes from a twenty-five-year-old man, one of the participants in Kohlberg's study:

[*What does the word morality mean to you?*] Nobody in the world knows the answer. I think it is recognizing the right of the individual, the rights of other individuals, not interfering with those rights. Act as fairly as you would have them treat you. I think it is basically to preserve the human being's right to existence. I think that is the most important. Secondly, the human being's right to do as he pleases, again without interfering with somebody else's rights.

[*How have your views on morality changed since the last interview?*] I think I am more aware of an individual's rights now. I used to be looking at it strictly from my point of view, just for me. Now I think I am more aware of what the individual has a right to.

Kohlberg[6] cites this man's response as illustrative of the principled conception of human rights that exemplifies his fifth and sixth stages. Commenting on the response, Kohlberg says: 'Moving to a perspective outside of that of his society, he identifies morality with justice (fairness, rights, the Golden Rule), with recognition of the rights of others as these are defined naturally or intrinsically. The human's being right to do as he pleases without interfering with somebody else's rights is a formula defining rights prior to social legislation'.[7]

The second response comes from a woman who participated in the rights and responsibilities study. She also was twenty-five and, at the time, a third-year law student:

[*Is there really some correct solution to moral problems, or is everybody's opinion equally right?*] No, I don't think everybody's opinion is equally right. I think that in some situations there may be opinions that are equally valid, and one could conscientiously adopt one of several courses of action. But there are other situations in which I think there are right and wrong answers, that sort of inhere in the nature of existence, of all individuals here who need to live with each other to live. We need to depend on each other, and hopefully it is not only a physical need but a need of fulfillment in ourselves, that a person's life is enriched by cooperating with other people and striving to live in harmony with everybody else, and to that end, there are right and wrong, there are things which promote that end and that move away from it, and in that way it is possible to choose in certain cases among different courses of action that obviously promote or harm that goal.

[*Is there a time in the past when you would have thought about these things differently?*] Oh, yeah, I think that I went through a time when I thought that things were pretty relative, that I can't tell you what to do and you can't tell me what to do, because you've got your conscience and I've got mine.

[*When was that?*] When I was in high school. I guess that it just sort of dawned on me that my own ideas changed, and because my own judgment changed, I felt I couldn't judge another person's judgment. But now I think even when it is only the person himself who is going to be affected, I say it is wrong to the extent it doesn't cohere with what I know about human nature and what I know about you, and just from what I think is true about the operation of the universe, I could say I think you are making a mistake.

[*What led you to change, do you think?*] Just seeing more of life, just recognizing that there are an awful lot of things that are common among people. There are certain things that you come to learn promote a better life and better relationships and more personal fulfillment than other things that in general tend to do the opposite, and the things that promote these things, you would call morally right.

This response also represents a personal reconstruction of morality following a period of questioning and doubt, but the reconstruction of moral understanding is based not on the primacy and universality of individual rights, but rather on what she describes as a 'very strong sense of being responsible to the world'. Within this construction, the moral dilemma changes from how to exercise one's rights without interfering with the rights of others to how 'to lead a moral life which includes obligations to myself and my family and people in general'. The problem then becomes one of limiting responsibilities without abandoning moral concern. When asked to describe herself, this woman says that she values 'having other people that I am tied to, and also having people that I am responsible to. I have a very strong sense of being responsible to the world, that I can't just live for my enjoyment, but just the fact of being in the world gives me an obligation to do what I can to make the world a better place to live in, no matter how small a scale that may be on.' Thus while Kohlberg's subject worries about people interfering with each other's rights, this woman worries about 'the possibility of omission, of your not helping others when you could help them'.

The issue that this woman raises is addressed by Jane Loevinger's fifth 'autonomous' stage of ego development, where autonomy, placed in a context of relationships, is defined as modulating an excessive sense of responsibility through the recognition that other people have responsibility for their own destiny. The autonomous stage in Loevinger's account witnesses a relinquishing of moral dichotomies and their replacement with 'a feeling for the complexity and multifaceted character of real people and real situations'.[8] Whereas the rights conception of morality that informs Kohlberg's principled level (stages five and six) is geared to arriving at an objectively fair or just resolution to moral dilemmas upon which all rational persons could agree, the responsibility conception focuses instead on the limitations of any particular resolution and describes the conflicts that remain.

Thus it becomes clear why a morality of rights and noninterference may appear frightening to women in its potential justification of indifference and unconcern. At the same time, it becomes clear why, from a male perspective, a morality of responsibility appears inconclusive and diffuse, given its insistent contextual relativism. Women's moral judgments thus elucidate the pattern observed in the description of the developmental differences between the sexes, but they also provide an alternative conception of maturity by which these differences can be assessed and their implications traced. The psychology of women that has consistently been described as distinctive in its greater orientation toward relationships and interdependence implies a more contextual mode of judgment and a different moral understanding. Given the differences in women's conceptions of self and morality, women bring to the life cycle a different point of view and order human experience in terms of different priorities. [. . .]

In view of the evidence that women perceive and construe social reality differently from men and that these differences center around experiences of attachment and separation, life transitions that invariably engage these experiences can be expected to involve women in a distinctive way. And because women's sense of integrity appears to be entwined with an ethic of care, so that to see themselves as women is to see themselves in a relationship of connection, the major transitions in women's lives would seem to involve changes in the understanding and activities of care. Certainly the shift from childhood to adulthood witnesses a major redefinition of care. When the distinction between helping and pleasing frees the activity of taking care from the wish for approval by others, the ethic of responsibility can become a self-chosen anchor of personal integrity and strength.

In the same vein, however, the events of mid-life—the menopause and changes in family and work—can alter a woman's activities of care in ways that affect her sense of herself. If mid-life brings an end to relationships, to the sense of connection on which she relies, as well as to the activities of care through which she judges her worth, then the mourning that accompanies all life transitions can give way to the melancholia of self-deprecation and despair. The meaning of mid-life events for a woman thus reflects the interaction between the structures of her thought and the realities of her life. [. . .]

Thus women not only reach mid-life with a psychological history different from men's and face at that time a different social reality having different possibilities for love and for work, but they also make a different sense of experience, based on their knowledge of human relationships. Since the reality of connection is experienced by women as given rather than as freely contracted, they arrive at an understanding of life that reflects the limits of autonomy and control. As a result, women's development delineates the path not only to a less violent life but also to a maturity realized through interdependence and taking care. [. . .]

There seems at present to be only partial agreement between men and women about the adulthood they commonly share. In the absence of mutual understanding, relationships between the sexes continue in varying degrees of constraint, manifesting the 'paradox of egocentrism' which Piaget describes, a mystical respect for rules combined with everyone playing more or less as he pleases and paying no attention to his neighbor.[9] For a life-cycle understanding to address the development in adulthood of relationships characterized by cooperation, generosity, and care, that understanding must include the lives of women as well as of men.

Among the most pressing items on the agenda for research on adult development is the need to delineate *in women's own terms* the experience of their adult life. My own work in that direction indicates that the inclusion of women's experience brings to developmental understanding a new perspective on relationships that changes the basic constructs of interpretation. The concept of identity expands to include the experience of interconnection. The moral domain is similarly enlarged by the inclusion of responsibility and care in relationships. And the underlying epistemology correspondingly shifts from the Greek ideal of knowledge as a correspondence between mind and form to the Biblical conception of knowing as a process of human relationship.

Given the evidence of different perspectives in the representation of adulthood by women and men, there is a need for research that elucidates the effects of these differences in marriage, family, and work relationships. My research suggests that men and women may speak different languages that they assume are the same, using similar words to encode disparate experiences of self and social relationships. Because these languages share an overlapping moral vocabulary, they contain a propensity for systematic mistranslation, creating misunderstandings which impede communication and limit the potential for cooperation and care in relationships. At the same time, however, these languages articulate with one another in critical ways. Just as the language of responsibilities provides a weblike imagery of relationships to replace a hierarchical ordering that dissolves with the coming of equality, so the language of rights underlines the importance of including in the network of care not only the other but also the self.

As we have listened for centuries to the voices of men and the theories of development that their experience informs, so we have come more recently to notice not only the silence of women but the difficulty in hearing what they say when they speak. Yet in the different voice of women lies the truth of an ethic of care, the tie between relationship and responsibility, and the origins of aggression in the failure of connection. The failure to see the different reality of women's lives and to hear the differences in their voices stems in part from the assumption that there is a single mode of social experience and interpretation. By positing instead two different modes, we arrive at a more complex rendition of human experience which sees the truth of separation and attachment in the lives of women and men and recognizes how these truths are carried by different modes of language and thought.

To understand how the tension between responsibilities and rights sustains the dialectic of human development is to see the integrity of two disparate modes of experience that are in the end connected. While an ethic of justice proceeds from the premise of equality—that everyone should be treated the same—an ethic of care rests on the premise of nonviolence—that no one should be hurt. In the representation of maturity, both perspectives converge in the realization that just as inequality adversely affects both parties in an unequal relationship, so too violence is destructive for everyone involved. This dialogue between fairness and care not only provides a better understanding of relations between the sexes but also gives rise to a more comprehensive portrayal of adult work and family relationships.

As Freud and Piaget call our attention to the differences in children's feelings and thought, enabling us to respond to children with greater care and respect, so a recognition of the differences in women's experience and understanding expands our vision of maturity and points to the contextual nature of developmental truths. Through this expansion in perspective, we can begin to envision how a marriage between adult development as it is currently portrayed and women's development as it begins to be seen could lead to a changed understanding of human development and a more generative view of human life.

[*In a Different Voice* (Cambridge, Mass.: Harvard University Press, 1982), 1–22, 171–4.]

NANCY HARTSOCK

22 The Feminist Standpoint: Developing the Ground for a Specifically Feminist Historical Materialism

I will attempt to develop, on the methodological base provided by Marxian theory, an important epistemological tool for understanding and opposing all forms of domination—a feminist standpoint.

Despite the difficulties feminists have correctly pointed to in Marxian theory, there are several reasons to take over much of Marx's approach. First, I have argued elsewhere that Marx's method and the method developed by the contemporary women's movement recapitulate each other in important ways.[1] This makes it possible for feminists to take over a number of aspects of Marx's method. Here, I will adopt his distinction between appearance and essence, circulation and production, abstract and concrete, and use these distinctions between dual levels of reality to work out the theoretical forms appropriate to each level when viewed not from the standpoint of the proletariat but from a specifically feminist standpoint. [. . .]

I set off from Marx's proposal that a correct vision of class society is available from only one of the two major class positions in capitalist society. On the basis of this meta-theoretical claim, he was able to develop a powerful critique of class domination. The power of Marx's critique depended on the epistemology and ontology supporting this meta-theoretical claim. Feminist Marxists and materialist feminists more generally have argued that the position of women is structurally different from that of men, and that the lived realities of women's lives are profoundly different from those of men.[2] They have not yet, however, given sustained attention to the epistemological consequences of such a claim. [...]

A standpoint is not simply an interested position (interpreted as bias) but is interested in the sense of being engaged. It is true that a desire to conceal real social relations can contribute to an obscurantist account, and it is also true that the ruling gender and class have material interests in deception. A standpoint, however, carries with it the contention that there are some perspectives on society from which, however well-intentioned one may be, the real relations of humans with each other and with the natural world are not visible. This contention should be sorted into a number of distinct epistemological and political claims: (1) Material life (class position in Marxist theory) not only structures but sets limits on the understanding of social relations. (2) If material life is structured in fundamentally opposing ways for two different groups, one can expect that the vision of each will represent an inversion of the other, and in systems of domination the vision available to the rulers will be both partial and perverse. (3) The vision of the ruling class (or gender) structures the material relations in which all parties are forced to participate, and therefore cannot be dismissed as simply false. (4) In consequence, the vision available to the oppressed group must be struggled for and represents an achievement which requires both science to see beneath the surface of the social relations in which all are forced to participate, and the education which can only grow from struggle to change those relations. (5) As an engaged vision, the understanding of the oppressed, the adoption of a standpoint exposes the real relations among human beings as inhuman, points beyond the present, and carries a historically liberatory role.

The concept of a standpoint structures epistemology in a particular way. Rather than a simple dualism, it posits a duality of levels of reality, of which the deeper level or essence both includes and explains the 'surface' or appearance, and indicates the logic by means of which the appearance inverts and distorts the deeper reality. In addition, the concept of a standpoint depends on the assumption that epistemology grows in a complex and contradictory way from material life. Any effort to develop a standpoint must take seriously Marx's injunction that 'all mysteries which lead theory to mysticism find their rational solution in human practice and in the comprehension of this practice'.[3] Marx held that the source both for the proletarian standpoint and the critique of capitalism it makes possible is to be found in practical activity itself. The epistemological (and even ontological) significance of human activity is made clear in Marx's argument not only that persons are active but that reality itself consists of 'sensuous human activity, practice'. Thus Marx can speak of products as crystallized or congealed human activity or work, of products as conscious human activity in another form. He can state that even plants, animals, light, etc. constitute theoretically a part of human consciousness, and a part of human life and activity.[4] As Marx and Engels summarize their position.

As individuals express their life, so they are. What they are, therefore, coincides with their production, both with *what* they produce and with *how* they produce. The nature of individuals thus depends on the material conditions determining their production.[5] [...]

Women's work in every society differs systematically from men's. I intend to pursue the suggestion that this division of labor is the first and in some societies the only division of labor, and moreover, that it is central to the organization of social labor more generally. On the basis of an account of the sexual division of labor, one should be able to begin to explore the oppositions and differences between women's and men's activity and their consequences for epistemology. While I cannot attempt a complete account, I will put forward a schematic and simplified account of the sexual division of labor and its consequences for epistemology. [...]

Women's activity as institutionalized has a double aspect—their contribution to subsistence, and their contribution to childrearing. Whether or not all of us do both, women as a sex are institutionally responsible for producing both goods and human beings and all women are forced to become the kinds of people who can do both. Although the nature of women's contribution to subsistence varies immensely over time and space, my primary focus here is on capitalism, with a secondary focus on the Western class societies which preceded it. In capitalism, women contribute both production for wages and production of goods in the home, that is, they like men sell their labor power and produce both commodities and surplus value, and produce use-values in the home. Unlike men, however, women's lives are institutionally defined by their production of use-values in the home. [...]

Let us trace both the outlines and the consequences of woman's dual contribution to subsistence in capitalism. Women's labor, like that of the male worker, is contact with material necessity. Their contribution to subsistence, like that of the male worker, involves them in a world in which the relation to nature and to concrete human requirements is central, both in the form of interaction with natural substances whose quality, rather than quantity is important to the production of meals, clothing, etc., and in the form of close attention to the natural changes in these substances. Women's labor both for wages and even more in household production involves a unification of mind and body for the purpose of transforming natural substances into socially defined goods. This too is true of the labor of the male worker.

There are, however, important differences. First, women as a group work more than men. We are all familiar with the phenomenon of the 'double day', and with indications that women work many more hours per week than men.[6] Second, a larger proportion of women's labor time is devoted to the production of use-values than men's. Only some of the goods women produce are commodities (however much they live in a society structured by commodity production and exchange). Third, women's production is structured by repetition in a different way than men's. While repetition for both the woman and the male worker may take the form of production of the same object, over and over—whether apple pies or brake linings—women's work in housekeeping involves a repetitious cleaning. [. . .]

The female contribution to subsistence, however, represents only a part of women's labor. Women also produce/reproduce men (and other women) on both a daily and a long-term basis. This aspect of women's 'production' exposes the deep inadequacies of the concept of production as a description of women's activity. One does not (cannot) produce another human being in anything like the way one produces an object such as a chair. Much more is involved, activity which cannot easily be dichotomized into play or work. Helping another to develop, the gradual relinquishing of control, the experience of the human limits of one's action—all these are important features of women's activity as mothers. Women as mothers even more than as workers, are institutionally involved in processes of change and growth, and more than workers, must understand the importance of avoiding excessive control in order to help others grow. The activity involved is far more complex than the instrumental working with others to transform objects. (Interestingly, much of women's wage work—nursing, social work, and some secretarial jobs in particular—requires and depends on the relational and interpersonal skills women learned by being mothered by someone of the same sex.)

This aspect of women's activity too is not without consequences. Indeed, it is in the production of men by women and the appropriation of this labor and women themselves by men that the opposition between feminist and masculinist experience and outlook is rooted, and it is here that features of the proletarian vision are enhanced and modified for the woman and diluted for the man. The female experience in reproduction represents a unity with nature which goes beyond the proletarian experience of interchange with nature. As another theorist has put it, 'reproductive labor might be said to combine the functions of the architect and the bee: like the architect, parturitive woman knows what she is doing; like the bee, she cannot help what she is doing'. And just as the worker's acting on the external world changes both the world and the worker's acting nature, so too 'a new life changes the world and the consciousness of the woman'.[7] In addition, in the process of producing human beings, relations with others may take a variety of forms with deeper significance than simple cooperation with others for common goals—forms which range from a deep unity with another through the many-leveled and changing connections mothers experience with growing children. Finally, the female experience in bearing and rearing children involves a unity of mind and body more profound than is possible in the worker's instrumental activity.

Motherhood in the large sense, i.e. motherhood as an institution rather than experience, including pregnancy and the preparation for motherhood almost all female children receive as socialization, results in the construction of female existence as centered with a complex relational nexus. One aspect of this relational existence is centered on the experience of living in a female rather than male body. There are a series of boundary challenges inherent in the female physiology—challenges which make it impossible to maintain rigid separation from the object world. Menstruation, coitus, pregnancy, childbirth, lactation—all represent challenges to bodily boundaries.[8] Adrienne Rich has described the experience of pregnancy as one in which the embryo was both inside and

daily more separate, on its way to becoming separate from me and of-itself. In early pregnancy the stirring of the fetus felt like ghostly tremors of my own body, later like the movements of a being imprisoned in me; but both sensations were *my* sensations, contributing to my own sense of physical and psychic space.[9]

In turn, the fact that women but not men are primarily responsible for young children means that the infant first experiences itself as not fully differentiated from the mother, and then as an I in relation to an it that it later comes to know as female.[10]

Jane Flax and Nancy Chodorow have argued that the object relations school of psychoanalytic theory puts forward a materialist psychology, one which I propose to treat as a kind of empirical hypothesis. If the account of human development provided by object relations is correct, one ought to expect to find consequences—both psychic, and social. According to object relations theory, the process of differentiation from a woman by both male and female children reinforces boundary confusion in female egos and boundary strengthening in males. Individuation is far more conflictual for male than for female children, in part because both mother and son experience the other as a definite 'other'. The experience of oneness on the part of both mother and infant seems to last longer with girls.[11] [. . .]

The construction of the self in opposition to another who threatens one's very being reverberates throughout the construction of both class society and the masculinist world view and results in a deepgoing and hierarchical dualism. First, the male experience is characterized by the duality of concrete versus abstract. Material reality as experienced by the boy in the family provides no model, and is unimportant in the attainment of masculinity. Nothing of value to the boy occurs with the family, and masculinity becomes an abstract ideal to be achieved over the opposition of daily life. Masculinity must be attained by means of opposition to the concrete world of daily life, by escaping from contact with the female world of the household into the masculine world of public life. This experience of two worlds, one valuable, if abstract and deeply unattainable, the other useless and demeaning, if concrete and necessary, lies at the heart of a series of dualisms—abstract/ concrete, mind/body, culture/nature, ideal/real, stasis/change. And these dualisms are overlaid by gender: only the first of each pair is associated with the male.

Dualism, along with the dominance of one side of the dichotomy over the other, marks phallocentric society and social theory. These dualisms appear in a variety of forms—in philosophy, technology, political theory, and the organization of class society itself. One can, for example, see them very clearly worked out in Plato, although they appear in many other forms.[12] There, the concrete/abstract duality takes the form of an opposition of material to ideal, and a denial of the relevance of the material world to the attainment of what is of fundamental importance: love of knowledge, or philosophy (masculinity). The duality between nature and culture takes the form of a devaluation of work or necessity, and the primacy instead of purely social interaction for the attainment of undying fame. Philosophy itself is separate from nature, and indeed, exists only on the basis of the domination of (at least some) of the philosopher's own nature.[13] Abstract masculinity, then, can be seen to have structured Western social relations and the modes of thought to which these relations give rise at least since the founding of the polis.

The oedipal roots of these hierarchical dualisms are memorialized in the overlay of female and male connotations: it is not accidental that women are associated with quasi-human and non-human nature, that the female is associated with the body and material life, that the lives of women are systematically used as examples to characterize the lives of those ruled by their bodies rather than their minds.

Both the fragility and fundamental falseness of the masculinist ideology and the deeply problematic nature of the social relations from which it grows are apparent in its reliance on a series of counterfactual assumptions and contentions. Consider how the following contentions are contrary to lived experience: the body is both irrelevant and in opposition to the (real) self, an impediment to be overcome by the mind; the female mind either does not exist (Do women have souls?) or works in such incomprehensible ways as to be unintelligible (the 'enigma of woman'); what is real and primary is imperceptible to the senses and impervious to nature and natural change. What is remarkable is not only that these contentions have absorbed a great deal of philosophical energy, but, along with a series of other counterfactuals, have structured social relations for centuries.

[...] In sum, then, the male experience when replicated as epistemology leads to a world conceived as, and (in fact) inhabited by, a number of fundamentally hostile others whom one comes to know by means of opposition (even death struggle) and yet with whom one must construct a social relation in order to survive.

The female construction of self in relation to others leads in an opposite direction—toward opposition to dualisms of any sort, valuation of concrete, everyday life, sense of a variety of connectednesses and continuities both with other persons and with the natural world. If material life structures consciousness, women's relationally defined existence, bodily experience of boundary challenges, and activity of transforming both physical objects and human beings must be expected to result in a world view to which dichotomies are foreign. Women experience others and themselves along a continuum whose dimensions are evidenced in Adrienne Rich's argument that the child carried for nine months can be defined 'neither as me or as not-me', and she argues that inner and outer are not polar opposites but a continuum.[14] What the sexual division of labor defines as women's work turns on issues of change rather than stasis, the changes involved in producing both use-values and commodities, but more profoundly in the activity of rearing human beings who change in both more subtle and more autonomous ways than any inanimate object. Not only the qualities of things but also the qualities of people are important in women's work: quantity becomes peripheral. In addition, far more than the instrumental cooperation of the workplace is required; the mother–child relation and the maintenance of the family, while it has instrumental aspects, is not defined by them. Finally, the unity of mental and manual labor, and the directly sensuous nature of much of women's work leads to a more profound unity of mental and manual labor, social and natural worlds, than is experienced by the male worker in capitalism. The unity grows from the fact that women's bodies, unlike men's, can be themselves instruments of production: in pregnancy, giving birth or lactation, arguments about a division of mental from manual labor are fundamentally foreign.

That this is indeed women's experience is documented in both the theory and practice of the contemporary women's movement and needs no further development here. The more important question here is whether female experience and the world view constructed by female activity can meet the criteria for a standpoint. If we return to the five claims carried by the concept of a standpoint, it seems clear that women's material life activity has important epistemological and ontological consequences for both the understanding and construction of social relations. Women's activity, then, does satisfy the first requirement of a standpoint.

I can now take up the second claim made by a standpoint: that the female experience not only inverts that of the male, but forms a basis on which to expose abstract masculinity as both partial and fundamentally perverse, as not only occupying only one side of the dualities it has constructed, but reversing the proper valuation of human activity. The partiality of the masculinist vision and of the societies which support this understanding is evidenced by its confinement of activity proper to the male to only one side of the dualisms. [. . .]

Feminists have only begun the process of revaluing female experience, searching for common threads which connect the diverse experiences of women, and searching for the structural determinants of the experiences. The difficulty of the problem faced by feminist theory can be illustrated by the fact that it required a struggle even to define household labor, if not done for wages, as work, to argue that what are held to be acts of love instead must be recognized as work whether or not wages are paid. Both the valuation of women's experience, and the use of this experience as a ground for critique are required. A feminist standpoint may be present on the basis of the common threads of female experience, but it is neither self-evident nor obvious.

Finally, because it provides a way to reveal the perverseness and inhumanity of human relations, a standpoint forms the basis for moving beyond these relations. Just as the proletarian standpoint emerges out of the contradiction between appearance and essence in capitalism, understood as essentially historical and constituted by the relation of capitalist and worker, the feminist standpoint emerges both out of the contradiction between the systematically differing structure of male and female life activity in Western cultures. It expresses female experience at a particular time and place, located within a particular set of social relations. Capitalism, Marx noted, could not develop fully until the notion of human equality achieved the status of universal truth.[15] Despite women's exploitation both as unpaid reproducers of the labor force and as a sex-segregated labor force available for low wages, then, capitalism poses problems for the continued oppression of women. Just as capitalism enables the proletariat to raise the possibility of a society free from class domination, so too, it provides space to raise the possibility of a society free from all forms of domination. The articulation of a feminist standpoint based on women's relational self-definition and activity exposes the world men have constructed and the self-understanding which manifests these relations as partial and perverse. More importantly, by drawing out the potentiality available in the actuality and thereby exposing the inhumanity of human relations, it embodies a distress which requires a solution. The experience of continuity and relation—with others, with the natural world, of mind with body—provides an ontological base for developing a non-problematic social synthesis, a social synthesis which need not operate through the denial of the body, the attack on nature, or the death struggle between the self and other, a social synthesis which does not depend on any of the forms taken by abstract masculinity.

What is necessary is the generalization of the potentiality made available by the activity of women—the defining of society as a whole as propertyless producer both of use-values and of human beings. To understand what such a transformation would require we should consider what is involved in the partial transformation represented by making the whole of society into propertyless producers of use-values—i.e. socialist revolution. The abolition of the division between mental and manual labor cannot take place simply by means of adopting worker-self-management techniques, but instead requires the abolition of private property, the seizure of state power, and lengthy post-revolutionary class struggle. Thus, I am not suggesting that shared parenting arrangements can abolish the sexual division of labor. Doing away with this division of labor would of course require institutionalizing the participation of both women and men in childrearing; but just as the rational and conscious control of the production of goods and services requires a vast and far-reaching social transformation, so the rational and conscious organization of reproduction would entail the transformation both of *every* human relation, and of human relations to the natural world. The magnitude of the task is apparent if one asks what a society without institutionalized gender differences might look like.

['The Feminist Standpoint: Developing the Ground for a Specifically Feminist Historical Materialism', in Sandra Harding and Merrell Hintikka (eds.), *Discovering Reality* (Dordrecht, Holland: Reidel Publishing Company, 1983), 283–305.]

SANDRA HARDING

23 Is there a Feminist Method?

Over the last two decades feminist inquirers have raised fundamental challenges to the ways social science has analyzed women, men, and social life. From the beginning, issues about method, methodology, and epistemology have been intertwined with discussions of how best to correct the partial and distorted accounts in the traditional analyses. Is there a distinctive feminist method of inquiry? How does feminist methodology challenge—or complement—traditional methodologies? On what grounds would one defend the assumptions and procedures of feminist researchers? Questions such as these have generated important controversies within feminist theory and politics, as well as curiosity and anticipation in the traditional discourses.

The most frequently asked question has been the first one: is there a distinctive feminist method of inquiry? [...]

One reason it is difficult to find a satisfactory answer to questions about a distinctive feminist method is that discussions of method (techniques for gathering evidence) and methodology (a theory and analysis of how research should proceed) have been intertwined with each other and with epistemological issues (issues about an adequate theory of knowledge or justificatory strategy) in both the traditional and feminist discourses. This claim is a complex one and we shall sort out its components. But the point here is simply that 'method' is often used to refer to all three aspects of research. Consequently, it is not at all clear what one is supposed to be looking for when trying to identify a distinctive 'feminist method of research'. This lack of clarity permits critics to avoid facing up to what *is* distinctive about the best feminist social inquiry. It also makes it difficult to recognize what one must do to advance feminist inquiry.

A research *method* is a technique for (or way of proceeding in) gathering evidence. One could reasonably argue that all evidence-gathering techniques fall into one of the following three categories: listening to (or interrogating) informants, observing behavior, or examining historical traces and records. In this sense, there are only three methods of social inquiry. [...] [F]eminist researchers use just about any and all of the methods, in this concrete sense of the term, that traditional androcentric researchers have used. Of course, precisely how they carry out these methods of evidence gathering is often strikingly different. For example, they listen carefully to how women informants think about their lives and men's lives, and critically to how traditional social scientists conceptualize women's and men's lives. They observe behaviors of women and men that traditional social scientists have not thought significant. They seek examples of newly recognized patterns in historical data.

There is both less and more going on in these cases than new methods of research. The 'less' is that it seems to introduce a false sense of unity to all the different 'little things' feminist researchers do with familiar methods to conceptualize these as 'new feminist research methods'. However, the 'more' is that it is new methodologies and new epistemologies that are requiring these new uses of familiar research techniques. If what is meant by a 'method of research' is just this most concrete sense of the term, it would undervalue the transformations feminist analyses require to characterize these in terms only of the discovery of distinctive methods of research. [...]

A *methodology* is a theory and analysis of how research does or should proceed; it includes accounts of how 'the general structure of theory finds its application in particular scientific disciplines'.[1] For example, discussions of how functionalism (or Marxist political economy, or phenomenology) should be or is applied in particular research areas are methodological analyses.[2] Feminist researchers have argued that traditional theories have been applied in ways that make it difficult to understand women's participation in social life, or to understand men's activities as gendered (vs. as representing 'the human'). They have produced feminist versions of traditional theories. Thus we can find examples of feminist methodologies in discussions of how phenomenological approaches can be used to begin to understand women's worlds, or of how Marxist political economy can be used to explain the causes of women's continuing exploitation in the household or in wage labor. But these sometimes heroic efforts raise questions about whether even feminist applications of these theories can succeed in producing complete and undistorted accounts of gender and of women's activities. And they also raise epistemological issues.

An *epistemology* is a theory of knowledge. It answers questions about who can be a 'knower' (can women?); what tests beliefs must pass in order to be legitimated as knowledge (only tests against men's experiences and observations?); what kinds of things can be known (can 'subjective truths' count as knowledge?), and so forth. Sociologists of knowledge characterize epistemologies as strategies for justifying beliefs: appeals to the authority of God, of custom and tradition, of 'common sense', of observation, of reason, and of masculine authority are examples of familiar justificatory strategies. Feminists have argued that traditional epistemologies, whether intentionally or unintentionally, systematically exclude the possibility that women could be 'knowers' or *agents of knowledge*; they claim that the voice of science is a masculine one; that history is written from only the point of view of men (of the dominant class and race); that the subject of a traditional sociological sentence is always assumed to be a man. They have proposed alternative theories of knowledge that legitimate women as knowers.[3] [. . .] In summary, there are important connections between epistemologies, methodologies, and research methods. But I am arguing that it is *not* by looking at research methods that one will be able to identify the distinctive features of the best of feminist research. [. . .]

The traditional philosophy of science argues that the origin of scientific problems or hypotheses is irrelevant to the 'goodness' of the results of research. It doesn't matter where one's problems or hypotheses come from—from gazing into crystal balls, from sun worshipping, from observing the world around us, or from critical discussion with the most brilliant thinkers. There is no logic for these 'contexts of discovery', though many have tried to find one. Instead, it is in the 'context of justification', where hypotheses are tested, that we should seek the 'logic of scientific inquiry'. It is in this testing process that we should look for science's distinctive virtues (for its 'method'). But the feminist challenges reveal that the questions that are asked—and, even more significantly, those that are not asked—are at least as determinative of the adequacy of our total picture as are any answers that we can discover. Defining what is in need of scientific explanation only from the perspective of bourgeois, white men's experiences leads to partial and even perverse understandings of social life. One distinctive feature of feminist research is that it generates its problematics from the perspective of women's experiences. It also uses these experiences as a significant indicator of the 'reality' against which hypotheses are tested.

Recognition of the importance of using women's experiences as resources for social analysis obviously has implications for the social structures of education, laboratories, journals, learned societies, funding agencies— indeed, for social life in general. And it needs to be stressed that it is *women* who should be expected to be able to reveal *for the first time* what women's experiences are. Women should have an equal say in the design and admin- istration of the institutions where knowledge is produced and distributed for reasons of social justice: it is not fair to exclude women from gaining the benefits of participating in these enterprises that men get. But they should also share in these projects because only partial and distorted understandings of ourselves and the world around us can be produced in a culture which systematically silences and devalues the voices of women.

Notice that it is 'women's experiences' *in the plural* which provide the new resources for research. This formulation stresses several ways in which the best feminist analyses differ from traditional ones. For one thing, once we realized that there is no universal *man*, but only culturally different men and women, then 'man's' eternal companion—'woman'—also disappeared. That is, women come only in different classes, races, and cultures: there is no 'woman' and no 'woman's experience'. Masculine and feminine are always categories within every class, race, and culture in the sense that women's and men's experiences, desires, and interests differ within every class, race, and culture. But so, too, are class, race, and culture always categories within gender, since women's and men's experiences, desires, and interests differ according to class, race, and culture. This leads some theorists to propose that we should talk about our 'feminisms' only in the plural, since there is no one set of feminist principles or understandings beyond the very, very general ones to which feminists in every race, class, and culture will assent. Why should we have expected it to be any different? There are very few principles or understandings to which sexists in every race, class, and culture will assent!

Not only do our gender experiences vary across the cultural categories; they also are often in conflict in any one individual's experience. My experi- ences as a mother and a professor are often contradictory. Women scientists often talk about the contradictions in identity between what they experience as women and scientists. Dorothy Smith writes of the 'fault line' between women sociologists' experience as sociologists and as women. The hyphenated state of many self-chosen labels of identity—black feminist, socialist feminist, Asian-American feminist, lesbian feminist—reflects this challenge to the 'identity politics' which has grounded Western thought and public life. These fragmented identities are a rich source of feminist insight.

Finally, the questions an oppressed group wants answered are rarely requests for so-called pure truth. Instead, they are queries about how to change its conditions; how its world is shaped by forces beyond it; how to win over, defeat, or neutralize those forces arrayed against its emancipation, growth, or development; and so forth. Consequently, feminist research projects originate primarily not in any old 'women's experiences', but in women's experiences in political struggles. (Kate Millett and others remind us that the bedroom and the kitchen are as much the site of political struggle as are the board room or the polling place.[4] It may be that it is only through such struggles that one can come to understand oneself and the social world. [. . .]

There are a number of ways we could characterize the distinctive subject matter of feminist social analysis. While studying women is not new, studying them from the perspective of their own experiences so that women can understand themselves and the world can claim virtually no history at all. It is also novel to study gender. The idea of a systematic social construction of masculinity and femininity that is little, if at all, constrained by biology, is very recent. Moreover, feminist inquiry joins other 'underclass' approaches in insisting on the importance of studying ourselves and 'studying up', instead of 'studying down'. While employers have often commissioned studies of how to make workers happy with less power and pay, workers have rarely been in a position to undertake or commission studies of anything at all, let alone how to make employers happy with less power and profit. Similarly, psychiatrists have endlessly studied what they regard as women's peculiar mental and behavioral characteristics, but women have only recently begun to study the bizarre mental and behavioural characteristics of psychiatrists. If we want to understand how our daily experience arrives in the forms it does, it makes sense to examine critically the sources of social power.

The best feminist analysis goes beyond these innovations in subject matter in a crucial way: it insists that the inquirer her/himself be placed in the same critical plane as the overt subject matter, thereby recovering the entire research process for scrutiny in the results of research. That is, the class, race, culture, and gender assumptions, beliefs, and behaviors of the researcher her/himself must be placed within the frame of the picture that she/he attempts to paint. This does not mean that the first half of a research report should engage in soul searching (though a little soul searching by researchers now and then can't be all bad!). Instead, as we will see, we are often explicitly told by the researcher what her/his gender, race, class, culture is, and sometimes how she/he suspects this has shaped the research project—

though of course we are free to arrive at contrary hypotheses about the influence of the researcher's presence on her/his analysis. Thus the researcher appears to us not as an invisible, anonymous voice of authority, but as a real, historical individual with concrete, specific desires and interests.

This requirement is no idle attempt to 'do good' by the standards of imagined critics in classes, races, cultures (or of a gender) other than that of the researcher. Instead, it is a response to the recognition that the cultural beliefs and behaviors of feminist researchers shape the results of their analyses no less than do those of sexist and androcentric researchers. We need to avoid the 'objectivist' stance that attempts to make the researcher's cultural beliefs and practices invisible while simultaneously skewering the research objects' beliefs and practices to the display board. Only in this way can we hope to produce understandings and explanations which are free (or, at least, more free) of distortion from the unexamined beliefs and behaviors of social scientists themselves. Another way to put this point is that the beliefs and behaviors of the researcher are part of the empirical evidence for (or against) the claims advanced in the results of research. *This* evidence too must be open to critical scrutiny no less than what is traditionally defined as relevant evidence. Introducing this 'subjective' element into the analysis in fact increases the objectivity of the research and decreases the 'objectivism' which hides this kind of evidence from the public. [...]

Once we undertake to use women's experience as a resource to generate scientific problems, hypotheses, and evidence, to design research for women, and to place the researcher in the same critical plane as the research subject, traditional epistemological assumptions can no longer be made. These agendas have led feminist social scientists to ask questions about who can be a knower (only men?); what tests beliefs must pass in order to be legitimated as knowledge (only tests against men's experiences and observations?); what kinds of things can be known (can 'subjective truths', ones that only women—or only some women—tend to arrive at, count as knowledge?); the nature of objectivity (does it require 'point-of-viewlessness'?); the appropriate relationship between the researcher and her/his research subjects (must the researcher be disinterested, dispassionate, and socially invisible to the subject?); what should be the purposes of the pursuit of knowledge (to produce information *for* men?). [...]

A major source of feminist challenge to traditional epistemologies arises from the following problem. Feminism is a political movement for social change. Looked at from the perspective of science's self-understanding, 'feminist knowledge', 'feminist science', 'feminist sociology'—or psychology or economics—should be a contradiction in terms. Scientific knowledge-seeking is supposed to be value-neutral, objective, dispassionate, disinterested, and so forth. It is supposed to be protected from political interests, goals, and desires (such as feminist ones) by the norms of science. In particular, science's 'method' is supposed to protect the results of research from the social values of the researchers. And yet it is obvious to all that many claims which clearly have been generated through research guided by feminist concerns, nevertheless appear more plausible (better supported, more reliable, less false, more likely to be confirmed by evidence, etc.) than the beliefs they replace. How can politicized inquiry be increasing the objectivity of inquiry?

Feminist Empiricism

The main response to this problem by social researchers has been feminist empiricism. In research reports one frequently finds the argument that the sexist and androcentric claims to which the researcher objects are caused by social biases. Social biases are conceptualized as prejudices that are based on false beliefs (due to superstition, custom, ignorance, or miseducation) and hostile attitudes. These prejudices enter research particularly at the stage when scientific problems are being identified and defined, but they also can appear in the design of research and in the collection and interpretation of data. Feminist empiricists argue that sexist and androcentric biases are eliminable by stricter adherence to the existing methodological norms of scientific inquiry; it is 'bad science' or 'bad sociology', etc, which is responsible for these biases in the results of research.

But how can the scientific community (the sociological one, psychological one, etc.) come to see that more than individual biases are the problem here—that its work *has* been shaped by culture-wide androcentric prejudices? Here is where we can see the importance of movements for social liberation, such as the women's movement. As Marcia Millman and Rosabeth Moss Kanter have pointed out, movements for social liberation 'make it possible for people to see the world in an enlarged perspective because they remove the covers and blinders that obscure knowledge and observation.' The women's movement has generated just such possibilities. Furthermore, feminist empiricists often point out that the women's movement creates the opportunity for more women researchers, and for more feminist researchers (male and female), who are more likely than sexist men to notice androcentric biases.

This justificatory strategy is by no means uncontroversial. Nevertheless, it is often thought to be the least threatening of the feminist epistemologies for two reasons. Most importantly, it appears to leave intact much of science's self-understanding of the principles of adequate scientific research as they are taught to students, quoted to Congress, and viewed on television (regardless of whether scientists actually believe them). This justificatory strategy appears to challenge mainly the incomplete way empiricism has been practiced, not the norms of empiricism themselves: mainstream inquiry has not rigorously enough adhered to its own norms. To say this in other words, it is thought that social values and political agendas can raise new issues that enlarge the scope of inquiry and reveal cause for greater care in the conduct of inquiry, but that the logic of explanation and research still conforms to standard empiricist rules. [...]

Though feminist empiricism appears in these ways to be consistent with empiricist tendencies, further consideration reveals that the feminist component deeply undercuts the assumptions of traditional empiricism in three ways: feminist empiricism has a radical future.[5] In the first place, feminist empiricism argues that the 'context of discovery' is just as important as the 'context of justification' for eliminating social biases that contribute to partial and distorted explanations and understandings. Traditional empiricism insists that the social identity of the observer is irrelevant to the 'goodness' of the results of research. It is not supposed to make a difference to the explanatory power, objectivity, and so on of the research's results if the researcher or the community of scientists are white or black, Chinese or British, rich or poor in social origin. But feminist empiricism argues that women (or feminists, male and female) as a group are more likely than men (nonfeminists) as a group to produce claims unbiased by androcentrism, and in that sense objective results of inquiry. It argues that the authors of the favored social theories are not anonymous at all: they are clearly men, and usually men of the dominant classes, races, and cultures. The people who identify and define scientific problems leave their social fingerprints on the problems and their favored solutions to them.

Second, feminist empiricism makes the related claim that scientific method is not effective at eliminating social biases that are as wide-spread as androcentrism. This is especially the case when androcentrism arrives in the inquiry process through the identification and definition of research problems. Traditional empiricism holds that scientific method will eliminate any social biases as a hypothesis goes through its rigorous tests. But feminist empiricism argues that an androcentric picture of nature and social life emerges from the testing by men only of hypotheses generated by what men find problematic in the world around them. The problem here is not only that the hypotheses which would most deeply challenge androcentric beliefs are missing from those alternatives sexists consider when testing their favored hypotheses. It is also that traditional empiricism does not direct researchers to locate themselves in the same critical plane as their subject matters. Consequently, when nonfeminist researchers gather evidence for or against hypotheses, 'scientific method'—bereft of such a directive—is impotent to locate and eradicate the androcentrism that shapes the research process.

Finally, feminist empiricists often exhort social scientists to follow the existing research norms more rigorously. On the other hand, they also can be understood to be arguing that it is precisely following these norms that contributes to androcentric research results. The norms themselves have been constructed primarily to produce answers to the kinds of questions men ask about nature and social life and to prevent scrutiny of the way beliefs which are nearly or completely culture-wide in fact cannot be eliminated from the results of research by these norms. A reliable picture of women's worlds and of social relations between the sexes often requires alternative approaches to inquiry that challenge traditional research habits and raise profound questions which are no longer marginalized as deviant.

Thus feminist empiricism intensifies recent tendencies in the philosophy and social studies of science to problematize empiricist epistemological assumptions.[6] There is a tension between the feminist uses of empiricist justificatory strategies and the parental empiricist epistemology. However, empiricism is not the only resource that has been used to justify the intimate relationship between the politics of the women's movement and the new research on women and gender.

The Feminist Standpoint

A second response to the question about how to justify the results of feminist research is provided by the feminist standpoint theorists. Knowledge is supposed to be based on experience, and the reason the feminist claims can turn out to be scientifically preferable is that they originate in, and are tested against, a more complete and less distorting kind of social experience. Women's experiences, informed by feminist theory, provide a potential grounding for more complete and less distorted knowledge claims than do men's. Thus the standpoint theorists offer a different explanation than do feminist empiricists of how research that is directed by social values and political agendas can nevertheless produce empirically preferable results of research.

This justificatory approach originates in Hegel's insight into the relationship between the master and the slave, and the development of Hegel's perceptions into the 'proletarian standpoint' by Marx, Engels, and Lukacs. The argument here is that human activity, or 'material life', not only structures but also sets limits on human understanding: what we do shapes and constrains what we can know. As Nancy Hartsock argues, if human activity is structured in fundamentally opposing ways for two different groups (such as men and women), 'one can expect that the vision of each will represent an inversion of the other, and in systems of domination the vision available to the rulers will be both partial and perverse'. Men in the ruling classes and races reserve for themselves the right to perform only certain kinds of human activity, assigning the balance to women and men in other subjugated groups. What they assign to others they rationalize as merely natural activity—

whether this be manual labor, emotional labor, or reproduction and child care—in contrast to what they regard as the distinctively cultural activity that they reserve for themselves. Of course, their 'ruling' activities (in our society, management and administration) could not occur unless others were assigned to perform the social labors they disdain.

For these theorists, knowledge emerges for the oppressed only through the struggles they wage against their oppressors. It is through feminist struggles against male domination that women's experience can be made to yield up a truer (or less false) image of social reality than that available only from the perspective of the social experience of men of the ruling classes and races. Thus a feminist standpoint is not something anyone can have by claiming it, but an achievement. (A standpoint differs in this respect from a perspective.) To achieve a feminist standpoint one must engage in the intellectual and political struggle necessary to see nature and social life from the point of view of that disdained activity which produces women's social experiences instead of from the partial and perverse perspective available from the 'ruling gender' experience of men.

Like feminist empiricism, the feminist standpoint reveals key problems in its paternal discourse. Where Marxism suggests that sexism is entirely a consequence of class relations, a problem within only the superstructural social institutions and bourgeois ideology, the feminist version sees sexual relations as at least as causal as economic relations in creating forms of social life and belief. Like feminist empiricism, the standpoint approach takes women and men to be fundamentally sex classes. In contrast to Marxist assumptions, they are not merely or perhaps even primarily members of economic classes, though class, like race and culture, also mediates women's opportunities to gain empirically adequate understandings of nature and social life. Just as feminist empiricism's radical future pointed toward epistemological assumptions that empiricism could not accommodate, so, too, the feminist standpoint's radicalism points toward epistemological assumptions that Marxism cannot contain.

The reader needs to remember at this point that standpoint theorists are not defending any form of relativism. [. . .] [F]eminist researchers are never proposing that women's and men's characteristic social experiences provide *equal* grounds for reliable knowledge claims. This kind of relativist claim is not being advanced at the level of these epistemologies or justificatory strategies. [. . .] For instance, it is not *equally true* that men's experiences provide the only legitimate origin of scientific problems, as traditional social science has assumed, and also that women's experiences provide a legitimate origin of scientific problems, let alone *the best* origin, as the standpoint theorists argue. For the standpoint theorists, this inequality is due to the fact that the activities of men shape the horizons of their knowledge and support interests in ignorance of the misery generated by the domination of women.

Should one have to choose between feminist empiricism and the feminist standpoint as justificatory strategies? I think not. A justificatory strategy is intended to convince, and it is important to notice that these two are likely to appeal to quite different audiences. Feminist empiricism is useful precisely because it stresses the continuities between traditional justifications of scientific research and feminist ones, as these would be understood by social scientists. In contrast, the feminist standpoint stresses the continuities between the radical upheavals in social understanding created by nineteenth-century class struggles and those created by feminist inquiry. These can be appreciated by political economists and those familiar with the post-Kuhnian histories and sociologies of science. The two epistemologies also appear locked into dialogue with each other. The relationship they have to each other reflects the struggles in mainstream discourses between liberal and Marxist theories of human nature and politics. Perhaps choosing one over the other insures choosing more than feminism should want of those paternal discourses; we are shaped by what we reject as well as by what we accept.

The tensions between the two feminist epistemologies and the tensions within each one suggest their transitional natures. They are *transitional epistemologies*, and there are good reasons to see that as a virtue.

['Introduction: Is there a Feminist Method?' and 'Conclusion: Epistemological Questions', in *Feminism and Methodology* (Bloomington: Indiana University Press, 1986), 1–13, 181–6]

JANE FLAX

24 Postmodernism and Gender Relations in Feminist Theory

I think there are currently three kinds of thinking that best present (and represent) our own time 'apprehended in thought': psychoanalysis, feminist theory, and postmodern philosophy. These ways of thinking reflect and are partially constituted by Enlightenment beliefs still prevalent in Western (especially American) culture. At the same time they offer ideas and insights that are only possible because of the breakdown of Enlightenment beliefs under the cumulative pressure of historical events such as the invention of the atomic bomb, the Holocaust, and the war in Vietnam.

Each of these ways of thinking takes as its object of investigation at least one facet of what has become most problematic in our transitional state: how to understand and (re-)constitute the self, gender, knowledge, social relations, and culture without resorting to linear, teleological, hierarchical, holistic, or binary ways of thinking and being.

My focus here will be mainly on one of these modes of thinking: feminist theory. I will consider what it could be and reflect upon the goals, logics, and problematics of feminist theorizing as it has been practiced in the past fifteen years in the West. I will also place such theorizing within the social and philosophical contexts of which it is both a part and a critique.

I do not mean to claim that feminist theory is a unified or homogeneous discourse. Nonetheless, despite the lively and intense controversies among persons who identify themselves as practitioners concerning the subject matter, appropriate methodologies, and desirable outcome of feminist theorizing, it is possible to identify at least some of our underlying goals, purposes, and constituting objects.

A fundamental goal of feminist theory is (and ought to be) to analyze gender relations: how gender relations are constituted and experienced and how we think or, equally important, do not think about them. The study of gender relations includes but is not limited to what are often considered the distinctively feminist issues: the situation of women and the analysis of male domination. Feminist theory includes an (at least implicit) prescriptive element as well. By studying gender we hope to gain a critical distance on existing gender arrangements. This critical distance can help clear a space in which re-evaluating and altering our existing gender arrangements may become more possible.

Feminist theory by itself cannot clear such a space. Without feminist political actions theories remain inadequate and ineffectual. However, I have come to believe that the further development of feminist theory (and hence a better understanding of gender) also depends upon locating our theorizing within and drawing more self-consciously upon the wider philosophic contexts of which it is both a part and a critique. In other words, we need to think more about how we think about gender relations or any other social relations and about how other modes of thinking can help or hinder us in the development of our own discourses. In this paper, I will be moving back and forth between thinking about gender relations and thinking about how I am thinking—or could think—about them.

Feminist theory seems to me to belong within two, more inclusive, categories with which it has special affinity: the analysis of social relations and postmodern philosophy.[1] Gender relations enter into and are constituent elements in every aspect of human experience. In turn, the experience of gender relations for any person and the structure of gender as a social category are shaped by the interactions of gender relations and other social relations such as class and race. Gender relations thus have no fixed essence; they vary both within and over time.

As a type of postmodern philosophy, feminist theory reveals and contributes to the growing uncertainty within Western intellectual circles about the appropriate grounding and methods for explaining and/or interpreting human experience. Contemporary feminists join other postmodern philosophers in raising important metatheoretical questions about the possible nature and status of theorizing itself. Given the increasingly fluid and confused status of Western self-understandings, it is not even clear what would constitute the basis for satisfactory answers to commonly agreed upon questions within feminist (or other forms of social) theory.

Postmodern discourses are all 'deconstructive' in that they seek to distance us from and make us skeptical about beliefs concerning truth, knowledge, power, the self, and language that are often taken for granted within and serve as legitimation for contemporary Western culture.

Postmodern philosophers seek to throw into radical doubt beliefs still prevalent in (especially American) culture but derived from the Enlightenment, such as:

1. The existence of a stable, coherent self. Distinctive properties of this Enlightenment self include a form of reason capable of privileged insight into its own processes and into the 'laws of nature'.

2. Reason and its 'science'—philosophy—can provide an objective, reliable, and universal foundation for knowledge.

3. The knowledge acquired from the right use of reason will be 'True'—for example, such knowledge will represent something real and unchanging (universal) about our minds and/or the structure of the natural world.

4. Reason itself has transcendental and universal qualities. It exists independently of the self's contingent existence (e.g. bodily, historical, and social experiences do not affect reason's structure or its capacity to produce atemporal knowledge).

5. There are complex connections between reason, autonomy, and freedom. All claims to truth and rightful authority are to be submitted to the tribunal of reason. Freedom consists in obedience to laws that conform to the necessary results of the right use of reason. (The rules that are right for me as a rational being will necessarily be right for all other such beings.) In obeying such laws, I am obeying my own best transhistorical part (reason) and hence am exercising my own autonomy and ratifying my existence as a free being. In such acts, I escape a determined or merely contingent existence.

6. By grounding claims to authority in reason, the conflicts between truth, knowledge, and power can be overcome. Truth can serve power without distortion; in turn, by utilizing knowledge in the service of power both freedom and progress will be assured. Knowledge can be both neutral (e.g. grounded in universal reason, not particular 'interests') and also socially beneficial.

7. Science, as the exemplar of the right use of reason, is also the paradigm for all true knowledge. Science is neutral in its methods and contents but socially beneficial in its results. Through its process of discovery we can utilize the 'laws of nature' for the benefit of society. However, in order for science to

progress, scientists must be free to follow the rules of reason rather than pander to the 'interests' arising from outside rational discourse.

8. Language is in some sense transparent. Just as the right use of reason can result in knowledge that represents the real, so, too, language is merely the medium in and through which such representation occurs. There is a correspondence between 'word' and 'thing' (as between a correct truth claim and the real). Objects are not linguistically (or socially) constructed, they are merely *made present* to consciousness by naming and the right use of language.

The relation of feminist theorizing to the postmodern project of deconstruction is necessarily ambivalent. Enlightenment philosophers such as Kant did not intend to include women within the population of those capable of attaining freedom from traditional forms of authority. Nonetheless, it is not unreasonable for persons who have been defined as incapable of self-emancipation to insist that concepts such as the autonomy of reason, objective truth, and beneficial progress through scientific discovery ought to include and be applicable to the capacities and experiences of women as well as men. It is also appealing, for those who have been excluded, to believe that reason will triumph—that those who proclaim such ideas as objectivity will respond to rational arguments. If there is no objective basis for distinguishing between true and false beliefs, then it seems that power alone will determine the outcome of competing truth claims. This is a frightening prospect to those who lack (or are oppressed by) the power of others.

Nevertheless, despite an understandable attraction to the (apparently) logical, orderly world of the Enlightenment, feminist theory more properly belongs in the terrain of postmodern philosophy. Feminist notions of the self, knowledge, and truth are too contradictory to those of the Enlightenment to be contained within its categories. The way(s) to feminist future(s) cannot lie in reviving or appropriating Enlightenment concepts of the person or knowledge.[2]

Feminist theorists enter into and echo postmodernist discourses as we have begun to deconstruct notions of reason, knowledge, or the self and to reveal the effects of the gender arrangements that lay beneath their 'neutral' and universalizing facades. Some feminist theorists, for example, have begun to sense that the motto of Enlightenment, *sapere aude*—Have courage to use your own reason',[3] rests in part upon a deeply gender-rooted sense of self and self-deception. The notion that reason is divorced from 'merely contingent' existence still predominates in contemporary Western thought and now appears to mask the embeddedness and dependence of the self upon social relations, as well as the partiality and historical specificity of this self's existence. What Kant's self calls its 'own' reason and the methods by which reason's contents become present or 'self-evident', it now appears, are no freer from empirical contingency than is the so-called phenomenal self.

In fact, feminists, like other postmodernists, have begun to suspect that all such transcendental claims reflect and reify the experience of a few persons—mostly white, Western males. These transhistoric claims seem plausible to us in part because they reflect important aspects of the experience of those who dominate our social world.

This excursus into metatheory has now returned us to the opening of my paper—that the fundamental purpose of feminist theory is to analyze how we think, or do not think, or avoid thinking about gender. Obviously, then, to understand the goals of feminist theory we must consider its central subject—gender.

Here, however, we immediately plunge into a complicated and controversial morass. For among feminist theorists there is by no means consensus on such (apparently) elementary questions as: What is gender? How is it related to anatomical sexual differences? How are gender relations constituted and sustained (in one person's lifetime and more generally as a social experience over time)? How do gender relations relate to other sorts of social relations such as class or race? Do gender relations have a history (or many)? What causes gender relations to change over time? What are the relationships between gender relations, sexuality, and a sense of individual identity? What are the relationships between heterosexuality, homosexuality, and gender relations? Are there only two genders? What are the relationships between forms of male dominance and gender relations? Could/would gender relations wither away in egalitarian societies? Is there anything distinctively male or female in modes of thought and social relations? If there is, are these distinctions innate and/or socially constituted? Are gendered distinctions socially useful and/or necessary? If so, what are the consequences for the feminist goal of attaining gender justice?

Confronted with such a bewildering set of questions, it is easy to overlook the fact that a fundamental transformation in social theory has occurred. The single most important advance in feminist theory is that the existence of gender relations has been problematized. Gender can no longer be treated as a simple, natural fact. The assumption that gender relations are natural, we can now see, arose from two coinciding circumstances: the unexamined identification and confusion of (anatomical) sexual differences with gender relations, and the absence of active feminist movements. [...]

'Gender relations' is a category meant to capture a complex set of social relations, to refer to a changing set of historically variable social processes. Gender, both as an analytic category and a social process, is relational. That is, gender relations are complex and unstable processes (or temporary 'totalities' in the language of dialectics) constituted by and through interrelated parts. These parts are interdependent, that is, each part can have no meaning or existence without the others.

Gender relations are differentiated and (so far) asymmetric divisions and attributions of human traits and capacities. Through gender relations two types of persons are created: man and woman. Man and woman are posited as exclusionary categories. One can be only one gender, never the other or both. The actual content of being a man or woman and the rigidity of the categories themselves are highly variable across cultures and time. Nevertheless, gender relations so far as we have been able to understand them have been (more or less) relations of domination. That is, gender relations have been (more) defined and (imperfectly) controlled by one of their interrelated aspects—the man.

These relations of domination and the existence of gender relations themselves have been concealed in a variety of ways, including defining women as a 'question' or the 'sex' or the 'other' and men as the universal (or at least without gender). In a wide variety of cultures and discourses, men tend to be seen as free from or as not determined by gender relations. Thus, for example, academics do not explicitly study the psychology of men or men's history. Male academics do not worry about how being men may distort their intellectual work, while women who study gender relations are considered suspect (of triviality, if not bias). Only recently have scholars begun to consider the possibility that there may be at least three histories in every culture—'his', 'hers', and 'ours'. 'His' and 'ours' are generally assumed to be equivalents, although in contemporary work there might be some recognition of the existence of that deviant—woman (e.g. women's history).[4] However, it is still rare for scholars to search for the pervasive effects of gender relations on all aspects of a culture in the way that they feel obligated to investigate the impact of relations of power or the organization of production.

To the extent that feminist discourse defines its problematic as 'woman', it, too, ironically privileges the man as unproblematic or exempted from determination by gender relations. From the perspective of social relations, men and women are both prisoners of gender, although in highly differentiated but interrelated ways. That men appear to be and (in many cases) are the wardens, or at least the trustees within a social whole, should not blind us to the extent to which they, too, are governed by the rules of gender. [. . .]

[. . .] [I]n order for gender relations to be useful as a category of social analysis we must be as socially and self-critical as possible about the meanings usually attributed to those relations and the ways we think about them. Otherwise, we run the risk of replicating the very social relations we are attempting to understand. We have to be able to investigate both the social and philosophical barriers to our comprehension of gender relations.

One important barrier to our comprehension of gender relations has been the difficulty of understanding the relationship between gender and 'sex'. In this context, sex means the anatomical differences between male and female. Historically (at least since Aristotle), these anatomical differences have been assigned to the class of 'natural facts' of biology. In turn, biology has been equated with the pre- or nonsocial. Gender relations then become conceptualized as if they are constituted by two opposite terms or distinct types of being—man and woman. Since man and woman seem to be opposites or fundamentally distinct types of being, gender cannot be relational. If gender is as natural and as intrinsically a part of us as the genitals we are born with, it follows that it would be foolish (or even harmful) to attempt either to change gender arrangements or not to take them into account as a delimitation on human activities.

Even though a major focus of feminist theory has been to 'denaturalize' gender, feminists as well as nonfeminists seem to have trouble thinking through the meanings we assign to and the uses we make of the concept 'natural.' What after all, is the 'natural' in the context of the human world? There are many aspects of our embodiedness or biology that we might see as given limits to human action which Western medicine and science do not hesitate to challenge. For example, few Westerners would refuse to be vaccinated against diseases that our bodies are naturally susceptible to, although in some cultures such actions would be seen as violating the natural order. [. . .] More and more the 'natural' ceases to exist as the opposite of the 'cultural' or social. Nature becomes the object and product of human action; it loses its independent existence. Ironically, the more such disenchantment proceeds, the more humans seem to need something that remains outside our powers of transformation. Until recently one such exempt area seemed to be anatomical differences between males and females. Thus in order to 'save' nature (from ourselves) many people in the contemporary West equate sex/biology/nature/gender and oppose these to the cultural/social/human. Concepts of gender then become complex metaphors for ambivalences about human action in, on, and as part of the natural world.

But in turn the use of gender as a metaphor for such ambivalences blocks further investigation of them. For the social articulation of these equations is not really in the form I stated above but, rather, sex/biology/nature/woman:cultural/social/man. In the contemporary West, women become the last refuge from not only the 'heartless' world but also an increasingly mechanized and fabricated one as well. What remains masked in these modes of thought is the possibility that our concepts of biology/nature are rooted in social relations; they do not merely reflect the given structure of reality itself.

Thus, in order to understand gender as a social relation, feminist theorists need to deconstruct further the meanings we attach to biology/sex/gender/nature. This process of deconstruction is far from complete and certainly is not easy. Initially, some feminists thought we could merely separate the terms 'sex' and 'gender'. As we became more sensitive to the social histories of concepts, it became clear that such an (apparent) disjunction, while politically necessary, rested upon problematic and culture-specific oppositions, for example, the one between 'nature' and 'culture' or 'body' and 'mind'. As some feminists began to rethink these 'oppositions', new questions emerged: does anatomy (body) have no relation to mind? What difference does it make in the constitution of my social experiences that I have a specifically female body?

Despite the increasing complexity of our questions, most feminists would still insist that gender relations are not (or are not only) equivalent to or a consequence of anatomy. Everyone will agree that there are anatomical differences between men and women. These anatomical differences seem to be primarily located in or are the consequence of the differentiated contributions men and women make to a common biological necessity—the physical reproduction of our species. [. . .]

A problem with all these apparently obvious associations is that they may assume precisely what requires explanation—that is, gender relations. We live in a world in which gender is a constituting social relation and in which gender is also a relation of domination. Therefore, both men's and women's understanding of anatomy, biology, embodiedness, sexuality, and reproduction is partially rooted in, reflects, and must justify (or challenge) preexisting gender relations. In turn, the existence of gender relations helps us to order and understand the facts of human existence. In other words, gender can become a metaphor for biology just as biology can become a metaphor for gender. [. . .]

The enterprise of feminist theory is fraught with temptations and pitfalls. Insofar as women have been part of all societies, our thinking cannot be free from culture-bound modes of self-understanding. We as well as men internalize the dominant gender's conceptions of masculinity and femininity. Unless we see gender as a social relation, rather than as an opposition of inherently different beings, we will not be able to identify the varieties and limitations of different women's (or men's) powers and oppressions within particular societies. Feminist theorists are faced with a fourfold task. We need to (1) articulate feminist viewpoints of/within the social worlds in which we live; (2) think about how we are affected by these worlds; (3) consider the ways in which how we think about them may be implicated in existing power/knowledge relationships; and (4) imagine ways in which these worlds ought to/can be transformed.

Since within contemporary Western societies gender relations have been ones of domination, feminist theories should have a compensatory as well as a critical aspect. That is, we need to recover and explore the aspects of social relations that have been suppressed, unarticulated, or denied within dominant (male) viewpoints. We need to recover and write the histories of women and our activities into the accounts and stories that cultures tell about themselves. Yet, we also need to think about how so-called women's activities are partially constituted by and through their location within the web of social relations that make up any society. That is, we need to know how these activities are affected but also how they effect, or enable, or compensate for the consequences of men's activities, as well as their implication in class or race relations. [...]

Any feminist standpoint will necessarily be partial. Thinking about women may illuminate some aspects of a society that have been previously suppressed within the dominant view. But none of us can speak for 'woman' because no such person exists except within a specific set of (already gendered) relations—to 'man' and to many concrete and different women.

Indeed, the notion of *a* feminist standpoint that is truer than previous (male) ones seems to rest upon many problematic and unexamined assumptions. These include an optimistic belief that people act rationally in their own interests and that reality has a structure that perfect reason (once perfected) can discover. Both of these assumptions in turn depend upon an uncritical appropriation of the Enlightenment ideas discussed earlier. Furthermore, the notion of such a standpoint also assumes that the oppressed are not in fundamental ways damaged by their social experience. On the contrary, this position assumes that the oppressed have a privileged (and not just different) relation and ability to comprehend a reality that is 'out there' waiting for our representation. It also presupposes gendered social relations in which there is a category of beings who are fundamentally like each other by virtue of their sex—that is, it assumes the otherness men assign to women. Such a standpoint also assumes that women, unlike men, can be free of determination from their own participation in relations of domination such as those rooted in the social relations of race, class, or homophobia.

I believe, on the contrary, that there is no force or reality 'outside' our social relations and activity (e.g. history, reason, progress, science, some transcendental essence) that will rescue us from partiality and differences. Our lives and alliances belong with those who seek to further decenter the world—although we should reserve the right to be suspicious of their motives and visions as well. Feminist theories, like other forms of postmodernism, should encourage us to tolerate and interpret ambivalence, ambiguity, and multiplicity as well as to expose the roots of our needs for imposing order and structure no matter how arbitrary and oppressive these needs may be.

If we do our work well, 'reality' will appear even more unstable, complex, and disorderly than it does now. In this sense, perhaps Freud was right when he declared that women are the enemies of civilization.[5]

['Postmodernism and Gender Relations in Feminist Theory', *Signs: Journal of Women in Culture and Society*, 12/4 (University of Chicago, 1987), 621–43.]

25 Thoroughly Postmodern Feminist Criticism

Psychoanalytic criticism, unlike any other criticism, offers feminist critics a way of looking at sexually differentiated subjects, giving access to the subjectivity of women in writing and in all forms of discursive practice. But when feminism takes up psychoanalysis it also takes on postmodernism: like postmodernism, it is interested in the shifting of boundaries, the undoing of binary oppositions, but at the same time it offers postmodernism a politics to be conducted in the literary and artistic field. Without feminism, psychoanalysis and literature were locked into what has turned out to be a somewhat barren embrace: there has been little movement since Shoshana Felman's important advance in the 1970s, namely that literature and psychoanalysis were each to be the 'unthought' of the other: where psychoanalysis points to the unconscious of literature, literature points to the unconscious of psychoanalysis.[1] In other words, while literature was to be probed for its theories in fiction, psychoanalysis was to be investigated for its literariness, its slippages of meaning, which would reveal that there was fiction in theory.

Postmodernist theory provides feminism with an additional framework, enabling it to articulate the diversity and contradictions that spring up not only *between* various positions but also *within* various positions. In order to elaborate on the intersection of feminism and postmodernism I need to chart the main lines of the current debate. This seems to divide into a number of camps: (1) those who see postmodernism as a contamination of modernism, whose proponents (Bataille, Foucault, Derrida, are cited) 'claim as their own the revelations of a decentred subjectivity, emancipated from the imperatives of work and usefulness';[2] (2) those who similarly see it as negative, but for other reasons, namely, its reinforcement of 'the logic of consumer capitalism',[3] or its tendency to mime and parody 'the formal resolution of art and social life attempted by the avant garde, while remorselessly emptying it of its political content';[4] (3) those who see it as positive, welcoming the postmodern as a triumph of heterogeneity over consensus, artist and writer 'working without rules in order to formulate the rules for what *will have been done*' after the event has happened,[5] thereby able to resist capture by any form of ideology.

The notion of resistance to any form of reified meaning is central to the project of those who believe in the radical potential of postmodernism, but is this enough? Or is it not even counterproductive in that to lay stress on the marginal in experience undermines any sense of collectivity? The feminist critique of patriarchy and the postmodernist critique of representation intersect most fruitfully where the issue goes beyond a mere critique of representation. To stick within a particular problematic debating the pros and cons of representation has damaging consequences for a postmodern politics, 'where the power of representation is something sought, indeed passionately struggled for, by groups that consider themselves dominated by alien and alienating representations'.[6]

Feminism confronts this aporia by trying to do more than merely form a new alliance with theory. Feminists have taken up the struggle over the production, distribution, and transformation of meaning in a number of specific cultural practices as a focus of political intervention and opposition in order to challenge the forms of representation which constrain and oppress them. In this there is an analogy with the discourse of postmodernism as a discourse which attempts to conceive difference without opposition. The kind of simultaneous activity on many fronts (essentialist, culturalist, linguistic, psychoanalytic, anti-psychoanalytic) is already compatible with postmodern thought. The fact that feminist artists are forging a new alliance with theory certainly has radical effects. Postmodernist feminist projects deliberately break across the boundaries of the discourses of art, criticism, and theory.[7] [...] But are the politics inherent in these issues sufficiently positive?

One specific area where feminism and postmodernism engage in a mutual sexual politics is through their involvement with film theory, which enables them to challenge the way fantasy is put in the service of the oppressive ideology of capitalism. Film theory has certainly offered feminists a way of launching a substantial critique against the production and reproduction of fetishized images of women, constructed according to the male look. The postmodern has surrendered the belief in vision as a privileged mode of access to reality. Psychoanalysis has here enabled feminists to launch a critique on vision as sexually biased: in the Freudian scenario it is the look which determines the child's discovery of sexual difference and establishes the phallus as the privileged signifier of sexual identity. Film theory examines the cinematic manipulation of the gaze: the camera is conceptualized as an instrument of the gaze, which controls the spectator's eye. British and American feminist film theory has followed the control of the look in classical Hollywood films and shown how it is construed as a male patriarchal one and how it constitutes in turn the look of a spectator in the male field of vision. Feminist film theory articulates ways of countermanding the patriarchal system of the look, where the woman is always in front of the camera and the man behind it. Mulvey proposes the destruction of narrative and visual pleasure as the foremost aim of women's cinema,[8] and Koch suggests a move not to a 'feminist aesthetic', but a 'feminist deaesthetic'.[9] This suggests that women's cinema, in common with postmodernism, has rejected an avant-garde aesthetic of subversion for a resistance to (filmic) representation, requiring the abandonment of traditional notions of the 'aesthetic'.[10] [...]

[. . .] [W]hat is most striking about the postmodernist feminist project is [. . .] its transgression of the boundaries between art, criticism, and theory, an undertaking which modernism, with its stress on the autonomy of the aesthetic, would not have sanctioned. Lacanian-influenced feminist writers, such as Kristeva and Cixous, practise a postfeminist writing at the same time as they elaborate a theory; although this practice is not exclusive to feminist writing it is here that it is at its most overtly political.

The problem, however, is that so far there has been no way of reconciling the notion of the feminine as a general issue for both sexes (linking up with the postmodernist critique of binarism and the need to rethink difference) with the historical need for women to find a collective voice in an oppressive phallocentric reality. Sandra Harding, writing a theoretical discourse, *The Science Question in Feminism*,[11] tentatively suggests that there can be a feminism which is both united in its universal commitment to the exploring and overthrowing of women's oppression under patriarchy, and polyvocal in its representation of a diversity of positive feminist movements, encompassing differences of race, colour, and class. By the same token she rejects the ideal of a value-free objective science, conducted from a spuriously neutral standpoint, preferring one that is critically aware of the inescapable bond between scientific and moral and political commitment, thus accepting the continual need for dialectical adjustments. In acknowledging the presence of dialectics within itself, science becomes postmodernist. Science has been *par excellence* the paradigm of a phallogocentric idealized system, and the challenge to it exemplifies feminism's project of the diversification of its modes of enquiry.

The feminist project entails that the worlds that have encoded projections of woman be subject to a general decipherment: feminism examines the processes whereby woman is given or refused access to discourse, and at the same time inaugurates a new way of thinking, writing, and speaking. There is now a plethora of women's writing springing up from all kinds of communities. In some areas, such as North America, women's studies are changing the face of university departments. What the diversity of feminist literary criticisms, backed by a rereading of psychoanalysis, shows, is that discourses are not merely about producing definitions but that they determine the 'nature' of the bodies and minds of the subjects they aim to govern. Thus feminist literary critics do not merely provide subversive readings of traditional and modern literary texts and modify the received images of femininity. They also offer a continual challenge to the prevailing power structure and its claims of impartiality, showing that there is nothing impartial under the sun, including the discourse of feminism itself, whose most vivid sign of life is its thriving on the difference within.

['Thoroughly Postmodern Feminist Criticism', in Teresa Brennan (ed.), *Between Feminism and Psychoanalysis* (London: Routledge, 1989), 146–50.]

26 Feminism and Psychoanalytic Theory

In the early period of the contemporary feminist movement, feminists searched for a grand theory. This single cause, or dominant factor, theory would explain a sexual inequality, hierarchy, and domination that were omnipresent and that defined and circumscribed entirely the experience and organization of gender and sexuality. For some theorists, gender oppression inhered in capitalist relations of work and exploitation, in the state or the family, in divisions among women or alliances among men, or in male violence and control of women's reproductive and sexual capacities. For others, women were entrapped through their own reproductive anatomy, the objectification of their bodies, the mothering relation or the marriage relation, compulsory heterosexuality, the cultural or ideological construction of 'woman', location in the domestic sphere, or association with nature.

For members of the feminist subculture that developed out of the New Left, Marxism presented the hegemonic theoretical claim to explain oppression. Yet as I reflected during the late 1960s upon the historical and cross-cultural record, it seemed clear that women's oppression well preceded class society and that its dynamics did not inhere exclusively or dominantly in material relations of work. I turned to psychological anthropology for an alternative to the Marxist account of women's oppression that would still privilege actual social relations as an explanatory underpinning. I concluded [...] that women's mothering generated, more or less universally, a defensive masculine identity in men and a compensatory psychology and ideology of masculine superiority. This psychology and ideology sustained male dominance. [...]

The advantages of a psychoanalytic feminist approach were substantial. In psychoanalytic theory, as in psychological anthropology and anthropological kinship theory, explicit attention to sex and gender, though not approached from a feminist perspective, has been central and basic to both theory and practice. It would be difficult for a psychoanalyst to ignore completely an analysand's sexuality or gender or to argue that a theory of sexuality or gender was irrelevant to the field. In other disciplines that feminists have tried to reshape, the argument for gender neutrality or irrelevance has been more easily sustained by traditionalists.

I argued that this centrality of sex and gender in the categories of psychoanalysis, coupled with the tenacity, emotional centrality, and sweeping power in our lives of our sense of gendered self, made psychoanalysis a particularly apposite source of feminist theorizing. I suggested that our experiences as men and women come from deep within, both within our pasts and, relatedly, within the deepest structures of unconscious meaning and the most emotionally moving relationships that help constitute our daily lives. I showed that the selves of women and men tend to be constructed differently—women's self more in relation and involved with boundary negotiations, separation and connection, men's self more distanced and based on defensively firm boundaries and denials of self-other connection. This emotional meaningfulness has something to do more generally with the continuing theoretical appeal of psychoanalytic feminism and with the emotional–intellectual engrossment of psychoanalytic feminists. [. . .]

Like all theoretical approaches within the feminist project, psychoanalytic feminism does specific things and not others. First, like the theory from which it derives, it is not easily or often historically, socially, or culturally specific. It tends toward universalism and can be read, even if it avoids the essentialism of psychoanalysis itself, to imply that there is a psychological commonality among all women and among all men. Psychoanalytic feminism has not tried enough to capture the varied, particular organizations of gender and sexuality in different times and places, nor has it made the dynamics of change central. The dominant theoretical lexicon of psychoanalysis includes gender but not class, race, or ethnicity. Accordingly, psychoanalytic feminism has not been especially attuned to differences among women—to class, racial, and ethnic variations in experience, identity, or location in social practices and relations. Feminist theory and practice, of course, need to be culturally and historically specific, and it would be useful if psychoanalysis had the data and theory to differentiate genders and sexualities finely across history and culture. Psychoanalytic feminism would also be considerably enriched by clinical, theoretical, or psychoanalytically informed phenomenological and experiential accounts of gender identity, self, and relation among women and men of color and of non-dominant classes.

It is a serious mistake, however, to conflate this delimitation of the contribution of psychoanalysis to feminism with a dismissal of its importance. People everywhere have emotions that they care about, connections to others, sexual feelings, and senses of self, self-esteem, and gender. People everywhere form a psyche, self, and identity. These are everywhere profoundly affected by unconscious fantasies as well as by conscious perceptions that begin as early as infancy. Psychoanalysis is the method and theory directed toward the investigation and understanding of how we develop and experience these unconscious fantasies and of how we construct and reconstruct our felt past in the present. Historically, this method and theory have not often been applied in a socially or culturally specific manner, but there is not a basic antagonism between psychoanalytic thinking and social specificity. Psychoanalysis uses universal theoretical categories—distinguishing conscious from unconscious mental processes, labelling and analyzing defenses, arguing that basic ego or self feelings are a product of and constructed by early experienced object relations—but it need not (though it may in some versions) prescribe the content of unconscious fantasy, the inevitable invocation of particular defenses, or particular developmental or self stories. As factors of race, class, culture, or history enter either into a labelled (conscious or unconscious) identity, or as they shape particular early object-relational and family patterns and forms of subjectivity, psychoanalytic tools should be able to analyze these. Until we have another theory which can tell us about unconscious mental processes, conflict, and relations of gender, sexuality, and self, we had best take psychoanalysis for what it does include and can tell us rather than dismissing it out of hand. We might also bear in mind that on some kinds of differences among women, psychoanalysis already has great interpretive potential experientially and clinically on the individual case level, if not theoretically—that is, as a general developmental theory. I think here of differences of sexual orientation and identity, of sexual victimization and its sequelae, of married and single, of mother and not-mother.

[. . .] My drawing upon psychoanalysis, in some sense the creation of a single individual, during that period was itself in the context of, and remains a sort of carryover from, feminist grand theory days.

Now, however, when I speak of feminist theory, I mean something more holistic and pluralistic—encompassing a number of organizational axes—and at the same time not absolute. In my current view, feminist understanding requires a multiplex account—perhaps not as acausal as thick description, but yet not necessarily claiming causal explanatory status—of the dynamics of gender, sexuality, sexual inequality, and domination. It is the focus on relations among elements, or dynamics, along with an analysis and critique of male dominance, which define an understanding of sex and gender as feminist, and not just the exclusive focus on male dominance itself. I no longer think that one factor, or one dynamic, can explain male dominance (even if I still have my own predilections for particular theoretical contenders). An open web of social, psychological, and cultural relations, dynamics, practices, identities, beliefs, in which I would privilege neither society, psyche, nor culture, comes to constitute gender as a social, cultural, and psychological phenomenon. This multiplex web composes sexual inequality, but, at the same time, feminist understanding encompasses relations of gender and sexuality not immediately comprehended in terms of hierarchy, domination, or inequality or by concepts like patriarchy, male dominance, or the law of the father. Gender and sexuality are more fragmentary, so that some differences are not implicated in dominance, and the complex of gender may include benefits to women as well as liabilities. This complex is manifold, constituted by multiple, often contradictory, locations and identities. There are times when gender itself as well as sexual inequality are more or less relevant to our experiences or the conclusions of our investigations. Such complexity is

among other things a necessary correlate to the multiple social, psychological, and cultural identities of different women and to the polyvocality we find
in women's accounts of their lives and situations. These accounts show that
psychological, cultural, and social constructions of gender vary and that
gender varies in its link to the self and in how and when it is invoked. [. . .]

This global shift in my general view of feminist theory has substantive
import for my psychoanalytic feminist analysis. My early writing, in articles
[. . .] and in my book, *The Reproduction of Mothering*, implied that women's
mothering was *the* cause or prime mover of male dominance.[1] I would now
argue that these writings document and delineate one extremely important,
and previously largely unexamined, aspect of the relations of gender and the
psychology of gender. My focus on the mother and the pre-Oedipal period
must also be understood historically and contextually, as a reaction to and
dialogue with the nearly exclusive Freudian focus on the father and the
Oedipus complex. That we are mothered by women, that in all societies
women rather than men have primary parenting responsibilities, is an important social and cultural fact that still bears remarking and analyzing. In
those individual and cultural cases where we have some insight into human
emotions and psychodynamics, this fact also seems to have significant import
for people's constructions of self and interpersonal relations, for their emotions, their fantasies, and their psychological apprehensions of gender.
Women's inequality may be multiply caused and situated, but I have yet to
find a convincing explanation for the virulence of masculine anger, fear, and
resentment of women, or of aggression toward them, that bypasses—even if
it does not rest with—the psychoanalytic account, first suggested by Horney,
that men resent and fear women because they experience them as powerful
mothers.

To emphasize the emotional (and even social, cultural, or political) power
of the mother, which I have done, following psychoanalytic object-relations
theory, does not preclude a recognition of the father's social, cultural, and
political (and even emotional) power. However, although such a position is
not incompatible with a view that locates power in the father, it is incompatible with arguments that the father, either as actual or symbolic presence,
controls the mother–child relation entirely, or that motherhood is solely an
institution that sustains women's powerlessness, or that we can only understand the mother–daughter relation as it is experienced in the domain of the
father. Fathers are not only socially and culturally dominant; they can be
personally domineering, seductive, and exciting, often as an alternative to the
taken-for-granted mother. Mothers can, in contrast to such fathers, be perceived as submissive, self-effacing, and powerless.

My position here is consonant with modern, more decentered, views of
theory in general and feminist theory in particular—views of the multiplicities of gender(ed) experience which include varied axes of power and

powerlessness and dimensions of gender which do not encode power. The complexity of the emotional and personal is best captured by decentered views, such that attempts to polarize personal and emotional experiences as all bad, or to valorize them as all good, are often insufficient. Such a perspective enables us to understand that one can both valorize feminine qualities like women's self in relation and see them as products of inequality. As a result of investigating how the relational development of self differs for women and men, I have criticized men's denial of relatedness and individualism in social and psychoanalytic theory. I have implied that women's self in relation is a potential strength. But such critique does not mean that I do not acknowledge many women's very difficult problems with establishing differentiated selfhood, autonomy, and an agentic subjectivity.

There is a second change in my project from the period when I wrote *The Reproduction of Mothering*, and that is a greater interest in writing about psychoanalysis for its own sake. As I now see feminist theory as a more multiplex account of relations in many domains, I care less to justify my interests by arguing that psychoanalysis is *the* feminist theory. I am more convinced even than I was during an earlier period that psychoanalysis describes a significant level of reality that is not reducible to, or in the last instance caused by, social or cultural organization. I would not, as I believe I do in *Reproduction*, give determinist primacy to social relations that generate certain psychological patterns or processes but would argue that psychology itself is equally important to, constitutive and determinative of, human life. If I were to discover that the 'central dynamic' or 'cause' of women's oppression were located outside of the personal, interiorized, subjective, and intersubjective realm of psychic life and primary relationships that psychoanalysis describes, I would still be concerned with this realm and its relation to gender, sexuality, and self.

Part of the explanation for this shift may lie in the particular psychoanalytic feminist approach that I chose. Object-relations theory is originally a set of accounts about the constitution of self in the context of primary emotional relationships. It is not primarily a theory of gender. This branch of psychoanalytic feminism in some sense imposed a non-explicitly gendered object-relational account on gender and the gender-infused relations of parenting and heterosexual intimacy. As a result, some of my writings more easily grew to encompass an independent interest in self or subjectivity, as these experiences are and are not so gender-related. [. . .]

For some readers and colleagues, this direct fascination with—what I sometimes consider this experience of being passionately 'hooked on'—psychoanalytic theory may make my more recent writing less powerful as feminist theory, which should in their opinion focus unswervingly on gender domination.[2] My own view, of course, is that such a position is wrong. I continue to locate important experiences and oppressions of gender in emotional and intrapsychic life and in the arena of primary relations. This personal sphere is psychologically, culturally, and socially meaningful, even if we now understand that our cultural legacy conceptualizing such a sphere as separate is historically and structurally inaccurate. I certainly recognize relations of gender and male dominance in the community, the economy, and the state, and I think that feminist politics and analysis in these arenas are extremely important. But I do not agree with the strand of feminist theory that argues that the central arena of gender oppression in the modern period has moved from the family and the personal to the public and social realm.[3] Moreover, it does seem to me that the most heatedly contested gender politics concern what we conceptualize and experience as the personal and familial—abortion, marriage, divorce, the regulation of sexuality, parenting.

I would stress, probably more now than in my earliest writings, the extent to which concerns in the emotional realm, gender related or not, are tied up with (at least our own society's) notions of human fulfillment—selfhood, agency, meaningful relationship, depth and richness of experience, a comfortable centering in our bodies and in our sexuality. Psychoanalysis enables us to understand such experiences particularly well, to recognize their acute intensity and yet to analyze them in their full multilayered complexity. Such concerns are a natural extension of my interests in object-relations theory. [...]

As a psychoanalytic theorist, I part company with most American psychoanalysts in my reliance on object-relations theory and in that I have always seen psychoanalysis as an interpretive and not a medical or scientific enterprise. However, I differ from many academic humanists in seeing psychoanalysis as a social science that is a theoretically grounded but nonetheless empirically infused study of lives. Recently, as I have been training as a psychoanalyst, I have become more concerned than formerly with claims psychoanalysts, both in their traditional identities and as feminists, make about gender. [...] [O]ften what psychoanalysts have to say is narrowly delimited—the little details of how men and women empirically *are*. This is not rich enough or broadsweeping enough, or enough imbued with an understanding of gender as a relation, for the average academic feminist. Even writing by self-defined feminist psychoanalysts sometimes seems too closely focussed on the details of masculinity and femininity, assuming only in a general way that there is something problematic about the larger situation of gender but having no specific analytic categories to invoke to explain or characterize this situation. Reciprocally, the sweeping generalizations of psychoanalytic feminists sometimes seem well beyond utility for the clinical practitioner. I have felt in the middle, and as a result there is often a sense, in the concluding chapters, of someone feeling buffeted around the disciplines, reacting rather than creating.

I have not, in this brief introduction, been able exhaustively to describe contemporary psychoanalytic feminism or to place my ideas within it, and the volume as a whole has the task of documenting and arguing for the psychoanalytic feminist project. In the ten or more years since the major statement I put forth in *Reproduction*, the psychoanalytic–feminist project has proliferated and become more intricate. Psychoanalytic feminism has also become much more institutionalized and has developed a number of pro-ponents (and antagonists) in a variety of academic fields and from a variety of psychoanalytic perspectives. We can now count ourselves, even as we dis-agree, as part of a collaborative and growing project. The essays that follow provide my own contribution to that rich and complex endeavor.

[*Feminism and Psychoanalytic Theory* (Cambridge: Polity Press, 1989), 1–19.]

ALISON JAGGAR

27 Love and Knowledge: Emotion in Feminist Epistemology

Within the Western philosophical tradition, emotions have usually been considered potentially or actually subversive of knowledge.[1] From Plato until the present, with a few notable exceptions, reason rather than emotion has been regarded as the indispensable faculty for acquiring knowledge.[2]

Typically, although again not invariably, the rational has been contrasted with the emotional, and this contrasted pair then often linked with other dichotomies. Not only has reason been contrasted with emotion, but it has also been associated with the mental, the cultural, the universal, the public and the male, whereas emotion has been associated with the irrational, the physical, the natural, the particular, the private and, of course, the female.

Although Western epistemology has tended to give pride of place to reason rather than emotion, it has not always excluded emotion completely from the realm of reason. In the *Phaedrus*, Plato portrayed emotions, such as anger or curiosity, as irrational urges (horses) that must always be controlled by reason (the charioteer). On this model, the emotions were not seen as needing to be totally suppressed, but rather as needing direction by reason: for example, in a genuinely threatening situation, it was thought not only irrational but foolhardy not to be afraid.[3] The split between reason and emotion was not absolute, therefore, for the Greeks. Instead, the emotions were thought of as providing indispensable motive power that needed to be channelled appropriately. Without horses, after all, the skill of the charioteer would be worthless.

The contrast between reason and emotion was sharpened in the seven-teenth century by redefining reason as a purely instrumental faculty. For both the Greeks, and the medieval philosophers, reason had been linked with value in so far as reason provided access to the objective structure or order of reality, seen as simultaneously natural and morally justified. With the rise of modern science, however, the realms of nature and value were separated: nature was stripped of value and reconceptualized as an inanimate mechanism of no intrinsic worth. Values were relocated in human beings, rooted in their preferences and emotional responses. The separation of supposedly natural fact from human value meant that reason, if it were to provide trustworthy insight into reality, had to be uncontaminated by or abstracted from value. Increasingly, therefore, though never universally,[4] reason was reconceptualized as the ability to make valid inferences from premises established elsewhere, the ability to calculate means but not to determine ends. The validity of logical inferences was thought independent of human attitudes and preferences; this was now the sense in which reason was taken to be objective and universal.

The modern redefinition of rationality required a corresponding reconceptualization of emotion. This was achieved by portraying emotions as nonrational and often irrational urges that regularly swept the body, rather as a storm sweeps over the land. The common way of referring to the emotions as the 'passions' emphasized that emotions happened to or were imposed upon an individual, something she suffered rather than something she did.

The epistemology associated with this new ontology rehabilitated sensory perception that, like emotion, typically had been suspected or even discounted by the Western tradition as a reliable source of knowledge. British empiricism, succeeded in the nineteenth century by positivism, took its epistemological task to be the formulation of rules of inference that would guarantee the derivation of certain knowledge from the 'raw data' supposedly given directly to the senses. Empirical testability became accepted as the hallmark of natural science; this, in turn, was viewed as the paradigm of genuine knowledge. Often epistemology was equated with the philosophy of science, and the dominant methodology of positivism prescribed that truly scientific knowledge must be capable of intersubjective verification. Because values and emotions had been defined as variable and idiosyncratic, positivism stipulated that trustworthy knowledge could be established only by methods that neutralized the values and emotions of individual scientists.

Recent approaches to epistemology have challenged some fundamental assumptions of the positivist epistemological model. Contemporary theorists of knowledge have undermined once rigid distinctions between analytic and synthetic statements, between theories and observations and even between facts and values. However, few challenges have been raised thus far to the purported gap between emotion and knowledge. [...]

As we have already seen, Western epistemology has tended to view emotion with suspicion and even hostility. This derogatory Western attitude toward emotion, like the earlier Western contempt for sensory observation, fails to recognize that emotion, like sensory perception, is necessary to human survival. Emotions prompt us to act appropriately, to approach some people and situations and to avoid others, to caress or cuddle, fight or flee. Without emotion, human life would be unthinkable. Moreover, emotions have an intrinsic as well as an instrumental value. Although not all emotions are enjoyable or even justifiable, as we shall see, life without any emotion would be life without any meaning.

[. . .] Several feminist theorists have argued that modern epistemology itself may be viewed as an expression of certain emotions alleged to be especially characteristic of males in certain periods, such as separation anxiety and paranoia[5] or an obsession with control and fear of contamination.[6]

Positivism views values and emotions as alien invaders that must be repelled by a stricter application of the scientific method. If the foregoing claims are correct, however, the scientific method and even its positivist construals themselves incorporate values and emotions. Moreover, such an incorporation seems a necessary feature of all knowledge and conceptions of knowledge. Therefore, rather than repressing emotion in epistemology it is necessary to rethink the relation between knowledge and emotion and construct conceptual models that demonstrate the mutually constitutive rather than oppositional relation between reason and emotion. Far from precluding the possibility of reliable knowledge, emotion as well as value must be shown as necessary to such knowledge. Despite its classical ante-cedents and as in the ideal of disinterested inquiry, the ideal of dispassionate inquiry is an impossible dream, but a dream none the less or perhaps a myth that has exerted enormous influence on Western epistemology. Like all myths, it is a form of ideology that fulfils certain social and political functions.

[. . .] Feminist theorists have pointed out that the Western tradition has not seen everyone as equally emotional. Instead, reason has been associated with members of dominant political, social, and cultural groups and emotion with members of subordinate groups. Prominent among those subordinate groups in our society are people of color, except for supposedly 'inscrutable orientals', and women.[7]

Although the emotionality of women is a familiar cultural stereotype, its grounding is quite shaky. Women appear to be more emotional than men because they, along with some groups of people of color, are permitted and even required to express emotion more openly. In contemporary Western culture, emotionally inexpressive women are suspect as not being real women, whereas men who express their emotions freely are suspected of being homosexual or in some other way deviant from the masculine ideal. Modern Western men, in contrast with Shakespeare's heroes, for instance, are required to present a façade of coolness, lack of excitement, even boredom, to express emotion only rarely and then for relatively trivial events, such as sporting occasions, where the emotions expressed are acknowledged to be dramatized and so are not taken entirely seriously. Thus, women in our society form the main group allowed or even expected to express emotion. A woman may cry in the face of disaster, and a man of color may gesticulate, but a white man merely sets his jaw. [. . .]

The previous section of this paper argued that dispassionate inquiry was a myth. This section has shown that the myth promotes a conception of epistemological justification vindicating the silencing of those, especially women, who are defined culturally as the bearers of emotion and so are perceived as more 'subjective', biased and irrational. In our present social context, therefore, the ideal of the dispassionate investigator is a classist, racist, and especially masculinist myth. [. . .]

The most obvious way in which feminist and other outlaw emotions can help in developing alternatives to prevailing conceptions of reality is by motivating new investigations. This is possible because, as we saw earlier, emotions may be long-term as well as momentary; it makes sense to say that someone continues to be shocked or saddened by a situation, even if she is at the moment laughing heartily. As we have seen already, theoretical investigation is always purposeful, and observation always selective. Feminist emotions provide a political motivation for investigation and so help to determine the selection of problems as well as the method by which they are investigated. Susan Griffin makes the same point when she characterizes feminist theory as following 'a direction determined by pain, and trauma, and compassion and outrage'.[8]

As well as motivating critical research, outlaw emotions may also enable us to perceive the world differently from its portrayal in conventional descriptions. They may provide the first indications that something is wrong with the way alleged facts have been constructed, with accepted understandings of how things are. Conventionally unexpected or inappropriate emotions may precede our conscious recognition that accepted descriptions and justifications often conceal as much as reveal the prevailing state of affairs. Only when we reflect on our initially puzzling irritability, revulsion, anger or fear may we bring to consciousness our 'gut-level' awareness that we are in a situation of coercion, cruelty, injustice or danger. Thus, conventionally inexplicable emotions, particularly though not exclusively those experienced by women, may lead us to make subversive observations that challenge dominant conceptions of the *status quo*. They may help us to realize that what are taken generally to be facts have been constructed in a way that obscures the reality of subordinated people, especially women's reality.

But why should we trust the emotional responses of women and other subordinated groups? How can we determine which outlaw emotions are to be endorsed or encouraged and which rejected? In what sense can we say that some emotional responses are more appropriate than others? [. . .]

Here I appeal to a claim for which I have argued elsewhere: the perspective on reality that is available from the standpoint of the subordinated, which in part at least is the standpoint of women, is a perspective that offers a less partial and distorted and therefore more reliable view.[9] Subordinated people have a kind of epistemological privilege in so far as they have easier access to this standpoint and therefore a better chance of ascertaining the possible beginnings of a society in which all could thrive. For this reason, I would claim that the emotional responses of subordinated people in general, and often of women in particular, are more likely to be appropriate than the emotional responses of the dominant class. That is, they are more likely to incorporate reliable appraisals of situations. [. . .]

The alternative epistemological models that I suggest would display the continuous interaction between how we understand the world and who we are as people. They would show how our emotional responses to the world change as we conceptualize it differently and how our changing emotional responses then stimulate us to new insights. They would demonstrate the need for theory to be self-reflexive, to focus not only on the outer world but also on ourselves and our relation to that world, to examine critically our social location, our actions, our values, our perceptions, and our emotions. The models would also show how feminist and other critical social theories are indispensable psychotherapeutic tools because they provide some insights necessary to a full understanding of our emotional constitution. Thus, the models would explain how the reconstruction of knowledge is inseparable from the reconstruction of ourselves. [. . .]

Finally, the recognition that emotions play a vital part in developing knowledge enlarges our understanding of women's claimed epistemic advantage. We can now see that women's subversive insights owe much to women's outlaw emotions, themselves appropriate responses to the situations of women's subordination. In addition to their propensity to experience outlaw emotions, at least on some level, women are relatively adept at identifying such emotions, in themselves and others, in part because of their social responsibility for caretaking, including emotional nurturance. It is true that women, like all subordinated peoples, especially those who must live in close proximity with their masters, often engage in emotional deception and even self-deception as the price of their survival. Even so, women may be less likely than other subordinated groups to engage in denial or suppression of outlaw emotions. Women's work of emotional nurturance has required them to develop a special acuity in recognizing hidden emotions and in understanding the genesis of those emotions. This emotional acumen can now be recognized as a skill in political analysis and validated as giving women a special advantage both in understanding the mechanisms of domination and in envisioning freer ways to live.

['Love and Knowledge: Emotion in Feminist Epistemology', *Inquiry*, 32 (1989), 151–72]

IRIS YOUNG

28 The Ideal of Impartiality and the Civic Public

A growing body of feminist-inspired moral theory has challenged the paradigm of moral reasoning as defined by the discourse of justice and rights. In this paradigm moral reasoning consists in adopting an impartial and impersonal point of view on a situation, detached from any particular interests at stake, weighing all interests equally, and arriving at a conclusion which conforms to general principles of justice and rights, impartially applied to the case at hand. Critics argue that this paradigm describes not moral reasoning as such, but the specific moral reasoning called for in the impersonal public contexts of law, bureaucracy, and the regulation of economic competition. This 'ethic of rights' corresponds poorly to the social relations typical of family and personal life, whose moral orientation requires not detachment from but engagement in and sympathy with the particular parties in a situation: it requires not principles that apply to all people in the same way, but a nuanced understanding of the particularities of the social context, and the needs particular people have and express within it. Philosophers should recognize that the paradigm of moral reasoning as the impartial application of general principles describes only a restricted field of moral life, and develop moral theories adequate to the private, personal, and informal contexts it ignores.

More recently some feminist theorists have begun to question this opposition between justice and care. The feminist critiques of traditional moral theory retain a distinction between public, impersonal institutional roles in which the ideal of impartiality and formal reason applies, on the one hand, and private, personal relations which have a different moral structure. Instead of retaining this public/private dichotomy, these criticisms of an ethic of rights should lead us to question the ideal of impartiality itself, as an appropriate ideal for any concrete moral context.

I argue that the ideal of impartiality in moral theory expresses a logic of identity that seeks to reduce differences to unity. The stances of detachment and dispassion that supposedly produce impartiality are attained only by abstracting from the particularities of situation, feeling, affiliation, and point of view. These particularities still operate, however, in the actual context of action. Thus the ideal of impartiality generates a dichotomy between universal and particular, public and private, reason and passion. It is, moreover, an impossible ideal, because the particularities of context and affiliation cannot and should not be removed from moral reasoning. Finally, the ideal of impartiality serves ideological functions. It masks the ways in which the particular perspectives of dominant groups claim universality, and helps justify hierarchical decisionmaking structures.

The ideal of impartial moral reason corresponds to the Enlightenment ideal of the public realm of politics as attaining the universality of a general will that leaves difference, particularity, and the body behind in the private realms of family and civil society. [. . .]

Recent feminist analyses of the dichotomy between public and private in modern political theory imply that the ideal of the civic public as impartial and universal is itself suspect. Modern political theorists and politicians proclaimed the impartiality and generality of the public and at the same time quite consciously found it fitting that some persons, namely, women, non-whites, and sometimes those without property, should be excluded from participation in that public. If this was not just a mistake, it suggests that the ideal of the civic public as expressing the general interest, the impartial point of view of reason, itself results in exclusion. By assuming that reason stands opposed to desire, affectivity, and the body, this conception of the civic public excludes bodily and affective aspects of human existence. In practice this assumption forces homogeneity upon the civic public, excluding from the public those individuals and groups that do not fit the model of the rational citizen capable of transcending body and sentiment. This exclusion has a twofold basis: the tendency to oppose reason and desire, and the association of these traits with kinds of persons.

In the social scheme expounded by Rousseau, and Hegel after him, women must be excluded from the public realm of citizenship because they are the caretakers of affectivity, desire, and the body. Allowing appeals to desires and bodily needs to move public debates would undermine public deliberation by fragmenting its unity. Even within the domestic realm, moreover, women must be dominated. Their dangerous, heterogeneous sexuality must be kept chaste and confined to marriage. Enforcing chastity on women will keep each family a separated unity, preventing the chaos and blood mingling that would be produced by illegitimate children. Only then can women be the proper caretakers of men's desire, by tempering its potentially disruptive impulses through moral education. Men's desire for women itself threatens to shatter and disperse the universal rational realm of the public, as well as to disrupt the neat distinction between the public and the private. As guardians of the private realm of need, desire, and affectivity, women must ensure that men's impulses do not remove them from the universality of reason. The moral neatness of the female-tended hearth, moreover, will temper the possessively individual-istic impulses of the particularistic realm of business and commence, which like sexuality constantly threatens to explode the unity of society.

The bourgeois world instituted a moral division of labor between reason and sentiment, identifying masculinity with reason and femininity with sentiment and desire. The sphere of family and personal life is as much a modern creation as the modern realm of state and law, and comes about as part of the same process. The impartiality and rationality of the state depend on containing need and desire in the private realm of the family. The public realm of citizens achieves unity and universality only by defining the civil individual in opposition to the disorder of womanly nature, which embraces feeling, sexuality, birth and death, the attributes that concretely distinguish persons from one another. The universal citizen is disembodied, dispassionate (male) reason. [...]

[...] [T]he ideal of normative reason, moral sense, stands opposed to desire and affectivity. Impartial civilized reason characterizes the virtue of the republican man who rises above passion and desire. Instead of cutting bourgeois man entirely off from the body and affectivity, however, the culture of the rational public confines them to the domestic sphere, which also confines women's passions and provides emotional solace to men and children. Indeed, within this domestic realm sentiments can flower, and each individual can recognize and affirm his particularity. Precisely because the virtues of impartiality and universality define the civic public, that public must exclude human particularity. Modern normative reason and its political expression in the idea of the civic public, then, attain unity and coherence through the expulsion and confinement of everything that would threaten to invade the polity with differentiation: the specificity of women's bodies and desire, differences of race and culture, the variability and heterogeneity of needs, the goals and desires of individuals, the ambiguity and changeability of feeling. [...]

Insistence on the ideal of impartiality in the face of its impossibility functions to mask the inevitable partiality of perspective from which moral deliberation actually takes place. The situated assumptions and commitments that derive from particular histories, experiences, and affiliations rush to fill the vacuum created by counterfactual abstraction: but now they are asserted as 'objective' assumptions about human nature or moral psychology. The ideal of impartiality generates a propensity to universalize the particular.

Where social group differences exist, and some groups are privileged while others are oppressed, this propensity to universalize the particular reinforces that oppression. The standpoint of the privileged, their particular experience and standards, is constructed as normal and neutral. If some groups experience differs from this neutral experience, or they do not measure up to those standards, their difference is constructed as deviance and inferiority. Not only are the experience and values of the oppressed thereby ignored and silenced, but they become disadvantaged by their situated identities. It is not necessary for the privileged to be selfishly pursuing their own interests at the expense of others to make this situation unjust. Their partial manner of constructing the needs and interests of others, or of unintentionally ignoring them, suffices. If oppressed groups challenge the alleged neutrality of prevailing assumptions and policies and express their own experience and perspectives, their claims are heard as those of biased, selfish special interests that deviate from the impartial general interest. Commitment to an ideal of impartiality thus makes it difficult to expose the partiality of the supposedly general standpoint, and to claim a voice for the oppressed.

The ideal of impartiality legitimates hierarchical decisionmaking and allows the standpoint of the privileged to appear as universal. The combination of these functions often leads to concrete decisions that perpetuate the oppression and disadvantage of some groups and the privilege of others. Positions of decisionmaking authority are usually occupied by members of privileged groups—white Anglo nominally heterosexual men—for access to such positions is part of their privilege. Based on assumptions and standards they claim as neutral and impartial, their authoritative decisions often silence, ignore, and render deviant the abilities, needs, and norms of others. The remedy for the domination and oppression that ensues is to dismantle the hierarchy. If normative reason is dialogic, just norms are most likely to arise from the real interaction of people with different points of view who are drawn out of themselves by being forced to confront and listen to others. Just decisionmaking structures must thus be democratic, ensuring a voice and vote to all the particular groups involved in and affected by the decisions.

If we give up the ideal of impartiality, there remains no moral justification for undemocratic processes of decisionmaking concerning collective action. Instead of a fictional contract, we require real participatory structures in which actual people, with their geographical, ethnic, gender, and occupational differences, assert their perspectives on social issues within institutions that encourage the representation of their distinct voices. Theoretical discussion of justice, then, requires theoretical discussion of participatory democracy. As Carole Pateman (1986) points out, however, many contemporary theorists of participatory democracy are no less committed to the ideal of the civic public than their classical forebears.[1]

This ideal of the civic public, I have argued, excludes women and other groups defined as different, because its rational and universal status derives only from its opposition to affectivity, particularity, and the body. Republican theorists insisted on the unity of the civic public: insofar as he is a citizen every man leaves behind his particularity and difference, to adopt a universal standpoint identical for all citizens, the standpoint of the common good or general will. In practice republican politicians enforced homogeneity by excluding from citizenship all those defined as different, and associated with the body, desire, or need influences that might veer citizens away from the standpoint of pure reason. [. . .]

The repoliticization of public life does not require the creation of a unified public realm in which citizens leave behind their particular group affiliations, histories, and needs to discuss a mythical 'common good'. In a society differentiated by social groups, occupations, political positions, differences of privilege and oppression, regions, and so on, the perception of anything like a common good can only be an outcome of public interaction that expresses rather than submerges particularities. Those seeking the democratization of politics in our society, in my view, should reconceptualize the meaning of public and private and their relation, to break decisively with the tradition of Enlightenment republicanism. While there are good theoretical and practical reasons to maintain a distinction between public and private, this distinction should not be constructed as a hierarchical opposition corresponding to opposition between reason and feeling, masculine and feminine, universal and particular. [. . .]

Instead of defining the private as what the public excludes, I suggest, the private should be defined, as in one strain of liberal theory, as that aspect of his or her life and activity that any person has a right to exclude others from. The private in this sense is not what public institutions exclude, but what the individual chooses to withdraw from public view. With the growth of both state and nonstate bureaucracies, the protection of privacy has become a burning public issue. In welfare capitalist society, the defense of personal privacy has become not merely a matter of keeping the state out of certain affairs, but of calling for positive state regulation to ensure that both its own agencies and nonstate organizations, such as corporations, respect the claims of individuals to privacy.

This manner of formulating the concepts of public and private, which is inspired by feminist confrontations with traditional political theory, does not deny their distinction. It does deny, however, a social division between public and private spheres, each with different kinds of institutions, activities, and human attributes. The concept of a heterogeneous public implies two political principles: (a) no persons, actions, or aspects of a person's life should be forced into privacy; and (b) no social institutions or practices should be excluded a priori from being a proper subject for public discussion and expression. [. . .]

[. . .] Challenging the traditional opposition between public and private that aligns it with oppositions between universality and particularity, reason and affectivity, implies challenging a conception of justice that opposes it to care. A theory that limits justice to formal and universal principles that define a context in which each person can pursue her or his personal ends without hindering the ability of others to pursue theirs entails not merely too limited a conception of social life, but too limited a conception of justice.

['The Ideal of Impartiality and the Civic Public', in *Justice and the Politics of Difference* (Princeton: Princeton University Press, 1990), 96–121; some of the material in this chapter originally appeared as 'Impartiality and the Civic Public: Some Implications of Feminist Critiques of Moral and Political Theory', in Seyla Benhabib and Drucilla Cornell (eds.), *Feminism as Critique* (Polity Press and University of Minnesota Press, 1987).]

PATRICIA HILL COLLINS

29 Toward an Afrocentric Feminist Epistemology

Black feminist thought, like all specialized thought, reflects the interests and standpoint of its creators. Tracing the origin and diffusion of any body of specialized thought reveals its affinity to the power of the group that created it. Because elite white men and their representatives control structures of knowledge validation, white male interests pervade the thematic content of traditional scholarship. As a result, Black women's experiences with work, family, motherhood, political activism, and sexual politics have been routinely distorted in or excluded from traditional academic discourse.

Black feminist thought as specialized thought reflects the thematic content of African-American women's experiences. But because Black women have had to struggle against white male interpretations of the world in order to express a self-defined standpoint, Black feminist thought can best be viewed as subjugated knowledge. The suppression of Black women's efforts for self-definition in traditional sites of knowledge production has led African-American women to use alternative sites such as music, literature, daily conversations, and everyday behavior as important locations for articulating the core themes of a Black feminist consciousness.

Investigating the subjugated knowledge of subordinate groups—in this case a Black women's standpoint and Black feminist thought—requires more ingenuity than that needed to examine the standpoints and thought of dominant groups. I found my training as a social scientist inadequate to the task of studying the subjugated knowledge of a Black women's standpoint. This is because subordinate groups have long had to use alternative ways to create independent self-definitions and self-valuations and to rearticulate them through our own specialists. Like other subordinate groups, African-American women have not only developed a distinctive Black women's standpoint, but have done so by using alternative ways of producing and validating knowledge.

Epistemology is the study of the philosophical problems in concepts of knowledge and truth. The techniques I use in this volume to rearticulate a

Black women's standpoint and to further Black feminist thought may appear to violate some of the basic epistemological assumptions of my training as a social scientist. In choosing the core themes in Black feminist thought that merited investigation, I consulted established bodies of academic research. But I also searched my own experiences and those of African-American women I know for themes we thought were important. My use of language signals a different relationship to my material than that which currently prevails in social science literature. For example, I often use the pronoun 'our' instead of 'their' when referring to African-American women, a choice that embeds me in the group I am studying instead of distancing me from it. In addition, I occasionally place my own concrete experiences in the text. To support my analysis, I cite few statistics and instead rely on the voices of Black women from all walks of life. These conscious epistemological choices signal my attempts not only to explore the thematic content of Black feminist thought but to do so in a way that does not violate its basic epistemological framework.

One key epistemological concern facing Black women intellectuals is the question of what constitutes adequate justifications that a given knowledge claim, such as a fact or theory, is true. In producing the specialized knowledge of Black feminist thought, Black women intellectuals often encounter two distinct epistemologies: one representing elite white male interests and the other expressing Afrocentric feminist concerns. Epistemological choices about who to trust, what to believe, and why something is true are not benign academic issues. Instead, these concerns tap the fundamental question of which versions of truth will prevail and shape thought and action. [...]

Africanist analyses of the Black experience generally agree on the fundamental elements of an Afrocentric standpoint. Despite varying histories, Black societies reflect elements of a core African value system that existed prior to and independently of racial oppression.[1] Moreover, as a result of colonialism, imperialism, slavery, apartheid, and other systems of racial domination, Black people share a common experience of oppression. These two factors foster shared Afrocentric values that permeate the family structure, religious institutions, culture, and community life of Blacks in varying parts of Africa, the Caribbean, South America, and North America.[2] This Afrocentric consciousness permeates the shared history of people of African descent through the framework of a distinctive Afrocentric epistemology.

Feminist scholars advance a similar argument by asserting that women share a history of gender oppression, primarily through sex/gender hierarchies. These experiences transcend divisions among women created by race, social class, religion, sexual orientation, and ethnicity and form the basis of a women's standpoint with a corresponding feminist consciousness and epistemology.[3]

Because Black women have access to both the Afrocentric and the feminist standpoints, an alternative epistemology used to rearticulate a Black women's standpoint should reflect elements of both traditions. The search for the distinguishing features of an alternative epistemology used by African-American women reveals that values and ideas Africanist scholars identify as characteristically 'Black' often bear remarkable resemblance to similar ideas claimed by feminist scholars as characteristically 'female'. This similarity suggests that the material conditions of race, class, and gender oppression can vary dramatically and yet generate some uniformity in the epistemologies of subordinate groups. Thus the significance of an Afrocentric feminist epistemology may lie in how such an epistemology enriches our understanding of how subordinate groups create knowledge that fosters resistance.

The parallels between the two conceptual schemes raise a question: Is the worldview of women of African descent more intensely infused with the overlapping feminine/Afrocentric standpoints than is the case for either African-American men or white women? While an Afrocentric feminist epistemology reflects elements of epistemologies used by African-Americans and women as groups, it also paradoxically demonstrates features that may be unique to Black women. On certain dimensions Black women may more closely resemble Black men; on others, white women; and on still others Black women may stand apart from both groups. Black women's both/and conceptual orientation, the act of being simultaneously a member of a group and yet standing apart from it, forms an integral part of Black women's consciousness. Black women negotiate these contradictions by using this both/and conceptual orientation.[4]

Rather than emphasizing how a Black women's standpoint and its accompanying epistemology are different from those in Afrocentric and feminist analyses, I use Black women's experiences to examine points of contact between the two. Viewing an Afrocentric feminist epistemology in this way challenges additive analyses of oppression claiming that Black women have a more accurate view of oppression than do other groups. Such approaches suggest that oppression can be quantified and compared and that adding layers of oppression produces a potentially clearer standpoint. One implication of standpoint approaches is that the more subordinated the group, the purer the vision of the oppressed group. This is an outcome of the origins of standpoint approaches in Marxist social theory, itself an analysis of social structure rooted in Western either/or dichotomous thinking. Ironically, by quantifying and ranking human oppressions, standpoint theorists invoke criteria for methodological adequacy characteristic of positivism. Although it is tempting to claim that Black women are more oppressed than everyone else and therefore have the best standpoint from which to understand the mechanisms, processes, and effects of oppression, this simply may not be the case.

Like a Black women's standpoint, an Afrocentric feminist epistemology is rooted in the everyday experiences of African-American women. In spite of diversity that exists among women, what are the dimensions of an Afrocentric feminist epistemology?

'My aunt used to say, "A heap see, but a few know" ', remembers Carolyn Chase, a 31-year-old inner-city Black woman.[5] This saying depicts two types of knowing—knowledge and wisdom—and taps the first dimension of an Afrocentric feminist epistemology. Living life as Black women requires wisdom because knowledge about the dynamics of race, gender, and class oppression has been essential to Black women's survival. African-American women give such wisdom high credence in assessing knowledge.

Allusions to these two types of knowing pervade the words of a range of African-American women. Zilpha Elaw, a preacher of the mid-1800s, explains the tenacity of racism: 'The pride of a white skin is a bauble of great value with many in some parts of the United States, who readily sacrifice their intelligence to their prejudices, and possess more knowledge than wisdom'.[6] In describing differences separating African-American and white women, Nancy White invokes a similar rule: 'When you come right down to it, white women just *think* they are free. Black women *know* they ain't free.'[7] Mabel Lincoln eloquently summarizes the distinction between knowledge and wisdom: 'To black people like me, a fool is funny—you know, people who love to break bad, people you can't tell anything to, folks that would take a shotgun to a roach.'[8]

African-American women need wisdom to know how to deal with the 'educated fools' who would 'take a shotgun to a roach'. As members of a subordinate group, Black women cannot afford to be fools of any type, for our objectification as the Other denies us the protections that white skin, maleness, and wealth confer. This distinction between knowledge and wisdom, and the use of experience as the cutting edge dividing them, has been key to Black women's survival. In the context of race, gender, and class oppression, the distinction is essential. Knowledge without wisdom is adequate for the powerful, but wisdom is essential to the survival of the subordinate.

For most African-American women those individuals who have lived through the experiences about which they claim to be experts are more believable and credible than those who have merely read or thought about such experiences. Thus concrete experience as a criterion for credibility frequently is invoked by Black women when making knowledge claims. For instance, Hannah Nelson describes the importance personal experience has for her: 'Our speech is most directly personal, and every black person assumes that every other black person has a right to a personal opinion. In speaking of grave matters, your personal experience is considered very good evidence.

With us, distant statistics are certainly not as important as the actual experience of a sober person.'⁹ Similarly, Ruth Shays uses her concrete experiences to challenge the idea that formal education is the only route to knowledge: 'I am the kind of person who doesn't have a lot of education, but both my mother and my father had good common sense. Now, I think that's all you need. I might not know how to use thirty-four words where three would do, but that does not mean that I don't know what I'm talking about. . . . I know what I'm talking about because I'm talking about myself. I'm talking about what I have lived.'¹⁰ Implicit in Ms. Shays's self-assessment is a critique of the type of knowledge that obscures the truth, the 'thirty-four words' that cover up a truth that can be expressed in three. [. . .]

In valuing the concrete, African-American women invoke not only an Afrocentric tradition but a women's tradition as well. Some feminist theorists suggest that women are socialized in complex relational nexuses where contextual rules versus abstract principles govern behavior.¹¹ This socialization process is thought to stimulate characteristic ways of knowing.¹² These theorists suggest that women are more likely to experience two modes of knowing: one located in the body and the space it occupies and the other passing beyond it. Through their child-rearing and nurturing activities, women mediate these two modes and use the concrete experiences of their daily lives to assess more abstract knowledge claims.

Although valuing the concrete may be more representative of women than men, social class differences among women may generate differential expression of this women's value. One study of working-class women's ways of knowing found that both white and African-American women rely on common sense and intuition.¹³ These forms of knowledge allow for subjectivity between the knower and the known, rest in the women themselves (not in higher authorities), and are experienced directly in the world (not through abstractions). [. . .]

'Dialogue implies talk between two subjects, not the speech of subject and object. It is a humanizing speech, one that challenges and resists domination', asserts bell hooks.¹⁴ For Black women new knowledge claims are rarely worked out in isolation from other individuals and are usually developed through dialogues with other members of a community. A primary epistemological assumption underlying the use of dialogue in assessing knowledge claims is that connectedness rather than separation is an essential component of the knowledge validation process.¹⁵

This belief in connectedness and the use of dialogue as one of its criteria for methodological adequacy has Afrocentric roots. In contrast to Western, either/or dichotomous thought, the traditional African worldview is holistic and seeks harmony. 'One must understand that to become human, to realize the promise of becoming human, is the only important task of the person', posits Molefi Asante. People become more human and empowered only in the context of a community, and only when they 'become seekers of the type of connections, interactions, and meetings that lead to harmony'.[16] The power of the word generally and dialogues specifically, allows this to happen.

Not to be confused with adversarial debate, the use of dialogue has deep roots in an African-based oral tradition and in African-American culture. [...]

The widespread use of the call-and-response discourse mode among African-Americans illustrates the importance placed on dialogue. Composed of spontaneous verbal and nonverbal interaction between speaker and listener in which all of the speaker's statements, or 'calls', are punctuated by expressions, or 'responses', from the listener, this Black discourse mode pervades African-American culture. The fundamental requirement of this interactive network is active participation of all individuals.[17] For ideas to be tested and validated, everyone in the group must participate. To refuse to join in, especially if one really disagrees with what has been said, is seen as 'cheating'.[18]

June Jordan's analysis of Black English points to the significance of this dimension of an alternative epistemology:

Our language is a system constructed by people constantly needing to insist that we exist.... Our language devolves from a culture that abhors all abstraction, or anything tending to obscure or delete the fact of the human being who is here and now/the truth of the person who is speaking or listening. Consequently, *there is no passive voice construction possible in Black English.* For example, you cannot say, 'Black English is being eliminated.' You must say, instead, 'White people eliminating Black English.' The assumption of the presence of life governs all of Black English ... every sentence assumes the living and active participation of at least two human beings, the speaker and the listener.[19]

Black women's centrality in families and community organizations provides African-American women with a high degree of support for invoking dialogue as a dimension of an Afrocentric feminist epistemology. However, when African-American women use dialogues in assessing knowledge claims, we might be invoking a particularly female way of knowing as well. Feminist scholars contend that men and women are socialized to seek different types of autonomy—the former based on separation, the latter seeking connectedness—and that this variation in types of autonomy parallels the characteristic differences between male and female ways of knowing. For instance, in contrast to the visual metaphors (such as equating knowledge with illumination, knowing with seeing, and truth with light) that scientists and philosophers typically use, women tend to ground their epistemological premises in metaphors suggesting finding a voice, speaking, and listening. The words of the Black woman who struggled for her education at Medgar Evers College resonate with the importance placed on voice: 'I was basically a shy and reserved person prior to the struggle at Medgar, but I found my voice—and I used it! Now, I will never lose my voice again!'[20]

While significant differences exist between Black women's family experiences and those of middle-class white women, African-American women clearly are affected by general cultural norms prescribing certain familial roles for women. Thus in terms of the role of dialogue in an Afrocentric feminist epistemology, Black women may again experience a convergence of the values of the African-American community and women's experiences.

'Ole white preachers used to talk wid dey tongues widdout sayin' nothin', but Jesus told us slaves to talk wid our hearts'.[21] These words of an ex-slave suggest that ideas cannot be divorced from the individuals who create and share them. This theme of talking with the heart taps the ethic of caring, another dimension of an alternative epistemology used by African-American women. Just as the ex-slave used the wisdom in his heart to reject the ideas of the preachers who talked 'wid dey tongues widdout sayin' nothin'', the ethic of caring suggests that personal expressiveness, emotions, and empathy are central to the knowledge validation process.

One of three interrelated components comprising the ethic of caring is the emphasis placed on individual uniqueness. Rooted in a tradition of African humanism, each individual is thought to be a unique expression of a common spirit, power, or energy inherent in all life. When Alice Walker 'never doubted her powers of judgment because her mother assumed they were sound', she invokes the sense of individual uniqueness taught to her by her mother.[22] The polyrhythms in African-American music, in which no one main beat subordinates the others, is paralleled by the theme of individual expression in Black women's quilting. Black women quilters place strong color and patterns next to one another and see the individual differences not as detracting from each piece but as enriching the whole quilt. This belief in individual uniqueness is illustrated by the value placed on personal expressiveness in African-American communities. Johnetta Ray, an inner-city resident, describes this Afrocentric emphasis on individual uniqueness: 'No matter how hard we try, I don't think black people will ever develop much of a herd instinct. We are profound individualists with a passion for self-expression'.[23]

A second component of the ethic of caring concerns the appropriateness of emotions in dialogues. Emotion indicates that a speaker believes in the validity of an argument. Consider Ntozake Shange's description of one of the goals of her work: 'Our [Western] society allows people to be absolutely neurotic and totally out of touch with their feelings and everyone else's feelings, and yet be very respectable. This, to me, is a travesty. . . . I'm trying to change the idea of seeing emotions and intellect as distinct faculties.'[24] The Black women's blues tradition's history of personal expressiveness heals this either/or dichotomous rift separating emotion and intellect. For example, in her rendition of 'Strange Fruit', Billie Holiday's lyrics blend seamlessly with the emotion of her delivery to render a trenchant social commentary on southern lynching. Without emotion, Aretha Franklin's (1967) cry for 'respect' would be virtually meaningless.

A third component of the ethic of caring involves developing the capacity for empathy. Harriet Jones, a 16-year-old Black woman, explains to her interviewer why she chose to open up to him: 'Some things in my life are so hard for me to bear, and it makes me feel better to know that you feel sorry about those things and would change them if you could'.[25] Without her belief in his empathy, she found it difficult to talk. Black women writers often explore the growth of empathy as part of an ethic of caring. [. . .]

These components of the ethic of caring—the value placed on individual expressiveness, the appropriateness of emotions, and the capacity for empathy—pervade African-American culture. [. . .]

An ethic of personal accountability is the final dimension of an alternative epistemology. Not only must individuals develop their knowledge claims through dialogue and present them in a style proving their concern for their ideas, but people are expected to be accountable for their knowledge claims. Zilpha Elaw's description of slavery reflects this notion that every idea has an owner and that the owner's identity matters: 'Oh, the abominations of slavery! . . . Every case of slavery, however lenient its inflictions and mitigated its atrocities, indicates an oppressor, the oppressed, and oppression'[26]. For Elaw abstract definitions of slavery mesh with the concrete identities of its perpetrators and its victims. African-Americans consider it essential for individuals to have personal positions on issues and assume full responsibility for arguing their validity.

Assessments of an individual's knowledge claims simultaneously evaluate an individual's character, values, and ethics. African-Americans reject the Eurocentric, masculinist belief that probing into an individual's personal viewpoint is outside the boundaries of discussion. Rather, all views expressed and actions taken are thought to derive from a central set of core beliefs that cannot be other than personal.[27] 'Does Aretha really *believe* that Black women should get "respect", or is she just mouthing the words?' is a valid question in an Afrocentric feminist epistemology. Knowledge claims made by individuals respected for their moral and ethical connections to their ideas will carry more weight than those offered by less respected figures. [. . .]

Alternative knowledge claims in and of themselves are rarely threatening to conventional knowledge. Such claims are routinely ignored, discredited, or simply absorbed and marginalized in existing paradigms. Much more threatening is the challenge that alternative epistemologies offer to the basic process used by the powerful to legitimate their knowledge claims. If the epistemology used to validate knowledge comes into question, then all prior knowledge claims validated under the dominant model become suspect. An alternative epistemology challenges all certified knowledge and opens up the question of whether what has been taken to be true can stand the test of alternative ways of validating truth. The existence of a self-defined Black women's standpoint using an Afrocentric feminist epistemology calls into question the content of what currently passes as truth and simultaneously challenges the process of arriving at that truth.

['Toward an Afrocentric Feminist Epistemology', in *Black Feminist Thought: Knowledge, Consciousness, and the Politics of Empowerment* (London and New York: Routledge, 1991), 201–19.]

PATRICIA WAUGH

30 Modernism, Postmodernism, Gender: The View from Feminism

The discourses of feminism clearly arise out of and are made possible by those of Enlightened modernity and its models of reason, justice and autonomous subjectivity as universal categories. Feminist discourses, however, have been powerful forces in exposing some of the most entrenched and disguised contradictions and limitations of Enlightenment thought. Simply in articulating issues of sexual difference, the very existence of feminist discourses weakens the rootedness of Enlightenment thought in the principle of sameness; it exposes the ways in which this 'universal' principle is contradicted by Enlightenment's construction of a public/private split which consigns women to the 'private' realm of feeling, domesticity, the body, in order to clarify a public realm of Reason as masculine. In this sense at least, feminism can be seen to be an intrinsically 'postmodern' discourse. Until very recently, however, debates within feminism have tended to be ignored within discussions of Postmodernism and vice versa. Things have begun to change. Feminist theory has developed a self-conscious awareness of its own hermeneutic perspectivism based on the recognition of a central contradiction in its attempts to define an epistemology: that women seek equality and recognition of a gendered identity which has been constructed through the very culture and ideological formations which feminism seeks to challenge and dismantle. Awareness of such contradictions, in fact, start to emerge as early as 1971 with the publication by Kristeva of the essay 'Women's Time'.[1] The concept of a 'woman's identity' functions in terms both of affirmation and negation, even within feminism itself. There can be no simple legitimation for feminists in throwing off 'false consciousness' and revealing a true but 'deeply' buried female self. Indeed, to embrace the essentialism of this notion of 'difference' is to come dangerously close to reproducing that very patriarchal construction of gender which feminists have set out to contest as *their* basic project of modernity.

Feminism of late, therefore, has developed a self-reflexive mode: questioning its own legitimating procedures in a manner which seems to bring it close to a Postmodernism which has absorbed the lessons of post-structuralism and consists at the most general level of a crisis of legitimation across culture, politics and aesthetic theory and practice. The slogan 'Let us wage war against totality', however, could be seen as Postmodernism's response to that earlier slogan of the feminist movement, 'the personal is political'. But if the latter can be seen as a rallying cry, the former implies a hostile attitude towards its implicit ideals of collectivism and community. The feminist cry situated its politics firmly within what Lyotard wishes to denounce and Habermas to affirm in modified form as the 'project of modernity'. In fact, at this point in my argument, I will have tó declare my own situatedness and argue that if feminism can learn from Postmodernism it has finally to resist the logic of its arguments or at least to attempt to combine them with a modified adherence to an epistemological anchorage in the discourses of Enlightened modernity. Even if feminists have come to recognise in their own articulations some of the radical perspectivism and thoroughgoing epistemological doubt of the postmodern, feminism cannot sustain itself as an emancipatory movement unless it acknowledges its foundation in the discourses of modernity. It seems to me, however, it is possible to draw on the aesthetics of Postmodernism as strategies for narrative disruption of traditional stories and construction of new identity scripts, without embracing its more extreme nihilistic or pragmatist implications. Surely to assume otherwise is in itself to embrace a naively reflectionist aesthetic which sees representation as necessarily reflective of prior structures or ideologies. A number of questions arise out of this: can feminism remain opposed to Postmodernism's circular tendency to project itself onto the contemporary world and thus, not surprisingly, to find in that world an affirmation of its own theoretical presuppositions? Can it resist the implicitly religious vocabulary of apocalypse while acknowledging the force of its critique of Enlightenment epistemology as rooted in the instrumental domination of inert object (body, world, nature, woman), by a detached and transcendent subject (mind, self, science, man).

These issues can usefully be approached, it seems to me, through further consideration of that central Enlightenment concept, autonomy, and its role in the construction of various models of subjectivity. What the preceding discussion has suggested is that the epistemological and ethical contradictions now confronting postmodernists and feminists are fundamentally issues about identity and difference. Subjective transformation has been central to feminist agendas for political change. Similarly, over the last thirty years, the deconstruction of liberal individualism and the dissolution of traditional aesthetic conceptualisations of character have been central to postmodern art and theory. Like feminism, Postmodernism (in theoretical and artistic modes), has been engaged in a re-examination of the Enlightenment concepts of subjectivity as autonomous self-determination; the human individual as defined without reference to history, traditional values, God, nation. Both have assaulted aesthetic or philosophical notions of identity as pure autonomous essence. Ethical and epistemological contradictions have crowded onto the modern scene. [. . .]

One hears much in Postmodernism about the subject as myth and the notion that the master narratives of history are redundant illusions. Yet, I often have the feeling, as I read postmodernist writing, that its apocalyptic nihilism about the possibility of ethical and imaginative subjective existence is still grounded in a nostalgia for the ideal autonomous self as presented in Enlightenment thought. Nostalgia rewrites history in the terms of desire. In the case of apocalyptic postmodernism, it may be that its schizophrenic fragmentation is a response to a continuing obsession with an impossible ideal. Postmodernism, in this mode, may itself have rigidified autonomy into an absolute identity. Autonomy has been a powerful concept in philosophical and aesthetic writing, but even as they ascribe to the theory most people know it cannot be lived absolutely in this ideal form. Certainly, few women have attempted to live it, because women have been more or less excluded from its applications. They have developed alternative models of self-identity. A problem for feminists in relating to Postmodernism, is that they are highly unlikely to bear this sort of relationship to history or to the ideal autonomous self central to the discourses of modernity. Those who have been systematically excluded from the constitution of that so-called universal subject— whether for reasons of gender, class, race, sexuality—are unlikely either to long nostalgically for what they have never experienced or possessed (even as an illusion) or to revel angrily or in celebratory fashion in the 'jouissance' of its disintegration. To recognise the limitations of an ideal which was never one's own is to bear a very different relationship to its perceived loss.

The decentred and fragmented subject of the 'postmodern condition' is one which has been created, at least in part, by Postmodernism itself. It is in part the consequence of an inability to rethink a self not premised in some way on the pure idealism of the autonomous subject of Enlightenment thought, German Idealist philosophy and Kantian aesthetics. It is present in much postmodern writing at least as a structure of feeling. Recent feminist scholarship has shown why women are unlikely to have experienced history in this form. For feminists, therefore, the goals of agency, personal autonomy, self-expression and self-determination, can neither be taken for granted nor written off as exhausted. They are ideals which feminism has helped to reformulate, modify and challenge. Feminism needs coherent subjects and has found a variety of ways of articulating them which avoid the fetishisation of Pure Reason as the locus of subjecthood and the irrationalism born out of the perceived failure of this ideal. [...]

I want to suggest, somewhat tentatively, that despite differences in the theoretical construction of modernity and postmodernity, common to them both is the inheritance of a particular ideal of subjectivity defined in terms of transcendence and pure rationality. Postmodernism can be seen as a response to the perceived failure of this ideal. This notion of subjectivity, whether expressed through Descartes' rational 'I' and refined into Kant's categorical imperatives, or through Nietzsche's 'übermensch' or Lacan's phallogocentric symbolic order, has not only excluded women but has made their exclusion on the grounds of emotionality, failure of abstract intellect or whatever, the basis of its own identity. This position has been reproduced across philosophy, psychoanalysis and literature. In viewing this situation as fundamentally unchanged, I am, in effect, repudiating the postmodern notion that there are no longer any generally legitimated metanarratives. What I am saying is that patriarchal metanarratives function just as effectively within our so-called 'postmodern age' as in any other age and in its metaphorical play on notions of the feminine they continue insidiously to function powerfully within postmodern theory itself. [...]

In my view it is the identification of self with an impossible ideal of autonomy which can be seen to produce the failure of love and relationship in so many texts by male modernist and postmodernist writers. Can one rethink the self outside of this concept without abandoning subjectivity to dispersal and language games? Not only do I believe that one can, I also believe that many feminist writers have done so. This is the really 'grand and totalising' part of my argument. It seems to me that autonomy defined as transcendence, impersonality and absolute independence, whether an idealised goal or a nostalgic nihilism, whether informing the aesthetics of Modernism or those of Postmodernism, is not a mode with which most feminists, nor indeed, most women, can very easily identify. Feminist theory, though drawing on anti-humanist discourses to sharpen its understanding of social processes, has emphasised that 'impersonal' historical determinants are lived out through experience. This distance from anti-humanist discourse has allowed feminist academics to connect with grass roots activists outside the academy. Their own historical experience has tended to develop in women strongly 'humanist' qualities in the broader sense of the term and feminism has always been rooted in women's subjective experience of the conflicting demands of home and work, family and domestic ties and the wider society.

[...] According to most psychoanalytic theories and their popularly disseminated forms, subjecthood is understood as the achievement of separation. Maturity is seen to be reached when the dependent infant comes to regard its primary caretaker (nearly always a woman) as simply an object through which it defines its own identity and position in the world. This is then maintained through the defensive patrolling of boundaries. Implicit then in most theories of identity is the assumption that the 'otherness' analysed by feminists from de Beauvoir on, is the necessary condition of women— certainly as long as women mother. Separation and objectivity rather than relationship and connection become the markers of identity. Freudian theory has been used to support this view. Both the liberal self and the postmodern 'decentred subject' can be articulated through Freud's notion of the unconscious, dominated by instinctual and universal drives seeking impossible gratification. In the liberal version, ego as rationality can master the drives either intrapsychically or with the help of the silent, impersonal and objective analyst who will be uncontaminated by countertransference. In the postmodern version, rationality breaks down and the anarchy of desire as impersonal and unconscious energy is unleashed either in the freeplay of the signifier of the avant-garde text or that of the marketplace of Late Capitalism. Freud's infant hovers behind both: an autoerotic isolate, inherently aggressive and competitive, its sexuality and identity oedipally resolved only by fear, seeking to discharge libidinal energy which is necessarily in conflict with 'rational' and 'enlightened' concern for others and for society as a whole.

Can we imagine alternative models of subjectivity? If knowledge is inextricably bound up with experience then it seems that we certainly can, for this is not a description of universal experience. In fact Freud himself hints at other possibilities in less familiar parts of his writings. In the paper 'On Narcissism', for example, he says: 'A strong egotism is a protection against falling ill, but in the last resort we must begin to love in order not to fall ill and we are bound to fall ill if in consequence of frustration, we are unable to love' (1914: 85).[2] In fact, in the development of selfhood, the ability to conceive of oneself as separate from and mutually independent with the parent develops with the ability to accept one's dependency and to feel secure enough to relax the boundaries between self and other without feeling one's identity to be threatened. Why, then, is autonomy always emphasised as the goal of maturity? Why not emphasise equally the importance of maintaining connection and intersubjectivity? As Joan Rivière has argued 'There is no such thing as a single human being pure and simple, unmixed with other human beings . . . we are members one of another.'[3] Parts of other people, the parts we have had relationships with, are parts of us, so the self is both constant and fluid, ever in exchange, ever redescribing itself through its encounters with others. It seems to be this recognition of mediation as that which renders total self-determination impossible which so many male modernist and postmodernist writers find unacceptable. Yet much women's, particularly feminist, writing has been different in that it has neither attempted to transcend relationship through the impersonal embrace of Art

as formal autonomy or sacred space nor through rewriting its own Apocalyptic sense of an ending.

Returning to psychoanalysis, however, one can see some of the reasons
why the definition of subjectivity as transcendence and autonomy has been so
powerful and why it has come to be seen not as a description of the
experience of most white, Western males, but of universal structures of
subjectivity. In psychoanalytic terms, if subjectivity is defined as separateness,
its acquisition will involve radical disidentification with women in a society
where women are normally the exclusive caretakers of children. This will be
true even for girls who, at the level of gender, will also seek to identify with
the mother. Fathers are not perceived as threatening non-identity for in
classical analysis they are seen as outside the pre-oedipal world of primary
socialisation with its intense ambivalences and powerful Imagos. They are
from the start associated with the clear, rational world of work and secondary
socialisation. Object relations theorists like Nancy Chodorow,[4] however, have
pointed out that the desire for radical disidentification with the mother will
be more acute for boys for the perception of women as mothers will be
bound up with pre-oedipal issues of mergence and potential loss of identity
requiring a culturally reinforced masculine investment in denial and separation. The world of secondary socialisation associated with the father comes
to be seen as superior and as inherently male. Subjectivity thus comes to be
seen as autonomy or as role-definition through work. Truth is defined as
objectivity and transcendence. Science in the form of an instrumental technology will be overvalued and defined in terms of objectivity; philosophy
comes to deal only with universal and metaphysical truths (whatever the
theoretical challenges to these notions). Women (or the 'feminine') come to
be identified in Cartesian or post-structuralist philosophy with all that cannot
be rationally controlled and thus threatening dissolution or non-identity:
mortality, the body, desire, emotionality, nature. Post-structuralist 'femininity' is simply another way of making actual femininity safe, of controlling
through a process of naming which in post-structuralist fashion prises the
term utterly away from the anatomical body of woman.

If the female sex thus represents, in Sartre's words 'the obscenity... of
everything which gapes open',[5] then men seem to be justified in their
instrumental attitude to women and to everything, including nature, which
has been 'feminised' and which must therefore be distanced, controlled,
aestheticised, subdued (one might call this the Gilbert Osmond syndrome).
Women appear threatening in this way because they carry the culture's more
widespread fear of loss of boundaries, of the uncontrollable, more threatening because unconsciously split off in order to retain the purity of a subjectivity, a human-ness defined as autonomy, pure reason and transcendence.
Cartesian dualism thus persists along with strict empiricism in science and
impersonality and formalism in literary theory and criticism.

What I have tried to argue here, therefore, is that an examination of alternative feminist models of identity can add a further and important dimension to the debates considered earlier about the construction of Modernism in terms of formal autonomy. The exclusion of gender from postmodern discussions has left its theorists largely blind to the possibilities of challenging autonomy through a relational concept of identity. If women's identity has tended, broadly, and allowing for differences across this, to be experienced in terms which do not necessarily see separation gained only at the expense of connection, one would expect some sense of this to be expressed in discourses other than the theoretical and psychoanalytic. Women's sense of identity is more likely, for psychological and cultural reasons, to consist of a more diffuse sense of the boundaries of self and their notion of identity understood in relational and intersubjective terms. I am certainly not claiming that this is exclusive to women, for clearly gender is a continuum, and there are several theoretical models often invoked in the postmodern debate which articulate a similar sense of identity. [. . .] If ego is the product of culture, as Freud argued, and if ego may only be defined in terms of separateness, impersonality, containment and pure reason, then culture has produced only divided and deformed human beings. Feminist discourses suggest that the dissolution of containment into irrational desire or the dispersal of jouissance are not the only alternatives to a discredited Enlightenment. My hope is that these perspectives may be fairly represented in future accounts of the postmodern debate and the condition of late modernity.

['Modernism, Postmodernism, Gender', in *Practising Postmodernism/Reading Modernism* (London: Edward Arnold, 1992), 119–35.]

SEYLA BENHABIB

31 The Generalized and the Concrete Other

Can there be a feminist contribution to moral philosophy? That is to say, can those men and women who view the gender-sex system of our societies as oppressive, and who regard women's emancipation as essential to human liberation, criticize, analyze and when necessary replace the traditional categories of moral philosophy in order to contribute to women's emancipation and human liberation? By focussing on the controversy generated by Carol Gilligan's work, this chapter seeks to outline such a feminist contribution to moral philosophy.

Carol Gilligan's research in cognitive, developmental moral psychology recapitulates a pattern made familiar to us by Thomas Kuhn.[1] Noting a discrepancy between the claims of the original research paradigm and the data, Gilligan and her co-workers first extend this paradigm to accommodate anomalous results. This extension then allows them to see some other problems in a new light; subsequently, the basic paradigm, namely the study of the development of moral judgment, according to Lawrence Kohlberg's model, is fundamentally revised. Gilligan and her co-workers now maintain that Kohlbergian theory is valid only for measuring the development of one aspect of moral orientation, which focusses on justice and rights. [. . .]

Let me describe two conceptions of self–other relations that delineate both moral perspectives and interactional structures. I shall name the first the standpoint of the 'generalized'[2] and the second that of the 'concrete' other. In contemporary moral theory these conceptions are viewed as incompatible, even as antagonistic. These two perspectives reflect the dichotomies and splits of early modern moral and political theory between autonomy and nurturance, independence and bonding, the public and the domestic, and more broadly, between justice and the good life. The content of the generalized as well as the concrete other is shaped by this dichotomous characterization, which we have inherited from the modern tradition.

The standpoint of the generalized other requires us to view each and every individual as a rational being entitled to the same rights and duties we would want to ascribe to ourselves. In assuming the standpoint, we abstract from the individuality and concrete identity of the other. We assume that the other, like ourselves, is a being who has concrete needs, desires and affects, but that what constitutes his or her moral dignity is not what differentiates us from each other, but rather what we, as speaking and acting rational agents, have in common. Our relation to the other is governed by the norms of *formal equality* and *reciprocity*: each is entitled to expect and to assume from us what we can expect and assume from him or her. The norms of our interactions are primarily public and institutional ones. If I have a right to X, then you have the duty not to hinder me from enjoying X and conversely. In treating you in accordance with these norms, I confirm in your person the rights of humanity and I have a legitimate claim to expect that you will do the same in relation to me. The moral categories that accompany such interactions are those of right, obligation and entitlement, and the corresponding moral feelings are those of respect, duty, worthiness and dignity.

The standpoint of the concrete other, by contrast, requires us to view each and every rational being as an individual with a concrete history, identity and affective-emotional constitution. In assuming this standpoint, we abstract from what constitutes our commonality, and focus on individuality. We seek to comprehend the needs of the other, his or her motivations, what she searches for, and what s/he desires. Our relation to the other is governed by the norms of *equity* and *complementary reciprocity*: each is entitled to expect and to assume from the other forms of behavior through which the other feels recognized and confirmed as a concrete, individual being with specific needs, talents and capacities. Our differences in this case complement rather than exclude one another. The norms of our interaction are usually, although not exclusively private, noninstitutional ones. They are norms of friendship, love and care. These norms require in various ways that I exhibit more than the simple assertion of my rights and duties in the face of your needs. In treating you in accordance with the norms of friendship, love and care, I confirm not only your *humanity* but your human *individuality*. The moral categories that accompany such interactions are those of responsibility, bonding and sharing. The corresponding moral feelings are those of love, care and sympathy and solidarity. [. . .]

The distinction between the generalized and the concrete other raises questions in moral and political theory. It may be asked whether, without the standpoint of the generalized other, it would be possible to define a moral point of view at all. Since our identities as concrete others are what distinguish us from each other according to gender, race, class, cultural differentials, as well as psychic and natural abilities, would a moral theory restricted to the standpoint of the concrete other not be a racist, sexist, cultural relativist and discriminatory one? Furthermore, without the standpoint of the generalized other, a political theory of justice suited for modern, complex societies is unthinkable. Certainly rights must be an essential component of any such theory. Finally, the perspective of the 'concrete other' defines our relations as private, noninstitutional ones, concerned with love, care, friendship and intimacy. Are these activities so gender specific? Are we not all 'concrete others'?

The distinction between the 'generalized' and the 'concrete' other, as drawn in this chapter so far, is not a *prescriptive* but a *critical* one. My goal is not to prescribe a moral or political theory consonant with the standpoint of the concrete other. As I have argued throughout part I, my purpose is to develop a universalistic moral theory that defines the 'moral point of view' in light of the reversibility of perspectives and an 'enlarged mentality'. Such a moral theory allows us to recognize the dignity of the generalized other through an acknowledgement of the moral identity of the concrete other. Substitutionalist universalism dismisses the concrete other behind the facade of a definitional identity of all as rational beings, while interactive universalism acknowledges that every generalized other is also a concrete other. [. . .]

Neither the concreteness nor the otherness of the 'concrete other' can be known in the absence of the *voice* of the other. The viewpoint of the concrete other emerges as a distinct one only as a result of self-definition. It is the other who makes us aware both of her concreteness and her otherness. Without engagement, confrontation, dialogue and even a 'struggle for recognition' in the Hegelian sense, we tend to constitute the otherness of the other by projection and fantasy or ignore it in indifference. I therefore trust much less than Okin (and even Gilligan) the sentiments of empathy and benevolence; for, as Arendt also has noted,[3] the capacity for exercising an 'enlarged mentality', the ability to take the standpoint of the other into account is not empathy although it is related to it. Empathy means the capacity to 'feel with, to feel together'. Yet precisely very empathetic individuals may also be the ones lacking an 'enlarged mentality', for their empathetic nature may make it difficult for them to draw the boundaries between self and other such that the standpoint of the 'concrete other' can emerge. Ironically, I agree here much more with Rawls than with either Okin or Gilligan that 'because the objects of benevolence'—and I would add empathy—oppose one another, one needs principles, institutions and procedures to enable articulation of the voice of 'others'.[4] [. . .]

[I]t is Carol Gilligan's lasting contribution to moral theory and moral psychology that she has made us aware of the implicit models of selfhood, autonomy, impartiality and justice sustained and privileged by such dichotomous reasoning. The ideal of autonomy in universalistic moral theories from the social contract tradition down to Rawls's and Kohlberg's work is based upon an implicit politics which defines the 'personal', in the sense of the intimate/domestic sphere, as ahistorical, immutable and unchanging, thereby removing it from discussion and reflection. Needs, interests, as well as emotions and affects, are then considered properties of individuals which moral philosophy recoils from examining on the grounds that it may interfere with the autonomy of the sovereign self. What Carol Gilligan has heard are those mutterings, protestations and objections voiced by women who were confronted with ways of posing moral dilemmas that seemed alien to them and who were faced with visions of selfhood which left them cold. Only if we can understand why this voice has been so marginalized in moral theory, and how the dominant ideals of moral autonomy in our culture, as well as the privileged definition of the moral sphere, continue to silence women's voices, do we have a hope for moving to a more integrated vision of ourselves and of our fellow humans as generalized as well as 'concrete others'.

[*Situating the Self: Gender, Community and Postmodernism in Contemporary Ethics* (Cambridge: Polity Press, 1992), 148–70.]

Section 3

Subjectivities

INTRODUCTION

> In 'woman' I see something that cannot be represented, something that
> is not said, something above and beyond nomenclatures and ideologies.
>
> Julia Kristeva

The following debate between social constructivist and essentialist theorists
highlights the issues at stake in the invocation of the category of 'woman'.
How do we represent sexual, or social difference, without returning to dual
hierarchicized oppositions? Do new subject positions impact on form—are
we dealing here with metaphor, representation, or some kind of 'real'?

'Ain't I a woman?': Sojourner Truth's insistent question haunts feminist
discourses still. Defying most of the characteristics defined as paradigmatic of
white womanhood in 1851, Black American freed slave Sojourner Truth
asserted her corporeal presence as evidence of her status as woman. Claiming
the name of woman is no less contentious amongst feminists today: 'concentration on and a refusal of the identity of "women" are essential', asserts
Denise Riley over a century later, 'to feminism'. As testament to this claim, all
the pieces in this section explore the tension—central to current feminist
theory—between claiming and refusing an identity as woman. From an
assertion that real concrete women share an essential 'Womanness' which
is to be celebrated and emancipated, to the theoretically sophisticated but—
some fear—politically challenged notion of contingent, fluctuating post-
gendered subjectivities, the issue of subjectivity has become of vital significance to feminist debate.

The problem of trying to capture all the nuances of notions of 'Woman',
'woman', or even 'women' in any categorical grouping has propelled many
feminists away from the empirical quagmire and towards the twin extremes
of transcendence or deconstruction (where women become essence or fiction
respectively). Amidst this debate Denise Riley suggests: 'we could try another
train of speculations: that "women" is indeed an unstable category, that this
instability has a historical foundation, and that feminism is the site of the
systematic fighting-out of that instability' (p. 244). In other words, there is a
productive tension between essentialist, constructivist, and deconstructivist
understandings of gendered subjectivity which has proved to be constitutive
of a field of feminist theory. Taking this as our starting point, we have

compiled in this section those pieces which have most eloquently engaged with this process of fighting the instability.

'How does experience guarantee political authenticity and the ownership of identity?' asks Kadiatu Kanneh. It is perhaps worth initially debunking the presumption that there is a straightforward split in responses to this question between a politically engaged feminism and an academically ensconced one: that any form of political action requires a stable category of women in whose name one speaks and acts, and that only those distanced from such realities might consider deconstructing the very subject of feminism. On reflection it is evident that actions taken in the name of women have always adopted a politically expedient construction of that category (implicitly delimited by other fluctuating identities such as nationality, religion, sexuality, race, wealth, etc.). The more significant division is perhaps—to refer back to the discussion of the previous section—the extent to which one is self-reflexive about these strategies: in other words, whether such identifications and exclusions are made knowingly.

So, whilst feminist perspectives regarding subjectivity are frequently characterized as being either essentialist or social constructivist, in theory and in practice, most feminists are both essentialists and constructionists. Within theoretical debates some have constructed schemas that label liberal, radical, and Marxist feminists as essentialists and post-structuralist feminists as constructionists, but detailed reading reveals much more ambivalent affiliations than this allows. Luce Irigaray, for example, is a post-structuralist who might be considered essentialist, whilst Monique Wittig might be categorized as either radical or Marxist feminist (depending on one's definitional categories) but explicitly endorses social constructivism. Others, such as Gayatri Spivak, have argued for a strategic essentialism for the most effective political stance open to contingent clusters of fluctuating identities.

Although, in steadfastly claiming the title 'working-class lesbian', Liz Stanley indicates her personal and political unease at the self-reflexivity proposed by such an ironic politics—believing it to undermine the achievement of those who have 'gone through much to have named oneself thus and to have recovered something of the history of one's foremothers' (p. 276)— the initial apparent opposition between constructivists and essentialists has surely begun to blur. For, as Diana Fuss argues, 'the deconstruction of essentialism, rather than putting essence to rest, simply raises the discussion to a more sophisticated level...' (p. 257). Despite the apparent gulf and political hostility between radical and postmodern feminists over the question of subjectivity, it could be that the debate is not best formulated as one for or against essential female subjectivity, but rather between authentic and ironic understandings of such identities.

Whether ironic, strategic, or authentic, the notion of essentialism draws our attention to the issue of power. For, as Morag Shiach notes, ' "feminism" is, after all, a political term, an interrogation of power and of the possibility of change, and not just a matter of technique' (p. 270). Who determines what makes a text woman's writings? As Gunew points out, after Derrida this seems an impossible question because how can one still argue for writing in conjunction with any notion of authenticity. Who determines or validates the production of new literature forms and new narratives for the representation of difference? Why should we insist on the rights of individuals to construct their own stories? Who determines when similarities are to be emphasized, when differences are to be articulated? Who delineates the criteria of inclusion and exclusion, for what reasons, and to what effect? These are complex and politically charged questions: 'Women of colour', comments Elizabeth Spelman, 'have been distrustful of white women who point to similarities between them when it seems politically expedient to do so and to dissimilarities when it does not' (p. 235). The issue Spelman notes, is 'not so much a metaphysical one as a political one'. In other words, in attempting to define what might constitute 'woman', what matters most is not shared transcendental essence, but politically determined perceptions of pertinent similarities and differences.

The 'systematic fighting-out' of the instability of the category of women has, to date, involved battles too numerous to mention, though the most deeply fought have perhaps been those over race, nation, sexuality, and class. On the issue of sexuality Monique Wittig proclaims: 'not only is there no natural group "women" (we lesbians are living proof of it), but as individuals as well we question "woman", which for us . . . is only a myth' (p. 220). For Wittig forced assimilation to a dominant norm, ignoring sexuality as a pertinent difference, acts as a political constraint—not only misrecognizing but more substantially oppressing those who would be different (though note, interestingly, that Wittig presumes to speak for all lesbians in a paradoxically analogous manner). This type of critique represents a serious political challenge to many forms of universalizing feminisms.

The cumulative result of many such challenges has resulted in the current unease about articulating any stable notion of female identity. But what then of the feminist political project? How can one campaign as a woman if the very category has been deconstructed? Here the writing of Judith Butler has been influential, working to bridge the gap between non-essentialist ontological positions and practical politics. 'If a stable notion of gender no longer proves to be the foundational premise of feminist politics,' she reflects, 'perhaps a new sort of feminist politics is now desirable to contest the very reifications of gender and identity, one that will take the variable construction of identity as both a methodological and normative prerequisite, if not a political goal' (p. 279). Such a politics will inevitably involve relinquishing any presumption of solidarity and jettisoning the unity of the category of woman: 'identities can come into being and dissolve depending on the concrete practices that constitute them'. But whilst holding great appeal to some, this notion of the political remains troubling for others. As Kate Soper reflects, 'feminism, like any other politics, has always implied a banding together, a movement based on solidarity and sisterhood of women, who are linked by perhaps very little else than their sameness and "common cause" as women' (p. 289).

The question for contemplation then, is how these debates concerning subjectivity impact upon the political ambitions of feminist practice: do the challenges to essentialism offer us 'a new sort of feminist politics', or might they rather—as Soper considers—lead us from solidarity to individualism and ultimately dispersion?

32 One is not Born a Woman

A materialist feminist[1] approach to women's oppression destroys the idea that women are a 'natural group': 'a racial group of a special kind, a group perceived *as natural*, a group of men considered as materially specific in their bodies'.[2] What the analysis accomplishes on the level of ideas, practice makes actual at the level of facts: by its very existence, lesbian society destroys the artificial (social) fact constituting women as a 'natural group'. A lesbian society[3] pragmatically reveals that the division from men of which women have been the object is a political one and shows that we have been ideologically rebuilt into a 'natural group'. In the case of women, ideology goes far since our bodies as well as our minds are the product of this manipulation. We have been compelled in our bodies and in our minds to correspond, feature by feature, with the *idea* of nature that has been established for us. Distorted to such an extent that our deformed body is what they call 'natural', what is supposed to exist as such before oppression. Distorted to such an extent that in the end oppression seems to be a consequence of this 'nature' within ourselves (a nature which is only an *idea*). What a materialist analysis does by reasoning, a lesbian society accomplishes practically: not only is there no natural group 'women' (we lesbians are living proof of it), but as individuals as well we question 'woman', which for us, as for Simone de Beauvoir, is only a myth. She said: 'One is not born, but becomes a woman. No biological, psychological, or economic fate determines the figure that the human female presents in society: it is civilization as a whole that produces this creature, intermediate between male and eunuch, which is described as feminine.'[4]

However, most of the feminists and lesbian-feminists in America and elsewhere still believe that the basis of women's oppression *is biological as well as* historical. Some of them even claim to find their sources in Simone de Beauvoir.[5] The belief in mother right and in a 'prehistory' when women created civilization (because of a biological predisposition) while the coarse and brutal men hunted (because of a biological predisposition) is symmetrical with the biologizing interpretation of history produced up to now by the class of men. It is still the same method of finding in women and men a biological explanation of their division, outside of social facts. For me this could never constitute a lesbian approach to women's oppression, since it assumes that the basis of society or the beginning of society lies in heterosexuality. Matriarchy is no less heterosexual than patriarchy: it is only the sex of the oppressor that changes. Furthermore, not only is this conception still imprisoned in the categories of sex (woman and man), but it holds onto the idea that the capacity to give birth (biology) is what defines a woman.

Although practical facts and ways of living contradict this theory in lesbian society, there are lesbians who affirm that 'women and men are different species or races (the words are used interchangeably): men are biologically inferior to women; male violence is a biological inevitability. . . .'[6] By doing this, by admitting that there is a 'natural' division between women and men, we naturalize history, we assume that 'men' and 'women' have always existed and will always exist. Not only do we naturalize history, but also consequently we naturalize the social phenomena which express our oppression, making change impossible. For example, instead of seeing giving birth as a forced production, we see it as a 'natural', 'biological' process, forgetting that in our societies births are planned (demography), forgetting that we ourselves are programmed to produce children, while this is the only social activity 'short of war'[7] that presents such a great danger of death. Thus, as long as we will be 'unable to abandon by will or impulse a lifelong and centuries-old commitment to childbearing as *the* female creative act',[8] gaining control of the production of children will mean much more than the mere control of the material means of this production: women will have to abstract themselves from the definition 'woman' which is imposed upon them.

A materialist feminist approach shows that what we take for the cause or origin of oppression is in fact only the *mark*[9] imposed by the oppressor: the 'myth of woman',[10] plus its material effects and manifestations in the appropriated consciousness and bodies of women. Thus, this mark does not predate oppression: Colette Guillaumin has shown that before the socio-economic reality of black slavery, the concept of race did not exist, at least not in its modern meaning, since it was applied to the lineage of families. However, now, race, exactly like sex, is taken as an 'immediate given', a 'sensible given', 'physical features', belonging to a natural order. But what we believe to be a physical and direct perception is only a sophisticated and mythic construction, an 'imaginary formation',[11] which reinterprets physical features (in themselves as neutral as any others but marked by the social system) through the network of relationships in which they are perceived. (They are seen as *black*, therefore they *are* black; they are seen as *women*, therefore, they *are* women. But before being *seen* that way, they first had to be *made* that way.) Lesbians should always remember and acknowledge how 'unnatural', compelling, totally oppressive, and destructive being 'woman' was for us in the old days before the women's liberation movement. It was a political constraint, and those who resisted it were accused of not being 'real' women. But then we were proud of it, since in the accusation there was already something like a shadow of victory: the avowal by the oppressor that 'woman' is not something that goes without saying, since to be one, one has to be a 'real' one. We were at the same time accused of wanting to be men. Today this double accusation has been taken up again with enthusiasm in the context of the women's liberation movement by some feminists and also, alas, by some lesbians whose political goal seems somehow to be becoming more and more 'feminine'. To refuse to be a woman, however, does not mean that one has to become a man. Besides, if we take as an example the perfect 'butch', the classic example which provokes the most horror, whom Proust would have called a woman/man, how is her alienation different from that of someone who wants to become a woman? Tweedledum and Tweedledee. At least for a woman, wanting to become a man proves that she has escaped her initial programming. But even if she would like to, with all her strength, she cannot become a man. For becoming a man would demand from a woman not only a man's external appearance but his consciousness as well, that is, the consciousness of one who disposes by right of at least two 'natural' slaves during his life span. This is impossible, and one feature of lesbian oppression consists precisely of making women out of reach for us, since women belong to men. Thus a lesbian *has to* be something else, a not-woman, a not-man, a product of society, not a product of nature, for there is no nature in society.

The refusal to become (or to remain) heterosexual always meant to refuse to become a man or a woman, consciously or not. For a lesbian this goes further than the refusal of the *role* 'woman'. It is the refusal of the economic, ideological, and political power of a man. This, we lesbians, and nonlesbians as well, knew before the beginning of the lesbian and feminist movement. However, as Andrea Dworkin emphasizes, many lesbians recently 'have increasingly tried to transform the very ideology that has enslaved us into a dynamic, religious, psychologically compelling celebration of female biological potential'.[12] Thus, some avenues of the feminist and lesbian movement lead us back to the myth of woman which was created by men especially for us, and with it we sink back into a natural group. Having stood up to fight for a sexless society,[13] we now find ourselves entrapped in the familiar deadlock of 'woman is wonderful'. Simone de Beauvoir underlined particularly the false consciousness which consists of selecting among the features of the myth (that women are different from men) those which look good and using them as a definition for women. What the concept 'woman is wonderful' accomplishes is that it retains for defining women the best features (best according to whom?) which oppression has granted us, and it does not radically question the categories 'man' and 'woman', which are political categories and not natural givens. It puts us in a position of fighting within the class 'women' not as the other classes do, for the disappearance of our class, but for the defence of 'woman' and its reenforcement. It leads us to develop with complacency 'new' theories about our specificity: thus, we call our passivity 'nonviolence', when the main and emergent point for us is to fight our passivity (our fear, rather, a justified one). The ambiguity of the term 'feminist' sums up the whole situation. What does 'feminist' mean? Feminist is formed with the word 'femme', 'woman', and means: someone who fights for women. For many of us it means someone who fights for women as a class and for the disappearance of this class. For many others it means someone who fights for woman and her defense—for the myth, then, and its reenforcement. But why was the word 'feminist' chosen if it retains the least ambiguity? We chose to call ourselves 'feminists' ten years ago, not in order to support or reenforce the myth of woman, nor to identify ourselves with the oppressor's definition of us, but rather to affirm that our movement had a history and to emphasize the political link with the old feminist movement.

It is, then, this movement that we can put in question for the meaning that it gave to feminism. It so happens that feminism in the last century could never resolve its contradictions on the subject of nature/culture, woman/ society. Women started to fight for themselves as a group and rightly considered that they shared common features as a result of oppression. But for them these features were natural and biological rather than social. They went so far as to adopt the Darwinist theory of evolution. They did not believe like Darwin, however, 'that women were less evolved than men, but they did believe that male and female natures had diverged in the course of evolutionary development and that society at large reflected this polarization'.[14] The failure of early feminism was that it only attacked the Darwinist charge of female inferiority, while accepting the foundations of this charge—namely, the view of woman as "unique".[15] And finally it was women scholars—and not feminists—who scientifically destroyed this theory. But the early feminists had failed to regard history as a dynamic process which develops from conflicts of interests. Furthermore, they still believed as men do that the cause (origin) of their oppression lay within themselves. And therefore after some astonishing victories the feminists of this first front found themselves at an impasse out of a lack of reasons to fight. They upheld the illogical principle of 'equality in difference', an idea now being born again. They fell back into the trap which threatens us once again: the myth of woman.

Thus it is our historical task, and only ours, to define what we call oppression in materialist terms, to make it evident that women are a class, which is to say that the category 'woman' as well as the category 'man' are political and economic categories not eternal ones. Our fight aims to suppress men as a class, not through a genocidal, but a political struggle. Once the class 'men' disappears, 'women' as a class will disappear as well, for there are no slaves without masters. Our first task, it seems, is to always thoroughly dissociate 'women' (the class within which we fight) and 'woman', the myth. For 'woman' does not exist for us: it is only an imaginary formation, while 'women' is the product of a social relationship. We felt this strongly when everywhere we refused to be called a 'woman's liberation movement'. Furthermore, we have to destroy the myth inside and outside ourselves. 'Woman' is not each one of us, but the political and ideological formation which negates 'women' (the product of a relation of exploitation). 'Woman' is there to confuse us, to hide the reality 'women'. In order to be aware of being a class and to become a class we first have to kill the myth of 'woman' including its most seductive aspects (I think about Virginia Woolf when she said the first task of a woman writer is to kill 'the angel in the house'). But to become a class we do not have to suppress our individual selves, and since no individual can be reduced to her/his oppression we are also confronted with the historical necessity of constituting ourselves as the individual subjects of our history as well. I believe this is the reason why all these attempts at 'new' definitions of woman are blossoming now. What is at stake (and of course not only for women) is an individual definition as well as a class definition. For once one has acknowledged oppression, one needs to know and experience the fact that one can constitute oneself as a subject (as opposed to an object of oppression), that one can become *someone* in spite of oppression, that one has one's own identity. There is no possible fight for someone deprived of an identity, no internal motivation for fighting, since, although I can fight only with others, first I fight for myself.

The question of the individual subject is historically a difficult one for everybody. Marxism, the last avatar of materialism, the science which has politically formed us, does not want to hear anything about a 'subject'. Marxism has rejected the transcendental subject, the subject as constitutive of knowledge, the 'pure' consciousness. All that thinks per se, before all experience, has ended up in the garbage can of history, because it claimed to exist outside matter, prior to matter, and needed God, spirit, or soul to exist in such a way. This is what is called 'idealism'. As for individuals, they are only the product of social relations, therefore their consciousness can only be 'alienated'. (Marx, in *The German Ideology*, says precisely that individuals of the dominating class are also alienated, although they are the direct producers of the ideas that alienate the classes oppressed by them. But since they draw visible advantages from their own alienation they can bear it without too much suffering.) There exists such a thing as class consciousness, but a consciousness which does not refer to a particular subject, except as participating in general conditions of exploitation at the same time as the other subjects of their class, all sharing the same consciousness. As for the practical class problems—outside of the class problems as traditionally defined—that one could encounter (for example, sexual problems), they were considered 'bourgeois' problems that would disappear with the final victory of the class struggle. 'Individualistic', 'subjectivist', 'petit bourgeois', these were the labels given to any person who had shown problems which could not be reduced to the 'class struggle' itself.

Thus Marxism has denied the members of oppressed classes the attribute of being a subject. In doing this, Marxism, because of the ideological and political power this 'revolutionary science' immediately exercised upon the workers' movement and all other political groups, has prevented all categories of oppressed peoples from constituting themselves historically as subjects (subjects of their struggle, for example). This means that the 'masses' did not fight for themselves but for *the* party or its organizations. And when an economic transformation took place (end of private property, constitution of the socialist state), no revolutionary change took place within the new society, because the people themselves did not change.

For women, Marxism had two results. It prevented them from being aware that they are a class and therefore from constituting themselves as a class for a very long time, by leaving the relation 'women/men' outside of the social order, by turning it into a natural relation, doubtless for Marxists the only one, along with the relation of mothers to children, to be seen this way, and by hiding the class conflict between men and women behind a natural division of labor (*The German Ideology*). This concerns the theoretical (ideological) level. On the practical level, Lenin, *the* party, all the communist parties up to now, including all the most radical political groups, have always reacted to any attempt on the part of women to reflect and form groups based on their own class problem with an accusation of divisiveness. By uniting, we women are dividing the strength of the people. This means that for the Marxists women *belong* either to the bourgeois class or to the proletariat class, in other words, to the men of these classes. In addition, Marxist theory does not allow women any more than other classes of oppressed people to constitute themselves as historical subjects, because Marxism does not take into account the fact that a class also consists of individuals one by one. Class consciousness is not enough. We must try to understand philosophically (politically) these concepts of 'subject' and 'class consciousness' and how they work in relation to our history. When we discover that women are the objects of oppression and appropriation, at the very moment that we become able to perceive this, we become subjects in the sense of cognitive subjects, through an operation of abstraction. Consciousness of oppression is not only a reaction to (fight against) oppression. It is also the whole conceptual reevaluation of the social world, its whole reorganization with new concepts, from the point of view of oppression. It is what I would call the science of oppression created by the oppressed. This operation of understanding reality has to be undertaken by every one of us: call it a subjective, cognitive practice. The movement back and forth between the levels of reality (the conceptual reality and the material reality of oppression, which are both social realities) is accomplished through language.

It is we who historically must undertake the task of defining the individual subject in materialist terms. This certainly seems to be an impossibility since materialism and subjectivity have always been mutually exclusive. Nevertheless, and rather than despairing of ever understanding, we must recognize the *need* to reach subjectivity in the abandonment by many of us to the myth 'woman' (the myth of woman being only a snare that holds us up). This real necessity for everyone to exist as an individual, as well as a member of a class, is perhaps the first condition for the accomplishment of a revolution, without which there can be no real fight or transformation. But the opposite is also true; without class and class consciousness there are no real subjects, only alienated individuals. For women to answer the question of the individual subject in materialist terms is first to show, as the lesbians and feminists did, that supposedly 'subjective', 'individual', 'private' problems are in fact social problems, class problems; that sexuality is not for women an individual and subjective expression, but a social institution of violence. But once we have shown that all so-called personal problems are in fact class problems, we will still be left with the question of the subject of each singular woman—not the myth, but each one of us. At this point, let us say that a new personal and subjective definition for all humankind can only be found beyond the categories of sex (woman and man) and that the advent of individual subjects demands first destroying the categories of sex, ending the use of them, and rejecting all sciences which still use these categories as their fundamentals (practically all social sciences).

To destroy 'woman' does not mean that we aim, short of physical destruction, to destroy lesbianism simultaneously with the categories of sex, because lesbianism provides for the moment the only social form in which we can live freely. Lesbian is the only concept I know of which is beyond the categories of sex (woman and man), because the designated subject (lesbian) is *not* a woman, either economically, or politically, or ideologically. For what makes a woman is a specific social relation to a man, a relation that we have previously called servitude,[16] a relation which implies personal and physical obligation as well as economic obligation ('forced residence',[17] domestic corvée, conjugal duties, unlimited production of children, etc.), a relation which lesbians escape by refusing to become or to stay heterosexual. We are escapees from our class in the same way as the American runaway slaves were when escaping slavery and becoming free. For us this is an absolute necessity; our survival demands that we contribute all our strength to the destruction of the class of women within which men appropriate women. This can be accomplished only by the destruction of heterosexuality as a social system which is based on the oppression of women by men and which produces the doctrine of the difference between the sexes to justify this oppression.

['One is not Born a Woman' (1981), in *The Straight Mind* (Hemel Hempstead: Harvester Wheatsheaf, 1992), 9–20.]

33 Black Women and Feminism

More than a hundred years have passed since the day Sojourner Truth stood before an assembled body of white women and men at an anti-slavery rally in Indiana and bared her breasts to prove that she was indeed a woman. To Sojourner, who had traveled the long road from slavery to freedom, the baring of her breasts was a small matter. She faced her audience without fear, without shame, proud of having been born black and female. Yet the white man who yelled at Sojourner, 'I don't believe you really are a woman,' unwittingly voiced America's contempt and disrespect for black womanhood. In the eyes of the 19th century white public, the black female was a creature unworthy of the title woman; she was mere chattel, a thing, an animal. When Sojourner Truth stood before the second annual convention of the women's rights movement in Akron, Ohio, in 1852, white women who deemed it unfitting that a black woman should speak on a public platform in their presence screamed: 'Don't let her speak! Don't let her speak! Don't let her speak!' Sojourner endured their protests and became one of the first feminists to call their attention to the lot of the black slave woman who, compelled by circumstance to labor alongside black men, was a living embodiment of the truth that women could be the work-equals of men.

It was no mere coincidence that Sojourner Truth was allowed on stage after a white male spoke against the idea of equal rights for women, basing his argument on the notion that woman was too weak to perform her share of manual labor—that she was innately the physical inferior to man. Sojourner quickly responded to his argument, telling her audience:

Well, children, whar dar is so much racket dar must be something out o' kilter. I tink dat 'twixt de niggers of de Sout and de women at de Norf all a talkin 'bout rights, de white men will be in a fix pretty soon. But what's all dis here talkin 'bout? Dat man ober dar say dat women needs to be helped into carriages, and lifted ober ditches, and to have de best places . . . and ain't I a woman? Look at me! Look at my arm! . . . I have plowed, and planted, and gathered into barns, and no man could head me—and ain't I a woman? I could work as much as any man (when I could get it), and bear de lash as well—and ain't I a woman? I have borne five children and I seen 'em mos all sold off into slavery, and when I cried out with a mother's grief, none but Jesus hear—and ain't I a woman?

Unlike most white women's rights advocates, Sojourner Truth could refer to her own personal life experience as evidence of woman's ability to function as a parent; to be the work equal of man; to undergo persecution, physical abuse, rape, torture; and to not only survive but emerge triumphant.

['Black Women and Feminism', in *Ain't I a Woman* (London: Pluto Press, 1982), 159–60.]

> Up until now philosophers have only interpreted the world. The point
> now is to change it.
>
> Karl Marx and Friedrich Engels, *Theses on Feuerbach*

> The delusions (*Wahnbildungen*) of patients appear to me to be the
> equivalents of the [interpretive] constructions which we build up in the
> course of an analytic treatment—attempts at explanation and cure.
>
> Sigmund Freud, 'Constructions in Analysis'

[...] Academic discourse, and perhaps American university discourse in
particular, possesses an extraordinary ability to absorb, digest and neutralize
all of the key, radical or dramatic moments of thought, particularly a fortiori,
of contemporary thought. Marxism in the United States, though marginalized, remains deafly dominant and exercizes a fascination that we have not
seen in Europe since the Russian *Proletkult* on the 1930s. Post-Heideggerian
'deconstructivism', though esoteric, is welcomed in the United States as an
antidote to analytic philosophy or, rather, as a way to valorize, through
contrast, that philosophy. Only one theoretical breakthrough seems consistently to *mobilize* resistances, rejections and deafness; psychoanalysis—not as
the 'plague' allowed by Freud to implant itself in America as a 'commerce in
couches' but rather as that which, with Freud and after him, has led the
psychoanalytic decentring of the speaking subject to the very foundations of
language. It is this latter direction that I will be exploring here, with no other
hope than to awaken the resistances and, perhaps, the attention of a concerned few, after the event (*après coup*).

For I have the impression that the 'professionalism' discussed throughout
the 'Politics of Interpretation' conference is never as strong as when professionals denounce it. In fact, the same pre-analytic rationality unites them all,
'conservatives', and 'revolutionaries'—in all cases, jealous guardians of their
academic 'chairs' whose very existence, I am sure, is thrown into question and
put into jeopardy by psychoanalytic discourse. I would therefore schematically summarize what is to follow in this way:

1. There are political implications inherent in the act of interpretation
itself, whatever meaning that interpretation bestows. What is the meaning,
interest and benefit of the interpretive position itself, a position from which I
wish to give meaning to an enigma? To give a political meaning to something
is perhaps only the ultimate consequence of the epistemological attitude
which consists, simply, of the desire *to give meaning*. This attitude is not
innocent but, rather, is rooted in the speaking subject's need to reassure

himself of his image and his identity faced with an object. Political interpretation is thus the apogee of the obsessive quest for A Meaning.

2. The psychoanalytic intervention within Western knowledge has a fundamentally deceptive effect. Psychoanalysis, critical and dissolvant, cuts through political illusions, fantasies and beliefs to the extent that they consist in providing only one meaning, an uncriticizable ultimate Meaning, to human behaviour. If such a situation can lead to despair within the polis, we must not forget that it is also a source of lucidity and ethics. The psychoanalytic intervention is, from this point of view, a counterweight, an antidote, to political discourse which, without it, is free to become our modern religion: the final explanation.

3. The political interpretations of our century have produced two powerful and totalitarian results: Fascism and Stalinism. Parallel to the socio-economic reasons for these phenomena, there exists as well another, more intrinsic reason: the simple desire to give a meaning, to explain, to provide the answer, to interpret. In that context I will briefly discuss Louis Ferdinand Céline's texts in so far as the ideological interpretations given by him are an example of political delirium in avant-garde writing.

I would say that interpretation as an epistemological and ethical attitude began with the Stoics. In other words, it should not be confused with *theory* in the Platonic sense, which assumes a prior knowledge of the ideal Forms to which all action or creation is subordinate. Man, says Epictetus, is 'born to contemplate God and his works, and not only to contemplate them but also interpret them (kai ou monon teatin, ala kai exegetin auton)'. 'To interpret' in this context, and I think always, means 'to make a connection'. Thus the birth of interpretation is considered the birth of semiology, since the semiological sciences relate a sign (an event-sign) to a signified in order to *act* accordingly, consistently, consequently.

Much has been made of the circularity of this connection which, throughout the history of interpretive disciplines up to hermeneutics, consists in enclosing the enigmatic (interpretable) object within the interpretive theory's pre-existent system. Instead of creating an object, however, this process merely produces what the interpretive theory had pre-selected as an object within the enclosure of its own system. Thus it seems that one does not interpret something outside theory but rather that theory harbours its object within its own logic. Theory merely projects that object on to a theoretical place at a distance, outside its grasp, thereby eliciting the very possibility of interrogation (Heidegger's *Sachverhalt*).

We could argue at length about whether interpretation is a circle or a spiral: in other words, whether the interpretable object it assigns itself is simply constituted by the interpretation's own logic or whether it is recreated, enriched and thus raised to a higher level of knowledge through the unfolding of interpretive discourse. Prestigious work in philosophy and logic is engaged in this investigation. I will not pursue it here. Such a question, finally, seems to me closer to a Platonic idea of interpretation (i.e. theorization) than it does to the true innovation of the Stoics' undertaking. This innovation is the reduction, indeed the elimination, of the distance between theory and action as well as between model and copy. What permits this elimination of the distance between nature (which the Stoics considered interpretable) and the interpreter is the extraordinary opening of the field of subjectivity. The person who does the interpretation, the subject who makes the connection between the sign and the signified, is the Stoic sage displaying, on the one hand, the extraordinary architectonics of his *will* and, on the other, his mastery of *time* (both momentary and infinite).

I merely want to allude to this Stoic notion of the primordial interdependence of *interpretation*, subjective *will* and mastery of *time*. For my own interest is in contemporary thought which has rediscovered, in its own way, that even if interpretation does no more than establish a simple logical connection, it is nevertheles played out on the scene of speaking subjectivity and the moment of speech. Two great intellectual ventures of our time, those of Marx and Freud, have broken through the hermeneutic tautology to make of it a *revolution* in one instance and, in the other, a *cure*. We must recognize that all contemporary political thought which does not deal with technocratic administration—although technocratic purity is perhaps only a dream—uses interpretation in Marx's and Freud's sense: as transformation and as cure. Whatever *object* one selects (a patient's discourse, a literary or journalistic text, or certain socio-political behaviour), its interpretation reaches its full power, so as to tip the object towards the *unknown* of the interpretive theory or, more simply, toward the theory's *intentions*, only when the interpreter *confronts* the interpretable object.

It is within this field of confrontation between the object and the subject of interpretation that I want to pursue my investigation. I assume that at its resolution there are two major outcomes. First, the object may succumb to the interpretive intentions of the interpreter, and then we have the whole range of domination from suggestion to propaganda to revolution. Or second, the object may reveal to the interpreter the unknown of his theory and permit the constitution of a new theory. Discourse in this case is renewed; it can begin again: it forms a new object and a new interpretation in this reciprocal transference.

Before going any further, however, I would like to suggest that another path, post-hermeneutic and perhaps even post-interpretive, opens up for us within the lucidity of contemporary discourse. Not satisfied to stay within the interpretive place which is, essentially, that of the Stoic sage, the contemporary interpreter renounces the game of *indebtedness*, *proximity* and *presence* hidden within the connotations of the concept of interpretation. (*Interpretare* means 'to be mutually indebted'; *prêt*: from popular Latin *praestus*, from the classical adverb *praesto*, meaning 'close at hand', 'nearby'; *praesto esse*: 'to be present, attend' *praestare*: 'to furnish, to present (as an object, e.g. money)'.) The modern interpreter avoids the presentness of subjects to themselves and to things. For in this presentness a strange object appears to speaking subjects, a kind of currency they grant themselves—interpretation—to make certain that they are really there, close by, within reach. Breaking out of the enclosure of the presentness of meaning, the *new* 'interpreter' no longer interprets: he speaks, he 'associates', because there is no longer an object to interpret; there is, instead, the setting-off of semantic, logical, phantasmatic and indeterminable sequences. As a result, a fiction, an uncentred discourse, a subjective polytopia come about, cancelling the metalinguistic status of the discourses currently governing the post-analytic fate of interpretation.

The Freudian position on interpretation has the immense advantage of being midway between a classic interpretive attitude—that of providing meaning through the connection of two terms from a stable place and theory—and the questioning of the subjective and theoretical stability of the interpretant which, in the act of interpretation itself, establishes the theory and the interpreter himself as interpretable objects. The dimension of *desire*, appearing for the first time in the citadel of interpretive will, steals the platform from the Stoic sage, but at the same time it opens up time, suspends Stoic suicide and confers not only an interpretive power but also a transforming power to these new, unpredictable signifying effects which must be called *an imaginary*. I would suggest that the wise interpreter give way to delirium so that, out of his desire, the imaginary may join interpretive closure, thus producing a perpetual interpretive creative force.

['Psychoanalysis and the Polis', *Critical Inquiry*, 9/1 (Sept. 1982), 25–39.]

HÉLÈNE CIXOUS

35   Sorties

Where is she?
Activity / Passivity
Sun / Moon
Culture / Nature
Day / Night

Father / Mother
Head / Heart
Intelligible / Palpable
Logos / Pathos.

Form, convex, step, advance, semen, progress.

Matter, concave, ground—where steps are taken, holding- and dumping-ground.

Man
_____

Woman

Always the same metaphor: we follow it, it carries us, beneath all its figures, wherever discourse is organized. If we read or speak, the same thread or double braid is leading us throughout literature, philosophy, criticism, centuries of representation and reflection.

Thought has always worked through opposition,

Speaking/Writing

Parole/Écriture

High/Low

Through dual, hierarchical oppositions. Superior/Inferior. Myths, legends, books. Philosophical systems. Everywhere (where) ordering intervenes, where a law organizes what is thinkable by oppositions (dual, irreconcilable; or sublatable, dialectical). And all these pairs of oppositions are *couples*. Does that mean something? Is the fact that Logocentrism subjects thought—all concepts, codes and values—to a binary system, related to 'the' couple, man/woman?

Nature/History

Nature/Art

Nature/Mind

Passion/Action

Theory of culture, theory of society, symbolic systems in general—art, religion, family, language—it is all developed while bringing the same schemes to light. And the movement whereby each opposition is set up to make sense is the movement through which the couple is destroyed. A universal battlefield. Each time, a war is let loose. Death is always at work.

Father/son   Relations of authority, privilege, force.

The Word/Writing   Relations: opposition, conflict, sublation, return.

Master/slave   Violence. Repression.

We see that 'victory' always comes down to the same thing: things get hierarchical. Organization by hierarchy makes all conceptual organization subject to man. Male privilege, shown in the opposition between *activity* and *passivity*, which he uses to sustain himself. Traditionally, the question of sexual difference is treated by coupling it with the opposition: activity/passivity.

There are repercussions. Consulting the history of philosophy—since philosophical discourse both orders and reproduces all thought—one notices[1] that it is marked by an absolute *constant* which orders values and which is precisely this opposition, activity/passivity. [...]

Writing Femininity Transformation

And there is a link between the economy of femininity—the open, extravagant subjectivity, that relationship to the other in which the gift doesn't calculate its influence—and the possibility of love; and a link today between this 'libido of the other' and writing.

At the present time, *defining* a feminine practice of writing is impossible with an impossibility that will continue; for this practice will never be able to be *theorized*, enclosed, coded, which does not mean it does not exist. But it will always exceed the discourse governing the phallocentric system; it takes place and will take place somewhere other than in the territories subordinated to philosophical-theoretical domination. It will not let itself think except through subjects that break automatic functions, border runners never subjugated by any authority. But one can begin to speak. Begin to point out some effects, some elements of unconscious drives, some relations of the feminine Imaginary to the Real, to writing.

What I have to say about it is also only a beginning, because right from the start these features affect me powerfully.

First I sense femininity in writing by: a privilege of *voice: writing and voice* are entwined and interwoven and writing's continuity/voice's rhythm take each other's breath away through interchanging, make the text gasp or form it out of suspenses and silences, make it lose its voice or rend it with cries.

In a way, feminine writing never stops reverberating from the wrench that the acquisition of speech, speaking out loud, is for her—'acquisition' that is experienced more as tearing away, dizzying flight and flinging oneself, diving. Listen to woman speak in a gathering (if she is not painfully out of breath): she doesn't 'speak', she throws her trembling body into the air, she lets herself go, she flies, she goes completely into her voice, she vitally defends the 'logic' of her discourse with her body; her flesh speaks true. She exposes herself. Really she makes what she thinks materialize carnally, she conveys meaning with her body. She *inscribes* what she is saying because she does not deny unconscious drives the unmanageable part they play in speech.

Her discourse, even when 'theoretical' or political, is never simple or linear or 'objectivized', universalized; she involves her story in history.

Every woman has known the torture of beginning to speak aloud, heart beating as if to break, occasionally falling into loss of language, ground and language slipping out from under her, because for woman speaking—even just opening her mouth—in public is something rash, a transgression.

A double anguish, for even if she transgresses, her word almost always falls on the deaf, masculine ear, which can only hear language that speaks in the masculine.

We are not culturally accustomed to speaking, throwing signs out toward a scene, employing the suitable rhetoric. Also, it is not where we find our pleasure: indeed, one pays a certain price for the use of a discourse. The logic of communication requires an economy both of signs—of signifiers—and of subjectivity. The orator is asked to unwind a thin thread, dry and taut. We like uneasiness, questioning. There is waste in what we say. We need that waste. To write is always to make allowances for superabundance and uselessness while slashing the exchange value that keeps the spoken word on its track. That is why writing is good, letting the tongue try itself out—as one attempts a caress, taking the time a phrase or a thought needs to make oneself loved, to make oneself reverberate.

It is in writing, from woman and toward woman, and in accepting the challenge of the discourse controlled by the phallus, that woman will affirm woman somewhere other than in silence, the place reserved for her in and through the Symbolic. May she get out of booby-trapped silence! And not have the margin or the harem foisted on her as her domain!

In feminine speech, as in writing, there never stops reverberating something that, having once passed through us, having imperceptibly and deeply touched us, still has the power to affect us—song, the first music of the voice of love, which every woman keeps alive.

The Voice sings from a time before law, before the Symbolic took one's breath away and reappropriated it into language under its authority of separation. The deepest, the oldest, the loveliest Visitation. Within each woman the first, nameless love is singing.

In woman there is always, more or less, something of 'the mother' repairing and feeding, resisting separation, a force that does not let itself be cut off but that runs codes ragged. The relationship to childhood (the child she was, she is, she acts and makes and starts anew, and unties at the place where, as a same she even others herself), is no more cut off than is the relationship to the 'mother', *as it consists of* delights and violences. Text, my body: traversed by lilting flows; listen to me, it is not a captivating, clinging 'mother'; it is the equivoice that, touching you, affects you, pushes you away from your breast to come to language, that summons *your* strength; it is the rhyth-me that laughs you; the one intimately addressed who makes all metaphors, all body(?)—bodies(?)—possible and desirable, who is no more describable than god, soul, or the Other; the part of you that puts space between yourself and pushes you to inscribe your woman's style in language. Voice: milk that could go on forever. Found again. The lost mother/bitter-lost. Eternity: is voice mixed with milk.

Not the origin: she doesn't go back there. A boy's journey is the return to the native land, the *Heimweh* Freud speaks of, the nostalgia that makes man a being who tends to come back to the point of departure to appropriate it for himself and to die there. A girl's journey is farther—to the unknown, to invent.

How come this privileged relationship with voice? Because no woman piles up as many defenses against instinctual drives as a man does. You don't prop things up, you don't brick things up the way he does, you don't withdraw from pleasure so 'prudently'. Even if phallic mystification has contaminated good relations in general, woman is never far from the 'mother' (I do not mean the role but the 'mother' as no-name and as source of goods). There is always at least a little good mother milk left in her. She writes with white ink.

Voice! That, too, is launching forth and effusion without return. Exclamation, cry, breathlessness, yell, cough, vomit, music. Voice leaves. Voice loses. She leaves. She loses. And that is how she writes, as one throws a voice—forward, into the void. She goes away, she goes forward, doesn't turn back to look at her tracks. Pays no attention to herself. Running breakneck. Contrary to the self-absorbed, masculine narcissism, making sure of its image, of being seen, of seeing itself, of assembling its glories, of pocketing itself again. The reductive look, the always divided look returning, the mirror economy; he needs to love himself. But she launches forth; she seeks to love. Moreover, this is what Valéry sensed, marking his Young Fate in search of herself with ambiguity, masculine in her jealousy of herself: 'seeing herself see herself', the motto of all phallocentric speculation/specularization, the motto of every Teste; and feminine in the frantic descent deeper deeper to where a voice that doesn't know itself is lost in the sea's churning.

['Sorties', in Hélène Cixous and Catherine Clement, *The Newly Born Woman*, tr. Betsy Wing (Manchester: Manchester University Press, 1986), 66–79.]

ELIZABETH SPELMAN

36   Woman: The One and the Many

[...] [W]omen of color have been distrustful of white women who point to similarities between them when it seems politically expedient to do so and to dissimilarities when it does not.[1] They have wanted to know just why and when white women become interested in similarities and differences among women. At issue is not so much whether there are or are not similarities or differences, but about how white middle-class feminists try to use claims about similarity and differences among women in different directions, depending on what they believe such similarity or dissimilarity implies. For example, as we have seen, sometimes feminists have insisted on the similarity between the treatment of 'women' and that of 'slaves'; other times they have insisted that the situation of free women and slave women is different enough that the situation of slave women cannot be a useful guide to that of free women. The issue is thus not so much a metaphysical one as a political one. [...]

We have begun to realize that I don't necessarily correct my picture of what is true of women 'as women' by doing 'empirical research' rather than simply generalizing from my own case. For I can't simply 'look and see' to find out what we have or don't have in common. First of all, I have to have decided what kind of similarity or difference I am interested in. It makes no sense to ask simply whether women are similar or different—I have to specify in what way they might be similar or different. Moreover, I have to employ criteria of sameness and difference—I have to use some measure by which I decide whether they are the same or different in the specified way. And finally, I have to determine the significance of the similarities and differences I find. [...]

[...] [P]ositing an essential 'womanness' has the effect of making women inessential in a variety of ways. First of all, if there is an essential womanness that all women have and have always had, then we needn't know anything about any woman in particular. For the details of her situation and her experience are irrelevant to her being a woman. Thus if we want to understand what 'being a woman' means, we needn't investigate her individual life or any other woman's individual life. All those particulars become inessential to her being and our understanding of her being a woman. And so she also becomes inessential in the sense that she is not needed in order to produce the 'story of woman'. If all women have the same story 'as women', we don't need a chorus of voices to tell the story.

Moreover, to think of 'womanness' in this way obscures three related facts about the meaning of being a woman: first of all, that whatever similarities there are between Angela Davis and me, they exist in the context of differences between us; second, that there is ongoing debate about what effect such differences have on those similarities (different arrangements of the doors express different positions on this matter); third, not all participants in that debate get equal air time or are invested with equal authority.

The problem with the 'story of man' was that women couldn't recognize themselves in it. So those who produce the 'story of woman' want to make sure they appear in it. The best way to ensure that is to be the storyteller and hence to be in a position to decide which of all the many facts about women's lives ought to go into the story, which ought to be left out. Essentialism works well in behalf of these aims, aims that subvert the very process by which women might come to see where and how they wish to make common cause. For essentialism invites me to take what I understand to be true of me 'as a woman' for some golden nugget of womanness all women have as women; and it makes the participation of other women inessential to the production of the story. How lovely: the many turn out to be one, and the one that they are is me.

[*Inessential Woman: Problems of Exclusion in Feminist Thought* (London: The Women's Press, 1988), 138–9, 140, 158–9.]

37 Authenticity and the Writing Cure: Reading Some Migrant Women's Writing

Feminism, while infinite in its variations, is finally rooted in the belief that women's truth-in-experience-and-reality is and has always been different from men's . . .[1]

> My sealed tomb
> Travels in my dreams . . .[2]

The title of this essay expresses a contradiction which has been haunting me for some time. It was prompted initially by such questions as: when does one start, or stop, writing as a migrant (an immigrant to Australia from a non-Anglo-Celtic culture), or 'as' anything? A related version was: what makes a text migrant writing, or women's writing? After Derrida, this seems an impossible question because how can one still argue for writing in conjunction with any notion of authenticity? Authenticity has traditionally been located in speech and in the self purportedly fully present behind the utterance. Writing, in Derrida's scheme, has to do with an orphaned textuality and a free play of language which goes beyond presence or the individual writer, whereas authenticity is associated with speech and voice and functions to reinforce precisely 'the' individual.[3] My oxymoronic title is an attempt to encapsulate a paradox at the heart of postmodernist feminism, also expressed in the opening quotation from Alice Jardine's recent book. It is a paradox which continues to surface in various guises in many of the debates around feminist theory. It can be posed in other terms: why should we read anyone in particular? Why should we insist on the rights of particular individuals to construct their own stories? How, indeed, might anyone be said to 'own' a story if in writing we are dealing with a free play of signification? And what do we hope to see/hear when our ways of thinking about ourselves as fixed entities have been profoundly unsettled?

How, in the wake of postmodernism, is it possible to theorize or clear a necessary space for the writings of particular subjects? For example, for those who derive part of their subjectivity from belonging to minority groups, from those who are disadvantaged by signifying practices which privilege a majority as being the arbiters of public meaning, that is to say, of what circulates as public meaning. As Catherine Belsey reminds us in her recent study of the subject:

Subjectivity is discursively produced and is constrained by the range of subject-positions defined by the discourses in which the concrete individual participates . . . In this sense existing discourses determine not only what can be said and understood, but the nature of subjectivity itself, what it is possible to be. Subjects as agents act in accordance with what they are, 'work by themselves' to produce and reproduce the social formation of which they are a product . . . signifying practice is also the location of resistances. Since meaning is plural, to be able to speak is to be able to take part in the contest for meaning which issues in the production of new subject-positions, new determinations of what it is possible to be.[4]

But how might one argue for those 'new determinations' and resistances as coming from a particular group, privileging that group, without returning to or reconsolidating the humanist subject? And why indeed do we not want that unified subject? Because, as origin of meaning, that subject is traditionally constituted as male, bourgeois, European and universal (speaking for all). And he keeps reappearing, even in such sensitively anti-imperialist studies of the 'other' as Todorov's recent book, *The Conquest of America*.[5]

To explain feminist interrogations of the unified subject: a few years ago, in our efforts to clear a space for women's writing in general, there was a great deal of debate over whether or not one could claim the authority to write on the basis of a difference which had apparently not yet been represented. As Anne Freadman has argued, 'Theories of representation . . . assume the world itself to be the arbiter of accuracy',[6] and, indeed, women's writing claimed its legitimation on the grounds of a prior world, woman's own experiential truths. This controversy over whether or not women write differently simply by belonging to an unproblematic category, 'woman', still surfaces.[7] What became increasingly clear is that this strategy landed us back with biological essentialism and thus imprisoned us in a determination which precluded social change. Such arguments reinforce the concept of the passive and unreflective 'feminine' which has always been an oppositional, binary category in the writings of men. This was arguably so even when it took the subtle form of *écriture féminine*, as Toril Moi has argued concerning the work of Hélène Cixous.[8] Women did not write differently by virtue of being born with wombs but because they had learnt to become women. This counter-thesis was rooted in de Beauvoir's famous and elegantly concise dictum, but later versions gained strength from Christine Delphy's argument for a materialist feminism[9] and from Teresa de Lauretis's redefinition of 'experience', which is worth quoting in full:

by experience, I do not mean the mere registering of sensory data, or a purely mental (psychological) relation to objects and events, or the acquisition of skills and competences by accumulation or repeated exposure. I use the term not in the individualistic, idiosyncratic sense of something belonging to one and exclusively her own even though others might have 'similar' experiences; but rather in the general sense of a process by which, for all social beings, subjectivity is constructed. Through that process one places oneself or is placed in social reality, and so perceives and comprehends as subjective (referring to, even originating in, oneself) those relations—material, economic, and interpersonal—which are in fact social and, in a larger perspective, historical. The process is continuous, its achievement unending or daily renewed. *For each person*, therefore, *subjectivity is an ongoing construction*, not a fixed point of departure or arrival from which one then interacts with the world. On the contrary, it is the effect of that interaction which I call *experience*; and thus it *is produced* not by external ideas, values, or material causes, but *by one's personal, subjective, engagement in the practices, discourses, and institutions that lend significance* (value, meaning, and affect) *to the events of the world.*[10]

The focus is increasingly on materialism (in the sense of the continuous worldly construction of subjectivity) rather than biologism. In other words, women write and read differently in so far as they live out their lives as socially categorized women and in so far as their texts circulate or are consumed differently from those stamped with male signatures. Even those women whose writings / readings have been superficially indistinguishable from those of men nonetheless negotiate a different kind of access to signifying practices and to discursive formations. What they might be seen as practising is a type of mimicry which, even when self-consciously executed, could be argued as being limited in its subversive effects.[11] Current projects of redefining the interactions between the somatic and psychic body promise to push yet further, using new theoretical arguments supporting the specificities of women's writing while assiduously avoiding any biological essentialism.[12]

These developments in feminist materialisms are important in the face of a growing feminist orthodoxy which has been circulating in the last few years and which might be described as the emergence of a unified female subject who is the flipside of the humanist (male) subject referred to earlier. Of course, what else! In response to what I am loosely calling postmodernism and in the face of increasing critiques from so-called marginal women's groups, the feminist subject was seen to be just as ethnocentric and exclusive, just as imperialist and bourgeois, as her male counterpart in claiming to speak on behalf of all women.[13]

As a result of such critiques and the recognition that the oppositional model will always seesaw between contending unified subjects, it seemed more expedient than ever that the emphasis should shift to a decentred subject or to subjects-in-process in order to open up different kinds of discursive resistances, resulting, as Belsey argues, in different possibilities for social meanings. Whether we label this shift modernist, structuralist, or postmodernist is not my central concern here, and I derive comfort from the last paragraph of Elizabeth Grosz's recent article:

When the postmodern can be understood more directly in its cultural and historical context, as a reaction, within theory, to the anti-historical yet subversive materiality of structuralism (i.e. as a form of poststructuralism); as a renunciation of the values to which modernity committed itself (individuality, technocracy, historicism, organic or romantic autonomy of the work of art); its search for the ineffable; as anti-modernism which nevertheless acknowledges its foundations in or as modernism; and as a mode of development from and beyond the transgressive, dispersing material experimentation of the fin de siècle avant garde; where it is positioned as a mode of representational interrogation of dominant norms, the postmodern may be seen as more than just the 'latest' Parisian fashion.[14]

My own use of the term 'postmodernism' derives from a reading of Lyotard and from being struck by his definition of this term as registering an 'incredulity toward metanarratives' accompanied by a concomitant movement toward 'local determinism'[15] (these local determinisms I see as being related to Belsey's discursive resistances). I am not of course in any way asserting that postmodernism represents a total break with modernism. Rather my emphasis is on heterogeneous narratives which come from outside known canons and literary traditions.

In the last decade feminist scholars have recovered many lost female writers, and this archaeological project has resulted in the formation of a female great tradition; I cannot deny that, like all of us, I derive great pleasure from my expanding shelves of women writers. But, simultaneously, I have become conscious of exclusions—symptomatic, of course, of any canon formation. Even when those exclusions are noted and there is a scramble to read, for example, varieties of non-European women writers, the *way* in which they are read is often derived from familiar and eurocentric perspectives. At the same time the market-place is attempting to capture ever more exotic 'outsiders' and recruit them for publishers' lists. The effect has been ambiguous. On the one hand there has been the welcome diversification of eurocentric and bourgeois literary canons, but, on the other hand, those writings have also served to consolidate the genre of the first-person confessional novel (the promulgation of the truth-speaking subject) to which all women's writing had initially been attached. Woman as Truth has returned in the guise of working-class, black, lesbian and other varieties of minority women, and has been constructed in opposition to hegemonic women as much as to hegemonic men.

The delineations of oppression and silencing contained in these texts served to reinforce, renew and legitimate the original claims for promoting women's writing which were offered in the 1960s and 1970s. The more women's writing there was, the less our claims of being silenced or textually absent rang true, so that new witnesses to oppression were required. Not that I'm saying that the struggle to introduce women's texts into teaching institutions is by any means over (we know it's not and we all have tales of continuing battles to tell); but I am arguing that a nervousness has crept over us as we have registered the spectacular marketing success which women's writing has enjoyed. As ever, we are alert to the spectre of recuperation. My further claim, therefore, is that the emphasis should now be on rereading these newly conscripted texts and on being alert to their differences in order not to see them as a chorus of women's voices blended in undifferentiated sisterhood. That impulse to blend is a feminist version of imperialism.

['Authenticity and the Writing Cure: Reading some Migrant Women's Writing', in Susan Sheridan (ed.), *Grafts: Feminist Cultural Criticism* (London: Verso, 1988), 111–15.]

DENISE RILEY

38 Am I That Name? Feminism and the Category of 'Women' in History

DESDEMONA. Am I that name, Iago?
IAGO. What name, fair lady?
DESDEMONA. Such as she says my lord did say I was.

William Shakespeare, *Othello*, IV. ii. 1622

The black abolitionist and freed slave, Sojourner Truth, spoke out at the Akron convention in 1851, and named her own toughness in a famous peroration against the notion of woman's disqualifying frailty. She rested her case on her refrain 'Ain't I a woman?' It's my hope to persuade readers that a new Sojourner Truth might well—except for the catastrophic loss of grace in the wording—issue another plea: 'Ain't I a fluctuating identity?' For both a concentration on and a refusal of the identity of 'women' are essential to feminism. This its history makes plain.

The volatility of 'woman' has indeed been debated from the perspective of psychoanalytic theory; her fictive status has been proposed by some Lacanian work,[1] while it has been argued that, on the other hand, sexual identities are ultimately firmly secured by psychoanalysis.[2] From the side of deconstruction, Derrida among others has advanced what he calls the 'undecidability' of woman.[3] I want to sidestep these debates to move to the ground of historical construction, including the history of feminism itself, and suggest that not only 'woman' but also 'women' is troublesome—and that this extension of our suspicions is in the interest of feminism. That we can't bracket off either Woman, whose capital letter has long alerted us to her dangers, or the more modest lower-case 'woman', while leaving unexamined the ordinary, inno-cent-sounding 'women'.

This 'women' is not only an inert and sensible collective; the dominion of fictions has a wider sway than that. The extent of its reign can be partly revealed by looking at the crystallisations of 'women' as a category. To put it schematically: 'women' is historically, discursively constructed, and always relatively to other categories which themselves change; 'women' is a volatile collectivity in which female persons can be very differently positioned, so that the apparent continuity of the subject of 'women' isn't to be relied on;

'women' is both synchronically and diachronically erratic as a collectivity, while for the individual, 'being a woman' is also inconstant, and can't provide an ontological foundation. Yet it must be emphasised that these instabilities of the category are the *sine qua non* of feminism, which would otherwise be lost for an object, despoiled of a fight, and, in short, without much life.

But why should it be claimed that the constancy of 'women' can be undermined in the interests of feminism? If Woman is in blatant disgrace, and woman is transparently suspicious, why lose sleep over a straightforward descriptive noun, 'women'? Moreover, how could feminism gain if its founding category is also to be dragged into the shadows properly cast by Woman? And while, given the untidiness of word use, there will inevitably be some slippery margins between 'woman' and 'women', this surely ought not to worry any level-headed speaker? If the seductive fraud of 'woman' is exposed, and the neutral collectivity is carefully substituted, then the ground is prepared for political fights to continue, armed with clarity. Not woman, but women—then we can get on with it.

It is true that socialist feminism has always tended to claim that women are socially produced in the sense of being 'conditioned' and that femininity is an effect. But 'conditioning' has its limits as an explanation, and the 'society' which enacts this process is a treacherously vague entity. Some variants of American and European cultural and radical feminism do retain a faith in the integrity of 'women' as a category. Some proffer versions of a female nature or independent system of values, which, ironically, a rather older feminism has always sought to shred to bits,[4] while many factions flourish in the shade cast by these powerful contemporary naturalisms about 'women'. Could it be argued that the only way of avoiding these constant historical loops which depart or return from the conviction of women's natural dispositions, to pacifism for example, would be to make a grander gesture—to stand back and announce that there *aren't any* 'women'? And then, hard on that defiant and initially absurd-sounding assertion, to be scrupulously careful to elaborate it—to plead that it means that all definitions of gender must be looked at with an eagle eye, wherever they emanate from and whoever pronounces them, and that such a scrutiny is a thoroughly feminist undertaking. The will to support this is not blandly social-democratic, for in no way does it aim to vault over the stubborn harshness of lived gender while it queries sexual categorisation. Nor does it aim at a glorious indifference to politics by placing itself under the banner of some renewed claim to androgyny, or to a more modern aspiration to a 'post-gendered subjectivity'. But, while it refuses to break with feminism by naming itself as a neutral deconstruction, at the same time it refuses to identify feminism with the camp of the lovers of 'real women'.

Here someone might retort that there are real, concrete women. That what Foucault did for the concept of 'the homosexual' as an invented classification just cannot be done for women, who indubitably existed long before the nineteenth century unfolded its tedious mania for fresh categorisations. That historical constructionism has run mad if it can believe otherwise. How can it be overlooked that women are a natural as well as a characterised category, and that their distinctive needs and sufferings are all too real? And how could a politics of women, feminism, exist in the company of such an apparent theoreticist disdain for reality, which it has mistakenly conflated with ideology as if the two were one?

A brief response would be that unmet needs and sufferings do not spring from a social reality of oppression, which has to be posed against what is said and written about women—but that they spring from the ways in which women are positioned, often harshly or stupidly, *as* 'women'. This positioning occurs both in language, forms of description, and what gets carried out, so that it is misleading to set up a combat for superiority between the two. Nor, on the other hand, is any complete identification between them assumed.

It is true that appeals to 'women's' needs or capacities do not, on their own, guarantee their ultimately conservative effects any more than their progressivism; a social policy with innovative implications may be couched in a deeply familial language, as with state welfare provision at some periods. In general, which female persons under what circumstances will be heralded as 'women' often needs some effort of translation to follow; becoming or avoiding being named as a sexed creature is a restless business.

Feminism has intermittently been as vexed with the urgency of disengaging from the category 'women' as it has with laying claim to it; twentieth-century European feminism has been constitutionally torn between fighting against over-feminisation and against under-feminisation, especially where social policies have been at stake. Certainly the actions and the wants of women often need to be fished out of obscurity, rescued from the blanket dominance of 'man', or 'to be made visible'. But that is not all. There are always too many invocations of 'women', too much visibility, too many appellations which were better dissolved again—or are in need of some accurate and delimiting handling. So the precise specifying of 'women' for feminism might well mean occasionally forgetting them—or remembering them more accurately by refusing to enter into the terms of some public invocation. At times feminism might have nothing to say on the subject of 'women'—when their excessive identification would swallow any opposition, engulfing it hopelessly.

This isn't to imply that every address to 'women' is bad, or that feminism has some special access to a correct and tolerable level of feminisation. Both these points could generate much debate. What's suggested here is that the volatility of 'women' is so marked that it makes feminist alliances with other tendencies as difficult as they are inescapable. A political interest may descend to illuminate 'women' from almost anywhere in the rhetorical firmament, like lightning. This may happen against an older, slower backdrop of altering understandings as to what sexual characterisations are, and a politician's fitful concentration on 'women' may be merely superimposed on more massive alterations of thought. To understand all the resonances of 'women', feminist tactics would need to possess not only a great elasticity for dealing with its contemporary deployments, but an awareness of the long shapings of sexed classifications in their post-1790s upheavals.

This means that we needn't be tormented by a choice between a political realism which will brook no nonsense about the uncertainties of 'women', or deconstructionist moves which have no political allegiances. No one needs to believe in the solidity of 'women'; doubts on that score do not have to be confined to the giddy detachment of the academy, to the semiotics seminar rooms where politics do not tread. There are alternatives to those schools of thought which in saying that 'woman' is fictional are silent about 'women', and those which, from an opposite perspective, proclaim that the reality of women is yet to come, but that this time, it's we, women, who will define her. Instead of veering between deconstruction and transcendence, we could try another train of speculations: that 'women' is indeed an unstable category, that this instability has a historical foundation, and that feminism is the site of the systematic fighting-out of that instability—which need not worry us.

It might be feared that to acknowledge any semantic shakiness inherent in 'women' would plunge one into a vague whirlpool of 'postgendered' being, abandoning the cutting edges of feminism for an ostensibly new but actually well-worked indifference to the real masteries of gender, and that the known dominants would only be strengthened in the process. This could follow, but need not. The move from questioning the presumed ahistoricity of sexed identities does not have to result in celebrating the carnival of diffuse and contingent sexualities. Yet this question isn't being proposed as if, on the other hand, it had the power to melt away sexual antagonism by bestowing a history upon it. [. . .]

If it is fair to speculate that 'women' as a category does undergo a broadly increasing degree of sexualisation between the late seventeenth and the nineteenth centuries, what would constitute the evidence? To put clear dates to the long march of the empires of gender over the entirety of the person would be difficult indeed. My suggestion isn't so much that after the seventeenth century a change in ideas about women and their nature develops; rather that 'women' itself comes to carry an altered weight, and that a re-ordered idea of Nature has a different intimacy of association with 'woman' who is accordingly refashioned. It is not only that concepts are forced into new proximities with one another—but they are so differently shot through with altering positions of gender that what has occurred is something more fundamental than a merely sequential innovation—that is, a reconceptualisation along sexed lines, in which the understandings of gender both re-order and are themselves re-ordered.

The nineteenth-century collective 'women' is evidently voiced in new ways by the developing human sciences of sociology, demography, economics, neurology, psychiatry, psychology, at the same time as a newly established realm of the social becomes both the exercising ground and the spasmodic vexation for feminism. The resulting modern 'women' is arguably the result of long processes of closure which have been hammered out, by infinite mutual references, from all sides of these classifying studies; closures which were then both underwritten and cross-examined by nineteenth- and twentieth-century feminisms, as they took up, or respecified, or dismissed these productions of 'women'.

'Women' became a modern social category when their place as newly re-mapped entities was distributed among the other collectivities established by these nineteenth-century sciences. 'Men' did not undergo any parallel re-alignments. But 'society' relied on 'man' too, but now as the opposite which secured its own balance. The couplet of man and society, and the ensuing riddle of their relationship, became the life-blood of anthropology, sociology, social psychology—the endless problem of how the individual stood *vis-à-vis* the world. This was utterly different from the ways in which the concept of the social realm both encapsulated and illuminated 'women'. When this effectively feminised social was then set over and against 'man', then the alignments of the sexes in the social realm were conceptualised askew. It was not so much that women were omitted, as that they were too thoroughly included in an asymmetrical manner. They were not the submerged opposite of man, and as such only in need of being fished up; they formed, rather, a kind of continuum of sociality against which the political was set. [. . .]

Feminism of late has emphasised that indeed 'women' are far from being racially or culturally homogeneous, and it may be thought that this corrective provides the proper answer to the hesitations I've advanced here about 'women'. But this is not the same preoccupation. Indeed there is a world of helpful difference between making claims in the name of an annoyingly generalised 'women' and doing so in the name of, say, 'elderly Cantonese women living in Soho'. Any study of sexual consolidations, of the differing metaphorical weightings of 'women', would have to be alerted to the refine-ments of age, trade, ethnicity, exile, but it would not be satisfied by them. However the specifications of difference are elaborated, they still come to rest on 'women', and it is the isolation of this last which is in question.

It's not that a new slogan for feminism is being proposed here—of feminism without 'women'. Rather, the suggestion is that 'women' is a simultaneous foundation of and an irritant to feminism, and that this is constitutionally so. It is true that the trade-off for the myriad namings of 'women' by politics, sociologies, policies and psychologies is that at this cost 'women' do, sometimes, become a force to be reckoned with. But the caveat remains: the risky elements to the processes of alignment in sexed ranks are never far away, and the very collectivity which distinguishes you may also be wielded, even unintentionally, against you. Not just against you as an individual, that is, but against you as a social being with needs and attributions. The dangerous intimacy between subjectification and subjection needs careful calibration. There is, as we have repeatedly learned, no fluent trajectory from feminism to a truly sexually democratic humanism; there is no easy passage from 'women' to 'humanity'. The study of the historical development and precipitations of these sexed abstractions will help to make sense of why not. That is how Desdemona's anguished question, 'Am I that name?', may be transposed into a more hopeful light.

[*Am I that Name? Feminism and the Category of 'Women' in History* (New York: Macmillan, 1988), 1–17.]

TORIL MOI

39 Feminist, Female, Feminine

Over the past decade, feminists have used the terms 'feminist', 'female' and 'feminine' in a multitude of different ways. [...] I will suggest that we distinguish between 'feminism' as a political position, 'femaleness' as a matter of biology and 'femininity' as a set of culturally defined characteristics.

The words 'feminist' or 'feminism' are political labels indicating support for the aims of the new women's movement which emerged in the late 1960s. 'Feminist criticism', then, is a specific kind of political discourse: a critical and theoretical practice committed to the struggle against patriarchy and sexism. [...]

If feminist criticism is characterised by its *political* commitment to the struggle against all forms of patriarchy and sexism, it follows that the very fact of being *female* does not necessarily guarantee a feminist approach. As a political discourse feminist criticism takes its *raison d'être* from outside criticism itself. It is a truism, but it still needs to be said that not all books written by women on women writers exemplify anti-patriarchal commitment. This is particularly true for many early (pre-1960s) works on women writers, which often indulge in precisely the kind of patriarchal stereotyping feminists want to combat. A female tradition in literature or criticism is not necessarily a feminist one. [...]

If the confusion of *female* with *feminist* is fraught with political pitfalls, this is no less true of the consequences of the collapse of *feminine* into *female*. Among many feminists it has long been established usage to make 'feminine' (and 'masculine') represent *social constructs* (patterns of sexuality and behaviour imposed by cultural and social norms), and to reserve 'female' and 'male' for the purely biological aspects of sexual difference. Thus 'feminine' represents nurture, and 'female' nature in this usage. 'Femininity' is a cultural construct: one isn't born a woman, one becomes one, as Simone de Beauvoir puts it. Seen in this perspective, patriarchal oppression consists of imposing certain social standards of femininity on all biological women, in order precisely to make us believe that the chosen standards for 'femininity' are *natural*. Thus a woman who refuses to conform can be labelled both *unfeminine* and *unnatural*. It is in the patriarchal interest that these two terms (femininity and femaleness) stay thoroughly confused. Patriarchy, in other words, wants us to believe that there is such a thing as an essence of femaleness, called femininity. Feminists, on the contrary, have to disentangle this confusion, and must therefore always insist that though women undoubtedly are *female*, this in no way guarantees that they will be *feminine*. This is equally true whether one defines femininity in the old patriarchal ways or in a new feminist way. Essentialism (the belief in a given female nature) in the end always plays into the hands of those who want women to conform to predefined patterns of femininity. In this context *biologism* is the belief that such an essence is biologically given. It is not less *essentialist*, however, to hold that there is a historically or socially given female essence.

But if, as suggested, we define *feminism* as a political position and *femaleness* as a matter of biology, we are still confronted with the problem of how to define *femininity*. 'A set of culturally defined characteristics' or a 'cultural construct' may sound irritatingly vague to many. It would seem that any content could be poured into this container; it does not read like a 'proper' definition. The question is, however, whether it is desirable for feminists to try to fix the meaning of femininity at all. Patriarchy has developed a whole series of 'feminine' characteristics (sweetness, modesty, subservience, humility, etc.). Should feminists then really try to develop another set of 'feminine' virtues, however desirable? And even if we did want to define femininity normatively, would it then not just become a part of the metaphysical binary oppositions Hélène Cixous rightly criticises? There is also a danger of turning a positive, feminist definition of femininity into a definition of femaleness, and thereby falling back into another patriarchal trap. Gratifying though it is to be told that women really are strong, integrated, peace-loving, nurturing and creative beings, this plethora of new virtues is no less essentialist than the old ones, and no less oppressive to all those women who do not want to play the role of Earth Mother. It is after all patriarchy, not feminism, which has always believed in a true female/feminine nature: the biologism and essentialism which lurk behind the desire to bestow feminine virtues on all female bodies necessarily plays into the hands of the patriarchs. [. . .]

But doesn't all this theory leave feminists in a kind of double impasse? Is it really possible to remain in the realm of deconstruction when Derrida himself acknowledges that we still live in a 'metaphysical' intellectual space? And how can we continue our political struggle if we first have to deconstruct our own basic assumption of an opposition between male power and female submission? One way of answering these questions is to look at the French-Bulgarian linguist and psychoanalyst Julia Kristeva's considerations on the question of femininity. Flatly refusing to define 'femininity', she prefers to see it as a *position*. If femininity then can be said to have a definition at all in Kristevan terms, it is simply as 'that which is marginalised by the patriarchal symbolic order'. This relational 'definition' is as shifting as the various forms of patriarchy itself, and allows her to argue that men can also be constructed as marginal to the symbolic order, as her analyses of male avant-garde artists (Joyce, Céline, Artaud, Mallarmé, Lautréamont) have shown.[1]

Kristeva's emphasis on femininity as a patriarchal construct enables feminists to counter all forms of biologistic attacks from the defenders of phallocentrism. To posit all women as necessarily feminine and all men as necessarily masculine, is precisely the move which enables the patriarchal powers to define, not femininity, but all *women* as marginal to the symbolic order and to society. If, as Cixous has shown, femininity is defined as lack, negativity, absence of meaning, irrationality, chaos, darkness—in short, as non-Being—Kristeva's emphasis on marginality allows us to view this repression of the feminine in terms of *positionality* rather than of essences. What is perceived as marginal at any given time depends on the position one occupies. A brief example will illustrate this shift from essence to position: if patriarchy sees women as occupying a marginal position within the symbolic order, then it can construe them as the *limit* or borderline of that order. From a phallocentric point of view, women will then come to represent the necessary frontier between man and chaos, but because of their very marginality they will also always seem to recede into and merge with the chaos of the outside. Women seen as the limit of the symbolic order will in other words share in the disconcerting properties of *all* frontiers: they will be neither inside nor outside, neither known nor unknown. It is this position which has enabled male culture sometimes to vilify women as representing darkness and chaos, to view them as Lilith or the Whore of Babylon, and sometimes to elevate them as the representatives of a higher and purer nature, to venerate them as Virgins and Mothers of God. In the first instance the borderline is seen as part of the chaotic wilderness outside, and in the second it is seen as an inherent part of the inside: the part which protects and shields the symbolic order from the imaginary chaos. Needless to say, neither position corresponds to any essential truth of woman, much as the patriarchal powers would like us to believe that they did.[2]

Such a positional perspective on the meaning of femininity would seem to be the only way of escaping the dangers of biologism (conflation with femaleness). But it does not answer our basic political questions. For if we now have deconstructed the *female* out of existence, it would seem that the very foundations of the feminist struggle have disappeared. In her article 'Women's Time', Kristeva advocates a deconstructive approach to sexual difference. The feminist struggle, she argues, must be seen historically and politically as a three-tiered one, which can be schematically summarised as follows:

1. Women demand equal access to the symbolic order. Liberal feminism. Equality.
2. Women reject the male symbolic order in the name difference. Radical feminism. Femininity extolled.
3. Women reject the dichotomy between masculine and feminine as metaphysical. (This is Kristeva's own position.)

The third position is one that has deconstructed the opposition between masculinity and femininity, and therefore necessarily challenges the very notion of identity. Kristeva writes:

In this third attitude, which I strongly advocate—which I imagine?—the very dichotomy man/woman as an opposition between two rival entities may be understood as belonging to *metaphysics*. What can 'identity', even 'sexual identity', mean in a new theoretical and scientific space where the very notion of identity is challenged?[3]

The relationship between these three positions requires some comments. Elsewhere in her article Kristeva clearly states that she sees them as simultaneous and non-exclusive positions in contemporary feminism, rather than as a feminist version of Hegel's philosophy of history. To advocate position 3 as exclusive of the first two is to lose touch with the political reality of feminism. We still need to claim our place in human society as equals, not as subordinate members, and we still need to emphasise that difference between male and female experience of the world. But that difference is shaped by the patriarchal structures feminists are opposing; and to remain faithful to it, is to play the patriarchal game. Nevertheless, as long as patriarchy is dominant, it still remains *politically* essential for feminists to defend women *as* women in order to counteract the patriarchal oppression that precisely despises women *as* women. But an 'undeconstructed' form of 'stage 2' feminism, unaware of the metaphysical nature of gender identities, runs the risk of becoming an inverted form of sexism. It does so by uncritically taking over the very metaphysical categories set up by patriarchy in order to keep women in their places, despite attempts to attach new feminist values to these old categories. An adoption of Kristeva's 'deconstructed' form of feminism therefore in one sense leaves everything as it was—our positions in the political struggle have not changed; but in another sense, it radically transforms our awareness of the nature of that struggle. A feminist appropriation of deconstruction is therefore both possible and politically productive as long as it does not lead us to repress the necessity of incorporating Kristeva's two first stages into our perspective. [. . .]

['Feminist, Female, Feminine', in Catherine Belsey and Jane Moore (eds.), *The Feminist Reader: Essays in Gender and the Politics of Literary Criticism* (London: Macmillan, 1989), 117–32.]

DIANA FUSS

40   The 'Risk' of Essence

One of the prime motivations behind the production of this book is the desire to break or in some way to weaken the hold which the essentialist/construc-tionist binarism has on feminist theory. It is my conviction that the deadlock created by the long-standing controversy over the issue of human essences (essential femininity, essential blackness, essential gayness . . .) has, on the one hand, encouraged more careful attention to cultural and historical specifi-cities where perhaps we have hitherto been too quick to universalize but, on the other hand, foreclosed more ambitious investigations of specificity and difference by fostering a certain paranoia around the perceived threat of essentialism. It could be said that the tension produced by the essentialist/ constructionist debate is responsible for some of feminist theory's greatest insights, that is, the very tension is constitutive of the field of feminist theory. But it can also be maintained that this same dispute has created the current impasse in feminism, an impasse predicated on the difficulty of theorizing the social in relation to the natural, or the theoretical in relation to the political. The very confusion over whether or not the essentialist/constructionist tension is beneficial or detrimental to the health of feminism is itself over-determined and constrained by the terms of the opposition in question.

One needs, therefore, to tread cautiously when mapping the boundaries of this important structuring debate for feminism. [. . .]

Essentialism is classically defined as a belief in true essence—that which is most irreducible, unchanging, and therefore constitutive of a given person or thing. This definition represents the traditional Aristotelian understanding of essence, the definition with the greatest amount of currency in the history of Western metaphysics.[1] In feminist theory, essentialism articulates itself in a variety of ways and subtends a number of related assumptions. Most obviously, essentialism can be located in appeals to a pure or original femininity, a female essence, outside the boundaries of the social and thereby untainted (though perhaps repressed) by a patriarchal order. It can also be read in the accounts of universal female oppression, the assumption of a totalizing symbolic system which subjugates all women everywhere, throughout history and across cultures. Further, essentialism underwrites claims for the autonomy of a female voice and the potentiality of a feminine language (notions which find their most sophisticated expression in the much discussed concept of *écriture féminine*).[2] Essentialism emerges perhaps most strongly within the very discourse of feminism, a discourse which presumes upon the unity of its object of inquiry (women) *even* when it is at pains to demonstrate the differences within this admittedly generalizing and imprecise category.

Constructionism, articulated in opposition to essentialism and concerned with its philosophical refutation, insists that essence is itself a historical construction. Constructionists take the refusal of essence as the inaugural moment of their own projects and proceed to demonstrate the way previously assumed self-evident kinds (like 'man' or 'woman') are in fact the effects of complicated discursive practices. Anti-essentialists are engaged in interrogating the intricate and interlacing processes which work together to produce all seemingly 'natural' or 'given' objects. What is at stake for a constructionist are systems of representations, social and material practices, laws of discourses, and ideological effects. In short, constructionists are concerned above all with the *production* and *organization* of differences, and they therefore reject the idea that any essential or natural givens precede the processes of social determination.

Essentialists and constructionists are most polarized around the issue of the relation between the social and the natural. For the essentialist, the natural provides the raw material and determinative starting point for the practices and laws of the social. For example, sexual difference (the division into 'male' and 'female') is taken as prior to social differences which are presumed to be mapped on to, *a posteriori*, the biological subject. For the constructionist, the natural is itself posited as a construction of the social. In this view, sexual difference is discursively produced, elaborated as an effect of the social rather than its *tabula rasa*, its prior object. Thus while the essentialist holds that the natural is *repressed* by the social, the constructionist maintains that the natural is *produced* by the social. The difference in philosophical positions can be summed up by Ernest Jones's question: 'Is woman born or made?' For an essentialist like Jones, woman is born not made; for an anti-essentialist like Simone de Beauvoir, woman is made not born.

Each of these positions, essentialism and constructionism, has demonstrated in the range of its deployment certain analytical strengths and weaknesses. The problems with essentialism are perhaps better known. Essentialist arguments frequently make recourse to an ontology which stands outside the sphere of cultural influence and historical change. 'Man' and 'woman', to take one example, are assumed to be ontologically stable objects, coherent signs which derive their coherency from their unchangeability and predictability (there have *always* been men and women it is argued). No allowance is made for the historical production of these categories which would necessitate a recognition that what the classical Greeks understood by 'man' and 'woman' is radically different from what the Renaissance French understood them to signify or even what the contemporary postindustrial, postmodernist, post-structuralist theoretician is likely to understand by these terms. 'Man' and 'woman' are not stable or universal categories, nor do they have the explanatory power they are routinely invested with. Essentialist arguments are not necessarily ahistorical, but they frequently theorize history as an unbroken continuum that transports, across cultures and through time, categories such as 'man' and 'woman' without in any way (re)defining or indeed (re)constituting them. History itself is theorized as essential, and thus unchanging; its essence is to generate change but not itself to *be* changed.

Constructionists, too, though they might make recourse to historicity as a way to challenge essentialism, nonetheless often work with uncomplicated or essentializing notions of history. While a constructionist might recognize that 'man' and 'woman' are produced across a spectrum of discourses, the categories 'man' and 'woman' still remain constant. Some minimal point of commonality and continuity necessitates at least the linguistic retention of these particular terms. The same problem emerges with the sign 'history' itself, for while a constructionist might insist that we can only speak of *histories* (just as we can only speak of feminisms or deconstructionisms) the question that remains unanswered is what motivates or dictates the continued semantic use of the term 'histories'? This is just one of many instances which suggest that essentialism is more entrenched in constructionism than we previously thought. In my mind, it is difficult to see how constructionism can *be* constructionism without a fundamental dependency upon essentialism.

It is common practice in social constructionist argumentation to shift from the singular to the plural in order to privilege heterogeneity and to highlight important cultural and social differences. Thus, woman becomes women, history becomes histories, feminism becomes feminisms, and so on. While this maneuver does mark a break with unitary conceptual categories (eternal woman, totalizing history, monolithic feminism), the hasty attempts to pluralize do not operate as sufficient defenses or safeguards against essentialism. The plural category 'women', for instance, though conceptually signaling heterogeneity nonetheless semantically marks a collectivity; constructed or not, 'women' still occupies the space of a linguistic unity. It is for this reason that a statement like 'American women are "*x*" ' is no less essentializing than its formulation in the singular, 'The American woman is "*x*".' The essentialism at stake is not countered so much as *displaced*.

If essentialism is more entrenched in constructionist logic than we previously acknowledged, if indeed there is no sure way to bracket off and to contain essentialist maneuvers in anti-essentialist arguments, then we must also simultaneously acknowledge that there is no essence to essentialism, that essence *as* irreducible has been *constructed* to be irreducible. Furthermore, if we can never securely displace essentialism, then it becomes useful for analytical purposes to distinguish between *kinds* of essentialisms, as John Locke has done with his theory of 'real' versus 'nominal' essence. Real essence connotes the Aristotelian understanding of essence as that which is most irreducible and unchanging about a thing; nominal essence signifies for Locke a view of essence as merely a linguistic convenience, a classificatory fiction we need to categorize and to label. Real essences are discovered by close empirical observation; nominal essences are not 'discovered' so much as assigned or produced—produced specifically by language. This specific distinction between real and nominal essence corresponds roughly to the broader oppositional categories of essentialism and constructionism: an essentialist assumes that innate or given essences sort objects naturally into species or kinds, whereas a constructionist assumes that it is language, the names arbitrarily affixed to objects, which establishes their existence in the mind. To clarify, a rose by any other name would still be a rose—for an essentialist; for a constructionist, a rose by any other name would not be a rose, it would be something altogether rather different.

Certainly, Locke's distinction between real and nominal essence is a useful one for making a political wedge into the essentialist/constructionist debate. When feminists today argue for maintaining the notion of a *class* of women, usually for political purposes, they do so I would suggest on the basis of Locke's nominal essence. It is Locke's distinction between nominal and real essence which allows us to work with the category of 'women' as a *linguistic* rather than a natural kind, and for this reason Locke's category of nominal essence is especially useful for anti-essentialist feminists who want to hold onto the notion of women as a group without submitting to the idea that it is 'nature' which categorizes them as such. And yet, however useful the 'real' versus 'nominal' classification may be for clarifying the relation between essence and language (transposing essence as an effect of language), the distinction it proposes is far from an absolute one. Real essence is itself a nominal essence—that is, a linguistic kind, a product of naming. And nominal essence is still an essence, suggesting that despite the circulation of different kinds of essences, they still all share a common classification *as essence*. I introduce the Lockean theory of essence to suggest both that it is crucial to discriminate between the ontological and linguistic orders of essentialism and that it is equally important to investigate their complicities as types of essentialisms, members of the same semantic family.

My point here [. . .] is that social constructionists do not definitively escape the pull of essentialism, that indeed essentialism subtends the very idea of constructionism. Let me take another example, one often cited as the exemplary problem which separates the essentialist from the constructionist: the question of 'the body'. For the essentialist, the body occupies a pure, pre-social, pre-discursive space. The body is 'real', accessible, and transparent; it is always *there* and directly interpretable through the senses. For the constructionist, the body is never simply there, rather it is composed of a network of effects continually subject to sociopolitical determination. The body is 'always already' culturally mapped; it never exists in a pure or uncoded state. Now the strength of the constructionist position is its rigorous insistence on the production of social categories like 'the body' and its attention to systems of representation. But this strength is not built on the grounds of essentialism's demise, rather it works its power by strategically deferring the encounter with essence, displacing it, in this case, onto the concept of sociality.

To say that the body is always already deeply embedded in the social is not by any sure means to preclude essentialism. Essentialism is embedded in the idea of the social and lodged in the problem of social determination (and even [...] directly implicated in the deconstructionist turn of phrase 'always already'). Too often, constructionists presume that the category of the social automatically escapes essentialism, in contradistinction to the way the category of the natural is presupposed to be inevitably entrapped within it. But there is no compelling reason to assume that the natural is, in essence, essentialist and that the social is, in essence, constructionist. If we are to intervene effectively in the impasse created by the essentialist/constructionist divide, it might be necessary to begin questioning the *constructionist* assumption that nature and fixity go together (naturally) just as sociality and change go together (naturally). In other words, it may be time to ask whether essences can change and whether constructions can be normative.

It has often been remarked that biological determinism and social determinism are simply two sides of the same coin: both posit an utterly passive subject subordinated to the shaping influence of either nature or culture, and both disregard the unsettling effects of the psyche. There is a sense in which social constructionism can be unveiled as merely a form of sociological essentialism, a position predicated on the assumption that the subject is, in essence, a social construction. It may well be that at this particular historical moment it has become imperative to retrieve the subject from a total subordination to social determination. Perhaps that is why so many feminist theorists have turned to psychoanalysis as a more compelling, less essentializing account of the constructionist process. Psychoanalysis is in many ways the anti-essentialist discourse *par excellence* in that sexual difference is taken as something to be *explained* rather than assumed. But even psychoanalysis cannot do its work without making recourse to certain essentialist assumptions.

This is an important point since, next to deconstruction, psychoanalysis is generally the discourse most strongly identified as sufficiently able to repudiate metaphysical idealism and its reliance upon essentialism. Lacan refuses all treatments of the subject which take as self-evident an essential, pre-given identity; he is more concerned with displacing the classical humanist subject by demonstrating the production of the subject in language. [...] I am interested in whether an account of the subject based on language can fully detach itself from the essentialist notions it claims so persistently to disinherit. I locate three main areas where Lacan leans heavily on essentialist underpinnings in order to advance an anti-essentialist argument: his emphasis on the speaking subject; his much heralded return to Freud; and, finally, his controversial theory of woman. [...] Even a necessarily abbreviated account of Lacan's sophisticated and complex theory of the psyche will underscore the immense importance of his work for social constructionists.

[...] In his theory of woman as 'not all', Lacan posits the essence of woman as an enigmatic excess or remainder. In this regard, woman remains for Lacan the enigma she was for Freud. In fact, essence operates in Lacan as a leftover classical component which re-emerges in his theory of woman precisely because it is woman who escapes complete subjection to the Symbolic and its formative operations. In her inscription as not all (as Truth, lack, Other, *objet a*, God) woman becomes for Lacan the very repository of essence.

And what of Derrida's theory of essence? Does Derrida 'transcend' essentialism more successfully than Lacan, and if not, where is it inscribed and what implications might it hold for the most rigorous anti-essentialist discourse of all: deconstruction? My position here is that the possibility of any radical constructionism can only be built on the foundations of a hidden essentialism. Derrida would, of course, be quick to agree that despite the dislocating effects of deconstruction's strategies of reversal/displacement we can never get beyond metaphysics, and therefore, since all of Western metaphysics is predicated upon Aristotle's essence/accident distinction, we can never truly get beyond essentialism. This is why we should not be surprised to see certain metaphysical holds operative in Derrida's own work, supporting even his relentless pursuit of binary oppositions and phenomenological essences. My interest in exploring what Derrida calls 'fringes of irreducibility'[3] as they operate in deconstruction itself is motivated not by a desire to demonstrate that Derrida is a *failed* constructionist (this would be a pointless exercise, given the terms of my argument) but by an interest in uncovering the ways in which deconstruction deploys essentialism against itself, leans heavily on essence in its determination to displace essence. Derrida's theory of woman is one place to start [...] essentialism works its logic through a number of important 'Derrideanisms', including the emphasis upon undecidability and the related notions of contradiction and heterogeneity. [...]

Despite the uncertainty and confusion surrounding the sign 'essence', more than one influential theorist has advocated that perhaps we cannot do without recourse to irreducibilities. One thinks of Stephen Heath's by now famous suggestion, 'the risk of essence may have to be taken'.[4] It is post-structuralist feminists who seem most intrigued by this call to risk essence. Alice Jardine, for example, finds Stephen Heath's proclamation (later echoed by Gayatri Spivak) to be 'one of the most thought-provoking statements of recent date'.[5] But not all poststructuralist feminists are as comfortable with the prospect of re-opening theory's Pandora's box of essentialism. Peggy Kamuf warns that calls to risk essentialism may in the end be no more than veiled defences against the unsettling operations of deconstruction:

How is one supposed to understand essence as a *risk* to be run when it is by definition the non-accidental and therefore hardly the apt term to represent danger or risk? Only over against and in impatient reaction to the deconstruction of the subject can 'essence' be made to sound excitingly dangerous and the phrase 'the risk of essence' can seem to offer such an appealing invitation. . . . 'Go for it,' the phrase incites. 'If you fall into "essence," you can always say it was an accident.'[6]

In Kamuf's mind, risking essence is really no risk at all; it is merely a clever way of preserving the metaphysical safety net should we lose our balance walking the perilous tightrope of deconstruction.

But the call to risk essence is not merely an 'impatient reaction' to decon-struction (though it might indeed be this in certain specific instances); it can also operate as a deconstructionist strategy. 'Is not strategy itself the real risk?' Derrida asks in his seminar on feminism.[7] To the deconstructionist, strategy of any kind is a risk because its effects, its outcome, are always unpredictable and undecidable. Depending on the historical moment and the cultural context, a strategy can be 'radically revolutionary or deconstructive' or it can be 'dan-gerously reactive'. What is risky is giving up the security—and the fantasy—of occupying a single subject-position and instead occupying two places at once. In a word, 'we have to negotiate'. For an example of this particular notion of 'risk' we can turn to Derrida's own attempts to dare to speak as woman. For a male subject to speak as woman can be radically de-essentializing; the trans-gression suggests that 'woman' is a social space which any sexed subject can fill. But because Derrida never specifies *which* woman he speaks as (a French bourgeois woman, an Anglo-American lesbian, and so on), the strategy to speak as woman is simultaneously re-essentializing. The risk lies in the difficult negotiation between these apparently contradictory effects.

It must be pointed out here that the constructionist strategy of specifying more precisely these sub-categories of 'woman' does not necessarily preclude essentialism. 'French bourgeois woman' or 'Anglo-American lesbian', while crucially emphasizing in their very specificity that 'woman' is by no means a monolithic category, nonetheless reinscribe an essentialist logic at the very level of historicism. Historicism is not always an effective counter to essentialism if it succeeds only in fragmenting the subject into multiple identities, each with its own self-contained, self-referential essence. The constructionist impulse to specify, rather than definitively counteracting essentialism, often simply redeploys it through the very strategy of historicization, rerouting and dispersing it through a number of micropolitical units or sub-categorical classifications, each presupposing its own unique interior composition or metaphysical core.

There is an important distinction to be made, I would submit, between 'deploying' or 'activating' essentialism and 'falling into' or 'lapsing into' essentialism. 'Falling into' or 'lapsing into' implies that essentialism is inherently reactionary—inevitably and inescapably a problem or a mistake. 'Deploying' or 'activating', on the other hand, implies that essentialism may have some strategic or interventionary value. What I am suggesting is that the political investments of the sign 'essence' are predicated on the subject's complex positioning in a particular social field, and that the appraisal of this investment depends not on any interior values intrinsic to the sign itself but rather on the shifting and determinative discursive relations which produced it. [...] [T]he radicality or conservatism of essentialism depends, to a significant degree, on *who* is utilizing it, *how* it is deployed, and *where* its effects are concentrated.

It is important not to forget that essence is a sign, and as such historically contingent and constantly subject to change and to redefinition. Historically, we have never been very confident of the definition of essence, nor have we been very certain that the definition of essence is to *be* the definitional. Even the essence/accident distinction, the inaugural moment of Western metaphysics, is by no means a stable or secure binarism. The entire history of metaphysics can be read as an interminable pursuit of the essence of essence, motivated by the anxiety that essence may well be accidental, changing and unknowable. Essentialism is not, and has rarely been, monolithically coded. Certainly it is difficult to identify a single philosopher whose work does not attempt to account for the question of essentialism in some way; the repeated attempts by these philosophers to fix or to define essence suggest that essence is a slippery and elusive category, and that the sign itself does not remain stationary or uniform.

The deconstruction of essentialism, rather than putting essence to rest, simply raises the discussion to a more sophisticated level, leaps the analysis up to another higher register, above all, keeps the sign of essence in play, even if (indeed *because*) it is continually held under erasure. Constructionists, then, need to be wary of too quickly crying 'essentialism'. Perhaps the most dangerous problem for anti-essentialists is to see the category of essence as 'always already' knowable, as immediately apparent and naturally transparent. Similarly, we need to beware of the tendency to 'naturalize' the category of the natural, to see this category, too, as obvious and immediately perceptible *as such*. Essentialism may be at once more intractable and more irrecuperable than we thought; it may be essential to our thinking while at the same time there is nothing 'quintessential' about it. To insist that essentialism is always and everywhere reactionary is, for the constructionist, to buy into essentialism in the very act of making the charge; *it is to act as if essentialism has an essence.*

[*Essentially Speaking: Feminism, Nature and Difference* (New York: Routledge, 1989), 1–22.]

RACHEL BOWLBY

41 Still Crazy After All These Years

To begin at the end, then, an excessively clear and schematic summary of the current state of play (or the permanent state of play) for the two protagonists. Psychoanalysis and feminism, it seems, have been together for a long time now, fixed into what seems to have become a virtually interminable relationship, marked repeatedly by expressions of violent feeling on both sides. Passionate declarations are followed by calm periods and then by the breaking out or resurgence of desperate denunciations and pleas once again. Past periods or episodes—Freud and the hysterics, the 'great debate' of the 1920s and 1930s—are dimly glimpsed or resuscitated, long-forgotten dates, taking on renewed if not new meanings from the perspective of contemporary interests. Vehement denials and vehement advocacy characterize the proposals of both parties. 'We were made for each other', says one partner in the first flush of rapture; only to be followed at a later, more bitter stage by a transformed insistence that 'the relationship was doomed from the start'. The one constant seems to be that neither side ever lets go: even when far apart, between their scattered blind dates—the 1890s, the 1920s and 1930s, the 1970s and 1980s—they have always somewhere been on each other's mind.

Both sides accuse the other of conforming to cultural edicts which they should rather be challenging. For the anti-psychoanalysts, an awesome 'Freudianism' represents the reimposition of the law of patriarchy by which women have always been oppressed, and so is detrimental to the cause of women's emancipation. These feminists see in psychoanalysis an endorsement, rather than a critique, of just what makes patriarchal society unbearable for women. For the pro-psychoanalytic feminists, the problem lies rather with (the rest of) feminism's assumption that the identity of women as women (and men as men, for that matter) is unproblematically given, or that difficulties of sexuality and conflicts of subjectivity are no more than the effect of contingent social oppression. Psychoanalytic feminism takes non-psychoanalytic feminism to be too simple in its notion of subjectivity for it to be capable of achieving the very political goals it sets itself; while anti-psychoanalytic feminism sees in the psychoanalytic stress on subjectivity a needless detour from feminism's real concerns, if not a pernicious undermining of the tough, coherent agents needed to carry through political action with a subjectivity united at both the individual and the collective level.[1]

It is thus not only that feminisms for and against psychoanalysis have trouble in knowing how they feel about each other, but that these difficulties come to be related to problems of how they identify each other's position. The psychoanalysis that one side sees as the cure, or at least as an account of the workings of the disease, is seen by the other as just another instance of the same infection, all the more insidious for being misrecognized as its mitigation. Psychoanalytic feminism claims that feminism needs an extra edge of questioning that only psychoanalysis can supply, while non-psychoanalytic feminism argues in its turn that feminism is quite radical enough on its own and would only fall back into the very traps from which it is trying to free women by taking up with a psychoanalysis irretrievably tainted with conservative, masculine norms.

The issue, repeatedly, revolves around deciding what is to be considered truly political for feminism: one of the baselines of the argument is the implied legitimation in terms of the gesture of 'more political than thou'. And it is in relation to this that the double question of origins and ends arises: Where are women's difficulties supposed to have started; and where does feminism think it is going? Is psychoanalysis a time-wasting diversion from the principal goal; or (from the other side) has the feminism that ignores psychoanalysis taken a short cut that will only return it to the same questions in the long run? [. . .]

Trivial Pursuits

The possibility, or inevitability, of mistaken identification—each side seeing in the other what it longs for or what it dreads—seems to be built in to the structure of this case. Perhaps there is no relationship between psychoanalysis and feminism. [. . .] If the couple are unknown to each other, there is first the possibility for boundless expectations in the imagining of what the other party may have to offer. Disappointment gives place to disillusionment; but then, after a period of temporary forgetting, the whole thing can start up again, with both partners blind to the fact that they have ever met before. What becomes more disturbing in this perpetual restaging of the same passionate drama, the same old serial, is that it might be quite literally a programmed repeat, with no differences at all. If every move, every question, and every answer is entirely given in advance, a perfect copy of an unchanging script, then the joke of the blind date is not only on the hapless participants, but on the spectators trying in vain to maintain their belief in the 'live' spontaneity of the proceedings—or perhaps, finally, not caring one way or the other. An allusion to Cilla Black's infamous television show, where the jokes are all pre-written and the blind dates are spectacularly predictable, may seem out of place in the serious context of the dates, or rather debates, between psychoanalysis and feminism. I bring her on stage, or onto the screen, provocatively, as the doubtful *dea ex machina* who will guide me to what I want to suggest is a serious question about triviality.[2]

Both psychoanalysis and feminism throw into confusion ordinary conceptions of what is to be considered as 'merely' trivial; and not least—though not necessarily from the same angle—in terms of what constitutes the basis for the 'obvious', everyday distinction between the sexes. Freud says towards the beginning of his 'Introductory lecture' on 'Femininity': 'When you meet someone, the first distinction you make is "male or female?" and you are accustomed to make this distinction with unhesitating certainty.'[3] This is the distinction which is so automatic, so 'unhesitating', as to go without saying; and for that very reason, as he will go on to suggest, all the more liable to question. The triviality of the example—any everyday encounter with an unknown person—reverses the implications of the 'accustomed' grid, the habit becoming suspect precisely because it is habitual.

But there is more to triviality than this. The word is derived not from a binary but from a triple distinction: the Latin 'trivium', *tris viae*, 'three ways'. In the context of psychoanalytic stories, this indicates a further step back, from Latin into Greek and Sophocles' play about Oedipus, where the event that may or may not have taken place when the hero, travelling many years before, killed an old man at the intersection of a 'triple way', $\tau\rho\iota\pi\lambda\eta$ $\sigma\delta\eta$, becomes a question of the utmost importance.[4]

There is another point at which psychoanalysis comes upon a crossroads at which three ways, three roads, lead off. This is none other than the crucial original encounter with that other person as 'male or female': the mythical moment of 'fright' at first sight when the meaning of sexual difference impinges upon the child.[5] And at this juncture, each of the two trivially obvious sides of the distinction turns out to be broken down into three different possible ways. For the boy, the realization of the girl's lack sends him off along one of three lines—homosexuality, fetishism, or 'normality'— which respond to his newfound vulnerability. Feminist priorities mean that we do not have time to follow the boy's adventures further. For the girl, there are also three possible 'lines of development'—to neurosis, to the 'masculine protest', or to 'normal' femininity—and we shall have occasion to return to them later on.

Boy meets Girl?

One of the difficulties in bringing about or rejecting the desirability of a final union between psychoanalysis and feminism has been precisely that of identifying the sexes of the two parties. From the point of view of anti-psychoanalytic feminism, the person of Freud as a Victorian patriarch is usually taken as the ground for assuming an inescapably anti-feminist stance built into the texts and the practice of psychoanalysis ever since. 'Dora', who walked out before the conclusion of her analysis by a Freud who had not recognized his own interest in seeing her desire as simply heterosexual, can be regarded from this point of view as the first heroine of feminist protest against a psychoanalysis which was doing no more than reconfirming the prevailing sexual norms. From the other side, that of pro-psychoanalytic feminism, Freud's early researches into hysteria mark the starting point of what was to be an undoing of every bourgeois or patriarchal assumption as to the biological naturalness of heterosexual attraction, or the masculinity and femininity predicated of men and women.

The first *OED Supplement* example for the word 'feminism' may possibly be enlightening here. It dates from 1895, and reads: 'Her intellectual evolution and her coquettings with the doctrines of "feminism" are traced with real humour.' This might alert the reader to a possible danger in assuming too easily a convenient equality or symmetry in the origins of psychoanalysis and feminism in Britain. Here, as the inaugurating example, the 'very first' instance which will set the terms for the established meanings of the word, we have something that appears to be just the same old misogynist bar-room joke. Not only is feminism in quotation marks, but it is something merely to flirt with—temporarily, perhaps, on the way to a womanhood that would have nothing to do with 'feminism'. The relation between the 'intellectual evolution' and the 'coquettings with "feminism"' is not specified. They might be complementary, reinforcing each other as reason and emotion. They might both be taken as delaying the arrival at normal femininity, but only in the sense of predictable 'phases' to be treated with indulgent paternal 'humour'. Or feminism might be considered the principal deviant: all intellectually evolved women are likely to go through a feminist 'phase'. As a last possibility, the two might be antagonistic, the feminism militating against the intellectual development or the 'coquettings' distracting the brain.

The exemplary first occurrence of feminism (or rather 'feminism') begins, on closer scrutiny, to look more and more like a miniature illustration of the questions surrounding the psychoanalytic account of femininity. Does this vignette postulate the implied relationship between intellect, feminism, coquetting, and the acquisition of a 'normal' femininity as something that calls for explanation, or rather as a matter of course, obvious as the difference of the sexes? Is the choice of a first citation for feminism in which these moments are said to be treated with 'real humour' an exposé of the standard smutty jokes at women's expense whose structure Freud lays bare, or is it just one more example of them?[6]

Oddly or inevitably enough, 1895 is also the date of the publication of Freud's and Breuer's *Studies in Hysteria*, in which the 'cases' analysed raise all the same questions as does this questionable 'case' of feminism as to the pertinence of the psychoanalytic account of feminine development. Either the hysterical women analysed by Freud and Breuer open the way to a general understanding of the typical structures which make femininity difficult for women, or they inaugurate an ineradicable complicity of psychoanalysis with the same notions that make all women into aberrant 'cases' for masculine correction or contempt, and make feminism into a permanent joke between men.

It is perhaps quite appropriate that the English girl should be 'coquetting' with feminism, the word carrying with it all the quintessentially English connotations of its Frenchness. 'Feminism' is French too, according to the dictionary; the pair seem to be well-matched, and heterosexually, since it is with men that girls are supposed to coquette. And further investigations with the French dictionary reveal that feminism is in fact ultimately a masculine word—not only by grammatical gender, but in that Fourier is specifically named as its (male) inventor: 'Le mot "féminisme" fut créé par Fourier.'[7] This makes feminism's kinship with Dr Freud's personalized psychoanalysis take on different implications. In its origin, as in Freud's interpretation of it, it apparently represents a 'masculine' line of development. Or, like psychoanalysis, its beginnings seem to have the form of the father's kindly intervention to set the dissatisfied girl to rights. An investigation of the source of the coquetting quotation makes things no simpler; but we will not allow ourselves to be waylaid by this here.

The question of the relationship between intellectual evolution and femininity is one that is broached by Freud, too, quite soon after this, for instance in a footnote to the 'Dora' case, where he refers to 'her declaration that she had been able to keep abreast with her brother up to the time of her first illness, but that after that she had fallen behind him in her studies'. He goes on:

It was as though she had been a boy up till that moment, and had then become girlish for the first time. She had in truth been a wild creature; but after the 'asthma' she became quiet and well-behaved. That illness formed the boundary between two phases of her sexual life, of which the first was masculine in character, and the second feminine.[8]

It is also significant that at the time when Dora was presented to Freud for analysis, she 'employed herself... with attending lectures for women and with carrying on more or less serious studies'.[9] Read with hindsight, the passage can be seen as foreshadowing what will later become the definitive Freudian account of femininity as predicated on the giving up of what is first of all, but equally with hindsight, a masculinity shared by children of both sexes. In the meantime, the structures of castration and the Oedipus complex have been fully installed in Freud's theory, to make the 'boundary' between the 'two phases' of the girl's life acquire all the sharper a distinction. [...]

A Thicker Entanglement

In view of this loaded background in the texts of Freud, it is intriguing that 'repudiation' is a word which has often appeared or recurred in arguments over the proper relationship between psychoanalysis and feminism. To begin with the opening page of Juliet Mitchell's Psychoanalysis and Feminism, the book which launched the present engagement: 'It seems to me that we have turned things on their head by accepting Reich's and Laing's analyses and repudiating Freud's.'[10] Then Jane Gallop, analysing Mitchell's criticisms of those who criticize Freud on biographical grounds declares: 'Interestingly, the repudiation of the trivial ad hominem argument returns continually'.[11] In Jacqueline Rose's fine reply to Elizabeth Wilson's criticisms of psychoanalysis, the word occurs a few times in relation to both the British left and British feminism, in their joint or separate 'repudiation' of psychoanalysis. What Rose calls 'a fairly consistent repudiation of Freud' is also a fairly consistent application of the term 'repudiation' by those who are for psychoanalysis to those who are not.[12]

Given the cluster of associations which link repudiation and femininity in the Standard Edition, it may well be worth examining the implications of this recurrent charge in some detail. For 'repudiation', even aside from its Freudian uses, is not, after all, just any old word. It is strong language, and seems to imply not just rejection or refusal, but also that what is rejected is somehow a part of the repudiator: that it is illegitimately cast off. Repudiation's five emphatic syllables seem to proclaim their refusal a little too loudly. There is the implication that what you repudiate really belongs to you, stays behind to haunt you, however hard you try to get rid of it. Repudiation carries the suggestion of an arbitrary gesture which is not concerned with arguing in terms of moral rights or logic. In this respect, the word is precisely differentiated from its near homonymic neighbour 'refutation', which has—or had, until it began recently to be used as synonymous with 'disagree'—just that dispassionate reason which repudiation lacks. Or put the other way round, repudiation has all the emotional conviction to which refutation is indifferent.

Returning to the OED for more rational or impartial enlightenment, we find that there are further layers to be uncovered. The primary meaning, now defunct, of the verb 'repudiate' is specific and revealing. It is 'to divorce', and it was used in English of a man in relation to a woman but not the other way around. In the expansion that follows the initial definition, we have first: 'Of a husband: To put away or cast off (his wife): to divorce, dismiss'; and then 'cast off, disown (a person or thing)'. If we put this piece of information back into the context of the relation between psychoanalysis and feminism, the situation seems all the more confusing. To say that feminism repudiates psychoanalysis is to put feminism in the position of a man rejecting his wife, in a gesture that could not be reciprocated. It means that the feminist rejection of psychoanalysis is equivalent to an exemplary instance of the exercise of patriarchal power; it means also that there is no position other than that of an identification with patriarchal authority from which it can be done. And if repudiation connotes the putting asunder, at the instigation of one of them, of two 'persons or things' which were to have been joined together for life, it suggests a newly literal side to what are claimed as the 'fatal' consequences that would ensue on feminism's refusal to couple itself with psychoanalysis.[13]

The use of the term 'repudiation' by advocates of psychoanalysis seems then to have the effect of a double bind—or rather, a forced marriage. It accuses feminism of acting with the arbitrary prerogatives of a representative of patriarchy, of inserting itself into precisely the paradigm from which it wants to free women, and on the side of masculine power. If feminism accuses psychoanalysis of merely validating the established forms whereby women are supposed to find their fulfilment as wives and mothers, psychoanalysis turns this back on feminism by declaring it already married to a psychoanalysis from which it can only be separated by itself re-enacting or reinstalling those structures of patriarchal authority: repudiation is just one of the lesser known and more patriarchal of the fifty accredited ways to leave your lover.

Bearing in mind all these complexities, some old-fashioned 'feminine' sympathy is perhaps not out of place for the heroine or victim of one of the dictionary's examples of the word, taken from the *Edinburgh Review* of 1803: 'She does not appear even to have understood what they meant by repudiation.' Now this poor lady so patronizingly chided is in fact none other than Madame Suzanne Necker, the mother of Madame de Staël and the wife of Louis XVI's minister, Jacques Necker. In 1794 she published from exile in Switzerland a book on divorce. But we don't have time to pursue this lead any further...

There are still further layers to be uncovered: we have not reached 'bedrock' yet. The English 'repudiation' is a direct import from the Latin *repudium*, which is in turn cognate with *pudor*, meaning 'shame', whence in English the (still Latin, euphemistic) *pudenda*. Literally, the *pudenda* are simply 'parts for which shame should be felt'; the use of the word (in Latin as later in English) to refer only to the female genitals is an interesting case of the figure of part for whole (or rather hole for whole). A single instance of nebulous neuter 'things for which shame is appropriate' comes to take the place of the entire class. Both the euphemistic equivocation and the generality of the *pudenda* serve as a thin veil for the word which in practice can mean only one thing. It is the female genitals, in their lack by comparison with those of the man, which figure as the ultimate cause in Freud for the disparagement of femininity, for the determination on the part of protesting men and women to be exempt from such a meagre and shameful endowment.

All this leaves us with some contradictory consequences. In psychoanalytic theory, supported by linguistic fossils if not by human anatomy, there is apparently no case of repudiation which is not, at bottom, at rock-bottom, a repudiation of feminity. There is further no attitude to feminity which is not that of repudiation: thus no place, once past the crossroads where the question 'male or female?' is first posed or imposed, that does not imply the repudiation of femininity, including the place of femininity itself, which is *repudianda*, to be repudiated, for feminine women and feminists alike. And this merely repeats the fate of the *pudenda*, themselves concealed inside the word: there are no shameful parts other than the parts which are those which distinguish, or rather diminish, the woman. Repudiation implies the taking of a masculine position and the rejection of a feminine one; at the same time there is no escape from that femininity which is everyone's cast-off or ex-wife, be they man, feminist, or lady.

So where does this leave psychoanalysis and feminism? If repudiation is always the repudiation of femininity, then in its own terms psychoanalysis can hardly blame feminism for an attitude which it has identified as inevitable. This is perhaps just a different inflection of that old psychoanalytic saw about Dostoevsky's 'knife that cuts both ways', to which Freud alludes in a footnote about nothing other than feminist objections to psychoanalysis: any objection to psychoanalysis can always be interpreted psychoanalytically, as can the psychoanalytic account of femininity, which then leads to 'no decision'. Psychoanalytically, it is impossible to adopt psychoanalysis (which is what the sceptics are being urged to do): it cannot but be repudiated. To put it bluntly, the knife that cuts both ways is also the three ways that fork only one way. You can't refute it; to which we may now add: you can only repudiate it.

All this may provide some kind of explanation for the interminability of the courtship of psychoanalysis and feminism. Psychoanalysis is certainly accusing feminism of taking a masculine stance. But even more significantly, it is putting itself in the impossible place of the woman. For just as they are locked into a state of mutual denunciation, each accusing the other of acting like a man, so they come straight back together in their joint claim that something should speak from the position of the cast-off woman.

Three Words in a Boat

But further discoveries await us. So far we have been assuming that there is some kind of textual justification for the connection we have been making between the various Freudian feminine repudiations. But if we go back behind the familiar words of the Strachey translation to take a look at the original language of psychoanalysis, a startling revelation awaits us. For it turns out that the German word translated by 'repudiation' is different in each of the three cases noted above. In the 'Femininity' lecture, it is *verwerfen*, meaning 'to throw away' or 'discard'. In the 'Analysis' essay, 'repudiation' translates *ablehnen*: 'to decline, refuse, remove'. And in the 'Female homosexuality' text, it is *weisen*, in a construction where it means 'to exile, expel, or banish'. These words are not identical in meaning or in force. In fact, the mildest word, *ablehnen*, is the one which occurs in the most intractable, most often cited passage, the one which makes the repudiation of femininity into the 'biological "bedrock" '. In view of the fact that 'the repudiation of femininity' has become one of the most familiar phrases in anglophone discussions of Freud and femininity, this assimilation on the part of the translator, deliberate or not, seems to be worth some attention. 'Repudiation' covers three different German words in the same context of an attitude to femininity; the three words are themselves used elsewhere in Freud without being translated by 'repudiation'.

Just as in Freudian theory the obviousness of 'male or female?' must be broken down to show the three ways offered to each sex at the point of that initial separation, so the 'repudiation' of femininity which has turned out to dominate, even to block, all the possible paths seems now to be itself made up of three different words, hitherto unsuspected beneath the familiar, unified cover. Arguably, then, the decision can be seen retrospectively to have marked a turning point in the future possibilities for discussions of psychoanalysis and feminism. Perhaps, indeed, it may have inaugurated a distinctively English, or anglophone, 'line of development': 'No femininity please, we're British'.

We could then carry this to the limit, and ask what it would mean if 'the repudiation of femininity' were nothing but an error of translation, a bad English dream that has been marring the fates of femininity and feminism ever since. What a momentous difference would then turn out to have ensued when psychoanalysis crossed the Channel and arrived in Britain: at one stroke, we might then have found the answer to why psychoanalysis has never made its way into British culture, or why English-speaking feminists have been reluctant to adopt it as a theory. What a relief, or a shock, after all these years, if the trouble could all be blamed on an idiosyncratic predilection, say, for that satisfying and rare five-syllable word—or else just on the slightest assimilating slip of the Strachey pen. Legend has it—and I have not been able, despite earnest researches, to find the source—that when Freud arrived in the United States to deliver a series of lectures in 1909, he said of his new science and its new destination: 'We are bringing them the plague'. It would be a nice irony if the plague with which the Standard Edition infected the English-speaking world was not Freud's psychoanalysis at all.

But the problem cannot be put in quite such clear-cut terms—all the more so since the clearness of the cut is precisely what is at issue. Instead, the multiple origin of 'repudiation' raises more general questions about the necessary interpretation and distortion that accompany the translating and the transporting of theories from one language and culture to another. There are also the issues surrounding the gesture of a 'return' to the texts of Freud—questions which are particularly risky at this point because one of the German words translated as 'repudiation', *verwerfen*, is also the word from one of whose uses in Freud Lacan extracts the concept of foreclosure associated with psychosis.[14] It might be argued that there is a crucial difference in the two moves: Lacan is openly admitting that he is drawing out implications which are not thematized in the master text, whereas Strachey, who says nothing about what he is up to, is smuggling in his plague upon women by the back port, in the guise of a direct rendering. But the moral terms of this could just as easily be put the other way round: Strachey is the simpleton who does not realize the significance of what he is doing, while Lacan is claiming as faithfully Freudian something which is actually not there in the original. Putting the issue like this sets up dividing lines which only send the question back to the problem of the master text: to distinguish between the honest importer and the pirate, between the judicious and the blind interpretation, involves just the same appeal to the initial text as the rock which harbours the pure ore of indisputable meaning. The straight and the stray become indistinguishable in the 'Strachey' translation. Even if it could somehow be demonstrated that 'the repudiation of femininity' did not correspond to 'what Freud really said' or 'really meant', this would not cancel out all the arguments about psychoanalysis in English that have been carried on in the meantime: it would simply be the vehicle of a further stage in them.

Now that the rock of repudiation has been shattered, or at least its impenetrability put in question, do the three German words that lie beneath it offer us any potential way out of the impasse of femininity? One meaning of *die Verwerfung* is that of a geological fault: using the translator's licence in reverse, we could put this back into the passage from 'Analysis terminable and interminable'. In this sense, it would seem that 'the biological "bedrock"' was not the repudiation of femininity but the faulting of femininity, leaving open, in the slide between the strata, the possibility that there might be further to go after all, a still more 'basic fault' that had previously not been seen.

The gap between German and English takes us back to the meaning of *weisen von sich*, 'to exile or banish', in the passage from the 'Female homosexuality' case. The word 'repudiation' has itself exiled, repudiated, the femininity that might not have been so utterly ruled out in the German original. This story of a forced exile is also, of course, that of the girl's sudden and shattering realization of the significance of her sex and her doomed departure on a one-way ticket to the far land of femininity that never comes, or at which she never arrives.

And what of the time before that? For Freud uses the motif of feminine exile in an explicit and famous simile: 'Our insight into this early, pre-Oedipus, phase in girls comes to us as a surprise, like the discovery, in another field, of the Minoan–Mycenaean civilization behind the civilization of Greece.'[15] Let us pause for a moment with this Minoan–Mycenaean civilization that was producing such archaeological excitement in Freud's time, the layers of an even more ancient Greece below the one that had previously been thought to be the bedrock, the furthest back or down that there could be. It is generally dated about 1400–1100 BC, and has been the source of much evidence for the society from which the Homeric poems and the legends of Greek tragedy then turned out originally—in their first, orally transmitted, form—to derive. It had been thought that this society was non-literate; then came the discoveries of tablets with writing, and the eventual deciphering after many years of the script known as Linear B. Here are some Linear B ideograms:[16]

It is from this other Greece that Freud takes his analogy for the world of the girl before the discovery of her castration.

Imagine, then, lovely Rita, the psychoanalytic girl, her illusions ruined, forced to emigrate from the world of Mycenae into civilization, having to make that choice between three journeys that is no choice after all. The travel agent, who has seen it all before, demands the usual excessive price and explains the various options. 'It will be the trip of a lifetime'. He hands her the standard brochure. It is in twenty-four blue volumes, very heavy for travelling. She takes one look and casts it back in disgust: 'It's all English to me.' But it is too late—the ship is already pulling away and her mother is bidding her goodbye with a repressive wave from the quayside.

Now imagine, several millennia later, the psychoanalytic girl, still travelling. She has been to Phrygia, to Protest City. She has been to Vienna, to Berlin, to Paris; she has crossed the sea to London and sailed across the ocean to New York. Then she was in France again, and lately she has been attending many international gatherings. Never has she come anywhere near to the promised destination of Normal, in the state of Femininity, and in any case she has never been able to avoid the feeling that it does not sound like a place where she would like to end up. She is tired out and disappointed with the trip that cost her so much, longing for home in spite of it all; she is inclined to think that the agent ripped her off. With great difficulty, she procures a passage back to Mycenae, telling herself that she might have been mistaken in the reasons for leaving which seemed so pressing at the time.

She travels for many miles, and eventually the landscape starts to seem familiar. The old town looks the same as she steps down from the train, except that the station seems to have been modernized. There is no more grass, but there is a big tree, to which some zealous bureaucrat has pointlessly attached a label bearing the word 'tree'. And what do those signs mean on the doors over there? She never saw them (were they there?) when she was a girl, but now in a flash it hits her that they must be the same as the ones she has seen at every stop on her journey. Just in time, with a well-trained feminist instinct, she jumps back into the compartment, and away she goes again.

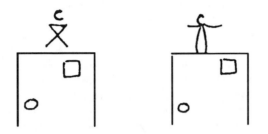

She thought she loved, she thought she was full of love. This was her idea of herself. But the strange brightness of her presence, a marvellous radiance of intrinsic vitality, was a luminousness of supreme repudiation, repudiation, nothing but repudiation.

Yet ... this state of constant unfailing repudiation, was a strain, a suffering also ...

... why need she trouble, why repudiate any further. She was free of it all, she could seek a new union elsewhere.[17]

['Still Crazy After All These Years', in Teresa Brennan (ed.), *Between Feminism and Psychoanalysis* (London: Routledge, 1989), 42–7, 50–9; repr. in *Still Crazy After All These Years: Women, Writing, and Psychoanalysis* (London: Routledge), 1992.]

MORAG SHIACH

42 Their 'symbolic' exists, it holds power—we, the sowers of disorder, know it only too well

The title of this paper is a quotation from 'The laugh of the Medusa' by Hélène Cixous. The quotation mobilizes terms that are central both to Cixous's work over the last twenty years and to this collection on psychoanalysis and feminism. Focusing on questions of 'the symbolic', of power, and on the politics of disorder, Cixous's work suggests new sorts of solutions to the relationship between psychoanalytic theory and feminist practice. It allows us to analyse what we mean by feminist theory or feminist criticism and to consider the implications of a theoretical practice that begins with an articulated politics: 'feminism' is, after all, a political term, an interrogation of power and of the possibility of change, and not just a matter of technique.

Cixous begins by evoking the symbolic, which points us towards the discourse of psychoanalysis. But she puts it in quotation marks, and thus questions its ontological status: are we dealing with metaphor, with representation, or with some kind of real? She also describes it as 'their' symbolic. It is thus a term from which she invites women to take a certain distance, even if only rhetorically, and she implicitly offers the possibility of another symbolic, one that would be 'ours'.

The complicated nature of this invocation of the language of psychoanalysis is, as we shall see, typical of Cixous's work. Notions such as 'the imaginary', 'the symbolic', and 'lack' recur in her writing, but are constantly undermined. Having stated the problem of power and 'the symbolic', Cixous then insists that 'we are in no way obliged to deposit our lives in their banks of lack'.[1] The observation is rhetorical, and the obligation, as Cixous knows, is real enough: but that does not mean it is not open to attack. At other times, Cixous develops a critique of the language of psychoanalysis which engages with the sort of arguments made by Naomi Segal [. . .] about the contingent nature of the narratives mobilized by psychoanalysis. Cixous argues that 'they've theorized their desire for reality', and that psychoanalysis 'reproduces the masculine view, of which it is one of the effects'.[2] She thus distances the political and theoretical project of feminism from the partial accounts of subjectivity and sexual identity offered by psychoanalysis. [. . .]

Cixous does not simply theorize the possibility of writing which undermines a dual hierarchized structure of oppositions; she also produces such writing. I will thus now look at Cixous's theatrical writing as an attempt to produce new forms, and new narratives, for the representation of difference. This writing constitutes part of Cixous's own engagement with a politics of the symbolic.

The problem that is explored in Cixous's theatrical texts is the possibility of representing sexual, or indeed social, difference, without returning to the dual hierarchized oppositions explored in The Newly Born Woman. Cixous writes about difference, but not as something given, natural, or essential. She offers us neither such security, nor such paralysis. Instead, she struggles to represent the fact of difference, as process, as structure, and as constitutive of social and sexual identities.

The theorization of difference, a difference which does not return to the implied judgements of 'different from', is perhaps best known in terms of the writing of Jacques Derrida. In Margins of Philosophy Derrida explains his use of the concept, or rather the process, of différance. He insists that difference cannot be thought in relation to a fixed structure of positive terms. Différance is that which allows the production of meaning. It involves a plethora of relationships across time. Meaning is always constituted by both structural differences and temporal deferrals—and this temporal element is what we have lost in our concept of 'difference'. Derrida argues that: '*différer* in this sense is to temporize, to take recourse, consciously or unconsciously, in the temporal and temporizing mediation of a detour that suspends the accomplishment or fulfilment of "desire" or "will" '.[3] This *différance*, difference with no positive terms, is further described by Derrida as 'the becoming-time of space and the becoming-space of time'. The question then becomes how such a complex relation can be representable: '*Différance* as temporization, *différance* as spacing. How are they to be joined?'[4] One answer, I believe, lies in theatre, which organizes its representations explicitly along both temporal and spatial axes: thus, the attraction of the form of theatre in terms of Cixous's attempts to rewrite, to retheorize, difference.

Cixous has discussed the importance of the temporal aspect of theatre: the spectator 'moves forward [through a play] with a beating heart, not knowing what is going to happen next'.[5] Everyone is in this state of alertness to the existence of time, confronted by its opacity. No one in the theatre can have prior, or superior, knowledge. Each spectator is caught in the play of differences, and the production of meaning.

Cixous has written of her commitment to the poetic over the novelistic. Novelists are the 'allies of representationalism' who try to produce coherence, fixity, and transparency, whereas poets are committed to complexity, to the density of language, and to the power of the unconscious.[6] This commitment to the 'poetic' can also make sense of the terms in which Cixous uses the medium of the theatre: her use of gesture and of image, in order to complicate, or undermine, the stability of narrative. She uses theatre as a means to represent intertextuality, in her constant allusions to and quotations from other theatrical and mythical texts. This foregrounding of the ways in which both 'action' and 'character' are produced through a negotiation with existing texts forces a questioning of the 'natural' bases of character and identity. Cixous produces multivocal forms of theatre, where voices echo each other, contradict each other, and constitute each other. She represents, theatrically, the power of history to disturb, to question, the certainty of the present. All of these strategies can be related to her insistence that writing 'should infinitely dynamize by an incessant process of exchange from one subject to another'.[7] Theatre is speech rather than writing, or at least it is written speech, but it represents exactly such an exchange of subjectivities.

This claim that the basis of Cixous's commitment to, and use of, the form of theatre is *theoretical* should not, perhaps, come as a great surprise. 'Theatre' and 'theory' share a common linguistic origin. Both derive from the concept of 'spectacle', of 'looking', and, as we know, it is not only theatre that can be spectacular! 'Theatre' and 'theory', then, share a lot, but it is the 'something more', the 'poetic' that is offered by the theatre that explains the power of Cixous's theatrical texts. As Jane Gallop observes:

Perhaps in a theoretical text one can never do more than say 'there is more, there is love and beauty' which is a necessary affirmative supplement to the murderous negation that theory must be. But in *Portrait de Dora*, in the theatrical text...this is not a problem, the affirmative is interwoven in various patterns with the negative.[8]

And Cixous is always on the side of the affirmative, against the murderous.

Theatre, then, can be used to represent the process, and the possibility, of *différance*. Cixous further observes the close relation between theatre and psychoanalysis, both in terms of the theatricality of the process of psychoanalysis (its origins in 'family dramas') and in terms of the ways in which theatre represents the relation between, and the constitution of, subjectivities. It is this nexus that leads Cixous to explore, theatrically, questions of sexual difference.

This exploration is carried on in the opera *Le Nom d'Oedipe* (*The Name of Oedipus*), whose title places it immediately at the intersection of theatre and psychoanalysis: Oedipus' drama, after all, became one of the founding narratives of psychoanalysis. Cixous says that in *Le Nom d'Oedipe* she aims to bring 'splitting', to bring sexual difference, to the stage.[9] *Le Nom d'Oedipe* dramatizes sexual difference, explores the relation between masculine and feminine subjectivity, and retells a myth.

Le Nom d'Oedipe speaks, and sings, in many voices, which contrast with, harmonize with, or disturb each other. The opera explores the sexual encounter between Oedipus and Jocasta, his mother, as observed by the bisexual and prophetic figure of Tiresias. Jocasta struggles to relate to Oedipus, without the use of names, or words that will reveal their relationship and make their love impossible. Her own identity is uncertain: 'I, who was you yesterday.' Jocasta declares that 'words escape me', insists that she loves Oedipus 'with my flesh and my soul—and without names'. Tiresias encourages her, 'don't say the delicious old words, spit them out'. But this is too much disruption, the old words reassert themselves, the Law is put in place and Jocasta dies. Oedipus, however, who, as the choir suggests 'is a man, like all other men, their desire is always the same', is left alive, but unsure of his own identity, without the comforting mirror of devoted love: 'who am I if you don't tell me?' Oedipus, throughout the opera, seeks to repress his name, his place in the symbolic order. He tries to repress the existence of the Law, in order to assure his complete possession of Jocasta: 'Promise you will never have another lover...I alone want to be your child, your father if you wish'. But the imposition of the Law does not lead to Oedipus' death. He is left with speech, with language. We are left in no doubt as to who has most interest in challenging the Law that supports the symbolic order, but we also see that the stakes are high, that murder is possible.

Portrait de Dora also explores the construction of sexual identities, the drawing of portraits, and it also retells an old story. Cixous's treatment of Freud's case history explores the relation between power and language and the silencing of Dora, the hysteric whose only power is absence and refusal. Cixous has already warned us of the way in which portraits function to produce fixity and identity, and of the complicity of psychoanalysis in this process: 'hold still, we're going to do your portrait, so that you can begin looking like it right away'.[10]

Dora is constantly being constructed within narratives, 'she is no longer a child', she 'could have taken the place of [their] mother'. She is caught in the determinations of narratives and dramas that circulate around her and through her. The staging, and the structure, of *Portrait de Dora* represent infinite mirroring, the repetition of relations that function to erase the feminine, except as 'nothingness' and silence.

This mirroring theme, so crucial to the formation of subjectivity, is reflected in the dialogue of the play. Freud tells that 'each time Dora's father was asked about her health his eyes filled with tears' and Frau K. tells Dora that 'your father cannot speak about you without tears coming into his eyes'. Language is quotation, is repetition, and identity is always precarious. As Freud says, 'Who is in whose place in this story?' Frau K. is occasionally in Freud's place. She, after all, delivers his observation from the Dora Case History about openness and frankness, 'J'appelle un chat un chat'. Frau K. and Freud are linked, as objects of Dora's love. Cixous, however, *represents* what Freud had only hinted at: Dora's love for Frau K.

The equation of women and nothingness circulates throughout the play: Dora says of her father that 'my mother is nothing for him', and quotes Herr K. as saying that 'you know my wife is nothing to me'. 'Woman' becomes an empty sign. Dora knows that within these narratives and repetitions she has only one place: that is a place within the structure of exchange of women. This is what she refuses. She undermines the transparency and immediacy of the stories she is told, and by which she is placed, when she says to Freud, 'I "knew" you would say that'. She 'knows' the basis of his certainty: she understands the ways in which she is placed by Freud's narrative.

Dora tries to take up a place within the symbolic, as a means to end the perpetual mirroring in which she is caught. She challenges Freud, who has told her that the body speaks, asking, 'Why do you turn your pen over seven times before speaking to me?' But Freud is not to be caught: 'you know perfectly well I'm an institution', 'keep to the rules'.

Cixous stages these encounters, offering us spatial and temporal representations of the dynamics of Freud's exploration of hysteria, of female sexuality. The mechanics of Freud's narratives are made explicit, the 'transparency' of his discourse is undermined by the physical presence of its object.

The play represents mirroring and repetition, it stages the power relations in which Dora is caught. At the end of the play Dora walks out on Freud, she takes her revenge by choosing to go it alone. But for this action Dora pays a high price. Freud asks her to write to him (a frequent amorous ploy) but Dora replies, 'write—that's not my business'—and she's right.

Dora's refusal, her 'dismissal' of Freud, is disruptive. Freud is bereft, but it leaves the symbolic order intact—and unavailable to Dora. Within the narratives and compulsive repetitions that constitute the 'portrait' of Dora, there is no place for Dora to write, to speak, or to construct a different and less murderous identity. Nothing comes of nothing.

So, Cixous has tried to stage the process of sexual differentiation, to show the possibility of refusal, of transgression, of moving beyond the Law. In both *Le Nom d'Oedipe* and *Portrait de Dora*, we are offered exhilaration, difference, and disruption, but the rest, unfortunately, is silence. In both plays the symbolic reasserts itself, a little battered but not destroyed. In more recent plays, however, Cixous has represented the process of differentiation in more social terms, and has offered the possibility of more hopeful conclusions: the construction of new sorts of identity, which cut across 'dual *hierarchized* oppositions'. This move, from painful marginality to new sorts of unity which respect the facts of difference, is represented as possible, but as infinitely fragile. Cixous has argued that theatre is uniquely placed to construct such identities, which do not repeat the dominant hierarchical system of difference. She says that theatre offers recognition and new identification, an intersubjectivity that is elsewhere impossible.[11]

['Their "symbolic" exists, it holds power—we, the sowers of disorder, know it only too well', in Teresa Brennan (ed.), *Between Feminism and Psychoanalysis* (London: Routledge, 1989), 153–65.]

LIZ STANLEY

43 Recovering *Women* in History from Feminist Deconstructionism

Denise Riley's (1988) speculative deliberation on the category of *women* in history raises a major epistemological debate that confronts contemporary feminism and, although in a somewhat different form, also confronts contemporary mainstream history and sociology too. Her thesis is that the category *women* (as well as the more obviously contentious *Woman*) is 'historically, discursively constructed, and always relatively to other categories which themselves change'.[1] This argument is more than an emphasis on conditioning or socialisation, for what it disputes is the existence of any reality beneath or within the constructions (and thus it parallels or rather repeats Michel Foucault's (1976) argument about 'the homosexual'). [. . .]

The conclusion and starting point both of Denise Riley's argument is that feminism has gone through continual historical loops in its political arguments and actions, necessarily oscillating between equality and difference as it has claimed that women's difference needs recognition, but also that women are equal and should be treated so. Her declared aim is to provide an intellectual route out from what she sees as the impasse of either under-feminisation or over-feminisation of the category *women*.

Denise Riley's intention is to prepare the ground for a feminism that neither accepts any notion of real or essential women (lying, as it were, somewhere beneath present distorting categorisations), nor propounds a supposedly neutral deconstructionism that eschews any political commitment. Along the way she rejects a number of alternatives to feminist deconstructionism, including the making of a feminist history of the collectivity men. Her first reason for such a rejection is the conviction that it is *women* which has been both a condition of and a trial to feminist history and politics. Her second reason is contained in the argument that it is the category *women* which has been subject to an increased degree of sexualisation as an altered weight, reordered in relation to a changing categorisation of nature brought into increasing association with women; and relatedly, *women* has also been reordered in relation to the emergent category of *the social*, of society. This latter category, she argues, is one that has encapsulated women, but men stand outside of it and debate their relationship to it.

The implicit argument here is that, somehow, *women* is categorised while *men* is not because it is never apparently sexualised in the way that *women* has been. However, at this point a feminist sociologist working with historical materials begins to get restless. I would certainly want to argue that, in sexualising women, the parallel and symbiotically related process at work is of the *apparent only* desexualisation of *men* as rational, ordered, denatured, minded. It is simply not possible that constructions of *women* do not also and thereby impact upon constructions of *men*. Unless, of course, the commentator fails to note that here heterosexuality acts as a binding agent between the two categories, or as Monique Wittig suggests, as a metanarrative.[2]

Heterosexuality is central to definitions of sex both as a supposedly entirely biological category and also as a genital sexual activity between such category members and defined as a release of the self-same biology. It is important to insist that once implied heterosexuality is noted as a defining attribute of the category *female*, the implications for the category *male* are obvious and *must* be included in any sensible analysis. Certainly Denise Riley notes that *women* is always defined relational to other categories (but naming these as nature and society only); so the later denial of the equal need for a historically located deconstruction of *men* is perplexing unless she does indeed fail to see *women* and *men* as heterosexually constructed.

My argument is that at least as much as feminism requires the categorical deconstructionism of *women*, it also requires a hand-in-hand analysis of the part played by men (or *men*, for those who suppose I am arguing some biologically unchanging essentialism here rather than some men as some men presently are) in the accompanying sexualisation of *men* over and against the sexualisation of *women*. [...]

Other reservations concern Denise Riley's too easy ascription of essentialism to anyone invoking *women* as a category—and indeed what seems to be a covert implicit rejection of all arguments sociological. She uses the term in at least two different senses: one is the sociology of those involved in the National Association for the Promotion of Social Science (NAPSS), in latter-day terms a social theory containing a broad amalgam of social policy, social administration, and social work concerns; the other is any analysis using categories. Her rejection is seemingly of all uses of categories as a mode of analysis as at basis essentialist. However, I wonder whether anyone invoking the category *the working class* would really be accused, by deconstructionist feminists or anyone else, of essentialism? Surely when feminist sociologists and fellow travellers use the phrase we know that it stands for the social construction of a particular set of people facing—albeit with large internal differences—a common material reality because one based in a common oppression/exploitation: and the key here is the rootedness of this category of people in a common oppression. Similarly so when *black people* is invoked as a category. And equally similarly so with feminist sociological uses of the word *women*. We know that we use it to stand for the social construction of *women* as a particular set of people who face—albeit with large and important internal differences—a common material reality rooted in oppression; and by material oppression here I of course mean categorisations or representations as much as physical material circumstances.

And, in contradistinction to what Denise Riley implies, most radical feminists, certainly those active in academic life, would echo my words here. Essentialism, biological invocations and ellisions there certainly are within feminism (as within life), but I doubt that we would find them in academic feminist writings howsoever positioned in feminist terms. [...]

Welcoming difference, nonetheless Denise Riley's feminist deconstructionist argument implicitly portrays as essentialism the differing and sometimes multiple identities painstakingly *constructed* in the very recent past, by lesbians, older women, women of colour, disabled women, and working-class women (to name only some). What must it be like to be a black women, having gone through much to have named oneself thus and to have recovered something of the history of one's foremothers, to have it implied that this is not only not enough but an intellectual error, an ontological over-simplification to have done so? As a working-class lesbian (for so I continue to name myself this different kind of woman), and thus having gone through comparable, if not similar, struggles to name, I sigh another bitter sigh at yet another, although surely unintended, theoretical centrism: the resurgeance of Theory from those who were once the certificated namers of other women's experiences and who are now likely to become the certificated deconstructors of the same.

What is needed—and indeed must be insisted upon by those of us who are black, lesbian, aged, disabled, working class—is that *all* difference must be attended to *equally*. In particular, there must be an end to the now ritual invocation of 'and black women' as the only such difference seen but which actually goes no further than a formula of words that leaves untouched actual relations of power between differently situated groups of black and white women, and which also masks a refusal to see that *black women* is itself no unitary category, but one internally differentiated on grounds of age, class, able-bodiedness, and sexuality. [. . .]

What has come to be described as the feminist standpoint epistemology— feminist social science research should start from the material experience of actual women and theorise from out of this—is itself a fractured position. Sandra Harding[3] suggests that once one feminist standpoint, as a materially experientially grounded epistemology, is admitted to exist, then we need to consider two related possibilities. One is that other standpoints, as women of colour, of age, of class, lesbian women, disabled women, and so on, exist. The other is that there are no *a priori* epistemological grounds for deciding a hierarchy of standpoints—of the superordinate right or correct one over and against subordinate standpoints. Oppressions cannot be weighted against each other; those feminists who do attempt to put oppressions into a hierarchy against each other need to have the moral and political, as well as intellectual, dubiousness of this pointed out to them.

This opens up possibilities (and closes down dubious assumptions) for feminism. No longer claiming 'I am right, you are wrong', we necessarily move into the realm of the ethically/morally/politically *preferable*, into the realm of minded choice. It simultaneously enables us to reject the role of anyone—theorists of grand feminist theory, poets of feminist common language, feminist deconstructors of the category *women*—to name and not to name on our behalves. This is not to dismiss, nor even to deconstruct, feminist deconstructionism. Rather, it is to welcome its strengths but also to recognise that, as Sandra Harding says in the same discussion referred to above, although feminist standpoint approaches and feminist deconstructionism may be contradictory and even work towards somewhat different feminist ends, nonetheless we need them both.

['Recovering *Women* in History from Feminist Deconstructionism', *Women's Studies International Forum*, 13/1–2 (1990), 151–4.]

44 Subjects of Sex/Gender/Desire

> One is not born a woman, but rather becomes one.
> Simone de Beauvoir

> Strictly speaking, 'women' cannot be said to exist.
> Julia Kristeva

> Woman does not have a sex.
> Luce Irigaray

> The deployment of sexuality... established this notion of sex.
> Michel Foucault

> The category of sex is the political category that founds society as heterosexual.
> Monique Wittig

[T]here is the political problem that feminism encounters in the assumption that the term *women* denotes a common identity. Rather than a stable signifier that commands the assent of those whom it purports to describe and represent, *women*, even in the plural, has become a troublesome term, a site of contest, a cause for anxiety. As Denise Riley's title suggests, *Am I That Name?* is a question produced by the very possibility of the name's multiple significations.[1] If one 'is' a woman, that is surely not all one is; the term fails to be exhaustive, not because a pregendered 'person' transcends the specific paraphernalia of its gender, but because gender is not always constituted coherently or consistently in different historical contexts, and because gender intersects with racial, class, ethnic, sexual, and regional modalities of discursively constituted identities. As a result, it becomes impossible to separate out 'gender' from the political and cultural intersections in which it is invariably produced and maintained.

The political assumption that there must be a universal basis for feminism, one which must be found in an identity assumed to exist cross-culturally, often accompanies the notion that the oppression of women has some singular form discernible in the universal or hegemonic structure of patriarchy or masculine domination. The notion of a universal patriarchy has been widely criticized in recent years for its failure to account for the workings of gender oppression in the concrete cultural contexts in which it exists. Where those various contexts have been consulted within such theories, it has been to find 'examples' or 'illustrations' of a universal principle that is assumed from the start. That form of feminist theorizing has come under criticism for its efforts to colonize and appropriate non-Western cultures to support highly

Western notions of oppression, but because they tend as well to construct a 'Third World' or even an 'Orient' in which gender oppression is subtly explained as symptomatic of an essential, non-Western barbarism. The urgency of feminism to establish a universal status for patriarchy in order to strengthen the appearance of feminism's own claims to be representative has occasionally motivated the shortcut to a categorial or fictive universality of the structure of domination, held to produce women's common subjugated experience.

Although the claim of universal patriarchy no longer enjoys the kind of credibility it once did, the notion of a generally shared conception of 'women', the corollary to that framework, has been much more difficult to displace. Certainly, there have been plenty of debates: Is there some commonality among 'women' that preexists their oppression, or do 'women' have a bond by virtue of their oppression alone? Is there a specificity to women's cultures that is independent of their subordination by hegemonic, masculinist cultures? Are the specificity and integrity of women's cultural or linguistic practices always specified against and, hence, within the terms of some more dominant cultural formation? If there is a region of the 'specifically feminine', one that is both differentiated from the masculine as such and recognizable in its difference by an unmarked and, hence, presumed universality of 'women'? The masculine/feminine binary constitutes not only the exclusive framework in which that specificity can be recognized, but in every other way the 'specificity' of the feminine is once again fully decontextualized and separated off analytically and politically from the constitution of class, race, ethnicity, and other axes of power relations that both constitute 'identity' and make the singular notion of identity a misnomer.[2][...]

Is the construction of the category of women as a coherent and stable subject an unwitting regulation and reification of gender relations? And is not such a reification precisely contrary to feminist aims? To what extent does the category of women achieve stability and coherence only in the context of the heterosexual matrix? If a stable notion of gender no longer proves to be the foundational premise of feminist politics, perhaps a new sort of feminist politics is now desirable to contest the very reifications of gender and identity, one that will take the variable construction of identity as both a methodological and normative prerequisite, if not a political goal.

To trace the political operations that produce and conceal what qualifies as the juridical subject of feminism is precisely the task of *a feminist genealogy* of the category of women. [...]

Although the unproblematic unity of 'women' is often invoked to construct a solidarity of identity, a split is introduced in the feminist subject by the distinction between sex and gender. Originally intended to dispute the biology-is-destiny formulation, the distinction between sex and gender serves the argument that whatever biological intractability sex appears to have, gender is culturally constructed: hence, gender is neither the causal result of sex nor as seemingly fixed as sex. The unity of the subject is thus already potentially contested by the distinction that permits of gender as a multiple interpretation of sex.

If gender is the cultural meanings that the sexed body assumes, then a gender cannot be said to follow from a sex in any one way. Taken to its logical limit, the sex/gender distinction suggests a radical discontinuity between sexed bodies and culturally constructed genders. Assuming for the moment the stability of binary sex, it does not follow that the construction of 'men' will accrue exclusively to the bodies of males or that 'women' will interpret only female bodies. Further, even if the sexes appear to be unproblematically binary in their morphology and constitution (which will become a question), there is no reason to assume that genders ought also to remain as two.[3] The presumption of a binary gender system implicitly retains the belief in a mimetic relation of gender to sex whereby gender mirrors sex or is otherwise restricted by it. When the constructed status of gender is theorized as radically independent of sex, gender itself becomes a free-floating artifice, with the consequence that *man* and *masculine* might just as easily signify a female body as a male one, and *woman* and *feminine* a male body as easily as a female one.

This radical splitting of the gendered subject poses yet another set of problems. Can we refer to a 'given' sex or a 'given' gender without first inquiring into how sex and/or gender is given, through what means? And what is 'sex' anyway? Is it natural, anatomical, chromosomal, or hormonal, and how is a feminist critic to assess the scientific discourses which purport to establish such facts for us? Does sex have a history?[4] Does each sex have a different history, or histories? Is there a history of how the duality of sex was established, a genealogy that might expose the binary options as a variable construction? Are the ostensibly natural facts of sex discursively produced by various scientific discourses in the service of other political and social interests? If the immutable character of sex is contested, perhaps this construct called 'sex' is as culturally constructed as gender; indeed, perhaps it was always already gender, with the consequence that the distinction between sex and gender turns out to be no distinction at all.[5]

It would make no sense, then, to define gender as the cultural interpretation of sex, if sex itself is a gendered category. Gender ought not to be conceived merely as the cultural inscription of meaning on a pregiven sex (a juridical conception); gender must also designate the very apparatus of production whereby the sexes themselves are established. As a result, gender is not to culture as sex is to nature; gender is also the discursive/cultural means by which 'sexed nature' or 'a natural sex' is produced and established as 'prediscursive', prior to culture, a politically neutral surface *on which* culture acts. [. . .]

Is there 'a' gender which persons are said *to have*, or is it an essential attribute that a person is said *to be*, as implied in the question 'What gender are you?' When feminist theorists claim that gender is the cultural interpretation of sex or that gender is culturally constructed, what is the manner or mechanism of this construction? If gender is constructed, could it be constructed differently, or does its constructedness imply some form of social determinism, foreclosing the possibility of agency and transformation? Does 'construction' suggest that certain laws generate gender differences along universal axes of sexual difference? How and where does the construction of gender take place? What sense can we make of a construction that cannot assume a human constructor prior to that construction? On some accounts, the notion that gender is constructed suggests a certain determinism of gender meanings inscribed on anatomically differentiated bodies, where those bodies are understood as passive recipients of an inexorable cultural law. When the relevant 'culture' that 'constructs' gender is understood in terms of such a law or set of laws, then it seems that gender is as determined and fixed as it was under the biology-is-destiny formulation. In such a case, not biology, but culture, becomes destiny.

On the other hand, Simone de Beauvoir suggests in *The Second Sex* that 'one is not born a woman, but, rather, becomes one'.[6] For Beauvoir, gender is 'constructed', but implied in her formulation is an agent, a *cogito*, who somehow takes on or appropriates that gender and could, in principle, take on some other gender. Is gender as variable and volitional as Beauvoir's account seems to suggest? Can 'construction' in such a case be reduced to a form of choice? Beauvoir is clear that one 'becomes' a woman, but always under a cultural compulsion to become one. And clearly, the compulsion does not come from 'sex'. There is nothing in her account that guarantees that the 'one' who becomes a woman is necessarily female. If 'the body is a situation',[7] as she claims, there is no recourse to a body that has not always already been interpreted by cultural meanings; hence, sex could not qualify as a prediscursive anatomical facticity. Indeed, sex, by definition, will be shown to have been gender all along.[8]

The controversy over the meaning of *construction* appears to founder on the conventional philosophical polarity between free will and determinism. As a consequence, one might reasonably suspect that some common linguistic restriction on thought both forms and limits the terms of the debate. Within those terms, 'the body' appears as a passive medium on which cultural meanings are inscribed or as the instrument through which an appropriative and interpretive will determines a cultural meaning for itself. In either case, the body is figured as a mere *instrument* or *medium* for which a set of cultural meanings are only externally related. But 'the body' it itself a construction, as are the myriad 'bodies' that constitute the domain of gendered subjects. Bodies cannot be said to have a signifiable existence prior to the mark of their gender; the question then emerges: To what extent does the body *come into being* in and through the mark(s) of gender? How do we reconceive the body no longer as a passive medium or instrument awaiting the enlivening capacity of a distinctly immaterial will?

Whether gender or sex is fixed or free is a function of a discourse which, it will be suggested, seeks to set certain limits to analysis or to safeguard certain tenets of humanism as presuppositional to any analysis of gender. The locus of intractability, whether in 'sex' or 'gender' or in the very meaning of 'construction', provides a clue to what cultural possibilities can and cannot become mobilized through any further analysis. The limits of the discursive analysis of gender presuppose and preempt the possibilities of imaginable and realizable gender configurations within culture. This is not to say that any and all gendered possibilities are open, but that the boundaries of analysis suggest the limits of a discursively conditioned experience. These limits are always set within the terms of a hegemonic cultural discourse predicated on binary structures that appear as the language of universal rationality. Constraint is thus built into what that language constitutes as the imaginable domain of gender. [. . .]

What can be meant by 'identity', then, and what grounds the presumption that identities are self-identical, persisting through time as the same, unified and internally coherent? More importantly, how do these assumptions inform the discourses on 'gender identity'? It would be wrong to think that the discussion of 'identity' ought to proceed prior to a discussion of gender identity for the simple reason that 'persons' only become intelligible through becoming gendered in conformity with recognizable standards of gender intelligibility. Sociological discussions have conventionally sought to understand the notion of the person in terms of an agency that claims ontological priority to the various roles and functions through which it assumes social visibility and meaning. Within philosophical discourse itself, the notion of 'the person' has received analytic elaboration on the assumption that whatever social context the person is 'in' remains somehow externally related to the definitional structure of personhood, be that consciousness, the capacity for language, or moral deliberation. Although that literature is not examined here, one premise of such inquiries is the focus of critical exploration and inversion. Whereas the question of what constitutes 'personal identity' within philosophical accounts almost always centers on the question of what internal feature of the person establishes the continuity or self-identity of the person through time, the question here will be: To what extent do *regulatory practices* of gender formation and division constitute identity, the internal coherence of the subject, indeed, the self-identical status of the person? To what extent is 'identity' a normative ideal rather than a descriptive feature of experience? And how do the regulatory practices that govern gender also govern culturally intelligible notions of identity? In other words, the 'coherence' and 'continuity' of 'the person' are not logical or analytic features of personhood, but, rather, socially instituted and maintained norms of intelligibility. Inasmuch as 'identity' is assured through the stabilizing concepts of sex, gender, and sexuality, the very notion of 'the person' is called into question by the cultural emergence of those 'incoherent' or 'discontinuous' gendered beings who appear to be persons but who fail to conform to the gendered norms of cultural intelligibility by which persons are defined.

'Intelligible' genders are those which in some sense institute and maintain relations of coherence and continuity among sex, gender, sexual practice, and desire. In other words, the spectres of discontinuity and incoherence, themselves thinkable only in relation to existing norms of continuity and coherence, are constantly prohibited and produced by the very laws that seek to establish causal or expressive lines of connection among biological sex, culturally constituted genders, and the 'expression' or 'effect' of both in the manifestation of sexual desire through sexual practice.

The notion that there might be a 'truth' of sex, as Foucault ironically terms it, is produced precisely through the regulatory practices that generate coherent identities through the matrix of coherent gender norms. The heterosexualization of desire requires and institutes the production of discrete and asymmetrical oppositions between 'feminine' and 'masculine', where these are understood as expressive attributes of 'male' and 'female'. The cultural matrix through which gender identity has become intelligible requires that certain kinds of 'identities' cannot 'exist'—that is, those in which gender does not follow from sex and those in which the practices of desire do not 'follow' from either sex or gender. 'Follow' in this context is a political relation of entailment instituted by the cultural laws that establish and regulate the shape and meaning of sexuality. Indeed, precisely because certain kinds of 'gender identities' fail to conform to those norms of cultural intelligibility, they appear only as developmental failures or logical impossibilities from within that domain. Their persistence and proliferation, however, provide critical opportunities to expose the limits and regulatory aims of that domain of intelligibility and, hence, to open up within the very terms of that matrix of intelligibility rival and subversive matrices of gender disorder.

Before such disordering practices are considered, however, it seems crucial to understand the 'matrix of intelligibility'. Is it singular? Of what is it composed? What is the peculiar alliance presumed to exist between a system of compulsory heterosexuality and the discursive categories that establish the identity concepts of sex? If 'identity' is an *effect* of discursive practices, to what extent is gender identity, construed as a relationship among sex, gender, sexual practice, and desire, the effect of a regulatory practice that can be identified as compulsory heterosexuality? Would that explanation return us to yet another totalizing frame in which compulsory heterosexuality merely takes the place of phallogocentrism as the monolithic cause of gender oppression? [. . .]

The articulation 'I feel like a woman' by a female or 'I feel like a man' by a male presupposes that in neither case is the claim meaninglessly redundant. Although it might appear unproblematic *to be* a given anatomy (although we shall later consider the way in which that project is also fraught with difficulty), the experience of a gendered psychic disposition or cultural identity is considered an achievement. Thus, 'I feel like a woman' is true to the extent that Aretha Franklin's invocation of the defining Other is assumed: 'You make me feel like a natural woman.' This achievement requires a differentiation from the opposite gender. Hence, one is one's gender to the extent that one is not the other gender, a formulation that presupposes and enforces the restriction of gender within that binary pair.

Gender can denote a *unity* of experience, of sex, gender, and desire, only when sex can be understood in some sense to necessitate gender—where gender is a psychic and/or cultural designation of the self—and desire— where desire is heterosexual and therefore differentiates itself through an oppositional relation to that other gender it desires. The internal coherence or unity of either gender, man or woman, thereby requires both a stable and oppositional heterosexuality. That institutional heterosexuality both requires and produces the univocity of each of the gendered terms that constitute the limit of gendered possibilities within an oppositional, binary gender system. This conception of gender presupposes not only a causal relation among sex, gender, and desire, but suggests as well that desire reflects or expresses gender and that gender reflects or expresses desire. The metaphysical unity of the three is assumed to be truly known and expressed in a differentiating desire for an oppositional gender—that is, in a form of oppositional heterosexuality. Whether as a naturalistic paradigm which establishes a causal continuity among sex, gender, and desire, or as an authentic-expressive paradigm in which some true self is said to be revealed simultaneously or successively in sex, gender, and desire, here 'the old dream of symmetry', as Irigaray has called it, is presupposed, reified, and rationalized.

This rough sketch of gender gives us a clue to understanding the political reasons for the substantializing view of gender. The institution of a compulsory and naturalized heterosexuality requires and regulates gender as a binary relation in which the masculine term is differentiated from a feminine term, and this differentiation is accomplished through the practices of heterosexual desire. The act of differentiating the two oppositional moments of the binary results in a consolidation of each term, the respective internal coherence of sex, gender, and desire. [. . .]

If it is possible to speak of a 'man' with a masculine attribute and to understand that attribute as a happy but accidental feature of that man, then it is also possible to speak of a 'man' with a feminine attribute, whatever that is, but still to maintain the integrity of the gender. But once we dispense with the priority of 'man' and 'woman' as abiding substances, then it is no longer possible to subordinate dissonant gendered features as so many secondary and accidental characteristics of a gender ontology that is fundamentally intact. If the notion of an abiding substance is a fictive construction produced through the compulsory ordering of attributes into coherent gender sequences, then it seems that gender as substance, the viability of *man* and *woman* as nouns, is called into question by the dissonant play of attributes that fail to conform to sequential or causal models of intelligibility.

The appearance of an abiding substance or gendered self, what the psychiatrist Robert Stoller refers to as a 'gender core',[9] is thus produced by the regulation of attributes along culturally established lines of coherence. As a result, the exposure of this fictive production is conditioned by the deregulated play of attributes that resist assimilation into the ready made framework of primary nouns and subordinate adjectives. It is of course always possible to argue that dissonant adjectives work retroactively to redefine the substantive identities they are said to modify and, hence, to expand the substantive categories of gender to include possibilities that they previously excluded. But if these substances are nothing other than the coherences contingently created through the regulation of attributes, it would seem that the ontology of substances itself is not only an artificial effect, but essentially superfluous.

In this sense, *gender* is not a noun, but neither is it a set of free-floating attributes, for we have seen that the substantive effect of gender is performatively produced and compelled by the regulatory practices of gender coherence. Hence, within the inherited discourse that is, constituting the identity it is purported to be. In this sense, gender is always a doing, though not a doing by a subject who might be said to preexist the deed. The challenge for rethinking gender categories outside of the metaphysics of substance will have to consider the relevance of Nietzsche's claim in *On the Genealogy of Morals* that 'there is no "being" behind doing, effecting, becoming; "the doer" is merely a fiction added to the deed—the deed is everything'.[10] In an application that Nietzsche himself would not have anticipated or condoned, we might state as a corollary: There is no gender identity behind the expressions of gender; that identity is performatively constituted by the very 'expressions' that are said to be its results.

[*Gender Trouble* (New York and London: Routledge, 1990), 1–25.]

45 Feminism, Humanism, Postmodernism

Postmodernist argument (or the argument of 'modernity' as others have wanted to call it)[1] has issued a number of challenges: to the idea that we can continue to think, write and speak of our culture as representing a continuous development and progress; to the idea that humanity is proceeding towards a telos of 'emancipation' and 'self-realization'; to the idea that we can invoke any universal subjectivity in speaking about the human condition. Lyotard has argued, for example, that neither of the two major forms of *grands récits* ('grand narratives') by which in the past we have legitimated the quest for knowledge can any longer perform that function. Neither the instrumental narrative of emancipation which justifies science and technology by reference to the poverty and injustice they must eventually eliminate, nor the purist defence of knowledge accumulation as something inherently beneficial, can any longer command the belief essential to warding off scepticism about the purpose and value of the technosciences. With this scepticism has gone a loss of confidence in the whole idea of human 'progress' viewed as a process more or less contemporaneous with Western-style 'civilization', and a calling into question of the emancipatory themes so central to the liberal, scientific and Marxist/socialist discourses of the nineteenth century.

This loss of credulity is in turn associated with the collapse of 'humanism'. There are two aspects to the collapse, both of them registered in much of the writing, theoretical and literary, of recent times. Firstly (though this aspect of the critique of humanism was launched by the humanist Karl Marx, and continued within a tradition of socialist-humanist thinking), there is an acknowledgement of the partial and excluding quality of the supposedly universal 'we' of much humanist discourse. Secondly, and partly as a consequence of this exposure of liberal hypocrisies and the ethnocentricity of Western humanism, there has been a refusal of the 'we' which lurks in the unifying discourse of the dialectic: a rejection of all attempts to find a sameness in otherness. Instead, we have been witness to a theoretical celebration of difference, a resistance to all synthesizing discourse, an assertion of an indefinite and multiplying plurality of particulars and specificities.

Insistence on the specificity of 'woman' or the 'feminine' has by no means been confined to the latter wave of criticism. An initial feminist 'deconstruction' of the humanist subject was made as long ago as 1792 by Mary Wollstonecraft in her demand for women to be included within the entitlements claimed by the 'Rights of Man'. But it is only in comparatively recent times that feminists have gone beyond an exposure of the maleness of the supposedly universal subject invoked by humanist rhetoric, to denounce the 'masculinism' of humanism as such. Whereas in the past, the call of feminist critiques of liberal humanism was for women to be recognized as 'equal' subjects of that discourse, equally entitled to the 'rights' which were claimed for 'all men',[2] what is more at issue today is the maleness of the subject place to which these earlier feminists were staking their claim. Today there is a whole body of feminist writing which would shy away from an 'equality' which welcomed women (at last) as human subjects on a par with men. For this 'human' subject, it is argued, must always bear the traces of the patri-archal ordering which has been more or less coextensive with the 'human' condition as such: a patriarchal culture in the light of whose biased and supposedly 'masculine' values (of rationality, symbolic capacity, control over nature) the 'human' is at the 'beginning' of 'culture' defined in opposition to the 'animal', and the discourse of 'humanism' itself first given currency. As so conceived, 'feminism' and 'humanism' would appear to aspire to incompat-ible goals, for 'feminism' is the quest for the registration and realization (though quite in what language and cultural modes it is difficult to say...) of feminine 'difference': of that ineffable 'otherness' or negation of human culture and its symbolic order (and gender system), *which is not the human* as this human is spoken to in humanism. Humanism, inversely, according to this way of thinking is the discourse which believes or wishes or pretends that there is no such difference.

[...] Here, for the time being, let us stay with the arguments of the so-called 'difference' feminists: with those who, in varying ways, have ques-tioned any ultimate compatibility. Two of the more prominent voices here are those of Hélène Cixous and Luce Irigaray. To these one might very tentatively add the name of Julia Kristeva: very tentatively because she herself has forcefully criticized 'difference' feminisms, and is opposed to all theoret-ical moves which tend to an essentialism, of 'femininity', and hence to a 'denegation of the symbolic' and removal of the 'feminine' from the order of language.[3] On the other hand, her own position is very equivocal. For insofar as she is concerned to forestall any discourse on femininity which implies the 'ineffability' of the 'feminine' at the level of the Symbolic, and to remind us that if the 'feminine' exists it only does so within the order of meaning and signification, she is herself implicitly invoking a feminine 'otherness'. [...]

Irigaray and Cixous, on the other hand, have rejected the Lacanian eter-nalization of the cultural 'negativity' of women; but their challenge, none-theless, to the supposed inevitability of masculine preeminence relies on an invocation of feminine difference which would seem to offer no better guarantee of outlet from a phallocentric universe. For the difference in question refers us to the difference in the female body and body experience in a manner which arguably reintroduces the masculine Symbolic identifica-tion of sexuality with genitality,[4] and essentializes the maternal function (particularly so in the case of Cixous's inflated celebrations of the plenitude, richness and fecundity of the feminine body). As has been pointed out in respect of Kristeva's appeal to the maternal,[5] this tends to an elision of symbolic and empirical features which is theoretically confusing: after all, if feminine difference is being defined in terms of maternal function, then many actual, empirical, women are going to find themselves cast out from femininity insofar as they are not mothers nor intending to become so. At the same time, the association of the feminine with the maternal or with the feminine body is deeply problematic for many feminists who see in this precisely the male cultural signification which they are attempting to contest, and which, they would argue, has been the justification for a quite unreasonable and unfair domestication of women and a very damaging social and economic division of labour from the point of view of female self-fulfilment and self-expression.

In a more general way, we must surely also contest the reductionism of the argument found in different forms in both Irigaray's and Cixous's theories of the feminine (in Irigaray's advocacy of *parler femme* and Cixous's notion of *écriture féminine* as speaking to a kind of feminine unconscious) that language, whether spoken or written, directly mirrors physical morphology. It is a radical misunderstanding of the nature of signs to suppose that the two lips of the vulva or breast milk or menstrual blood are 'represented' in contiguous statements or in the unencodable libidinal gushings of a feminine prose *in any but a purely metaphorical sense*. But if we treat the supposed representation as purely metaphorical, then 'feminine writing' is being defined in terms of a certain image or metaphor of itself, and we end up with a purely tautological argument. [...]

At any rate, the important point would seem to be that where the appeal to difference is made, it tends to an essentialism of the female physique and function which reproduces rather than surpasses the traditional male–female divide and leaves 'woman' once again reduced to her body—and to silence—rather than figuring as a culturally shaped, culturally complex, evolving, rational, engaged and noisy opposition. The total disengagement of the feminine in the position of Cixous and Irigaray,[6] the complete severence of any masculine–feminine cultural intercourse, removes this opposition to the point where one might say there was no longer any feminist critique of patriarchy but only a self-absorption in the feminine.

On the other hand, if difference is not given this kind of anchorage in the feminine body and function, it is not clear why there is any reason, once set on the path of difference, for feminism to call a halt. In other words, if one disallows the feminine universal of a common bodily essence, then the commitment to difference ought to move one into a deconstruction of feminine difference itself. Having exposed the 'masculinity' of humanism in the name of feminine difference, one must surely go on, by the same logic, to expose the generalizing and abstract (and quasi-humanist) appeal to feminine difference in the name of the plurality of concrete differences between

women (in their nationality, race, class, age, occupation, sexuality, parenthood status, health, and so on...) For on this argument 'woman' can no
more be allowed to stand in for all women than can 'man' be allowed to stand
for all members of the human species. The way, then, of course, lies open to
an extreme particularism in which all pretensions to speak (quasi-humanis-
tically) in general for this or that grouping, or to offer an abstract and
representative discourse on behalf of such putative groups, must give way
to a hyper-individualism.[7] From this standpoint any appeal to a collectivity
would appear to be illegitimate—yet another case of 'logocentric imperialism', to use the inflated rhetoric of poststructuralism.

But at this point one is bound to feel that feminism as theory has pulled the
rug from under feminism as politics. For politics is essentially a group affair,
based on the idea of making 'common cause', and feminism, like any other
politics, has always implied a banding together, a movement based on the
solidarity and sisterhood of women, who are linked by perhaps very little else
than their *sameness* and 'common cause' as women. If this sameness itself is
challenged on the grounds that there is no 'presence' of womanhood,
nothing that the term 'woman' immediately expresses, and nothing instan-
tiated concretely except particular women in particular situations, then the
idea of a political community built around women—the central aspiration of
the early feminist movement—collapses. I say the 'idea', for women do still
come together in all sorts of groups for feminist purposes, and will doubtless
continue to do so for a good while to come even if their doing so transgresses
some Derridean conceptual rulings. But *theoretically* the logic of difference
tends to subvert the concept of a feminine political community of 'women' as
it does of the more traditional political communities of class, Party, Trade
Union, etc. And theory does, of course, in the end get into practice, and
maybe has already begun to do so: one already senses that feminism as a
campaigning movement is yielding to feminism as discourse (and to discourse
of an increasingly heterogeneous kind).

In the face of this dispersion, with its return from solidarity to individualism, it is difficult not to feel that feminism itself has lost its hold, or at any rate
that much of contemporary theory of the feminine is returning us full circle
to those many isolated, and 'silent' women, from which it started—and for
whom it came to represent, precisely, a 'common voice'. It is a *renversement*,
moreover, which leaves feminism exposed to the temptations of what are
arguably deeply nostalgic and conservative currents of postmodernist
thinking. [...]

In conclusion, then, I would pursue the charge of political conservatism a
little further, offering some arguments both in defence but also in mitigation
of it.

I have already indicated my main reason for thinking that 'maternal'
feminism and *écriture féminine* are open to this charge. But my objection is

not only to the fact that the emphasis on the distinctness of the female body and its reproductive and erotic experience comes so close to reinforcing patriarchal conceptions of gender difference. I would also argue that despite its avant-gardist pretensions, the style in which this feminism is couched is disquietingly confirming of traditional assumptions about the 'nature' of feminine thought and writing. The dearth of irony; the fulsome self-congratulation; the resistance to objectivity; the sentimentalization of love and friendship and the tendency always to reduce these relations to their sexual aspect; the focus on the 'erotic' conceived as an amorphous, all-engulfing, tactile, radically unintellectual form of experience; the overblown poetics and arbitrary recourse to metaphor (which so often lack the hardness of crystalline meaning as if exactitude itself must be avoided as inherently 'male' . . .): all this, which is offered in the name of allowing 'woman' to discover her 'voice', itself voices those very conceptions of female selfhood and self-affection which I believe are obstacles to cultural liberation. And the reason I find them obstacles is not simply because they so directly lend themselves to a patriarchically constructed ideology of femininity and its modes of self-expression, but because the ideology is, like all ideologies, at best partial in its representation and therefore illegitimately generalizing of a certain specific form of understanding. Moreover, when this understanding relates so directly to images of selfhood and subjectivity, it is peculiarly offensive and arrogant—to the point, in fact, of operating a kind of theft of subjectivity or betrayal of all those who fail to recognize themselves in the mirror it offers. At the same time, because ideologies of their nature are always fractured reflections of society, exploded in the very moment which reveals their ideological status, those who cling to them and reinforce their decaying hold are also always marginalizing their own discourse; ensuring that it cannot be taken seriously in the world at large. [. . .]

[A] more important difficulty with the strategy of 'in-difference' is that it recommends changes at the level of discourse and consciousness rather than at the level of material—economic and social—circumstance, and like all such recommendations is open to the charge that it is politically conservative because it is too little dialectical. Because it refuses to discriminate between 'world' and 'text', between the 'material' and the 'discursive' it follows that it has no theoretical purchase on the interdependency and mutual conditioning between the two. Of course, these arguments themselves can have no purchase on a position which eschews the metaphysical vocabulary of materialism and idealism. There is simply here no common discourse and all that one can do is to charge poststructuralist 'idealism' with lacking the conceptual apparatus for marking important distinctions between different areas or modalities of social life. Adopting this critical position, however, I would argue that there are many material circumstances firmly in place which tend to the disadvantaging of women and whose correction is not obviously going to be achieved simply by a revaluation of theory on the part of a poststructuralizing feminist elite. In fact there are some concrete and universal dimensions of women's lives which seem relatively unaffected by the transformation of consciousness already achieved by the women's movement. To give one example: despite the indisputable gains of feminist theory and action, the fact remains that women live in fear of men and men do not live in fear of women. When I say 'live in fear' of men, I do not mean that we live our lives in a continual and conscious anxiety, or that we think an attack on our persons is very likely (it isn't statistically and we are rational enough to accept it). I mean that women live in a kind of alertness to the possibility of attack and must to some degree organize their lives in order to minimize its threat. In particular, I think, this has constraints—from which men are free—on our capacity to enjoy solitude. As a woman, one's reaction to the sight of a male stranger approaching on a lonely road or country walk is utterly different from one's reaction to the approach of a female stranger. In the former case there is a frisson of anxiety quite absent in the latter. This anxiety, of course, is almost always confounded by the man's perfectly friendly behaviour, but the damage to the relations between the sexes has already been done—and done not by the individual man and woman—but by their culture. This female fear and the constraints it places on what women can do—particularly in the way of spending time on their own—has, of course, its negative consequences for men too, most of whom doubtless deplore its impact on their own capacities for spontaneous relations with women. (Thus, for example, the male stranger has to think twice about smiling at the passing woman/exchanging the time of day with her, etc. for fear he will either alarm her or be misinterpreted in his intentions . . .) But the situation all the same is not symmetrical: resentment or regret is not as disabling as fear; and importantly it does not affect the man's capacity to go about on his own.

This, then, is one example of the kind of thing I have in mind in speaking of 'material circumstances' which have been relatively unaffected by changes at a discursive and 'Symbolic' level. They are circumstances which relate to conditions which are experienced by both sexes, and in the most general sense are therefore culturally universal. But they are conditions which are differently experienced simply in virtue of which sex you happen to be, and in that sense they are universally differentiated between the sexes: *all* men and *all* women are subject to them *differently*. It is this sex-specific but universal quality of certain conditions of general experience which justifies and gives meaning to collective gender categories. To put the point in specifically feminist terms: there are conditions of existence common to all women which the policy of in-difference—with its recommendation not to focus on *female* experience—is resistant to registering in theory and therefore unlikely to correct in practice.

The implication of these rather open-ended remarks, I think, is that feminism should proceed on two rather contrary lines: it should be constantly moving towards 'in-difference' in its critique of essentializing and ghettoizing modes of feminist argument; but at the same time it should also insist on retaining the gender-specific but universal categories of 'woman' or 'female experience' on the grounds that this is essential to identifying and transforming all those circumstances of women's lives which the pervasion of a more feminist consciousness has left relatively unaffected. In short, feminism should be both 'humanist' and 'feminist'—for the paradox of the post-structuralist collapse of the 'feminine' and the move to 'in-difference' is that it reintroduces—though in the disguised form of an aspiration to no-gender—something not entirely dissimilar from the old humanistic goal of sexual parity and reconciliation. And while one can welcome the reintroduction of the goal, it may still require some of the scepticism which inspired its original deconstruction.

['Feminism, Humanism, Postmodernism', in *Troubled Pleasures: Writings on Gender, Politics and Hedonism* (London: Verso, 1990), 1–25.]

KADIATU KANNEH

46 Love, Mourning and Metaphor: Terms of Identity

The obsession of feminist theories with the body as the conclusive image of identity and the site of political struggle has led to a proliferation of unspoken conflations, confusions and invisibilities in the field of gender studies. Where love is fractured by violence and subjectivity is an unstable and threatening arena, a keen and painful listening to the conflicting pasts and languages which constitute Woman seems an obvious and difficult imperative. Within the terms of experience and desire I envisage an ongoing feminist battle which demands consideration.

Focusing eclectically on a variety of feminisms—previous, current, white and black—I intend to scrutinize the role of the body as metaphor, how the fusion of desire and language theorizes and politicizes love and suffering. How does experience guarantee political authenticity and the ownership of identity? [...]

The privileging of the body in the writing of Cixous and Irigaray as the focal point for a radical subversion is in many ways, however, a dangerous political move. It is undeniably crucial to revalorize the female body, to rescue it from the vilification which, for centuries, has been practised against it through oppressive codes and institutions. When men are degrading women sexually, hating them carnally and violently, it is positive to reclaim and revalue the female body. To see the body as a source of potential power and intense pleasure is a needed reaction to the kind of anti-female sadism which is explored by Benoîte Groult in 'Night Porters',[1] and is the sad fate of the heroine in The Story of O. It is highly important, however, to determine which aspects of this femininity should be held up for celebration, and to sort out just what would be the political ramifications of such a move.

Lacan's insistence that there is no feminine outside language is useful here in that it marks out the difficulties into which Cixous and Irigaray fall. Cixous's description in 'The Laugh of the Medusa' of the painful moment of a woman speaking in public is an example of the dubious valorizations upon which she relies. The description concentrates upon the interplay of language and body which is the peculiarly feminine mode of discourse: 'She doesn't "speak", she throws her trembling body forward; she lets go of herself, she flies; all of her passes into her voice, and it's with her body that she vitally supports the "logic" of her speech.'[2] Here the woman is seen bursting from the 'snare of silence' and flying free in the *jouissance* of her own natural self-expression, a form of expression which spills out of the definite structures of 'masculine' discourse: 'Her speech, even when "theoretical" or political is never simple or linear or "objectified", generalized.' There is another way of reading this moment, however, which would be to examine the causes for such a manner of public address from a social viewpoint. Surely, this tremor which seizes the woman from the depths of her lungs, this irresistible use of the body to complement the unmanageable ipple of her voice, is an accurate account not of an inherent feminine essence but of the direct results of social marginalization and intolerable sexual visibility. Not conditioned to wear mastery in a public scene or to forget the role of her body in a voyeuristic male society, the female public speaker acts, in this prototypical case, with a shivering uncertainty, handling the language of politico-theoretical discourse with stumbling skill. Celebrating this part of feminine activity and so following the rallying cry of Marguerite Duras, 'We must move on to the rhetoric of women, one that is anchored in the organism, in the body',[3] Cixous runs on the same tracks as the 'Wages for Housework' campaign which, finding women incarcerated in the kitchen, rushes to sing the kitchen's praise.

This same danger recurs throughout 'The Laugh of the Medusa', where women's supposed empathy with nature, their removal from the construction of civilizations and their innate maternal instinct—'In women there is always more or less of the mother who makes everything all right, who nourishes'—are merely valorizations of spaces into which women have been coerced by dint of a social world which will not tolerate women as law-givers. This quotation from Questions Féministes, which Deborah Cameron includes in her Feminism and Linguistic Theory, adequately pinpoints the risk that women run by celebrating an area of 'femininity' which is merely the very point of ineffectiveness outside and beneath social control to which they have been driven: 'To advocate a direct relation to the body is therefore not subversive because it is equivalent to denying the reality and the strength of social mediations, the very same ones that oppress us in our bodies.'[4]

Determinism through body language—the self at the centre of the orgasm and its roots in the unconscious—relies upon a belief in a pre-linguistic reality, a way of experiencing and understanding the self which is prior to the symbolic. The falsity of this search and its prescription for a Utopian future is evident in Simone de Beauvoir's *Memoirs of a Dutiful Daughter*, in which she recalls the bliss of a childhood perception uninitiated into words:

White was only rarely totally white, and the blackness of evil was relieved by lighter touches; I saw greys and half-tones everywhere. Only as soon as I tried to define their muted shapes, I had to use words, and found myself in a world of bony-structured concepts.[5]

The memory here is of an understanding which is wholly informed by the senses, which runs intuitively with a flow of sensation that needs no translation into a socially conceptual language. Simone de Beauvoir imagines a period where her body articulated lights and shadows, safety and fear, joy and pain through a dreamtime in tune with the flooding nuances of life. Language arrives as a dam against the flow, where meaning comes up against more concrete definitions. However, this passage upon a mode of experience which is born with the body has a neutrality to the social world and history which has already placed white in direct opposition to black and qualified each according to the scale which is lodged in Western ideology: white as a purity far uperior to 'the blackness of evil'. This recalls Jacqueline Rose's intimation (*Sexuality in the Field of Vision*) that 'the effects of the unconscious are tied to the key fantasies operating at the heart of institutions'. Seeping into de Beauvoir's 'pre-linguistic' experience and already forming her conceptions are the institutionalized values appraised by Sista Roots in her poem 'Dictionary Black', which apprehends the loaded metaphors of a deeply racist Western culture:

A Darky is a Negro
Not fair—atrocious—evil
And the Prince of Darkness
Is the Devil . . .
. . . So I turn to 'white'
All sweetness and light.[6]

The spine of white culture also supports Hélène Cixous's 'The Laugh of the Medusa', the work being animated from within the nerve centre of a Western post-colonial backbone. Cixous consistently upholds her argument that women inhabit a pre-civilizational world which is closer to the pulse of nature and the rhythms of sensuality, a world which can be found in the germinating moments of childhood sexuality, by drawing a sustained analogy with black Africa. She stakes a claim for a true female identity by linking women's position with that of people outside Western culture, people whose land and bodies have suffered systematic vilification, thrown under a cloak of fear and mystery: 'they can be taught that their territory is black: because you are Africa, you are black. Your continent is dark. Dark is dangerous.' The principle for revaluing such a space is to celebrate its apparent 'natural' qualities: 'We the precocious, we the repressed of culture, our lovely mouths gagged with pollen, our wind knocked out of us, we the labyrinths, the ladders, the trampled spaces, the bevies . . . we are black and we are beautiful.'[7]

This reference to African peoples in order to underline the position of women outside history and culture, beyond the self-conscious, adult world of reason and politics, is in indirect collusion with the deliberate policies of the Western colonial countries which aim to wipe out the achievements and the intricate pasts of the colonized. Ngũgĩ Wa Thiong'o (in *Decolonizing the Mind*) attacks just this Eurocentric myopia in Western philosophy, for instance 'Hegel with his Africa comparable to a land of childhood still enveloped in the dark mantle of the night as far as the development of self-conscious history was concerned'.[8]

If we apply this approach to the white feminist practice of hoarding accounts of black subjectivity in order to mark out a common linguistic ground we face a tricky political situation which pivots itself on questions of language, experience and identity. The fusion of metaphor and body, identity and experience is both a political choice and a historical coercion which, I believe, cannot be either swept aside by poetic licence or blindly embraced as immutable. Cixous legitimizes her use of black historical metaphors, based on references to colonialism, slavery and racism, by claiming that, 'In woman, personal history blends together with the history of all women, as well as ational and world history.' The call for a feminine culture which sees itself as separate from the history of wars and colonialisms is validated by the asser-tion that women had nothing to do with all of this: 'This is known by the colonised people of yesterday, the workers, the nations, the species off whose backs the history of *men* has made its gold' (my emphasis).[9]

Liberating the female body from language creates flesh out of words. Desire explodes the social, sex subverses and recreates the political Upholding a female experience which cannot—biologically/psychically—slide into the male and yet can slide racially and class-wise, Cixous and Irigaray legitimize a flagrant fluidity of metaphor. The question of who owns which metaphor is tied closely into an ongoing struggle over the past, over history, which will inevitably be a matter of eclectic analogy and constructions of fantasy. How-ever, this eclecticism has definite political meaning in that the oppressions of the present are very often fixed in ways of perceiving the body—through race—as a personification of the past. The unconscious use of geography and time in understanding identity through the body is made conscious by Cixous's defiant attempts to disengage the specificity of historical metaphor, releasing women from the grip of time and placing a radical feminine identity beyond the tyrannies of race and class, 'so as to prevent the class struggle, or any other struggle for the liberation of a class or people, from operating as a form of repression, pretext for postponing the inevitable'. The joyous fervour with which Cixous cries for the blowing up of the past, of history and of political struggles outside the unconscious and the body relies on her understanding of difference as variations of sensual pleasure between women. Her drive to unlock women from a history she labels as exclusively male manages to lock all women into a history free-floating between images of black subjection and imperialist domination. Sensuality and the body suck in figurations of power drawn from colonial ideas of land and nature. Female masturbation is a 'unique empire', the unconscious is 'that other limitless country', and 'the Dark Continent' of the female psyche 'is neither dark nor unexplorable'.

The idea that women should ignore the divisions between themselves and sweep together across class, race and national boundaries to create a post-historical Utopian home, bypasses the knowledge that racial oppression has always created the body from obsessive fantasies of biology and environment. The power of Cixous's metaphors comes precisely from their continuing life in present ideologies of race. Black women are not in a position to bypass the histories and divisions, both of class and race, which block the development of a unified feminist movement.

For black feminists there can be no easy separation between blackness and womanhood, just as there cannot be a simple slicing apart of white racial identity and womanhood. This reality informs a black feminist approach to the body, sensual pleasure and political language. Chrystos, for example (in *This Bridge Called My Back*), writes in her poem 'I Walk in the History of My People', that her body and her relationship to it is also a communion with the culture and history of which she is a part. Like Cixous's celebration of white witchery, Chrystos becomes the living embodiment of centuries of anger:

> There are women locked in my joints
> for refusing to speak to the police
> my red blood full of those
> arrested, in flight, shot
> My tendons stretched brittle with anger.[10]

Sensual pleasure has as much to do with cultural identity as it has to do with physical sensation, and the articulation of the erotic for black women is the marker of a certain socio-historical belonging as much as it is for white women. From Sonia Sanchez's 'you and i exploding in | our blue black skins' ('Haiku'),[11] to Grace Nichols' 'Even Tho', the environment and the social sense of self is an indissoluble part of the erotic:

I'm all watermelon
and star-apple and plum
when you touch me...
...You be banana
I be avocado[12]

The experiences entailed in being black or white are both cultural and psychological, and any thoughtless separation by white feminists of the powerlessness which is engendered by a socially constructed racial 'inferiority' or victimization seriously denies black women's sense of reality. Merle Collins's poem 'Same But Different' (in *Watchers and Seekers*) expresses the double sense of fear which is invested in black women by a racist society. Comparing her experience to a white friend who has reciprocal nightmares of 'rapists and robbers' at every lonely step of the night, Collins's persona must also contend with the terror of racial violence: 'Each sudden shadow│was a threat of the National Front'.[13]

Toni Morrison's *The Bluest Eye* traces the extent to which racism affects the identity, the fantasies and the sexuality of black women (and men). The development of desire and understanding, of self-articulation and its source is expressed in Pecola Breedlove's childhood and adolescent encounters. Living in a world which is run by white domination, which informs the discourses of 'normality' of beauty and of worth, Pecola is continually slammed up against an image of herself which is sharply at odds with the white 'norm'. The novel opens with the script of a child's story-book: 'Here is the house. It is green and white. It has a red door. It is very pretty. Here is the family. Mother, Father, Dick, and Jane live in the green and white house. They are very happy.'[14] This is the doorway through which black and white children will enter into the social discourse, a discourse which will run into the mind of a childish imagination, forming the shape of a child's contact with the world around her. The script is repeated three times, each time letting the words seep closer together until a tightly woven fabric is created, a fabric which will run threads through the unconscious too deep to eradicate: 'othermotherisverynicemotherwillyouplaywith-Janemotherlaughslaughmotherseefatherheisbigandstrongfather'. If this is 'normality' with which a black child must identify, the result can only be a deep sense of alienation, a low, encrusted sense of worthlessness, a dizzying cellophane barrier between the self and the world, created by the standard literary discourse. Ngũgĩ Wa Thiong'o, in *Decolonizing the Mind*, writes that:

the second aspect of language as culture is as an image-forming agent in the mind of the child.... But our capacity to confront the world creatively is dependent on how those images correspond or not to that reality, how they distort or clarify the reality of our struggles.... Language is mediating in my very being.[15]

Looking around her, Pecola sees only images that are disjointed from the language of her reading. She sees a black father enraged with the impotence which burned in his body when white men enacted a vicious visual rape, a black mother whose fancied identity with the white film stars of the dark cinemas smashed along with her front tooth, and a grey and ugly home.

One of the effects of a discourse which makes blackness a concept of excruciating visibility is the suffocation of all other differentiation beneath it. If there is no place at which to position the self within this discourse, the result is a form of self-annihilation which, beginning in the mirror of white society, becomes a conscious and then an internalized unconscious activity. Pecola's visit to the sweet shop, owned by a white shopkeeper, is an episode which reveals the role of blackness in the formation of identity:

> But she has seen interest, disgust, even anger in grown male eyes. Yet this vacuum is not new to her. It has an edge; somewhere in the bottom lid is the distaste. She has seen it lurking in the eyes of all white people. So the distaste must be for her, her Blackness. All things in her are flux and anticipation. But her blackness is static and dread. And it is the blackness that accounts for, that creates, the vacuum edged with distaste in white eyes.[16]

At this point Pecola is aware of the white gaze as an outside force, translating who she is by virtue of her skin and features. Within her, another awareness ebbs and flows, the same awareness which appraised the dandelions on the edge of cultivation as 'pretty' and which gave her an immeasurable joy in her own reality. She knows the language her mind speaks, the 'codes and touch-stones' which are available to her, the beauty upon which she relies and understands as her own: 'And owning them made her part of the world and the world part of her.' The part of the world she is able to articulate, however, has no corresponding moment in white consciousness and before the white shopkeeper she finds herself robbed of language and dumb in the loneliness of her perceptions: 'He cannot see her view—the angle of his vision, the slant of her finger, makes it incomprehensible to him.'

Such is the power of white discourse that it forces its values deeper than the surface, making Pecola internalize the scales of worth which are held before her. As her shame heats up the surface of her skin, the 'dread' black-ness melts down through her pores, filling up the cracks of her imagination with the 'vacuum-edged distaste' that 'white eyes' attached to it: 'The shame wells up again, its muddy rivulets seeping into her eyes.' Believing in the ugliness in her mirror, just as she is coerced into believing that the dandelions after-all 'are ugly. They are weeds', Pecola's first move is self-extermination. [. . .]

Any feminist approach to language will commit serious errors of judge-ment unless there is a full appreciation of the position of all women as regards language. To state vapidly that women across national, racial, geographic and class boundaries have the same access to and alienation from the language of social discourse, and to leap from here into the belief in a common feminine identity, reveals a sad lack of awareness as to how language operates and how deeply all women are implicated in colonial history and present-day racism. The minefield of emotions, histories and identifications which arise from the battle over metaphors points, I believe, not to a theory of impossible owner-ships but to a heightened awareness of the relationship between body and word, the past and the racial politics of the present. Meiling Jin's poem 'Strangers in a Hostile Landscape' (in *Watchers and Seekers*) outlines the bitterness and anger which burns deep beneath the 'Invisible-Ness' brought about by white culture. With a resistance that will linger beyond death, Jin's persona stores up the intense concentration of her identity, born beyond the Occident, and her gaze will redirect the scorching, alienating and maddening gaze of a Western racist world back upon the Occident through the continu-ing of herself in her people. This is nearer the Utopia envisaged by black women, this is the sweet concentration of delight which lies waiting at the closest throb of a long bruised collective consciousness:

> and when I die
> I shall return
> to a place I call my own
> Only my eyes will remain
> to watch and to haunt,
> and to turn your dreams to chaos.[17]

['Love, Mourning and Metaphor: Terms of Identity', in Isobel Armstrong (ed.), *New Feminist Discourses: Critical Essays in Theories and Texts* (London: Routledge, 1992), 139–52.]

ELIZABETH GROSZ

47 Psychoanalysis and the Imaginary Body

This [. . .] is part of a larger project: [. . .] an attempt to rethink the terms in which subjectivity is usually understood in feminist theory. Subjectivity has tended to be conceptualised in terms that privilege and affirm the primacy of mind over body, a conceptual opposition that has characterised Western philosophy since its inception in ancient Greece. Even psychoanalytic theory has been generally understood, by feminists and others, as an account of the psychical production of masculine and feminine subjects, as if this can some-how occur or make any sense in isolation from the (cultural and social) specificities of sexed bodies. This [. . .] is an attempt to explain how psycho-analytic theory may be read as precisely an account of the psychosocial signification and lived reality of sexed bodies, rather than as an account of the genesis and functioning of the abstract processes of masculinity and femininity. [. . .]

The Ego as Corporeal Projection

Freud presents a startling account of the ego as a corporeal projection. This view confirms his claims in 'On Narcissism' (1914) that the subject only acquires a sense of unity and cohesion, that is, becomes an ego, over and above the disparate, heterogeneous sensations that comprise its experiences as a result of an intervention into nature. If the subject were merely a perceiving and experiencing being then there could be no way of unifying its experiences as the experiences of a single being, no way of asserting some kind of propriety over those experiences, no way of taking otherwise disconnected perceptual events, which give it no index of the existence of objects or the world. Before the advent of primary narcissism, the child is a (passive) conglomerate of fleeting experiences, at the mercy of organic and social excitations to which it may respond but over which it has no agency or control.

For Freud, the ego is what brings unity to the vast and overwhelming diversity of perceptions. It is a consequence of a perceptual surface: it is produced and grows only relative to this surface. Freud argues that the ego does not result from a preordained biological order, but is the result of a psychosocial intervention into the child's hitherto natural development:

We are bound to suppose that a unity comparable to the ego has to be developed. . . . there must be something added to auto-eroticism—a new psychical action—in order to bring about narcissism.[1]

This new action engenders primary narcissism (or what Lacan calls the mirror stage) at around six months of age. Narcissism, as Freud understands it, is a form of self-love, a mode of investing libido or sexual energy into one's own ego. Primary narcissism, that stage that engenders the existence of the ego, consists in a relative stabilization of the circulation of libido in the child's body, so that the division between subject and object (even the subject's capacity to take itself as an object) becomes possible for the first time. The ego is the result of a series of identificatory relations with the images of other subjects, particularly the mother or even its own image in the mirror. These identifications, which constitute what Lacan calls the imaginary,[2] are introjected or internalised, brought into the psychical sphere of influence of the ego in the form of the ego-ideal, the idealised model of itself to which the ego strives. At the same time, the ego is also a consequence of a blockage or rechannelling of libidinal impulses in the subject's own body in the form of a narcissistic attachment to a part or the whole of its body. In this sense, the ego is the meeting-point, the point of conjunction, between the body and the social. It is constituted from *internal* libidinal intensities and their relative stabilisation, and external identificatory inscriptions.

The subject cannot remain neutral or indifferent to its own body and body-parts. The body is libidinally invested. The human subject always maintains a relation of love (or hate) towards its own body because it must always maintain a certain level of psychical and libidinal investment, or more technically, cathexis. No person lives his or her own body merely as a functional instrument or a means to an end. Its value is never functional, for it has a (libidinal) value in itself. It is for this reason that 'Man' must be distinguished from animals. No animal kills itself in the presence of life-preserving conditions, no animal starves itself to death when food is readily available. The human subject is capable of suicide, of anorexia, because the body is *meaningful*, has significance, because it is in part constituted both for the subject and for others in terms of meanings and significances. The body can never be a mere object or instrument for consciousness, never a matter of indifference or insignificance.

Freud claims that the genesis of the ego is dependent on the construction of a psychical map of the body's libidinal intensities: the ego is not so much a self-contained entity or thing as a kind of bodily tracing, a cartography of the erotogenic intensity of the body, an internalised image of the degrees of the intensity of sensations in the child's body. He backs up his claims with reference to the 'cortical homunculus', a much-beloved idea circulating in neurological and medical circles in the nineteenth century:

The ego is first and foremost a bodily ego: it is not merely a surface entity, but is itself the projection of a surface. If we wish to find an anatomical analogy for it we can best identify it with the 'cortical homunculus' of the anatomists, which stands on its head in the cortex, sticks up its heels, faces backwards and as we know, has its speech-area on the left hand side.[3]

The ego is a mapping, not of the real or anatomical body, but of the degree of libidinal cathexis or sexual energy the subject has invested in its own body:

We can decide to regard erotogencity as a general characteristic of all organs and may then speak of an increase or decrease of it in a particular part of the body. For every such change in the erotogenicity of libidinal zones there might be a parallel change in the ego.[4]

The amount of libidinal intensity invested in the erotogenic zones—mouth, anus, genitals, eyes, including possibly even the entire surface of the skin—which Freud describes as 'erotogenicity', the sites from which libido eman-ates, parallels changes that occur in the shape and form of the ego itself. If the ego is a libidinal reservoir, its 'shape' and contours vary both according to its libidinal investments in other objects, and according to the quantities of libidinal excitation that circulate in the subject's own body which are available for object-love through the sexual drives, which in their turn find their sources in the different erotogenic zones of the body.

The ego is ultimately derived from bodily sensations, chiefly from those springing from the surface of the body. It may thus be regarded as a mental projection of the surface of the body.[5]

Freud attributes a privileged role to the erotogenic zones, for it is clear that they play a disproportionately significant role in the formation of the sensori-motor homunculus, a mapping or registration of the passive (or sensory) and active (motor) interrelations between the subject's body and the world. The homunculus, the tiny 'manikin' registered in the brain, most notably in the cerebral cortex, is inverted like a mirror-image, but instead of being a point-for-point projection of the outside of the body, an accurate description of the body as it 'really' is, certain points of intensity are stressed above all others, leaving little or no room for the registration of other bodily zones. For example, the homunculus is usually regarded as highly overdeveloped in oral, manual and genital representations; it is particularly significant that there is no mention made in the relevant literature, of the female homunculus, and the ways in which it differs from the male. Hysteria can, in a way, be seen as a response to this absence of representation, especially of autonomous representations of women. In much of the relevant literature, the homunculus is *explicitly* described as male, and there is no mention of what this means for women.

Hysteria is a somatisation of psychical conflict, an acting out of resistance rather than its verbal articulation or conceptual representation. It is, according to Freud, a largely feminine neurosis. This may help explain how anorexia, a sub-branch of hysteria, is also an overwhelmingly feminine neurosis. It is a form of protest against and resistance to cultural investments defining what the 'proper' body is for women. (It is significant that there is no such 'proper' image for men. A wide variety of body-images remain perfectly tolerable.) The problem is not to provide women with *positive self-images*, but with *self-defined* images, whatever they might be—a much less patronising and more difficult project.

Although information can be provided by any of the sense organs, the surface of the body is in a particularly privileged position to receive information and excitations from both the interior and the exterior of the organism. This may help explain why the orifices are especially privileged in the establishment of erotogenic zones, and why the infant's psychosexual stages are part of the process of maturation which relies disproportionately on the cutaneous openings of the body's surface. However, in any case, the skin and the various sensations which are located at the surface of the body are the most primitive, essential and constitutive of all sources of sensory stimulation. The information provided by the surface of the skin is both internal and external, active and passive, receptive and expressive.

The surface of the body, the skin, moreover, provides the ground for the articulation of orifices, erotogenic rims, cuts on the body's surface, loci of exchange between the inside and the outside, points of conversion of the outside into the body, and of the inside out of the body.

These are sites not only for the reception and transmission of information but also for bodily secretions, on-going processes of sensory stimulation which require some form of signification and sociocultural and psychical representation. These cuts on the body's surface create a kind of 'landscape' of that surface, providing it with 'regions', 'zones' capable of erotic significance; it serves as a kind of gridding for erotic investments in the body in uneven distributions.

The ego, then, is something like an internal screen onto which the illuminated and projected images of the body's outer surface are directed. It is the site for the gathering together and unification of otherwise disparate and scattered sensations provided by the various sense organs in all their different spaces and registers. It is also a registration or mapping of the body's inner surface, the surface of sensations, intensities and affect, the 'subjective experience' of bodily excitations and sensations.

The ego is not a map, photograph or a point for point projection of the body's surface, but an outline or representation of the degrees of erotogenicity of the bodily zones and organs. It is derived from two kinds of 'surface': on the one hand, the ego is on the 'inner' surface of the psychical agencies; on the other hand, it is a projection or representation of the body's 'outer' surface. In both cases, the surface is perceptual. Perception thus provides both the contents of the ego, and, to begin with, the earliest sexual 'objects' for the child. Moreover, in the establishment of the ego, perceptual processes are themselves sexualised, libidinally invested.

The ego is a representation of the varying intensities of libidinal-investment in the various bodily parts, and the body as a whole. Significantly, this notion of the body as a whole is dependent on the recognition of the totality and autonomy of the body of the other. The ego is thus *both* a map of the body's surface and a reflection of the image of the other's body. The other's body provides the frame for the representation of one's own. In this sense, the ego is an image of the body's significance or meaning for the subject and for the other. It is thus as much a function of fantasy and desire as it is of sensation and perception; it is a taking over of sensation and perception by a fantasmatic dimension. This significatory, cultural dimension implies that bodies, egos, subjectivities are not simply *reflections* of their cultural context and associated values, but are constituted as such by them, marking bodies in their very 'biological' configurations with sociosexual inscriptions.

It is significant that the two neuroses traversing the mind/body split, hysteria and hypochondria, in which there is a somatisation of psychical conflicts, are 'feminine' neuroses in which it is precisely the status of the female body that is causing psychical conflict. Anorexia is itself a kind of sexualisation (in a mode of renunciation) of the eating process, a displacement of genital sexuality. The body image becomes bloated, extended as the biological reality of the body becomes thinner and more frail.

Why is it that women are more likely to somatise their conflicts than men? Does this have anything to do with the female body-image? With the problematic rift of mind and body which women, even less than men, are able to live out and live with?

The ego is not simply bounded by the 'natural' body. The 'natural body', insofar as there is one, is continually augmented by the products of history and culture, which it readily incorporates into its own intimate space. In this, according to Freud, 'man' must be recognised as a 'prosthetic god', approaching the fantasy of omnipotence, or at least of a body well beyond its physical, geographical and temporal immediacy. If the ego is a mapping of the body, and if the body is able to incorporate a host of instrumental supplements, the ego (or at least its ideal) aspires to a megalomania worthy of gods:

With every tool [man] is perfecting his own organs, whether motor or sensory, or is removing the limits to their functioning. Motor power places gigantic forces at his disposal, which, like his muscles, he can employ in any direction; thanks to ship and aircraft neither water nor air can hinder his movements...Man has, as it were, become a kind of prosthetic God. When he puts on all his auxiliary organs he is truly magnificent, but these organs have not grown onto him and they still give him much trouble at times.[6]

The once clear boundary between the mind and the body, nature and culture, becomes increasingly eroded. The very organ whose function it is to distinguish biological or id impulses from sociocultural pressures, the ego, is always already the intermingling of both insofar as it is the consequence of the cultural, that is, significatory effects of the body, the meaning and love of the body that is projected to produce the form of the ego.

Lacan and the Imaginary Anatomy

Like Freud, Lacan claims that the ego has no *a priori* status. It comes into being in the mirror stage, a phase in human development that occurs between about six and eighteen months, in which the infant comes to recognise its own image in a mirror. The mirror stage provides the matrix or ground for the development of human subjectivity, the place and time from which the ego emerges. He seems to take Freud's comments about the ego being a bodily extension or projection very seriously. For Lacan, the ego is not an outline or projection of the real, anatomical and physiological body but is the body insofar as it is imagined and represented for the subject through the image of others (including its own reflection in a mirror). The mirror stage provides the child with an anticipatory image of his own body as a *Gestalt* or externalised and totalised image. The earliest recognition by the child of its bodily unity, that is, the recognition that its skin is the limit of its spatial location, is at the same time a misrecognition insofar as the image with which the child identifies belies the child's own sensory and motor incapacities. Lacan makes it clear that the mirror stage institutes 'an essential libidinal relationship with the body-image'.

The imaginary anatomy is an internalised image or map of the meaning that the body has for the subject, for others in its social world, and for a culture as a whole. It is an individual and collective fantasy of the body's forms and modes of action. This, Lacan claims, helps to explain the peculiar, nonorganic connections formed in hysteria, including anorexia, and in such phenomena as the phantom limb. It also helps to explain why there are distinct waves of particular forms of hysteria, some even call them 'fashions', i.e. why hysterics commonly exhibited forms of breathing difficulty (e.g. fainting, *tussis nervosa*, breathlessness and so on) in the nineteenth century, which today have relatively disappeared and taking their place as the most 'popular' forms of hysteria today are eating disorders, anorexia nervosa and bulimia in particular. [. . .]

Masculine and Feminine

The question of biology and of the mind/body relation is raised once again, and in a most crucial and complex fashion, in Freud's account of the differences between the sexes. This is clearly the location of the most controversial and contested elements of his work. Yet even here, and in spite of Freud's clear biologism, there are also concepts and ideas which indicate a considerably more sophisticated understanding of sexual difference than many views commonly attributed to him. This is not to deny that there are still very major problems regarding his understanding of the differences between the sexes and particularly of female sexuality. Although this cannot be examined in detail, it is worthwhile indicating some of the major areas of feminist concern as well as those places in Freud's writing where, perhaps without his own knowledge or awareness, his position entails much that could be of value to feminist theory regarding the body and sexual difference.

Freud's account of the acquisition of masculine and feminine psychical positions can plausibly be interpreted as an account of the ways in which the male and female bodies are given meaning, and structured with reference to their relative social positions. Freud himself is not really concerned with the question of anatomy *per se*, seeking instead the psychical implications of anatomical differences. Nevertheless, he justifies his claims regarding the order of psychical events with recourse to a kind of confrontation the child has with (the meaning of) anatomy. His position can be best understood in terms of how meanings, values and desires construct male and female bodies (and particularly how their differences are represented). His postulation of the Oedipus complex and the castration threat can be read as an analysis and explanation of the social construction of women's bodies as a lack, and the correlative (and dependent) constitution of the male body as phallic.

The notions of phallic and castrated are not simply superimposed on pregiven bodies, an added attribute that could, in other cultural configurations, be removed to leave 'natural' sexual differences intact. Rather, the attribution of a phallic or a castrated status to sexually different bodies is an internal condition of the ways those bodies are lived and given meaning right from the very start (with or without the child's knowledge or compliance). There is no natural body to return to, no pure sexual difference one could gain access to if only the distortions and deformations of patriarchy could be removed or transformed. The phallus binarizes the differences between the sexes, dividing up a sexual-corporeal continuum into two mutually exclusive categories which in fact belie the multiplicity of bodies and body-types.

Although most psychoanalysts do not attribute sexual difference to the pre-Oedipal stages, and do not discuss the question of the sex of the body-image or the ways in which the body image does or does not include the sex of the body, it seems incontestable that the type of genitals (and later, secondary sexual characteristics) one has must play a major role in the type of body image one has, and the type of self-conception directly linked to the social meaning and value of the sexed body. Indeed, an argument could be made that the much beloved category of 'gender' so commonly used in feminist theory should be understood, not as the attribution of social and psychological categories to a biologically given sex, i.e. in terms of a mind/body split, but in terms that link gender much more closely to the specificities of sex. Gender is not an ideological superstructure added to a biological base; rather, gender is the inscription, and hence also the production, of the sexed body. Masculine or feminine gender cannot be neutrally attributed to bodies of either sex: the 'masculinity' of the male body cannot be the same as the 'masculinity' of the female body, because the kind of body inscribed makes a difference to the meanings and functioning of gender that emerges.[7]

Lacan says explicitly what is implied in Freud's understanding of sexual difference: while it makes perfect sense for the young boy, before he understands the anatomical differences between the sexes, to see others on a model derived from his own body morphology or representation, it makes no sense at all to claim that the girl too sees the whole world on a model derived from the *boy's* experience. Indeed it is the site of an amazing blindness on the part of these founding fathers of psychoanalytic feminism to claim that both the boy and the girl regard themselves, each other and the others in their world as phallic unless the phallus has an *a priori* privilege in the constitution of the body image. This is precisely Lacan's claim:

All the phenomena we are discussing [that is, the various manifestations of the body image in psychical life] seem to exhibit the laws of *Gestalt*; the fact that the penis is dominant in the shaping of the body image is evidence of this, though this may shock the sworn champions of the autonomy of female sexuality, such dominance is a fact and one moreover which cannot be put down to cultural influences alone.[8]

Among Lacan's most deliberately provocative statements (in a body of work that abounds in provocation), it is unclear that the 'laws of *Gestalt*' entail the dominance of the penis in the body-image *unless* female sexuality is already, even in the pre-Oedipal stages when the body-image is being formed, construed as castrated. Now, in one sense this is true. If patriarchy requires that female sexual organs be regarded more as the absence or lack of male organs than in any autonomous terms, then, for the others in the child's social world, the child's female body is lacking. But for the child herself to understand her body as such requires her to accept castration long before the castration threat. What Lacan says is clear for the boy: insofar as the body image is a unified, externalised and totalising representation of the body, and insofar as the penis is 'part' of the male body, it clearly plays some role, even if not yet a dominant one in shaping the boy's body-image. But how it does so in the case of the girl is entirely obscure. When the penis takes on the function of the phallus which is only possible as a result of the Oedipal classification of female sexuality as castrated, as lacking the phallus, only then can it be said to be dominant in the shaping of the body-image for girls as well as boys. And even then, clearly the phallus does not have the same meaning for the girl as it does for the boy: at best, for the girl it represents a form of nostalgic fantasy for her pre-Oedipal and pre-castrated position, the position that I believe the anorexic tenaciously clings to, as the only period in which the female body is regarded as whole and intact; but for the boy it represents the social valorisation of the penis, an actual and not simply a fantasised part of the body.

If women do not lack in any ontological or biological sense (there is no lack in the real, as Lacan is fond of saying), men cannot be said to have. In this sense, patriarchy requires that female bodies and sexualities be socially producted a lack. This, in some social contexts is taken literally but also occurs at an imaginary and symbolic level, that is, at the level of the body's morphology and the body image. Psychoanalysis describes how this mutilated body image comes about, thus explaining the socially authorised social and sexual positions and behaviours appropriate to and expected from women: but it is unable to explain how this occurs (not only because it is unable to see that its analyses find their context in patriarchal culture and not just neutral 'civilization', but above all, because it is unable to see that its own pronouncements and position are masculine). On such a model, anorexia may be seen as a resistance to the castrated status accorded to women in our culture. It can be regarded as a mode of confirmation and acceptance of femininity only if the contradictory status of women and the female body in patriarchal cultures is ignored. It is a way of trying (often unsuccessfully) to negotiate a place in culture as a subject (and not just as a body).

What psychoanalytic theory makes clear is that the body is literally written on, inscribed by desire and signification, at the anatomical, physiological and neurological levels. The body is in no sense naturally or innately psychical, sexual or sexed. It is indeterminate and indeterminable outside its social constitution as a body of a particular type. This implies that the body which it presumes and helps to explain is an open-ended, pliable set of significations, capable of being rewritten, reconstituted in quite other terms than those which mark it, and consequently the forms of sexed identity and psychical subjectivity at work today. This project of rewriting the female body as a positivity rather than as a lack entails two related concerns: reorganisation and reframing the terms by which the body has been socially represented (a project in which many feminists are presently engaged in the variety of challenges feminism poses in literary, visual, and filmic representational systems): and challenging the discourses which claim to analyse and explain the body and subject scientifically—biology, psychology, sociology—to develop different perspectives that may be able to better represent women's interests.

['Psychoanalysis and the Imaginary Body', in Penny Florence and Dee Reynolds (eds.), *Feminist Subjects, Multimedia. Cultural Methodologies* (Manchester: Manchester University Press, 1995), 183–96.]

LUCE IRIGARAY

48 The Other: Woman

Issues to do with women's liberation generate a good deal of misunderstanding, confusion and pointless conflict. I would like to try to interpret a few of these associated with my own work. To do this, I will take three interrelated examples: (1) the meaning of the title and subtitle of *Speculum*, (2) the view or belief that I changed theoretical and political direction with *An Ethics of Sexual Difference*, (3) accusations that I have been untrue or a traitor to the women's cause owing to my work with certain mixed-sex political groups, the Italian Communist Party among them.

In the title of *Speculum*, as throughout the whole book, I played on words, on meanings, to enable a different truth to appear. Thus, *speculum* denotes a gynecological instrument, though at an earlier period in our culture this term was used to denote the most faithful expression of reality possible. *Speculum mundi*, for example, was not an uncommon title and was what I had in mind. It signifies mirror of the world—not so much the reflection of the world in a mirror as the thought of the reality or objectivity of the world through a discourse. Unfortunately, this second meaning, the most important in terms of what I intended, is less well-known. My primary intention is, therefore, generally poorly understood, which is especially obvious in the interpretations and translations given to the subtitle: *De l'autre femme*.

Naturally, I took risks in writing the title and sub-title in the way I did in French. It might have been less ambiguous if I had written it like this: *Speculum, De l'autre: femme*. Then the title of this first book dealing with female identity could have been, in Italian, for example: *Speculum, A proposito de l'altro in quanto donna*, or, *Speculum, De l'altro: donna*. The actual translation: *L'altra donna* does not correspond to the meaning of my thought and the English translation: *Speculum, Of the other woman*, is clearly even further from what I intended; *Speculum, On the other woman*. would have been a more suitable choice, or better still, *On the other: woman*. The same goes for the Spanish translation of the title. The German translators opted for *Speculum, Spiegel des andere Geschlecht*. This option might seem preferable since it avoids the possible insistence upon a relation between two women but there is still too much emphasis on the mirror and it leaves out the allusion to a dialectical relation between a woman and herself as other.

My intention in choosing the title and subtitle of *Speculum, De l'autre femme*, related to the project of constituting the world—and not only the specular world—of the other as a woman. There was no question, then, of my holding up some mirror so that it reflects an other or the other woman. In *Speculum*, the question of the mirror figures as interpretation and criticism of the enclosure of the Western subject in the *Same*, even in those propositions concerning the need to use a different mirror for the constitution of female identity.

The meaning of the title and subtitle: *Speculum, De l'autre femme*, does not, therefore, refer to a purely empirical relation between (two?) women, nor to an already constituted relation of Luce Irigaray with *L'autre femme* (l'altra donna, the other woman, and so on). Who would this other woman be given that no female generic yet exists as representation or as content of an ideality for woman?

The other—*De l'autre femme*—should be taken as a substantive. In French, the other is supposed to denote man and woman, just as it is in other languages, such as Italian and English. In the subtitle of *Speculum*, I wanted to indicate that the other is not in fact neuter, either grammatically or semantically, and that it is not, or is no longer, possible to use the same words indiscriminately for the masculine and the feminine. Now this practice is widespread in philosophy, religion, and politics. There is talk of the other's existence, love of the other, concern for the other, etc., without it being asked whom or what this other represents. This lack of definition of the alterity of the other has left all thought, the dialectical method included, in a state of paralysis, in an idealistic dream appropriate to a single subject (the male), in the illusion of a unique absolute, and has left religion and politics to an empiricism profoundly lacking in ethics when it comes to respect between persons. For if the other is not defined in his or her actual reality, there is only an other me, not real others: the other may then be *more* or *less* than I am, might have *more* or *less* than me. And so it may represent (my) absolute perfection or greatness, the Other: God, Master, *logos*; it might denote the most insignificant or the most destitute: children, the ill, the poor, the outsider; it might name the one I consider to be my equal. It is not the other we are really dealing with but the same: inferior, superior, or equal to me.

However, before wishing to make the other one's equal, I think it is fair to ask: who am I who asks the other to be my equal? And then: in accordance with which measure, which order, which power, which Other (?) will these so-called equals be brought together and organized socially?

Between man and woman, there really is otherness: biological, morphological, relational. To be able to have a child constitutes a difference, but also being born a girl or a boy of a woman, who is of the same or the other gender as oneself, as well as to be or to appear corporeally with differing properties and qualities. Some of our prosperous or naive contemporaries, women and men, would like to wipe out this difference by resorting to monosexuality, to the unisex and to what is called identification: even if I am bodily a man or woman, I can identify with, and so be, the other sex. This new opium of the people annihilates the other in the illusion of a reduction to identity, equality and sameness, especially between man and woman, the ultimate anchorage of real alterity. The dream of dissolving material, corporeal or social identity leads to a whole set of delusions, to endless and unresolvable conflicts, to a war of images or reflections and to powers being accredited to somebody or other more for imaginary or narcissistic reasons than for their actual abilities. Unless money itself is becoming the sole stake in ideality.

Man and woman should not be abandoned to a mode of functioning in which woman is hierarchically inferior to man—to positively construct alterity between them is a task for our time. The aim of *Speculum* is to construct an objectivity that facilitates a dialectic proper to the female subject, meaning specific relations between her nature and her culture, her same and her other, her singularity and the community, her interiority and her exteriority, etc. *Speculum* and my other works insist upon the irreducibility—either subjective or objective—of the sexes to one another, which requires us to establish a dialectic of the relation of woman to herself and of man to himself, a double dialectic therefore, enabling a real, cultured and ethical relation between them.¹ It is both a philosophical and a political task. It should not be confused with autobiographical narrative, with theoretical propositions that ignore the labor of the negative vis-à-vis elementary subjectivity, with immediate affect, with self-certainty, mimetic or recapitulative intuitive truth, with historical narrative, etc.

Having commented at some length on the title of *Speculum*, I believe I have explained why *An Ethics of Sexual Difference* followed on from *Speculum*, as well as why it was quite logical for me to want to work with the Italian Communist Party, in that they recognize the importance of the other, as a woman, (*l'altro in quanto donna*) for the operation of a just dialectic in History. Moreover, History cannot do without the existence of two human subjects, man and woman, if it is to get away from master–slave relationships.

Making the difference between the sexes the motor of the dialectic's becoming also means being able to renounce death as sovereign master so that we may at last give our care to the expansion of life: natural and spiritual, individual and collective, life.

But many women, and men for that matter, still do not believe that woman can be anything other than the complement to man, his inverse, his scraps, his need, his other. Which means that she cannot be truly other. The other that she is remains trapped in the economy or the horizon of a single subject. In *Speculum*, I wanted to question this female alterity defined from a male subject's point of view. I questioned myself as identified in this way: the other of/for man and man alone.

Asked about my method for initiating the thinking of sexual difference, I could say that I have several or that I try to find the most suitable one, but there is one method that I used to write *Speculum* and continue to use regularly—inversion. It is a method used by more recent philosophers: Marx inverts Hegel, Nietzsche inverts Platonism, and the problematics of the return—present in other philosophies, such as Heidegger's—are in some respect problematics of inversion. There is a notable difference, though, in that Marx inverts Hegel, Nietzsche inverts Platonism, the problematics of the return invert History, and so on. Thus it is a case of inverting something exterior to oneself and already constituted as such. In Freudian terms, we might say that it approximates to the murder of the father, the overthrow of the ancestor or his *oeuvre* by a son wishing to become an adult.

In my case, it was more a question of inverting myself. I was the other of/for man, I attempted to define the objective alterity of myself for myself as belonging to the female gender. I carried out an inversion of the femininity imposed upon me in order to try to define the female corresponding to my gender: the in-and-for-itself of my female nature. This process is extremely difficult to carry out and explains most of the misunderstandings about my work and thought. Unlike most women, (see Simone de Beauvoir's introduction to *The Second Sex*), I did not want to speak of the other: woman as the other-woman of/for man, of the other-woman in the male and patriarchal horizon of our culture. Nor did I want, as some have thought or written, to enact the parricide of one of my supposed masters. Not at all, I wanted to begin to define what a woman is, thus myself as a woman—and not only *a* woman but as freely belonging to the female gender or generic—by carrying out a partial process of limitation or negation relative to my natural immediacy, and relative to the representation I had been given of what I was as a woman, that is, the other of/for man, the other of male culture. Hence, I attempted to sketch out a spirituality in the feminine, and in doing so, of course, I curbed my own needs and desires, my natural immediacy, especially by thinking myself as half and only half the world, but also by calling into question the spirituality imposed on me in the culture appropriate to the male or to patriarchy, a culture in which I was the other of the Same.

Most of the works by women today aim to describe what a woman is within the horizon of a male subject's culture. In which case, some women, some of the one + one + one . . . (*une + une + une . . .*) women describe or tell their life stories. This is indeed speaking out. But then there is a plurality that seems to elude the definition of a unity: *woman*, except perhaps insofar as it is determined by man or as possible natural immediacy. More often than not, these women, or rather this female identity, still apparently originates in man. As our tradition dictates, man originates from God, and woman from man. As long as the female generic—woman—is not determined as such, this will be true. Women will remain men's or Man's creatures. With respect to themselves, and among themselves, they are unable to create, create (for) themselves, especially an ideal, for want of an identity and of mediations. They will be able to criticize their condition, complain, reject themselves or one another, but not establish a new era of History or of culture.

But some of the strongest resistance, indeed the greatest resistance, to the construction of new relations between women, and between women and men, arises wherever a new model of female identity is to be elaborated. This resistance is upheld by men in the name of their culture: they must not lose their monopoly of the model of human kind, the privilege of representing the ideal for human kind. Thus they are Man, he, He, the human generic, and women are the one + one + one (*un/e/ + un/e/ + un/e/*) of this human kind, which is, in fact, male. The resistance is also perpetuated by women who are not used to defining themselves in human terms as women and have difficulty in acknowledging a female model of identity. They are often the most virulent in calling for equality with men and for the neutralization of female identity and the female ideal. Thus, women have a strange idea of democracy. As they have no rights proper to them, democracy is often, in their view, the reduction of women to the lowest common denominator. Rarely do they recognize in a woman's value a possible model of identity, whether this be the person herself or in her theory or thought. Unfortunately, women are the first to say that woman does not exist and cannot do so. Which means they refuse to accept a generic identity for the female. This denial eliminates the possibility of constituting a culture of two sexes, two genders. We remain in the horizon in which man is the model of human kind, and within this human kind, there are empirical women or there are natural entities without an identity of their own.

Women's liberation, and indeed the liberation of humanity, depends upon the definition of a female generic, that is, a definition of what woman is, not just this or that woman. For women to get away from a model of hierarchical submission to male identity we need to define the female gender, the generic identity of women.

To be able to attain this generic identity, we need to attribute value to the pronouns *he* and *she* and to their plural forms[2] as an expression of gender and we need to accord positive value to the pronoun *she* as that which designates the female gender.

It's fairly easy to state that the *I* and the *you* are not used in the same way depending upon whether the speaking subjects are women or men. Men tend to speak out more than women. In addition, men say *I* more, designate themselves as subjects of the discourse, action or condition that is being expressed more frequently than women do. Analysis of their respective statements reveals that men use *I*, women *you/the other*, but these *I* and *you* are situated within one single problematic where there are not two subjects but rather the workings of the incomplete economy of a single subject.

That said, subjectivity cannot be reduced to saying *I*; it is also signified by means of the objective generic representation of the speaking subject: *he* and *she*. Yet in the history of culture—in philosophy, theology, even linguistics—much is said about *I* and *you* and very little about *he* or *she*. With the result that we are no longer sure who *I* and *you* are in a concrete situation, since *I* and *you* are always sexed and the loss of this dimension obscures the identity of who is speaking and of the person to whom the message is addressed. Consequently, we do not have an *I* and *you* that are clearly determined and stand for a meaning, nor do we have the possibility of *we*.

To come to this *we*, consideration has to be given to how *he* and *she* operate in exchanges. *He* and *she* are figures forgotten in the history of philosophy, censured by theology, and poorly defined in linguistics, where these real partners hobble along, one foot in culture, the other in nature. While men and women do not speak out equally, if man says *I* more and woman *you* more, the gap is even greater between the use of *he* and *she* in the discourse of women and men.

Of course, in this case usage is directly induced by cultural models and codes, especially linguistic ones, which have not been thought through in terms of sexual difference: (*a*) the human generic is designated by *he* and *he* alone; (*b*) the mixed plural is expressed by the masculine plural, which means that in a mixed group, even with just two people, a woman has to endorse the *il(s)*,[3] especially in love; of lovers, one has to say: *ils s'aiment* (they love each other), *ils sont beaux* (they are beautiful), *ils out fait un grand voyage* (they took a long trip), and so on. The same goes for generation: *ils out fait un bel enfant* (they have had a lovely baby), *ils ont décidé d'avoir un enfant cette année* (they have decided to have a child this year), and so on; the woman's relationship to herself, women's relationships among themselves, and especially the relationship between mother and daughter, are thus wiped out in all mixed-sex situations; (*c*) the masculine gender is valorized at the expense of the feminine, which means not only that *he* always takes precedence over *she* but also that masculine gender words, things belonging to the masculine gender, are valued more highly than those designating the feminine: *la secrétaire du patron* (the boss's secretary), for example, compared with *le secrétaire de l'État* (the Secretary of State).[4]

How can this be explained on a speculative level?

Language and its values reflect the social order and vice versa.

Language functions as a sort of inversion of the situation of the engendering of *he* in *she*. Language presents itself as a technique of appropriating *she/they* (*elles*) in *he/they* (*ils*) or an inverted hierarchy vis-à-vis the power of maternal gestation. Father-*logos* claims to be the overall engenderer compared to mother-nature. But, in this gesture—which is similar to the *fort-da* of little Hans with his bobbin[5]—man has not really thought out his relation to engendering, to the fact of being engendered: he denies it by affirming the all-powerful status of language, of his language, which cancels out the difference between the sexes, the genders and is conveyed by setting up a transcendence corresponding to a monosexual code, a Law-making-God-the-Father, etc. Which can equate to an absolute transcendence only insofar as it is appropriated to male identity, and entails reductions with respect to the constitution of female identity.

Just as the masculine's transcendence is problematic in terms of what it annuls of the reality of engendering, the establishment of this culture, which is called patriarchal, denies transcendence in the feminine. Everything that is of the feminine gender is thus less valued in this logic because it lacks any possible dimension of transcendence. Christianity's cult of mother and son is not a sign of respect for feminine transcendence, unless it is given a different interpretation.

It is this that makes a spiritual relationship between the sexes an impossibility.

Now *he* and *she* designate the objectivity of two sexed subjects. Not to give them an equally valid linguistic status is to:

—To say that as subject *I* and *you*, they do not have the same value.

—To deprive the two pronouns, the two genders, of their meanings since one term is defined by the other.

—To rule out a dialectic of the sexed subject; thus the female subject who can say *I* but without *she* remains in a subjectivism without a subjectivity—objectivity dialectic. Furthermore, an *I–you* relation between the sexes needs to go through a subjectivity–objectivity dialectic for each sex.

We need to go through this valorizing of the two pronouns *he* and *she* in order to uphold the intentionality of the *I* that operates in the relation between *I* and *you*; otherwise it becomes pathological.

In order to constitute a free and active temporality, the *I*-woman needs a *she* that is valorized as a pole of intentionality between *she* and *she*, *I-she* and *she-herself*.

['The Other: Woman', *I Love to You: Sketch for a Felicity Within History* (London: Routledge, 1996).]

Section 4

Sexualities

INTRODUCTION

> 'Coitus can scarcely be said to take place in a vacuum; although of itself
> it appears a biological and physical activity, it is set so deeply within the
> larger context of human affairs that it serves as a charged microcosm of
> the variety of attitudes and values to which culture subscribes.'
>
> Kate Millett

The pieces in this section reflect upon sexuality as a domain of exploration, pleasure, and agency as well as a domain of restriction, repression, and danger. Opposing attitudes to sexuality—hetero, homo, bi, and queer—within feminist discourses have proved so intense and enduring that it is perhaps this issue above all else that, as Lynne Segal argues, 'produced the final and fundamental rift between feminists at the end of the 1970s and which shattered any potential unity about the nature, direction and goal of feminism'.[1] Central areas of disagreement focus upon the questions of whether sexuality should be viewed as natural or as social constructed; whether there are universal forms of male and female sexuality; the extent to which sexuality should be viewed as central, both to women's oppression and to our expression of agency; how one should view the relation between sex and violence; and how one should define and respond to pornography. Whilst there are a wide diversity of perspectives on each of these issues, debate does tend to polarize into two very broad camps commonly perceived as radical and its critics.

Radical feminist perspectives characteristically castigate heterosexuality as an oppressive socially constructed patriarchal institution forcibly imposed upon women. Heterosexuality is perceived to be the primary sphere of male power, male control of female sexuality being foundational to patriarchal power. The perspective frequently includes a central preoccupation with pornography, viewed as one of the key manifestations and mechanisms of this system of control. Heterosexuality, from this perspective, is a patriarchal construct serving to oppress women. To speak of heterosexuality is to speak of sexual violence and danger.

Broadly defined radical feminist perspectives are represented here by the writings of Adrienne Rich, Andrea Dworkin, and Catharine MacKinnon, whose writings have both inspired and mobilized a substantial feminist following and generated intense disagreement, refutation, and even condemnation in other feminist quarters (as manifest in the writings in this section by Eve Kosofsky Sedgwick, Lynne Segal, and Wendy Brown). The various articulations of such radical feminist analyses of sexuality, though dominant in the 1970s, were largely eclipsed (in terms of sheer numbers of publications at least) in the 1980s by disparate critical voices which found early radical feminist accounts of sexuality to be overly reductive. It is such critical voices which perhaps best characterize feminist writings of sexuality since 1980, hence their predominance in this section. As Liz Kelly notes in her piece, 'A shift away from the feminist challenge to previously "taken for granted" perspectives on sexuality is evident in some of the current focus on pleasure' (p. 348). These previously taken for granted perspectives are precisely those which result in the depiction, challenged by Lynne Segal in her extract, of feminism as anti-heterosexual pleasure and heterosexual pleasure as anti-woman. More frequently articulated during recent years are those perspectives that stress the importance of individual choice and sexual pleasure rather than (or sometimes in addition to) structural oppression and sexual danger. It is perhaps the fact that MacKinnon continues to develop and defend a particularly sophisticated version of the radical feminist understanding of sexuality against this prevailing trend that accounts for the controversy that her writings engender. As Wendy Brown reflects, MacKinnon successfully deployed 'a militant feminism during the 1980s, a decade markedly unsympathetic to all militancies to the left of centre' (p. 379).

At odds with those feminist analyses which view heterosexual and romantic passion and pleasure as simply oppressive, a more exploratory engagement has come to prevail. Increasingly, we find the recognition that sexuality is a domain of exploration and agency as well as one of restriction and repression. Vance's 1984 collection signalled a general shift within feminism towards a focus on pleasure. Viewing heterosexuality as simply a manifestation of male power came to be seen by many as problematic in that it encouraged all women to identify themselves as the victim of all men, and risked making speech about sexual pleasure taboo. Cultural, literary, and psychoanalytic theory were drawn upon to develop alternative analyses of sexualities and their representations. Alison Light, for example, counters that feminist reading of romance fiction which assumes it to be solely comprised of coercive and stereotyping narratives working to oppress women. Offering a more upbeat account, Light explores the pleasure of the texts of romance fictions for women. This approach involves not only a different perception of sexuality but also, crucially, a different understanding of strategies of visual and narrative representation and reception. Rather than viewing readers as passive victims of patriarchal strategies of control, such analysis posits a more interactive and indeterminate relationship between text and reader, image and viewer.

This form of exploration of the relation between the real, representation, and fantasy is directly at odds with the tendency within the writings of Dworkin, MacKinnon, and others of a radical feminist persuasion to argue a causal realism: for Dworkin 'pornography is not imagery in some relation to a reality elsewhere. It is not a distortion, reflection, projection, expression, fantasy, representation or symbol either. It is sexual reality.' In direct opposition to this assertion psychoanalytic and deconstructivist forms of feminism work to interrogate the complex relations between symbols and 'the real'. Eve Kosofsky Sedgwick, for example, suggests that rather than characterizing sexual fantasies as simple internalization and endorsement of oppressive sexual norms, they might better be viewed as symptomatic, oppositional responses to the experience of oppression. In such claims one can see the extent to which psychoanalytic frameworks take pleasure and fantasy seriously, enriching the debate between those who argue that sexual desire is best understood as false consciousness and those who perceive it as an expression of free agency and individual choice.

The goal of 'sexual liberation' does not then disperse in the face of these refutations of more radical feminist assumptions, analyses, and strategies: it is, to use Segal's phrase, 'differently conceived'. Rather than struggling to combat the repression of a female sexual essence, sexual liberation is understood by those who adopt more postmodern or psychoanalytic perspectives as the struggle to recognize the pleasure of multiple sexualities. These feminist voices of sexual exploration emphasize the extent to which existing mechanisms of heterosexuality not only require a subordinate other in homosexuality, but also serve to occlude possibilities for an expansive spectrum of sexualities. Queer theorists such as Cherry Smyth claim that the dominant feminist agenda of the 1970s and 1980s served as a disciplinary discourse, blocking attempts to understand the interconnections between lesbian and gay male desires. Challenging earlier prescriptive feminist politics, queer politics rejects structuralist analyses which resulted in hierarchies of oppression and simply celebrates diversity.

Moves to resist all dualisms and constructions of otherness are rife in contemporary politics and theory. In the field of sexuality this leads to a project to deconstruct the hetero/homosexual split. Bisexuality and queer politics become modish radical gestures in a manner akin to the assertion of political lesbianism in previous decades. But these newer sexual politics stand in a different relation to feminism. Whereas the earlier radical accounts of sexuality claimed to provide a basis for a feminist theory, queer politics would seem to some to undermine the basis for an engagement with feminism, replacing as it does a collective gender-based politics with aestheticized individual assertions of identity politics. Mary McIntosh offers a resolution to this apparent tension by proposing that these are two distinct but mutually supportive theories; Susan Sturgis suggests a more integrated approach.

Elizabeth Wilson posits an overt tension between the two in that individual acts of defiance may be 'personally liberating', but they cannot deal with 'the systematic or structural nature of oppressive institutions'. The central issue here is whether the transgression of all sexual norms, ignoring the whole issue of gender, offers a radical means to deconstruct oppressive identities, or whether such a strategy—adopted in our highly hierarchical society—effectively legitimizes existing power imbalances. Can one really celebrate difference without attending to dominance, and still claim a feminist politics? What is the relation between personal acts of transgression and collective acts of liberation?

'The right to define our sexuality' was demarcated a key demand of the women's movement back in 1978. All that has transpired since acts as testament to the fact that the apparent simplicity of the statement belies the complexity of its realization. It is for the reader to decide whether the 'current focus on pleasure' noted by Kelly and manifest in the selection of extracts in this section, is a nuanced and mature recognition of this complexity, or a problematic retreat to an individualistic and compliant acceptance of the status quo.

49 Compulsory Heterosexuality and Lesbian Existence

Feminist theory can no longer afford merely to voice a toleration of 'lesbian-ism' as an 'alternative life-style', or make token allusion to lesbians. A feminist critique of compulsory heterosexual orientation for women is long overdue. In this exploratory paper, I shall try to show why. [. . .]

I will begin by way of examples, briefly discussing books that have appeared in the last few years, written from different viewpoints and political orientations, but all presenting themselves, and favorably reviewed, as feminist.[1] [. . .]

Nancy Chodorow does come close to the edge of an acknowledgement of lesbian existence. [. . .] Chodorow believes that the fact that women, and women only, are responsible for child care in the sexual division of labor has led to an entire social organization of gender inequality, and that men as well as women must become primary carers for children if that inequality is to change. In the process of examining, from a psychoanalytic perspective, how mothering-by-women affects the psychological development of girl and boy children, she offers documentation that men are 'emotionally secondary' in women's lives; that 'women have a richer, ongoing inner world to fall back on. . . . men do not become as emotionally important to women as women do to men'.[2] Chodorow concludes that because women have women as mothers, 'The mother remains a primary internal object [sic] to the girl, so that heterosexual relationships are on the model of a nonexclusive, second relationship for her, whereas for the boy they recreate an exclusive, primary relationship.' According to Chodorow, women 'have learned to deny the limitations of masculine lovers for both psychological and practical reasons'.[3]

But the practical reasons (like witch burnings, male control of law, theology, and science, or economic nonviability within the sexual division of labor) are glossed over. Chodorow's account barely glances at the constraints and sanctions which, historically, have enforced or insured the coupling of women with men and obstructed or penalized our coupling or allying in independent groups with other women. She dismisses lesbian existence with the comment that 'lesbian relationships do tend to re-create mother–daughter emotions and connections, but most women are heterosexual' (implied: more mature, having developed beyond the mother–daughter connection). She then adds: 'This heterosexual preference and taboos on homosexuality, in addition to objective economic dependence on men, make the option of primary sexual bonds with other women unlikely—though more prevalent in recent years.'[4] The significance of that qualification seems irresistible—but Chodorow does not explore it further. [. . .] Chodorow leads us implicitly to conclude that heterosexuality is *not* a 'preference' for women;

that, for one thing, it fragments the erotic from the emotional in a way that women find impoverishing and painful. Yet her book participates in mandating it. Neglecting the covert socializations and the overt forces which have channelled women into marriage and heterosexual romance, pressures ranging from the selling of daughters to postindustrial economics to the silences of literature to the images of the television screen, she, like Dinnerstein, is stuck with trying to reform a man-made institution—compulsory heterosexuality—as if, despite profound emotional impulses and complementarities drawing women toward women, there is a mystical/biological heterosexual inclination, a 'preference' or 'choice' which draws women toward men.

Moreover, it is understood that this 'preference' does not need to be explained, unless through the tortuous theory of the female Oedipus complex or the necessity for species reproduction. It is lesbian sexuality which (usually, and, incorrectly, 'included' under male homosexuality) is seen as requiring explanation. This assumption of female heterosexuality seems to me in itself remarkable: it is an enormous assumption to have glided so silently into the foundations of our thought.

The extension of this assumption is the frequently heard assertion that in a world of genuine equality, where men were nonoppressive and nurturing, everyone would be bisexual. Such a notion blurs and sentimentalizes the actualities within which women have experienced sexuality; it is the old liberal leap across the tasks and struggles of here and now, the continuing process of sexual definition which will generate its own possibilities and choices. (It also assumes that women who have chosen women have done so simply because men are oppressive and emotionally unavailable: which still fails to account for women who continue to pursue relationships with oppressive and/or emotionally unsatisfying men.) I am suggesting that heterosexuality, like motherhood, needs to be recognized and studied as a *political institution*—even, or especially, by those individuals who feel they are, in their personal experience, the precursors of a new social relation between the sexes.

If women are the earliest sources of emotional caring and physical nurture for both female and male children, it would seem logical, from a feminist perspective at least, to pose the following questions: whether the search for love and tenderness in both sexes does not originally lead toward women; *why in fact women would ever redirect that search*; why species-survival, the means of impregnation, and emotional/erotic relationships should ever have become so rigidly identified with each other; and why such violent strictures should be found necessary to enforce women's total emotional, erotic loyalty and subservience to men. I doubt that enough feminist scholars and theorists have taken the pains to acknowledge the societal forces which wrench women's emotional and erotic energies away from themselves and other women and from woman-identified values. These forces [...] range from literal physical enslavement to the disguising and distorting of possible options.

[...] The chastity belt; child marriage; erasure of lesbian existence (except as exotic and perverse) in art, literature, film; idealization of heterosexual romance and marriage—these are some fairly obvious forms of compulsion, the first two exemplifying physical force, the second two control of consciousness. While clitoridectomy has been assailed by feminists as a form of woman-torture,[5] Kathleen Barry first pointed out that it is not simply a way of turning the young girl into a 'marriageable' woman through brutal surgery: it intends that women in the intimate proximity of polygynous marriage will not form sexual relationships with each other; that—from a male, genital-fetishist perspective—female erotic connections, even in a sex-segregated situation, will be literally excised.[6] [...]

The assumption that 'most women are innately heterosexual' stands as a theoretical and political stumbling block for many women. It remains a tenable assumption, partly because lesbian existence has been written out of history or catalogued under disease; partly because it has been treated as exceptional rather than intrinsic; partly because to acknowledge that for women heterosexuality may not be a 'preference' at all but something that has had to be imposed, managed, organized, propagandized, and maintained by force, is an immense step to take if you consider yourself freely and 'innately' heterosexual. Yet the failure to examine heterosexuality as an institution is like failing to admit that the economic system called capitalism or the caste system of racism is maintained by a variety of forces, including both physical violence and false consciousness. To take the step of questioning heterosexuality as a 'preference' or 'choice' for women—and to do the intellectual and emotional work that follows—will call for a special quality of courage in heterosexually identified feminists but I think the rewards will be great: a freeing-up of thinking, the exploring of new paths, the shattering of another great silence, new clarity in personal relationships.

I have chosen to use the terms *lesbian existence* and *lesbian continuum* because the word *lesbianism* has a clinical and limiting ring. *Lesbian existence* suggests both the fact of the historical presence of lesbians and our continuing creation of the meaning of that existence. I mean the term *lesbian continuum* to include a range—through each woman's life and throughout history—of woman-identified experience; not simply the fact that a woman has had or consciously desired genital sexual experience with another woman. If we expand it to embrace many more forms of primary intensity between and among women, including the sharing of a rich inner life, the bonding against male tyranny, the giving and receiving of practical and political support [...] we begin to grasp breadths of female history and psychology which have lain out of reach as a consequence of limited, mostly clinical, definitions of 'lesbianism'. [...]

Lesbians have historically been deprived of a political existence through 'inclusion' as female versions of male homosexuality. To equate lesbian existence with male homosexuality because each is stigmatized is to deny and erase female reality once again. To separate those women stigmatized as 'homosexual' or 'gay' from the complex continuum of female resistance to enslavement, and attach them to a male pattern, is to falsify our history. Part of the history of lesbian existence is, obviously, to be found where lesbians, lacking a coherent female community, have shared a kind of social life and common cause with homosexual men. But this has to be seen against the differences: women's lack of economic and cultural privilege relative to men; qualitative differences in female and male relationships, for example, the prevalence of anonymous sex and the justification of pederasty among male homosexuals, the pronounced ageism in male homosexual standards of sexual attractiveness, etc. In defining and describing lesbian existence I would hope to move toward a dissociation of lesbian from male homosexual values and allegiances. I perceive the lesbian experience as being, like motherhood, a profoundly *female* experience, with particular oppressions, meanings, and potentialities we cannot comprehend as long as we simply bracket it with other sexually stigmatized existences. Just as the term 'parenting' serves to conceal the particular and significant reality of being a parent who is actually a mother, the term 'gay' serves the purpose of blurring the very outlines we need to discern, which are of crucial value for feminism and for the freedom of women as a group.

As the term 'lesbian' has been held to limiting, clinical associations in its patriarchal definition, female friendship and comradeship have been set apart from the erotic, thus limiting the erotic itself. But as we deepen and broaden the range of what we define as lesbian existence, as we delineate a lesbian continuum, we begin to discover the erotic in female terms: as that which is unconfined to any single part of the body or solely to the body itself, as an energy not only diffuse but, as Audre Lorde has described it, omnipresent in 'the sharing of joy, whether physical, emotional, psychic', and in the sharing of work; as the empowering joy which 'makes us less willing to accept powerlessness, or those other supplied states of being which are not native to me such as resignation, despair, self-effacement, depression, self-denial'.[7] [...]

A feminism of action, often, though not always, without a theory, has constantly reemerged in every culture and in every period. We can then begin to study women's struggle against powerlessness, women's radical rebellion, not just in male-defined 'concrete revolutionary situations'[8] but in all the situations male ideologies have not perceived as revolutionary: for example, the refusal of some women to produce children, aided at great risk by other women; the refusal to produce a higher standard of living and leisure for men (Leghorn and Parker show how both are part of women's unacknowledged, unpaid, and ununionized economic contribution); that female antiphallic sexuality which, as Andrea Dworkin notes, has been 'legendary', which, defined as 'frigidity' and 'puritanism', has actually been a form of subversion of male power—'an ineffectual rebellion, but . . . rebellion nonetheless'.[9] We can no longer have patience with Dinnerstein's view that women have simply collaborated with men in the 'sexual arrangements' of history; we begin to observe behavior, both in history and in individual biography, that has hitherto been invisible or misnamed; behavior which often constitutes, given the limits of the counterforce exerted in a given time and place, radical rebellion. And we can connect these rebellions and the necessity for them with the physical passion of woman for woman which is central to lesbian existence: the erotic sensuality which has been, precisely, the most violently erased fact of female experience.

Heterosexuality has been both forcibly and subliminally imposed on women, yet everywhere women have resisted it, often at the cost of physical torture, imprisonment, psychosurgery, social ostracism, and extreme poverty. [. . .]

Woman-identification is a source of energy, a potential springhead of female power, violently curtailed and wasted under the institution of heterosexuality. The denial of reality and visibility to women's passion for women, women's choice of women as allies, life companions, and community; the forcing of such relationships into dissimulation and their disintegration under intense pressure have meant an incalculable loss to the power of all women *to change the social relations of the sexes, to liberate ourselves and each other*. The lie of compulsory female heterosexuality today afflicts not just feminist scholarship, but every profession, every reference work, every curriculum, every organizing attempt, every relationship or conversation over which it hovers. It creates, specifically, a profound falseness, hyprocrisy, and hysteria in the heterosexual dialogue, for every heterosexual relationship is lived in the queasy strobelight of that lie. However we chose to identify ourselves, however we find ourselves labeled, it flickers across and distorts our lives. [. . .]

The question inevitably will arise: Are we then to condemn all heterosexual relationships, including those which are least oppressive? I believe this question, though often heartfelt, is the wrong question here. We have been stalled in a maze of false dichotomies which prevents our apprehending the institution as a whole: 'good' versus 'bad' marriages; 'marriage for love' versus arranged marriage; 'liberated' sex versus prostitution; heterosexual intercourse versus rape; Liebeschmerz versus humiliation and dependency. Within the institution exist, of course, qualitative differences of experience; but the absence of choice remains the great unacknowledged reality, and in the absence of choice, women will remain dependent upon the chance or luck of particular relationships and will have no collective power to determine the meaning and place of sexuality in their lives. As we address the institution itself, moreover, we begin to perceive a history of female resistance which has never fully understood itself because it has been so fragmented, miscalled, erased. It will require a courageous grasp of the politics and economics, as well as the cultural propaganda, of heterosexuality to carry us beyond individual cases or diversified group situations into the complex kind of overview needed to undo the power men everywhere wield over women, power which has become a model for every other form of exploitation and illegitimate control.

['Compulsory Heterosexuality and Lesbian Existence' *Signs*, 5/4 (1980), 631–60 (first published as a pamphlet by Onlywomen Press, London, 1979).]

ANDREA DWORKIN

50 Pornography

The word *pornography*, derived from the ancient Greek *porne* and *graphos*, means 'writing about whores'. *Porne* means 'whore', specifically and exclusively the lowest class of whore, which in ancient Greece was the brothel slut available to all male citizens. The *porne* was the cheapest (in the literal sense), least regarded, least protected of all women, including slaves. She was, simply and clearly and absolutely, a sexual slave. *Graphos* means 'writing, etching, or drawing'.

The word *pornography* does not mean 'writing about sex' or 'depictions of the erotic' or 'depictions of sexual acts' or 'depictions of nude bodies' or 'sexual representations' or any other such euphemism. It means the graphic depiction of women as vile whores. In ancient Greece, not all prostitutes were considered vile: only the *porneia*.

Contemporary pornography strictly and literally conforms to the word's root meaning: the graphic depiction of vile whores, or, in our language, sluts, cows (as in: sexual cattle, sexual chattel), cunts. The word has not changed its meaning and the genre is not misnamed. The only change in the meaning of the word is with respect to its second part, *graphos*: now there are cameras— there is still photography, film, video. The methods of graphic depiction have increased in number and in kind: the content is the same; the meaning is the same; the purpose is the same; the status of the women depicted is the same; the sexuality of the women depicted is the same; the value of the women depicted is the same. With the technologically advanced methods of graphic depiction, real women are required for the depiction as such to exist.

The word *pornography* does not have any other meaning than the one cited here, the graphic depiction of the lowest whores. Whores exist to serve men sexually. Whores exist only within a framework of male sexual domination. Indeed, outside that framework the notion of whores would be absurd and the usage of women as whores would be impossible. The word *whore* is incomprehensible unless one is immersed in the lexicon of male domination. Men have created the group, the type, the concept, the epithet, the insult, the industry, the trade, the commodity, the reality of woman as whore. Woman as whore exists within the objective and real system of male sexual domination. The pornography itself is objective and real and central to the male sexual system. The valuation of women's sexuality in pornography is objective and real because women are so regarded and so valued. The force depicted in pornography is objective and real because force is so used against women. The debasing of women depicted in pornography and intrinsic to it is objective and real in that women are so debased. The uses of women depicted in pornography are objective and real because women are so used. The women used in pornography are used in pornography. The definition of women articulated systematically and consistently in pornography is objective and real in that real women exist within and must live with constant reference to the boundaries of this definition. The fact that pornography is widely believed to be 'sexual representations' or 'depictions of sex' emphasizes only that the valuation of women as low whores is widespread and that the sexuality of women is perceived as low and whorish in and of itself. The fact that pornography is widely believed to be 'depictions of the erotic' means only that the debasing of women is held to be the real pleasure of sex. [...] The idea that pornography is 'dirty' originates in the conviction that the sexuality of women is dirty and is actually portrayed in pornography; that women's bodies (especially women's genitals) are dirty and lewd in themselves. Pornography does not, as some claim, refute the idea that female sexuality is dirty: instead, pornography embodies and exploits this idea; pornography sells and promotes it.

In the United States, the pornography industry is larger than the record and film industries combined. In a time of widespread economic impoverishment, it is growing: more and more male consumers are eager to spend more and more money on pornography—on depictions of women as vile whores. Pornography is now carried by cable television; it is now being marketed for home use in video machines. The technology itself demands the creation of more and more *porneia* to meet the market opened up by the technology. Real women are tied up, stretched, hanged, fucked, gang-banged, whipped, beaten, and begging for more. In the photographs and films, real women are used as *porneia* and real women are depicted as *porneia*. To profit, the pimps must supply the *porneia* as the technology widens the market for the visual consumption of women being brutalized and loving it. One picture is worth a thousand words. The number of pictures required to meet the demands of the marketplace determines the number of *porneia* required to meet the demands of graphic depiction. The numbers grow as the technology and its accessibility grow. The technology by its very nature encourages more and more passive acquiescence to the graphic depictions. Passivity makes the already credulous consumer more credulous. He comes to the pornography a believer; he goes away from it a missionary. The technology itself legitimizes the uses of women conveyed by it.

In the male system, women are sex; sex is the whore. The whore is *porne*, the lowest whore, the whore who belongs to *all* male citizens: the slut, the cunt. Buying her is buying pornography. Having her is having pornography. Seeing her is seeing pornography. Seeing her sex, especially her genitals, is seeing pornography. Seeing her in sex is seeing the whore in sex. Using her is using pornography. Wanting her means wanting pornography. Being her means being pornography.

> [*Pornography* (London: Women's Press, 1981), 191–202 (originally published by Perigee Books, New York, 1981).]

CAROLE VANCE

51 Pleasure and Danger: Toward a Politics of Sexuality

The tension between sexual danger and sexual pleasure is a powerful one in women's lives. Sexuality is simultaneously a domain of restriction, repression, and danger as well as a domain of exploration, pleasure, and agency. To focus only on pleasure and gratification ignores the patriarchal structure in which women act, yet to speak only of sexual violence and oppression ignores women's experience with sexual agency and choice and unwittingly increases the sexual terror and despair in which women live.

The juxtaposition of pleasure and danger has engaged the attention of feminist theorists and activists in both the nineteenth and twentieth centuries, just as it has been an ongoing subject in the lives of individual women who must weigh the pleasures of sexuality against its cost in their daily calculations, choices, and acts. For some, the dangers of sexuality—violence, brutality, and coercion, in the form of rape, forcible incest, and exploitation, as well as everyday cruelty and humiliation—make the pleasures pale by comparison. For others, the positive possibilities of sexuality—explorations of the body, curiosity, intimacy, sensuality, adventure, excitement, human connection, basking in the infantile and non-rational—are not only worthwhile but provide sustaining energy. Nor are these positions fixed, since a woman might chose one perspective or the other at different points in her life in response to external and internal events.

[. . .] The second wave of feminism demanded and won increased sexual autonomy for women and decreasing male 'protection', still within a patriarchal framework. Amid this flux, many women have come to feel more visible and sexually vulnerable. Despite the breakdown in the old bargain, which placed sexual safety and sexual freedom in opposition, women's fear of reprisal and punishment for sexual activity has not abated.

This sense of vulnerability has been played on by the Right. The conservative attack on feminist gains has taken the form of a moral crusade. In its campaign against the evils of abortion, lesbian and gay rights, contraceptive education and services, and women's economic independence, the Right is attempting to reinstate traditional sexual arrangements and the formerly inexorable link between reproduction and sexuality. In this, the Right offers a comprehensive plan for sexual practice which resonates in part with women's apprehension about immorality and sexual danger. To respond convincingly as feminists, we cannot abandon our radical insights into sexual theory and practice. Instead, we must deepen and expand them, so that more women are encouraged to identify and act in their sexual self-interest.

[. . .] As feminists, we need to draw on women's experience of pleasure in imagining the textures and contours that would unfurl and proliferate in a safer space. What we want is not a mystery, not a blank. The clues to it are found in our daily experience already.

One clue lies in an obvious form of danger—the sexual violence committed by men against women: rape, sexual harassment, incest. As women began to speak out, it became clear that these apparently taboo acts were far from uncommon, and their damage to women was great. Beyond the actual physical or psychological harm done to victims of sexual violence, the threat of sexual attack served as a powerful reminder of male privilege, constraining women's movement and behavior. The cultural mythology surrounding sexual violence provided a unique and powerful route for it to work its way into the heart of female desire. A rag-bag of myths and folk knowledge that the contemporary feminist movement opposed depicted male lust as intrinsic, uncontrollable, and easily aroused by any show of female sexuality and desire. The main features of this ideology have been roundly critiqued by feminists, primarily for blaming the female victim while letting men off the hook, but its corollaries are equally pernicious. If female sexual desire triggers male attack, it cannot be freely or spontaneously shown, either in public or in private. [. . .]

The second wave of feminism mounted a major critique of male sexual violence, indicting the complicity of state institutions and the cultural ideologies that justify it. However, feminism is newly beginning to appreciate the intra-psychic effects of a gender system that places pleasure and safety in opposition for women. Sexual constriction, invisibility, timidity, and uncuriosity are less the signs of an intrinsic and specific female sexual nature and more the signs of thoroughgoing damage. The resulting polarization of male and female sexuality is a likely product of the prevailing gender system, which is used to justify women's need for a restricted, but supposedly safe space and highly controlled sexual expression. The horrific effects of gender inequality may include not only brute violence, but the internalized control of women's impulses, poisoning desire at its very root with self-doubt and anxiety. The subtle connection between how patriarchy interferes with female desire and how women experience their own passion as dangerous is emerging as a critical issue to be explored. [. . .]

The hallmark of sexuality is its complexity: its multiple meanings, sensations, and connections. It is all too easy to cast sexual experience as either wholly pleasurable or dangerous; our culture encourages us to do so. Women are encouraged to assent that all male sexuality done to them is pleasurable and liberatory: women really enjoy being raped but can't admit it, and the often horrid cartoons in *Hustler* are just a lighthearted joke. In a countermove, the feminist critique emphasized the ubiquity of sexual danger and humiliation in a patriarchal surround. Initially useful as an ideological interruption, this critique now shares the same undialectical and simplistic focus as its opposition. Women's actual sexual experience is more complicated, more difficult to grasp, more unsettling. Just as agreeing not to mention danger requires that one's sexual autobiography be recast, agreeing not to speak about pleasure requires a similar dishonest alchemy, the transmutation of sexuality into unmitigated danger and unremitting victimization.

The truth is that the rich brew of our experience contains elements of pleasure and oppression, happiness and humiliation. Rather than regard this ambiguity as confusion or false consciousness, we should use it as a sourcebook to examine how women experience sexual desire, fantasy, and action. We need to sort out individually and together what the elements of our pleasure and displeasure are. What, for instance, is powerful, enlivening, interesting in our experience? Our task is to identify what is pleasurable and under what conditions, and to control experience so that it occurs more frequently. To begin, we need to know our sexual histories, which are surely greater than our own individual experience, surely more diverse than we know, both incredible and instructive. To learn these histories, we must speak about them to each other. And for speech to flourish, there must be tolerance for diversity and curiosity, which Joan Nestle calls 'the respect that one life pays to another'.[1] Without women's speech, we fall back on texts and myths, prescriptive and overgeneralized.

Even some feminist analysis runs the risk of overemphasizing sexual danger, following the lead of the larger culture. The anti-pornography movement in a sense restates the main premises of the old gender system: the dominant cultural ideology elaborates the threat of sexual danger, so the anti-pornography movement responds by pushing for sexual safety via the control of public expression of male sexuality. Although this would seem in certain respects a decisive break with an oppressive system—sexual danger is being directly challenged—in other respects the focus continues unchanged in that sexual pleasure for women is still minimized and the exploration of women's pleasurable experience remains slight. Feminism has succeeded in making public previously unmentionable activities like rape and incest. But the anti-pornography movement often interprets this as an indicator of rising violence against women and a sign of backlash against feminism. The net effect has been to suggest that women are less sexually safe than ever and that discussions and explorations of pleasure are better deferred to a safer time.

Women are vulnerable to being shamed about sex, and the anti-pornography ideology makes new forms of shaming possible. Traditional objections that women's concern with sex is unimportant are restated in suggestions that sexuality is trivial, diversionary, or not political. If sexual desire is coded as male, women begin to wonder if they are really ever sexual. Do we distrust our passion, thinking it perhaps not our own, but the construction of patriarchal culture? Can women be sexual actors? Can we act on our own behalf? Or are we purely victims, whose efforts must be directed at resisting male depredations in a patriarchal culture? Must our passion await expression for a safer time? When will that time come? Will any of us remember what her passion was? Does exceeding the bounds of femininity—passivity, helplessness, and victimization—make us deeply uncomfortable? Do we fear that if we act on our most deeply felt sexual passion that we will no longer be women? Do we wish, instead, to bind ourselves together into a sisterhood which seeks to curb male lust but does little to promote female pleasure? Sex is always guilty before proven innocent, an expensive undertaking considering the negative sanctions it easily evokes.

The overemphasis on danger runs the risk of making speech about sexual pleasure taboo. Feminists are easily intimidated by the charge that their own pleasure is selfish, as in political rhetoric which suggest that no woman is entitled to talk about sexual pleasure while any woman remains in danger—that is—never. Some also believe that sexuality is a privileged topic, important only to affluent groups, so to talk of it betrays bad manners and bad politics on the part of sexual betters toward the deprived, who reputedly are only interested in issues that are concrete, material, and life-saving, as if sexuality were not all of these. The result is that sexual pleasure in whatever form has become a great guilty secret among feminists. [. . .]

Much feminist work on sexuality starts from the premise that sex is a social construction, articulated at many points with the economic, social, and political structures of the material world. Sex is not simply a 'natural' fact, as earlier, essentialist theories would suggest. Although sexuality, like all human cultural activity, is grounded in the body, the body's structure, physiology, and functioning do not directly or simply determine the configuration or meaning of sexuality; were this so, we would expect to find great uniformity across the world's cultures. Yet the sexual diversity we see is startling: activities condemned in one society are encouraged in another, and ideas about what is attractive or erotic or sexually satisfying or even sexually possible vary a great deal.

Nor is the role of culture confined to choosing some sexual acts (by praise, encouragement, or reward) and rejecting others (by scorn, ridicule, or condemnation), as if selecting from a sexual buffet. The social construction of sexuality is far more thorough-going, encompassing the very way sex is conceptualized, defined, labeled, and described from time to time and from culture to culture.[2] Although we can name specific physical actions like anal sex, heterosexual intercourse, kissing, fellatio, or masturbation, it is clear that the social and personal meanings attached to each of these acts in terms of sexual identity and sexual community have varied historically. Without denying the body, we note that the body and its actions are understood according to prevailing codes of meaning. Recent work on the history of male homosexuality shows, for instance, that although sodomy occurred and was punished in earlier periods in Europe and America, it was viewed as the result of carnal lust to which any mortal could fall prey, not as an act committed by a particular type of individual, the 'homosexual'. The classification of sexual types awaited the late nineteenth century, when capitalism and urban development made it possible for individuals to exist beyond the sphere of the extended family as a productive and reproductive unit.[3] Historians have also traced the outlines of changing definitions of women's intimacy. In the nineteenth century, two women who shared the same household and bed were usually perceived as close friends; by the twentieth century, such women were increasingly viewed as lesbians.[4] Doubtless, modern forms of heterosexuality have a history to be written as well.[5]

One might expect that feminists would be especially receptive to a social construction approach to sexuality, since in many ways it is analogous to social construction theories about gender: that the body is the agent of human activity, but the body's configuration does not literally determine it. Scientific 'knowledge' or folklore suggesting that the dominant cultural arrangements are the result of biology—and therefore intrinsic, eternal, and unchanging—are usually ideologies supporting prevailing power relations. Deeply felt personal identities—for example, masculinity/femininity or heterosexuality/homosexuality—are not private or solely the product of biology, but are created through the intersection of political, social, and economic forces, which vary over time.

Yet social construction theory remains a radical view of sexuality which poses a range of unsettling questions for feminists and other thinkers brought up on an essentialist view of sexuality. What is the nature of the relationship between the arbitrariness of social construction and the immediacy of our bodily sensations and functions? Is sexuality not a unitary, ongoing phenomenon with an essential core, but something created differently at each time and place? If sexuality is not a transhistorical, transcultural essence whose manifestations are mildly shaped by cultural factors, must we then consider the possibility that desire is not intrinsic but itself constituted or constructed, and if so, by what mechanisms? [. . .]

In examining these domains in which women's sexuality is described or represented [. . .] the observer, interpreter, or scholar is striving to understand what the various representations mean—that is, what their relationship is to women's thought and experience at the time of their creation. To answer this question, the analyst applies an interpretive frame, through which meaning can be detected and inferred. Do we assume that all women share this interpretive frame? That it is universal? [. . .]

If we want to study sexuality, we need more information about individual responses to symbol and image. We need to know what the viewer brings with her to make an interpretation: a cultural frame, resonances, connections, and personal experience. The question of context is important too, since viewers read symbols differently depending on the material they are embedded in and the relationship they have to other symbols, as well as individual interpretive frames which are somewhat idiosyncratic.

To assume that symbols have a unitary meaning, the one dominant culture assigns them, is to fail to investigate the individuals' experience and cognition of symbols, as well as individual ability to transform and manipulate symbols in a complex way which draws on play, creativity, humor, and intelligence. This assumption grants mainstream culture a hegemony it claims, but rarely achieves. To ignore the potential for variation is to inadvertently place women outside of culture except as passive recipients of official symbol systems. It continues to deny what mainstream culture has always tried to make invisible—the complex struggles of disenfranchised groups to grapple with oppression using symbolic, as well as economic and political, resistance. Mainstream symbols may be used to both reveal and mock dominant culture. [. . .]

It is no accident that recent feminist sexual controversies about pornography, S/M, and butch/femme all demonstrate a need for a more developed analysis of symbolic context and transformation, especially difficult in regard to visual material where our education, vocabulary, and sophistication are far less developed than in regard to literary texts. Our visual illiteracy renders the image overpowering. The emotion aroused by an image is easily attached to rhetorical arguments, overwhelming more subtle analysis and response, and the audience as well, by manipulative imagery, as in polemical slide shows mounted by Right to Life groups or some feminist anti-pornography groups. In each case, the shock induced by the image of a fetus in a bottle or a woman in chains is effectively used to propel viewers to the desired conclusion. [. . .]

A sophisticated analysis of sexual symbols requires that we look beyond easy generalization. Feminist scholarship has delivered a scathing critique of an androcentric and falsely universalizing history in which the historical Everyman, like his authors, was male, white, heterosexual, and affluent. Such accounts omitted women as both subjects of inquiry and as self-conscious historical actors. Corrective research indicates that social characteristics modify the perception and experience of historical events, with gender a significant social marker. Despite its critique of false universals, feminist scholarship and inquiry has not escaped the same sin. Until recently challenged, feminist descriptions and analyses have often assumed that women are white, middle- or upper-class, heterosexual, able-bodied, and moderately youthful, or that the experiences and perspectives of these women are shared by all. The term 'woman' used in feminist discourse often substituted part of women's experience for the whole, a 'deadly metonymy' in Hortense Spillers's words, relegating the experience of some women to silence. The experience of those standing outside both mainstream culture and 'women's culture' has been excluded from the feminist canon as well. Self-criticism of feminist parochialism has proliferated in recent years and has been persuasive in showing why feminist analysis must attempt to include the experience of diverse groups of women, with conclusions specific to particular groups identified as such. [. . .]

Although a portion of feminist reluctance to acknowledge differences among women derives from arrogance on the part of mainstream feminists, a significant part derives from another source: the fear of difference among women. If women organize around their oppression by and through differentiation from men, should they not maintain a united front, stressing their shared and unifying characteristic, femaleness? Does the admission of women's cross-cutting allegiances and links to groups containing men weaken the universal sisterhood? Once differences are admitted, what is to prevent them from becoming bitter and divisive, fracturing the base for shared political action? In a society that structures and maintains group antagonisms, what model do we have for acknowledging difference and working together? Exploration of differences has, in fact, been a painful experience, beginning with lesbian and heterosexual differences in the early stages of the women's movement and continuing in recent years to differences involving class, religion, ethnicity, and race. Although some have retreated to doctrines which emphasize women's commonality on the one hand, or women's total separation by factors of race and class on the other, many feminists see the importance of dealing with difference, while they remain wary and uncertain of how to do so.

Our discomfort with difference is especially evident around questions of sexual variation, which have expanded beyond the topic of lesbian and heterosexual difference to include all the ways women can obtain pleasure.

Sexual orientation is not the only, and may not be the most significant, sexual difference among women.[6] Our ability to think about sexual difference is limited, however, by a cultural system that organizes sexual differences in a hierarchy in which some acts and partners are privileged and others are punished. Privileged forms of sexuality, for example, heterosexuality, marriage, and procreation, are protected and rewarded by the state and subsidized through social and economic incentives. [. . .] Less privileged forms of sexuality are regulated and interdicted by the state, religion, medicine, and public opinion. [. . .]

What directions might a feminist politics on sex take in the future? Above all, feminism must be a movement that speaks to sexuality, that does not forfeit the field to reactionary groups who are more than willing to speak. We cannot be cowardly, pretending that feminism is not sexually radical. Being a sex radical at this time, as at most, is less a matter of what you do, and more a matter of what you are willing to think, entertain, and question.

Feminism must, of course, continue to work for material changes that support women's autonomy, including social justice, economic equality, and reproductive choice. At the same time, feminism must speak to sexuality as a site of oppression, not only the oppression of male violence, brutality, and coercion which it has already spoken about eloquently and effectively, but also the repression of female desire that comes from ignorance, invisibility, and fear. Feminism must put forward a politics that resists deprivation and supports pleasure. It must understand pleasure as life-affirming, empowering, desirous of human connection and the future, and not fear it as destructive, enfeebling, or corrupt. Feminism must speak to sexual pleasure as a fundamental right, which cannot be put off to a better or easier time. It must understand that the women to whom it speaks, and those it hopes to reach, care deeply about sexual pleasure and displeasure in their daily lives; that sexuality is a site of struggle—visceral, engaging, riveting—and not a domain of interest only to a narrow, small, and privileged group.

Feminism should encourage women to resist not only coercion and victimization, but also sexual ignorance, deprivation and fear of difference. Feminism should support women's experiments and analyses, encouraging the acquisition of knowledge. We can begin by examining our own experience, sharing it with each other, knowing that in sexuality as in the rest of social life, our adventures, risks, impulses, and terrors provide clues to the future. Feminism must insist that women are sexual subjects, sexual actors, sexual agents; that our histories are complex and instructive; that our experience is not a blank, nor a mere repetition of what has been said about us, and that the pleasure we have experienced is as much a guide to future action as the brutality.

In doing so, we admit that it is not safe to be a woman, and it never has been. Female attempts to claim pleasure are especially dangerous, attacked not only by men, but by women as well. But to wait until a zone of safety is established to begin to explore and organize for pleasure is to cede it as an arena, to give it up, and to admit that we are weaker and more frightened than our enemies ever imagined.

Social movements, feminism included, move toward a vision; they cannot operate solely on fear. It is not enough to move women away from danger and oppression; it is necessary to move toward something: toward pleasure, agency, self-definition. Feminism must increase women's pleasure and joy, not just decrease our misery. It is difficult for political movements to speak for any extended time to the ambiguities, ambivalences, and complexities that underscore human experience. Yet movements remain vital and vigorous to the extent that they are able to tap this wellspring of human experience. Without it, they become dogmatic, dry, compulsive, and ineffective. To persist amid frustrations and obstacles, feminism must reach deeply into women's pleasure and draw on this energy.

['Pleasure and Danger: Toward a Politics of Sexuality', in Carole S. Vance (ed.), *Pleasure and Danger: Exploring Female Sexuality* (London: Pandora, 1992), 1–24 (originally published London: Routledge, 1984).]

ALISON LIGHT

52 'Returning to Manderley'—Romance Fiction, Female Sexuality and Class

Last night I dreamt I went to Manderley again.

Thus opens Daphne du Maurier's *Rebecca*, published in 1938. With thirty-nine impressions and translations into twenty languages in as many years, *Rebecca* was and still is an enormous bestseller. Hitchcock made a film of the novel in 1940, its latest TV serialization was only a couple of years ago and even more recently it has been the subject of an opera. [. . .] [I]t's clear that *Rebecca* speaks as much to readers in the 1980s as it did to those in the 1940s. The story of the plain, genteel orphan girl—we never learn her name—who marries the aristocratic widower has got everything a romance needs and more: jealously, mystery, adultery and murder.

Jealousy and envy of her husband's first wife—the beautiful, upper-class Rebecca—propels the nameless heroine down the dark corridors of Rebecca's past. But in unlocking the secrets of Rebecca's character, the girl gets more than she bargained for: her husband turns out to have murdered Rebecca himself. All is not lost, however, for the heroine's bourgeois virtue triumphs and in the end she manages to save both her husband and her marriage. *Rebecca* is a rewrite of *Jane Eyre* amidst a nostalgia for the waning of the British Empire and the decline of its aristocracy. It's a lingering farewell to the world of Monte Carlo and of paid companions, to splendid breakfasts and devoted servants, the ease and arrogance of life in a stately home like Manderley, the Cornish mansion of the suave gentleman-hero, Maximilian de Winter. Obviously, it is a ripping yarn. But apart from that how do feminists and socialists account for the continued popularity and appeal of a book like this?

In the aftermath of Charles and Di, a lot of critical attention has been turned toward romance and its fictions, from Mills and Boon to 'boddice rippers' and the latest high-gloss consumerist fantasies.[1] At the centre of the discussion has been the question of the possible political effects of reading romances—what, in other words, do they do to you? Romances have on the whole, been condemned by critics on the Left (although Janet Batsleer's piece is a notable exception). They are seen as coercive and stereotyping narratives which invite the reader to identify with a passive heroine who only finds true happiness in submitting to a masterful male. What happens to women readers is then compared to certain Marxist descriptions of the positioning of all human subjects under capitalism. Romance thus emerges as a form of oppressive ideology, which works to keep women in their socially and sexually subordinate place.

I want to begin by registering the political dangers of this approach to romance fiction and then to suggest that we should come at the question of its effects rather differently. [. . .] Feminists must baulk at any such conclusion which implies that the vast audience of romance readers (with the exception of a few up-front intellectuals) are either masochistic or inherently stupid. Both text and reader are more complicated than that. It is conceivable, say, that reading Barbara Cartland could turn you into a feminist. Reading is never simply a linear con-job but a process of interaction, and not just between text and reader, but between reader and reader, text and text. It is a process which helps to query as well as endorse social meanings and one which therefore remains dynamic and open to change.

In other words, I think we need critical discussions that are not afraid of the fact that literature is a source of pleasure, passion *and* entertainment. This is not because pleasure can then explain away politics, as if it were a panacea existing outside of social and historical constraints. Rather it is precisely because pleasure is experienced by women and men within and despite those constraints. We need to balance an understanding of fictions as restatements (however mediated) of a social reality, with a closer examination of how literary texts might function in our lives as imaginative constructions and interpretations. It is this meshing of the questions of pleasure, fantasy and language which literary culture takes up so profoundly and which makes it so uniquely important to women. Subjectivity—the ways in which we come to express and define our concepts of our selves—then seems crucial to any analysis of the activity of reading. Far from being 'inward-looking' in the dismissive sense of being somehow separate from the realities of the state or the marketplace, subjectivity can be recognized as the place where the operations of power and the possibilities of resistance are also played out.

A re-emphasis on the imaginative dimensions of literary discourse may then suggest ways in which romance, as much because of its contradictory effects as despite them, has something positive to offer its audience, as readers and as *women* readers. It must at the very least prevent our 'cultural politics' becoming a book-burning legislature, a politics which is doomed to fail since it refuses ultimately to see women of all classes as capable of determining or transforming their own lives.

Romance fiction deals above all with the doubts and delights of hetero-sexuality, an institution which feminism has seen as problematic from the start. In thinking about this 'problem' I myself have found the psychoanalytic framework most useful since it suggests that the acquisition of gendered subjectivity is a process, a movement towards a social 'self', fraught with conflicts and never fully achieved. Moreover, psychoanalysis takes the ques-tion of pleasure seriously, both in its relation to gender and in its under-standing of fictions as fantasies, as the explorations and productions of desires which may be in excess of the socially possible or acceptable. It gives us ways into the discussion of popular culture which can avoid the traps of moralism or dictatorship. [. . .]

How then does *Rebecca* say anything at all about the formulaic fiction in which frail flower meets bronzed god? I would like to see *Rebecca* as the absent subtext of much romance fiction, the crime behind the scenes of Mills and Boon. For it seems to me that perhaps what romance tries to offer us is a 'triumph' over the unconscious, over the 'resistance to identity which lies at the very heart of psychic life'.[2] *Rebecca* acts out the process of repression which these other texts avoid by assuming a fully-achievable, uncomplicated gendered subject whose sexual desire is not in question, not produced in struggle, but given. Above all, romance fiction makes heterosexuality easy, by suspending history in its formulae (whether costume, hospital or Caribbean drama) and by offering women readers a resolution in which submission and repression are not just managed without pain or humiliation but man-aged at all.

Thus although women are undoubtedly represented as sexual objects, there might be a sense in which women are also offered unique opportunities for reader-power, for an imaginary control of the uncontrollable in the fiction of romance. Within that scenario of extreme heterosexism can be derived the pleasure of reconstructing any heterosexuality which is not 'difficult'. Romance offers us relations impossibly harmonized; it uses unequal hetero-sexuality as a dream of equality and gives women uncomplicated access to a subjectivity which is unified and coherent *and* still operating within the field of pleasure.

Perhaps then the enormous readership of romance fiction, the fact that so many women find it deeply pleasurable, can be registered in terms other than those of moralizing shock. Romance is read by over fifty per cent of all women, but it is no coincidence that the two largest audiences are those of young women in their teens and 'middle-aged housewives'.[3] I would suggest that these are both moments when the *impossibility* of being successfully feminine is felt, whether as a 'failure' ever to be feminine enough—like the girl's in *Rebecca*—or whether in terms of the gap between fulfilling social expectations (as wife and mother) and what those roles mean in reality. That women read romance fiction is, I think, as much a measure of their deep dissatisfaction with heterosexual options as of any desire to be fully identified with the submissive versions of femininity the texts endorse. Romance imagines peace, security and ease precisely because there is dissension, insecurity and difficulty. In the context of women's lives, romance reading might appear less a reactionary reflex or an indication of their victimization by the capitalist market, and more a sign of discontent and a technique for survival. All the more so because inside a boring or alienating marriage, or at the age of fifteen, romance may be the only popular discourse which speaks to the question of women's sexual pleasure. Women's magazines, for example, do at least prioritize women and their lives in a culture where they are usually absent or given second place.

Patterns of romance reading are also revealing. Readers often collect hundreds, which are shared and recycled amongst friends. Reading romance fiction means participating in a kind of subculture, one which underlines a collective identity as women around the issue of women's pleasure and which can be found outside a political movement. As Janet Batsleer has pointed out, romances are not valued because like 'Great Art' they purport to be unrepeatable stories of unique characters, they are valued precisely as ritual and as repetition. It is difficult then to assume that these narratives are read in terms of a linear identification—it is not real and rounded individuals who are being presented and the endings are known by *readers* to be a foregone conclusion. Romance offers instead of closure a postponement of fulfillment. They are addictive because the control they gesture toward is always illusory, always modified and contained by the heterosexuality which they seek to harmonize. In a sense the activity of reading repeats the compulsion of desire and testifies to the limiting regulation of female sexuality. Romances may pretend that the path to marriage is effortless (obstacles are there to be removed) but they have to cry off when the action really starts—after marriage. The reader is left in a permanent state of foreplay, but I would guess that for many women this is the best heterosexual sex they ever get.

I want to suggest then that we develop ways of analysing romances and their reception as 'symptomatic' rather than simply reflective. Romance reading then becomes less a political sin or moral betrayal than a kind of 'literary anorexia' which functions as a protest against, as well as a restatement of, oppression. Their compulsive reading makes visible an insistent search on the part of readers for more than what is on offer. This is not, of course, any kind of argument for romance fictions being somehow progressive. Within the realities of women's lives, however, they may well be *trans*-gressive. Consumerist, yes; a hopeless rebellion, yes; but still, in our society, a forbidden pleasure—like cream cakes. Romance does write heterosexuality in capital letters but in so doing it is an embarrassment to the literary establishment since its writers are always asking to be taken seriously. Their activity highlights of course the heterosexism of much orthodox and important Literature. For, leaving aside the representation of femininity, what other models are available *anywhere* for alternative constructs of masculinity? Romance is not being wilfully different in its descriptions of virility as constituted around positions of authority, hierarchy and aggression. Male, left-wing critics might do well to address themselves to projects which set out to deconstruct 'normal' male heterosexuality—a phenomenon which does after all exist outside war-stories and cowboy books. [. . .]

If I have a soft spot for romance fiction then it is because nothing else speaks to me in the same way. It is up to us as feminists to develop a rigorous and compassionate understanding of how these fictions work in women's lives, keeping open the spaces for cultural and psychic pleasure whilst rechanneling the dissatisfactions upon which they depend. That then would seem to me to be the point of returning to Manderley.

['Returning to Manderley—Romance Fiction, Female Sexuality and Class', *Feminist Review*, 16 (1984), 7–23.]

EVE KOSOFSKY SEDGWICK

53   Sexual Politics and Sexual Meaning

What does it mean—what difference does it make—when a social or political relationship is sexualized? [. . .] [W]hat theoretical framework do we have for drawing any links between sexual and power relationships?

This question, in a variety of forms, is being posed importantly by and for the different gender-politics movements right now. Feminist along with gay male theorists, for instance, are disagreeing actively about how direct the relation is between power domination and sexual sadomasochism. Start with two arresting images: the naked, beefy motorcyclist on the front cover, or the shockingly battered nude male corpse on the back cover, of the recent so-called 'Polysexuality' issue of *Semiotext(e)*[1]—which, for all the women in it, ought to have been called the semisexuality issue of *Polytext*. It seemed to be a purpose of that issue to insist, and possibly not only for reasons of radical-chic titillation, that the violence imaged in sadomasochism is not mainly theatrical, but is fully continuous with violence in the real world. Women Against Pornography and the framers of the 1980 NOW Resolution on Lesbian and Gay Rights share the same view, but without the celebratory glamor: to them too it seems intuitively clear that to sexualize violence or an image of violence is simply to extend, unchanged, its reach and force. But, as other feminist writers have reminded us, another view is possible. For example: is a woman's masochistic sexual fantasy really only an internalization and endorsement, if not a cause, of her more general powerlessness and sense of worthlessness? Or may not the sexual drama stand in some more oblique, or even oppositional, relation to her political experience of oppression?

The debate in the gay male community and elsewhere over 'man–boy love' asks a cognate question: can an adult's sexual relationship with a child be simply a continuous part of a more general relationship of education and nurturance? Or must the inclusion of sex quantatively alter the relationship, for instance in the direction of exploitiveness? In this case, the same NOW communiqué that had assumed an unbroken continuity between sexualized violence and real, social violence, came to the opposite conclusion on pedophilia: that the injection of the sexual charge *would* alter (would corrupt) the very substance of the relationship. Thus, in moving from the question of sadomasochism to the question of pedophilia, the 'permissive' argument and the 'puritanical' argument have essentially exchanged their assumptions about how the sexual relates to the social.

So the answer to the question 'what difference does the inclusion of sex make' to a social or political relationship, is—it varies: just as, for different groups in different political circumstances, homosexual activity can be either supportive of or oppositional to homosocial bonding. [...] It is clear that there is not some ahistorical *Stoff* of sexuality, some sexual charge that can be simply added to a social relationship to 'sexualize' it in a constant and predictable direction, or that splits off from it unchanged. Nor does it make sense to *assume* that the sexualized form epitomizes or simply condenses a broader relationship. [...]

Instead, an examination of the relation of sexual desire to political power must move along two axes. First, of course, it needs to make use of whatever forms of analysis are most potent for describing historically variable power asymmetries, such as those of class and race, as well as gender. But in conjunction with that, an analysis of representation itself is necessary. Only the model of representation will let us do justice to the (broad but not infinite or random) range of ways in which sexuality functions as a signifier for power relations. The importance of the rhetorical model in this case is not to make the problems of sexuality or of violence or oppression sound less immediate and urgent; it is to help us analyze and use the really very disparate intuitions of political immediacy that come to us from the sexual realm.

For instance, a dazzling recent article by Catharine MacKinnon, attempting to go carefully over and clear out the grounds of disagreement between different streams of feminist thought, arrives at the following summary of the centrality of sexuality per se for every issue of gender:

> Each element of the female *gender* stereotype is revealed as, in fact, *sexual*. Vulnerability means the appearance/reality of easy sexual access; passivity means receptivity and disabled resistance...; softness means pregnability by something hard.... Woman's infantilization evokes pedophilia; fixation on dismembered body parts... evokes fetishism; idolization of vapidity, necrophilia. Narcissism insures that woman identifies with that image of herself that man holds up....Masochism means that pleasure in violation becomes her sensuality.

And MacKinnon sums up this part of her argument: 'Socially, femaleness means femininity, which means attractiveness to men, which means sexual attractiveness, which means sexual availability on male terms.'[2]

There's a whole lot of 'mean'-ing going on. MacKinnon manages to make every manifestation of sexuality mean the same thing, by making every instance of 'meaning' mean something different. A trait can 'mean' as an element in a semiotic system such as fashion ('softness means pregnability'); or anaclitically, it can 'mean' its complementary opposite ('Woman's infantilization evokes pedophilia'); or across time, it can 'mean' the consequence that it enforces ('Narcissism insures that woman identifies.... Masochism means that pleasure in violation becomes her sensuality'). MacKinnon concludes, 'What defines woman as such is what turns men on.' But what defines 'defines'? That every node of sexual experience is in *some* signifying relation to the whole fabric of gender oppression, and vice versa, is true and important, but insufficiently exact to be of analytic use on specific political issues. The danger lies, of course, in the illusion that we do know from such a totalistic analysis where to look for our sexuality and how to protect it from expropriation when we find it. [...]

Let me take an example from the great ideological blockbuster of white bourgeois feminism, its apotheosis, the fictional work that has most resonantly thematized for successive generations of American women the constraints of the 'feminine' role, the obstacles to and the ravenous urgency of female ambition, the importance of the economic motive, the compulsiveness and destructiveness of romantic love, and [...] the centrality and the total alienation of female sexuality. Of course, I am referring to *Gone With the Wind*. As MacKinnon's paradigm would predict, in the life of Scarlett O'Hara, it is expressly clear that to be born female is to be defined entirely in relation to the role of 'lady', a role that does take its shape and meaning from a sexuality of which she is not the subject but the object. For Scarlett, to survive as a woman does mean learning to see sexuality, male power domination, and her traditional gender role as all meaning the same dangerous thing. To absent herself silently from each of them alike, and learn to manipulate them from behind this screen as objects or pure signifiers, as men do, is the numbing but effective lesson of her life.

However, it is *only* a white bourgeois feminism that this view apotheosizes. As in one of those trick rooms where water appears to run uphill and little children look taller than their parents, it is only when viewed from one fixed vantage in any society that sexuality, gender roles, and power domination can seem to line up in this perfect chain of echoic meaning. From an even slightly more ec-centric or disempowered perspective, the *dis*placements and *dis*continuities of the signifying chain come to seem increasingly definitive. For instance, if it is true in this novel that all the women characters exist in some meaning-ful relation to the role of 'lady', the signifying relation grows more tortuous—though at the same time, in the novel's white bourgeois view, more totally determining—as the women's social and racial distance from that role grows. Melanie is a woman as she is a lady; Scarlett is a woman as she is required to be and pretends to be a lady; but Belle Watling, the Atlanta prostitute, is a woman not in relation to her own role of 'lady', which is exiguous, but only negatively, in a compensatory and at the same time parodic relation to Melanie's and Scarlett's. And as for Mammy, her mind and life, in this view, are *totally* in thrall to the ideal of the 'lady', but in a relation that excludes herself entirely: she is the template, the support, the enforcement, of Scarlett's 'lady' role, to the degree that her personal femaleness loses any meaning whatever that is not in relation to Scarlett's role. Whose mother is Mammy?

At the precise intersection of domination and sexuality is the issue of rape. *Gone With the Wind*—both book and movie—leaves in the memory a most graphic image of rape:

> As the negro came running to the buggy, his black face twisted in a leering grin, she fired point-blank at him. . . . The negro was beside her, so close that she could smell the rank odor of him as he tried to drag her over the buggy side. With her own free hand she fought madly, clawing at his face, and then she felt his big hand at her throat and, with a ripping noise, her basque was torn open from breast to waist. Then the black hand fumbled between her breasts, and terror and revulsion such as she had never known came over her and she screamed like an insane woman.[3]

In the wake of this attack, the entire machinery by which 'rape' is signified in this culture rolls into action. Scarlett's menfolk and their friends in the Ku Klux Klan set out after dark to kill the assailants and 'wipe out that whole Shantytown settlement', with the predictable carnage on both sides. The question of how much Scarlett is to blame for the deaths of the white men is widely mooted, with Belle Watling speaking for the 'lady' role—'She caused it all, prancin' bout Atlanta by herself, enticin' niggers and trash'—and Rhett Butler, as so often, speaking from the central vision of the novel's bourgeois feminism, assuring her that her desperate sense of guilt is purely superstitious (chs. 46, 47). In preparation for this central incident, the novel had even raised the issue of the legal treatment of rape victims (ch. 42). And the effect of that earlier case, the classic effect of rape, had already been to abridge Scarlett's own mobility and, hence, personal and economic power: it was to expedite her business that she had needed to ride by Shantytown in the first place.

The attack on Scarlett, in short, fully means rape, both *to her* and to all the forces in her culture that produce and circulate powerful meanings. It makes no difference at all that one constituent element of rape is missing; but the missing constituent is simply sex. The attack on Scarlett had been for money; the black hands had fumbled between the white breasts because the man had been told that was where she kept her money; Scarlett knew that; there is no mention of any other motive; but it does not matter in the least, the absent sexuality leaves no gap in the character's, the novel's, or the society's discourse of rape.

Nevertheless, *Gone With the Wind* is not a novel that omits enforced sexuality. We are shown one actual rape in fairly graphic detail; but when it is white hands that scrabble on white skin, its ideological name is 'blissful marriage'. '[Rhett] had humbled her, used her brutally through a wild mad night and she had gloried in it' (ch. 54). The sexual predations of white men on Black women are also a presence in the novel, but the issue of force vs. content is never raised there; the white male alienation of a Black woman's sexuality is shaped differently from the alienation of the white woman's, to the degree that rape ceases to be a meaningful term at all. And if forcible sex ever did occur between a Black male and female character in this world, the sexual event itself would have no signifying power, since Black sexuality 'means' here only as a grammatic transformation of a sentence whose true implicit subject and object are white.

We have in this protofeminist novel, then, in this ideological microcosm, a symbolic economy in which both the meaning of rape and rape itself are insistently circulated. Because of the racial fracture of the society, however, *rape and its meaning circulate in precisely opposite directions*. It is an extreme case; the racial fracture is, in America, more sharply dichotomized than others except perhaps for gender. Still, other symbolic fractures such as class (and by fractures I mean the lines along which the quantitative differentials of power may in a given society be read as qualitative differentials with some other name) are abundant and actively disruptive in every social constitution. The signifying relation of sex to power, of sexual alienation to political oppression, is not the most stable, but precisely the most volatile of social nodes, under this pressure.

Thus, it is of serious political importance that our tools for examining the signifying relation be subtle and discriminate ones, and that our literary knowledge of the most crabbed or oblique paths of meaning not be over-simplified in the face of panic-inducing images of real violence, especially the violence of, around, and to sexuality. To assume that sex signifies power in a flat, unvarying relation of metaphor or synecdoche will always entail a blind-ness, not to the rhetorical and pyrotechnic, but to such historical categories as class and race. Before we can fully achieve and use our intuitive grasp of the leverage that sexual relations seem to offer on the relations of oppression, we need more—more different, more complicated, more diachronically apt, more off-centered—more daring and prehensile applications of our present understanding of what it may mean for one thing to signify another. [. . .]

The choice of sexuality as a thematic emphasis [. . .] makes salient and problematical a division of thematic emphasis between Marxist-feminist and radical-feminist theory as they are now practiced. Specifically, Marxist femi-nism, the study of the deep interconnections between on the one hand historical and economic change, and on the other hand the vicissitudes of gender division, has typically proceeded in the absence of a theory of sexu-ality and without much interest in the meaning or experience of sexuality. Or more accurately, it has held implicitly to a view of female sexuality as some-thing that is essentially of a piece with reproduction, and hence appropriately studied with the tools of demography; or else essentially of a piece with a simple, prescriptive hegemonic ideology, and hence appropriately studied through intellectual or legal history. Where important advances have been made by Marxist-feminist-oriented research into sexuality, it has been in areas that were already explicitly distinguished as deviant by the society's legal discourse: signally, homosexuality for men and prostitution for women. Marxist feminism has been of little help in unpacking the historical meanings of women's experience of heterosexuality, or even, until it becomes legally and medically visible in this century, of lesbianism.

Radical feminism, on the other hand, in the many different forms I am classing under that head, has been relatively successful in placing sexuality in a prominent and interrogative position, one that often allows scope for the decentered and the contradictory. Kathleen Barry's *Female Sexual Slavery*, Susan Griffin's *Pornography and Silence*, Gilbert and Gubar's *The Madwoman in the Attic*, Jane Gallop's *The Daughter's Seduction*, and Andrea Dworkin's *Pornog-raphy: Men Possessing Women* make up an exceedingly heterogeneous group of texts in many respects—in style, in urgency, in explicit feminist identifica-tion, in French or American affiliation, in 'brow'-elevation level. They have in common, however, a view that sexuality is centrally problematical in the formation of women's experience. And in more or less sophisticated formulations, the subject as well as the ultimate object of female heterosexuality within what is called patriarchal culture are seen as male. Whether in literal interpersonal terms or in internalized psychological and linguistic terms, this approach privileges sexuality and often sees it within the context of the structure that Lévi-Strauss analyzes as 'the male traffic in women'.

This family of approaches has, however, shared with other forms of structuralism a difficulty in dealing with the diachronic. It is the essence of structures viewed as such to reproduce themselves; and historical change from this point of view appears as something outside of structure and threatening—or worse, *not* threatening—to it, rather than in a formative and dialectical relation with it. History tends thus to be either invisible or viewed in an impoverishingly glaring and contrastive light. Implicitly or explicitly, radical feminism tends to deny that the meaning of gender or sexuality has ever significantly changed; and more damagingly, it can make future change appear impossible, or necessarily apocalyptic, even though desirable. Alternatively, it can radically oversimplify the prerequisites for significant change. In addition, history even in the residual, synchronic form of class or racial difference and conflict becomes invisible or excessively coarsened and dichotomized in the universalizing structuralist view.

As feminist readers, then, we seem poised for the moment between reading sex and reading history, at a choice that appears (though, it must be, wrongly) to be between the synchronic and the diachronic. We know that it must be wrongly viewed in this way, not only because in the abstract the synchronic and the diachronic must ultimately be considered in relation to one another, but because specifically in the disciplines we are considering they are so mutually inscribed: the narrative of Marxist history is so graphic, and the schematics of structuralist sexuality so narrative.

[*Between Men: English Literature and Male Homosocial Desire* (Columbia University Press, 1985), xx–xx.]

LIZ KELLY

54   A Central Issue: Sexual Violence and Feminist Theory

There are two interlinked aspects of feminist theory which connect analysis of sexuality with male violence: first, the proposition that male control of women's sexuality is a key factor in women's oppression; and second, that sexuality as it is currently constructed is based on men's experiences and definitions, which legitimate the use of force or coercion within heterosexual encounters.

One of the major disagreements between feminists is the location of the primary site of women's oppression. Catharine MacKinnon presents the most complex formulation of a strand of radical feminism which sees sexuality, broadly defined, as occupying this position.

Feminism fundamentally identifies sexuality as the primary social sphere of male power. The centrality of sexuality emerges not from Freudian conceptions but from feminist practice on diverse issues including abortion, birth control, sterilization abuse, domestic battery, rape, incest, lesbianism, sexual harassment, prostitution, female sexual slavery and pornography... producing a feminist political theory centering on sexuality; its social determination, daily construction, birth to death expression, and ultimately male control.[1]

Whilst having much sympathy with this view, a number of Black feminists and feminists of Colour have suggested that sexuality does not have the same significance for women in all cultures, or all women in a particular culture. These critiques do not question the importance of sexuality in gender relations but assert that other forms of inequality may be the primary organizing focus for certain groups of women.

The definition and depiction of women as primarily sexual beings has increased this century, particularly in western capitalist countries. What has been called 'the eroticization of dominance'[2] has been perceived as central by a number of white, middle-class, western women. Whilst classism and racism inform these definitions and depictions and undoubtedly affect white working-class women and Black women, other forms of oppression may be experienced by them as more urgent. In fact, multiple levels of oppression may fuse into a complex totality which makes their separation problematic in both theory and individual experience. This is reflected in Ruth Hall's discussion of 'racist sexual violence' where she argues that, for Black women, assaults by white men often involve the fusion of racial and sexual violence.[3]

It is not, however, merely the distorting effects of racism and classism which led feminist theorists to give such a central place to sexuality. Diana Gittins suggests: 'It is in sexual relations that the essence of patriarchy... becomes manifest'.[4] Adrienne Rich has attempted to integrate an analysis of sexual violence within a broader framework of the enforcement of compulsory heterosexuality.[5] She argues that heterosexuality must be examined, historically and cross-culturally, as a social institution within which a variable range of forms of control, coercion and force are used by men to ensure sexual access to women.

The concept of sexual access, as used by feminist theorists, refers to the range of processes through which women are defined as sexual objects available to men. These processes are legitimized through a naturalistic ideology of sex which presents heterosexuality as the only 'normal' form of sexual practice and male sexuality as determined by biological 'drives'. The concept has been applied by feminists in two related contexts.

First, it is argued that men assume sexual access to women they do not know (or with whom they have slight acquaintance) by, for example, making sexual approaches or remarks. The extreme form of this is sexual assault or rape by strangers. Diana Scully's and Joseph Marolla's research on convicted rapists suggests that many of the men saw sex as a male entitlement and the justifications they offered for their actions were 'buttressed by the cultural view of women as sexual commodities, dehumanized and devoid of autonomy and dignity'.[6] Extending this analysis, it has been suggested that men sexualize all relationships with women. This is implicit in Catharine MacKinnon's analysis of sexuality as the main area through which men express power over and attempt to control women. The increasing entry of women into the public sphere of work and the revival of feminist campaigning for sexual equality has undoubtedly been accompanied by an increased public sexualization of women throughout the mass media. Several feminist researchers have suggested that increasing demands from women for greater autonomy and equality will increase sexual violence in the short-term as men attempt to reassert their dominance; Diana Russell and Laura Lederer see the recent increase in the sale, availability and acceptability of pornography as a patriarchal response to campaigns for women's liberation.[7]

The second context in which the concept of sexual access is used is within intimate relationships. Here the focus is the assumed rights of men to sexual access with wives and lovers and, in some cases, to daughters. There are remnants of the historical status of women and children in men's proprietorial attitudes which are most clearly legitimized in marital rape exemption clauses. Sexual access, like other resources, is determined by relational power. The more power a man can claim over a particular women, the greater his claim to exclusive access. The greater his perceived right to exclusive sexual access, the more likely it is that some level of sexual aggression will be considered legitimate.

Feminist analysis of the social construction of sexuality has directly challenged naturalistic, biologically determinist theories of sexuality whilst acknowledging that gender currently determines, to a large extent, beliefs about and experiences of sexuality. Nancy Hartsock maintains that 'sexuality in our society is defined almost exclusively in masculine terms and, moreover, hostility and domination are central to the construction of masculine sexuality'.[8] Masculinity, as it is currently constructed in western culture, draws on notions of virility, conquest, power and domination and these themes are reflected in gender relations and heterosexual practice; sex and aggression are linked for most men. To suggest otherwise, Hartsock argues, is to recreate the myth that heterosexual relationships are based on intimacy and mutuality, disguising the reality of hostility and domination that feminism set out to challenge.

A shift away from the feminist challenge to previously 'taken for granted' perspectives on sexuality is evident in some of the current focus on pleasure. A number of feminists, strongly influenced by sexual liberation perspectives and/or psychoanalysis, argue that there has been too much emphasis on danger and too little on pleasure in recent feminist theory and practice.[9] The issues raised by other feminists, namely that 'pleasure' is a problematic concept for women in a context in which for many men pleasure coincides with endangering women and where male ideology encourages women to see fear, pain and power over others as potentially pleasurable, are seldom directly addressed. These theorists seem to want to reassert the western emphasis on sex as the most important site of pleasure that many feminists questioned in the early 1970s. The sexual liberationist influence is evident in the assertion that women have a 'right' to 'pleasure'. The concept of a 'rights' and the unproblematic usage of terms such as 'pleasure' and 'desire' represent a return to an individualistic stance and the implicit suggestion that we possess fundamental characteristics which can be abstracted from social circumstances.

Feminist analysis of power and sexuality leads to an understanding that social control is the purpose, and may also be the outcome, of gendered social relations. The threat and reality of sexual violence may result in women developing strategies for self-protection which result in apparently voluntary limitations of mobility, territory and encounters. It is also the case, however, that the threat and reality of sexual violence may prompt both individual and collective resistance to men's power.

Betsy Stanko's recent discussion of women's greater fear of crime extends the focus on the threat of rape to the many forms of sexual violence women experience and/or fear.[10] She shows how women's lives are structured around personal safety and is currently researching the range of 'precautionary strategies' which women employ. Whilst not all women live in constant fear, many of women's routine decisions and behaviour are almost automatic measures taken to protect themselves from potential sexual violence. Michele Cliff describes the constant presence of the threat of sexual violence in women's lives as 'the force that does not kill' and likens women's lives to a state of siege.[11]

A number of feminists have used the terms terrorism and/or colonization to describe the impact on women's lives of sexual violence.[12] Kathleen Barry's analysis in *Female Sexual Slavery* demonstrates how her definition of sexual slavery, developed whilst studying forced prostitution, applies equally to a range of forms of sexual violence.

Female sexual slavery is present in *all* situations where women or girls cannot change the immediate conditions of their existence; where regardless of how they got into those conditions they cannot get out; and where they are subject to sexual violence and exploitation.[13]

She stresses that her use of the term 'slavery' is not rhetorical but, describes 'an objective social condition of sexual exploitation and violence'. Like Catharine MacKinnon, she defines male control of female sexuality as the foundation of patriarchal societies and the result of this is sex colonization.

Female sexual slavery, in all its forms, is the mechanism for controlling women through the sex-is-power ethic, either directly through enslavement or indirectly using enslavement as a threat held over all other women. This is the generalized condition of sex colonization. Enslavement or potential slavery is rarely seen as such by either its aggressors potential aggressors or by its victims/potential victims. That is the subtlety of long-term sex colonization.[14]

Jill Radford, in developing the analysis of how sexual violence functions as a form of social control, has called it a form of policing.[15] She argues that much of men's interaction with women involves routine behaviour of the type that characterizes police work: watching, supervising, segregating and changing women's behaviour. The state's role in policing women is, in her view, residual, confined to defining the limits of acceptable behaviour and deciding which women are legitimate targets for male sexual aggression. MacKinnon, on the other hand, sees the state as having a critical role in western patriarchal societies where, she maintains, it has become an institutionalized agency of male control over women. [. . .]

A considerable amount of attention has been paid in feminist writing and campaigning to challenging limited definitions of particular forms of sexual violence. Kathleen Barry's definition of 'female sexual slavery' is, however, one of very few attempts to link a number of forms of sexual violence within a broader definition. It does not, however, cover all possible forms of sexual violence as it is intentionally limited to situations where women are trapped in relationships or situations where they are repeatedly violated.

One way of developing a feminist definition is to examine the range of behaviour that feminists have included within the category of violence in the light of the dictionary definition of the word. The *Oxford English Dictionary* defines violence as involving damage to the self. The damage may be physical, emotional, psychological and/or material. Violation can be of the body, of the mind or of trust. The exercise of violence involves the denial of the victims' will and autonomy. Interestingly, this definition emphasizes the impact on the person violated, making little reference to the imputed intentions of the violator.

Clearly, acts committed by individual men which result in physical, emotional and/or psychological damage are covered by this definition. It is also possible to include institutional or sociostuctural factors. Miriam Hirsch, for example, includes medical violence in her book on male violence.[16] She sees male control of the medical profession as denying women autonomy and resulting in particular forms of abuse that damage women physically and emotionally. The recent discussion of 'the feminization of poverty' raises the possibility of defining gendered economic deprivation as violence which results in material damage.[17] Whilst the dictionary definition could accommodate a wide range of actions on the individual and societal levels within the category of violence against women, such a wide definition is likely to prove less than helpful in developing feminist analysis. All forms of male power, individual and institutional, are potentially definable as violence.

I intend to explore a definition in terms of the conjunction of the words sexual and violence. [. . .] Kathleen Barry herself begins from this premise in a more recent article. 'Crimes against women are defined as those acts of violence which are directed at women because of their female sexual definition.' However, in her development of this theme she arrives at a much more limited definition than is implied in the first sentence: 'In committing a crime against women, sexual satisfaction, usually in the form of orgasm, is one of the intended outcomes of sexual violence for the aggressor who unites sex and violence to subdue, humiliate, degrade and terrorize his female victim.'[18] Here sexual violence is restricted to only those forms of abuse where ejaculation is possible or intended, where power is used to get sex. [. . .] I would argue that much sexual violence uses sex to get power.

Dorothy Klein maintains that a feminist definition of sexual violence must distance itself from legal codes which focus on the extreme and less frequent forms of violence, thereby obscuring 'the subtler and more pervasive forms of abuse of women which are woven into the fabric of our society'.[19] Cross-culturally, words describing women's bodies or sexuality are often used as insults, often containing associations with hurt and devaluation. Sandra Bartky maintains that language and images which portray women as inferior are the result of stereotyping, cultural domination and sexual objectification.[20] She notes that such attitudes and images are habitually used in everyday life and function to deny women autonomy; there are few places where women are safe from threat, insult or affront.

The social meaning of pornography and whether or not it constitutes a form of sexual violence has been the most contested aspect of the analysis of violence against women within feminism. In fact, the debate has focused less on the content and meaning of pornography and more on its importance as an issue and the strategies some feminists have suggested for opposing it. Whatever an individual feminist's perspective on these issues, few dispute that pornography presents women as objects available to be acted upon by men and as enjoying rape or coercive sex. It is also incontrovertible that the pornography industry has grown rapidly over the past ten years. Within this debate, however, there is disagreement about how pornography should be analysed.

Andrea Dworkin and Robin Morgan argue that pornography represents the ideology of patriarchal domination.[21] This analysis is premised on seeing men's attempts to control women's sexuality as the fundamental basis of patriarchy. Feminists who question this analysis are likely to see women's place in the social organization of production and reproduction as the determining factor in women's subordination. Elizabeth Wilson, for example, questions the connection between pornographic images and acts of sexual violence implicit in Robin Morgan's phrase 'pornography is the theory, rape is the practice'.[22] Much recent feminist opposition to pornography has, however, focused on the fact that, whether or not causal connections between it and acts of sexual violence can be proven, it constitutes a form of sexual violence in itself.

To complicate the issue of definition further, a feminist definition must be sensitive to woman's perceptions and understandings. Whilst the definition I have come to is rather lengthy, it does attempt to reflect both the extent and range of sexual violence and to include women's perceptions within it. Sexual violence includes *any physical, visual, verbal or sexual act that is experienced by the woman or girl, at the time or later, as a threat, invasion or assault, that has the effect of hurting her or degrading her and/or takes away her ability to control intimate contact.*

[*Surviving Sexual Violence* (Cambridge: Polity Press, 1988), 20–42.]

CATHARINE MACKINNON

55   Toward a Feminist Theory of the State

What is it about women's experience that produces a distinctive perspective on social reality? How is an angle of vision and an interpretive hermeneutics of social life created in the group, women? [...]

How are the qualities we know as male and female socially created and enforced on an everyday level? Sexual objectification of women—first in the world, then in the head, first in visual appropriation, then in forced sex, finally in sexual murder—provides answers.

Male dominance is sexual. Meaning: men in particular, if not men alone, sexualize hierarchy; gender is one. As much a sexual theory of gender as a gendered theory of sex, this is the theory of sexuality that has grown out of consciousness raising. Recent feminist work, both interpretive and empirical, on rape, battery, sexual harassment, sexual abuse of children, prostitution and pornography, support it. These practices, taken together, express and actualize the distinctive power of men over women in society; their effective permissibility confirms and extends it. If one believes women's accounts of sexual use and abuse by men; if the pervasiveness of male sexual violence against women substantiated in these studies is not denied, minimized, or excepted as deviant or episodic; if the fact that only 7.8 percent of women in the United States are not sexually assaulted or harassed in their lifetimes is considered not ignorable or inconsequential; if the women to whom it happens are not considered expendable; if violation of women is understood as sexualized on some level—then sexuality itself can no longer be regarded as unimplicated. Nor can the meaning of practices of sexual violence be categorized away as violence not sex. The male sexual role, this information and analysis taken together suggest, centers on aggressive intrusion on those with less power. Such acts of dominance are experienced as sexually arousing, as sex itself. They therefore are. The new knowledge on the sexual violation of women by men thus frames an inquiry into the place of sexuality in gender and of gender in sexuality.

A feminist theory of sexuality based on these data locates sexuality within a theory of gender inequality, meaning the social hierarchy of men over women. To make a theory feminist, it is not enough that it be authored by a biological female, nor that it describe female sexuality as different from (if equal to) male sexuality, or as if sexuality in women ineluctably exists in some realm beyond, beneath, above, behind—in any event, fundamentally untouched and unmoved by—an unequal social order. A theory of sexuality becomes feminist methodologically, meaning feminist in the post-marxist sense, to the extent it treats sexuality as a social construct of male power: defined by men, forced on women, and constitutive of the meaning of gender. Such an approach centers feminism on the perspective of the subordination of women to men as it identifies sex—that is, the sexuality of dominance and submission—as crucial, as a fundamental, as on some level definitive, in that process. Feminist theory becomes a project of analyzing that situation in order to face it for what it is, in order to change it. . . .

A distinctively feminist theory conceptualizes social reality, including sexual reality, on its own terms. The question is, what are they? If women have been substantially deprived not only of their own experience but of terms of their own in which to view it, then a feminist theory of sexuality which seeks to understand women's situation in order to change it must first identify and criticize the construct 'sexuality' as a construct that has circumscribed and defined experience as well as theory. This requires capturing it in the world, in its situated social meanings, as it is being constructed in life on a daily basis. It must be studied in its experienced empirical existence, not just in the texts of history (as Foucault does), in the social psyche (as Lacan does), or in language (as Derrida does). Sexual meaning is not made only, or even primarily, by words and in texts. It is made in social relations of power in the world, through which process gender is also produced. In feminist terms, the fact that male power has power means that the interests of male sexuality construct what sexuality as such means, including the standard way it is allowed and recognized to be felt and expressed and experienced, in a way that determines women's biographies, including sexual ones. Existing theories, until they grasp this, will not only misattribute what they call female sexuality to women as such, as if it were not imposed on women daily; they will also participate in enforcing the hegemony of the social construct 'desire', hence its product, 'sexuality', hence its construct 'woman', on the world.

The gender issue, in this analysis, becomes the issue of what is taken to be 'sexuality'; what sex means and what is meant by sex, when, how, with whom, and with what consequences to whom. [. . .]

Sexuality, in feminist light, is not a discrete sphere of interaction or feeling or sensation or behavior in which pre-existing social divisions may or may not be played out. It is a pervasive dimension of social life, one that permeates the whole, a dimension along which gender occurs and through which gender is socially constituted; it is a dimension along which other social divisions, like race and class, partly play themselves out. Dominance eroticized defines the imperatives of its masculinity, submission eroticized defines its femininity. So many distinctive features of women's status as second class—the restriction and constraint and contortion, the servility and the display, the self-mutilation and requisite presentation of self as a beautiful thing, the enforced passivity, the humiliation—are made into the content of sex for women. Being a thing for sexual use is fundamental to it. This approach identifies not just a sexuality that is shaped under conditions of gender inequality but reveals this sexuality itself to be the dynamic of the inequality of the sexes. It is to argue that the excitement at reduction of a person to a thing, to less than a human being, as socially defined, is its fundamental motive force. It is to argue that sexual difference is a function of sexual dominance. It is to argue a sexual theory of the distribution of social power by gender, in which this sexuality that is sexuality is substantially what makes the gender division be what it is, which is male dominant, wherever it is, which is nearly everywhere.

Across cultures, in this perspective, sexuality is whatever a given culture or subculture defines it as. The next question concerns its relation to gender as a division of power. Male dominance appears to exist cross-culturally, if in locally particular forms. Across cultures, is whatever defines women as 'different' the same as whatever defines women as 'inferior' the same as whatever defines women's 'sexuality'? Is that which defines gender inequality as merely the sex difference also the content of the erotic, cross-culturally? In this view, the feminist theory of sexuality is its theory of politics, its distinctive contribution to social and political explanation. To explain gender inequality in terms of 'sexual politics' is to advance not only a political theory of the sexual that defines gender but also a sexual theory of the political to which gender is fundamental. . . .

[. . .] [C]rucial feminist questions [include]: What do sexuality and gender inequality have to do with each other? How do dominance and submission become sexualized, or, why is hierarchy sexy? How does it get attached to male and female? Why does sexuality center on intercourse, the reproductive act by physical design? Is masculinity the enjoyment of violation, femininity the enjoyment of being violated? Is that the social meaning of intercourse? Do 'men love death'? Why? What is the etiology of heterosexuality in women? Is its pleasure women's stake in subordination?

Taken together and taken seriously, feminist inquiries into the realities of rape, battery, sexual harassment, incest, child sexual abuse, prostitution, and pornography answer these questions by suggesting a theory of the sexual mechanism. Its script, learning, conditioning, developmental logos, imprinting of the microdot, its deus ex machina, whatever sexual process term defines sexual arousal itself, is force, power's expression. Force is sex, not just sexualized; force is the desire dynamic, not just a response to the desired object when desire's expression is frustrated. Pressure, gender socialization, withholding benefits, extending indulgences, the how-to books, the sex therapy are the soft end; the fuck, the fist, the street, the chains, the poverty are the hard end. Hostility and contempt, or arousal of master to slave, together with awe and vulnerability, or arousal of slave to master—these are the emotions of this sexuality's excitement. [...]

To be clear: what is sexual is what gives a man an erection. Whatever it takes to make a penis shudder and stiffen with the experience of its potency is what sexuality means culturally. Whatever else does this, fear does, hostility does, hatred does, the helplessness of a child or a student or an infantilized or restrained or vulnerable woman does, revulsion does, death does. Hierarchy, a constant creation of person / thing, top / bottom, dominance / subordination relations, does. What is understood as violation, conventionally penetration and intercourse, defines the paradigmatic sexual encounter. The scenario of sexual abuse is: you do what I say. These textualities and these relations, situated within as well as creating a context of power in which they can be lived out, become sexuality. All this suggests that what is called sexuality is the dynamic of control by which male dominance—in forms that range from intimate to institutional, from a look to a rape—eroticizes and thus defines man and woman, gender identity and sexual pleasure. It is also that which maintains and defines male supremacy as a political system. Male sexual desire is thereby simultaneously created and serviced, never satisfied once and for all, while male force is romanticized, even sacralized, potentiated and naturalized, by being submerged into sex itself. [...]

Women often find ways to resist male supremacy and to expand their spheres of action. But they are never free of it. Women also embrace the standards of women's place in this regime as 'our own' to varying degrees and in varying voices—as affirmation of identity and right to pleasure, in order to be loved and approved and paid, in order just to make it through another day. This, not inert passivity, is the meaning of being a victim. The term is not moral: who is to blame or to be pitied or condemned or held responsible. It is not prescriptive; what we should do next. It is not strategic: how to construe the situation so it can be changed. It is not emotional: what one feels better thinking. It is descriptive: who does what to whom and gets away with it. [. . .]

Nor is homosexuality without stake in this gendered sexual system. Putting to one side the obviously gendered content of expressly adopted roles, clothing, and sexual mimicry, to the extent the gender of a sexual object is crucial to arousal, the structure of social power which stands behind and defines gender is hardly irrelevant, even if it is rearranged. Some have argued that lesbian sexuality—meaning here simply women having sex with women, not with men—solves the problem of gender by eliminating men from women's voluntary sexual encounters. Yet women's sexuality remains constructed under conditions of male supremacy; women remain socially defined as women in relation to men; the definition of women as men's inferiors remains sexual even if not heterosexual, whether men are present at the time or not. To the extent gay men choose men because they are men, the meaning of masculinity is affirmed as well as undermined. It may also be that sexuality is so gender marked that it carries dominance and submission with it, whatever the gender of its participants. . . .

Male sexuality is apparently activated by violence against women and expresses itself in violence against women to a significant extent. If violence is seen as occupying the most fully achieved end of a dehumanization continuum on which objectification occupies the least express end, one question that is raised is whether some form of hierarchy—the dynamic of the continuum—is currently essential for male sexuality to experience itself. If so, and if gender is understood to be a hierarchy, perhaps the sexes are unequal so that men can be sexually aroused. To put it another way, perhaps gender must be maintained as a social hierarchy so that men will be able to get erections; or, part of the male interest in keeping women down lies in the fact that it gets men up. Maybe feminists are considered castrating because equality is not sexy. [. . .]

What effect does the pervasive reality of sexual abuse of women by men have on what are deemed the more ordinary forms of sexual interaction? [. . .]

Consider women. Recall that more than one-third of all girls experience sex, perhaps are sexually initiated, under conditions that even this society recognizes are forced or at least unequal. Perhaps they learn this process of sexualized dominance as sex. Top–down relations feel sexual. Is sexuality throughout life then ever not on some level a reenactment of, a response to, that backdrop? Rape, adding more women to the list, can produce similar resonance. Sexually abused women—most women—seem to become either sexually disinclined or compulsively promiscuous or both in series, trying to avoid the painful events, or repeating them over and over almost addictively, or both, in an attempt to reacquire a sense of control or to make them come out right. Women also widely experience sexuality as a means to male approval; male approval translates into nearly all social goods. Violation can be sustained, even sought out, to this end. Sex can, then, be a means of trying to feel alive by redoing what has made one feel dead, of expressing a denigrated self-image seeking its own reflection in self-action in order to feel fulfilled, or of keeping up one's stock with the powerful.

Many women who have been sexually abused (like many survivors of concentration camps and ritual torture) report having distanced and split themselves as a conscious strategy for coping with the abuse. With women, this dissociation often becomes a part of their sexuality per se and of their experience of the world, especially their experience of men. Women widely report having this sensation during sex. Not feeling pain, including during sex, has a similar etiology. [...]

All women live in sexual objectification the way fish live in water. Given the statistical realities, all women live all the time under the shadow of the threat of sexual abuse. The question is, what can life as a woman mean, what can sex mean, to targeted survivors in a rape culture? Given the statistical realities, much of women's sexual lives will occur under post-traumatic stress. Being surrounded by pornography—which is not only socially ubiquitous but often directly used as part of sex—makes this a relatively constant condition. Women cope with objectification through trying to meet the male standard, and measure their self-worth by the degree to which they succeed. Women seem to cope with sexual abuse principally by denial or fear. On the denial side, immense energy goes into defending sexuality as just fine and getting better all the time, and into trying to make sexuality feel all right, the way it is supposed to feel. Women who are compromised, cajoled, pressured, tricked, blackmailed, or outright forced into sex (or pornography) often respond to the unspeakable humiliation, coupled with the sense of having lost some irreplaceable integrity, by claiming that sexuality as their own. Faced with no alternatives, the strategy to acquire self-respect and pride is: I chose it.

Consider the conditions under which this is done. This is a culture in which women are socially expected—and themselves necessarily expect and want—to be able to distinguish the socially, epistemologically, indistinguishable. Rape and intercourse are not authoritatively separated by any difference between the physical acts or amount of force involved but only legally, by a standard that centers on the man's interpretation of the encounter. Thus, although raped women, that is, most women, are supposed to be able to feel every day and every night that they have some meaningful determining part in having their sex life—their life, period—not be a series of rapes, the most they provide is the raw data for the man to see as he sees it. And he has been seeing pornography. Similarly, 'consent' is supposed to be the crucial line between rape and intercourse, but the legal standard for it is so passive, so acquiescent, that a woman can be dead and have consented under it. The mind fuck of all of this makes liberalism's complicitous collapse into 'I chose it' feel like a strategy for sanity. It certainly makes a woman at one with the world.

On the fear side, if a woman has ever been beaten in a relationship, even if 'only once', what does that do to her everyday interactions, or her sexual interactions, with that man? With other men? Does her body ever really forget that behind his restraint he can do that any time she pushes an issue, or for no reason at all? Does her vigilance ever really relax? If she tried to do something about it, as many women do, and if nothing was done, as it usually is not, does she ever forget that that is what can be done to her at any time and nothing will be done about it? Does she smile at men less—or more? If she writes at all, does she imitate men less—or more? If a woman has ever been raped, ever, does a penis ever enter her without some body memory, if not a flashback then the effort of keeping it back; or does she hurry up or keep trying, feeling something gaining on her, trying to make it come out right? If a woman has ever been raped, does she ever fully regain the feeling of physical integrity, of self-respect, of having what she wants count somewhere, of being able to make herself clear to those who have not gone through what she has gone through, of living in a fair society, of equality?

Given the effects of learning sexuality through force or pressure or imposition; given the constant roulette of sexual violence; given the daily sexualization of every aspect of a woman's presence—for a woman to be sexualized means constant humiliation or threat of it, being invisible as human being and center stage as sex object, low pay, and being a target for assault or being assaulted. Given that this is the situation of all women, that one never knows for sure that one is not next on the list of victims until the moment one dies (and then, who knows?), it does not seem exaggerated to say that women are sexual, meaning that women exist, in a context of terror. [. . .]

The general theory of sexuality emerging from this feminist critique does not consider sexuality to be an inborn force inherent in individuals, nor cultural in the Freudian sense, in which sexuality exists in a cultural context but in universally invariant stages and psychic representations. It appears instead to be culturally specific, even if so far largely invariant because male supremacy is largely universal, if always in specific forms. Although some of its abuses (like prostitution) are accentuated by poverty, it does not vary by class, although class is one hierarchy it sexualizes. Sexuality becomes, in this view, social and relational, constructing and constructed of power. Infants, though sensory, cannot be said to possess sexuality in this sense because they have not had the experiences (and do not speak the language) that give it social meaning. Since sexuality is its social meaning, infant erections, for example, are clearly sexual in the sense that this society centers its sexuality on them, but to relate to a child as though his erections mean what adult erections have been conditioned to mean is a form of child abuse. Such

erections have the meaning they acquire in social life only to observing adults.
[. . .]

There may be a feminist unconscious, but it is not the Freudian one.
Perhaps equality lives there. Its laws, rather than a priori, objective, or
universal, might as well be a response to the historical regularities of sexual
subordination, which under bourgeois ideological conditions require that the
truth of male dominance be concealed in order to preserve the belief that
women are sexually self-acting: that women want it. The feminist psychic
universe certainly recognizes that people do not always know what they
want, have hidden desires and inaccessible needs, lack awareness of motivation, have contorted and opaque interactions, and have an interest in obscuring what is really going on. But this does not essentially conceal that what
women really want is more sex. It is true, as Freudians have persuasively
observed, that many things are sexual that do not present themselves as such.
But in ways Freud never dreamed. [. . .]

So long as sex inequality remains unequal and sexual, attempts to value
sexuality as women's, possessive as if women possess it, will remain part of
limiting women to it, to what women are now defined as being. Outside of
truly rare and contrapuntal glimpses (which most people think they live
almost their entire sex life within), to seek an equal sexuality without political
transformation is to seek equality under conditions of inequality. Rejecting
this, and rejecting the glorification of settling for the best that inequality has
to offer or has stimulated the resourceful to invent, are what Ti-Grace
Atkinson meant to reject when she said: 'I do not know any feminist worthy
of that name who, if forced to choose between freedom and sex, would
choose sex. She'd choose freedom every time.'

[*Towards a Feminist Theory of the State* (Cambridge, Mass.: Harvard University Press, 1989),
127–54.]

ROSALIND COWARD

56 Slim and Sexy: Modern Woman's Holy Grail

It is inevitable, when considering the subject of how and why women accept
traditional sexual roles, that the subject of sexual behaviour itself should also
come up. After all, this is the point where men and women come together
and where the foundation for later sexual roles is laid. Traditionalists have it
that underneath our complex social structure there is a simple natural
instinct, saying we should look no further for an explanation as to why
women collude with men in keeping to predictable male and female roles.
It ought to be easy to challenge such simplistic biological explanations, but
some aspects of recent sexual behaviour make this challenge harder. For in

sexual behaviour there seems to be evidence of a backlash against attempts to transform sexual relations—a backlash greater than in any other aspect of male–female relations.

In this allegedly post-feminist era there has been little sign that women no longer care about male sexual approval and the forms of personal adornment that go with that. Instead, over the last ten years or so, women seem to have become more, rather than less, preoccupied with being seen as 'sexy'. The increase in the number of 'successful' women over the last ten years has not been accompanied by a rejection of female sexual wiles and devices, a straight swap of public prestige for sexual prestige. On the contrary, the ultimate accolade for a contemporary woman is that she is not only a successful career woman but sexy to boot.

Is this continuing female preoccupation with 'sexiness' confirmation of the belief that we are all still creatures of biology whose main task is to attract a mate and create a secure environment for our young? Or is it a sign that women are as much as ever tied to male approval, too scared to bring about a situation where our own needs and feelings as *people* come before our need for sexual approval? Of course, there are those who tell us that contemporary women *are* free of concern about male responses. They tell us that contemporary expressions of female sexuality, including sometimes the wearing of all the old trappings of female exploitation, have nothing to do with pleasing men and everything to do with sexual self-definition and self-gratification. In short, they would have us believe that the Utopia envisaged by feminism, where women define their own sexual needs and styles, has already arrived.

The question of women's sexual self-definition was central in the first onrush of the feminist movement. Then it was argued that women had no real sexual rights, let alone sexual freedom. Sexual choice was supposed to reflect women's economic and social dependency on men, a dependency that was played out in sexual and emotional ways. Not only did women want to attract men who could support them, but in order to do so they were prepared to mould themselves to men's desires. Women, it was said, acceded to the male definition of sexiness, and to the policing of their sexuality inside and outside the bedroom. Women displaying sexuality beyond the confines of a monogamous heterosexual unit risked exposure to men's hostility and contempt. Even in the 1960s, when feminism began to gain ground, women were vulnerable to a sexual double standard. They were still liable to be deemed 'slags', 'whores' and 'prostitutes' if they asserted their right to enjoy sex and acted in characteristically 'male' ways.

Feminism asserted that at the heart of all this was a hostility to women's sexual feelings. Men wanted to control or obliterate women's sexuality, or at the very least put it in the service of men. Feminism tapped into a torrent of resentment about this. Women revealed that they felt ignorant of their bodies' functions, controlled by men's interpretation of their sexual history, and belittled or demeaned by prevailing images of sexual desirability. Such discontent fuelled the women's movement, where the call for sexual self-definition was central and where men's control of sexual imagination and imagery was challenged.

For a while these challenges fitted under the broad heading of a call for 'sexual liberation' or, more specifically, women's liberation. But this soon came to be seen as problematic. Women's liberation was something which was all too easily accommodated by an increasingly 'permissive' society. Without a more fundamental challenge to women's economic dependency and prevailing sexual standards, increased sexual expression for women seemed doomed to make them even more vulnerable to men's sexual needs and double standards. Increasingly, women felt that 'liberation' was too limited. Discovering your own sexual needs would be only one part of a wider social and economic independence for women—the real source of security.

Nobody quite knew what a free, self-defined women's sexuality would be like, but many suggestions were made. Some envisaged a sort of unisexual, androgynous sexuality, some the nurturing, natural body of an earth mother. Others suggested that the only free expression of women's sexuality would be with other women. There were other, more nebulous ideas which tried to find ways of making women's preoccupation with sexual attraction less central; women were to concentrate more on their 'sisters', or were to give less time to make-up and trivia. But all these different emphases agreed on one thing: a 'true', free expression of female sexuality would be quite unlike anything that preceded it.

But as the term 'liberation' disappeared, to be replaced by a myriad of different (often competing) descriptions and prescriptions for the problem of sexual redefinition, so too did the groundswell of female opinion cease to call for changes on the sexual front. While many women identified with feminism's economic goals, they were anxious to distance themselves from a *sexual* antagonism to men and from a sexual revolution which they saw as undermining their 'femininity'. The feminist vision of a new sexuality came to be seen as the fevered imaginings of man-haters.

Through the 1980s we heard men and women telling us how it was quite natural for women to enjoy being sexy, quite natural to want to be sexy for men. Only 'uptight lesbian feminists' had a problem with that. As one woman said to me, 'Of course I want men to find me attractive. We all do, don't we? I try to make the best of my appearance and I like it when men respond.' Now, although there may be a much greater variety of female styles, the concern with desirability to men is still uppermost in women's self-presentation. Women backed off from what they saw as a sexual confrontation with men.

In fact, the vision of an egalitarian society, where women would no longer have to use sex to gain power, couldn't be further from what happened in the

1980s. Far from sexuality becoming less central, it seems to have become more so. Far from using the greater equality between the sexes to determine their own sexual image, we have seen women reaffirming the notion that what is most important to a woman is her sexual allure. Madonna is often held up as the young woman's icon of self-defined female sexuality, but she has done nothing to challenge this traditional notion that being sexually desirable is the *ultimate* source of power for women.

So what is the truth behind the contemporary expression of women's sexuality? Is this desire to be desired the fundamental truth of female sexuality or further evidence of a deep collusion, by which women are failing to challenge the traditional exchanges between men and women? [. . .]

In Julie Burchill's *Ambition* (1991), the career woman's bonkbuster, the narrative impetus comes not so much from the heroine's quest for career advancement as from the humiliation planned for her by the newspaper magnate who desires her. He says, 'I'm sick of breaking bimbos—it's no fun, no challenge. Strong, hard, career girls—they're the new *filet mignon* of females. They're the new frontier. Girls like you. Oh, I'm going to have fun breaking you, Susan.' This is a new version of the Mills and Boon romance, where the powerful man sets about subduing the girl. Still the greatest power for women is sexual power, being desired. What is different is the belief that somehow being a successful career woman, being rich and powerful in your own right, means that you can wear the sexual mantle of a masochist without being oppressed by it.

Jessica Benjamin, an American psychoanalyst, shows how much these new images are still an expression of a deep passivity, however actively they are pursued:

Once sexuality is cut loose from reproduction, a goal the era of sexual liberation has urged upon our imagination, womanhood can no longer be equated with mother-hood. But the alternative images of the *femme fatale* does not signify an active subjectivity either; the sexy woman—an image that intimidates women whether or not they strive to conform to it—is sexy, but as object, not as subject. She expresses not so much *her* desire as her pleasure in being desired; what she enjoys is her capacity to evoke desire in the other, to attract. Her power does not reside in her own passion, but in her acute desirability. Neither the power of the mother nor that of the sexy woman can, as in the case of the father, be described as the power of the sexual subject. (*The Bonds of Love*, 1990)

Benjamin believes this to be a fundamental truth that still underlies what she calls women's desire. Not only is women's greatest power still seen as sex, but that sexual power is still essentially passive, courting the approval and response of men. And with the increasing sexualization of culture, a woman is under contradictory pressures: she is still essentially a passive subject, yet she is expected more and more to be defined by her ability to provoke and satisfy a sexual response in men. [. . .]

What is startling is how little headway women have made on the sexual front. Not only have they accepted the increasing sexualization of their world—of motherhood, of working life, of old age—but they appear to have accepted it as an inevitable part of female desire. Women have only themselves to blame if they continue to accept willingly that sexual value is women's greatest value. It is true that women are in a situation where the goal posts are constantly being moved—first we have to be sexually free, then sexual *and* careerist, then sexual *and* careerist *and* a mother—but few women are challenging this. Naomi Wolf's *The Beauty Myth* is the only real sign that there is any resistance to the coercive belief that sexual desirability is overwhelmingly important. Yet she recycles the old feminist analysis that women are the dupes of men's needs. The real problem lies in women's readiness to buy into the myths of sexual desirability as the ultimate source of female potency, as if for women the only power they can wield is sexual power.

[*Our Treacherous Hearts: Why Women Let Men Get Their Way* (London: Faber and Faber, 1992), 147–63.]

CHERRY SMYTH

57 Queer Notions

Each time the word 'queer' is used it defines a strategy, an attitude, a reference to other identities and a new self-understanding. (And queer can be qualified as 'more queer', 'queerer' or 'queerest' as the naming develops into a more complex process of identification.) For many, the term marks a growing lack of faith in the institutions of the state, in political procedures, in the press, the education system, policing and the law. Both in culture and politics, queer articulates a radical questioning of social and cultural norms, notions of gender, reproductive sexuality and the family. We are beginning to realise how much of our history and ideologies operate on a homo-hetero opposition, constantly privileging the hetero perspective as normative, positing the homo perspective as bad and annihilating the spectrum of sexualities that exists. [...]

The attraction of queer for some lesbians is flavoured by a rebellion against a prescriptive feminism that had led them to feel disenfranchised by the lesbian feminist movement. There was a feeling that the importance of identifying politically as a lesbian had obscured lesbianism as a sexual identity. 'Acceptable' ideas of lesbian sexuality and desire were constructed around notions of sameness and a desexed androgyny, and anyone who disagreed with the 'right on' line, regardless of her sexual practice, would be dismissed at best as an SM dyke and at worst as a fascist. While the ground gained by identity politics in promoting equal representation and access to resources were important achievements of feminism, the rigid hierarchies of oppression rhetoric that privileged certain oppressions above others were considered divisive and futile. [. . .]

The gender-polarised feminism of the 60s and 70s blocked any attempts to understand how lesbian and gay male desires and identities might be mapped against each other. Lesbian sex was posited as loving and monogamous, in false opposition to gay male sex, which was deemed abusive, exploitative and promiscuous. The split was compounded by a moralistic feminist separatism that declared that the further women got from the penis, the better lesbians they became. Many gay men felt that their sexual practices and ethics were reviled and policed, thereby blocking almost all discussion about shared oppression. The situation for black lesbians and gay men, as outlined in the previous chapter, was often different as the fight against racism was given priority.

At the same time, lesbian feminism rejected modes of behaviour and appearance that were encoded as 'feminine', idealising instead an androgyny (based on a masculine aesthetic) that was somehow promoted as both 'natural' and progressive. Butch and femme were outlawed as a replay of heterosexist power imbalances. The silencing of anything but 'right on' forms of sexual expression led to a failure to negotiate issues of desire and power, as lesbian feminists propagated the belief that women did not objectify each other sexually and that lust was a gentle wild orchid. The anxiety about what constituted correct 'feminist' sexual desire resulted, in extreme cases, in a ludicrous sexual code that forbade even finger penetration.

One of the key sites of the battles between feminists was, and continues to be, pornography. To watch, never mind admit to enjoying porn, was deemed equal to treacherous collusion with the most sinister component of hetero-patriarchy. Anti-porn campaigners often conflated sexually explicit images with violence against women, so that instead of analysing the social con-struction of male sexual violence, campaigns focused on the battle for censor-ship, even though the links between male violence and pornography are far from proven. Perhaps because porn is visible and explicit, it became an easy target on which to focus the fight against sexism and racism. [. . .]

In 1984, anti-pornographers Andrea Dworkin and Catharine MacKinnon introduced the Minneapolis Ordinance, which allowed women to take civil action against anyone involved in the production, sale or distribution of pornography on the grounds that the prosecutor had been harmed by the image of women's sexuality portrayed. The definition of pornography was dangerously broad, and the alliance of the campaign with the American right was a worrying indicator of what might follow. FACT (Feminist

Anti-Censorship Task Force) was set up in the US and FAC (Feminists Against Censorship) was founded in London in 1989. FAC's first leaflet argued: 'We need a feminism willing to tackle issues of class and race and to deal with the variety of oppressions in the world, not to reduce all oppressions to pornography.'

For some lesbian feminists, the threat of increased censorship at a time of new openness in the discussion of sexual practice and a newly created demand for and production of sexually explicit material was bad news. The nub of the censorship debate for dykes came in 1985, when the London Lesbian and Gay Centre (now the site of a blooming mixed SM club...due to queer, or simply the weariness of the radfem lobby?) declared that SM groups and anyone wearing 'SM clothes' would be banned. (Although access was finally won, even as recently as March 1991, a gay man wearing half a handcuff on his leather jacket was denied entry. The fact that he lost the other half to the Metropolitan Police while participating in an AIDS demo was considered irrelevant.)

It is important to highlight the SM sex battle as it signifies why so many dykes developed a dissatisfaction and disaffection for 'lesbian feminism' and consequently feel attracted to the transgressive elements putatively offered by queer. The issues at stake were not specifically about SM practices; instead, these became the focus for a growing need to discuss desire, fantasies and sexual practices without being policed or labelled 'post-feminist'.

[*Lesbians Talk Queer Notions* (London: Scarlet Press, 1992), 20, 26, 36–8.]

MARY MCINTOSH

58 Queer Theory and the War of the Sexes

Feminism is a form of politics deeply rooted in humanism. Its project is liberatory, its subjects women. To be a feminist necessarily involves a belief that women and men are intrinsically free and equal and that women's oppression lies in the denial of the development of our full capacities. This is why the question of defining women, in terms other than those of biological reductionism, has been so important. And this is why differences between women—along lines of race, class, sexuality and so on—have been so divisive. For in recent years, liberatory projects have lent themselves to identity politics, privileging the lived experience of oppression, so that feminism is only for women, anti-racism only for black people, and so on. In a context of humanism, the way to avoid the divisiveness of identity politics is through theorizing the various oppressions and their interrelationships at a structural level. But this has proved a particularly difficult task where the groups concerned have a biological as well as a social definition. The difficulties, and especially the need to break with commonsense biological reductionism, have led to forms of theory that appear abstract, tortuous and only available to an intellectual élite. With the eclipse of Marxism and rise of Thatcherite individualism, too, structural theories and coherent political strategies have been less popular than identity politics and tactical alliances.

Queer politics, on the other hand, is rooted (albeit rather shallowly) in a queer theory that is deconstructive of categories and subjectivities. Queer theory has no time for disputes about whether bisexuals are really gay or transsexuals really women; it has no time for hierarchies of oppression or for all the divisiveness of identity politics that beset the movement in the 1980s. Kobena Mercer has spoken of the need to get away from binary thinking: 'binary thinking ends up with the static concept of identity rather than the more volatile concept of identification'.[1] Certainly the binary thinking involved in the terms of sex and gender has plagued feminist theory; feminism rejects gender divisions, yet much of its theory is concerned with drawing attention to gender and its inequalities and oppressions. The queer project is different. As a leaflet circulated in London in 1991 put it:

Queer means to fuck with gender. There are straight queers, biqueers, tranny queers, lez queers, fag queers, SM queers, fisting queers in every single street in this apathetic country of ours.[2]

Queer is a form of resistance, a refusal of labels, pathologies and moralities. It is defined more by what it is against than what it is for. Its slogan is not 'get out of my face' (let alone 'gay is good'), but rather, 'in your face'. [...]

The question is: can queer thinking, rooted in resistance rather than identity, transcend the binary divisions between women and men in the gay movement? Can we—and should we?—move beyond socially given identities towards politically formulated identifications? [...]

In the decade or so prior to the advent of queer theory, the dominant approach among lesbian and gay theorists was that of social constructionism, the idea that sexualities are not given in nature and biology but are mediated by history and culture.[3] Social constructionist theories of sexual orientation and identity have their origin in two very different observations. The first is that historical and anthropological evidence shows that the socially recognized categories of sexual orientation vary from one culture and one period to another. While there may well be homosexual *behaviour* in all societies, it is commonly not recognized as a penchant of particular individuals, so that *the* lesbian or *the* homosexual does not exist as a deviant type or as an alternative identity. This means that no one is a heterosexual or a homosexual independently of culture. The second observation is that, even within a culture such as ours where these categories are well entrenched, patterns of sexual behaviour are not neatly polarized into the categories 'heterosexual' and 'homosexual'. This means that relatively few people actually are behaviourally heterosexual or homosexual in the way that the culture supposes. Many fall in between, or move to and fro during their lifetime, yet the bisexual is scarcely recognized as a social type.

Though social constructionism can be applied to both women's and men's sexuality, lesbian and gay male theorists have tended to use it rather differently. [. . .]

[. . .] [T]he separate development of lesbian and gay male history reveals that each of them could have learned a great deal from one other. One of the most striking things about them is the abject acceptance of gender stereotypes on both sides. In lesbian history the *status quo ante* is often assumed to be romantic friendships between women, not involving genital sexuality; in the case of men it is usually sodomy and other 'abominations', conceived as without a desiring subject. Yet it seems probable that women who engaged in sexual relations were not a complete figment of male pornographic imagination. [. . .] And it is certain that men were once able to form closer, more intimate friendships and to sleep in the same bed without being subjected to the taint of homosexuality. It is hard to believe that at roughly the same period women-loving women became translated from the sphere of the whole personality to that of the specifically sexual while men were translated from the specifically sexual to the whole personality. There must have been some connection between the two, and also some greater similarity between the two transformations than either side has acknowledged. Yet the history of male homosexuality has assumed a parallel completely modelled on its version of the male transition and the history of lesbianism has assumed no connection at all.

Another major divergence is over the kind of social constructionism espoused in the two traditions. A thoroughgoing rejection of essentialism marks much of the male homosexual history. In the case of the interactionists, this stems from a principled anti-positivism, in the case of the Foucauldians, from a principled anti-humanism. Among the radical-feminist historians of lesbianism, the rejection of essentialism has come from a very different source: not so much from a principled anti-essentialism as from a critique of the naturalizing labels that men have put upon women. This means that 'queer theory' has an odd relationship to pre-existing lesbian and gay male theory. For queer theory, being *de*constructionist, has much in common with the more radical forms of social constructionism represented in the male gay tradition. Indeed, queer theory may be said to be a development of that tradition, which has simply laid claim to a more all-encompassing status.

If so, this is horribly reminiscent of what feminists have often found about 'male-stream thought'. But I have argued that lesbian theory ought in any case to have learnt something from gay male theory. It should have learnt something of the importance of the sexual and of sexual transgression in the making of the lesbian. This is not to say that women's sexuality or women's transgression has been the same as men's—it has in fact been specifically womanly and has had to contest gender boundaries from the other side—but that an important element in the construction of the lesbian has been sexual and has been transgressive.[4] On the other side, queer theory should not forget that the heterosexuality in terms of which we are defined as other is a highly gendered one, so that our otherness and the forms and meanings of our dissidence are also gendered.

Lesbian and gay theorists are among the first and the foremost critics of those feminist theories that see a deep gender chasm at the psychic, cultural and structural levels and a complete congruence, or mutual determination, between those three levels. If gender is a neatly wrapped parcel in which sexual orientation is tied up with gender identity, then it leaves us out of the account altogether. So, for instance, film theory that sees subjectivity as constructed through cinematic representation may leave no space for indeterminacy between levels. And insofar as it relies on psychoanalytic theory, there is a danger that 'it *presumes* heterosexuality to such a degree that it often seems to *demand* it', as Bad Object-Choices put it.[5] Juliet Mitchell sought to defend psychoanalysis as 'not a recommendation *for* a patriarchal society, but an analysis of one.'[6] The problem is as Cora Kaplan has pointed out, that 'Freudian theory... emphasises, perhaps too heavily, the unalterable distance between gender positions so that they remain... stuck at distant poles'.[7] If this is true of psychoanlysis, it is equally true of much other feminist theory, though it can be argued that the concept of gender offers more ways out than the concept of sexual difference.[8]

But the fact that some feminist theory may have been too determinist and failed to take account of the actual heterogeneity of identities does not mean that we can ignore the whole issue of gender, as Simon Watney has proposed.[9] This position was notoriously taken to its logical extreme by Monique Wittig when she declared that 'Lesbians are not women', on the grounds that ' "woman" has meaning only in heterosexual systems of thought and heterosexual economic systems'.[10] This challenging proposition is, of course, both true and not true in terms of our identity. It is usually false as a statement of how we are socially defined by others. Its value as a political position depends very much on the alignments that are available at any particular conjuncture. But Wittig espoused a 'materialist lesbianism', recognizing a need for an economic and political transformation of the relations between women and men, as well as a change in language. So when she said 'If we as lesbians and gay men continue to speak of ourselves and to conceive of ourselves as women and as men, we are instrumental in maintaining heterosexuality',[11] she was speaking of a prefigurative 'transformation of the key concepts', rather than clinging to an infantile belief in the omnipotence of thought. Her words, intended to shock us out of complacent binary thinking, have been taken too literally—not least by herself. We should not be misled into pursuing a political strategy that might be called 'androgyny in one ghetto', unless we do it in ways that actively challenge the social reality of gender divisions both within and beyond the queer ghetto.

Queer theory and queer politics, I conclude, are important for feminists. They do not replace feminism, which remains as a humanist and liberatory project with its own more structural theories. But, on the one side, queer theory provides a critique of the heterosexual assumptions of some feminist theory and, on the other, feminists must agitate for an awareness of gender in queer thinking.

['Queer Theory and the War of the Sexes', in Joseph Bristow and Angela Wilson (eds.), *Activating Theory: Lesbian, Gay and Bisexual Politics* (London: Lawrence and Wishart, 1993), 30–52.]

ELIZABETH WILSON

59 Is Transgression Transgressive?

[T]he demand for the recognition of bisexuality challenges the foundations of the lesbian and gay movement, which for better or worse, is predicated on the assumption that the lesbian/gay identity is at least relatively fixed. We might argue for or believe in the possibility, or indeed the existence in many cases, of more fluid sexualities. Yet we must also recognise the problems this poses for political activism, and the bisexual movement in its demand for recognition primarily from the lesbian and gay movement has been insensitive to these difficulties.

In addition, bisexuality has come forward at a particular moment in time, and we must understand it in that context. It is explicitly posed as transgressive, as an extract from an article in the US magazine *Outlook* demonstrates:

When I strap on a dildo and fuck my male partner, we are engaging in 'heterosexual' behaviour, but I can tell you that it feels altogether *queer*, and I'm sure my grandmother and Jesse Helms would say the same.[1]

For this couple, ironically, *heterosexuality* has become the transgressive act against the stifling norms of political correctness, radical feminist separatism and binary oppositions. Yet, no matter how queer these two subjectively feel (and that's fine), unless they dress in a very extreme way or proclaim their sexual behaviour in some other fashion, so far as the world is concerned they are still a heterosexual couple—it's just that they are a *kinky* heterosexual couple. And we have to question whether sexual experiment on its own is necessarily political or subversive at all. As Inge Blackman said (in a discussion of this paper), it's happening all over the suburbs all the time. We aren't exactly seeing a social revolution as a result.

This illustrates a more general weakness and a political inadequacy in the way in which 'transgression' has operated or may operate, or rather can't operate: it can't deal with the systematic or structural nature of oppressive institutions. On the contrary, it reaffirms and may even reinforce them. An act of defiance may be personally liberating and may indeed make an important ideological statement, but whether it can do anything more seems uncertain. Like those other words I mentioned—dissidence, subversion, resistance—it is a word of weakness. We can rage against the fading of the light, we can shake our fist at society or piss on it, but that is all.

There is another disturbing aspect of the discourse around transgression. Like another contested term, queer, transgression sometimes operates as a rebellion against our own history—or at least against a part of the political history of lesbianism: the feminist part. For some lesbians and gay men feminism, seems to have become the wicked stepmother, originator of the hated political correctness against which it's become so important to rebel. In this, significantly, what has been occluded is socialist feminism, which opposed the political thought police of separatist feminism, and which was always in favour of working politically with men (and indeed of sleeping with them). [. . .]

Yet we still need to ask: *why* is it that some forms of political protest appear more effective when couched in aesthetic terms? Why are there periods, like now, or the early to mid-1960s, when politics seems to have to be expressed in aesthetic terms? Why have there always been bohemians, punks, a tradition of protest that precisely has never fitted into established political categories? I cannot claim to have answers to these questions. But they prevent me from taking any sort of absolute view, or from rejecting transgression out of hand. And I believe that these aesthetic forms of protest are valuable, and that we ought to hang on to them. It's also clear that the lesbian and gay movement has exploited them more successfully, perhaps, than any other group. [. . .]

Finally, while I would never reject the importance or impact of transgression, it can only be a tactic, never a total politics. And anyway, at present, it seems often to act as a substitute for politics. While I have always been suspicious of utopianism, I believe that no political movement can develop or grow without some idea of how society ought to be. We transgress in order to insist that we are there, that we exist, and to place a distance between ourselves and the dominant culture. But we have to go further— we have to have an idea of how things could be different, otherwise transgression ends in mere posturing. In other words, transgression on its own leads eventually to entropy, unless we carry within us some idea of transformation.

It is therefore not transgression that should be our watchword, but trans-formation.

['Is Transgression Transgressive?', in Joseph Bristow and Angela Wilson (eds.), *Activating Theory: Lesbian, Gay and Bisexual Politics* (London: Lawrence and Wishart, 1993), 107–16]

LYNNE SEGAL

60 Sexual Liberation and Feminist Politics

'There is feminism and then there's fucking', declares the bulimic and alco-holic ex-feminist literary critic Maryse, in the Canadian film *A Winter Tan* (1987), based on the published letters of Maryse Holder, *Give Sorrow Words*. Maryse tells her audience that she is taking a holiday from feminism to indulge herself and her 'natural sluttishness' with young Mexican men—one of whom eventually murders her. After gloomily absorbing this narrative, I found it hard to decide whether it was Maryse's notion of feminism or her own (and her killer's) predatory view of sex which was the more depressing in this harrowing tale of one woman's neurotic self-destruction. The fact that many feminists would proudly endorse Maryse Holder's dual depiction of feminism as anti-heterosexual pleasure and heterosexual pleasure as anti-woman (a dangerous, if not deadly pursuit), only adds to my sinking spirits. Some of us expect cautionary tales warning women of the price we must pay for sexual pleasure to come from our would-be patriarchal 'protectors', determined to stamp out the rich and hopeful dreams of women's liberation. It is harder to know what to think when the same message comes from our own side. (*A Winter Tan* was produced, written, directed and performed by Jackie Boroughs, a leading feminist figure in Canadian film and theatre for the last twenty-five years.)

One thing is clear, however, at least to me. The way to fight the continuing victimization of women cannot be to abandon notions of sexual liberation, or to make women's pursuit of heterosexual pleasure incompatible with women's happiness. It was not only the generation who came of age in the affluent 1960s who discovered that the fight against sexual hypocrisy and for sexual openness and pleasure could inspire both personal and political enthu-siasm for creative and co-operative projects of diverse kinds. Such sexual openness lay at the root of the politicization of women and gay people in the 1970s, suddenly fully aware that pleasure was as much a social and a political as a personal matter; well before they discovered Foucault, and his genealogy of the cultural institutions and discourses dictating the norms and regimes of 'sexuality'. It was seeing and hearing the dominant language and iconography of the joys of sex focussed on the power and activity of straight men, while subordinating and disparaging straight women (as 'chics') and gay men and lesbians (as 'queers'), that inspired the women's and the gay liberation movements into a battle against both sexism and heterosexism.

The ramifications of this battle take us all the way from opposing gender hierarchies to challenging the very conception of 'gender' itself. From the extensive debate about the care and treatment of women in relation to fertility control and childbirth, alongside pressure on men to share the full responsibilities of household tasks and parenting, to the subsequent highly successful 'safer sex' strategies pioneered by gay communities against the spread of HIV and AIDS, the struggle for sexual liberation has played a crucial role in changing patterns of life in Western countries. Indeed, it was the repression of any moment or movements of sexual liberation in the former Eastern European 'state socialist' countries that constituted the most significant aspect of the oppression of women there. Despite greater access to childcare facilities and extensive participation in the workforce, Eastern Europe saw almost no politicization of interpersonal relationships or sexual experience, making sexism, violence against women and exclusive maternal responsibility for childcare and housework as unchallenged as it was ubiquitous.[1]

Even in these days of greater insecurity, it is the rediscovering of the pleasures to be found in our bodies and the joy of bringing pleasure to others (of desiring and feeling desired) which, when things go well, feeds personal optimism and strength: 'Oh, when I was in love with you | Then I was clean and brave', as Housman wrote of his own homosexual passion, mourning its passing, and the resurrection of that gloomy tyrant—his old self.[2] The idea of sexual liberation, as Bob Connell has recently written, may seem 'good mainly for a horse-laugh, or a nanosecond of nostalgia in the world of the new puritanism', but in fact it 'should come back from the dead; we still need it'.[3] We need it, if only because, while many left and feminist radicals have forsaken their former enthusiasm for sexual liberation, the right have stuck doggedly to their task of opposing it. In these 'post-modern' times, we may not see sexual liberation as the struggle to combat the repression of some sexual essence. But we might usefully see it as the struggle to combat the manipulation of people's fears and anxieties around gender and sexuality in a climate of increasing confusion for men, with its accompanying homophobia and violence against women. [...]

As feminists, we play into the hands of our enemies if we downplay, rather than seek fully to strengthen, ideas of women's sexual liberation. Nor can we leave the goal of expanding personal liberation to a commodity consumer culture eager to expand its markets, whatever its sometimes 'dissident', playful or progressive moments. Women, like gays and lesbians, still need a political movement and agenda of our own, that continues to make demands on the state while providing its own diverse networks of support and cultural resistance.

Two trends have been highlighted in Western surveys of changing sexual patterns over the last few decades (usually undertaken in the USA): the increasing levels of sexual activity outside marriage, and the lowering of double standards as women's sexual experiences draw closer to men's.[4] Both, quite obviously, reflect a decline in men's control over women's sexuality. As the latest survey of sexual behaviour in Britain has concluded (the survey which Margaret Thatcher tried to prevent by withdrawing its promised funding), quite contrary to traditionalists' dire warnings and secret hopes, sex is far safer and less fraught for women today. The importance of female 'virginity' before marriage has all but disappeared as an issue for most groups of women and men, and younger people are far more likely to have used contraception during their first sexual intercourse: over 80 per cent of women, and over 70 per cent of men, had their first heterosexual intercourse with the man using a condom in 1990—two to three times higher than in preceding decades. Around 90 per cent of women gave either love, curiosity or 'natural follow on' as the main factor leading to their first intercourse, with the majority of women and men feeling it occurred at about the right time; although one in four women, against one in eight men, thought they had had sex too early. Serial monogamy is now the dominant pattern for both sexes. There seems to be 'a genuine long-term decline in the number of men who visit prostitutes'.[5]

By arguing for women's sexual autonomy, fertility rights and the education and resources necessary for each person to encounter or care for themselves and for others in ways that enhance the possibilities for pleasure, mutuality, responsibility and comfort, feminists today would be continuing to participate in changes which they once helped to set in motion. Sexual pleasure is far too significant in our lives and culture for women not to be seeking to express our agency through it. The task confronting feminists today, as yesterday, is to uncover the social forces which ensure that women's sexual agency is suppressed in contexts of significant gender inequality, and to fight to change them. It is also to uncover and challenge the cultural forces which disparage women and gay men through meanings roping gender to sexuality via conceptions of 'masculinity' as 'activity' and 'dominance' coded into heterosexual coitus, however shaky the symbolism at interpersonal levels. It is these tasks which keep sexuality a social and political issue and 'sexual liberation' a goal for which we have still to struggle. There is cause for genuine optimism, yet so much more to be done.

[...] Campaigns like those of Zero Tolerance, publicly exposing and condemning men's use of violence against women, have been launched by several local councils in Glasgow and London. Feminists have also continued to make important interventions and recommendations drawing media and state attention to the absurdly low levels of rape convictions (only 14 per cent of reported rapes result in conviction, on Home Office figures for 1991), with many violent men being acquitted over and over again, and women victims continuing to be subjected to humiliating treatment in court, especially when their attackers were already known to them.[6]

Worryingly, however, there is also some official backing for new anti-pornography legislation to 'protect' us from the 'harm' caused by images of 'sexually explicit subordination'.[7] While strengthening the agenda of moral conservatives, this does nothing to rid us of the ubiquitous non-sexually explicit gender imagery depicting men as dominant and aggressive, women as subordinate and servicing in cultural representation generally (the feminine/effeminate/homosexual remain subordinate identities, in and out of their clothes). Since images are read and responded to differently depending upon their framing, context, and the meanings they carry within the milieu in which they are consumed, sexual minorities and dissidents of all sorts rightly fear it is their representations of sexuality which will be censored by any new legislation, just as they have always been. Certainly 'safer sex' campaigning material and sex education generally, in both Britain and the USA has been grotesquely hampered by accusations of 'pornography'.[8] Most significantly, proposing anti-pornography legislation is a cheap diversion from doing anything useful about violence against women. Those most at risk from sexual brutality—overwhelmingly women who feel trapped in relationships with men, as well as prostitutes and gay men (lesbians are less vulnerable, unless occupying one of the first two categories)—need real solutions. These involve increasing women's financial independence, encouraging rather than stigmatizing or trying to penalize 'single' mothers who have fled violent partnerships, as well as combatting homophobia.

Given the poverty of resistance and imagination coming from mainstream political parties, it is campaigning groups, community networks and subcultural consolidations which are going to be the main focus for reflection and struggles around sexuality and personal life in the short term. Sexual freedoms have, however, proved one of the few issues capable of drawing people into progressive collective action in recent years, providing radicals of the Left with the best of reasons for addressing them, even as our opponents mobilize their counter-attack. The Clause 28 legislation, ironically, backfired completely in its goal of reaffirming the sanctity of the family, and silencing its feminist and gay critics. Instead, as many have celebrated, sexual dissidents of every sort, including heterosexuals, took to the streets in their tens of thousands to support 'Stop the Clause' campaigns and marches, and benefits, meetings and publicity stunts occurred throughout the country.[9] With well known media figures like Ian McKellan and Michael Cashman deciding it was time to come out and organize openly for full gay rights, and more gay and lesbian programmes finding their way into mainstream television, debates and struggles around sexuality seemed to have become the most successful area of dissent in the late 1980s. [. . .]

For those of us who want to see the recognition of women's equality and agency in every sphere of life, [hetero]'sexuality' as confirmation of 'manhood' is an idea we must attack. Its discursive displacement is central to the battle against the hierarchical gender relations which it serves to symbolize. It will only fade away with the passing of that gender order, as we continue to fashion new concepts and practices of gender based upon the mutual recognition of similarities and differences between women and men, rather than upon notions of their opposition. In the meantime, we can continue to insist, with all the passion we can muster, that there is no necessary fit between maleness, activity and desire; any more than there is a fit between femaleness, passivity and sexual responsiveness.

Straight sex, with its tactile, olfactory, oral and visual bodily connections, can be no less 'perverse' than its 'queer' alternatives. Ridiculing hierarchies of sexuality and gender, it too can serve as a body-blow to the old male order of things. There is feminism and there is fucking. As I see it, they can fit together quite as smoothly (or as painfully) as feminism and any other human activity. Straight feminists, like gay men and lesbians, have everything to gain from asserting our non-coercive desire to fuck if, when, how and as we choose.

[*Straight Sex: The Politics of Pleasure* (London: Virago Press, 1994), 309–18.]

PAULA TREICHLER

61 AIDS, Identity, and the Politics of Gender

This essay begins with a joke:

Joe is a regular at his neighborhood bar. One night he tells his buddies he's going to have sex-change surgery. 'I just feel there's a woman inside me,' he says, 'and I'm going to let her out.' A few months later Joe—or rather Jane—shows up at the bar and introduces herself to her old buddies. Once they're over their amazement, they greet her warmly, buy a pitcher, and start asking her about the surgery.

'What hurt the most?' they ask. 'Was it when they cut your penis?' 'No,' says Jane, 'that wasn't what hurt the most.' 'Was it when they cut your balls?' 'No, that wasn't what hurt the most.' 'So, what was it that hurt the most?' 'What hurt the most,' says Jane, 'was when they cut my salary.'

When I shared this with a medical school colleague, he got huffy: 'That's not a joke,' he said, 'that's feminism!' Indeed; it's feminism that turns on an important paradox of identity: When does 'Joe' become 'Jane'? And even *does* Joe become Jane?

If someone is called a 'woman', what criterion is being treated as essential? Are there specific characteristics, qualities, behaviors that count as female? Feature X but not feature Y? X chromosome but not Y? Recent reports on the gender testing of Olympic athletes ('chick tests') assure us that these are all unreliable criteria. 'For all its dazzling discoveries about the genes that guide a human embryo along its path to maleness or femaleness,' wrote Gina Kolata in the *New York Times*, 'science, it appears, cannot provide a simple answer'.[1] How about having a vagina, then? Or having a 'real' vagina as opposed to a constructed one? One feminist publishing house refused to allow a feminist researcher to use the pronoun 'she' in reference to a male-to-female transsexual. Is birth sex forever? What if someone with a penis wears a dress, uses the ladies room, and is universally taken as female? Are these criteria independent of each other, or is one fundamental? When Joe changes, does something 'in' him stay the same? Note that Joe's pals didn't treat Jane as a stranger, nor as a single woman in a bar, but as someone familiar, a drinking buddy. Yet when did Joe become Jane? When does 'he' become 'she'? Does it all come down to the moment 'she' picks up her paycheck?

Questions of gender and identity also emerge in narratives of the AIDS epidemic. Indeed, as a small sample of media headlines reveal, familiar identities were ready and waiting for women from the beginning: the loyal companion who stands by her man ('AIDS VICTIM TO WED IN ST. PATRICK'S CATHEDRAL'); the scheming carrier who deliberately infects her male victim ('WIFE MURDERS HUBBY WITH AIDS COCKTAIL'); the protector of morals, whose draconian proposals offer the illusion of control; the Madonna ('BLESSED VIRGIN CURED MY AIDS, MAN SAYS'); the whore ('CINCY PROSTITUTES FEARED SPREADING AIDS'); the innocent victim ('Her sickness would have been easier to accept if she'd been a slut or a drug user', said Kimberley Bergalis's father, 'But she had done everything right'); the transparent vessel ('AIDS CARRIER'S BABY NOT INFECTED, HOSPITAL STATES'); and above all, the loving mom, wife, or caretaker whose presence serves to humanize and desexualize the infected (gay) man, a role she shares in photographs with stuffed animals and pets.

An effective response to an epidemic (as to any widespread cultural crisis) depends on the existence of identities for whom that epidemic is meaningful and stories that take up those identities and give them life. Though plentiful, the identities AIDS scripts for women have rarely worked to expand women's own awareness of the epidemic or to further social change. Rather, facts, information campaigns, even stories of sickness have served, sometimes inadvertently, to discourage women from engaging seriously with the epidemic. Women lack access not only to clear information, in other words, but also to the subject positions, narratives, and identities that could make sense of that information and act on it. And if we, ourselves, cannot make sense of AIDS, articulate its influence upon our lives, and shape interventions that embody our interests and perspectives, history holds out little promise that anyone else will do it for us. Instead, the direction of the epidemic will be influenced by the prevailing stereotypes and ongoing confusions about identity that still, after more than a decade of documented cases among women, encourage women to feel immune to a 'gay male disease'.

Perhaps we should not be surprised that the crisis of women and AIDS has been systematically neglected. As Clay Stephens has written, 'Most of the problems are not new; they are simply viewed through another set of distorted lenses. AIDS is a paradigm for the condition of women within our society.'[2] But it is now imperative that we look closely at AIDS commentary on gender and end that neglect. Without intervention, it is hard to be optimistic about women and AIDS in the United States. The current state of affairs is that we lack knowledge, social policy, and cultural consensus—in part because we lack conceptual coherence about the role of gender in HIV transmission and about the epidemic's impact on women, families, and society at large. Women are studied in the scholarly literature on AIDS as an index to something else: total numbers infected, extent of heterosexual spread, impact on childbearing and caretaking, clues to patterns of disease transmission, or proof that women of the 1990s are not what they seem. In the popular literature, AIDS primarily provides a new occasion for recycling old narratives out of women's historical role in epidemics and disease. [. . .]

[. . .] [L]ongstanding identity of AIDS as a 'gay disease' and a 'man's disease' has the effect of placing the burden on women themselves to prove their own significance—as spokespersons, as persons at risk, as objects worthy of scientific and medical inquiry, and as agents of social justice and political change. [. . .] [T]his has proved very difficult to do. The negative consequences are material and immediate: women encounter barriers to diagnosis and care, exclusion from treatment and social support programs, lack of information about sexuality and reproduction, lack of preventive technologies designed for women, and lack of resources and support services for women, children, and families. There are long-term consequences as well. Even as the AIDS crisis reveals the unreliability of everyday categories, those categories are being further codified in policies and regulations for special classes of women, including sex workers, poor women, lesbians, women in Third World countries, IV drug users, inmates, and childbearing women at large. The AIDS epidemic fuels a conservative agenda for women—marriage, family, children—and amplifies already vocal calls for protection and surveillance. For women, this includes court-ordered caesarean sections, penalties for health-care providers who provide contraceptive information, incarceration for drug-using pregnant women, and an end to legal abortion. Electing a new president and a different political party will not erase many years of successful conservative efforts—that will require organized collective political responses by and for women.

Fortunately, such a response appears to be underway at last. A number of projects suggest strategies for creating a strong political voice for women and, in the process, identities that enable them to address the AIDS epidemic effectively. One of the clearest examples was provoked by Gould's 1988 *Cosmopolitan* article.[3] Women in the New York chapter of the activist organization AIDS Coalition to Unleash Power (ACT UP) identified errors of fact, flawed assumptions, outdated statistics, and claims contradicted by their own knowledge and experience. To challenge Gould's misleading advice to women they began with their knowledge that women *were* infected with HIV and *were* dying of AIDS. Picketing the offices of *Cosmopolitan*'s New York publisher, they asserted that 'The COSMO girl CAN get AIDS', distributed flyers countering Gould's claims with extensive documentation, and urged the public to just 'Say No to Cosmo' by boycotting the magazine. To follow up, the women in ACT UP produced and distributed a documentary video called *Doctors, Liars, and Women: AIDS Activists Say No to* Cosmo, which recorded the debate as it continued in local and national media; they formed the ACT UP Women's Caucus, which organized subsequent actions; and they produced the book *Women, AIDS, and Activism*.[4]

The *Cosmopolitan* action marks a significant step forward in identifying the AIDS epidemic as an urgent women's health problem, as a significant social and political crisis, and as a premier symbolic battleground of our times where battles today shape policies that will affect us all tomorrow. *Doctors, Liars, and Women* proclaims women's right to represent themselves and tell their side of the story: *Women, AIDS, and Activism* places the AIDS epidemic within a broad feminist framework, relates AIDS issues to ongoing scientific, clinical, and social issues for women, and spells out the epidemic's negative impact on civil rights, equality in the workplace, childbearing and reproductive freedom, and other areas. [. . .]

At the heart of the joke about Joe and Jane with which I opened this essay is the question of identity, a complicated phenomenon we know less about than we think we do. Problems of identity—problems, that is, of whether or not something is 'the same as' something else—underlie many seemingly unrelated issues with regard to women and AIDS/HIV. As I have tried to suggest here, the fluidity, ambiguity, and questioning posited by the joke—not to mention the brutal social reality embodied by its punch line—are absent from most conceptions of gender that inform AIDS discourse, whether in medical journals, epidemiological surveillance reports, or popular culture. As I said at the outset, an effective response to an epidemic (as to any widespread cultural crisis) depends on the existence of identities for whom that epidemic (or crisis) is meaningful—and stories in which those identities are taken up and animated. I have also sought to show how identities and narratives about women and AIDS have tended to discourage an effective response. Although many identities for women are readily available in relation to AIDS, they are rarely useful or meaningful. Despite sporadic efforts at clarification, the question of gender and AIDS/HIV remains a problematic component in most domains of AIDS discourse, where established conceptions of women shape a cycle of research, representation, and analysis that perpetuates a view of AIDS as a man's disease and discourages sustained focus on women's issues. In the culture at large, flourishing stereotypes generate simultaneous visions of women as impervious to infection and diseased fantasy figures.

With a few notable exceptions, I have argued, women and AIDS is also a problematic component of feminist discourse. While many women's magazines and feminist journals have dutifully published their 'what women should know about AIDS' articles, the epidemic is still represented rather narrowly as a personal health risk which basic precautions can virtually eliminate. Faced with inconclusive data, conflicting media reports, and increasingly difficult efforts to preserve a working definition of sisterhood and feminist identity, women remain confused and, despite the rising body count, reluctant to add AIDS to an already overburdened agenda. Put another way, in feminist discourse the categories 'women with AIDS' and 'women with HIV' languish in the divide between foundationalist and constructionist accounts of gender.

What can we do? One challenge before us is to acknowledge the legitimacy and usefulness of treating identity as complicated, as something to be investigated rather than assumed. At the same time, we must take responsibility for the growing social, material reality of women with HIV and AIDS, a category strikingly unified by its predictable and negative social consequences. In the process of becoming Jane, Joe's identity may be negotiable; but when Jane picks up her paycheck, negotiation stops. These social consequences constitute another challenge we must reckon with. Finally, we must assert that the AIDS epidemic is a premiere symbolic battleground where war will be waged incessantly, where language and reality will continue to shape each other, where we can see the health-care system in action and work to change it, and where women's futures will in part be determined. Informed by a feminist analysis that takes its historical and cultural context seriously and specifies its tasks carefully, we must come to see the story of women and AIDS as a dense narrative about women's health and American society; economic opportunity and political power; sexuality and safety; law and transgression; individual autonomy and reproductive freedom; the right to social services and health-care resources; the deformities of the American health-care system; alliances with others; and about the significance of identity—including our own—in everyday life.

['AIDS, Identity, and the Politics of Gender', in Gretchen Bender and Timothy Druckrey, *Culture on the Brink: Ideologies of Technology* (Seattle: Bay Press, 1994), 129–43.]

This effort to apprehend the *rhetorical* power of Catharine MacKinnon's social theory of gender is compelled by an aim that exceeds critique of her depiction of women as always and only sexually violable, her pornography politics, or her arguments about the First Amendment. Insofar as MacKinnon's work has extraordinary political purchase, this essay seeks to discern something of the composition and constituency of this power in her theoretical project. How and why does MacKinnon's complicatedly radical political analysis and voice acquire such hold? And what are the possibilities that other feminisms could rival such power with analysis more multivalent in their representation of gender subordination and gender construction, more attentive to the race and class of gender, more compatible with the rich diversity of female sexual experience, more complex in their representations of sexuality and sexual power, more extravagant and democratic in their political vision? In other words, while MacKinnon might be 'wrong' about Marxism, gender, sexuality, power, the state, or the relation between freedom and equality, those issues are of less concern here than the potent order of 'truth' she produces. How did MacKinnon so successfully deploy a militant feminism during the 1980s, a decade markedly unsympathetic to all militancies to the left of center?

[...] Can a radical postfoundationalist feminist political discourse about women, sexuality, and the law—with its necessarily partial logics and provisional truths, situated knowledges, fluid subjects, and decentered sovereignty—work to claim power, or to contest hegemonic power, to the degree that MacKinnon's discourse does? Or do the commitments of postfoundationalist feminist analysis condemn it to a certain political marginalization, to permanent gadfly status, to a philosopher's self-consolation that she is on the side of 'truth' rather than power? In the domain of late modern political life, and especially the domain of the law, can political-theoretical strategies of subversion, displacement, proliferation, and resignification compare or compete with the kinds of systematic and ontological claims MacKinnon makes about the condition of women and the good for women?

[...] MacKinnon's thesis mirrors a hyperbolic expression of gender as sexuality in the late-twentieth-century United States and reveals the extent to which construction and regulation of gender by a panoply of discourses, activities, and distinctions other than sexuality have been sharply eroded and destabilized. These would include the privatization and pervasive feminization of reproductive work; a gendered division of labor predicated on the exchange between household labor and socialized production; gendered religious, political, and civic codes; and other sharply gendered spheres of activity and social norms—in short, all elements of the construction of gender that are institutionalized, hence enforced, elsewhere than through the organization of desire. The destabilization of these other domains of the production and regulation of gender lead not only MacKinnon but feminist theorists putatively quite different from her—those theorizing gender as performativity vis-à-vis heterosexual norms, for example—to read gender as almost wholly constituted by the (heterosexual) organization of *desire*.

While a clearly delineated and complexly arrayed sexual division of labor may have constituted regimes of gender—gendered social locations, productions of subjectivity, and mechanisms of subordination—more profoundly in other times and places, the culturally normative heterosexual organization of desire, including its pornographic commercial expression, emerges most fiercely inscribed in our own. [. . .]

I am suggesting that MacKinnon's theory of gender as fully constituted by sexuality and of pornography as the ultimate expression of male dominance is itself historically produced by, on the one hand, the erosion of other sites of gender production and gender effects, and on the other, the profusion, proliferation, and radical deprivatization and diffusion of sexuality in the late twentieth century. The phenomenon Marcuse called repressive desublimation, which Foucault reconceived as the production of a specific regime of sexuality, is what we might call the pornographic age that MacKinnon's theory 'mirrors' rather than historically or analytically decodes. So, too, does her social theory of gender mirror rather than deconstruct the *subjects* of heterosexual male pornography—both the male consumer and the female model—subjects that, we may speculate, function largely (and futilely) to shore up or stabilize a sexual/gender dominance itself destabilized by the erosions of other elements of gender subordination in the late twentieth century.

In other words, if not only gendered divisions of labor and activity, but a regime of sexual binarism—heterosexuality—itself is decentered by the political-economic-cultural forces of late modernity, then MacKinnon's theory of gender unwittingly consolidates gender out of symptoms of a crisis moment in male dominance. In this way, MacKinnon formulates as the deep, universal, and transhistorical structure of gender what is really a hyperpornographic expression: indeed, it marks the crisis attendant upon the transmutation from overdetermined gender dualism and gender subordination (here underspecified) to a present and future characterized by the erosion of compulsory heterosexuality itself as constitutive of everyday gender constructions.[1]

MacKinnon's move to read gender off of pornography, her construction of a social theory of gender that mirrors heterosexual male pornography, not only convenes a pervasively, totally, and singly determined gendered subject, it encodes the pornographic age as the truth rather than the hyperbole of gender production: it fails to read the $10 billion a year porn industry as a 'state of emergency' (as Nietzsche spoke of the hyper-rationality of classical Greek philosophy) of a male dominant heterosexual regime.[2] More-over, her move to read pornography as the literal and essential representa-tion of gendered heterosexuality precisely identifies the pornographic male consumer and pornographic female subject as ontologically male and female. In arguing that 'pornography literally means what it says',[3] MacKinnon not only begs questions about the workings of representation and fantasy, of hermeneutics and interpellation, she ontologizes pornography *as* gender. In short, MacKinnon's theory of gender mirrors the straight male pornography it means to criticize, a mirroring that manifests in a number of ways.

First, in MacKinnon's theory of gender as in the heterosexual male porn she analyzes, the subject positions of male and female are depicted as relent-lessly dualistic and absolute, figured literally, not metaphorically or qualified-ly, as subject and object, person and thing, dominant and subordinate: or, as Drusilla Cornell puts it in *Beyond Accommodation*, 'fuckor and fuckee'.[4]

Second, in MacKinnon's theory of gender as in the heterosexual male porn she analyzes, the subject positions of male and female are formed only and totally by sexuality. Not only does gender lack other constituents, but the making of gender is not seen to vary substantively across other formations and vectors of power—for example, race—except insofar as these differences are expressed sexually. Sexuality may be racialized, racial subordination may be sexualized; but differences among women dissolve when sexuality is grasped as the universal axis of subordination. [...]

Third, in MacKinnon's theory as in the heterosexual male porn she ana-lyzes, the sexual subject positions of male and female are also made one with the *subjectivity* of male and female, with the consequence that male and female subjectivities are totalized, dichotomized, and pervasively sexualized. [...]

Fourth, in MacKinnon's theory as in the pornography she analyzes, hetero-sexuality is the past, present, and eternal future of gender. If gender is sexuality, sexuality is always gendered and women are sex for men, then, for example, lesbian sexuality either doesn't exist, is sex for men, or imitates heterosexuality—all of which are indeed tropes of lesbian representation in straight male porn as well as MacKinnon's account of lesbianism. [...]

Finally, and here the ground is more speculative, MacKinnon's social theory of gender mirrors pornography in its prose structure and rhetorical effect, in a fashion similar to what Baudrillard identified as Marxism's mirror-ing of the *code* of political economy. The pornographic rhetorical structure of MacKinnon's writing and speech would appear to inhere in the insistent and pounding quality of her prose: in the rhythmic pulses of her simple subject-verb-object sentences in which a single point is incessantly reiterated, reworked, driven, and thrust at its audience; in an overburdened syllogistic structure, which makes the syllogistic logic more proliferative, intoxicating, overstimulating, agitated, and less contestable; in the literalism and force of her abstract claims—'pornography is that way'—which simultaneously structure the scene and permit any (man) his own imaginative entry into the scene; in the use of simple, active verbs, hyperbolic adverbs, and strategically deployed sentence fragments; in the slippage between representation and action; in the direct and personalized form of address; in the repeated insistence on gender, sexuality, and representation as 'the real'; and in the personification and activation of things or concepts. [. . .]

In short, in its rehearsal of a powerful underground (pornographic) code of gender and sexuality, reinscribing and exploiting the power of this code even while denouncing its contents, MacKinnon's theory permits easy cultural identification and recognition, giving her 'radicalism' a seductively familiar rather than threatening resonance and cultural location. In this way, her putative radicalism simultaneously sustains the pleasure of the familiar, the pleasure of the illicit, the pleasure of moralizing against the illicit, and the comforts of conservatism—gender is eternal and sexual pleasure is opprobrious—in an era of despair about substantive political transformation. [. . .]

From this perspective, it would appear that the very structure and categories of her theory—its tautological and totalizing dimensions, its dualisms and absolutes, its strange syllogisms and forced equivalences—articulate a profound late modern anxiety, channeling it into a certain militance while doing nothing to resolve its constituents. Thus the rhetorical force of MacKinnon's theory of gender may inhere as much in its homological refiguring of a late modern political despair as in its pornographic cadences, and perhaps especially in the potentially fascistic interplay of manipulated despair and libidinal arousal.

[*States of Injury: Power and Freedom in Late Modernity* (Princeton: Princeton University Press, 1995), 77–95.]

SUSAN STURGIS

63 Bisexual Feminism: Challenging the Splits

Bisexual-conscious feminist theory and feminist-conscious bisexual theory have the potential to challenge western ways of thinking; and these western models form the basis not only of the oppression of bisexuals, lesbians and gay men, not only of women, but of the very construction of oppression. Western philosophy conceptualises the world along deep splits. Fragmenting human from animal, man from woman, mind from body, self from other, reason from emotion, culture from nature, enquirer from object of enquiry, and black from white, metaphysical dualism imposes polarities on what is in reality interconnected and interdependent. The splits are created in a context of domination, one half of each split pair privileged—and assigned gender. Human, mind, self, reason, culture, enquirer, white become masculine.

Animal, body, other, emotion, nature, object of enquiry, and black are deemed 'feminine', subordinate to their 'masculine' counterparts. A recent split, created by nineteenth century science, is heterosexual versus homosexual. Heterosexual is conceptualised as masculine, homosexual as feminine. This association of homosexuality—male homosexuality—with the feminine contributes to the cultural erasure of lesbianism.

By challenging this heterosexual/homosexual split and the construction of the 'sexual other', the bisexual movement provides a theoretical framework to resist all dualisms and constructions of 'otherness'—constructions which fracture our selves and society, and enable hatred and violence of all kinds to continue. That bisexuality resists these splits is hinted at in the anxieties bisexuals create for both heterosexuals and lesbians and gays. Biphobia is often articulated around fears of contamination, vividly demonstrated in the conflation of biphobia and AIDS phobia. Heterosexuals accuse bisexual men of spreading AIDS to them, while some lesbians accuse bisexual women of carrying AIDS into the lesbian community. The assumption on the part of both heterosexuals and lesbians here is that they exist in a world apart from each other, and that when bisexuals inappropriately cross the boundary, death results.

The destruction bisexuals are accused of wreaking is sometimes metaphorical: some lesbians and gay men, embracing the straight/queer split as a source of personal and community identity, accuse bisexuals of destroying the 'purity' of their movement and community through a presence which they biphobically view as confused, confusing, and straight-tainted. Much to the anxiety of those who imagine themselves on one or the other 'side', bisexual existence brings the straight and gay worlds together, attesting to the existence of a sexual continuum, rather than two separate worlds separated by an impenetrable fence.

After the medical establishment's creation of homosexuality as a phenomenon worthy of examination, mixed-gender relationships came to be seen as a biological 'truth' and same-gender relationships as a biological error. Homosexuality and bisexuality were viewed as illnesses. Heterosexuality became medically compulsory. In a curious parallel, in the late 1960s feminist resurgence, a strand of feminism emerged which viewed women's oppression as universal and fundamental. Radical feminism's emphasis on examining how women are oppressed through sex and reproduction gave it decidedly biological overtones, at times to the point of being as biologically determinist as conservative anti-feminism. Viewing men *qua* biological men as the problem naturally led to the political practice of separatism. Some radical feminists even came to see same-gender relationships as a political necessity and mixed-gender relationships as a political error, gender treachery. Thus radical feminism answered enforced heterosexuality with enforced homosexuality.

Both conservative anti-feminism and radical feminism demand that certain behaviour be determined by gender. But bisexual feminism resists this dualistic, polarised conception of gender. It queers up imposed gender order, rejecting the idea that the gender you fuck is determined by the gender you are. It broadens the zone of sexual liberation.

By its inherent rejection of gender separatism, bisexual feminism also avoids the radical feminist trap of biological determinism, in which the assumption is made that women are oppressed and men oppress because of their biology. Because it acknowledges that sexism is a basic problem and that men are a part of its world, bisexual feminism demands that men be included in any feminist change project. Bisexual feminism rejects the fatalism of both conservative anti-feminists and radical feminists. It rejects the conservative view that says women's oppression is biologically inevitable, so nothing can be done about it. Equally, because it insists on including men in our lives in deeply personal ways—out of choice, not out of compulsion—it requires political engagement with men in the hope that change is possible. In so doing bisexual feminism rejects the fatalism of radical feminists that says men's oppressiveness is biologically inevitable, with gender separatism the only option for freedom.

Some nonfeminist bisexuals might query the need for a bisexual *feminist* movement. If we are to work toward tearing down the divisions, why not bisexual *humanism*?

Embracing a 'we're-really-all-the-same humanism' obscures the very real power structure of male domination. Certainly men are also hurt by sexist dualism, just as whites are hurt by racism and straights by heterosexism. But to imply that men's experience of male domination is the same as women's, or whites' experience of racism is the same as blacks', is to trivialise the very real and immediate violence experienced by those who happen to fall on the subordinate side of the split. Men—and all of us who find ourselves on the privileged side of a division—need to acknowledge our privilege in order to struggle against it. Ignoring or denying the split won't make it, or the power imbalance, go away—that requires struggle conscious of existing realities. By embracing bisexual *feminism* over 'humanism', I acknowledge and challenge the existing power differential while at the same time challenging the structure that allows the imbalance to continue. [...]

The bisexual movement is burgeoning. It addresses cultural assumptions of dualism that obscure a real underlying continuum, while feminism challenges the power differentials resulting from dualism. A theory and movement— bisexual feminism—that combines these perspectives has the potential to disrupt the very structure of oppression.

['Bisexual Feminism: Challenging the Splits', in Sharon Rose, Cris Stevens, *et al.*, *Bisexual Horizons: Politics, Histories, Lives* (London: Lawrence and Wishart, 1996), 41–4.]

Section 5

Visualities

INTRODUCTION

> Feminist cultural theories of the image have moved...from an initial denunciation of stereotyped images of women to...an assessment of the productive role of representation in the construction of subjectivity, femininity and sexuality.
>
> Griselda Pollock

> **Visuality** (*Carlyle*) the quality or state of being visible to the mind: a mental picture.
>
> *Chambers Twentieth Century Dictionary*

'[T]o expose the fixed nature of sexual identity as a fantasy and, in the same gesture, to trouble, break up, or rupture the visual field before our eyes.' This, claims Jacqueline Rose, is one of the central tasks of an art which explores the 'presence of the sexual in representation' (p. 388). Such feminist explorations of sexuality in the image entail both political and aesthetic approaches. For scrutinizing the image involves not only holding 'the image accountable for the reproduction of norms', but also—shifting the focus from content to form—examining aesthetic structure. At stake in much feminist debate about visualities is the question of whether the former political evaluation of images works to veto engagement with the latter aesthetic response, thereby denying feminists the possibility of deriving pleasure from visual form. 'Is it possible', asks Annette Kuhn, 'for women/feminists to take pleasure in visual representation?' (p. 407). It is this question that has increasingly come to preoccupy feminist visual practice and criticism, but it was another—more politically direct question—which tended to dominate in earlier second-wave feminist debates over visual representation: 'What kinds of resistance to the normalizing effectivities of representation are available to feminism?' (p. 407–8).

Kuhn outlines three distinct feminist responses to this question: censorship; feminist practices of representation; feminist critical practice. Echoing Wendy Brown's critique of MacKinnon, Kuhn argues that the first of these strategies—censorship—is 'complicit in those very normalizing processes which feminism seeks to resist' (p. 408) by acknowledging and enforcing the power of the image. More productively, the second strategy—that of feminist practices of representation—requires a 'transformation of vision', resisting the normalizing discourses of gender through negotiation and subversion, rather than via simple refusal. For example, Abigail Solomon-Godeau writes: 'In choosing to assert rather than deny or avoid the fetish status of the female body, Woodman's photographs are vulnerable to the charge of collusion with those very operations. I would argue, however, that through strategies of defamiliarization and disruption—excess, displacement, disordering—Woodman exposes the overdetermination of the body as signifier, thereby significantly altering the spectator's relationship to it' (p. 435). The third strategy—that of feminist critical practice—is argued by Kuhn, echoing Flax's comments in Section 2 about the critical distance needed to bring about political change—to be a valuable political practice also.

In these second two strategies one can see an active feminist aesthetic and political intervention, distinct from the visual (though not political) passivity implicit in the censorship approach. The focus of feminist engagement with the image moves from women as observed, as passive object, as represented, to women as producer, as actively creative subject, as representing. Whereas political concerns tend to dominate aesthetic ones in the censorship approach, the adoption of transformative and critical visual strategies requires an integrated aesthetico-political engagement.

Such feminist visual practices require that one considers the issues of identity and authorship in relation to gender. For the move to actively creating feminist images signals a shift in focus away from the image itself to the complex dynamics surrounding the production and reception of the image. As Solomon-Godeau asks: 'Do women see differently, be it as artists or spectators . . . Is the act of looking or imaging, because active, inevitably a masculine position?' (p. 436). In asking these questions, and exploring their implications visually, feminists have drawn extensively on psychoanalytic models. For as Rose notes, 'the relationship between viewer and scene is always one of fracture, partial identification, pleasure and distrust' (p. 388). The psychoanalytic (primarily Freudian and Lacanian) emphasis on fantasy provides a sophisticated theoretical framework from which to interrogate these relationships.

Exploration of these questions is also argued to have worked to repoliticize the aesthetic. 'One of the most important achievements of the women's movement', states Rita Felski, 'has been to repoliticize art on the level of both production and reception' (p. 423). This politicization should not be viewed as a return to a reductive assumption that aesthetic categories merely or directly reflect political ideologies. Whilst this functionalist approach does constitute an element of recent feminist practices, considerations of plural signification and aesthetic pleasure are more symptomatic of recent feminisms. E. Ann Kaplan, for example, examines 'the deployment of television as itself a unique kind of apparatus, very different from the filmic one'. She considers, in particular, 'the implications of the television imaginary specifically for women' become integral rather than antithetical. As Felski argues, the relation between art and ideology is 'appropriately conceptualized in terms of a continuum in which the aesthetic function may be more or less dominant but always intermeshes with the ideological conditions governing the text's own historical location' (p. 425).

One image that is continuously and obsessively subject to transformation and critical evaluation is the female body itself—'a sort of bizarre art object' (p. 455) as Kate Chedgzoy says of Frida Kahlo's body. The visual recreation and representation of the female body—whether it be painterly (as discussed by Chedgzoy), physical (as discussed by Kuhn), or technological (as discussed by Kaplan)—is perhaps the primary site of both visual normalization and resistance for feminisms. As Kuhn points out, 'the naturalness of the body is called into question by its inscription within a certain kind of performance.' The dense network of visual discourses shaping the female body—a kind of perfected icon—attests to the impossibility of clearly distinguishing between representation and the real. 'In so far as the history of Cher's body has meaning at all,' writes Susan Bordo, 'it has meaning not as the "original" over which a false copy has been laid, but as a defect which has been corrected. It becomes constructed as "defect" precisely because the new image is the dominant reality, the normalising standard against which all else is judged' (p. 452). The history of the image in western culture reveals the contradictory aspects of the role of representation in the construction of subjectivity, femininity, and sexuality. In 'Just Like a Woman', Godeau points out how Woodman 'marks' the body 'in ways that conjure the impulse to debase and violate which parallels the impulse to worship and adore.' (p. 440). As both subject and object of the representational discourses of gendered identity, women constantly re-image/re-imagine themselves—not freely but within 'the cracks of dominant norms'. Feminist practices of representation embody a transformation of vision, seeking in different ways to expose or bridge the gap between women as spectacle and women as historical subjects. Recent feminist recognition of the political import of these aesthetic negotiations of the body may indeed go some way to addressing the issue—posed by Elizabeth Wilson in the previous section—as to why politics seems to have to be expressed in aesthetic terms. It also contextualizes the current feminist preoccupation with the new possibilities for such negotiations of the body opened by new technological developments.

Freud often related the question of sexuality to that of visual representation. Describing the child's difficult journey into adult sexual life, he would take as his model little scenarios, or the staging of events, which demonstrated the complexity of an essentially visual space, moments in which perception *founders* (the boy child refuses to believe the anatomical difference that he sees)[1] or in which pleasure in looking tips over into the register of *excess* (witness to a sexual act in which he reads his own destiny, the child tries to interrupt by calling attention to his presence).[2] Each time the stress falls on a problem of seeing. The sexuality lies less in the content of what is seen than in the subjectivity of the viewer, in the relationship between what is looked at and the developing sexual knowledge of the child. The relationship between viewer and scene is always one of fracture, partial identification, pleasure and distrust. As if Freud found the aptest analogy for the problem of our identity as human subjects in failures of vision or in the violence which can be done to an image as it offers itself to view. For Freud, with an emphasis that has been picked up and placed at the centre of the work of Jacques Lacan, our sexual identities as male or female, our confidence in language as true or false, and our security in the image we judge as perfect or flawed, are fantasies. And these archaic moments of disturbed visual representation, these troubled scenes, which expressed and unsettled our groping knowledge in the past, can now be used as theoretical prototypes to unsettle our certainties once again. Hence one of the chief drives of an art which today addresses the presence of the sexual in representation—to expose the fixed nature of sexual identity as a fantasy and, in the same gesture, to trouble, break up, or rupture the visual field before our eyes.

The encounter between psychoanalysis and artistic practice is therefore *staged*, but only in so far as that staging has *already taken place*. It is an encounter which draws its strength from that repetition, working like a memory trace of something we have been through before. It gives back to repetition its proper meaning and status: not lack of originality or something merely derived (the commonest reproach to the work of art), nor the more recent practice of appropriating artistic and photographic images in order to undermine their previous status; but repetition as insistence, that is, as the constant pressure of something hidden but not forgotten—something that can only come into focus now by blurring the field of representation where our normal forms of self-recognition take place. [. . .]

Artists engaged in sexual representation (representation *as* sexual) come in at precisely this point, calling up the sexual component of the image, drawing out an emphasis that exists *in potentia* in the various instances they inherit and of which they form a part.[3] Their move is not therefore one of (moral) corrective. They draw on the tendencies they also seek to displace, and clearly belong, for example, within the context of that postmodernism which demands that reference, in its problematised form, re-enter the frame. But the emphasis on sexuality produces specific effects. First, it adds to the concept of cultural artefact or stereotype the political imperative of feminism which holds the image accountable for the reproduction of norms. Secondly, to this feminist demand for scrutiny of the image, it adds the idea of a sexuality which goes beyond the issue of content to take in the parameters of visual form (not just what we see but how we see—visual space as more than the domain of simple recognition). The image therefore submits to the sexual reference, but only in so far as reference itself is questioned by the work of the image. And the aesthetics of pure from are implicated in the less pure pleasures of looking, but these in turn are part of an aesthetically extraneous political space. The arena is simultaneously that of aesthetics and sexuality, and art and sexual politics. The link between sexuality and the image produces a particular dialogue which cannot be covered adequately by the familiar opposition between the formal operations of the image and a politics exerted from outside.

The engagement with the image therefore belongs to a political intention. It is an intention which has also inflected the psychoanalytic and literary theories on which such artist draw. The model is not one of applying psycho-analysis to the work of art (what application could there finally be which does not reduce one field to the other or inhibit by interpretation the potential meaning of both?). Psychoanalysis offers a specific account of sexual differ-ence but its value (and also its difficulty) for feminism, lies in the place assigned to the woman in that differentiation. In his essay on Leonardo, Freud himself says that once the boy child sees what it is to be a woman, he will 'tremble for his masculinity' henceforth.[4] If meaning oscillates when a castrato comes onto the scene, our sense must be that it is in the normal image of the man that our certainties are invested and, by implication, in that of the woman that they constantly threaten collapse.

A feminism concerned with the question of looking can therefore turn this theory around and stress the particular and limiting opposition of male and female which any image seen to be flawless is serving to hold in place. More simply, we know that women are meant to *look* perfect, presenting a seamless image to the world so that the man, in that confrontation with difference, can avoid any apprehension of lack. The position of woman as fantasy therefore depends on a particular economy of vision (the importance of 'images of women' might take on its fullest meaning from this).[5] Perhaps this is also why only a project which comes via feminism can demand so unequivocally of the image that it renounce all pretensions to a narcissistic perfection of form.

At the extreme edge of this investigation, we might argue that the fantasy of absolute sexual difference, in its present guise, could be upheld only from the point when painting restricted the human body to the eye.[6] That would be to give the history of the image in Western culture a particularly heavy weight to bear. For, even if the visual image has indeed been one of the chief vehicles through which such a restriction has been enforced, it could only operate like a law which always produces the terms of its own violation. It is often forgotten that psychoanalysis describes the psychic law to which we are subject, but only in terms of its *failing*. This is important for a feminist (or any radical) practice which has often felt it necessary to claim for itself a wholly other psychic and representational domain. Therefore, if the visual image in its aesthetically acclaimed form serves to maintain a particular and oppressive mode of sexual recognition, it does so only partially and at a cost. Our previous history is not the petrified block of a singular visual space since, looked at obliquely, it can always be seen to contain its moments of unease.[7] We can surely relinquish the monolithic view of that history, if doing so allows us a form of resistance which can be articulated *on this side of* (rather than beyond) the world against which it protests.

Among Leonardo's early sketches, Freud discovers the heads of laughing women, images of exuberance which then fall out of the great canon of his art. Like Leonardo's picture of the sexual act, these images appear to unsettle Freud as if their pleasure somehow correlated with the discomfort of the sexual drawing (the sexual drawing through its failure, the heads of laughing women for their excess). These images, not well known in Leonardo's canon, now have the status of fragments, but they indicate a truth about the tradition which excludes them, revealing the presence of something strangely insistent to which these artists return. 'Teste di femmine, che ridono'[8]—laughter is not the emphasis here, but the urgent engagement with the question of sexuality persists now, as it did then. It can no more be seen as the beginning, than it should be the end, of the matter.

[*Sexuality in the Field of Vision* (London: Verso, 1986), 227–33.]

KAJA SILVERMANN

65 The Acoustic Mirror

Feminist film theory and criticism have manifested only an intermittent and fleeting interest in the status of authorship within the classic text. One of the earliest essays to approach authorship through a critique of sexual difference, was, of course, Laura Mulvey's 'Visual Pleasure and Narrative Cinema' (1975). Although the first half of that essay focuses on spectatorship, its second half uses the notion of the author as a mechanism for distinguishing between two very different specular regimes, regimes which exceed the 'intratextual' relations of which Nowell-Smith speaks, and which it associates with Sternberg and Hitchcock. Mulvey argues that there are moments in Sternberg's films when no fictional gaze mediates the spectator's access to Dietrich's image, and where the construction of that image as a fetish cannot be explained through an ideological spillage from the look of a character onto the look of the camera, implying instead an authorial eye behind the visual apparatus:

Sternberg plays down the illusion of screen depth; his screen tends to be one-dimensional, as light and shade, lace, steam, foliage, net, streamers, etc., reduce the visual field. There is little or no mediation through the eyes of the main protagonist. On the contrary, shadowy presences like La Bessière in *Morocco* act as surrogates for the director, detached as they are from audience identification.[1]

Mulvey also positions Hitchcock as the speaking subject of his films, attributing their voyeurism to the intensity of their author's obsessions, noting that 'Hitchcock has never concealed his interest in voyeurism, cinematic and noncinematic' (p. 15).

In an even earlier essay, 'Women's Cinema as Counter-Cinema' (1973), Claire Johnston emphasizes the importance of the *auteur* theory for feminism, suggesting that its polemics have 'challenged the entrenched view of Hollywood as monolithic', and have made it possible to see that the 'image of woman' does not assume the same status in all films made within that system of production.[2] Johnston also poses the possibility of female authorship within classic cinema by juxtaposing the names of Dorothy Arzner and Ida Lupino with the ubiquitous Howard Hawkes and John Ford.

In a monograph published in 1975, Johnston elaborates more fully upon the notion that Arzner's films bear the marks of female authorship. However, although she argues that what she calls 'the discourse of the woman' provides Arzner's work with its 'structural coherence', she is far from attributing to that discourse the systematicity which figures so centrally within Bellour's account of male authorship, or even the binary logic which Wollen identifies with the films of certain male *auteurs*. Johnston suggests that the female authorial voice makes itself heard only through disruptions and dislocations within the textual economy of classic cinema—i.e., *through breaks within its systematicity and binary logic*. Significantly, Johnston suggests that these disruptions and dislocations may occur at the level of the *histoire*, as well as at that of the *discours*.

In Arzner's work, the discourse of the woman, or rather her attempt to locate it and make it heard, is what gives the text its structural coherence, while at the same time rendering the dominant discourse of the male fragmented and incoherent. The central female protagonists react against and thus transgress the male discourse which entraps them.[3]

Sandy Flitterman has also suggested that feminist theory would do well to rethink authorship within the Hollywood text, which she conceptualizes in terms of discourse. In 'Woman, Desire, and the Look: Feminism and the Enunciative Apparatus in Cinema' (1978), she stresses the importance of Bellour's work on enunciation in *Marnie*, and argues that any foregrounding of authorship within the classic text functions at least momentarily to subvert 'the subject-effect that the apparatus is designed to produce and to conceal' by both raising and answering the question: 'Who is speaking?'[4]

However, one looks in vain to the feminist work published in *Camera Obscura* for a further elaboration of this point. Although that work is heavily indebted to Metz's and Bellour's notion of film-as-discourse, it largely occludes the role of the author within dominant narrative cinema. One of the most striking examples of this occlusion is Jacqueline Suter's 'Feminine Discourse in *Christopher Strong*'. Published in the same issue of *Camera Obscura* as 'Alternation, Segmentation, Hypnosis', that essay is in many respects a direct extension of Bellour's work on Hollywood cinema.[5] There is, however, one crucial difference: Suter makes absolutely no room in her discussion for the authorial subject. Indeed, the name 'Dorothy Arzner' is mentioned only once, along with the date of *Christopher Strong*. This is surprising, and not only because it marks a point of departure from the Bellourian model. Arzner was, after all, one of only two women to direct sound films in Hollywood during the studio period, a fact that would seem of some relevance to a feminist analysis of one of her films—especially when the stated aim of that analysis is to uncover a feminine discourse. However, instead of looking for ways in which Arzner might be said to 'speak' *Christopher Strong* differently from the ways in which Hitchcock 'speaks' *Marnie*, Suter focuses on two distinct and seemingly anonymous levels of the text—on what she calls the 'patriarchal discourse', and on what she calls the 'feminine discourse'.

Because of the way she conceptualizes each of these discourses, Suter's feminist reading would have to be characterized as dystopian. In effect, she associates the 'patriarchal discourse' with the film's formal and narrative articulation, and its 'feminine discourse' with the voices and transgressive desires of two of its female characters, Cynthia and Monica. Because Suter assumes enunciation to be absolutely coterminous with that formal and narrative articulation, the 'patriarchal discourse' emerges as a metalanguage, capable of neutralizing, any disruptions at the level of character or narrative, while the 'feminine discourse' is consigned in a completely unproblematical way to the inside of the diegesis. Suter at no point broaches the possibility that the latter discourse might also provide mechanisms through which an author 'outside' the text could 'speak' her subjectivity—the possibility, that is, that authorship might be inscribed not merely through the camera, or such an obviously reflexive diegetic indicator as the look, but through those forms of identification and textual organization which are generally assumed to be 'secondary', and which hinge upon a variety of characterological and narrative devices. Her theoretical model thus closely replicates the Hollywood model, which identifies the male voice with enunciative exteriority, and the female voice with diegetic interiority.

Suter's textual analysis is extremely persuasive, and it is difficult to argue with the conclusions she draws from it. However, the presupposition that *Christopher Strong* is enunciated like any other classic Hollywood film—i.e., from an exclusively male speaking position—guides and coerces her reading. The very different reading of Arzner's work proposed by Claire Johnston is clearly made possible by the assumption that an emphatically female authorial voice at least to some degree speaks Arzner's films, and that there can never be an absolutely smooth fit between such a voice and the dominant Hollywood model. This may very well be a situation where the cinematic apparatus in its complex totality speaks the film one way, in terms of the systematicity and binary logic that Suter notes, dominating and determining what has been widely taken to be the enunciative level, but where authorial desire seeks out another kind of language, finds a way of expressing itself through diegetic elements. The debate around *Christopher Strong* may also provide the occasion to rethink the absolute priority that recent film theory has given to cinematic specificity, particularly camera distance, angle, and movement and shot-to-shot relationships, and to consider whether there may not be enunciative elements elsewhere, as well—enunciative elements which can best be uncovered through returning to the issue of authorship, and by reposing the question: 'Who (or what) is speaking?' To assume, as Suter seems to do, that the cinematic apparatus is the only conceivable 'speaker' of a Hollywood film is to risk sealing over all kinds of localized resistance, which—as Foucault tells us—may well be the only form resistance can possibly take.[6]

Not surprisingly, this tendency to think of dominant cinema in monolithically phallic terms leads Suter to reject that cinema altogether:

Undoubtedly, the fact that we can locate certain formal transgressions in a film advances our knowledge of what might constitute a feminine discourse. But we should be aware that isolated interruptions do not necessarily deconstruct the narrative discourse in any significant way. It seems that a systematic rethinking of the entire terms of narrative logic, a reformulation of its elements into an order different from what has come to be known as the classic text, may allow the feminine to express itself more forcefully.[7]

What Suter proposes in place of *Christopher Strong* is *Jeanne Dielman, 23 Quai du Commerce, 1080 Bruxelles* (1975), a film whose formal as well as thematic operations deviate markedly from the classic paradigm. Significantly, the turn to experimental cinema marks the reemergence of the author. Chantal

Akerman figures conspicuously in this part of Suter's analysis, both as the director of *Jeanne Dielman* and as its enunciator ('Akerman, in showing a woman's daily routine in all its banality, breaks with convention because these images do not necessarily function to advance the narrative. . . . Akerman says that she found a plot *because* she wanted to show certain gestures in women's lives that are customarily left out of films').[8]

I have dwelt at such length upon Suter's extremely interesting essay for several reasons. To begin with, it gives new force to Bellour's suggestion that the systematicity of classic cinema 'operates very precisely at the expense of woman'—in this case, of the woman director. It may well be impossible to locate a female authorial voice within a Hollywood film by means of the strategies Bellour has devised for locating the male authorial voice. No film, after all, is entirely 'spoken' by its ostensible author, and in the case of dominant cinema, there are an enormous number of other productive elements, not the least of which is a whole textual system which often persists intransigently from one directorial corpus to another. Only a director 'speaking' from a position as smoothly aligned with the cinematic apparatus as Hitchcock—i.e., from a position of phallic dominance—would be able to identify his own 'vision' so fully with the textual system of Hollywood that the latter can seem the extension of the former. Other authorial subjects might well find themselves speaking against the weight of the textual system through which their films are largely articulated. What I am trying to suggest is that if authorial enunciation within the classic film text continues to be as insistently equated with that text's macrologic as it is within Bellourian segmentation, the theorist may quite simply be unable to 'hear' authorial voices that speak against the operations of dominant meaning, since those voices are much likelier to manifest themselves through isolated formal and diegetic irregularities than through formal systematicity.

A second reason why I have so conspicuously featured the Suter essay is that it dramatizes certain tendencies that are indicative of much recent writing on cinema by women. To the degree that feminist theory and criticism of the late seventies and the eighties have concerned themselves centrally with authorship, they have shifted attention away from the classic text to experimental cinema, and specifically to experimental cinema made by women. The author often emerges within the context of these discussions as a largely untheorized category, placed definitively 'outside' the text, and assumed to be the punctual source of its sounds and images. A certain nostalgia for an unproblematic agency permeates much of the writing to which I refer. There is no sense in which the feminist author, like her phallic counterpart, might be constructed in and through discourse—that she might be inseparable from the desire that circulates within her texts, investing itself not only in their formal articulation, but in recurring diegetic elements.

A brief essay by Janet Bergstrom on *Jeanne Dielman* is a case in point.[9] Bergstrom contends that there are two discourses in Akerman's film—one feminist, and the other deriving from a suppressed or 'acculturated' femininity. The first of these discourses is that 'spoken' by the director herself through the 'permissive' look of the camera, and the second is that associated with the character of Jeanne Dielman. Bergstrom argues that in eschewing the logic of the shot/reverse shot, the film works both to foreground the feminist discourse and to keep it separate from the feminine discourse. There would thus seem to be no possibility of 'contamination' or slippage from one side to the other. Bergstrom further isolates the author from her central female character by referring to her in quick succession as a 'marked controller' and a 'controlling eye'.[10]

I am not nearly as certain as Bergstrom that Jeanne Dielman manages to distinguish so sharply between feminism and femininity, or that the author 'outside' the text occupies the position of a transcendental seer, resting in easy detachment from the woman whose gestures are so meticulously recorded. To do Bergstrom justice, her own language ultimately works to erode the absoluteness of the division she draws, and to suggest that the feminist author is at least partially defined through her female protagonist. She characterizes the relationship between Akerman's stationary camera and Jeanne Dielman as 'obsessive' and 'fascinated',[11] adjectives which point to a certain psychic spillage between author and character. That spillage indicates that the ostensible object of speech is in this case also the subject of speech, and as such at least partly constitutive of the author-as-speaking-subject, even though the camera never adopts Jeanne Dielman's point of view.

As with most critiques, there is a barely concealed polemic here. I have been arguing over the last few pages for two rather contrary things—for a greater theoretical attentiveness to the ways in which authorship is both deployed and limited within the experimental text, and for the development of hermeneutic strategies capable of foregrounding rather than neutralizing female authorship within the classic film, where it is in danger of being occluded altogether. Of course, the obvious problem with respect to the second of these goals is that so few Hollywood films carry a female directorial signature. How is the feminist writer to proceed?

One possible solution to this difficulty is suggested by Tania Modleski in a chapter of her book *The Women Who Knew Too Much*. The chapter in question, 'Woman and the Labyrinth', focuses on the relationship between Hitchcock's *Rebecca* (1940) and the Daphne du Maurier novel on which it was based. Modleski comments upon Hitchcock's reluctance to claim that film, which was assigned to him by Selznick, as his own, and some of the subsequently deleted scenes in the script through which he attempted to 'vomit out' a 'whole school of feminine literature'.[12] What emerges from this discussion is a sense of the way in which even a classic film might be riven by conflicting authorial systems, in this case one 'male' and the other 'female'. But Modleski pushes her analysis even further than this, arguing that through his forced identification with du Maurier, Hitchcock found one of the great subjects of his later films—the 'potential terror involved in identification itself, especially identification with a woman'. This observation has important ramifications for our understanding of Hitchcock's status as *auteur*, indicating that his own authorial system may be far more heterogeneous and divided than Bellour can ever have imagined, and that it may, in fact, contain a female voice as one of its constituent although generally submerged elements.

Modleski bases her case not only on Truffaut's interview with Hitchcock, and the exchanges around the making of *Rebecca* that took place between Selznick and Hitchcock, but on the narrative organization of the film itself, which she persuasively shows to hinge upon the whole problematic of identification with the mother. The telling detail which brings this problematic definitively around again to the question of authorship is the fact that the character who most fully represents the mother—Rebecca—figures insistently throughout the film as an 'absent one' whose signature dominates the image track, but who herself escapes visibility. As such, it seems to me, she functions as a strikingly literal diegetic surrogate for the speaking subject, and hence very precisely as the subject of speech. What I am suggesting, in other words, is that Rebecca stands in for Hitchcock, in much the same way that Mark Rutland does in *Marnie*, and that in so doing she re-en-genders his authorial subjectivity.

Another strategy, deployed with very interesting results by Lea Jacobs in an article on *Now, Voyager*, is to shift the emphasis so sharply away from systematicity and textual macro-logic to disruption and contradiction as in effect to *reauthor* the classic film from the site of its (feminist) reception. This project has much in common with that Barthesian undertaking whereby the 'readerly' text yields to the *writerly* one, in that it shifts productivity away from the ostensible author to the side of the reader, and places itself on the side of heterogeneity and contradiction rather than unity. However, rather than working to disclose the chorus of cultural voices within the text, it strives to install the female voice at the site of a very qualified and provisional origin (and one which, I would argue, is once again defined through the subject of speech)—the voice, that is, of the female critic or theorist.

I speak of this project as though it were an overt and conscious one, but Jacob's reauthorship of Rapper's film can be glimpsed only indirectly, through the interpretive process whereby Charlotte is shown to supplant Dr. Jacquith as the speaker of her 'own' subjectivity. Her discussion focuses attention on that sequence in *Now, Voyager* where Charlotte looks at her image in the café window as the camera cuts back and forth between her and the reflected spectacle. This sequence, Jacobs argues, becomes the occasion whereby the female protagonist 'takes the enunciating position with respect to herself through an identification with a man', and so becomes 'a self-sufficient sexual and discursive configuration'—something which is seen as disturbing both to the shot-to-shot organization of the films, and to the constitution of the couple which is the form of narrative closure.[13] 'Now, Voyager: Some Problems of Enunciation and Sexual Difference' mimics this disturbance even as it in a sense creates it. Jacobs, in other words, enacts a discursive resistance to dominant cinema precisely through the resistance which she constitutes Charlotte as having. Charlotte thus functions not just as an enunciator within the diegesis, but as the subject of the speech whereby Jacobs rewrites Now, Voyager, and hence as a stand-in for the feminist theorist. [. . .]

Authorial subjectivity is inscribed into the cinematic text in two primary ways. The first kind of authorial inscription can best be described through a further elaboration of the Benvenistian model, with its distinction between the speaking subject and the subject of speech, but since it hinges upon a psychic mechanism about which linguistics has little to say—the psychic mechanism of identification—it will be necessary to supplement that model with psychoanalysis. The second kind of authorial inscription assumes a rather more dynamic and less easily localized form; it is the libidinal coherence that the films by a particular director can sometimes be said to have—the desire that circulates there, more or less perceptibly.

Insofar as a filmmaker can be said to function as one of the enunciators of the works that bear his or her name, those works will contain certain sounds, images, characterological motifs, narrative patterns, and/or formal configurations which provide the cinematic equivalent of the linguistic markers through which subjectivity is activated. However, the linguistic model is insufficient to account for the relationship which is thereby set up between the author 'inside' the text and the author 'outside' the text. Let us look, by way of example, at the most obvious of authorial references.

A director may turn the camera on his or her face, or the tape recorder on his or her voice, and incorporate the results into a film in the guise of a visual representation, a voice-over, a voice-off, or a synchronized sound and image 'totality'. Such an authorial citation would seem the closest of cinematic equivalents to the first-person pronoun. However, it also differs from that shifter in one crucial way: whereas the relation between 'I' and the speaker who deploys that signifier is based upon arbitrary convention, the relation between the cinematic image of a filmmaker and the actual filmmaker is based upon similitude; it is an iconic representation, and therefore more easily confused with what it designates.

Of course, this is not to suggest that the image is an ontological extension of the material reality it mimics. This is so far from being the case that it actually facilitates something which is in no way intrinsic to the 'original'—authorial subjectivity. Indeed, so far from being a mere reflection of the author 'outside' the text, it could reasonably be said to constitute him or her as such, in much the same way that the mirror reflection (retroactively) installs identity in the same child.

It is by now a truism of film theory that movies construct viewing subjects through identification. It seems to me that authorial subjects can be similarly constructed, albeit through a wider variety of textual supports than have been so far adduced for their spectatorial counterparts. Identity is, after all, impossible not only outside the symbolic, but outside the imaginary. Even an image which seems self-evidently part of the individual it depicts—which seems nothing more than his or her reflection or photographic imprint—can be claimed by that individual only through identification. And identification, as the writer of the *Ecrits* cautions us, inevitably turns upon misrecognition.

Through its intimate conflation of the author 'inside' the text with the author 'outside' the text, this kind of directorial 'appearance' often works to promote a second, much less inevitable misrecognition. It is the frequent site, that is, of a narcissistic idealization, through which the filmmaker speaks him- or herself as the point of absolute textual origin. Such is the case in *Marnie*, where Hitchcock not only makes his usual appearance on the image track, but turns to look boldly at the camera and the theater audience, as someone clearly in control of both.

Conversely, an authorial citation of this sort may also become the vehicle for an authorial diminution, a device for representing a film's director as a subject speaking from within history, ideology, and a particular social formation, as it is in *Far from Vietnam* (1967), where Godard turns the camera on himself, rather than 'going' to Southeast Asia. As important an authorial critique as this film provides, though, it never really qualifies the filmmaker's ostensible responsibility for its sounds and images, calls his masculinity into question, or suggests that his identity as a speaking subject is radically dependent upon the ways in which it is textually constituted. Although it lacks the reflexive complexity of either *Marnie* or *Far from Vietnam*, Chantal Akerman's voice-over in *News from Home* (1975) deprivileges the authorial voice much more profoundly by rendering it feminine, personal, and informal, and by stripping it of all transcendental pretense.

However, I can think of only one film—the Fassbinder section of *Germany in Autumn* (1978)—in which an authorial 'appearance' works not to subordinate the camera and voice-recording apparatuses to the filmmaker, but to subordinate *him* to *them*. It does so by placing at absolute center stage the irrecuperable figure of a director who is not just suffering, desiring, politically conflicted, unjust, and domineering, but a culturally, historically, and *textually* bound subject—by showing that his authorial subjectivity is kept in place only through a compulsive and frenetic productivity. *Germany in Autumn* also hystericizes the body of its author through a veritable theater of grotesque corporeality. This last dimension of the film is as exemplary as the other, since its insistence upon Fassbinder's sagging flesh, putrid breath, and drug and alcohol dependency locates him firmly on the side of a graceless but 'read-able' spectacle, making it impossible ever again to conflate him with a phallic exteriority. It thus openly declares the author 'outside' the text to be nothing more than an effect of discourse.

So far I have focused only on representations which so closely approximate the visual or sonorous features of the filmmaker as to be easily conflated with him or her—with representations which promote the kind of mirror recogni-tion that Lacan associates with 'primary narcissism'. However, authorial subjectivity can also be brought into play through what both Lacan and Metz would call 'secondary identification'—i.e., through identification with an anthropomorphic representation which is not, strictly speaking, his or her 'own', but that of an other who also happens in this case to be a fictional character. This kind of psychic alignment is brilliantly dramatized in *Scénario du Passion* (1982), where Godard once again turns the (video) camera on himself as he sits in an editing suite taking apart and recombining sounds and images from the film to which the title refers. At a key moment in the tape, he reaches out to the image of Jerzy, the character of the Polish expatriate filmmaker who is clearly a stand-in for Godard-as-director, and locks him in a narcissistic embrace. With that extraordinary gesture, the author who is sitting outside the text of *Passion* looking in is shown to derive all his subjective sustenance from a character who is firmly inside.

A director's relationship with the fictional character who 'stands in' for him or her textually may be predicated, as it is not only within *Marnie* but within many classic films, upon a kind of replication at the level of the fiction of those functions generally attributed to the cinematic apparatus—authorita-tive vision, hearing, and speech. Secondary identification can thus provide another vehicle leading to imaginary mastery and transcendence. Provided, at least, that the character who sustains this ambition is male, such an identification is completely compatible with dominant cinema. However, a filmmaker's secondary identifications may also depart from that paradigm altogether, and put in place a very different kind of authorial subjectivity— one which, for instance, is much more openly endangered and at risk. I think in this respect of Ulrike Ottinger's fascination with freaks of all sorts, or Marguerite Duras's investment in the figure of the exile. I will have much more to say about 'deviant' kinds of secondary identification when I come to Cavani, whose authorial subjectivity relies heavily upon her imaginary rela-tion to her male characters.

Finally, the author 'outside' the text may find the mirror for which he or she is looking in the 'body' of the text—in the way in which his or her films choreograph movement; compose objects within the frame; craft, disrupt, or multiply narrative; experiment with sound; create 'atmosphere'; articulate light and shadow; encourage or inhibit identification; use actors; or work with color. The kind of identification I am talking about here is the narcissistic correlative of that 'recognition' which permits a reasonably literate movie-goer to say after looking at several shots of *The Red and the White* that 'it's Jancso', or after viewing three or four minutes of a Peter Greenaway film that 'it's Greenaway'. Although the authorial citation is in this case a formal or narrative 'image', it is not any the less complexly imbricated with gender, ideology, or history.

Although directors such as Welles, Fassbinder, and Duras speak themselves through their films in virtually all of the ways in which it is possible to do so, other filmmakers may leave their signature only at random points within the diegesis. It would be a mistake to assume that there is no author 'inside' a particular corpus of films simply because they have no distinguishing formal trademark. There is little or nothing about the formal operations of either Arzner's or Cavani's work to distinguish it from other contemporaneous and culturally homogeneous work—little or nothing, indeed, to indicate a particular preoccupation on the part of either director with what generally passes for the level of enunciation. However, even at the level of the fiction, there can be all kinds of authorial spoors.

Of course, tracking these spoors is no simple matter. A reasonably experienced viewer can readily understand a heavy reliance on primary colors, collage techniques, and intertextuality to be devices with which Godard identifies, and even a naive viewer would immediately understand his 'appearance' in *Far from Vietnam* or *Scénario du Passion* to be an authorial trace. However, a filmmaker's imaginary relation to a given character is often much less evident, particularly so long as it is theoretically isolated from the closely related issue of desire. The moment has arrived when I must not only turn to the second of my authorial categories, but abandon the pretense that it can be so clearly separated from the first. Identification and desire are complexly imbricated with each other—so much so that it is often possible to uncover the former through the latter.

But what would the theorist be looking for if she wanted to find what gives a particular group of films their libidinal coherence? She would be searching not just for the author 'inside' the text, but for the text 'inside' the author—for the scenario for passion, or, to be more precise, the 'scene' of authorial desire. The 'scene' to which I refer is what Laplanche and Pontalis, in an inspired passage from *The Language of Psycho-analysis*, call the 'fantasmatic', and which they define as that unconscious fantasy or cluster of fantasies which structures not merely dreams and other related psychic formations, but object-choice, identity, and 'the subject's life as a whole'.[14] The fantasmatic generates erotic tableaux or *combinatoires* in which the subject is arrestingly positioned—whose function is, in fact, precisely to display the subject in a given place. Its original cast of characters would seem to be drawn from the familial reserve, but in the endless secondary productions to which the fantasmatic gives rise, all actors but one are frequently recast.

And even that one constant player may assume different roles on different occasions.

Freud has given us some idea of the kinds of fantasies that most frequently come to organize psychic life in this way. Not surprisingly, although he attempts to ground most of them in phylogenesis, all of his examples clearly derive from the Oedipus complex. The list is not, at first glance, very extensive; it includes only the fantasy of the primal scene, the fantasy of seduction, the fantasy of castration, and the fantasy of being beaten.[15] However, this list becomes extremely rich and varied once we have grasped the possible permutations of each fantasy—once all the instinctual vicissitudes have been factored in, the negative as well as the positive Oedipus complex has been taken into account,[16] and theoretical allowance has been made for the fantasizing subject to occupy more than one position in the imaginary tableau. Freud explores the multiple forms which the beating fantasy is capable of assuming for both the male and the female subject in 'A Child is Being Beaten', but we have barely begun to calibrate the textual range of any of the others.[17] And, of course, there may well be other fantasmatics than those to which Freud draws our attention.

Insofar as authorial desire manages to invade a particular corpus, it will be organized around some such structuring 'scene' or group of 'scenes'. It seems to me, for instance, that Fassbinder's cinema revolves around the beating fantasy, and that much of Bertolucci's work is libidinally motived by the male fantasy of maternal seduction. However, these generalizations indicate very little about the actual workings of desire in either body of work, since there are so many ways in which these two fantasies can be elaborated, each with its own consequences not only for object-cathexis, but for identity.

It is at this last juncture that my earlier distinction between authorial identification and authorial desire most completely collapses, since an author's identification with a fictional character will be determined by the subject-position the latter occupies not only within the narrative, but within the fantasmatic 'scene' which that narrative traces in some oblique and indirect way. This means that authorial identification and authorial desire are indeed mutually referential—that an investigation of one will sooner or later open on to the other.

Since the subject-position which the author occupies within the cinematic 'mise-en-scène'[18] may well transgress the biological gender of the author 'outside' the text, the question of whether the latter speaks with a 'male' or a 'female' voice can be answered only through an interrogation of the sort I have been urging. At the same time, this libidinal masculinity or femininity must be read in relation to the biological gender of the biographical author, since it is clearly not the same thing, socially or politically, for a woman to speak with a female voice as it is for a man to do so, and vice versa. All sorts of cultural imperatives dictate a smooth match between biological gender and subject-position, making any deviation a site of potential resistance to sexual difference. As stage 3 of the female version of the beating fantasy would indicate, where the subject sees herself as a group of boys being treated as if they were girls (i.e., occupying an erotically passive position in relation to the father),[19] biological gender can also figure in complex ways within the fantasmatic 'scene'.

Although this might seem the end point for an investigation of authorial desire, it is in many ways only the beginning. Laplanche and Pontalis make the crucial point that the fantasmatic is 'constantly drawing in new material' (p. 317), thereby indicating that it is far from closed—that, on the contrary, it is always absorbing the world outside. I would go even farther, and argue that it is being continually drawn into new social and political alignments, which may even lead to important 'scenic' changes. It is thus important to ask of any authorial desire: How has it assimilated history? And how might it be seen to have acted upon history?

One possible point of entry into the libidinal economy that helps to organize an authorial corpus would be through its nodal points. A nodal point might take the form of a sound, image, scene, place, or action to which that work repeatedly returns, such as Parma and its environs within the films of Bertolucci, dancing within the films of Yvonne Rainer or Sally Potter, or undressing within the films of Cavani. It might also assume the guise of a sound, image, scene, or sequence which is marked through some kind of formal 'excess', indicating a psychic condition such as rapture (the revolving door shot with which Leandro Katz's Splits concludes),[20] fixation (the frequent close-ups of Terence Stamp's crotch in Pasolini's Theorem), or intoxication (the vertiginous play of camera, set, and back projection during the final kiss in Hitchcock's Vertigo).

The authorial fantasmatic can also be tracked at the level of the story, at least within those films where story can be said to play even a vestigial role. Like Teresa de Lauretis, I believe that there is always desire 'in' narrative,[21] and that in certain cinematic instances that desire can reasonably be attributed to the author 'outside' the text. (There is also narrative in desire, or, to put it slightly differently, a fundamentally narrative bent to desire, which is so fully sustained by retrospection and anticipation.) Sometimes the fantasmatic 'scene' is sketched by the larger narrative trajectory which is repeatedly mapped by films with the same authorial signature. At other times, as in Duras's India Song, or in the films of Mark Rappaport, the fantasmatic 'scene' may give rise to an insistently scenic narrative structure.

['The Female Voice in Psychoanalysis and Cinema', in The Acoustic Mirror (Bloomington, Ind.: Indiana University Press, 1988), 205–18].

The Body and Cinema: Some Problems for Feminism

> Critique doesn't have to be the premise of a deduction which concludes:
> this then is what needs to be done. It should be an instrument for those
> who fight, those who resist and refuse what is....
>
> Michel Foucault[1]

It must be clear by now that representation—and visual representation in
particular—poses certain problems for both feminist thinking and feminist
politics. I want to take a look at one or two of these problems as they
presented themselves to me in the context of a recent cinema-going experience. Early in 1986, I attended a commercial screening in London of a film
called *Pumping Iron II—The Women*. The screening was organized for an all-
women audience and was followed by a discussion between the audience and
a panel, consisting of two film critics and a bodybuilder. It is possible there
were more critics and bodybuilders in the audience, but most of the women
present apparently fell into neither category. Though, being mostly feminists,
they were not the 'ordinary women' of the populist Imaginary, either.

Few 'ordinary women'—if such beings exist—would in any case have the
opportunity to see *Pumping Iron II*. Although the film received an enthusiastic
critical reception on its US and British releases, it has had no general release,
nor as far as I know has it been shown on television in Britain. And the video
version circulating in Britain for a while has now been withdrawn. None of
this matters very much in the present context, since the film figures here
largely as a peg or point of departure for a set of general observations on
visual representation and feminism. My argument, in other words, is applicable to more than this one film: and an argument based on *Pumping Iron II*
might even shed some light on cinema in general. [...]

In *Pumping Iron II*, for instance, an important source of pleasure for female
spectators must lie in its construction of the female body not only as strong
but also as capable of being shaped and defined by women themselves. And
yet while this film might evoke such new and technological narcissistic
identifications, the pleasure of this position may at the same time be undercut
in at least two ways: first of all, by a construction of the female body as
potentially monstrous; and secondly, as a consequence, by the fact that, for a
woman, assenting to the pleasures afforded by cinema is tantamount to
becoming caught up (to use Foucauldian terminology, on which I shall
elaborate later)[2] in certain relations of power, held in place by these relations
and by the constructs of sexuality they inscribe.

These power relations and their associated instabilities characterize a good
deal of classical cinema. *Pumping Iron II* is exceptional only in that it brings

such contradictions to the fore at the levels of both narrative and spectacle. For example, on both these levels the film is quite clearly 'about' the female body in ways that most films are not. That is to say, while—as feminist film theorists have argued—the female body may figure crucially in the production of both meaning and pleasure in classical cinema, *Pumping Iron II* transcends this inscription of the female body to interrogate that body and its limits. The film's narrative, I have suggested, is governed by the question of who will win the contest. But since in this context 'who?' must mean 'which body?', the trajectory of the narrative is harnessed to a further set of questions: What is a woman's body? Is there a point at which a woman's body becomes something else? What is the relationship between a certain type of body and 'femininity'?

These are challenging questions in a cultural context in which the body figures as an irreducible sign of the natural, the given, the unquestionable. Foremost among these cultural effectivities of the body is its function as a signifier of sexual difference. But the concept of sexual difference is itself an ideological battleground: it holds together—or tries to—a range of discourses and meanings centring on biological sex, social gender, gender identity and sexual object choice. The encapsulation of all these within constructs of sexual difference is a historically grounded ideological project which works to set up a heterogeneous and variably determinate set of biological, physical, social, psychological and psychic constructs as a unitary, fixed and unproblematic attribute of human subjectivity. One of the effects of this is that, at a social level at least, every human being gets defined as either male or female. From this fundamental difference flows a succession of discourses and powers centring upon identification and sexuality. *Pumping Iron II* can be read if not as actually unravelling this discursive formation, certainly as unpicking it a little around the edges.

The film does this most distinctively by constructing the body in a particular manner as *performance*. Performance is an activity that connotes pretence, dissimulation, 'putting on an act', assuming a role. In other words, in the notion of performance a distance of some sort is implied between the 'act' and the 'real self' concealed behind it. Performance proposes a subject which is at once both fixed in, and called into question by, this very distinction between assumed persona and authentic self. Performance, in other words, poses the possibility of a mutable self, of a fluid subjectivity. If performance proposes fluidity and the body connotes fixity, the combination of the two in the instance of bodybuilding confers a distinctly contradictory quality on the activity. For bodybuilding involves more than placing the body on display, more than simply passive exhibition. The fact that bodybuilding is an active production of the body, a process of acting upon and determining its contours, is impossible to ignore. In *Pumping Iron II*, for example, innumerable scenes emphasize the sheer hard work involved in the production of the

women's bodies. In bodybuilding—the willed construction of a certain physique—nature becomes culture.

Performance and the body are instrumental in the operations of classical
cinema as well; but rarely in ways which in the final instance challenge the
natural order of the body and its inscription of sexual difference. For in
cinema, performance is usually appropriated to the self-evidently cultural
and mutable instances of clothing and gesture.[3] In bodybuilding, muscles
function in much the same way as clothing does in other types of performance. But muscles, unlike clothes, are supposed to be natural. What happens,
then, when muscles enter the cultural domain? In a sense, of course, they
already do inhabit it, for muscles carry a heavy burden of cultural meanings.
Not least among these are meanings centred upon sexual difference and its
naturalness. Within such a discourse, muscles are constituted as 'essentially'
masculine.

Thus when women enter the arena of bodybuilding, a twofold challenge to
the natural order is posed. Not only is the naturalness of the body called into
question by its inscription within a certain kind of performance: but when
women have the muscles, the natural order of gender is under threat as well.
Muscles are rather like drag, for female bodybuilders especially: while
muscles can be assumed, like clothing, women's assumption of muscles implies a transgression of the proper boundaries of sexual difference. In *Pumping
Iron II*, the limits of the female body are the object of obsessive concern, to the
extent that the opposite poles of the issue are represented in the 'feminine'
body of Rachel McLish against the 'masculine' body of Bev Francis.

The woman's body as muscular may also be regarded as tantamount to a
fetish, a point which brings me back to the question of cinema. For it is an
axiom of feminist film theory that one of the masculine subject positions
available to the spectator in cinema is constructed through a fetishistic look, a
look which effects a disavowal of the threat of castration posed by woman.
The phallic woman imaged in this process of disavowal is either overvalued as
a glamorous figure, or punished as a monstrosity.[4] Such an operation, it is
argued, is characteristic of the spectator–text relations proposed by classical
cinema. Again, this operation is foregrounded in *Pumping Iron II*. In particular,
Bev Francis's body can only, within the terms of the body/gender/culture
problematic, be seen as 'masculine', or at least as 'not-feminine'. How is such
a disturbing body to be looked at when translated on to the cinema screen?
Indeed, can it be looked at?[5]

At the level of spectacle, then, the threatening quality of Bev's body can be
neutralized by its construction—in a fetishistic look—as monstrous. And yet
at the level of narrative, Bev figures as a key character—indeed as a sympathetic character—in the film. Whether she will receive her just narrative
deserts as a 'good person' or her just, 'specular' deserts as a phallic woman is a
question entirely central to the suspenseful trajectory of *Pumping Iron II*. In

the end, Bev loses the championship, coming in at a humiliating eighth place. But ultra-feminine Rachel McLish does not win, either: and of these two it is Bev who, by her magnanimity in defeat, scores the moral victory.

Carla Dunlap poses down in the final round

First prize, in fact, goes to Carla Dunlap, whose body is represented in the film as a midpoint between Bev's and Rachel's. But there is more to this resolution than mere compromise. Carla is set up as an outsider, as different from the other contestants—and not just by virtue of race: she is the most articulate of the group, a self-sufficient loner, the only one with no man to coach her and provide moral support. Carla's *dea ex machina* win does not so much answer the film's central question, then, as sidestep it. The issue of the appropriate body for a female bodybuilder is not actually resolved: rather it is displaced on to a set of discourses centring on—but also skirting—race, femininity and the body, a complex of discourses which the film cannot acknowledge, let alone handle. In *Pumping Iron II*'s terms. Carla's body can be 'read' only as a compromise: other major issues are left dangling.

These contradictions overdetermine the ways in which *Pumping Iron II* foregrounds a number of dilemmas facing female spectators at the cinema. Most especially, the film makes it clear that to adopt a narcissistic position in relation to the cinematic image is to run the risks of identifying with woman-as-fetish: of identifying with her over-idealization, certainly—and, more commonly, perhaps, in the cinema of the 1980s—with her victimization and punishment. The difficulties of such a mode of identification effectively become a topic of *Pumping Iron II*, so that the instability of femininity as a subject position, and the discomfort involved in identification with it, are liable to become evident in looking at this film in ways they are not when such relations are more embedded, more submerged in the text.

This brings me back to the question of the powers at work in cinema's relation of spectatorship: powers through which, it is argued, sexual difference—and indeed perhaps other kinds of difference, too[6]—are constructed. To take pleasure in cinema is to be seduced by these operations; to be subject to, to submit to, the powers they inscribe. The spectator becomes caught up in, and constituted by, a set of powers which produce (among other things) discursive constructs of femininity and masculinity. She/he is positioned, defined, set in place, within these powers and constructs. The gendered subjectivities so produced are not interchangeable, however. This is one reason—and a very important one—why visual representation presents special problems for feminist politics. In this context two questions present themselves: Is it possible for women/feminists to take pleasure in visual representation, particularly in cinema? And, more generally, what is to be done about the problems all this poses for feminism? Before tackling these issues, however, I want to subject the notion of the instrumentality of representation to a little more scrutiny, with a view to understanding it better in relation to women, to the feminine, indeed to feminism.

Representation, as I have suggested, sets in play certain relations of power through which, among other things, discourses around sexual difference and subjects in and for those discourses are ongoingly produced. In this sense, representation may be regarded, once more to adopt Foucauldian terminology, as a strategy of normalization. Representation participates in the various relations of power with which we are surrounded and in which we are always in one way or another implicated. Representation can be understood, then, as a form of regulation.

This theoretical position suggests that no one, no social group, no structure, can stand outside the powers and the normalizing instrumentality of representation. Therefore if 'women' are positioned and produced through these powers in specific ways as social subjects, it follows that they are not excluded from these powers. Nor, in the classic sense of the term, can women be regarded as 'oppressed' by them. For power, in this model, is not a thing, is not imposed from outside its subjects, but is rather a process, the outcome of a series of interacting and potentially contradictory relations in which these subjects are necessarily involved. If power operates in this way as a network of countervailing 'force relations', then resistance becomes an integral part of processes of power. Given this, what kinds of resistance to the normalizing effectivities of representation are available to feminism? In current circumstances, three sets of feminist strategies of resistance present themselves: censorship, feminist practices of representation, and feminist critical practice. My main concern here is with feminist critical practice, but a few words on the other two are perhaps in order first.

If censorship deserves attention, this is not because (at least in its legal or quasi-legal manifestations) it constitutes an important feminist strategy of resistance to the normalizing powers of representation: on the contrary, generally speaking it does not. However, since feminist protests against visual representations of women are often appropriated (in Britain and the US, at least) in support of pre-feminist and even anti-feminist arguments in favour of censorship, it might be worthwhile making a few distinctions here. While censorship—to the extent that it seeks to repress certain representations—can be regarded as a prohibitive operation, it can also be seen as productive.[7] At the most basic level, for example, it produces the 'unrepresentable' precisely as a set of images that should not be seen. What censorship both prohibits and produces is most especially that category of representations named the 'obscene'.

However, constructs of femininity produced by representation cannot simply be mapped directly on to constructs of the obscene produced by censorship. On the contrary, in fact: in both psychic and economic terms, 'femininity' may be regarded as exactly a condition of representation. If feminists and censors seem to be at one in objecting to certain images of women, the objects of their objections are in fact completely different. It might be added, moreover, that censorship, in inciting desire for the unrepresentable, in the final instance acknowledges and reinforces the power of the image. To this extent, censorship is complicit in those very normalizing processes which feminism seeks to resist.

Feminist practices of representation, on the other hand, embody—in the quest for a 'new voice', a transformation of vision—a wholly understandable desire to stand outside these powers. This is not necessarily an essentialist project, though given the appeals often made to an authentic feminine voice, 'writing the body' and suchlike, it certainly looks like it at times. A good deal of exciting and valuable work in film, as in other areas of cultural production, has appeared in recent years, some of it indeed claiming to speak a 'feminine voice'. Nevertheless, the search for new forms of expression is more productively seen in terms of resistance to the powers of representation than as taking place outside their 'field of force'.

This argument is more than just a corollary of the notion that power is all-pervasive: it also registers a discomfort with a distinction between feminist cultural production on the one hand and feminist theory and criticism on the other. Such a polarization perpetuates the assumption that while theory and criticism are of necessity implicated in 'discourses which negate or objectify [women] through their representations',[8] feminist cultural production is somehow capable of transcending these limitations. At stake here, of course, is a separation of theory and practices: precisely one of the dualisms of patriarchal thought which feminist thinking seeks to challenge.

This brings me to the third and final strategy of resistance, strategically termed in this context feminist critical practice. Feminist critics and theorists among my readers may be relieved to hear that, in arguing that criticism can be a political practice in its own right, I have masculine authority on my side. I refer here to the quotation from Foucault which heads this essay. If feminist critics can place themselves among those who, in Foucault's words, 'resist and refuse what is', we might well then ask: Where lies the specificity of feminist as against other forms of oppositional cultural practice? Perhaps it resides in the possibility that feminist critical practice may constitute not only a resistance to the powers of visual representation, but also an attempt to bridge the gap between woman as spectacle, as object of the look, and women as historical subjects. Alongside feminist cultural production, then, feminist critical practice

can be a fundamentally deconstructive strategy which questions the possibility of universals or absolute meanings and exposes the constitution of power at stake in their assertion.[9]

However, I shall not end with any fanfares, for one further question remains unanswered: can feminists (and indeed women in general) take pleasure in visual representations, and if so, how? I have suggested that the feminist audience at the screening of *Pumping Iron II* was uncomfortable with its own pleasure in the film. If this is so, then their discomfort was simultaneously expressed and dealt with in a process of disavowal. This is evident in the negative criticisms directed at—but actually missing—the film: and it may be seen in itself as a form of resistance to the film's powers of seduction and subjection. The question remains, though: Can there be a feminist critical position which neither refuses nor disavows the pleasures of cinema? Because I love cinema, I want to answer yes. In the end, though, perhaps a feminist critical practice can do no more than offer the—not inconsiderable—pleasure of resistance?

['The Body and Cinema: Some Problems for Feminism', in Susan Sheridan (ed.), *Grafts: Feminist Cultural Criticism* (London: Verso, 1988), 11–23.]

67 Whose Imaginary? The Televisual Apparatus, the Female Body and Textual Strategies in Select Rock Videos on MTV

The social Imaginary that I shall explore in Music Television (MTV)[1] has been constructed through the contradictory post-1960s historical moment in which rock videos arise as a mass popular culture form. It is the mapping in the 1980s of the new 1960s discourses about politics, sex and romance on to the increasingly high-tech stage of an already advanced capitalism that partly produces the extraordinary MTV Imaginary.

A symptom of the new high-tech stage of advanced capitalism is the deployment of television as itself a unique kind of apparatus, very different from the filmic one. Since MTV embodies in extreme form the characteristics of this apparatus, it is worth dwelling briefly on it, particularly as it has been described by Jean Baudrillard. Baudrillard points to television's cultural role in developing what he calls the new 'cold' universe of communication.[2] The universe involves marked changes in the relationship of subject to image; for while the movie screen harnesses the subject's desire through appearing momentarily to provide a longed-for plenitude,[3] the television screen keeps the subject in a position of alienation. The television screen's constantly changing 'texts', of whatever kind, provide the constant *promise* of plenitude, but this is for ever *deferred*. Instead of the illusory and temporary plenitude of the cinema, the television screen–spectator relationship mimics the subject's original discovery of split subjectivity before the mirror. The decentred, fragmented self that becomes the subject's human condition (although masked in daily life by the illusory construction of a permanent 'self') is duplicated in the processes of television watching; the crucial difference from daily life is the constant *expectation* of unity, oneness, in the *next* text-segment. [...]

I am interested in the myths, images and representations evident in the rock videos played on MTV as these might be seen as both reflecting unconscious changes in young people's 'real conditions of existence'[4] and as tapping into the unsatisfied desire remaining in the psyche from the Lacanian mirror-phase, in the manner suggested above. MTV at once embodies and then further develops major cultural changes. I shall extend these arguments by looking at how the televisual apparatus functions, and at the psychic processes it involves. I will then discuss the implications of the televisual imaginary specifically for women before undertaking some textual analyses of female representation in select rock videos by female stars.

By 'televisual apparatus,' I mean the complex of elements including the machine itself—its technological features (the way it produces and presents images); its various 'texts', including ads, commentaries, displays; the central relationship of programming to the sponsors, whose own texts—the ads—are arguably the real television texts;[5] the now various sites of reception from the living-room to the bathroom. Scholars may focus on problems of enunciation, that is of who speaks a text, and to whom it is addressed, which includes looking at the manner in which we watch television, its presence in the home, the so-called 'flow' of the programmes, the fragmentation of the viewing experience even within any one given programme, the unusual phenomenon of endlessly serialized programmes; or they may study the ideology embedded in the forms of production and reception, which are not 'neutral' or 'accidental,' but a crucial result of television's overarching commercial framework.

One of the still unresolved issues that work in this area has to address (whether explicitly or implicitly) is that of the degree to which theories of film are applicable to the very different 'televisual' apparatus. Since feminist film theory evolved very much in relation to the classic Hollywood cinema, it is particularly important for women approaching television to consider how far that theory is relevant to the different apparatus that television is; for example, do theories about the 'male gaze' apply to watching television, when usually there is no darkened room, where there is a small screen, and where viewing is often interrupted by commercials, people coming in, or by the viewer switching channels? To what extent is the television spectator addressed in the same manner as the film spectator? Do the same psycho-analytic processes of subject construction apply? Will semiotics aid in illuminating the processes at work? Is there a different form of interaction between the television text and the female viewer than between the cinema screen and the female spectator? What might that relation then be?

Much recent film theory has argued that one cannot make any distinction between the apparatus and the narrative, since it is the apparatus itself that produces certain inevitable 'narrative' effects (such as, in the film, the forced identification with the look of the camera). Thus, we need to know how the televisual apparatus is used in any one television genre to represent the female body—to see what possibilities there are for different kinds of female representation, and how bound by the limits of the apparatus are images of woman on television.

Let me first say something about the construction of what I have elsewhere called the 'decentred' spectator through the very rapid flow of what are comparatively short segments within a continuous, twenty-four-hour channel.[6] Here MTV carries to an extreme elements present in other TV programmes in the United States, particularly those that are also twenty-four-hour stations like continuous weather and news channels; but also those that are daily 'serials' in some form or another, for instance, game shows, talk shows, the soaps, and also the news (which is regularly slotted and so highly stylized as to be 'drama').[7]

All of these programmes exist on a kind of horizontal axis that is never ending, rather than consisting of discrete units consumed within a fixed two-hour limit, like the Hollywood movie, or other forms such as the novel, which also have a fixed, and clearly defined 'frame'. Television in a certain sense is not so bounded. Rather television texts resemble an endless film strip, turned on its side, in which the frames are replaced by episodes. Or, as Peggy Phelan has argued, perhaps a better model is that of Foucault's Panopticon, in which the guard surveys a series of prisoners through their windows.[8] Phelan is interested in setting up the television producer as the 'guard' and the individual television viewer as the 'prisoner' who watches in 'a sequestered and observed solitude'. But I think the guard metaphor works well also for the spectator's relationship to the various episodes that represent, in Foucault's words, 'a multiplicity that can be numbered and supervised': in fact, for the television viewer, that desire for plenitude, for complete knowledge is of course forever delayed, forever deferred. The television is seductive precisely because it speaks to a desire that is insatiable—it promises complete knowledge in some far distant and never-to-be-experienced future; its strategy is to keep us endlessly consuming in the hopes of fulfilling our desire; it hypnotizes us through addressing this desire, keeps us returning for more.

This strategy is particularly evident in MTV since the texts here are only four minutes long and so keep us for ever watching, for ever hoping to fulfil our desire with the next one that comes along. The mechanism of 'Coming Up Next . . .' that all programmes employ, and that is the staple of the serial, is an intricate aspect of the minute-by-minute watching of MTV. Lured by the seductiveness of the constant promise of immediate plenitude, we endlessly consume.

Now, the question is how does this decentring televisual apparatus position women? Are women necessarily addressed in specific ways by the apparatus, as was argued (at least initially) for the classic Hollywood film? Is there something inherent in the televisual apparatus that addresses woman's social positioning as absence and lack, as again was the case for the Hollywood film?

These questions take me beyond the confines of my topic, but it is possible that what is true for MTV is true also for other television programmes: namely, that instead of a more or less monolithic (and largely male) gaze as was found in the Hollywood film, there is a wide range of gazes with different gender implications. In other words, the apparatus itself, in its modes of functioning, is not gender specific *per se*; but across its 'segments,' be they soap opera segments, crime series segments, news segments, morning show segments, we can find a variety of 'gazes' that indicate an address to a certain kind of male or female Imaginary. If the address in some videos is not exactly genderless, people of both genders are often able to undertake multiple identifications.

What this implies is that the televisual Imaginary is more varied than the cinematic one; it does not involve the same regression to the Lacanian mirror-phase as theorists discovered in the filmic apparatus. In the case of MTV, for example, instead of the channel evoking aspects of the Lacanian mirror-phase Ideal Imago—a process that depends on sustained identification with a central figure in a prolonged narrative—issues to do with split sub-jectivity, with the alienation that the mirror image involves, are evoked instead. (See Chart 1.) In other words, filmic processes (at least for the male viewer) heal the painful split in subjectivity instituted during the mirror-phase, while MTV rather reproduces the decentred human condition that is especially obvious to the young adolescent.

MTV thus addresses the desires, fantasies and anxieties of young people growing up in a world in which traditional categories and institutions are apparently being questioned. I have elsewhere argued that there are five main types of video on MTV, and that a whole series of gazes replaces the broadly monolithic Hollywood gaze (see Chart 2 for summary of these types and of how the gaze affects female images). The plethora of gender positions on the channel arguably reflects the heterogeneity of current sex-roles, and the androgynous surface of many star-images indicates the blurring of clear lines between genders characteristic of many rock videos.[9]

Because of both the peculiarities of the televisual apparatus and the new phase of youth culture produced by the 1960s, most of the feminist methodologies that have emerged in television research so far are inappropri-ate for the rock videos on MTV. This is mainly because of the sophisticated, self-conscious and skewed stance that these television texts take toward their own subject matter. It is often difficult to know precisely what a rock video actually means, because its signifiers are not linked along a coherent, logical chain that produces an unambiguous message. The mode, to use Fredric Jameson's contrast, is that of *pastiche* rather than parody. By this Jameson means that whereas modernist texts often took a particular critical position *vis-à-vis* earlier textual models, ridiculing specific stances or attitudes in them, or offering a sympathetic, comic perspective on them, postmodernist works tend to use *pastiche*, a mode that lacks any clear positioning with regard to what it shows, or toward earlier texts that are used.[10]

This has implications for gender first because the source of address of the rock video text is often so unclear—consequently it is also unclear whether

Chart 1: Polarized Filmic Categories in Recent Film Theory

The classic text (Hollywood)	The avant-garde text
Realism/narrative	Non-realism/anti-narrative
History	Discourse
Complicit ideology	Rupture of dominant ideology

the male or the female discourse dominates; and second because attitudes toward sex and gender are often ambiguous. One finds oneself not knowing, for instance, whether or not a video like John Parr's 'Naughty Naughty', or John Cougar Mellencamp's 'Hurts So Good', are virulently sexist or merely pastiching an earlier Hollywood sexism. Even in the category that I call 'classical', where the gaze is clearly voyeuristic and male, there is a studied self-consciousness that makes the result quite different from that in the dominant commercial cinema.

A different but equally problematic ambiguity is just as prevalent in the videos made from lyrics by female stars as in those of white male stars featured on the channel. But, before going into that, let me note that it is precisely here that the cycling of videos featuring female singers across the video twenty-four-hour flow is important for understanding first the broad gender address of MTV and, related to this, the kind of Imaginary that predominates. Both issues are further linked to the overarching commercial framework of MTV, in that only those female representations considered the most 'marketable' are frequently cycled: and what is most marketable is obviously connected with dominant ideology, with the social Imaginary discussed above, and with the organization of the symbolic order around the phallus as signifier.

According to a recent quantifying study of MTV, videos featuring white males take up 83 per cent of the twenty-four-hour flow.[11] Only 12 per cent of MTV videos have central figures who are female: 11 per cent white, 1 per cent Black (the figure is 3 per cent for Black males). Brown and Campbell assert that 'white women are often shown in passive and solitary activity or are shown trying to gain the attention of a man who ignores them' (p. 104).

Chart 2: Types of Gaze in Music Television

		MODES (All use avant-garde strategies, especially self-reflexivity, play with the image, etc.)				
		Romantic	Socially conscious	Nihilist	Classical	Postmodernist
		Narrative	Elements varied	Performance Anti-narrative	Narrative	Pastiche No linear images
	Style	Loss and Reunion (Pre-Oedipal)	Struggle for autonomy: Love as prob-lematic	Sadism/maso-chism Homo-eroticism Androgyny (Phallic)	The male gaze (Voyeuristic, Fetishistic)	Play with Oedipal positions
MTV theme	*Love/sex*	Parent figures (positive)	Parent and public figures Cultural critique	Nihilism Anarchy Violence	Male as subject Female as object	Neither for nor against authority (ambiguity)

Among the 12 per cent of videos featuring women, the only ones frequently cycled are those in which the female star's position is ambiguous, where what we might call a post-feminist stance is evident.

Before discussing what I mean by this 'post-feminist' stance, I want first to note the other kinds of female representations that do appear on the channel, if only rarely. First, there are videos in the 'socially conscious' category that make the kind of statement one could call 'feminist' (for instance, Pat Benatar's 'Love Is a Battlefield', or her more recent 'Sex as a Weapon'; or Donna Summer's 'She Works Hard for the Money'); these have quite conventional narratives, although they do not adhere strictly to Hollywood codes. Second, there are occasional videos that appear to comment upon the objectifying male gaze (as perhaps does Tina Turner's 'Private Dancer') and whose visual strategies creatively embody those deconstructive aims. Finally, some videos attempt to set up a different gaze altogether, or to play with the male gaze, as arguably happens in the recent Aretha Franklin/Annie Lennox video 'Sisters Are Doin' It for Themselves'. Except for Benatar's 'Love Is a Battlefield', these videos remained in circulation for only a short period of time, and then not at a high density rate.

It is important that the channel's format of short, four-minute texts does permit gaps through which a variety of enunciative positions are made possible. I am thus able to 'stop the flow' as it were, in order to concentrate on constructions of the female body other than the prevailing 'post-feminist' or various 'male gaze' ones. But this is with full awareness that these isolated moments are in fact overridden by the plethora of texts presenting other positions. The various possibilities for 'seeing otherwise' in these different figurations of the female body are worth exploring as part of understanding what popular culture *can* do; but the ordinary MTV spectator will get little opportunity for this kind of 'seeing'. For such female images do not fit into the rich sensation of glossy surfaces, bright colours, rapid action, or the parade of bodies in contemporary clothing that the dominant videos offer.

Take, for example, the video, 'Material Girl', featuring Madonna, the female star who perhaps more than any other embodies the new post-feminist heroine in her odd combination of seductiveness and a gutsy sort of independence. 'Material Girl' is particularly useful as a point of discussion because it exemplifies a common rock-video phenomenon, namely the establishment of a unique kind of intertextual relationship with a specific Hollywood movie. For this reason, and because of difficulty of ensuring the text's stance toward what it shows and the blurring of many conventional boundaries, I would put the video in the 'postmodern' category in my chart, despite its containing more narrative than is usual in this type.

As is well known, 'Material Girl' takes off from the famous Marilyn Monroe dance/song sequence in *Gentlemen Prefer Blondes* (1953), 'Diamonds

Are a Girl's Best Friend'. The sequence occurs towards the end of the film when Esmond's father has severed Lorelei (Monroe) financially from Esmond, her fiancé, forcing her to earn her living by performing. In this sequence, having finally found Lorelei, Esmond is sitting in the audience watching the show. We thus have the familiar Hollywood situation in which the woman's performance permits her double articulation as spectacle for the male gaze (that is, she is object of desire for both the male spectator in the diegetic audience and for the spectator in the cinema watching the film). The strategy formalizes the mirror-phase situation by framing the female body within both the stage proscenium arch and the cinema screen. [...]

When we turn to the video inspired by the Monroe dance sequence, we see that the situation is far more complicated. (See Chart 3.) First, it is unclear who is 'speaking' this video, even on the remote 'authorial label' level, since credits are normally not provided. Is it perhaps Madonna, as historical star subject? Or is it one of the two narrative figures, Madonna I and Madonna II? (Madonna I is the movie-star protagonist within the diegesis that 'frames' the stage-performance plot about the 'material girl'; Madonna II is the figure within that dance performance, the 'material girl' of the video—and song's—title.) Is it the director who has fallen in love with her image and desires to possess her? Focusing first on the visual strategies and then on the sound-track, different and still more confusing answers emerge.

Visually, the director's gaze seems to structure some of the shots, but this is not consistent as it is in the Monroe sequence. And shots possibly structured by him (or in which he is later discovered to have been present) only occur at irregular intervals. The video begins by foregrounding the classic Hollywood male gaze: there is a close-up of the director, played by Keith Carradine (the video thus bows again to the classic film), whom we soon realize is watching rushes of a film starring 'Madonna I'. With an obsessed, glazed look on his face, he says, 'I want her, George.' George promises to deliver, as we cut to a two-shot of the men, behind whom we see the cinema screen and Madonna I's image, but as yet hear no sound from the performance. The camera closes in on her face, and on her seductive look first out to the camera then sideways to the men around her. As the camera now moves into the screen, blurring the boundaries between screening-room, screen and film set (the space of the performance that involves the story of the material girl, Madonna II), the 'rehearsal' (if that is what it was) ends and a rich lover comes on to the set with a large present for Madonna I.

This then is desire for the woman given birth through the cinematic apparatus, in classical manner; and yet, while the sequence seems to *fore-ground* those mechanisms, it does not appear to critique or in any way comment upon them. In Jameson's terms, the process is pastiche rather than parody, which puts it in the postmodernist mode. Considering the visual track

Chart 3: Summary Analysis of Madonna's 'Material Girl'

Level I: Madonna as historical subject, as star in consumerist circulation; this subject should be seen as multi-determined.

This level superimposes itself as a discourse on the discourse of the fictional world of the video.

Level II: Narrative strategies within the video:
(a) Use of diegetic 'spaces' pastiches classic realist codes:
    Spaces overlap, boundaries are not clearly marked
    Unclear whose gaze structures many shots; unorthodoz editing;
    Shifting enunciative strategies: who is speaking this text?

  Spaces and discourses that struggle for dominance:
  (1) The director's discourse and gaze;
        Spaces: Screening-room, dressing-room, outside studio;
  (2) Madonna I, protagonist/film star in love story (director wins her love).
        Spaces: Same as for director.
  (3) Madonna II, character within the performance of 'Material Girl' (presumably being filmed).
        Madonna II appears to assert her own desires, and, as the 'material girl', controls the discourse.
        Spaces: The studio stage-set.
(b) *Soundtrack:* primarily the song, 'Material Girl'.
    The studio-set story of the 'Material Girl' dominates the soundtrack, imposing itself even over the spaces for the director's and Madonna I's love story. Their story is only given two short pieces of dialogue.

The various diegetic spaces, thus, are not hierarchically ordered as in the usual classic text, where main story and framing story would be clearly marked. There is rather a conflation of narrative lines, or their flattening out on a single plane. Sound–image relations are not necessarily synchronized diegetically.

---

alone, the blurring of the diegetic spaces further suggests postmodernism, as does the ensuing confusion of enunciative stances. For while the director's gaze clearly constructed the first shot-series, it is not clear that his gaze structures the shot in which Madonna I receives the present. We still hear the whirring sound of a projector, as if this were still the screening-room space; and yet we are *inside* that screen—we no longer see the space around the frame, thus disorienting the viewer.

We cut to a close-up of a white phone ringing and a hand picking it up, and are again confused spatially. Where are we? Whose look is this? There has been no narrative preparation for the new space or for the spectator address: the phone monologue by Madonna I (the only time in the entire video that she speaks) establishes the space as her dressing-room. As she speaks, the camera behaves oddly (at least by standard Hollywood conventions), dollying back slowly to the door of her room, to reveal the director standing there. Was it then his gaze that structured the shot? At the moment of reaching him, the gaze certainly becomes his, and Madonna I is seen to be its object. The phone monologue that he overhears, as does the viewer, establishes that Madonna I has just received a diamond necklace. This causes the director to throw his present into the waste-paper basket that a janitor happens to be carrying out at that moment. It also establishes that Madonna I is *not* the 'material girl' of her stage role, since she offers the necklace to her (presumed) girlfriend on the phone.

We now cut back to the stage space that we assume to be the film set; it is not clear, because the diegesis does not foreground the processes of filming, and yet there is no audience space. Rather, Madonna II sets up a direct rapport with the camera filming the rock video and therefore with the television spectator, deliberately playing for her/him rather than for the man in the frame. But the spatial disorientation continues: there is a sudden cut to the rear of a flashy red car driving into the studio, followed by shots of Madonna I's elegant body in matching red dress (knees carefully visible), of her rich lover bending over her, and of her face and apparently dismissive reply. Whose gaze is this? Who is enunciating here? As Madonna I leaves her car, we discover the director again, but this series of shots could not have been structured by his gaze.

We cut back to the stage/film set for the most extended sequence of the performance in the video. This sequence follows the Monroe 'Diamonds' dance closely, and stands in the strange intertextual relationship already mentioned: we cannot tell whether or not the Monroe sequence is being commented upon, simply used, or ridiculed by exaggeration (which sometimes seems to be happening). Things are further complicated by the fact that *Gentlemen Prefer Blondes* is itself a comedy, mocking and exaggerating certain patriarchal gender roles. The situation is confused even more by occasional technical play with the image, destroying even the illusion of the stability of the stage/set space: at least once, a two-shot of Madonna II and one of the lovers is simply flipped over, in standard rock-video style but in total violation of classic codes that seek to secure illusionism.

Since there is no diegetic audience, the spectator is now in direct rapport with Madonna I's body, as she performs for the television spectator. There is again no diegetic source of enunciation, which continues to be the case until the end of the video, when the director and Madonna I finally are firmly situated in the same space: boy wins girl in a pastiche (perhaps) of the classical 'happy ending'. The spectator either remains disoriented, or secures a position through the body of the historical star, Madonna, implied as 'producing' the video or simply fixed on as a centring force.

This brief analysis of the main shots and use of diegetic spaces in 'Material Girl' demonstrates the ways in which conventions of the classic Hollywood film, which paradoxically provided the inspiration for the video, are routinely violated. The purpose here was to show how even in a video that at first appears precisely to remain within those conventions—unlike many other videos whose extraordinary and avant-garde techniques are immediately obvious—regular narrative devices are not adhered to. But the video violates classic traditions even more with its sound–image relations.

This raises the question of the rock video's uniqueness as an artistic form, namely as a form in which the sound of the song and the 'content' of its lyric exist prior to the creation of images which accompany music and words. While there are analogies with both opera and the Hollywood musical, neither prepares us for the rock video with its unique song–image relationship. The uniqueness has to do with a certain arbitrariness of the images used with any particular song, with the lack of conventional spatial limits, and with the frequent, extremely rapid, montage editing not found generally (if at all) in Hollywood musical song/dance sequences. It also has to do with the precise relationship of sound—both musical and vocal—to image. This latter relationship involves first the links between musical rhythms and significations of instrumental sounds and the images provided for them; and second links between the meanings of the song's actual *words* and the images conjured up to convey that 'content'.

This is obviously a very complex topic—which I can only touch on here— but I shall demonstrate some of the issues in relation to 'Material Girl', where again things are far simpler than in many other videos. We have seen that on the visual track there are two distinct but linked discourses, that involving the director's desire for Madonna I (his determined pursuit and eventual 'winning' of her), and that of Madonna I's performance, where she plays Madonna II, the 'material girl'. These discourses arc not hicrarchically arranged as in the Hollywood film, but rather exist on a horizontal axis, neither one being subordinated to the other. In terms of screen time, however, the performance is privileged.

When we turn to the soundtrack we find that, after the brief introductory scene in the screening-room (a scene, by the way, often excised from broadcasts of the video), the soundtrack consists entirely of the lyric for the song 'Material Girl'. This song deals with the girl who will only date boys who 'give her proper credit', and for whom love is reduced to money. Thus, none of the visuals pertaining to the director–Madonna I love story have any correlate on the soundtrack. We merely have two short verbal sequences (in the screening-room and the dressing-room) to carry the entire other story: in other words, sound-track and image track are not linked in those shots. An obvious example of this discrepancy is in the shot of Madonna I (arriving at the studio in the flashy car) rejecting her rich lover: Madonna lip-synchs 'That's right', from the 'Material Girl' song—a phrase that refers there to her only loving boys who give her money—in a situation where the opposite is happening: she *refuses* to love the man who is wealthy!

In other words, the video's soundtrack refers only to the stage performance and yet dominates the visuals depicting the framing story about Madonna I. The common device in the Hollywood musical of having the dance interlude simply as an episode in the main story seems here to be reversed: the performance is central while the love story is reduced to the status merely of a framing narrative. Significant here also is the disjunction between the two stories, the framing story being about a 'nice' girl, and the performance being about a 'bad' girl: but even these terms are blurred by the obvious seductiveness of the 'nice' girl, particularly as she walks toward the car at the end in a very 'knowing' manner.

Thus the usual hierarchical arrangement of discourses in the classic realist text is totally violated in 'Material Girl'. While Madonna I is certainly set up as object of the director's desire, in quite classical manner, the text refuses to let her be controlled by that desire. This is achieved by unbalancing the relations between framing story and performance story so that Madonna I is overridden by her stage figure, Madonna II, the brash, gutsy 'material girl'. The line between 'fiction' and 'reality' within the narrative is therefore blurred: this has severe consequences just because the two women are polar opposites.

In *Gentlemen Prefer Blondes*, on the other hand, no such confusion or discrepancy exists. From the start, the Monroe character's single-minded aim is to catch a rich man, and she remains fixed on that throughout. The function of her 'Diamonds Are a Girl's Best Friend' performance is to express what has been obvious to the spectator, if not to Esmond, all along, and to let Esmond get the idea, were he smart enough. Monroe sings a song that expresses her philosophy of life, but we are clear about the lines between the stage fiction and the context of its presentation on the one hand, and Monroe as a character in the narrative on the other. Part of the confusion in the Madonna video comes about precisely because the scene of the performance is not made clear and because the lines between the different spaces of the text are blurred.

The situation in 'Material Girl' is even more problematic because of the way that Madonna, as historical star subject, breaks through her narrative positions via her strong personality, her love of performing for the camera, her inherent energy and vitality. Madonna searches for the camera's gaze and for the television spectator's gaze that follows it because she relishes being desired. The 'roles' melt away through her unique presence and the logical narrative incoherence discussed above seems resolved in our understanding that Madonna herself, as historical subject, is really the 'material girl'!

It is perhaps Madonna's success in articulating and parading the desire to be desired in an unabashed, aggressive, gutsy manner (as against the self-abnegating urge to lose oneself in the male evident in the classic Hollywood film) that attracts the hordes of twelve-year-old fans who idolize her and crowd her concerts. The amazing 'look-alike' Madonna contests (for example, a recent Macy's campaign in New York) and the successful exploitation of the weird Madonna style of dress by clothing companies attests to this idolatry. It is significant that Madonna's style is a far cry from the conventional patriarchal feminine of the women's magazines—it is a cross between a bordello queen and a bag lady: young teenagers may use her as a protest against their mothers and the normal 'feminine' while still remaining very much within those modes (in the sense of spending a lot of money, time and energy on their 'look'; the 'look' being still crucial to their identities, still designed to attract attention, even if provocatively).

In some sense, then, Madonna represents the post-feminist heroine in that she combines unabashed seductiveness with a gutsy kind of independence. She is neither particularly male nor female identified, and seems mainly to be out for herself. This post-feminism is part of a larger postmodernist phenomenon which her video also embodies in its blurring of hitherto sacrosanct boundaries and polarities of the various kinds discussed. The usual bi-polar categories—male/female, high art/pop art, film/television, fiction/reality, private/public, interior/exterior—no longer apply to many rock videos, including 'Material Girl'. [. . .]

The televisual apparatus as a whole contributes to the prevalence of the ambiguous female image. To summarize: first, the main force of MTV as a cable channel is consumption on a variety of levels, ranging from the literal (selling the sponsors' goods, the rock stars' records, and MTV itself) to the psychological (selling the image, the 'look', the style). MTV is more obviously than other channels one nearly continuous advertisement, the flow being broken down merely into different *kinds* of advertisements. More than other channels, then, MTV positions the spectator in the mode of constantly hoping that the next ad segment (of whatever kind) will satisfy the desire for plenitude: the channel keeps the spectator in the consuming mode more intensely because its items are all so short.

Since the mode of address throughout is that of the advertisement, then like the advertisement the channel relies on engaging the spectator on the level of unsatisfied desire; this remains in the psyche from the moment of entry into the Lacanian symbolic, and is available for channelling in various directions. Given the organization of the Lacanian symbolic around the phallus as signifier, it is not surprising that MTV basically addresses the desire for the phallus remaining in the psyche of both genders. This partly accounts for the dominance on the channel of videos featuring white male stars.

Nevertheless, as Chart 2 shows, the male gaze is not monolithic on the channel: here again, the television apparatus enables the production of a variety of different gazes due to the arrangement of a series of short, constantly changing segments which replace the closure of the two-hour film, the classical novel and the theatrical play. There is no possibility within the four-minute segment for regression to the Freudian Oedipal conflicts in the manner of the classical narrative. What we have rather is a semi-comical play with Oedipal positions, as in the postmodern video, or a focus on one particular mode in the Oedipal complex in some of the other video-types outlined in the chart.

The implications of all this for a feminist perspective need close analysis. Feminism, particularly in America, has traditionally relied on a liberal- or left-humanist position. It is these ideologies that provided the stance from which feminists have been able to critique dominant practices and call them 'sexist' or 'patriarchal'. Humanist values, applied specifically to those humans called 'women' who often were not included in humanist cultural projections, formed the basis for arguments to improve women's conditions of existence. If Baudrillard is correct in seeing the television screen and the entire televisual apparatus as symbolizing a new era in which left/liberal humanism no longer has a place, then feminism needs to address the changed situation. Gender has been one of the central organizing categories of what Baudrillard calls the old 'hot' (as against the new 'cold') universe, but this category itself may be in the process of elimination, with unclear (and not necessarily progressive) results. It could be that women will no longer have the humanist position from which to critique what is going on; the new postmodern universe arguably makes impossible the critical position itself, making then irrelevant any 'feminist' stance.

Feminists then, in particular, need to explore television's part in the changed, and still changing, relationship of self to image. This change began at the turn of the century with the development of advertising and of the department-store window; it was then further affected by the invention of the cinematic apparatus, and television has, in its turn, produced more changes. The television screen now replaces the cinema screen as the central controlling cultural mode, setting up a new spectator–screen relationship which I have here begun to analyse in relation to MTV. For MTV constantly comments upon the self in relation to image (especially the television image), to such an extent that this may be seen as its main 'content'. The blurring of distinctions between a 'subject' and an 'image'—or the reduction of the old notion of 'self' to 'image'—is something for feminists to explore, even as we fear the coming of Baudrillard's universe of 'simulacra'.

The reduction of the female body to an 'image' is something that women have long endured: the phenomenon has been extensively studied by feminist film critics, who were able to assume a humanist position from which to critique film constructions. From that position the possibility of constructing other representations always existed. The new postmodern universe, however, with its celebration of the look, surfaces, textures, the self-as-commodity, produces an array of images/representations/simulacra that co-opts any possible critical position by the very incorporation of what were previously 'dissenting' images; this makes difficult the processes of foregrounding or exposing gender issues that feminist film-makers have used. As a cultural mode, postmodernism would eliminate gender difference as a significant category, just as it sweeps aside other polarities. Television, as a postmodern-ist apparatus—with its decentred address, its flattening out of things into a network or system that is endless, unbounded, unframed and whose parts all rely on each other—urgently requires more thorough examination, particularly in relation to its impact on women.

['Whose Imaginary? The Televisual Apparatus, the Female Body and Textual Strategies in Select Rock Videos on MTV', in E. Deirdre Pribram, *Female Spectators Looking at Film and Television* (London: Verso, 1988), 132–55.]

RITA FELSKI

68   The Dialectic of 'Feminism' and 'Aesthetics'

One of the most important achievements of the women's movement has been to repoliticize art on the level of both production and reception, and to question ruling ideologies of the text as a self-contained artifact which recur in both modernist aesthetics and formalist criticism. This repoliticization of the aesthetic sphere does not imply, in my view, that aesthetic categories are to be interpreted as a direct reflection of the interests of a political ideology, or that literary meaning is limited to its current political use-value for the women's movement, assumptions that lay themselves open to the obvious charge of reductionism. Rather, as evidenced by the current debates between American and French feminists, there exists a symptomatic tension in feminist literary theory between a pragmatic position, which seeks to repoliticize the literary text by reinserting it into the sphere of everyday communicative practices, and a simultaneous awareness of the potential limitations of a purely functionalist aesthetic, which stresses immediate political effects and is unable to address the specificity of literature as a site of plural signification and aesthetic pleasure which may resist as well as transmit dominant ideological positions.

Thus the assumption that literary meaning can in all cases be reduced to its immediate function in the transmission of an unambiguous political content fails to take into account the distinctive features of literary modes of signification, instead reading fiction as a one-dimensional articulation of existing ideological systems. The historical emergence of the category of literature as a relatively autonomous domain within bourgeois society allows a recognition of literary texts as polysemic symbolic structures governed by a high degree of self-referentiality; literature comes to function as a form of meta-language which may problematize referential meaning rather than transmit it, critically reflecting upon or playfully parodying the aesthetic conventions governing its own discourse. The increasing separation of the spheres of 'fact' and 'fiction' embodied in the self-differentiation of literature as a distinctive sphere governed by its own techniques and conventions makes it impossible to assume any automatic or self-evident equation between literary value and instrumental political value. This does not of course negate the possibility that particular individuals may find their own aesthetic responses entirely determined by moral or political factors, causing them to reject as works of art those texts which they consider 'ideologically unsound'. But any attempt to assert the *necessary* identity of political and aesthetic value in the context of a theory of feminist aesthetics runs into obvious problems, given the impossibility of revoking the relative autonomy of literature and art in modernity as embodied, for instance, in the capacity of readers to experience pleasure from texts they do not necessarily concur with on political grounds or texts whose ideological stance may not be immediately obvious.

In other words, while the relative autonomy of art is the product of a sociohistorical development, it does not follow that the differentiations which it serves to identify can be voluntaristically abolished or simply collapsed back into a socioeconomic or gender-determined base. Janet Wolff points out that critiques of aesthetics frequently rely upon a version of the 'genetic fallacy' and assume that an account of the historical and social determinants of a particular cultural formation constitutes an adequate basis for invalidating its claims. Wolff herself states that 'the sociology of art and the social history of art convincingly show the historical, ideological and contingent nature of a good deal of "aesthetics" and of many, if not all, "aesthetic judgements" '; nevertheless she argues against a reductionist standpoint which reads aesthetic categories as a direct expression of ideological interests, asserting the 'irreducibility of "aesthetic value" to social, political or ideological co-ordinates'.[1] To argue that art possesses a relative autonomy *within* society is not to suggest that it is independent *of* society, to employ Macherey's distinction,[2] or to argue that aesthetic judgments occur in some ideology-free suprahistorical realm. On the contrary, aesthetic judgments are necessarily and invariably mediated by the social and ideological contexts in which they occur. Thus, for example, the boundaries which separate what is considered art from nonart are shifting, unstable, and historically contingent and will be influenced by the ideologies and tastes of particular eras and social groups. Wolff has documented some of the numerous social, political, and ideological factors which have shaped the construction of artistic and literary canons.[3] Consequently, the criteria determining aesthetic judgments and values are by no means unproblematic and can be challenged or revised by oppositional movements capable of exposing their ideological basis.

Thus it has been possible for feminism to reveal numerous convincing instances of the influences of sexism on the evaluation of literary and artistic texts; a misogynist culture has shaped the practice of literary criticism at both individual and institutional levels. As Nina Baym points out, 'I cannot avoid the belief that "purely" literary criteria, as they have been employed to identify the best American works, have inevitably had a bias in favor of things male—in favor, say, of whaling ships rather than the sewing circle as a symbol of the human community.'[4] Consequently, feminist critics have succeeded in exposing and challenging the male prejudices which have denigrated women writers and artists and which have trivialized texts dealing with female concerns and centering on the domestic sphere. Any such approach is, however, unlikely to provide a convincing argument for the gender-based nature of *all* aesthetic judgments. Thus Michèle Barrett has questioned the assumption that a straightforward unilinear determining relationship can be established between aesthetic categories and sociopolitical structures, where the first term is reducible to an epiphenomenal function of the second.[5] Clearly, no text can in principle be exempt from an aesthetic reading, and all texts, whether 'fictional' or 'factual', are permeated to some degree by metaphor, narrative, and other figurative devices. Nevertheless, there remain important differences between texts in terms of their foregrounding of this poetic and self-referential dimension of signification, attained by means of the text's relative distance from the pragmatic constraints of everyday communicative practices. Because aesthetic criteria are produced within specific social and historical contexts, in other words, it does not follow that they are either completely arbitrary or can be construed as a one-dimensional reflection of gender or class biases.

The rejection of a reductionist aesthetic which seeks to subsume all forms of artistic production into a direct expression of particular ideological interests does not imply that a rigid division can be established between 'art' and 'ideology' as separate and antagonistic spheres. The relationship is more appropriately conceptualized in terms of a continuum in which the aesthetic function may be more or less dominant but always intermeshes with the ideological conditions governing the text's own historical location.[6] Thus the distinction between 'high' and 'popular' cultural texts cannot be adequately grasped in terms of an antithetical opposition between 'exceptional' texts which liberate multiple levels of meaning and formulaic fictions which merely serve to reinforce repressive ideological structures. Even the most overtly stereotypical and conventional of texts may articulate moments of protest and express utopian longings, while the most fragmented and aesthetically self-conscious of texts cannot escape its own ideological positioning. In turn, the relative significance and value assigned this aesthetic dimension is by no means constant and will change according to the priorities of particular social groups. At certain historical moments the urgency of political struggles may take priority over aesthetic considerations, which will be subordinated to specific didactic and ideological goals; in other instances (the example of Eastern bloc countries comes to mind) it becomes (politically) important to resist the instrumentalization of literature and to assert the validity of artistic experimentation and aesthetic pleasure and knowledge as legitimate goals in their own right.

In this context, one must realize that the ideological function of aesthetic autonomy in modern Western societies is a fundamentally ambivalent one, a crucial point ignored by those theorists who assume that it embodies a straightforward expression of ruling-class interests. On the one hand, an acknowledgment of aesthetic specificity has helped to encourage a mystification of art as a quasi-transcendental sphere, obscuring the historical and ideological determinants affecting the production of art and the dissemination of aesthetic values, and perpetuating the myth of the great artist as solitary genius. On the other hand, however, it has also formed the basis of a number of oppositional readings of literature; the formal complexity of the text is perceived to serve a potentially critical function by distancing and defamiliarizing the ideological frameworks within which it operates. A conception of literary discourse as a site of resistance to or subversion of ideology has been frequently drawn upon by both Marxist and feminist critics; the ambiguities and dissonances within the text reveal contradictions which enable a critical reading of prevailing ideologies. The text's relative autonomy, as embodied in its formally mediated relationship to ideology, can be appropriated by both conservative and radical positions, depending upon whether its affirmative/compensatory or its negative/contestatory function is foregrounded. Because the notion of aesthetic autonomy has been used by conservative critics to defend an ahistorical and apolitical reading of culture, feminism is not thereby obliged to respond by adopting a reductive theory of literary meaning. Rather, there is a need to acknowledge the formal complexity of the literary or artistic text while at the same time continuing to stress the socially mediated nature of both the text and responses to it.

This point has in fact been tacitly recognized in the interpretative practices of much contemporary feminist criticism. Whereas the earliest feminist readings concentrated upon the critique of sexist images in literature, an issue which still possesses relevance, particularly in the context of a theory of reception that relates texts to ordinary readers, it has become apparent that literary texts are governed by complex structural relations, which cannot always be reduced to a one-dimensional reflection of patriarchal ideology. Like Marxism, feminism has become increasingly aware of the problems involved in a reductionist approach to the analysis of culture, and feminist critics have consequently sought to address the specificity of literary signification by exploring the formal dissonances and contradictions within the individual work. At the same time, this potential 'openness' of the text, which defamiliarizes fixed ideological positions, does not in itself generate a specifically feminist knowledge: the polysemic work that allows for a feminist reading can by the same logic be equally well appropriated for a conservative one. The value of a text as art, if one means by this a self-reflexive symbolic structure which generates multiple meanings and is not directly reducible to ideological interests, does not therefore constitute a sufficient basis for the specific needs and interests of a feminist politics of culture, which also needs to situate itself more concretely in relation to the ideological dimension of the text and the praxis-oriented interests of an oppositional feminist public sphere.

There remains, then, both an interaction and an inevitable tension between the spheres of 'feminism' and 'aesthetics'. As Patrocinio Schweickart argues, feminist criticism is a necessarily contradictory enterprise; it produces tensions and problems which cannot be resolved by thinking either dualistically (whereby literature and ideology are separate spheres) or monistically (whereby literature is indistinguishable from political ideology): 'Feminist criticism must not imply the subordination of feminism to traditional literary criticism, or the subordination of aesthetic and literary concerns to politics, or a compromise between these opposing interests. Feminist criticism should be a dialectical mediation between them.'[7] My own analysis has tended to stress the 'feminist' side of the dialectic, given my interest in the politics of feminist fiction and my concern to show that this issue can be adequately addressed only by relating literary practices to the goals and interests of the women's movement, rather than relying upon an abstract fetishization of aesthetic modernism as a source of subversion. Instead of limiting itself to a reading of a few 'great works', whether those of Virginia Woolf or other canonical writers, feminist analysis can more usefully attempt to embrace an understanding of the full range of literary forms written and read by women in relation to a broader theorization of women's position in culture and society. In the case of feminist literature, this has entailed an investigation of the social importance and strategic value of contemporary women's writing in relation to the emancipatory claims of the women's movement. I have attempted to analyze some of the ways in which feminism has shaped attitudes toward the production and reception of literature and art. An investigation of some of the most representative genres of feminist literature has made it possible to elucidate in more detail the relationship between the ideological perspectives generated by feminism and the structures and themes of recent women's writing.

At the same time, it must be acknowledged that this reading offers only a partial and by no means comprehensive account of literary meaning, which cannot be collapsed into the social function it serves for a historically specific set of writers and readers without all the attendant problems of sociological reductionism. Literary theory had adequately demonstrated that literary texts, to varying degrees, possess the capacity to resist or transcend the interpretative schemata which are imposed upon them at any particular moment. Some examples of recent feminist writing foreground this polysemic dimension of literary discourse more clearly than others and continue

to generate multiple resonances well beyond the immediate historical conditions of their production. The works of Margaret Atwood, for example, have
inspired a large number of readings which go beyond any specific feminist
'message' her texts may be said to contain. Other examples of feminist fiction
that served an important purpose at the time of publication by articulating
women's discovery of their oppression may appear aesthetically naive or
excessively didactic at a historical distance.

The notion of a feminist aesthetics presupposes that these two dimensions
of textual reception can be unproblematically harmonized, assuming either
that an aesthetically self-conscious literature which subverts conventions of
representation forms a sufficient basis for a feminist politics of culture (a
position that can be regarded as both elitist and politically naive), or that texts
which have been politically important to the women's movement are automatically of aesthetic significance, a position that taken to its logical conclusion would rate *The Women's Room* as a better work of art than the writing of
Kafka, or indeed Woolf. A dialectical interaction between politics and aesthetics is compressed into an identity which attempts to construct a normative aesthetic on the basis of feminist interests.

Seen thus, the question of a feminist aesthetics, defined as a theory which
would subordinate all aesthetic categories to the interests of feminist ideology, reveals itself to be something of a nonissue, a chimera which feminist
critics have needlessly pursued. Rather than privileging the aesthetic, a
feminist cultural politics should concern itself with addressing the potential
value of forms from both high and mass culture in relation to the objectives of
a feminist public sphere. Because a particular form is formally conventional,
or marketed for profit, we may not automatically conclude that it is irre-
deemably compromised and cannot constitute a legitimate medium of oppositional cultural activity. The emergence of the feminist public sphere thus
calls into question the dichotomy that Bürger poses in his *Theory of the Avant-
Garde* and that reveals his continuing indebtedness to Adorno's position in
spite of his attempts to problematize it: between an autonomous art which
protests against society but remains elitist and ineffective, and the products of
the mass media, which encourage identification and blur the distinction
between art and life but with the loss of any critical dimension.[8] Much
feminist literature is both popular *and* oppositional; the importance of the
women's movement, along with other sites of resistance in contemporary
society which have generated a diversity of cultural forms, calls into question
the assumption underlying negative aesthetics that a literature which draws
on rather than problematizes conventional forms is invariably complicit with
a monolithic ruling ideology and serves as an apology for the status quo.

It should be stressed that this shift, from the pursuit of a single 'feminist
aesthetics' toward a situating of a range of literary and cultural forms in
relation to the politics of the women's movement, does not imply any kind of

uncritical assent to current feminist political and cultural practices. On the contrary, as I have tried to show, there exist problematic tendencies within feminism which need to be addressed, such as the trend toward an increasingly conservative and quietist politics grounded in a romantic celebration of a feminine sphere.[9] It is possible, moreover, that the diversity of contemporary feminism, often hailed as one of its main strengths, may well result in a gradual dissipation of its oppositional force; the women's movement appears to be splintering into conflicting factions, which may prove unable to articulate a systematic challenge to the increasing hegemony of neoconservatism in Western societies in the late 1980s. The significant ideological gains made by feminism in the last twenty years do not by any means provide grounds for unqualified optimism.

In any case, the question of the politics of feminist reading or writing is not a question which can be resolved at an aesthetic level alone; it is inextricably linked to the fate of the women's movement as a whole. I have argued that one of the most important strengths of feminism derives from the fact that it does not simply constitute an academic discourse but continues to inspire a social and cultural movement and that this issue must remain central to the discussion of the significance of feminist literature. Thus the political value and limitations of particular forms can be meaningfully assessed only in the context of a more general theoretical consideration of the relations among women, literature, and society. I am not suggesting that the function of literature is to reflect passively the already constituted needs of a female audience; on the contrary, literature and art can help to create new perceptions and new needs. In this sense there exists a dialectical relationship between audiences and texts which cannot be encompassed either by conceiving of literature as a mere reflection of existing social relations or by vaguely referring to the literary text as a form of radical intervention without specifying the text's particular relation to the social and historical contexts in which it is produced and received. My analysis has attempted to draw out the enabling function of feminist literature as a critique of values and as a source of positive fictions of female identity, while simultaneously insisting that feminist literature, like feminism itself, must be viewed not in isolation, but in relation to the social and ideological conditions within which it emerges and against which it defines itself.

['The Dialectic of "Feminism" and "Aesthetics"', in *Beyond Feminist Aesthetics: Feminist Literature and Social Change* (London: Hutchinson Radius, 1989), 175–82.]

69 Missing Women: Rethinking Early Thoughts on Images of Women

The political identity of the women's movement has been formed in large part by a critique of the representations of women that circulate through 'high' culture and the media, including film, television, advertising, and pornography. These 'images of women' have been denounced by some in the name of feminism. Yet they are difficult to disavow because of the potency of their formulations of femininity, their fascination, and their pleasures. We recognize a gap between idealized or debased versions of 'woman' and the lives and identities we ordinarily inhabit, but in spite of the gap, we cannot but acknowledge that to a certain extent our identities are formed through such imageries.

Feminist cultural theories of the image have moved along a trajectory from an initial denunciation of stereotyped images of women to a more exacting assessment of the productive role of representation in the construction of subjectivity, femininity, and sexuality. In this paper I want to revisit an article I wrote in 1977, at the beginning of my political and theoretical engagement with feminist studies of the image, entitled 'What's Wrong with "Images of Women"?' in order to draw out more clearly what has been gained by the substitution of one paradigm, 'images of women', for another, 'representation/sexuality/femininity'. As paradigms, they inhabit different theoretical universes, differently valorized by their advocates in terms of accessibility and relevance versus theoretical sophistication. My concern in 1977 was to establish a point of contact between women who had become conscious of the problem with 'images of women' and the theoreticians who were attempting to work the problem through. That dialogue is ongoing and continues to be relevant.

[...] I want now to reconsider some of the examples I used in the 1977 article. In trying to get a distance from the overwhelming naturalism of photographic imagery and the ideologies of woman, I looked at an advertisement for a large chemical company, which featured a series of seven ads. One of them showed a photograph of a young girl, nude. What I noted at the time was the elision of nakedness, bodyness, and woman, a combination which the reversal—using a man's body—made strange. In subsequent considerations of the original advertisement, much more complex readings became possible. The advertisement was composed of a large photograph accompanied by text which read:

Adolescence—a time of misgiving. Doubts about the site offered by parents to build a life on. Both head and heart subject to the tyranny of hormones. Youth under stress in search of an identity.

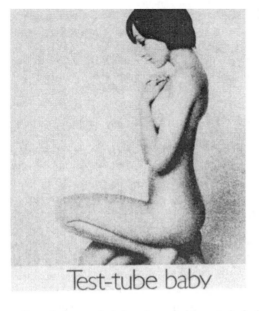

Detail from Bayer advertisement

Test-tube baby

Bayer is there to help her through this period of self-seeking. With textile fibers and die stuffs for the fashionable clothes she needs to wear... With raw ingredients for the cosmetics she uses to create her own personality. And simple remedies too. Like aspirin (a Bayer discovery) for the pain she will experience.

All of this was under two headings. The series was called the 'Seven Ages of Man'. This particular ad was labeled "Test Tube Baby'.

My first impulse was to point out that this was not only the single nude in the series, but the only woman. The combination seemed significant and sufficient (denunciation of the exploitative use of the female body). But close scrutiny of the text and its relation to the image generates something quite different. The whole of the text produces a tension between inner and outer, organic and artificial. Adolescence is the key condition; it is a moment of lack, waiting to be filled with meaning. It oscillates between notions of emptiness, a *tabula rasa* onto which personality and identity will be inscribed, and an imaginary fullness, the menstruating, fully dressed, and made-up woman. Femininity is to be mapped onto the body by cosmetics, fabric, fashion, which echo definitions of femininity as 'masquerade'. The body is also subject to another signification of femininity in which the feminine body is pathological, ill, in need of drugs as a direct result of the reproductive function with which it is so often elided. This body is both a trace of that maternal body and its disavowal through the fetishes of costume and the mask of makeup. Adolescence is posited as a period of transition between the lack and the completion. But completion is a kind of masquerade, and it is presented here as depending upon external interventions in the form of manufactured products. This psychosexual formation is thus articulated with commodity circulation. Bayer makes all the things this body needs to achieve 'her-ness'.

Yet Bayer is posited not merely as a producer of chemical commodities, but as a kind of midwife to the 'test tube baby'. It is there to help and provide. There is an implied identification with the place of the mother, as that nurturing, formative Other. At this point it is important to connect this text with the image. We might simply describe the image as a figure without clothes, in a kneeling posture, hands crossed over the chest, head inclined. But these body gestures and postures and the lack of clothing signify connotationally, outside the image, within the culture. 'Unclothed' is a willfully obscure way of not saying the obvious. This is a nude. The nude is a term of art (artifice, culture), but in that discourse, it is a signifier for an ideologically construed notion of a state of nature, innocence, ignorance. The term 'baby' implies a state of nature too, but the pose suggests another metaphor of the body as an organic entity. The pose may suggest an unfolding flower or bud. The pose and gesture are intensely rhetorical: the inclined head and crossed arms are both demure and submissive. We tend to associate these postures with woman, yet this body cannot be easily sexed. Indeed, its obvious sexual identity is carefully concealed by the legs and even the arms. The body is hairless and has no obvious signs of female gender, but it would be hard to dispute that most viewers would see it as a woman. Where does its femininity come from? From its submissiveness, its suggestion of unfurling flowers, its silence and to-be-done to-ness? In some senses the visual image is the opposite of the image conjured up by the text. The connotations of nature oppose the notion of the body as the site of chemical, that is, cultural transformation. The image has to sell the idea that someone needs Bayer products, that becoming a woman is a matter of intervention, construction, and artifice accomplished by using Bayer goods. The image also has to portray Bayer as a mere helper on the way to a process that is as natural as childbirth, yet naturally uses Bayer's test tube products. These contradictory impulses are at one level signified by the opposition between image-iconic message, and text-linguistic message. I do not think it is as simple as image being woman and the text signifying man (Bayer). The advertisement as a semantic field tries to knit into its complex pattern associations of birth and its feminine sphere, medicine and its supporting role, femininity and its artifice. The nude body is not a stable signifier for a given, simple notion of woman. It introduces into the play of the semantic field of the ad as a whole a series of possibilities that include a momentary recognition by the viewer of this as a female body. But the image does not work to fix that recognition, but rather to invoke and then destabilize it so that it can signify a lack that only Bayer can make good. Yet to put that lack on display involves defensive procedures to disavow that feminine body as a signifier of lack.

The text produces a body that lacks an identity, a self, and that needs Bayer to furnish those lacks, which will then produce 'woman'. Would there be pleasure in looking at a body signifying lack; does not the female body in Freud's schema represent lack in a most terrifying way, threatening the potential mutilation of that by which masculinity figures itself as lacking lack? It has been argued that woman's body is an extremely threatening sight, and that its visual display is conditional upon a series of defensive strategies by means of which the threat of lack this body evokes can be disavowed and allayed. Fetishism is the prime defense, turning from the lacking body to some comforting substitute for that which is missing. Indeed, under the regime of fetishism, the female body is converted into a sign for the phallus itself. When such fetishism is combined with a tendency to compensate for the fright the body could offer by building it up into an abstractly or formally beautiful object, the body we see can in no way be deemed to be a body of woman—rather it is a sign for phallus, an inscription of masculine anxieties and fears displaced by aesthetic beauty. Merely to denounce this body as impossibly glamorized is precisely to miss the conditions of its existence, which have nothing to do with women. It may, of course, address and solicit women viewers into complicity with the order of sexual difference that generated it, which it actively signifies to its viewers.

This suggests not only that we are not looking at an image of woman, but also that we are hardly looking at a body at all. We may be looking at traces of several body *signs*, which can simultaneously occupy the fictive space of the image—or perhaps we should now introduce the real site of meanings. The point at which all the traces and currents activated by the signifying elements in the text (iconic and linguistic or graphic) converge is the putative viewer, who carries with him or her the necessary baggage to move in and out and across the many dimensions of the image that such systematic decoding inevitably impoverishes. The viewer is the split subject of semiotics (since Kristeva) and of psychoanalysis. The split subject operates in two discontinuous fields. Both word and image must address the conflicting demands of conscious and unconscious registers. Photographic representation has particular potency in this field for it offers fictive fields for fantasy located in credible spaces, likely scenarios, and fantastic possibilities. It addresses the demand for the legible and visible while servicing the less prosaic signifying systems of the unconscious with its multiple displacements, substitutions, and playfulness.

Let me now turn to another example originally used in my 1977 article. It is an advertisement for Levi's jeans in which again an unclothed body appeared. Rather, I should be precise—the advertisement offered a *corps morcelé*, a body fragment. The best way to summon it up is to invoke the viewer. The viewer is presented with buttocks that are situated at eye level. One cheek is visible and the other cut off by the edge of the image. Also included is a section of the arm and half a hand. On the fully exposed buttock are drawn the outlines of the stitching of a pocket to which is attached the Levi's label. I assumed that this had to be read as a female body, until a colleague pointed out its clear references to one of art's most famous buttocks, those of *David* by Michelangelo.

The hand, then, is there to underline the quotation. Why then did I see it as female while my colleague saw it as male? Probably because I know this image in color and he saw only the black-and-white reproduction, which emphasized the sharp line that the divide and crease in the buttock make. The effect is obviously more like the masculine anatomy. In the color version, this perception is effaced by the golden glow that bathes and unifies the surface of the whole image. The light is softening and creates highlights that emphasize the curves. Softened forms and contours connote a difference in the sexually demarcated rhetories of representation, a difference signaled by the term 'woman'. The body is not sexed by reference to genital difference. The reading depends on the way light and color gloss the forms to convey feminine connotations. But to anyone for whom the reference to Michelangelo is available and vivid, the body would read as 'masculine'. The ambiguity is wholly to the point of the advertising campaign, which is serviced by an image that sells Levi's jeans both to men and women and can offer them to both kinds of consumer by pitching their desirability through a narrative of men looking at women's bums and women knowing that men find pleasure in looking at women's bums in tight jeans and thus imagine them without jeans, and so on. Jeans, moreover, have the added *frisson* of disrupting difference through confusing fixed-fashion codes for men and women. Yet this image has to be about desire and has to invoke it—a desire that will become attached to the commodity, which is itself here attached to the body as the site and figuring of desire. Could this image be read against this grain according to the viewer's sexual orientation? Its ambivalent gender identity only enhances that wide range of consumers. Yet without denying the potentiality of the images to be read variously according to the position of its viewers, there is a pressure within it towards a preferred reading. Color is vital here. Through it the body is drawn, photo-*graphy*. Yet at one point light signifies lack; between the legs there is a gap where the model's right thigh is clearly defined by the fall of light. The same lighting effaces the contours of the left buttock and thigh. In this dazzling brightness, form is obliterated. Does this create the void that signals a lack of masculine genitals, thus signifying a female body precisely as that which lacks? Does this bright shaft of light nonetheless stand in for what cannot be seen in its brightness? If it can erase the leg, what else has it merely erased?

More than a decade after writing my original essay, I still think that anyone brought up in western society would read the body in that image as a female body, an erotic proffering of a sexualized body part. But that hardly explains the success of this image or its possibility as an advertisement. The highly technical manufacture of this image, its management of scale and fragment, its play on disavowals and displacements, its use of saturated golden color, and the deployment of a phallic hand move us constantly back and forth over meanings generated by these specific elements in the image field and then out into a world of images, back across the fantasies of bodies and their sexualities and uses located in our psyches, in those unconscious formations of fantasy that are synonymous with the manufacture of sexuality and sexual difference itself.[1]

['Missing Women: Rethinking Early Thoughts on Images of Women', in Carol Squiers (ed.), *The Critical Image: Essays on Contemporary Photography* (London: Lawrence and Wishart, 1990), 202–16.]

ABIGAIL SOLOMON-GODEAU

70 Just Like a Woman

Running throughout the body of Woodman's work are three central and overarching themes. First, and perhaps most compelling, is Woodman's staging of herself as the model for herself, the artist. In this alternating movement between active, creative subject—a producer of meaning—and passive object—a receiver of meaning—are metaphorically enacted the difficulty and paradox that attend the activity of the woman artist. Moreover, this seesaw of subject/object positions involves another set of relations: those of the artist and the model to the camera. Accordingly, Woodman's work reckons with the camera as a third term in the construction of an elaborately coded femininity.

Another theme in Woodman's photography is the constant insistence on the woman's body as both a sight (a spectacle) and a site (of meaning, desire, projection). Last, Woodman appears wholly to have grasped, and taken as the very substance of her work, the operations of fetishism as they are mobilized in the metamorphosis of female flesh into image. In choosing to assert rather than deny or avoid the fetish status of the female body, Woodman's photographs are vulnerable to the charge of collusion with those very operations. I would argue, however, that through strategies of defamiliarization and disruption—excess, displacement, disordering—Woodman exposes the overdetermination of the body as signifier, thereby significantly altering the spectator's relationship to it.

There is a sense in which all three of Woodman's themes are integrally related, indivisibly bound. The youthful, beautiful Francesca Woodman experiences herself as the object of the gaze, magnet and locus of the desires and fantasies of others. And at the same time, as an artist, a photographer, she is the author of work that is specifically about the visual, the realm of the scopic. Her pictures, like those of any photographer, are produced by looking and arresting the look. The orchestration of these looks—those of the photographer, the camera, the spectator—functions of produce different subject positions. Feminist film theory, using psychoanalytic theory as a tool, has interpreted these positions through the operation of sexual difference.[1] These looks, these subject positions, are accordingly understood as *gendered*. Thus, active looking—the mastering look of the photographer, the voyeuristic or fetishistic look of the spectator (whose position is mandated by the photographer's and from which it cannot be separated)—is understood as occupying a masculine position. In her alternating occupancy of the active position of artist/photographer and the passive position of object/model. Woodman's activity raises many of the problems of feminine subjectivity and creativity, invoked, for example, in the question 'what (if anything) changes when it is a woman who wields the camera?' Implicit in such a rhetorical query are others: Do women see differently, be it as artists or spectators? What contradictions are described when women assume what is posited as a masculine position? Is the act of looking or imaging, because active, inevitably a masculine position?[2]

In placing herself, her body, in front of the lens, Woodman does in fact collapse the distinction between seer and seen, subject of the gaze and object of it, artist and model. But far from producing any ideal synthesis, or surmounting the terms of these positions, occupying them both serves only to reassert their essential difference.

By electing to function as her own model, by casting herself as an image (for there is no attempt at portrait-like characterization or psychological delineation), Woodman was adapting to her purposes a device shared by artists as dissimilar as Cindy Sherman, Les Krims, and Hannah Wilke. As such a grouping indicates, this strategy can yield entirely different results and be marshaled for wholly different purposes. Consequently, Woodman's use of it needs to be critically perceived in light of her other two overarching thematics. By staging her body in ways that appear deliberately calculated both to generate and emphasize what Laura Mulvey termed its 'to-be-looked-at-ness'.[3] Woodman links the psychic objectification she deliberately and literally enacts (self becoming other) with the specular objectification (human being becoming image) inherent in photographic representations. Further, in furnishing her image-self, or its surrogate, with the paraphernalia of fetishism (garter belts, boas, stockings, shells, eels, calla lilies, and so forth). Woodman constructs a metonymic chain that ultimately terminates in the imaged feminine body, presented to the spectator as itself the ur-fetish object. By way of example, we can consider a photograph dated 1979 which unambiguously adapts the conventional iconography of fetishism. The supine nude, stretched across a Victorian chaise lounge, offers her body to the gaze of surveillance, mastery, and imaginary possession. Here is presented a staple of erotica, with a pedigree as exalted as the Rokeby Venus or as debased as a *Playboy* centerfold. But by girding the torso with three garter belts instead of one, by suspending superfluous stockings from the wall, Woodman creates a disturbance in the field. The fantasy tableau, the little theater of the fetish, becomes deranged. Its familiar props, through a deceptively simple additive principle, now become strange and alienating. If a multiplication of phallic symbols signals castration fear, as Freud asserts, might not a multiplication of fetish paraphernalia evoke a comparable dread?

This interlocking network of fetishism and castration anxiety, as it constellates around the body of the woman, is frequently delineated in other of Woodman's images. A picture from the series *I Stopped Playing the Piano* (Providence, ca. 1977) depicts a knife-wielding woman, breast bared, a reptilian object cleaving to her chest. Another image in the series *Liza Used to Have Long Hair* confronts the viewer with a seated nude woman, cropped at the eyes, wisps and swatches of hair taped to her body. In another, the body of a nude is bisected by an inky swath of fur boa, obscuring the sex it simultaneously invokes. [. . .]

Overall, Woodman's variations on both the construction and the inscription of femininity do not stake out an identifiable position for either the male or female spectator. Arguably, it is precisely this ambiguity, the indeterminacy of subject and viewing positions, that charges Woodman's photographs with their unsettling admixture of seductiveness and affront. This ambiguity of address seems particularly apparent in the large number of Woodman's images that elaborate on that most venerable and recurrent topos, the conflation of the woman and her body with nature.

Consistent with her literalizing strategies that make manifest the latent dynamics of fetishism, Woodman renders the forms of this association explicit. One particular suite of images (MacDowell, Summer 1980) traces a successive slippage whereby the woman becomes progressively absorbed into the natural landscape with which she is mythically identified. The rolled birch bark clasped in one shot encases both of Woodman's arms in another. In a subsequent member of the series, the Daphne-like metamorphosis is accelerated; situated within the birch grove, the white verticals of the woman's raised arms become visually meshed with the trees. Similarly, in another member of the series, the woman's outstretched arm describes a boundary in which the real natural world—the conifers bordering the lake—and a 'natural' simulation—the ferns that mimic their reflection—are optically joined. What might otherwise be perceived as merely a playful trompe l'œil effect in photography is given an altogether different inflection by the use of the woman's body as a locus for this visual confusion. The familiarity and ubiquity of the conceptual collapse

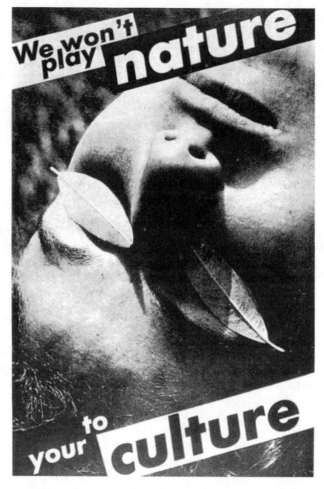

Barbara Kruger, Untitled, 1982, from *We Won't Play Nature to Your Culture* Catalogue

of woman into nature are here effectively bracketed, stalled, even short-circuited through the subtle suggestion of the nightmare facet of metamorphosis.

It is interesting in this context to compare a recent work such as Barbara Kruger's *We Won't Play Nature to Your Culture* to Woodman's approach. Kruger's confrontational address, effected both linguistically and formally, contributes to the construction of her work as an unambiguous act of radical refusal. Kruger's attempt to direct her work to a female spectator operates along the axis of language. We [women] refuse this relationship. Spectators are thus automatically differentiated and distinguished through the mode of address that constructs a feminine *us* and a masculine *them*. The purpose of Kruger's choice of purloined image—the woman's face with blinded, leaf-covered eyes—is to signify visually the implications of this putative relation-ship, characterized as both lethal and blinding. In contrast to Kruger's unmistakable stance, Woodman's production in general stages no act of defiant or militant negation, provides no guideposts for an alternate, meliorative construction, indicates no privileged space for the female specta-tor. Instead, Woodman relentlessly offers up the archetypal allusions, myth-ologies, emblems, and symbols adhering to the feminine, and infuses them—charges them—with dread, with dis-ease.

Woodman's art is thus a troubling and troubled one. Ridden with menace, its lapidary beauty and elegance function as a kind of lure. Nowhere is this clearer than in the numerous series that enact tableaux of entrapment, engulfment, or absorption of the woman in those spaces—both literal and metaphorical—to which she is conventionally relegated. In the *Space²* sequence (Providence, ca. 1975–76), for example, the body is depicted in, on, and around a glass museum display case. Here, the reified condition of the feminine as aestheticized object is made utterly explicit, as are the stakes. Variations on this theme include one in which the case contains an animal skull, another in which the corpse-like body of the model spills out of a Natural History display cabinet filled with stuffed specimens, birds, a raccoon.

But it is perhaps the *House* series (Providence, ca. 1975–77) where the gothic aspect of Woodman's work is most apparent. In these photographs the woman's body is physically devoured by the house. As in Charlotte Perkins Gilman's *The Yellow Wallpaper*, the space of woman's seclusion and worldly exclusion not only imprisons, it also consumes. Swallowed by the fireplace, layered over by the wallpaper, effaced, occulted, Woodman presents herself as

Francesca Woodman, from the *House* series, Nos. 3 and 4. Providence, R. I., 1975–6

the living sacrifice to the domus. The extremity and violence of these photographs are matched only by a grouping in which the woman's body is defaced—by dirt, by paint, by rubbish—and identified with the scabrous walls and corners against which she is impressed. The desecration of the woman's body that such images enact is tempered by the recognition that this is, after all, the flip side of its idealization. Woodman's linking of the woman's body to the walls and surfaces it seems bonded to repeats the theme of the body as itself a surface. The marking of this body in patriarchal culture, its incarnation as sign, is given a chilling embodiment when Woodman marks it in ways that conjure the impulse to debase and violate which parallels the impulse to worship and adore.

If the *House* photographs function on the register of nightmare, the astonishing blue-print works are conceived in the less charged modality of the oneiric. Thematically, they elaborate on ideas and motifs that surface regularly in Woodman's work: the 'found' morphological and formal resemblances between nature and culture, the animate and inanimate. Here as always, the image of woman is central insofar as it is her body that becomes the dictionary of form to which all others are metaphorically or metonymically linked. However, in one of these works, the figure of the woman is abolished, although the presence of masculine and feminine signifiers is nonetheless established. The triptych to which I refer, the 14-foot-long *Bridges and Tiaras*, is somewhat exceptional in the sense that it is constructed entirely from found images: a schematic rendering of an eighteenth-century bridge design, a filigree-work tiara, and a modern bridge. The three images, enlarged to the same grandiose scale, visually assert a condition of equivalence. Thus the decorative ornament, quintessence of the feminine, is the center image of the triptych, but, more crucially, it is presented in a way that insists on its equal importance. The masculine accomplishment of engineering and large-scale construction is similarly depicted as subject to gendered readings; the eighteenth-century bridge appears far more 'feminine' than its industrial-age successor. This relativizing of masculinity and femininity is comparatively rare in Woodman's work where the emphasis is placed so emphatically on the sexual, cultural, and aesthetic construction of femininity. Nonetheless, throughout her work there surface occasional explorations of sexual ambiguity or indeterminacy. This is manifest in suites of her images where sexual codes collide, where the boundaries and certainties of sexual difference are placed in unresolved play.

Reflecting on the range of Woodman's production in its entirety, I am struck by its encyclopedic recapitulation of images and symbols of and for the woman. But more impressive is Woodman's disturbance and denaturalizing of the attributes that are, in Bob Dylan's phrase, 'just like a woman'.

Consider, for example, the traditional iconographic coupling of the woman (or the goddess) with the mirror. As an attribute of vanity, or in our post-

Freudian age—narcissim—to which women are legendarily thought to be excessively prey, the mirror comes to connote femininity in a manner altogether self-evident. In Woodman's frequent use of mirrors, when they reflect the woman at all, what is produced is simply another image. Hence, the relationship constructed is not between the real woman and her image, but between the spectator and two equally unreal images. What the mirror reflects, or fails to reflect, is always thrown back on the spectator. Reading vanity, or narcissism, into the image is revealed as an interpretive—and thus projective—act. This seems to me to be at once the strength and the limit of Woodman's art. A feminine poetics or aesthetics must by definition presume the existence of a feminine subject whose perception, vision, and creativity are formed through and by her femininity. But if we acknowledge, as Woodman surely did, that femininity is a discursive construction, a social category, a constraining and psychically destructive process imposed from without and painfully internalized, a condition, moreover, defined by its alienation, how is that femininity to be authentically construed? Where, in short, do we locate and ground this femininity apart from the patriarchal structures that 'speak' it?

Alternatively, a feminist poetics or aesthetics tends to be far more tentative in its assumption of the mantle of femininity. The philosophy of the Other engenders a politics of the Other, and a feminist aesthetics must draw its mandate from both.[4] A feminist aesthetics can assume no given feminine, can only do its work by dislodging or intervening in the operations that have historically defined and imposed it.

Not the least part of the great accomplishment represented by the artistic legacy of Francesca Woodman is the way it both urgently and eloquently poses these complex issues of relationship between the definition of the feminine and the theories of the feminist. The identifications and projections the work summons or denies are inextricably joined to the investigation of both. The tragedy of Woodman's death is a fact and a given, but the work she produced is a living testimonial, a valuable bequest to other women. Its gravity and its extremity are a legacy of painful knowledge, but its sensuous beauty and dreamlike allusiveness assert, after all, the strength of the will, the pleasure of its maker. Alienated from language, from culture, from image, from body, the woman artist nonetheless manages to speak.

['Just Like a Woman', in Abigail Solomon-Godeau and Linda Nochlin (ed.), *Photography at the Dock: Essays on Photography, History, Institutions and Practices* (Minneapolis: University of Minnesota Press, 1991), 244–55.]

71 Getting Down to Basics: Art, Obscenity and the Female Nude

Immanuel Kant's *Critique of Aesthetic Judgement* (1790) was fundamental in the formation of European aesthetics and its influence is still easily discernible in art history and criticism today although usually in a somewhat 'hand-me-down' and popularized way.

The form/matter opposition governs the whole of the *Critique*.[1] Kant sought to distinguish sensory from contemplative pleasures. According to Kant, although the pleasure experienced in the beautiful is immediate, it involves a reflection on the object and this sets it apart from the merely sensuous pleasures which may be derived, for example, from eating or drinking. Aesthetic pleasure is thus more refined than physical forms of pleasure since it necessarily involves the 'higher' faculty of contemplation. Perhaps one of the most influential of Kant's ideas was the axiom that the individual object is detached in aesthetic judgement and considered simply for 'its own sake'. The art object should serve no ulterior purpose and aesthetic judgement itself should be disinterested; the observer's desires and ambitions should be held in abeyance in the act of pure contemplation. Kant also distinguished 'free' from 'dependent' beauty; the first derived without the aid of conceptualization, the second requiring an interest in the material existence of the object. For Kant the judgement of 'dependent' beauty is necessarily less pure or open to abstraction than the contemplation of 'free' beauty. Whereas examples of free beauty are found in nature they are rarely seen in art; art usually requires some conceptualization of the subject expressed. This system establishes a hierarchy of aesthetic experience. As far as possible, judgement should be free of interest both in relation to the material condition of the individual object and the aims and desires of the viewer, for it is only through this act of liberation from individual preference that a judgement may be claimed as universally valid for all rational beings.

This set of distinctions may seem clear enough but it has been devastatingly analysed and dismantled by Derrida in his essay entitled 'Parergon' included in the collection *The Truth in Painting*. Derrida makes an apparently simple observation: in order to make a 'pure' judgement you have to be able to judge what is intrinsic to the object and thus the proper concern of aesthetic judgement and what is extrinsic to the object and thus irrelevant. This permanent requirement, Derrida writes, structures all philosophical discourses on art and, most importantly, it 'presupposes a discourse on the limit between the inside and the outside of the art object, here a discourse on the frame'.[2]

So Kant's whole analytic of aesthetic judgement presupposes that you *can* distinguish rigorously between the intrinsic and the extrinsic. Judgement should properly bear upon intrinsic beauty (which is within the proper limits of art) and not upon mere decoration or sensuous appeal (which are outside the limits). According to Kant, [. . .] what is bad, what is outside or goes beyond aesthetic taste and judgement is matter, that which is motivated, sensory matter which seduces, which embarrasses or leads the viewer astray, away from the proper consideration of intrinsic form.

But how, or where, are these distinctions between form and matter, between intrinsic and extrinsic made? Derrida suggests that the critical place of judgement is not at the centre of the category where differences are most clear, but at the very limit, at the framing edge of the category where the surplus or secondary term most nearly belongs to the main subject. It is at these crucial edges where the distinction between inside and outside, inclusion and exclusion, acceptability and unacceptability, is most exquisite.

I have been taking this detour via Kant and Derrida because I believe that together they offer a way of understanding the critical importance of the female nude in the tradition of Western art. If we go back to the basic opposition of art and obscenity which I discussed earlier, we can now begin to place the female nude not only at the centre of the definition of art but also on the edge of the category, pushing against the limit, brushing against obscenity. The female nude is the border, the *parergon* as Derrida also calls it, between art and obscenity. The female body—natural, *un*structured— represents something which is outside the proper field of art and aesthetic judgement but artistic style—pictorial form—contains and regulates the body and renders it an object of beauty, suitable for art.

The frame, then, is a metaphor for the 'staging' of art, both in terms of surrounding the body with style and of marking the limit between art and not-art, that is, obscenity. Here, etymology seems to confirm the metaphor. The etymology of 'obscene' is disputed but it may be a modification of the Latin *'scena'*, so meaning literally what is off, or to one side of the stage, beyond presentation. Within this context, the art/obscenity pairing repre- sents the distinction between that which *can* be seen and that which is just beyond presentation. The female nude marks both the internal limit of art and the external limit of obscenity. This is why the representation of the female nude is critical. It is the internal structural link which holds art and obscenity and an entire system of meaning together. And whilst the female nude can behave well, it involves a risk and threatens to destabilize the very foundations of our sense of order.

There is just one more relationship which can be introduced to this system. The art/obscenity opposition can also be mapped on to Kant's distinction between the beautiful and the sublime. Following Edmund Burke, Kant differentiated between the experience of the sublime and the experience of the beautiful. He wrote in the *Critique*:

The beautiful in nature is a question of the form of the object, and this consists in limitation, whereas the sublime is to be found in an object even devoid of form, so far as it immediately involves, or else by its presence provokes, a representation of limitlessness.[3]

So whereas the form of the beautiful is seen to lie in limitation (e.g. in the contemplation of a framed picture), the sublime challenges this act of judgement by suggesting the possibility of form beyond limit. Whereas the sentiment of beauty is predicated on a sense of the harmony between man and nature and the rationality and intelligibility of the world, the sublime is conceived of as a mixture of pleasure, pain and terror which forces us to recognize the limits of rationality.[4] Kant specifies this relationship in terms of framing: the beautiful is characterized by the finitude of its formal contours, as a unity contained, limited, by its borders. The sublime, on the contrary, is presented in terms of excess, of the infinite; *it cannot be framed* and is therefore almost beyond presentation (in a quite literal sense, then, *obscene*). For Kant the sublime is encountered more readily in nature than in art. If art is defined as the limiting or framing of formed matter, then the sublime must necessarily be beyond or outside the parameters of art.

It is also significant that Kant expresses the distinction between the beautiful and the sublime in relation to the *viewer's experience* of the object. Whereas the pleasure provoked by the beautiful is one of life enhancement which may be united with the play of the imagination, the pleasure (Lüst) which is excited by the sublime is of a different and negative order. According to Kant, the feeling of the sublime arises indirectly; it is characterized by an inhibition of the vital forces and, as a result of this momentary retention, is followed by a 'discharge all the more powerful' (1911, p. 91). It is a violent, explosive experience; serious rather than playful, it goes beyond simple charms and attraction and is caught up in an alternating rhythm of attraction and repulsion.

We can find the echo of this Kantian differentiation of the beautiful and the sublime in Kenneth Clark's attempts to define art and obscenity. Clark describes the experience of beauty as a bringing together of delicate feelings but refers to the figure of the prostitute by Rouault as 'shattered and profaned'—broken up, out of shape; beyond art and yet conceived in a spirit of awe and inspiring fear. For Clark, the figure is sublime and almost beyond representation (obscene).

Of course, for Kant and other eighteenth-century writers on aesthetics, the sublime and the beautiful are clearly gendered. In a gesture towards fairness and balance, Kant observed:

It is not to be understood ... that woman lacks noble qualities, or that the male sex must do without beauty completely. On the contrary, one expects that a person of either sex brings both together, in such a way that all the other merits of a woman should unite solely to enhance the character of the beautiful, which is the proper reference point; and on the other hand, among the masculine qualities the sublime clearly stands as the criterion of his kind.[5]

Whereas the beautiful is associated with feminine attributes, the sublime is seen characterized by masculine traits. But in the light of this relationship between the sublime and the obscene we arrive at a new and more subtly nuanced understanding of the gendering of aesthetics. The sublime is not simply the site for the definition of masculinity but is also where a certain deviant or transgressive form of femininity is played out. It is where woman goes beyond her proper boundaries and gets out of place.

But in the final instance the beautiful and the sublime are primarily defined in terms of their effects upon the viewer. Whereas the experience of the sublime is seen to be kinetic, the pleasure of the beautiful is always contemplative. Kant writes: 'The mind feels itself *set in motion* in the representation of the sublime in nature; whereas in the aesthetic judgement upon what is beautiful therein it is in *restful* contemplation' (1911, p. 107).

This opposition of a quiet, contemplative pleasure and a form of excited arousal can be related back to the art/obscenity opposition. The axiom that the experience of high art should be static and reflective and that this differentiates it from the experience of non-artistic forms such as pornography recurs again and again in nineteenth- and twentieth-century European aesthetics. There is an interesting example in James Joyce's *A Portrait of the Artist as a Young Man* (published 1916). The novel presents a dramatized version of Joyce's own early aesthetic. In one passage Stephen Dedalus discusses the function of art with Lynch, a fellow undergraduate. The discussion is provoked by the fact that Lynch has scrawled graffiti on the bottom of the Venus of Praxiteles. Lynch argues that his action was stimulated by desire; Stephen replies:

The feelings excited by improper art are kinetic, desire or loathing. Desire urges us to possess, to go *to* something; loathing urges us to abandon, to go *from* something. The arts which excite them, pornographical or didactic, are therefore improper arts. The aesthetic emotion . . . is therefore static. The mind is arrested and raised above desire and loathing.[6]

And so we are back with the Greeks and the female nude as an icon of high art but also precariously at the edge of art and able to excite desire—graffiti scrawled on the bottom of the Venus of Praxiteles as the gesture which denies the aesthetic emotion.

There is a set of value oppositions which has dominated the philosophy of art before and since Kant and which organizes the way in which we conceive of the meaning of art and of meaning as such. And yet, as Derrida has shown categories, or frames, are: 'essentially constructed and therefore fragile'.[7] You cannot be certain of what is intrinsic and extrinsic, you can only engage in a ceaseless definition of contours and edges, limitations and frames. This is what is happening in Kenneth Clark's work; he takes the subject which is right on the edge—the nude—and embarks on a process of definition. We can agree or disagree with his judgements and opinions but this hardly seems the point. Unless we move beyond the traditional terms of the debate we can only engage in a meaningless tug-of-war concerning whether images are more or less obscene, beautiful, sensual, erotic and so on.

And so it is a question of 'getting down to basics' because an investigation of the female nude raises some of the most fundamental values which shape our attitudes to and judgements of art. I have argued that within the Western tradition, art is defined as the transmutation of matter into form and that, within this account, the female body—as nature, pure matter—becomes a most critical subject for art. The female nude stands as the perfect aesthetic achievement and yet also threatens to undo the very principles which structure and sustain the cultural values of art. In the meantime, however, mainstream art will never turn away from the female nude. It cannot afford to. The recent return to the life class is hardly surprising; it is a perpetual question (and I use the word knowingly) of *mastery* over matter.

['Getting Down to Basics: Art, Obscenity and the Female Nude', in Isobel Armstrong (ed.), *New Feminist Discourses: Critical Essays on Theories and Texts* (London and New York: Routledge, 1992), 216–20.]

PEGGY PHELAN

72 Broken Symmetries: Memory, Sight, Love

[B]elief is in itself the image: both arise out of the same procedures and through the same terms: *memory, sight,* and *love.*

Julia Kristeva[1]

The question of belief always enters critical writing and perhaps never more urgently than when one's subject resists vision and may not be 'really there' at all. Like the fantasy of erotic desire which frames love, the distortions of forgetting which infect memories, and the blind spots laced through the visual field, a believable image is the product of a negotiation with an unverifiable real. As a representation of the real the image is always, partially, phantasmatic. In doubting the authenticity of the image, one questions as well the veracity of she who makes and describes it. To doubt the subject seized by the eye is to doubt the subjectivity of the seeing 'I'. These words work both to overcome and to deepen the provocation of that doubt.

As Jacques Lacan repeatedly argued, doubt is a defense against the real.[2] And as basketball players know, sometimes the most effective offense is a good defense. Doubt can be temporarily overcome by belief, that old and slightly arthritic leap of faith. Like Jacob's struggle with the Angel who will not give him a proper name, *Unmarked* attempts to find a theory of value for that which is not 'really' there, that which cannot be surveyed within the boundaries of the putative real.

By locating a subject in what cannot be reproduced within the ideology of the visible, I am attempting to revalue a belief in subjectivity and identity which is not visibly representable. This is not the same thing as calling for greater visibility of the hitherto unseen. *Unmarked* examines the implicit assumptions about the connections between representational visibility and political power which have been a dominant force in cultural theory in the last ten years. Among the challenges this poses is how to retain the power of the unmarked by surveying it within a theoretical frame. By exposing the blind spot within the theoretical frame itself, it may be possible to construct a way of knowing which does not take surveillance of the object, visible or otherwise, as its chief aim.

Employing psychoanalysis and feminist theories of representation, I am concerned with marking the limit of the image in the political field of the sexual and racial other. I take as axiomatic the link between the image and the word, that what one can see is in every way related to what one can say. In framing more and more images of the hitherto under-represented other, contemporary culture finds a way to name, and thus to arrest and fix, the image of that other. Representation follows two laws: it always conveys more than it intends; and it is never totalizing. The 'excess' meaning conveyed by representation creates a supplement that makes multiple and resistant readings possible. Despite this excess, representation produces ruptures and gaps; it fails to reproduce the real exactly. Precisely because of representation's supplemental excess and its failure to be totalizing, close readings of the logic of representation can produce psychic resistance and, possibly, political change. (Although rarely in the linear cause-effect way cultural critics on the Left and Right often assume.)

Currently, however, there is a dismaying similarity in the beliefs generated about the political efficacy of visible representation. The dangerous complicity between progressives dedicated to visibility politics and conservatives patroling the borders of museums, movie houses, and mainstream broadcasting is based on their mutual belief that representations can be treated as 'real truths' and guarded or championed accordingly. Both sides believe that greater visibility of the hitherto under-represented leads to enhanced political power. The progressives want to share this power with 'others'; conservatives want to reserve this power for themselves. Insufficient understanding of the relationship between visibility, power, identity, and liberation has led both groups to mistake the relation between the real and the representational.

As Judith Butler points out,[3] the confusion between the real and the representational occurs because 'the real is positioned both before and after its representation; and representation becomes a moment of the reproduction and consolidation of the real' ('Force of Fantasy': 106). The real is read through representation, and representation is read through the real.

Each representation relies on and reproduces a specific logic of the real; this logical real promotes its own representation. The real partakes of and generates different imagistic and discursive paradigms. There is, for example, a legal real in which concepts such as 'the image' and 'the claimant' are defended and decided through recourse to pre-established legal concepts such as copyright, trademark, property, the contract, and individual rights.[4] Within the physical universe, the real of the quantum is established through a negotiation with the limitations of the representational possibilities of measuring time and space. To measure motion that is not predictable requires that one consider the uncertainty of both the means of measurement and the energy that one wants to measure. Within the history of theatre the real is what theatre defines itself against, even while reduplicating its effects.[5] Within Lacanian psychoanalysis the Real is full Being itself. Freud's mapping of the unconscious, as Lacan consistently insisted, makes the Real forever impossible to realize (to make real) within the frame of the Symbolic.[6] Within the diverse genre of autobiography the real is considered the motivation for self-representation.[7] Each of these concepts of the real contains within it a meta-text of exclusionary power. Each real believes itself to be the Real-real. The discourse of Western science, law, theatrical realism, autobiography, and psychoanalysis are alike in believing their own terms to be the most comprehensive, the most basic, the most fundamental route to establishing or unsettling the stability of the real. By employing each of them in *Unmarked* I hope to demonstrate that the very proliferation of discourses can only disable the possibility of a Real-real.

I know this sounds oh-so-familiar to the ears of weary poststructuralists. But what is less familiar is the way in which the visible itself is woven into each of these discourses as an unmarked conspirator in the maintenance of each discursive real. I want to expose the ways in which the visible real is employed as a truth-effect for the establishment of these discursive and representational notions of the real. Moreover, I want to suggest that by seeing the blind spot within the visible real we might see a way to redesign the representational real. If the visible real is itself unable to constitute a reliable representational real its use-value must lie elsewhere.

The pleasure of resemblance and repetition produces both psychic assurance and political fetishization. Representation reproduces the Other as the Same. Performance, insofar as it can be defined as representation without reproduction, can be seen as a model for another representational economy, one in which the reproduction of the Other *as* the Same is not assured.[8]

The relationship between the real and the representational, between the looker and the given to be seen, is a version of the relation between self and other. Cultural theory has thus far left unexamined the connection between the psychic theory of the relationship between self and other and the political and epistemological contours of that encounter. This relationship between self and other is a marked one, which is to say it is unequal. It is alluring and violent because it touches the paradoxical nature of psychic desire; the always already unequal encounter nonetheless summons the hope of reciprocity and equality; the failure of this hope then produces violence, aggressivity, dissent. The combination of psychic hope and political-historical inequality makes the contemporary encounter between self and other a meeting of profound romance and deep violence. While cultural theorists of the colonial subject and revisionary meta-anthropologists have thrown welcome light on the historical pattern of the violence of this encounter, we still have relatively little knowledge of the romance nestled within it.

Unmarked concerns the relationship between the self and the other as it is represented in photographs, paintings, films, theatre, political protests, and performance art. While the notion of the potential reciprocal gaze has been considered part of the 'unique' province of live performance, the desire to be seen is also activated by looking at inanimate art. Examining the politics of the exchange of gaze across these diverse representational mediums leads to an extended definition of the field of performance. The 'politics' of the imagined and actual exchange of gaze are most clearly exposed in relation to sexual difference. At once an attempt to stabilize 'difference' and an attempt to repress the 'sexual' itself, cultural representation seeks both to conceal and reveal a real that will 'prove' that sexual difference is a real difference. [. . .]

Oscar Wilde [. . .] gave us the added insight that criticism was the only civilized form of autobiography.[9]

For many years of my childhood in the heat of the summer my six brothers and sisters, two parents, the ghost of my dead sister and I drove from Long Island, New York to Carmel, Massachusetts in a green station wagon with brown sideboards. We'd all be crammed in the car, perched on the green vinyl seats, sweating to Massachusetts. On the roof of the car, like a precariously large hat, were three suitcases stacked from bottom to top. We divided ourselves into three sets of three, arranged left to right. My father drove and my mother sat in the front with my eldest brother. My next oldest brother and my two older sisters sat in the middle, while my next oldest sister, myself, and my younger brother sat in the 'way back' and faced the opposite direction of the rest of them and the way we were going.

When my mother couldn't stand us any longer she'd say, 'Let's have a keep quiet contest.' Whoever could keep quiet the longest won a prize. I can't remember what the prize was, but I remember trying very hard to listen to the sound of the tires on the asphalt, the sound of my sister's breath, the sound of the wind turning over as the car went through it. These contests had a strange tension for me, not so much because I was burning to speak, but because I thought my mother's weary sadness might infect us and render us all permanently mute. Eventually of course someone of us would break the silence. Sometimes one of my brothers would start tickling one of my sisters. Or my mother herself would speak to my father and we'd all yell with delight to see her undone by her own game. Sometimes she'd laugh at herself; sometimes she'd say it didn't count since she was the mother and the referee of the game, not a participant.

After years of this I realized that the games were meant to be lost at least as much as they were meant to be won. No one really expected nine people to drive six hours in silence. Part of 'losing' the game meant winning a certain kind of relief. A relief from the potential grief we all knew waited at my mother's elbow ready to carry her far away from us. And knowing when to lose the game—how to break the silence in such a way that we would not break our mother's temper—required a very specific intelligence, one schooled in the subtle calibrations of a substantive and mobile silence. An intelligence whose very expression, utterance itself, was hedged in on all sides by doubt.

In the years since I've spent a lot of time trying to understand what a captivating presence my sister's ghost was and is. There were nine of us in that car, but it was the one who was not with us that we worried about, thought about, remembered. In the clarity of her absence, we redefined ourselves. The real was the absence of her; we were representations of that loss. The incorporeal presence of my sister mattered to us I think because we were so bounded by the strange body we were—not octagonal and no longer pentagonal we were a nine-headed creature with a distressing sameness to our features. We were living maps of one another's physical history and future. The younger ones recorded the older ones' past; the older ones showed the younger ones their future. The girls showed the boys themselves as girls and the boys showed the girls themselves as boys. And no one, including our mother, got our names right. (My father evaded the whole thing by renaming us altogether.) The absolute break between the sign and the referent was a joke in our house, and the failure of the proper name to render an identity was an accepted fact. We recognized that distinct identities would not emerge from names which were so often misapplied, nor did we believe that within the tight resemblance of our physical bodies a singular image would tell us who we were. The similarity of our bodies, our uneasy sense of physical redundancy, made us especially conscious of my sister's swift escape from skin. And because we were so consciously caught up in the substitutional economy of the family (the string of wrong names that preceded your own address) she functioned as 'a ghost that is the phantom of no flesh' (Derrida, 'The Double Session', 206).[10] For while we were each reproducing one another's bodies across the unstable and always redoubled divide of time and gender, her non-corporeality reproduced our bodies as fleshless.

Even as we named my mother's sadness 'grief' and silently attributed it to the death of my sister, we also recognized, however dimly, the possibility that her silence had nothing at all to do with the loss of her child, but rather had to do with the enormous weight of her living children—or more distressing still, had nothing to do with any of us at all. Such thoughts could not be borne by us, so we did not try them out. Like our missing sister, they rested somewhere we could not often visit.

Identity cannot, then, reside in the name you can say or the body you can see—your own or your mother's. Identity emerges in the failure of the body to express being fully and the failure of the signifier to convey meaning exactly. Identity is perceptible only through a relation to an other—which is to say, it is a form of both resisting and claiming the other, declaring the boundary where the self diverges from and merges with the other. In that declaration of identity and identification, there is always loss, the loss of not-being the other and yet remaining dependent on that other for self-seeing, self-being.

['Broken Symmetries: Memory, Sight, Love', in *Unmarked: The Politics of Performance*
(London and New York: Routledge, 1993), 1–33.]

SUSAN BORDO

73 Normalisation and Resistance in the Era of the Image

Just how helpful [. . .] is an emphasis on creative agency in describing the relation of women and their bodies to the image industry of post-industrial capitalism, a context in which eating disorders and exercise compulsions are flourishing? Does the USA have a multi-million-dollar business in corrective, cosmetic surgery because women are asserting their racial and ethnic identities in resistance to prevailing norms, or because they are so vulnerable to the normalising power of those norms? Does an intellectual emphasis on 'resistance' really help us to describe and diagnose the politics of the body within the culture in which we live? Or, rather, does it participate in key mystifications of that culture? I will close this chapter by briefly addressing these questions.

Jean Baudrillard has suggested that a key characteristic of incessantly self-recreating, postmodern culture is the disappearance of the distinction between reality and appearance.[1] Today, all that is meaningful to us are our simulations. I think that Baudrillard is exactly right here. We all 'know' that Cher and virtually every other female star over the age of 25 is the plastic product of numerous cosmetic surgeries on face and body. Some of us can even remember what Cher *used* to look like. But in the era of the 'hyperreal' (as Baudrillard calls simulations) such historical 'knowledge' becomes faded and indistinct, unable to cast the merest shadow of doubt over the dazzling, compelling, utterly authoritative new images of Cher. Like the 'knowledge' of our own mortality when we are young and healthy, the knowledge that Cher as we see her today is a fabricated product is an empty abstraction; it simply does not compute. It is the present image that has the hold on our most vibrant sense of what is, what matters. In so far as the history of Cher's body has meaning at all, it has meaning not as the 'original' over which a false copy has been laid, but as a *defect* which has been corrected. It becomes constructed as 'defect' precisely because the new image is the dominant reality, the normalising standard against which all else is judged. This has tremendous implications for our relationship to physical appearance, which more and more has come to be understood not as a biological 'given' which we have to learn to accept, but as a plastic potentiality to be pressed into the service of image—to be arranged, re-arranged, constructed and deconstructed as we choose.[2] Cosmetic surgery is now a $1.75 billion-a-year industry in the United States, with almost 1.5 million people a year undergoing surgery of some kind, from face-lifts to call implants. These operations have become more and more affordable to the middle class (the average cost of a nose job is $2,500), and almost all can be done on an outpatient basis—some during the lunch hour. Lest it be imagined that most of these surgeries are to correct disfiguring accidents or birth defects, it should be noted that liposuction (vacuum extraction of 'surplus' fat) is the most frequently requested operation (average cost $1,500), with breast enlargement (average cost $2,000) a close second. More than two million women have received breast implants since they have been on the market.

Advocates of cosmetic surgery, as I noted earlier, argue that it is 'about' self-determination and choice, about 'taking one's life into one's hands'. But do we really choose the appearances that we reconstruct for ourselves? The images of beauty, power and success which dominate in US culture are generated out of Anglo-Saxon identifications and preferences and are images which, with some variations, are globally influential through the mass media. These images are still strongly racially, ethnically and heterosexually inflected—a reality that is continually effaced by the postmodern emphasis on resistant elements rather than dominant cultural forms. Products still promote 'hair that moves' and 'faded beauty' for black women; the slender-hipped, long-legged bodies of fashion models are infrequently produced by the Eastern European gene pool. Certainly, high-fashion images may contain touches of exotica: collagen-plumped lips or corn rows on white models, Barbra Streisand noses, 'butch' styles of dress. Consumer capitalism depends on the continual production of novelty, of fresh images to stimulate desire, and it frequently drops into marginalised neighbourhoods in order to find them. But such elements will be either explicitly *framed* as exotica, of, within the overall system of meaning, they will not be permitted to overwhelm the representation to establish a truly alternative or 'subversive' model of beauty or success. White models may collagen their lips, but black models are usually light-skinned and anglo-featured (unless, of course, their 'blackness' is being ideologically exploited, as in the many advertisments which code dark-skinned women with lust and animal desire). A definite (albeit not always fixed or determinate) system of normalising boundaries sets limits on the validation of cultural 'difference'. This system is reflected in the sorts of surgery people request; does anyone in this culture have her nose re-shaped to look more 'African' or 'Jewish'?

Popular culture offers few models of resistance to all this. Cher's public-relations image emphasises her individuality, honesty and defiance against norms. In the minds of many people, she (like Madonna) stands for female power, for rebellion against convention. Yet if we look past the 'discursive' hype to the message conveyed by her *body* we see that Cher's operations have gradually replaced a strong, decidely 'ethnic' look with a more symmetrical, delicate, 'conventional' (i.e. Anglo-Saxon) and ever-youthful version of female beauty. Cher admits to having had her breasts 'done', her nose bobbed and her teeth straightened; reportedly she has also had a rib removed, her buttocks re-shaped, and cheek implants. But whatever she has or has not done, the transformation from 1965 to 1992 is striking: in Foucauldian ter-minology, Cher has gradually 'normalised' herself. Her normalised image (the only 'reality' which counts) now acts as a standard against which other women will measure, judge, discipline and 'correct' themselves.

Such normalisation, to be sure, is continually mystified and effaced in our culture by the rhetoric of 'choice' and 'self-determination' which plays such a key role in commercial representations of diet, exercise, hair and eye-colour-ing and so forth. 'You get better or worse every day,' cautions Glen Frye on behalf of Bally Matrix Fitness, '*The choice is yours*.' (Yes, you are free to choose to be a lazy, self-indulgent slob?) 'The body you have is the body you inherited, but you must decide what to do with it', instructs Nike, offering glamorous shots of lean, muscled athletes to help us 'decide'. 'Now, choosing your very own eye colour is the most natural thing in the world', claims Durosoft (who does not market dark brown lenses). A recent television advertisment (featuring the 'new' Cher) even yokes the discourse on agency and self-determination to the selection of *Equal* over *Sweet 'N Low*; 'When I sit down to make a choice', explains Cher, 'I choose *Equal*.'

Rendered utterly invisible in the spa and exercise equipment advertisments, of course, is the coerciveness of the slenderness and fitness aesthetic (and ethic) itself. Rather, a nearly total inversion is effected, and the normalised body becomes *the* body of creative self-fashioning, even the body of cultural resistance. 'I believe' is the theme of a recent series of Reebok commercials, each of which features muscled, energetic women declaring their feminist rebellion as they exercise: 'I believe that babe is a four letter word', 'I believe in baying at the moon', 'I believe that sweat *is* sexy'. The last declaration—which 'answers' the man in a Secret deodorant advertisment who claims that, 'a woman just isn't sexy when she sweats'—not only rebels against gender ideology, but suggests resistance to the world of commercials itself (nice trick for a commercial!). Perhaps the most insidious of the series is a magazine advertisment which pictures a lean, highly toned, extremely attractive young woman, leaning against a wall, post-workout; 'I believe', the copy reads, 'that if you look at yourself and see what is right instead of what is wrong, that is the true mark of a healthy individual.' Now, those convinced that 'resistance is everywhere' might see this advertisment as offering a transgressive, subversive model of femininity: a women who is strong, fit and (unlike most women) *not* insecure about her body. What this reading neglects is that we have a visual message here as well: her body *itself*—probably the most potent 'representation' in the advertisment—is precisely the sort of perfected icon which women compare themselves to and of course see 'what is wrong'. The advertisment thus puts 'real' women in a painful double-bind. On the one hand, it encourages them to view themselves as defective; on the other hand, it chastises them for their insecurities. The offered resolution to this bind, of course, is to buy Reebok and become like the woman in the advertisment.

One might argue that an adequate analysis of advertisments such as those I have been discussing would take into account both their resistant elements and their normalising messages. (Weight-training and exercise, after all, often do have socially empowering results for women.) I have no problem granting this, so long as the normalising thrust of these advertisments *vis-à-vis* the politics of appearance is not obscured. In connection with this, we need to recognise that the symbols of resistance in these advertisements are included by advertisers in the profoundest of cynical bad faith; they pretend to reject the objectification of women and value female assertiveness, while attempting to convince women who *fail* to embody dominant ideas of (slender, youthful) beauty that they need to bring themselves into line. To resist *this* normalising directive is *truly* to 'go against the grain' of our culture, not merely in textual 'play', but at great personal risk—as the many women who have been sexually rejected for being 'too fat' and fired from their jobs for looking 'too old' know all too well. Subversion of dominant cultural forms, as bell hooks has said, 'happens much more easily in the realm of "texts" than in the world of human interaction ... in which such moves challenge, disrupt, threaten, where repression is real'.[3] The pleasure and power of 'difference' is hard-won; it does not freely bloom, insistently nudging its way through the cracks of dominant forms, Sexism, racism and 'ageism', while they do not determine human value and choices, while they do not deprive us of 'agency', remain strongly normalising within our culture.

The commercial texts that I have been examining, in contrast, participate in the illusion (which they share with other postmodern texts) that our 'differences' are already flourishing in the culture *as it is*, without need for personal struggle and social change—that we are already self-determining, already empowered to look in the mirror and see what is right, instead of what is wrong. The exposure of such mystifications, which should not be impeded by too facile a celebration of resistance, must remain central to a feminist politics of the body.

['Which Foucault for Feminism Today? Normalization and Resistance in the Era of the Image', in Caroline Ramazanoglu (ed.), *Up Against Foucault: Explorations of Some Tensions Between Foucault and Feminism* (London and New York: Routledge, 1993), 194–9.]

KATE CHEDGZOY

74 Frida Kahlo's 'Grotesque' Bodies

In a dark room she measures herself against a forgotten and idealised self-image. Her desire for wholeness is dislocated. Fragments of a former existence haunt her. Bound over to communicate an experience too uncomfortable to hear: expectations are unreliable.[1]

As soon as one steps out of the classroom . . . the dangers rather than the benefits of academic feminism . . . become more insistent. Institutional changes against sexism here . . . may mean nothing or, indirectly, further harm for women in the Third World. This discontinuity ought to be recognised and worked at. Otherwise, the focus remains defined by the investigator as subject. . . . I see no way to avoid insisting that there has to be a simultaneous other focus: not merely who am I? But who is the other woman? How am I naming her? How does she name me? Is this part of the problematic I discuss?[2]

In 1925, when she was an eighteen-year-old pre-medical student at the elite National Preparatory School in Mexico City, Frida Kahlo suffered terrible injuries as a result of a crash involving the bus she was travelling on. According to an eye-witness account, as Frida lay in the road, her pelvis crushed, pierced through the womb and vagina by a metal rod, somehow all her clothes were torn off and her naked body was showered with gold pigment which a fellow-passenger on the bus had been carrying. Even at this moment of utter physical pain and objection, her body was made into an object to be displayed and looked at. And if the objectivity of the account is questionable, it nevertheless testifies eloquently to the desire to convert Kahlo's lived existence into a sort of bizarre art object. In her own career, the visual recreation and reinterpretation of her body became the focus of her work as an artist, constantly transgressing and unfixing the possibility of a distinction between art and life. In her wide-ranging and provocative discussion of Kahlo's cultural status, Joan Borsa has warned that the critical preoccupation with Kahlo's representations of her body, particularly the body in pain, may have the effect of depoliticising the work by over-personalising it, reducing it to the status of solipsistic therapy, and thereby perpetuating a reactionary account of female artistic production:

I am not interested in demonstrating that . . . her art is the result of a life filled with physical and emotional pain or that her work somehow speaks of a truly female space. These approaches which now surround Kahlo's work further reinforce the myth of the artist as tortured genius and present the woman artist as victim—as if irreconcilably outside and other.[3]

During an interview recorded for a 1990 BBC *Omnibus* programme Madonna spoke of her intense emotional investment in Frida Kahlo's painting *My Birth*, which she said had come to fulfill the iconic function in her life to which the Catholic images of her childhood were no longer adequate. Later, a friend of mine who works with young women in crisis commented that a number of her clients lay claim to a similar fascination with this terrible yet haunting image, circulating reproductions of it among themselves as amulets or fetishes. As Jean Borsa has demonstrated, commodified images of Kahlo proliferate in western culture, on posters, book covers, and fashion spreads.[4] Moreover, the tone of much critical discourse about Kahlo seems to indicate that in her case the problematic question of the relationship between the artist's life and her work has a special significance for her commentators. Kahlo's uniquely iconic role is particularly striking in the context of feminist art criticism, where, as a woman artist whose primary subject matter was her own body, she has come to occupy a central but contested position. In what follows, I ask why this should be so.

My aims here are to offer a theory which can account for the unique intensity of the feminist critical response to Kahlo, and to provide a way of interpreting the special fascinations which her self-portraits offer feminist spectators, without personalising and pathologising these representations to an extent which would deny Kahlo's political location and agency as the subject of her own artistic practice. I hope to show that Kahlo used intimate representations of her body to make highly politicised public statements. Drawing on Julia Kristeva's theory of abjection,[5] and the Bakhtinian concept of carnival,[6] I locate my reading as a white western feminist of Kahlo's work both in the context of recent attempts to theorise the female body—particularly that body which is in some way disfigured, hystericised, or rendered 'grotesque'[7]—and of the related project of constructing a critical language which can speak of emotional and physical pain. I am not presuming to offer a definitive or comprehensive account of Kahlo's work, and I recognise that there are other, equally productive and appropriate contexts in which to locate an analysis of it.[8] Nevertheless, it seems to speak very directly to these preoccupations, which clearly have their origins in women's emotional and political experience. It has been suggested to me that there are political problems with the appropriation of Kahlo's self-portraits by western feminists as a way into understanding their own experience; but I would argue that turning a critical gaze on these problems can itself further our understanding of the culturally specific ways in which the female body is represented and encoded.

Although I use psychoanalytic concepts in an attempt to understand what is at stake for the viewer of Kahlo's art, I am aware that merely to psycho-analyse the traces of subjectivity which the viewer perceives in her paintings risks reinstating the colonising gestures of the Surrealists' appropriation of her work and persona. André Breton, who championed Kahlo in the 1930s, has been described as nurturing a fantasy of Mexico as 'the Surrealist place *par excellence*',[9] and chose to represent her as a naive and spontaneous genius who had stumbled on the tenets and practices of Surrealism by a process of intuition. Kahlo herself rejected the label of 'Surrealist', while astutely using Surrealist contacts to further her career, asserting that

I never knew I was a Surrealist till André Breton came to Mexico and told me.... And it is doubtless true that in many ways my painting is related to that of the Surrealists. But I never had the intention of creating a work that could be considered to fit in that classification.[10]

However, in the introduction to the brochure for her New York debut at Julien Levy's gallery in 1938, Breton wrote:

My surprise and joy were unbounded when I discovered on my arrival in Mexico that her work had blossomed forth, in her latest paintings, into pure Surreality, despite the fact that it had been conceived without any prior knowledge whatsoever of the ideas motivating the activities of my friends and myself.[11]

Whitney Chadwick comments that Breton here detaches Kahlo's work from its Mexican cultural (and, she might have added, political) context, and places it as confirming the work and theories of male Surrealists without developing them. In a gesture which is at once misogynist and racist, Kahlo is con-structed by Breton as the embodiment of femininity, the unconscious, and the exotic—all qualities which the Surrealist movement celebrated, but which nonetheless deny Kahlo agency as the subject of her own personal/political history and her artistic production. The danger that this gesture will be repeated in the western feminist movement's appropriation of Kahlo has already been noted:

The emphasis given in her work to the body, to personal emotion and to motherhood provided a visual counterpart to a growing feminist art history. However...she has also come to represent an archetypal image of woman as victim. As an artist

Frida Kahlo, *The Two Fridas* (1939)

she has been ascribed an almost naive self-absorption, and her admittedly great emotional and physical traumas have been seen as the major impetus of her art. Despite the laudable aims of such a reappraisal, it does little to address her active role in the formulation of a language of art which questioned neo-colonial cultural values. In fact her current status embodies both aspects of the modernist 'other', the feminine and the unconscious, which are consistently used to characterise Latin America itself.[12]

To use a concept like abjection, which has origins in psychoanalytic theory, to analyse Kahlo's work, may thus run the risk of confirming her association with the unconscious and the exotic, trapping her within an objectified identity constructed by the colonising discourses of western rationality. To avoid this, psychoanalytic theory can more profitably be used as a means of accounting for the fascination which Kahlo's paintings currently exert over the European female—or more precisely, feminist—viewer. Is this fascination

merely an exploitative pleasure in the contemplation of an exotic, unconscious and narcissistic femininity, whose display compensates for the sensual
deprivations of the puritan North? That is, are we using Kahlo's work to
assuage our own lack? Or is it possible that, in the recognition of the other
woman's subjectivity—be it suffering, self-absorbed, or revolutionary—which
Kahlo's work offers us, a more truly liberating and intersubjective dynamic
can come into being?

Jean Franco has noted that just such an intersubjective relation is already
embodied by the artistic form of Kahlo's doubled self-portraits (for example
Tree of Hope and *The Two Fridas*). These double portraits depict either a
Tehuana[13] and a European Frida, or a naked and a clothed Frida. In their
very form, these paintings undo the possibility of a facile identification of
Frida Kahlo (as the subject of her own work) with a single unconscious,
commodified object of the gaze. Franco's analysis undoes some of the easy
assumptions the viewer might be tempted to make about the potential
political meanings of conventional art forms; as she points out elsewhere in
her book, one way in which Kahlo's self-portraits can be said to challenge the
conventions of European art is that her 'mutilated body trespasses on the
place of the female nude':[14]

The unclothed body is not a 'self' but a socialised body, a body that is opened by
instruments, technologised, wounded, its organs displayed to the outside world.
The 'inner' Frida is controlled by modern society far more than the clothed Frida,
who often marks her deviation from a norm by defiantly returning the gaze of the
viewer. The naked Frida does not give the viewers what they want—the titillation of
female nakedness—but a revelation of what the examining eye does to the female
body.[15]

Franco's work is both persuasive and politically challenging. But one
limitation of her argument here is that it does not do enough to displace the
viewer—whose identity is not problematised—from a position as the unique
subject of this transaction. Although she makes a convincing argument for
the paintings' resistance to the colonizing gaze, Franco seems to imply that
this gaze is exclusively male, although this is not made explicit. For me, the
most pressing question still is: what is the relationship between Frida Kahlo's
body and the multiplicities of the western (European/North American) *female*
gaze?

To answer that question, I turn now to the theoretical concepts of abjection and carnival. Julia Kristeva's theory of abjection offers a psychoanalytic
understanding of the process by which the norms of embodied identity are
disrupted. It gives an account of the construction of desiring subjectivity
which stresses the faultlines, tensions and difficulties of achieving a stable
identity as the embodied subject of an unproblematic desire. In *Powers of
Horror*, Kristeva says:

The non-distinctiveness of inside and outside is unnameable, a border passable in both directions by pleasure and pain. Naming the latter, hence differentiating them, amounts to introducing language, which just as it distinguishes pleasure from pain, as it does all other oppositions, founds the separation inside/outside. And yet, there would be witnesses to the perviousness of the limit, artisans after a fashion who try to tap that pre-verbal beginning within a word which is flush with pleasure and pain.[16]

Frida Kahlo may be understood as just such a witness, such an artisan. Her paintings represent the moment of abjection which institutes a flickering in and out of existence of the frail, permeable boundaries between inside and outside, pleasure and pain. Kristeva's own writing on abjection is often marked by a sense of the inadequacy of language to record the extremes of psychic and physical experience. In Kahlo's paintings, what eludes language in this fashion is made visible: the representation of the body becomes the material realisation of abjection, enabling the artist to become a user, not of words, but of colours and forms capable of embodying the physical and psychic distress which exceeds or negates the expressive capacity of language. The pictorial image of the agonised abject body thus takes on an ironic and carnivalesque beauty, so that the ability of Kahlo's paintings to fascinate the gaze is seen to be generated by the tension between the pain and horror of what they represent, and the luscious visual pleasure which they offer the spectator. Abjection offers a possible way of understanding this disjunction because it shows how embodied subjectivity is constructed through the differentiation of pleasure and pain, while stressing the impossibility of ever fully achieving such a differentiation. According to Jacqueline Rose,

Abjection is a primordial fear situated at the point where the subject first splits from the body of the mother, finding at once in that body and in the terrifying gap that opens up between them the only space for the constitution of its own identity, the only distance which will allow it to become a user of words.... The body appears at the origin of language, not as idealisation, therefore, but as that which places both the subject and language most fundamentally at risk.[17]

The key themes in abjection are the construction of subjectivity over and against the desired and feared maternal body, which can never be fully repressed, but always returns to haunt the fragile, vulnerable subject; and the subject's experience, consequent on this inadequately achieved repression, of those liminal states in which the boundaries of the body, of the self, are blurred, transgressed, and refigured. The experience of abjection is also evoked by phenomena which inspire disgust or horror because of the threat which liminality poses to the attempt to stabilise—and thereby control—the categories we use to interpret meaning.[18] Both abjection and carnival (which I shall discuss in more detail below) share a tendency to take the body and subjectivity as ahistorical, transcendent givens, collapsing the feminine into the maternal, and taking the maternal body as the key image of embodiment as such. Reading this account against the grain, it becomes clear that abjection is a crucial component of the defensive fantasies which shape the body and the subjectivity of patriarchal masculinity. The female body is abjected as the Other of this masculine subjectivity, but can never be fully repressed or excluded. Abjection thus constitutes the theoretical embodiment of the way that patriarchal structures and subjects are always already infected by their worst fears.

While its psychoanalytic origins mean that abjection is primarily a theory of the formation of gendered and sexualised identity, its potential usefulness for analysing the construction of colonialist ideologies and racist subjectivities is clear.[19] Hence, while, as I suggested earlier, its use in this context entails political risks, it is also indispensable, in that it enables me, as an inescapably white and European subject, to become aware of and account for the dynamics of othering which may infect my fascination with Kahlo—that is, the process by which I ascribe to her work those aspects of my own identity which I experience as frightening and disruptive, but which I cannot bear to relinquish. Kristeva's work throughout the 1970s and in the early 1980s was preoccupied with precisely this question of the relationship between individual, subjective identity, and socio-political structures—including those which secure oppression on the grounds of racial or sexual difference. In *Powers of Horror*, she delineates the processes by which the maternally-connoted, pre-Oedipal realm of the semiotic and the symbolic law of patriarchal society are differentially constructed and maintained. Earlier, in *Revolution in Poetic Language*,[20] she had stressed that submission to the symbolic law of patriarchal society is essential, for it is the only means by which the infant can become socialised as a subject in language: the alternative of remaining in the pre-Oedipal semiotic realm precludes the possibility of social signification, and thus entails psychosis. Nevertheless, it is acknowledged that the semiotic can never be fully eliminated from subjectivity. It is conceived as an oppositional realm, associated with what is always alien, marginal, repressed, other; with those artistic practices and social instances which disrupt the symbolic by means of fragmentary, provisional, carnivalesque eruptions, thereby revealing the points of stress and instability in the symbolic realm and undermining its claim to mastery. The maternal is placed firmly on the side of this potentially revolutionary semiotic, because the semiotic is associated with the primary processes of the pre-Oedipal mother–child dyad. Kristeva describes it as, 'a modality which bears the most archaic memories of our link with the maternal body—of the dependence that all of us have *vis-à-vis* the maternal body, and where a sort of self-eroticism is indissociable from the experience of the (m)other'.[21] For me, this is an apt diagnosis of what is most powerful and haunting about Kahlo's work. It describes the emotional intensity which saturates paintings like *My Nurse and I*, or the dozens of self-portraits where so often this very eroticism is predicated on an acknowledgement of

Frida Kahlo, *My Nurse and I* (1937)

unassuageable loss and pain. In Kahlo's work, this narcissistic eroticism is inseparable from a sense of the loss of the (m)other and a constant yearning to recuperate it.

The necessary relationship of abjection to the maternal, which in Kristeva's work frequently stands as an image of femininity as such, means that the female body becomes the privileged signifier of abjection, emblem of the most agonising ambivalence of subjectivity: the desired and feared dissolution of identity which is associated with engulfment by the body of the mother, by sexual passion, or by the death drive. As Kristeva puts it, 'devotees of the abject, she as well as he, do not cease looking...for the desirable and terrifying, nourishing and murderous, fascinating and abject inside of the maternal body'.[22] The power of abjection lies precisely in this ambiguity; in the fact that what repels is also that which attracts most strongly. Hence its relevance to Kahlo's paintings: they body forth the experience of abjection which the subject normally excludes from its awareness, offering the viewer a temporary immersion in this horribly fascinating phase of the construction of subjectivity. Their troubling combination of beauty and horror enables the viewer to take pleasure in the lusciously depicted body and the returned gaze of the (m)other, while holding at bay—though only just—the loss of identity which normally accompanies this desired and feared fusion.

In a highly polemical critique of *Powers of Horror*, Jennifer Stone argues that the theory of abjection 'exchanges history for carnival and stamps on memory'.[23] However, a number of recent works have demonstrated that Kristeva's theories can usefully be deployed in the service of a more historically informed, materialist reading of culture, by means of a critical process which 'translocate[s] the issues of bodily exposure and containment, disguise and gender masquerade, abjection and marginality, parody and excess, to the field of the social, constituted as a symbolic system'.[24] The experience of embodiment and the workings of desire cannot be disentangled from social relations which are effects of hierarchical structures of power, gender, and wealth. The concept of carnival can be shown to expose the horror of abjection as a misogynist projection, and it provides a political and social framework for the ways in which women's bodies have been hystericised, idealised, or rendered grotesque. It is arguably this process which is explored in Kahlo's painting.

For Bakhtin, the carnival principle is embedded in the grotesque body, which is typified by events and activities—eating, defecation, birth, death, sex—in which the boundaries between bodies, and between bodies and the world, are obscured, eroded and displaced. He almost always speaks in very general, abstract terms of *the* body, regardless of factors like race and gender which we might see as important in contributing to differentiated constructions of embodiedness. And yet his descriptions of the grotesque body are replete with characteristics which have traditionally been coded as feminine, whereas the classical body to which it is opposed has certain conventionally masculine qualities:

One of the fundamental tendencies of the grotesque image of the body is to show two bodies in one: the one giving birth and dying, the other conceived, generated, and born. This is the pregnant and begetting body, or at least a body ready for conception and fertilisation, the stress being laid on the phallus or the genital organs. From one body a new body always emerges in some form or other.[25]

The characteristics of the grotesque body are clearly sexualised here, without questions of gender or sexuality ever being allowed to affect the conceptual framework which is being constructed. In another passage, woman is described, in a classically misogynist gesture, as being 'essentially related' to the 'material bodily lower stratum', which is a crucial aspect of the principle of carnival:

She is the incarnation of this stratum that degrades and regenerates simultaneously. She is ambivalent. She debases, brings down to earth, lends a bodily substance to things and destroys; but first of all, she is the principle that gives birth. She is the womb.   (p. 240)

This would seem to indicate clearly that the female body has a special relation (albeit not one which appears to offer great advantages to women) to the grotesque body. Nevertheless, this does not lead Bakhtin to work with gender as a conceptual category in his analyses of culture.

One of Bakhtin's most vivid images of the grotesque body is his description of the Kerch terracotta figurines representing senile, pregnant hags:

This is typical and very strongly expressed grotesque. It is ambivalent. It is pregnant death, a death that gives birth. There is nothing completed, nothing calm and stable in the bodies of these old hags. They combine senile, decaying and deformed flesh with the flesh of new life, conceived but as yet unformed. (pp. 25–6)

In some ways, Kahlo's work might seem to sanction this essentialist, bio-logically determined understanding of femininity. It has sometimes been claimed by feminist art critics as typifying a naively pictorial relationship to the external reality it supposedly represents, forming a celebratory testimo-nial to the unique power of female biology. I would argue, however, that Kahlo's paintings of birth, miscarriage, and the grotesque and suffering body, actually represent the process by which the female body is socialised, ren-dered abject by the technological gaze of patriarchal culture. These represen-tations are surely linked with her own painful and ambivalent experiences of both the biological potential (thwarted in her case) for motherhood, and the practices of technologised medicine. But the relationship between represen-tation and experience in this context is less straightforward than many commentators have assumed. Discussing the 1944 painting *Broken Column*, North American feminist art historians Karen Petersen and J. J. Wilson say, 'Frida wore this kind of brace and felt this kind of pain.'[26] No one, of course, can ever really know what another person's experience of pain is like; but this comment has a kind of distressing accuracy in so far as it testifies to the difficulty of finding an analytical language capable of dealing with the agony represented in *Broken Column*. It seems that words can only reiterate this pain, not account for it. The work of Petersen and Wilson played a vital historical role in the growth of feminist art criticism, but its drawback in this case is that it maps the artistic criteria of 1970s North American feminism (for example, the demand for a realistic representation of specifically female experience) onto Kahlo's work, erasing her agency as an artist and reducing her, in a somewhat colonialist move, to the naive and spontaneous illustrator of her own unproblematically self-present experience. In contrast, I would argue that Kahlo deployed the carnivalesque in order both to explore and problem-atise the relation between art and experience.

In an essay on Kahlo, Angela Carter has said that 'Women painters are often forced to make exhibitions of themselves in order to mount exhib-itions . . . Fame is not an end in itself but a strategy.'[27] Kahlo used her unique status as a celebrated icon of *Mexicanidad*—deriving partly from her relation-

Frida Kahlo, *Broken Column* (1944)

ship with the publicly idolised Marxist painter, Diego Rivera, who depicted her in his murals as a revolutionary distributing both arms and the weapon of literacy to the oppressed masses; and partly from her self-presentation as an incarnation of folk tradition—to carve out a context in which she could shape an identity for herself as an artist. Mary Russo has shown how the female grotesque is associated with 'making a spectacle [or as Carter says, perhaps even more appositely, an exhibition] out of oneself', connoting a certain shameful inadvertency; an embarrassing loss of control, loss of boundaries.[28] Conversely, I would argue that Kahlo's work reinscribes the grotesque in order to make a spectacle of herself in ways which actually enhanced her control over her art and life. Her own bodily experience was the main subject of her artwork, and at the same time she put enormous care into decorating and displaying her body as an artwork in itself. For example, her identification with the Tehuantepec people functions as a strategic identification with the most matriarchal of indigenous Mexican cultures. Even when confined to bed by pain or illness, she dressed herself in their lavish traditional costume. This is not merely to reproduce the female body as exotic object of display as it recurs in patriarchal, colonialist culture, however. Kahlo chose this style of dress in order to affirm publicly the previously devalued Mexican side of her dual heritage: art critic Michael Newman has argued that this kind of affirmation of *Mexicanidad* was a political gesture of reaction against the Europeanising policies of the pre-revolutionary regime.[29]

Biographical accounts of Kahlo have often been inclined to attribute her fascination with the creation of an elaborately decorated appearance to mere vanity, but this is clearly inadequate to account for the particular, over-determined and politically charged form in which her supposed vanity expressed itself. Late in life, she would decorate the plaster corsets which supported her disintegrating spine: one of the most striking of these juxta-poses the hammer and sickle, emblem of the revolutionary politics to which she was committed throughout her adult life, with an unborn foetus which seems to prefigure the central image of her 1945 painting, *The Birth of Moses*. Kahlo's interest in representing failed and frustrated maternity is often ascribed to a biographical origin in her own thwarted desire for motherhood, but works like this make clear that such desires and disappointments are always experienced in a political context. As Mara R. Witzling has recently said, 'Kahlo took her own private vision and externalized it vividly, in a public language that could not be misunderstood. In so doing, she took a step in moving the experience of the female subject from its marginal cultural position toward the center.'[30] This is what brought the once culturally marginal body of work which Kahlo's art constitutes to occupy a paradoxic-ally central position in feminist art criticism. Whilst this disconcerting

Frida Kahlo, *Corset with Hammer and Sickle* (1950)

centrality may sometimes have been achieved via a colonialist appropriation of the commodified figure of 'Frida Kahlo' as a symbol of exotic otherness, at its best her fascination for feminists has also enabled a salutary recognition of the subjectivity of the other woman; a subjectivity which western feminists must recognise as such if they are to resist their own personal and political abjection.

['Frida Kahlo's "Grotesque Bodies" ', in Penny Florence and Dee Reynolds (eds.), *Feminist Subjects, Multimedia, Cultural Methodologies* (Manchester: Manchester University Press, 1995), 39–53.]

Section 6

Technologies

INTRODUCTION

> The cyborg is our ontology; it gives us our politics.
>
> Donna Haraway

Is technology encoded in masculine terms? Signalling a clear break from 'technophobic' forms of ecofeminism, current feminist theory and practice reveals a keen determination to explore the productive possibilities for technological development. From explorations of emergent technologies concerned with promoting conception and with eliminating 'defects' in the unborn, to playful engagements with video technology and virtual reality, feminists are increasingly involved in moral and political struggles to negotiate the context and meaning of technological development.

Much of second-wave feminist engagement with technology has been characterized by the ecofeminist use of 'the ancient identity of nature as a nurturing mother' as a basis for claiming a deep alliance between the feminist and the ecological. Arguing that the 'uncontrolled growth associated with capitalism, technology and progress' has 'sanctioned the domination of both nature and women', ecofeminists assert the political importance of reclaiming both the natural and the female/maternal from the grips of an exploitative scientific patriarchalism.

Yet the simple assertion of women's historical association with nature leaves open the political question as to whether one chooses to valorize the association and accept it as the basis of one's identity, or whether one works to problematize it as a means of creating space for more plural forms of self-identification. When Maria Mies and Vandana Shiva claim that women have 'a deep and particular understanding' of the connection between patriarchal and ecological violence 'through our natures and our experience as women', they invoke both essentialist and materialist arguments for the association. In other words, women's 'special relation with nature' is viewed not as a patriarchal construct to be challenged, but as 'real' in both an a priori and an empirical sense. From this perspective the valorization of the connection is the only possible political option. Another strategy, first famously and polemically argued by Shulamith Firestone in *The Dialectic of Sex*, 1973, is to *embrace* the technological as a means of overthrowing the oppressive 'natural' conditions to which women have been subject. The assertion that it is not technology that is oppressive, but nature, represents the direct anti-thesis of the ecofeminist position.

Adopting more ambivalent approaches to developing technologies than either of the above, many feminists have conceived their project neither as the celebration of women's connection with the natural as a basis for condemning men's with the technological, nor as the simple embrace of the technological as a means to liberate ourselves from the natural, but rather as a renegotiation of both gendered identity and scientific rationalism. This approach opens up possibilities for more nuanced and productive engagements between feminist politics and emerging technologies. The question then becomes: in what ways are the associations of the feminine and the natural and the masculine and the scientific amenable to change? Pursuit of these questions has increasingly involved jettisoning totalizing rejections of the technological.

Recognition of the deeply ambivalent effects of technologies on the lives of contemporary women has led many to distance themselves from any presumed feminist technophobia. Notably, Michelle Stanworth argues that those analyses which conflate all manifestations of technology (real and fictional) and view all as the straightforward tools of patriarchy are so holistic that they fail to acknowledge women's positive engagements with, and resistance to, technologies. In contrast, many now feel that a feminist response to the technological involves the problematization rather than the celebration of 'the natural', the wresting back from nature that which has been constructed as 'natural'.

The presumed naturalness of reproduction is subject to particular critique. For Stanworth, for example, the project of revealing the cultural construction of the natural involves establishing 'pregnancy and childbirth not as a natural condition, the parameters of which are set in advance, but as an accomplishment which we can actively shape according to our own ends.' It also involves, as Sarah Franklin shows, questioning the naturalness of conceptions of biological life itself. Even our understanding of what constitutes life, the very point at which life is presumed to begin, is shaped by technological development. Visual strategies achieved through new technologies are shaping our political discourses concerning ontological status. 'What is at stake', Franklin argues, 'in both the discursive construction of the fetus in scientific accounts and the visual representation of it through scientific photography is the cultural construction of the natural facts of pregnancy.' If the natural itself is a cultural construct shaped by technological development, the strategy of rejecting the technological in the name of the natural is severely undermined. As Marilyn Strathern argues, it is not that new reproductive technologies 'interfere with nature' but rather that they interfere with 'the very idea of a natural fact' (p. 495). If the neat division between the natural and artificial is not tenable, claiming a special association between women and nature becomes paradoxical.

In the face of this paradox Donna Haraway famously invokes the image of the cyborg—'a cybernetic organism, a hybrid of machine and organism, a creature of social reality as well as a creature of fiction'—to articulate two central tenets: the rejection of universal, totalizing theory; and the replacement of a demonology of technology with an exploration of the breakdown of the boundaries between the natural and the technological. 'By the late twentieth century,' she reflects, 'we are all chimeras, theorized and fabricated hybrids of machine and organism: in short we are cyborgs.' Haraway's assertion that she would rather be a cyborg than a goddess clearly announces her distance from the ecofeminist perspective, and ushers in a tendency within feminism to positively explore the possibilities inherent in technological developments. This piece of writing, more than any other, is indicative of the fact that as a result of both the practical developments in reproductive and cybernetic technologies and the theoretical developments within feminist discourses, technologies have become subject to intense and often excited exploration.

The shift from spiritual ecofeminism to postmodern cyberfeminism represents yet another manifestation of the sea change that has characterized 1980s and 1990s feminism. There is now a significant body of feminist writing, represented here in Sadie Plant's piece, which is positively celebratory in its approach to the technological. The transition from Carolyn Merchant's 1980 claim that the simultaneous development of the women's movement and the ecology movement indicates some intrinsic link between their goals, to Sadie Plant's claim—of a decade later—that 'silicon and women's liberation track each other's development', is striking. Where Merchant assumes a link between ecological critiques of technological development and the women's movement, Plant gestures to a link between women's liberation and technological development itself. The gulf between these positions is indicative of the distance between eco- and cyberfeminist perspectives.

For some though, the price of this shift in feminist analyses of technology is a weakening of the feminist commitment to political struggle. Carole Stabile, for one, argues that in the process of rejecting universal, totalizing theory and celebrating the breakdown of boundaries, politics becomes 'a form of discursive engagement specific to intellectuals'. Haraway's call to take pleasure in the confusion of boundaries—as with the Queer challenge to earlier radical feminist analyses of sexuality—modishly counters certain rigidities in earlier feminist analyses allowing for greater theoretical complexity and individual flexibility, but in so doing invokes charges of obscurantism and élitism. Haraway's cyborg—resolutely committed to 'partiality, irony, intimacy and perversity'—is perhaps *the* icon of contemporary feminism. Yet Stabile's criticism of such cyborg politics echoes Elizabeth Wilson's reflection on the aestheticization of contemporary sexual politics: 'the cyborg feminist need not do anything in order to be political . . . the fact that the cyborg signifies is enough to guarantee her politics'. Once again, current feminist debate focuses on the appeal of the ambivalent and the aesthetic and the recurrent controversy as to whether this represents a changing understanding of political engagement or simple depoliticization.

This question is variously addressed in concrete form by Cynthia Cockburn and Ruža Fürst-Dilić, Constance Penley, and Sherry Turkle. Cockburn and Fürst-Dilić's explorations of increasing levels of technology within the home reveal ambivalent consequences of this increase for women's domestic status but indicate that there 'are clear pointers to a feminist strategy on technology'. In offering an account of Star Trek fandom Penley gives an example of the negotiation of political issues 'in everyday life outside the accepted languages of feminism and the left'; and by exploring gendered uses of the internet Sherry Turkle highlights that rather than to pursue pre-defined agendas for political change women are actively engaged in explorations of gender complexity: 'what is virtual gender-swapping all about?', she asks: 'For a man to present himself as female in a chat room, on an IRC channel, or in a MUD, only requires writing a description . . . But once they are on-line as female, they soon find that maintaining this fiction is difficult. To pass as a woman for any length of time requires understanding how gender inflects speech, manner, the interpretation of experience.' It is in precisely such practices—so frequently overlooked by those searching for sites of political struggle—that Penley claims we might find 'alternative and unexpected ways of thinking and speaking about women's relations to the new technologies of science, the body and the mind'. As examples of 'the tactical manoeuvres of the relatively powerless when attempting to resist, negotiate, or transform the system and products of the relatively powerful', these practices offer an insight into those forms of political engagement—positioned between the poles of structuralist materialism and ironic aestheticism—that a cyborgian ontology might generate.

We end with a piece by Rosi Braidotti which draws together many of the themes explored in the collection—the need to 'work towards a radical redefinition of political action', the importance of language and psychoanalytic theory to 'the project of exploring the dissymmetry of the sexes', the 'new and perversely fruitful alliance between technology and culture'—and articulates a sentiment that we hope the collection conveys: that the multiplicity and complexity of current feminisms should be seen not as 'a melancholy plunge into loss and decline, but rather the joyful opening up of new possibilities' (p. 523).

75 Women and Ecology

Women and nature have an age-old association—an affiliation that has persisted throughout culture, language, and history. Their ancient interconnections have been dramatized by the simultaneity of two recent social movements—women's liberation, symbolized in its controversial infancy by Betty Friedan's *Feminine Mystique* (1963), and the ecology movement, which built up during the 1960s and finally captured national attention on Earth Day, 1970. Common to both is an egalitarian perspective. Women are struggling to free themselves from cultural and economic constraints that have kept them subordinate to men in American society. Environmentalists, warning us of the irreversible consequences of continuing environmental exploitation, are developing an ecological ethic emphasizing the interconnectedness between people and nature. Juxtaposing the goals of the two movements can suggest new values and social structures, based not on the domination of women and nature as resources but on the full expression of both male and female talent and on the maintenance of environmental integrity. [. . .]

The ancient identity of nature as a nurturing mother links women's history with the history of the environment and ecological change. The female earth was central to the organic cosmology that was undermined by the Scientific Revolution and the rise of a market-oriented culture in early modern Europe. The ecology movement has reawakened interest in the values and concepts associated historically with the premodern organic world. The ecological model and its associated ethics make possible a fresh and critical interpretation of the rise of modern science in the crucial period when our cosmos ceased to be viewed as an organism and became instead a machine.

Both the women's movement and the ecology movement are sharply critical of the costs of competition, aggression, and domination arising from the market economy's *modus operandi* in nature and society. Ecology has been a subversive science in its criticism of the consequences of uncontrolled growth associated with capitalism, technology, and progress—concepts that over the last two hundred years have been treated with reverence in Western culture. The vision of the ecology movement has been to restore the balance of nature disrupted by industrialization and overpopulation. It has emphasized the need to live within the cycles of nature, as opposed to the exploitative, linear mentality of forward progress. It focuses on the costs of progress, the limits to growth, the deficiencies of technological decision making, and the urgency of the conservation and recycling of natural resources. Similarly, the women's movement has exposed the costs for all human beings of competition in the marketplace, the loss of meaningful productive economic roles for women in early capitalist society, and the view of both women and nature as psychological and recreational resources for the harried entrepreneur-husband. [...]

In investigating the roots of our current environmental dilemma and its connections to science, technology, and the economy, we must reexamine the formation of a world view and a science that, by reconceptualizing reality as a machine rather than a living organism, sanctioned the domination of both nature and women. The contributions of such founding 'fathers' of modern science as Francis Bacon, William Harvey, René Descartes, Thomas Hobbes, and Isaac Newton must be reevaluated. The fate of other options, alternative philosophies, and social groups shaped by the organic world view and resistant to the growing exploitative mentality needs reappraisal. To understand why one road rather than the other was taken requires a broad synthesis of both the natural and cultural environments of Western society at the historical turning point. [...]

By examining the transition from the organism to the machine as the dominant metaphor binding together the cosmos, society, and the self into a single cultural reality—a world view—I place less emphasis on the development of the internal content of science than on the social and intellectual factors involved in the transformation. Of course, such external factors do not cause intellectuals to invent a science or a metaphysics for the conscious purpose of fitting a social context. Rather, an array of ideas exists, available to a given age; some of these for unarticulated or even unconscious reasons seem plausible to individuals or social groups; others do not. Some ideas spread; others temporarily die out. But the direction and cumulation of social changes begin to differentiate among the spectrum of possibilities so that some ideas assume a more central role in the array, while others move to the periphery. Out of this differential appeal of ideas that seem most plausible under particular social conditions, cultural transformations develop.

Nor is the specific content of science determined by external factors. Instead social concerns serve consciously or unconsciously to justify a given research program and to set problems for a developing science to pursue. Cultural norms and social ideologies, along with religious and philosophical assumptions, form a less visible but nonetheless important component of the conceptual framework brought to the study of a scientific problem. Through dialectical interaction science and culture develop as an organic whole, fragmenting and reintegrating out of both social and intellectual tensions and tendencies.

Between 1500 and 1700, the Western world began to take on features that, in the dominant opinion of today, would make it modern and progressive. Now, ecology and the women's movement have begun to challenge the values on which that opinion is based. By critically reexamining history from these perspectives, we may begin to discover values associated with the premodern world that may be worthy of transformation and reintegration into today's and tomorrow's society.

['Women and Ecology', in *The Death of Nature: Women, Ecology and the Scientific Revolution* (San Francisco: Harper Row, 1980), pp. xix–xxiv.]

DONNA HARAWAY

76   A Manifesto for Cyborgs: Science, Technology, and Socialist Feminism in the 1980s

This chapter is an effort to build an ironic political myth faithful to feminism, socialism, and materialism. Perhaps more faithful as blasphemy is faithful, than as reverent worship and identification. Blasphemy has always seemed to require taking things very seriously. I know no better stance to adopt from within the secular-religious, evangelical traditions of U.S. politics, including the politics of socialist feminism. Blasphemy profects one from the Moral Majority within, while still insisting on the need for community. Blasphemy is not apostasy. Irony is about contradictions that do not resolve into larger wholes, even dialectically, about the tension of holding incompatible things together because both or all are necessary and true. Irony is about humor and serious play. It is also a rhetorical strategy and a political method, one I would like to see more honored within socialist feminism. At the center of my ironic faith, my blasphemy, is the image of the cyborg.

A cyborg is a cybernetic organism, a hybrid of machine and organism, a creature of social reality as well as a creature of fiction. Social reality is lived social relations, our most important political construction, a world-changing fiction. The international women's movements have constructed 'women's experience', as well as uncovered or discovered this crucial collective object. This experience is a fiction and fact of the most crucial, political kind. Liberation rests on the construction of the consciousness, the imaginative apprehension, of oppression, and so of possibility. The cyborg is a matter of fiction and lived experience that changes what counts as women's experience in the late twentieth century. This is a struggle over life and death, but the boundary between science fiction and social reality is an optical illusion. [. . .]

By the late twentieth century, our time, a mythic time, we are all chimeras, theorized and fabricated hybrids of machine and organism, in short, we are cyborgs. The cyborg is our ontology; it gives us our politics. The cyborg is a condensed image of both imagination and material reality, the two joined centers structuring any possibility of historical transformation. In the traditions of Western science and politics—the tradition of racist, male-dominant capitalism; the tradition of progress; the tradition of the appropriation of nature as resource for the productions of culture, the tradition of reproduction of the self from the reflections of the other, the relation between organism and machine has been a border war. The stakes in the border war have been the territories of production, reproduction, and imagination. This chapter is an argument for pleasure in the confusion of boundaries and for responsibility in their construction. It is also an effort to contribute to socialist-feminist culture and theory in a postmodernist, nonnaturalist mode and in the utopian tradition of imagining a world without gender, which is perhaps a world without genesis, but maybe also a world without end. The cyborg incarnation is outside salvation history. [. . .]

The cyborg is a creature in a postgender world; it has no truck with bisexuality, pre-Oedipal symbiosis, unalienated labor, or other seductions to organic wholeness through a final appropriation of all the powers of the parts into a higher unity. In a sense, the cyborg has no origin story in the Western sense: a 'final' irony since the cyborg is also the awful apocalyptic telos of the West's escalating dominations of abstract individuation, an ultimate self untied at last from all dependency, a man in space. An origin story in the Western humanist sense depends on the myth of original unity, fullness, bliss, and terror, represented by the phallic mother from whom all humans must separate; the task of individual development and of history, the twin potent myths inscribed most powerfully for us in psychoanalysis and Marxism. Hilary Klein has argued that both Marxism and psychoanalysis, in their concepts of labor and of individuation and gender formation, depend on the plot of original unity out of which difference must be produced and enlisted in a drama of escalating domination of woman / nature. The cyborg skips the step of original unity, of identification with nature in the Western sense. This is its illegitimate promise that might lead to subversion of its teleology as Star Wars.

The cyborg is resolutely committed to partiality, irony, intimacy, and perversity. It is oppositional, utopian, and completely without innocence. No longer structured by the polarity of public and private, the cyborg defines a technological polis based partly on a revolution of social relations in the oikos, the household. Nature and culture are reworked; the one can no longer be the resource for appropriation or incorporation by the other. The relationships for forming wholes from parts, including those of polarity and hierarchical domination, are at issue in the cyborg world. Unlike the hopes of Frankenstein's monster, the cyborg does not expect its father to save it through a restoration of the garden, that is, through the fabrication of a heterosexual male, through its completion in a finished whole, a city and cosmos. The cyborg does not dream of community on the model of the organic family, this time without the Oedipal project. The cyborg would not recognize the Garden of Eden; it is not made of mud and cannot dream of returning to dust. Perhaps that is why I want to see if cyborgs can subvert the apocalypse of returning to nuclear dust in the manic compulsion to name the Enemy. Cyborgs are not reverent; they do not remember the cosmos. They are wary of holism, but needy for connection—they seem to have a natural feel for united front politics, but without the vanguard party. The main trouble with cyborgs, of course, is that they are the illegitimate offspring of militarism and patriarchal capitalism, not to mention state socialism. But illegitimate offspring are often exceedingly unfaithful to their origins. Their fathers, after all, are inessential.

[...] I want to signal three crucial boundary breakdowns that make the following political fictional (political scientific) analysis possible. By the late twentieth century in United States, scientific culture, the boundary between human and animal, is thoroughly breached. The last beachheads of uniqueness have been polluted, if not turned into amusement parks—language, tool use, social behavior, mental events. Nothing really convincingly settles the separation of human and animal. Many people no longer feel the need of such a separation; indeed, many branches of feminist culture affirm the pleasure of connection with human and other living creatures. Movements for animal rights are not irrational denials of human uniqueness; they are clear-sighted recognition of connection across the discredited breach of nature and culture. Biology and evolutionary theory over the last two centuries have simultaneously produced modern organisms as objects of knowledge and reduced the line between humans and animals to a faint trace re-etched in ideological struggle or professional disputes between life and social sciences. Within this framework, teaching modern Christian creationism should be fought as a form of child abuse.

Biological-determinist ideology is only one position opened up in scientific culture for arguing the meanings of human animality. There is much room for radical political people to contest for the meanings of the breached boundary. The cyborg appears in myth precisely where the boundary between human and animal is transgressed. Far from signaling a walling off of people from other living things, cyborgs signal disturbingly and pleasurably tight coupling. Bestiality has a new status in this cycle of marriage exchange.

The second leaky distinction is between animal-human (organism) and machine. Pre-cybernetic machines could be haunted; there was always the specter of the ghost in the machine. This dualism structured the dialogue between materialism and idealism that was settled by a dialectical progeny called spirit or history, according to taste. But basically machines were not self-moving, self-designing, autonomous. They could not achieve man's dream, only mock it. They were not man, an author of himself, but only a caricature of that masculinist reproductive dream. To think they were otherwise was paranoid. Now we are not so sure. Late twentieth century machines have made thoroughly ambiguous the difference between natural and artificial, mind and body, self-developing and externally designed, and many other distinctions that used to apply to organisms and machines. Our machines are disturbingly lively, and we ourselves frighteningly inert.

Technological determinism is only one ideological space opened up by the reconceptions of machine and organism as coded texts through which we engage in the play of writing and reading the world. 'Textualization' of everything in poststructuralist, postmodernist theory has been damned by Marxists and socialist feminists for its utopian disregard for lived relations of domination that ground the 'play' of arbitrary reading. It is certainly true that postmodernist strategies, like my cyborg myth, subvert myriad organic wholes (e.g. the poem, primitive culture, the biological organism). In short, the certainty of what counts as nature—a source of insight and a promise of innocence—is undermined, probably fatally. The transcendent authorization of interpretation is lost and with it the ontology grounding Western epistemology. But the alternative is not cynicism or faithlessness, that is, some version of abstract existence, like the accounts of technological determinism destroying 'man' by the 'machine' or 'meaningful political action' by the 'text'. Who cyborgs will be is a radical question; the answers are a matter of survival. Both chimpanzees and artifacts have politics, so why shouldn't we?[1]

The third distinction is a subset of the second: The boundary between physical and nonphysical is very imprecise for us. Pop physics books on the consequences of quantum theory and the indeterminacy principle are a kind of popular scientific equivalent to the Harlequin romances as a marker of radical change in American white heterosexuality: They get it wrong, but they are on the right subject. Modern machines are quintessentially micro-electronic devices: They are everywhere and they are invisible. Modern machinery is an irreverent upstart god, mocking the Father's ubiquity and spirituality. The silicon chip is a surface for writing: it is etched in molecular scales disturbed only by atomic noise, the ultimate interference for nuclear scores. Writing, power, and technology are old partners in Western stories of the origin of civilization, but miniaturization has changed our experience of mechanism. Miniaturization has turned out to be about power; small is not so much beautiful as preeminently dangerous, as in Cruise missiles. Contrast the TV sets of the 1950s or the news cameras of the 1970s with the TV wristbands or hand-sized video cameras now advertised. Our best machines are made of sunshine; they are all light and clean because they are nothing but signals, electromagnetic waves, a section of a spectrum. These machines are eminently portable, mobile—a matter of immense human pain in Detroit and Singapore. People are nowhere near so fluid, being both material and opaque. Cyborgs are ether, quintessence. [...]

In this attempt at an epistemological and political position, I would like to sketch a picture of possible unity, a picture indebted to socialist and feminist principles of design. The frame for my sketch is set by the extent and importance of rearrangements in worldwide social relations tied to science and technology. I argue for a politics rooted in claims about fundamental changes in the nature of class, race, and gender in an emerging system of world order analogous in its novelty and scope to that created by industrial capitalism: we are living through a movement from an organic, industrial society to a polymorphous, information system—from all work to all play, a deadly game. Simultaneously material and ideological, the dichotomies may be expressed in the following chart of transitions from the comfortable old hierarchical dominations to the scary new networks I have called the informatics of domination:

Representation	Simulation
Bourgeois novel, realism	Science fiction, postmodernism
Organism	Biotic component
Depth, integrity	Surface, boundary
Heat	Noise
Biology as clinical practice	Biology as inscription
Physiology	Communications engineering
Small group	Subsystem
Perfection	Optimization
Eugenics	Population Control
Decadence, *Magic Mountain*	Obsolescence, *Future Shock*
Hygiene	Stress management
Microbiology, tuberculosis	Immunology, AIDS
Organic division of labor	Ergonomics/eybernetics of labor
Functional specialization	Modular construction
Reproduction	Replication
Organic sex role specialization	Optimal genetic strategies
Biological determinism	Evolutionary inertia, constraints
Community ecology	Ecosystem
Racial chain of being	Neo-imperialism, United Nations humanism
Scientific management in home/factory	Global factory/electronic cottage
Family/market/factory	Women in the integrated circuit
Family wage	Comparable worth
Public/private	Cyborg citizenship
Nature/culture	Fields of difference
Cooperation	Communications enhancement
Freud	Lacan
Sex	Genetic engineering
Labor	Robotics
Mind	Artificial intelligence
World War II	Star Wars
White capitalist patriarchy	Informatics of domination

This list suggests several interesting things. First, the objects on the right-hand side cannot be coded as 'natural', a realization that subverts naturalistic coding for the left-hand side as well. We cannot go back ideologically or materially. It's not just that 'god' is dead; so is the 'goddess'. Or both are revivified in the worlds charged with microelectronic and biotechnological politics. In relation to objects like biotic components, one must think not in terms of essential properties, but in terms of design, boundary constraints, rates of flows, systems logics, costs of lowering constraints. Sexual reproduction is one kind of reproductive strategy among many, with costs and benefits as a function of the system environment. Ideologies of sexual reproduction can no longer reasonably call on notions of sex and sex role as organic aspects in natural objects like organisms and families. Such reasoning will be unmasked as irrational, and ironically corporate executives reading *Playboy* and anti-porn radical feminists will make strange bedfellows in jointly unmasking the irrationalism.

Likewise for race, racist and anti-racist ideologies about human diversity have to be formulated in terms of frequencies of parameters. It is 'irrational' to invoke concepts like primitive and civilized. For liberals and radicals, the search for integrated social systems gives way to a new practice called 'experimental ethnography' in which an organic object dissipates in attention to the play of writing. At the level of ideology, we see translations of racism and colonialism into languages of development and underdevelopment, rates and constraints of modernization. Any objects or persons can be 'reasonably' thought of in terms of disassembly and reassembly: no 'natural' architectures constrain system design. The financial districts in all the world's cities, as well as the export-processing and free-trade zones, proclaim this elementary fact of 'late capitalism'. The entire universe of objects that can be known scientifically must be formulated as problems in communications engineering (for the managers) or theories of the text (for those who would resist). Both are cyborg semiologies.

One should expect control strategies to concentrate on boundary conditions and interfaces, on rates of flow across boundaries—and not on the integrity of natural objects. 'Integrity' or 'sincerity' of the Western self gives way to decision procedures and expert systems. For example, control strategies applied to women's capacities to give birth to new human beings will be developed in the languages of population control and maximization of goal achievement for individual decisionmakers. Control strategies will be formulated in terms of rates, costs of constraints, degrees of freedom. Human beings, like any other component or subsystem, must be localized in a system architecture whose basic modes of operation are probabilistic, statistical. No objects, spaces, or bodies are sacred in themselves; any component can be interfaced with any other if the proper standard, the proper code, can be constructed for processing signals in a common language. Exchange in this world transcends the universal translation effected by capitalist markets that Marx analyzed so well. The privileged pathology affecting all kinds of components in this universe is stress communications breakdown. The cyborg is not subject to Foucault's biopolitics; the cyborg simulates politics, a much more potent field of operations. Discursive constructions are no joke.

[...] One important route for reconstructing socialist-feminist politics is through theory and practice addressed to the social relations of science and technology, including crucially the systems of myth and meanings structuring our imaginations. The cyborg is a kind of disassembled and reassembled, postmodern collective and personal self. This is the self feminists must code.

Communications technologies and biotechnologies are the crucial tools recrafting our bodies. These tools embody and enforce new social relations for women worldwide. Technologies and scientific discourses can be partially understood as formalizations, that is, as frozen moments, of the fluid social interactions constituting them, but they should also be viewed as instruments for enforcing meanings. The boundary is permeable between tool and myth, instrument and concept, historical systems of social relations and historical anatomies of possible bodies, including objects of knowledge. Indeed, myth and tool mutually constitute each other.

Furthermore, communications sciences and modern biologies are constructed by a common move—the translation of the world into a problem of coding, a search for a common language in which all resistance to instrumental control disappears and all heterogeneity can be submitted to disassembly, reassembly, investment, and exchange.

In communications sciences, the translation of the world into a problem in coding can be illustrated by looking at cybernetic (feedback controlled) systems theories applied to telephone technology, computer design, weapons deployment, or data-base construction and maintenance. In each case, solution to the key questions rests on a theory of language and control; the key operation is determining the rates, directions, and probabilities of flow of a quantity called information. The world is subdivided by boundaries differentially permeable to information. Information is just that kind of quantifiable element (unit, basis of unity) which allows universal translation and so unhindered instrumental power (called effective communication). The biggest threat to such power is interruption of communication. Any system breakdown is a function of stress. The fundamentals of this technology can be condensed into the metaphor C^3I, command-control communication intelligence, the military's symbol for its operations theory.

In modern biologies, the translation of the world into a problem in coding can be illustrated by molecular genetics, ecology, sociobiological evolutionary theory, and immunobiology. The organism has been translated into problems of genetic coding and read-out. Biotechnology, a writing technology, informs research broadly. In a sense, organisms have ceased to exist as objects of knowledge, giving way to biotic components, that is, special kinds of information-processing devices. The analogous moves in ecology could be examined by probing the history and utility of the concept of the ecosystem. Immunobiology and associated medical practices are rich exemplars of the privilege of coding and recognition systems as objects of knowledge, as constructions of bodily reality for us. Biology here is a king of cryptography. Research is necessarily a kind of intelligence activity. Ironies abound. A stressed system goes awry; its communication processes break down; it fails to recognize the difference between self and other. Human babies with baboon hearts evoke national ethical perplexity—for animal-rights activists at least as much as for the guardians of human purity. In the United States gay men and intravenous drug users are the most 'privileged' victims of an awful immune-system disease that marks (inscribes on the body) confusion of boundaries and moral pollution.

But these excursions into communications sciences and biology have been at a rarefied level; there is a mundane, largely economic reality to support my claim that these sciences and technologies indicate fundamental transformations in the structure of the world for us. Communications technologies depend on electronics. Modern states, multinational corporations, military power, welfare-state apparatuses, satellite systems, political processes, fabrication of our imaginations, labor-control systems, medical constructions of our bodies, commercial pornography, the international division of labor, and religious evangelism depend intimately upon electronics. Microelectronics is the technical basis of simulacra, that is, of copies without originals.

Microelectronics mediates the translations of labor into robotics and word processing, sex into genetic engineering and reproductive technologies, and mind into artificial intelligence and decision procedures. The new biotechnologies concern more than human reproduction. Biology as a powerful engineering science for redesigning materials and processes has revolutionary implications for industry, perhaps most obvious today in areas of fermentation, agriculture, and energy. Communications sciences and biology are constructions of natural-technical objects of knowledge in which the difference between machine and organism is thoroughly blurred; mind, body, and tool are on very intimate terms. The 'multinational' material organization of the production and reproduction of daily life and the symbolic organization of the production and reproduction of culture and imagination seem equally implicated. The boundary maintaining images of base and superstructure, public and private, or material and ideal never seemed more feeble.

I have used Rachel Grossman's image of women in the integrated circuit to name the situation of women in a world so intimately restructured through the social relations of science and technology.[2] I use the odd circumlocution, 'the social relations of science and technology', to indicate that we are not dealing with a technological determinism, but with a historical system depending upon structured relations among people. But the phrase should also indicate that science and technology provide fresh sources of power, that we need fresh sources of analysis and political action. Some of the rearrangements of race, sex, and class rooted in high-tech-facilitated social relations can make socialist feminism more relevant to effective progressive politics. [...]

Cyborg imagery can help express two crucial arguments in this essay: (1) the production of universal, totalizing theory is a major mistake that misses most of reality, probably always, but certainly now; (2) taking responsibility for the social relations of science and technology means refusing an anti-science metaphysics, a demonology of technology, and so means embracing the skillful task of reconstructing the boundaries of daily life, in partial connection with others, in communication with all of our parts. It is not just that science and technology are possible means of great human satisfaction, as well as a matrix of complex dominations. Cyborg imagery can suggest a way out of the maze of dualisms in which we have explained our bodies and our tools to ourselves. This is a dream not of a common language, but of a powerful infidel heteroglossia. It is an imagination of a feminist speaking in tongues to strike fear into the circuits of the super savers of the New Right. It means both building and destroying machines, identities, categories, relationships, spaces, stories. Although both are bound in the spiral dance, I would rather be a cyborg than a goddess.

> ['A Manifesto for Cyborgs: Science, Technology, and Socialist Feminism in the 1980s', in Linda Nicholson (ed.), *Feminism/Postmodernism* (London and New York: Routledge, 1990), 190–233 (originally published in *Socialist Review*, 15/80 (1985), 65–107).]

MICHELLE STANWORTH

77 Reproductive Technologies: Tampering with Nature?

Technologies designed to intervene in the process of human reproduction fall, roughly speaking, into four groups. The first and most familiar group includes those concerned with fertility control—with preventing conception, frustrating implantation of an embryo, or terminating pregnancy. [...]

A second group of reproductive technologies is concerned with the 'management' of labour and childbirth. [...]

The third and one of the growth areas in reproductive technology is concerned with improving the health and the genetic characteristics of foetuses and of newborns—with the search for, as some have said, 'the perfect child'.

The fourth and perhaps most controversial group are the conceptive technologies, directed to the promotion of pregnancy through techniques for overcoming or bypassing infertility. [...]

Precisely because of the different and sometimes conflicting interests at stake in the application of reproductive technologies, women have not been content to leave the evaluation of the impact of technology to 'the experts', who are often the very people involved in their promotion. Instead, they have highlighted the ambivalent effects of reproductive technologies on the lives of women. Women in Western Europe and North America today, compared with their foremothers, have fewer pregnancies, bear fewer babies against their wishes, are less likely to die in childbirth and less often experience the death of their babies. This is no small matter—and it is due, in some part, to technologies for intervening in human reproduction. But the view that reproductive technologies have given women control over motherhood—and thereby over their own lives—simply will not do. [...]

[...] [M]edical and scientific advances in the sphere of reproduction—so often hailed as the liberators of twentieth-century women—have, in fact, been a double-edged sword. On the one hand, they have offered women a greater technical possibility to decide if, when and under what conditions to have children; on the other, the domination of so much reproductive technology by the medical profession and by the state has enabled others to have an even greater capacity to exert control over women's lives. Moreover, the 'technical possibility' of choosing an oral contraceptive or in-vitro fertilization is only a small aspect of reproductive freedom.[1] For some women, motherhood remains their only chance of creativity, while economic and social circumstances compel others to relinquish motherhood altogether.

Against the stark backcloth of the history of technologies for controlling fertility, pregnancy and birth, how are we to analyse the emergent technologies concerned with promoting conception and with eliminating 'defects' in the unborn? One powerful theoretical approach sees in these new techniques a means for men to wrest 'not only control of reproduction, but reproduction itself' from women.[2] Following O'Brien,[3] it is suggested that men's alienation from reproduction—men's sense of disconnection from their seed during the process of conception, pregnancy and birth—has underpinned through the ages a relentless male desire to master nature, and to construct social institutions and cultural patterns that will not only subdue the waywardness of women but also give men an illusion of procreative continuity and power. New reproductive technologies are the vehicle that will turn men's illusions of reproductive power into a reality. By manipulating eggs and embryos, scientists will determine the sort of children who are born—will make themselves the fathers of humankind. By removing eggs and embryos from some women and implanting them in others, medical practitioners will gain unprecedented control over motherhood itself. Motherhood as a unified biological process will be effectively deconstructed: in place of 'mother', there will be ovarian mothers who supply eggs, uterine mothers who give birth to children and, presumably, social mothers who raise them. Through the eventual development of artificial wombs, the capacity will arise to make biological motherhood redundant. Whether or not women are eliminated, or merely reduced to the level of 'reproductive prostitutes', the object and the effect of the emergent technologies is to deconstruct motherhood and to destroy the claim to reproduction that is the foundation of women's identity.

The problem with this analysis is not that it is too radical, as some have claimed; rather, in seeking to protect women from the dangers of new technologies, it gives too much away. There is a tendency to echo the very views of scientific and medical practice, of women and of motherhood, which feminists have been seeking to transform. This analysis entails, in the first instance, an inflated view of science and medicine, the mirror image of that which scientists and medical practitioners often try themselves to promote. By emphasizing the continuities between technologies currently in clinical use, and those that exist merely in the fantasies of scientific commentators; by insisting that the practices involved in animal husbandry or in animal experimentation can unproblematically be transferred to human beings; by ignoring the ways in which women have resisted abuses of medical power and techniques they found unacceptable: by arguing this way, science and medicine have been portrayed as realms of boundless possibility, in the face of which mere human beings have no choices other than total rejection or capitulation. Any understanding of the constraints within which science and medicine operate, and of the way these can be shaped for the greater protection of women and men, is effectively erased.

Also integral to this approach is a view of women that comes uncomfortably close to that espoused by some members of the medical professions. Infertile women are too easily 'blinded by science';[4] they are manipulated into 'full and total support of any technique which will produce those desired children';[5] the choices they make and even their motivations to choose are controlled by men.[6] In the case of doctors, it is the 'maternal instinct' that allows women's own assessments of what they want from their bodies or their pregnancies to be overlooked; in this analysis, it is patriarchal and pronatal conditioning that makes infertile women (and, by implication, all women) incapable of rationally grounded and authentic choice. I argued above that the ideology of motherhood attempts to press women in the direction of child-bearing, and that in this sense women's motivations are socially shaped. But 'shaped' is not the same as 'determined'; and a rejection of child-bearing (for infertile women or fertile) is not necessarily a more authentic choice. The very existence of a range of sanctions and rewards designed to entice women into marriage and motherhood indicates, not that

conformity is guaranteed, but that avoidance of motherhood (and autonomous motherhood) are genuine options, which efforts are made to contain.

Finally, this approach tends to suggest that anything 'less' than a natural
process, from conception through to birth, represents the degradation of
motherhood itself. The motherhood that men are attempting to usurp
becomes a motherhood that is biologically defined, and to which all women
are assumed to have the same relationship. While it is the case that the lives of
all women are shaped by their biological selves, and by their assumed or
actual capacity to bear children, our bodies do not impose upon us a common
experience of reproduction; on the contrary, our bodies stand as powerful
reminders of the differentiating effects of age, health, disability, strength and
fertility history. There is, moreover, little reason to assume that the biological
potential to give birth has an identical meaning for women, regardless of their
social circumstances or their wishes with regard to child-bearing. How can
the experience of women who have chosen to remain childfree be fitted into a
framework that sees the continuous biological process that culminates in
birth as the core of our identity as women? How can we make sense from this
perspective of women who value children and child-bearing highly, but who
experience pregnancy itself as merely an unpleasant reality *en route* to raising
children?[7] How can we explain the fact that fewer working-class women in
Britain attend antenatal clinics, demand natural childbirth or breast-feed their
infants? Luker's analysis (ibid.) suggests the possibility that while for many
middle-class women pregnancy may be a scarce resource—time out from
a hectic professional life to enjoy the sensations of being a woman—for a
greater proportion of working-class women pregnancy may be more a taken-
for-granted prelude to social motherhood, not an experience to be cherished
in itself. Far too many women have experienced the type of reproductive care
that is insensitive to their own wishes and desires; but shared reaction against
unsatisfactory medical treatment should not be allowed to mask differences
in women's own sense of what authentic motherhood might be. Women may
legitimately, as Rayna Rapp said, 'want other things from reproductive
technology than merely to get it off our backs'.[8]

Feminist critics of technologies have always and rightly insisted that
technologies derive their meaning from the social and political context in
which they emerge. But where the context that is invoked in connection with
reproductive technologies is the universal victimization of women, then it is
easy to underestimate the significance of political struggles concerning the
future of reproduction which are currently being waged. I wish to argue [. . .]
that reproductive technologies are controversial—not only amongst feminists, but among a wider public—because they crystallize issues at the heart
of contemporary controversies over sexuality, parenthood, reproduction and
the family; and that a concern for self-determination for women must
engage, above all, with these struggles. [. . .]

During the 1960s and early 1970s, campaigns around abortion provided an urgent focus for the women's movement. A great deal of energy went into exposing the 'motherhood mystique', and challenging the social conditions that sometimes made childcare isolating and exhausting, rather than enriching. By contrast, relatively little attention was given to physical aspects of reproduction: the experiences of conceiving, bearing and birthing children. Pregnancy and childbirth often seemed merely the brute biological backdrop to childcare, the physical rite of passage that signalled our individual entries into motherhood.

From the mid-1970s onwards, women have had the confidence to recognize pregnancy and childbirth as the accomplishments they are: to wrest them back from nature, to insist upon seeing them as part of a sphere of significant action as meaningful and as civilized as any of the accomplishments of men. This reclamation has not been a mere semantic exercise (if any semantic exercises are 'merely' that). It has involved campaigns to alter the conditions of reproduction and to ensure that women have the scope to develop the projects of pregnancy and childbirth, and relationships with children, in their own ways—as well as the freedom to refuse them altogether.

Since reproductive technologies so intimately affect women's bodies, our pregnancies, our children and our lives, we cannot avoid being actively involved in their appraisal. But the attempt to reclaim motherhood as a female accomplishment should not mean giving the natural priority over the technological—that pregnancy is natural and good, technology unnatural and bad. It is not at all clear what a 'natural' relationship to our fertility, our reproductive capacity, would look like. The early modern period in England—sometimes characterized as an era of 'natural fertility'—was a period when women and men (but especially women) were anything but laissez-faire where fertility was concerned.[9] They knew of, and drew upon, herbal, mechanical, dietary and behavioural remedies and safeguards in order to influence the timing of conceptions, the sex of a foetus, to prevent births or to ensure conceptions and they sought the services of midwives and other 'experts' to assist them in the application of these technologies. In today's world, the term 'natural' can hardly be applied to high rates of infertility exacerbated by potentially controllable infections, by occupational hazards and environmental pollutants, by medical and contraceptive mismanagement.[10] If it is not clear what a 'natural' relation to our fertility would look like, it is even less clear that it would be desirable: fertility undermined by poor nutrition or by gonorrhoea, unchecked by medical intervention; high birth rates, with population growth limited only by high infant and adult mortality; abstinence from intercourse for heterosexual people except when pregnancy was the immediately desired result?

The thrust of feminist analysis has been to rescue pregnancy from the status of 'the natural'—to establish pregnancy and childbirth not as a natural condition, the parameters of which are set in advance, but as an accomplishment which we can actively shape according to our own ends.[11] To call 'natural' the energy and commitment involved in achieving a wanted pregnancy, in carrying it safely to term and in creating a sense of relationship with the child-that-will-be, is to deny the very human investment that some women make in 'my baby'. In the feminist critique of reproductive technologies, it is not technology as an *'artificial* invasion of the human body' that is at issue—but whether we can create the political and cultural conditions in which such technologies can be employed by women to shape the experience of reproduction according to their own definitions.

['Reproductive Technologies and the Deconstruction of Motherhood', in Stanworth (ed.), *Reproductive Technologies: Gender, Motherhood and Medicine* (Cambridge: Polity Press, 1987), 10–35.]

SARAH FRANKLIN

78 Fetal Fascinations: New Dimensions to the Medical-Scientific Construction of Fetal Personhood

[T]he issue of fetal personhood or fetal rights has become increasingly significant within contemporary public debates over reproduction, and correspondingly within feminist analyses of these. [. . .]

Feminists such as Rosalind Petchesky and Janet Gallagher[1] were among the first to note this shift and to develop a feminist critique of its implications for women. Since the early 1980s, it has become an increasingly significant component of feminist analyses of various reproductive issues, from new reproductive technologies, such as prenatal diagnosis and *in vitro* fertilization, to fetal organ transplants, enforced Caesarian sections and, of course, the continuing struggle for abortion rights. [. . .]

Ontology is the philosophical study of being or existence. It is a necessary concept to describe that aspect of the cultural construction of personhood which concerns the essence and origins of a human being. In Western culture, the origin story of coming into being is a natural one, indeed a biological one, to be precise. Hence, persons 'originate' at conception: it is biological facts that cause them to be, to come into existence, as it were. Biology is also the dominant discourse informing our constructions of ontogeny, the development of the human individual, and phylogeny, the emergence of the human species (through the process of evolution). Consequently, the 'biological facts' of conception, pregnancy and fetal life are not only powerful as authoritative forms of *knowledge*, they are powerful *symbolically*, as key cultural resources in the construction of personhood. It is, therefore, not at all surprising that they should become such powerful sources of meaning in contemporary debates around abortion.

However, it is only since the fetus has emerged as a focus of increasing medical and biological attention that these areas of knowledge and expertise have become so much more valuable to the anti-abortion lobby. A shift away from a primary focus on maternal health within the medical literature was a prerequisite for the anti-abortion lobby to take up this discourse. [. . .]

The emergence of the fetus in the medical literature is the result of a significant shift away from the perception of it as a passive, semi-parasitic 'passenger' in the womb. As one fetologist describes this shift,

The fetus is thought of nowadays not as an inert passenger in pregnancy but, rather, as in command of it. The fetus, in collaboration with the placenta, (a) ensures the endocrine success of pregnancy, (b) induces changes in maternal physiology which make her a suitable host, (c) is responsible for solving the immunological problems raised by its intimate contact with its mother, and (d) determines the duration of pregnancy.[2]

Whereas a division of interests between the fetus and the mother had long been seen to exist, even if only as two different biological systems, the fetus was previously regarded as weakly parasitic, but essentially passive—'an inert passenger'. It is the complete reversal of this previous view which is most strikingly apparent in this passage. Not only is the fetus now the active partner, taking 'command' of pregnancy, but in fact it is the dominant partner, with a determining role in pregnancy. What is also evident in this passage is that the fetus is not only attributed agency, 'induc[ing] changes in maternal physiology', and individuality, but it is attributed a will of its own and even an ability to undertake responsibility for its own interests. In sum, the fetus is here defined as an individual agent, who is separate from the mother and has its own distinct interests of which it is both aware and capable of acting on. [. . .]

The emphasis on fetal autonomy evident in the medical scientific texts is visually achieved through the use of scientific photography, such as that of the Swedish photojournalist Lennart Nilsson. Nilsson's close-up colour photography of fetuses, many of which were recovered from late abortions, first became the subject of international acclaim in his photo-essay documenting early human development, published in *LIFE* magazine in 1965. Since then, it has featured centrally in the imagery of anti-abortion campaigns, [. . .] which drew heavily upon this source of potent photo-realist propaganda. Indeed, the bold, full-colour fetal portraits produced by Nilsson have proved to be an invaluable armature of emotive images, made to order for the anti-abortion-ists' crusade to make of fetal imagery an iconography of fetal innocence. In the face of these portraits of fetal tranquillity (actually portraits of fetal post-mortems), the spectre of bodily dismemberment strikes an especially powerful chord.

These photographs offer a specific set of points of identification with the fetus which are enhanced by the accompanying texts. The primary emphasis is on the miracle of fetal development and survival through the arduous journey of pregnancy. 'The little fetus that could' might have been the most appropriate subtitle for the article in this respect. The fetus is also presented as *physically very sensitive*, as continually under threat of *something going wrong* with its development, and hence as an agent responsible for the task of its own miraculous transformation from a kidney bean-sized encephaloid into a 'baby' at 28 weeks gestation where the story ends. [. . .]

The position of the spectator constructed by these images is most significantly defined by the structuring absence of the mother, who is replaced by empty space. Equally invisible are the means by which these images were produced, which must have involved highly invasive technological manoeuvres in order to produce 'the first portrait ever made of a living embryo inside its mother's womb', as is claimed in the article where they originally appeared.[3] Set against a black backdrop, these round fetal orbs resemble nothing more than a sort of organic spacecraft, floating in a void. Through this technique, the conditions for spectator recognition of and identification with the fetus are achieved on the basis of its separation and individuation from the mother. The fetus is here represented as autonomous, intact and at peace, in direct contrast to the [. . .] portrayal of the fetus in the woman's body as vulnerable to a violent disintegration.

In sum, the convergence between the scientific discourse of 'fetology' and the visual discourse of fetal autonomy produces a specific construction of fetal personhood which has proved highly compatible with the strategy of contemporary anti-abortionists to win state protection for the fetus and thus a ban on all abortions. These discourses have been skilfully popularized and widely disseminated by anti-abortion campaigners both in Britain and in the USA. What is at stake in both the discursive construction of the fetus in scientific accounts and the visual representation of it through scientific photography is the cultural construction of the natural facts of pregnancy. These 'natural facts' have been elaborated in such a manner as to produce a social category of fetal personhood which has an enhanced ontological validity and specificity, which is of particular value to the anti-abortionists because of its authoritative scientific pedigree.

Two components of this ontological construction are of particular importance to the contemporary debate around abortion. One is the extensive reliance upon high technology to construct this definition of fetal being, including both medical scientific and visual technologies. The second is the processes of separation involved in this construction: of the fetus from the mother, and of the social from the biological. The ontology of fetal being is entirely asocial. It is a definition of personhood constructed entirely out of 'natural facts', although these are themselves, of course, socially constructed. [...]

Patriarchal individualism holds together the construction of fetal personhood in a number of respects, including how it is constructed through power/ knowledge or discourse, how it is described through language and metaphor, how it is represented visually, how it is narrated and how it is positioned as a masculine subject. Examples of this include: the construction of the fetus as a patriarchal citizen, the construction of the fetus as the object of patriarchal science, the gendered construction of the fetus as the object of patriarchal science, the gendered construction of the fetal self as masculine, and the narration of the fetus in terms of masculine heroism and adventure.

The construction of the fetus as patriarchal citizen is clearly evident in the use of the language of rights and entitlements to state protection which have become staple arguments in anti-abortion rhetoric. This rhetoric of human rights, of liberal democratic values, of entitlement to protection by the state, is founded on the values of *liberté, égalité, fraternité* and the patriarchal 'social contract'. It has been argued by feminists that the model of individual citizenship implicit in the social contract is patriarchal to the extent that it excludes women on the basis of both their reproductive capacity and their sexuality.[4] Nowhere is this more clearly evident than in the assertion of fetal rights. By its very nature, such a concept threatens the bodily integrity, the individual autonomy and the right to bodily sovereignty of women. Fetal citizenship contradicts the citizenship of women; indeed, it contradicts their individuality. Endowing fetuses with full civil rights ironically confers upon them a status in relation to the patriarchal social contract *which women never had to begin with*. It is thus a double blow, extending feminine disenfranchise-ment from the patriarchal state, and locating within their bodies a citizen with greater rights to bodily integrity than they have.

The construction of fetal personhood also relies on the individualism of the scientific expert, whose independent, detached, objective stance is the basis for authority and claims to truth.[5] This too is a form of patriarchal individu-alism, rendered explicit in the long history of patriarchal science as a mascu-linist epistemology, inextricably bound up in the project of 'conquering' nature, and often most extreme at its points of encounter with women's reproductive capacity.[6] [...]

The fetus as bounded object of patriarchal science, through which the body of the woman in whom the fetus exists is rendered invisible, bears a strong, and not unremarked upon, resemblance to the bounded masculine self formed through a similar psychic process of disavowal of maternal depend-ence. Hence, the powerful drive to constitute fetal personhood in terms of separateness, independence and individuality must also be located in relation to these characteristic psychic requirements of 'successful' masculine individuation and identity formation. [. . .]

Certainly, the earlier description of the fetus-commander, preparing his defence-mechanisms against the hostile maternal environment speaks of a particularly militaristic genre of the masculine adventure narrative (*Rambo fetus*).

What is significant, therefore, is the extent to which the theme of patriarchal individualism holds together so many different versions of fetal personhood, while at the same time comprising one of the most exclusionary, masculinist perspectives from which to understand the process of reproduction. What is also significant is how deeply patriarchal these forms of individualism are, constituting the powerful mythology of masculine independence at the same time as they maintain the powerful institutions of patriarchal dominance.

The very term 'individual', meaning *one who cannot be divided*, can only represent the male, as it is precisely the process of one individual becoming two which occurs through a woman's pregnancy. Pregnancy is precisely about one body becoming two, two bodies becoming one, the exact antithesis of individuality. [. . .]

The centrality of patriarchal individualism to the construction of fetal personhood [. . .] poses a similar threat to women's reproductive control. The entire basis of this dominant patriarchal construction prohibits the possibility of a woman-centred perspective on pregnancy, in which the term 'individual' has no meaning.

As the abortion debate moves into the 1990s, a new language of reproductive politics must be foregrounded in terms that challenge the process of biologizing the social in the name of natural science and natural fact. In order to develop terms that are woman-centred and responsive to the realities of women's lives as mothers, workers and persons in society, reproduction must be reclaimed as a social process involving social persons, who are interdependent and whose right to exist is not bound up with notions of radical separateness. The construction of the fetus described in this section is one which mythologizes both the social and the biological, constructing of them categories which affirm a deeply patriarchal model of the reproductive process, both before and after birth. Moving beyond these accounts, and challenging the male-defined perspectives they both attempt to create and affirm, will be increasingly difficult as the state, the legal system and the medical profession converge with their versions of the fetal martyr/ victim/ hero. Shifting the terms of debate, however, is an increasingly significant component in the struggle to establish a woman-centred territory at the heart of reproductive politics.

['Fetal Fascinations: New Dimensions to the Medical-Scientific Construction of Fetal Personhood', in Sarah Franklin, Celia Lury, and Jackie Stacey (eds.), *Off-Centre: Feminism and Cultural Studies* (London: HarperCollins Academic, 1991), 190–204.]

79 Brownian Motion: Women, Tactics, and Technology

Women have been writing *Star Trek* pornography since at least 1976, mostly in the United States, but also in Britain, Canada, and Australia. The idea did not begin with one person who then spread it to others, but seems to have arisen spontaneously in various places beginning in the mid-seventies, as fans recognized, through seeing the episodes countless times in syndication and on their own taped copies, that there was an erotic homosexual subtext there, or at least one that could easily be *made* to be there. Most of the writers and readers started off in 'regular' *Star Trek* fandom, and many are still involved in it, even while they pursue their myriad activities in what is called 'K/S' or 'slash' fandom. [...]

It has also been argued, most recently by Sarah Lefanu in *Feminism and Science Fiction*, that science fiction offers women writers a freedom not available in mainstream writing because its generic form, with its overlooked roots in the female gothic novel and nineteenth-century feminist utopian literature, permits a fusing of political concerns with the 'playful creativity of the imagination'.[1] And this is so, she says, even though science fiction has been historically a male preserve. [...]

The women writers I want to discuss, however, are amateur writers, few of whom would be willing to identify themselves as feminists, even though their writing and their fan activity might seem to offer an indirect (and sometimes not so indirect) commentary on issues usually seen as feminist, such as women's lack of social and economic equality, their having to manage a double-duty work and domestic life, and their being held to much greater standards of physical beauty than men. The tension here between the feminist concerns of the fans and their unwillingness to be seen as feminists can teach those who work in the field of women and popular culture a great deal about how political issues get articulated in everyday life outside the accepted languages of feminism and the left. What is at issue here is not discovering in this female fan culture a pre- or protopolitical language that could then be evaluated from the perspective of 'authentic' feminist thought, but, rather, finding alternative and unexpected ways of thinking and speaking about women's relation to the new technologies of science, the body, and the mind.

Michel de Certeau uses the term 'Brownian motion' to describe the tactical maneuvers of the relatively powerless when attempting to resist, negotiate, or transform the system and products of the relatively powerful.[2] He defines *tactics* as guerrilla actions involving hit-and-run acts of apparent randomness. Tactics are not designed primarily to help users take over the system but to seize every opportunity to turn to their own ends forces that systematically exclude or marginalize them. These tactics are also *a way of thinking* and 'show the extent to which intelligence is inseparable from the everyday struggles and pleasures that it articulates'.[3] The only 'product' of such tactics is one that results from 'making do' (*bricolage*)—the process of combining already-existing heterogeneous elements. It is not a synthesis that takes the form of an intellectual discourse about an object; the form of its making is its intelligence. The K/S fans, however, seem to go de Certeau's 'ordinary man' one better. They are not just reading, viewing, or consuming in tactical ways that offer fleeting moments of resistance or pleasure while watching TV, scanning the tabloids, or selecting from the supermarket shelves (to use some of his examples). They are producing not just intermittent, cobbled-together acts, but real products (albeit ones taking off from already-existing heterogeneous elements)—zines, novels, artwork, videos—that (admiringly) mimic and mock those of the industry they are 'borrowing' from while offering pleasures found lacking in the original products. K/S fandom more than illustrates de Certeau's claim that consumption is itself a form of production. A mini-industry, but one that necessarily makes no money (the only thing keeping it from copyright suits), it has its own apparatuses of advertising and publishing; juried prizes (K/Star, Surak, and Federation Class of Excellence Awards); stars (the top editors, writers, and artists, but also fans who have become celebrities); house organ, *On the Double*; annual meetings, featuring charity fund-raisers (e.g. an art auction to support an animal shelter); music videos (with scenes from *Star Trek* reedited for their 'slash' meanings); brilliant built-in market research techniques (the consumers are the producers and vice versa, since almost all of the slash readers are also its writers); and, increasingly, the elements of a critical apparatus, with its own theorists and historians. [. . .]

Not only have they remade the *Star Trek* fictional universe to their own desiring ends, they have achieved it by enthusiastically mimicking the technologies of mass-market cultural production, and by constantly debating their own relation, as women, to those technologies, through both the way they make decisions about how to use the technological resources available to them and the way they rewrite bodies and technologies in their utopian romances.

The term *appropriate technology* refers to both everyday uses of technology that are appropriate to the job at hand and the way users decide how and what to appropriate. To avoid becoming dependent on sources that extract too high a price, or to ensure that the technology will be available to everyone, one appropriates only what is needed. The slashers (their name for themselves) are constantly involved in negotiating appropriate levels of technology for use within the fandom. The emphasis is on keeping the technology accessible and democratic, although this turns out to be easier said than done. [. . .]

One piece of technology about which the fans have no ambivalence whatever is the VCR, which, along with the zine publishing apparatus, is the lifeblood of the fandom. The ubiquitous VCR allows fans to copy episodes for swapping or for closer examination of their slash possibilities, and provides the basic technology for producing songtapes. Fans are deeply invested in VCR technology because it is cheap, widely available, easy to use, and provides both escape and a chance to criticize the sexual status quo. As one beautifully embroidered sampler at a fan art auction put it, 'The more I see of men, the more I love my VCR.'[. . .]

In slash fandom, then, and the writing practice that it supports, we find a bracing instance of the strength of the popular wish to think through and debate the issues of women's relation to the technologies of science, the mind, and the body, in both fiction and everyday life. I have argued that much can be learned from the way the slashers make individual and collective decisions about how they will use technology at home, at work, and at leisure, and how they creatively reimagine their world through making a tactics of technology itself.

> ['Brownian Motion: Women, Tactics, and Technology', in Constance Penley and Andrew Ross (eds.), *Technoculture* (Minneapolis: University of Minnesota, 1991), 135–59.]

MARILYN STRATHERN

80 Less Nature, More Technology

Technology, for those who are afraid of it, is a kind of culture without people. Meanwhile one is at the mercy of people. The reduction of naturally produced genetic material, like reduction in the diversity of the world's species, is symbolised in the fantasy that if those with the power in fact get their hands on the appropriate technology, they would produce versions of themselves over and again and/or counter versions such as drones and slaves. A particular individual would be reproduced—but its multiplication would be the very opposite of individuation. Diversity without individuality; individuality without diversity.

I have referred to the modern English opinion that kinship diminishes in importance over the generations. Perhaps this has fed the present-day feelings of being at a point at which there is actually 'less' nature in the world than there used to be. And here we come to a confusion. In one sense it would seem that 'more' technology means 'more' culture. But if more culture creates choice that is no choice, then with the reduction of diversity there is also 'less' culture. The mathematics does not work. The perception that there is less nature in the world is thus *also* joined to the feeling that there is less culture, and less society for that matter—less community, less tradition, less convention. Tradition was traditionally perceived as under assault from the individual who exercised choice, from innovation, from change that made the world a more varied place to be in. It is now individuality that is under assault from the over-exercise of individual choice, from innovations that reduce variation. 'More' choice seems less 'choice': with the engineering of genetic stock, the potential for long-term future variation may be reduced rather than enhanced. When diversity appears to depend literally on the vagaries of human individuals, it suddenly seems at risk; variation may not ensue.

In the modern epoch, kinship and family could play either nature to the individual's cultural creativity, or society to the individual's natural spirit of enterprise. But if that former symbolic order pitted natural givens against cultural choice, social convention against natural variation, then it no longer persuades. These perspectives will not play off against one another. The postplural nostalgia is for the simultaneous loss of convention *and* loss of choice.

At the root of current debate is a profound issue about the shape not just the English but Westerners in general give to ideas.[1] They have in the recent past used the idea of nature, including the idea of natural variation, as a vehicle for thinking about human organisation and its future potential. In its place is a late twentieth-century equivocation about the relationship between human and natural process. For every image of technological advance as increasing human potential lies a counter-image of profligate waste for trivial ends and of resource depletion. This includes Westerners' reproductive capacities. Artificial processes are seen to substitute for natural ones, and thus present themselves as 'interfering with nature'.[2] What is interfered with is the very idea of a natural fact. Or, to put it another way, of the difference between natural and cultural ones.

Schneider's *American Kinship*[3] depicted sexual intercourse as a core symbol: the diffuse enduring solidarity of close family relations was attributed to sharing substance through the act of procreation. Procreation was a natural fact of life. But that 'natural' image has lost its obviousness in a world where couples can seek assistance to beget offspring without intercourse. So too have the 'cultural' conventions of the union. The otherwise lawful connection of husband and wife may conceivably subsume a contract with a birthing mother or an agreement to obtain gametes by donation.

Yet change can always be denied. Some will seek comparisons with other cultures and other conventions, although the reassurance that these new modes are simply part of the manifold diversity of human ways of reproduction is [...] misleading. Others who cast their minds back to the science-fiction writers of earlier this century, or even to Mary Shelley's Frankenstein, will say, as it is said of individualism, that these things have always been with us. Human beings have always fantasised about creating life; there have always been ways of dealing with infertility; there have always been those who deplored the spoiling of the countryside, as the English Lakeland poets protested with horror at the railways that were to bring tourists to their beloved spots. It is, in fact, this very capacity to think one is perpetuating old ideas, simply doing again what has been done at other times and in other places, before, elsewhere, that is itself a profound engine for change.

Anthropologists have always had problems in the analysis of social change. Perhaps it is because social change sometimes comes about in a very simple way. As far as aspects of English culture are concerned, all that is required is what (middle class) people do all the time, namely that they do what they think can be done. Put into action, this becomes an effort to promote and implement current values. Values are acted upon; implicit assumptions become explicit, and that includes rendering culturally visible what may be perceived as natural process. [. . .]

The 1980s witnessed an interesting phenomenon. To a remarkable extent, British public discourse has become dominated by the metaphors and symbols of the government, by which I mean not a constitutional consciousness but the specific depiction of social and cultural life promoted by the political party in power. Its discourse generates a single powerful metaphor: that the way forward is also recovering traditional values. Tradition has become a reason for progress. The way forward is defined not as building a better society, for that smacks of the collective and state idioms against which the present ideology is constructed. For the way forward is a better life for individual persons, and that is to be achieved by promoting what is proclaimed as Britain's (England's) long lived 'individualism'. A return to Victorian Values is presented as at once evoking a decent, law-abiding citizenry, and as a retreat from state intervention interfering in individual choice and personal effort. Rather, as a consequence, enterprise must be privatised, and the government has indeed privatised one of the country's foremost plant-breeding institutes along with its seed bank. Such a projection of the past into the future is beautifully exemplified in the elision with Contemporary American: recapturing traditional values will bring the bright future promised by (what English fantasise as) American enterprise. In the 1980s, English pubs have become heavy with reinstated Victorian decor in high streets dominated by over-lit fast-food outlets.

As a piece of history, of course, the 'return to Victorian values' is nonsense. But it ought to interest social scientists. A traditional value is claimed for England's (Britain's) true heritage, and individualism promoted and encouraged in the name of returning to tradition.

Not only is the individualism promoted so actively in the late twentieth century radically different from its counterpart of a century ago, it would not be conceivable without the intervening era which made the state an explicit instrument of public welfare. For the target of present political discourse is the tyranny of the collective. Indeed, the way in which the present 'individual' is construed comes directly from values and ideas that belong to that collectivist era. This is also true of many of the ways in which anthropologists have thought about the study of kinship.

Schneider was right to celebrate 1984 with a critique of the idea of kinship. His book is an attack on the unthinking manner in which generations of anthropologists have taken kinship to be the social or cultural construction of natural facts. But underlying the attack is the recognition that this is how kinship has been constructed in anthropology from the start, and indeed that this is its identity.

The anthropological construction of kinship as a domain of study was formed in a specific epoch. It came initially from the modernism of Morgan's era, from the 1860s onwards, but flowered in England in the middle decades of the twentieth century. This was the era when the anthropological task was to understand other people's cultures and societies, being thereby directed to their modes of collectivisation and public welfare. The concept of kinship as a set of principles by which people organised their fundamental relations epitomised the anthropological capacity to describe cultural production on the one hand and the way people made collective and social life known to themselves on the other. It was thus no accident that kinship played such a part in the making of British Social Anthropology, which—and however hybrid the origins of their practitioners—between 1910–1960 was basically English anthropology. Kinship was above all seen to be concerned with what peoples did everywhere with the facts of human nature.

For the modern anthropologist the facts of kinship were simultaneously facts of nature and facts of culture and society. In this light, it is more than intriguing to look back on these mid-twentieth-century assumptions from a world that seems, if only from the ability for endless printout or in the timeless attributes of role-playing games, to post-date Society, and whose culture might no longer mould or modify nature but could be everything that is left once Nature has gone.

[*After Nature* (Cambridge: Cambridge University Press, 1992), 42–6.]

MARIA MIES AND VANDANA SHIVA

81 Ecofeminism

Ecofeminism, 'a new term for an ancient wisdom'[1] grew out of various social movements—the feminist, peace and the ecology movements—in the late 1970s and early 1980s. Though the term was first used by Francoise D'Eaubonne[2] it became popular only in the context of numerous protests and activities against environmental destruction, sparked-off initially by recurring ecological disasters. The meltdown at Three Mile Island prompted large numbers of women in the USA to come together in the first ecofeminist conference—'Women and Life on Earth: A Conference on Eco-Feminism in the Eighties'—in March 1980, at Amherst. At this conference the connections between feminism, militarization, healing and ecology were explored. As Ynestra King, one of the Conference organizers, wrote:

Ecofeminism is about connectedness and wholeness of theory and practice. It asserts the special strength and integrity of every living thing. For us the snail darter is to be considered side by side with a community's need for water, the porpoise side by side with appetite for tuna, and the creatures it may fall on with Skylab. We are a woman-identified movement and we believe we have a special work to do in these imperilled times. We see the devastation of the earth and her beings by the corporate warriors, and the threat of nuclear annihilation by the military warriors, as feminist concerns. It is the same masculinist mentality which would deny us our right to our own bodies and our own sexuality, and which depends on multiple systems of dominance and state power to have its way.[3]

Wherever women acted against ecological destruction or/and the threat of atomic annihilation, they immediately became aware of the connection between patriarchal violence against women, other people and nature, and that: 'In defying this patriarchy we are loyal to future generations and to life and this planet itself. We have a deep and particular understanding of this both through our natures and our experience as women.'[4]

The 'corporate and military warriors' aggression against the environment was perceived almost physically as an aggression against our female body. This is expressed by many women who participated in these movements. Thus, women in Switzerland who demonstrated against the Seveso poisoning wrote: 'We should think of controlling our bodies in a more global way, as it is not only men and doctors who behave aggressively towards our bodies, but also the multinationals! What more aggression against the body of women, against the children than that of La Roche-Givaudan at Seveso? From 10 July 1976, their entire lives have been taken over by the "accident" and the effects are going to last for a long time'.[5]

On the night of 2–3 December 1984, 40 tons of toxic gas were released from a Union Carbide pesticides plant in Bhopal, India; 3,000 people died during the disaster and of the 400,000 others who were exposed, many have since died, and the suffering continues. Women have been those most severely affected but also the most persistent in their demand for justice. The Bhopal Gas Peedit Mahila Udyog Sangathan, has continued to remind the Government of India, Union Carbide and the world that they still suffer, and that no amount of money can restore the lives and health of the victims. As Hami-dabi, a Muslim woman from one of the poor *bastis* which were worst hit in the disaster said, 'We will not stop our fight till the fire in our hearts goes quiet—this fire started with 3,000 funeral pyres—and it will not die till we have justice.' Or, as the women of Sicily who protested against the stationing of nuclear missiles in their country stated:

Our 'no' to war coincides with our struggle for liberation. Never have we seen so clearly the connection between nuclear escalation and the culture of the musclemen; between the violence of war and the violence of rape. Such in fact is the historical memory that women have of war... But it is also our daily experience in 'peacetime' and in this respect women are perpetually at war... It is no coincidence that the gruesome game of war—in which the greater part of the male sex seems to delight—passes through the same stages as the traditional sexual relationship: aggression, conquest, possession, control. Of a woman or a land, it makes little difference.[6]

The women who were a driving force in movements against the construction of nuclear power plants in Germany, were not all committed feminists, but to them also the connection between technology, war against nature, against women and future generations was clear. The peasant women who actively protested against the proposed construction of the nuclear power plant at Whyl in South-West Germany also saw the connection between technology, the profit-oriented growth mania of the industrial system and the exploitation of the 'Third World'. This connection was also most clearly spelt out by a Russian woman after the Chernobyl catastrophe in 1986: 'Men never think of life. They only want to conquer nature and the enemy.'

The Chernobyl disaster in particular provoked a spontaneous expression of women's outrage and resistance against this war technology and the general industrial warrior system. The illusion that atomic technology was malevolent when used in bombs but benevolent when used to generate electricity for the North's domestic appliances was dispelled. Many women too, also understood that their consumerist lifestyle was also very much part of this system of war against nature, women, foreign peoples and future generations.

The new developments in biotechnology, genetic engineering and reproductive technology have made women acutely conscious of the gender bias of science and technology and that science's whole paradigm is characteristically patriarchal, anti-nature and colonial and aims to dispossess women of their generative capacity as it does the productive capacities of nature. The founding of the Feminist International Network of Resistance to Genetic and Reproductive Engineering (FINRRAGE) in 1984, was followed by a number of important congresses: 1985 in Sweden and in Bonn, 1988 in Bangladesh, and 1991 in Brazil. This movement reached far beyond the narrowly defined women's or feminist movement. In Germany women from trade unions, churches and universities, rural and urban women, workers and housewives mobilized against these technologies; their ethical, economic, and health implications continue to be hotly debated issues. This movement was instrumental in preventing the establishment of a 'surrogate motherhood' agency in Frankfurt. The ecofeminist principle of looking for connections where capitalist patriarchy and its warrior science are engaged in disconnecting and dissecting what forms a living whole also informs this movement. Thus those involved look not only at the implications of these technologies for women, but also for animals, plants, for agriculture in the Third World as well as in the industrialized North. They understand that the liberation of women cannot be achieved in isolation, but only as part of a larger struggle for the preservation of life on this planet.

This movement also facilitates the creation of new connections and networks. An African woman at the Bangladesh congress, on hearing of these technologies exclaimed: 'If that is progress, we do not want it. Keep it!'

As women in various movements—ecology, peace, feminist and especially health—rediscovered the interdependence and connectedness of everything, they also rediscovered what was called the spiritual dimension of life—the realization of this interconnectedness was itself sometimes called spirituality. Capitalist and Marxist materialism, both of which saw the achievement of human happiness as basically conditional on the expansion of material goods' production, denied or denigrated this dimension. Feminists also began to realize the significance of the 'witch hunts' at the beginning of our modern era in so far as patriarchal science and technology was developed only after these women (the witches) had been murdered and, concomitantly, their knowledge, wisdom and close relationship with nature had been destroyed.[7] The desire to recover, to regenerate this wisdom as a means to liberate women and nature from patriarchal destruction also motivated this turning towards spirituality. The term 'spiritual' is ambiguous, it means different things to different people. For some it means a kind of religion, but not one based upon the continuation of the patriarchal, monotheistic religions of Christianity, Judaism or Islam, all of which are arguably hostile to women and to nature vis-a-vis their basic warrior traditions. Hence, some tried to revive or recreate a goddess-based religion; spirituality was defined as the Goddess.

Some call it the female principle, inhabiting and permeating all things— this spirituality is understood in a less 'spiritual', that is, less idealistic way. Although the spirit was female, it was not apart from the material world, but seen as the life-force in everything and in every human being: it was indeed the connecting principle. Spirituality in these more material terms was akin to magic rather than to religion as it is commonly understood. This interpretation of spirituality [...] is largely identical to women's sensuality, their sexual energy, their most precious life force, which links them to each other, to other life forms and the elements. It is the energy that enables women to love and to celebrate life. This sensual or sexual spirituality, rather than 'other-worldly' is centred on and thus abolishes the opposition between spirit and matter, transcendence and immanence. There is only immanence, but this immanence is not inert, passive matter devoid of subjectivity, life and spirit. The spirit is inherent in everything and particularly our sensuous experience, because we ourselves with our bodies cannot separate the material from the spiritual. The spiritual is the love without which no life can blossom, it is this magic which is contained within everything. The rediscovered ancient wisdom consisted of the old magic insight into the existence of these all-embracing connections and that through these, powerless women could therefore influence powerful men. This at least informed the thinking of the women who, in 1980, surrounded the Pentagon with their rituals and who formulated the first ecofeminist manifesto.[8]

The ecological relevance of this emphasis on 'spirituality' lies in the rediscovery of the sacredness of life, according to which life on earth can be preserved only if people again begin to perceive all life forms as sacred and respect them as such. This quality is not located in an other-worldly deity, in a transcendence, but in everyday life, in our work, the things that surround us, in our immanence. And from time to time there should be celebrations of this sacredness in rituals, in dance and song.

This celebration of our dependence to Mother Earth is quite contrary to the attitude promoted by Francis Bacon and his followers, the fathers of modern science and technology. For them this dependence was an outrage, a mockery of man's right to freedom on his own terms and therefore had forcefully and violently to be abolished. Western rationality, the West's paradigm of science and concept of freedom are all based on overcoming and transcending this dependence, on the subordination of nature to the (male) will, and the disenchantment of all her forces. Spirituality in this context endeavours to 'heal Mother Earth' and to re-enchant the world. This means to undo the process of disenchantment, which Max Weber saw as the inevitable outcome of the European rationalization process.

Ecofeminists in the USA seemingly put greater emphasis on the 'spiritual' than do those in Europe. For example, in Germany, particularly since the early 1980s this tendency has often been criticized as escapism, as signifying a withdrawal from the political sphere into some kind of dream world, divorced from reality and thus leaving power in the hands of men. But the 'spiritual' feminists argue that theirs is the politics of everyday life, the transformation of fundamental relationships, even if that takes place only in small communities. They consider that this politics is much more effective than countering the power games of men with similar games. In Germany, too this debate has to be seen against the background of the emergence of the Greens, who participated in parliamentary politics since 1978. Many feminists joined the Green Party, less out of ecological, than feminist concerns. The Greens, however, were keen to integrate these concerns too into their programmes and politics. The critique of the 'spiritual' stand within the ecofeminist movement is voiced mainly by men and women from the left. Many women, particularly those who combine their critique of capitalism with a critique of patriarchy and still cling to some kind of 'materialist' concept of history, do not easily accept spiritual ecofeminism, because it is obvious that capitalism can also co-opt the 'spiritual' feminists' critique of 'materialism'.

This, indeed, is already happening. The New Age and esoteric movement have created a new market for esoterica, meditation, yoga, magic, alternative health practices, most of which are fragments taken out of the context of oriental, particularly Chinese and Indian, cultures. Now, after the material resources of the colonies have been looted, their spiritual and cultural resources are being transformed into commodities for the world market.

This interest in things spiritual is a manifestation of Western patriarchal capitalist civilization's deep crisis. While in the West the spiritual aspects of life (always segregated from the 'material' world), have more and more been eroded, people now look towards the 'East', towards pre-industrial traditions in the search for what has been destroyed in their own culture.

This search obviously stems from a deep human need for wholeness, but the fragmented and commodified way in which it takes place is to be criticized. Those interested in oriental spiritualism rarely know, or care to know, how people in, for example India, live or even the socio-economic and political contexts from these which fragments—such as yoga or tai-chi—have been taken. It is a kind of luxury spirituality. It is as Saral Sarkar put it,[9] the idealist icing on top of the material cake of the West's standard of living. Such luxury spiritualism cannot overcome the dichotomies between spirit and matter, economics and culture, because as long as it fails to integrate this search for wholeness into a critique of the existing exploitative world system and a search for a better society it can easily be co-opted and neutralized.

For Third World women who fight for the conservation of their survival base this spiritual icing-on-the-cake, the divorce of the spiritual from the material is incomprehensible for them, the term Mother Earth does not need to be qualified by inverted commas, because they regard the earth as a living being which guarantees their own and all their fellow creatures survival. They respect and celebrate Earth's sacredness and resist its transformation into dead, raw material for industrialism and commodity production. It follows, therefore, that they also respect both the diversity and the limits of nature which cannot be violated if they want to survive. It is this kind of materialism, this kind of immanence rooted in the everyday subsistence production of most of the world's women which is the basis of our ecofeminist position. This materialism is neither commodified capitalist nor mechanical Marxist materialism, both of which are based on the same concept of humanity's relationship to nature. But the ecofeminist spirituality as we understand it is not to be confused with a kind of other-worldly spirituality, that simply wants 'food without sweat', not caring where it comes from or whose sweat it involves. [. . .] [O]ur basic understanding of ecofeminism starts from the fundamental necessities of life; we call this the subsistence perspective. Our opinion is that women are nearer to this perspective than men—women in the South working and living, fighting for their immediate survival are nearer to it than urban, middle-class women and men in the North. Yet all women and all men have a body which is directly affected by the destructions of the industrial system. Therefore, all women and finally also all men have a 'material base' from which to analyse and change these processes.

[*Ecofeminism* (London: Zed Books, 1993), 13–20.]

SADIE PLANT

82 Beyond the Screens: Film, Cyberpunk and Cyberfeminism

Machines and women have at least one thing in common: they are not men. In this they are not alone, but they do have a special association, and with recent developments in information technology, the relationship between women and machinery begins to evolve into a dangerous alliance. Silicon and women's liberation track each other's development. [...]

Cyberfeminism is information technology as a fluid attack, an onslaught on human agency and the solidity of identity. Its flows breach the boundaries between man and machine, introducing systems of control whose complexity overwhelms the human masters of history Secreted in culture, its future begins to come up on the screen, downloaded virally into a present still striving, with increasing desperation, to live in the past. Cyberfeminism is simply the acknowledgement that patriarchy is doomed. No one is making it happen: it is not a political project, and has neither theory nor practice, no goals and no principles. It has nevertheless begun, and manifests itself as an alien invasion, a program which is already running beyond the human.

The connection between women and technology has been sedimented in patriarchal myth: machines were female because they were mere things on which men worked: because they always had an element of unpredictability and tended to go wrong, break down. No matter how sophisticated, the machine is still nature, and therefore understood to be lacking in all the attributes of the man: agency, autonomy, self-awareness, the ability to make history and transform the world. Women, nature and machines have existed for the benefit of man, organisms and devices intended for the service of a history to which they are merely the footnotes. The text itself is patriarchy, the system within which women occupy a world of objects, owned by men and exchanged between them. After Oedipus, the connection between castration and blindness, the penis and sight, seals the fate of woman within the phallic organisation of a specular economy for which she is the sold as seen. As the French feminist theoretician Luce Irigaray suggests, this is a strategy which has meant that there is only one human species, and it is male homo sapiens. There are no other sapiens. Woman is a virtual reality.

Women, however, have always found ways of circumventing the dominant systems of communication which have marginalised their own speech. And while man gazed out, looking for the truth, and reflecting on himself, women have never depended on what appears before them. On the contrary, they have persisted in communicating with each other and their environment in ways which the patriarch has been unable to comprehend, and so has often been interpreted as mad, or hysterical. Now these lines of communication between women, long repressed, are returning in a technological form, Hypertext destroys linearity, allowing the user to enter the density of writing, and disrupting every conception of the straightforward narrative. The imme- diacy of women's communion with each other, the flashes of intuitive exchange, and the non-hierarchical systems which women have established in the networking practices of grass roots feminist organisations: all these become the instant access of telecommunication, the decentered circuits and dispersed networks of information. The screens of cinematic and televisual experience become touch sensitive, transforming the gaze and collapsing its vision into the tactile worlds of virtual reality.

When Freud named weaving as woman's sole achievement, a remnant of the veiling of her own desire, it had been automated for more than a century. Jacquard's loom was the first step to software, a vital moment in the devel- opment of the cybernetic machine. Ada Lovelace, the first computer pro- grammer, said of Babbage's Analytic Engine: it 'weaves algebraical patterns just as the Jacquard loom weaves flowers and leaves'.[1] Today the American photographer Esther Parada writes: 'I like to think of the computer as an electronic loom strung with a matrix image, into which I can weave other material . . . I hope to create an equivalent to Guatemalan textiles, in which elaborate embroidery plays against the woven pattern of the cloth'.[2] With digitalisation, weaving no longer screens woman's desire, but allows it to flow in the dense tapestries and complex depth of the computer image. The data streams and information flows of cybernetic machines are the transformation and return of sensuality and the extra-sensory perceptions denied by the rational speculations of human history.

Enlightenment history dreams of a world of its own design and institutes man as the privileged agent of change: the world must be answerable to him, and wherever possible, it is he who must be seen to be making it happen. In his ideal world, he really would be running the whole show, master of all he surveys; in the late Twentieth Century, this is the show which begins to go out of control. In spite of every attempt at domestication, the agents of history have now to contend with runaway economies, overheating atmos- pheres, computers which can beat them at chess, and gun-toting women like Thelma and Louise. These are occasions for regret to those nostalgic for the days when planning and mastery seemed unproblematic. They are also symptoms of an emerging cybernetic environment which, as Donna Haraway suggests in her *Cyborg Manifesto*, allow us to learn 'how not to be a Man, the embodiment of Western Logos'.[3]

There is no doubt that the wares of technology, hard and soft, old and new, are always intended as toys for the boys; technical development has always been a consequence of man's attempt to perpetuate and extend his dominion. This is the basis of many feminist critiques of technology, which is said to be developed without and against women, and used only as an extension of masculine power. And it is all true: fuelled by dreams of light and flight, the machinery which feeds into the cultural images of the late Twentieth Century has its roots in a struggle against nature which has also been the repression of the feminine: a drive for security inscribed in the militarisation of the planet. As Virilio points out, cinema has always been a spin-off from war,[4] video. High Definition TV and virtual reality are equally the after-images of the weapons and surveillance systems, networks of communications and intelligence developed for use in advanced theatres of war like the Persian Gulf.

Yet it is these technologies, the pinnacles of man's supremacy, the high-tide of his speculations, that leave his world vulnerable to cyberfeminist infection. Hooked up to the screens and jacked into decks, man becomes the user, the addict, who can no longer insist on his sovereign autonomy and separation from nature. Increasingly integrated with the environment from which he always considered himself distinguished, he finds himself travelling on networks he didn't even know existed, and entering spaces in which his conceptions of reality and identity are destroyed. This is the return of the repressed, the return of the feminine, perhaps even the revenge of nature. But that which returns is transformed: no longer passive and inert, nature has become an intelligent machine, a self-regulating system. Nature was always the matrix it becomes: once the passive womb, a space for man; now weaving itself on the integrated circuit. [. . .]

Virtual reality: the simulation of space, the pixelled manifestation of another zone. Bought on the street, VR is still crude: cyberspace is too jerky and as yet, the programmes are self-contained and overdetermined. Even within these limits, the VR machine begins to allow its users to choose their disguises and assume alternative identities: 'would madam like blue eyes or brown, round ears or pointed ones?' Enthusiasts celebrate this diversity as a liberation from necessity, and off-the-shelf identity is an exciting new adventure for the user of virtual reality. Women, who know all about disguise, are already familiar with this trip. Imitation and artifice, make-up and pretence: they have been role-playing for millennia: always exhorted to 'act like a woman', to 'be ladylike': always to be like something, but never to be anything in particular, least of all herself. There is as yet no such thing as being a real woman. To be truly human is to be a real man. 'Woman does not yet exist', except as she appears on the set: wife and mother, sister and daughter: always performing duties, keeping up appearances, the acting head of the household.

Women have of course been roped into the patriarchal privileging of identity, so that much feminist struggle has been devoted to the search for the true self, the missing ingredient which would give women a full and equal place in human society. Cyberfemininity is something quite different. It is not a subject lacking an identity, but a virtual reality, whose identity is a mere tactic of infiltration. VR is a disturbance of human identity far more profound than pointed ears, or even gender bending, or becoming a sentient octopus. Those who believe these to be the limits of its impact are duped by dissimulation and the present state of its development. Cyberspace certainly tempts its users with the ultimate fulfilment of the patriarchal dream, leaving the proper body behind and floating in the immaterial. But who is adrift in the data stream? All identity is lost in the matrix, where man does not achieve pure consciousness, final autonomy, but disappears on the matrix, his boundaries collapsed in the cybernetic net. Like women, all technologies have to be camouflaged as toys for the boys, and virtual reality is itself an alien in disguise.

The cyborg is also undercover: as *Robocop*, it masquerades as the vanguard of human security, the more real man, the military machine. But even this figure is already an inhuman mutation; neither man, machine, nor even man becoming machine, the cybernetic organism is itself a symptom of cyberfeminist invasion, the introduction of the cybernetic system to even the most sacrosanct of organisms: the human. This destruction of the human identity boundary is also the vanguard of attempts to secure its dominion. The muscular cyborgs of popular film are creatures of law enforcement, security, policing, and surveillance: deployed, like Eve VIII, to safeguard the values and interests of human security, this is a mission they accomplish only by complicating control and proliferating chaos, disrupting security in the very process of reinforcing it. The cyborg betrays every patriarchal illusion, dragging the human into an alien future in which all its systems of security are powerless. This is the runaway auto-immunity of a humanity that is no longer itself: the frontier of patriarchy's automated defence networks has already become cybernetic, and so female. Even the Robocop heroes of a generation are already cut-ups of man and machine, intruders from virtual posthumanity. The cores of identity become the ones and zeros of a digital printout: the programming is revealed, the camouflage is slipping away. 'To become the cyborg, to put on the seductive and dangerous cybernetic space like a garment, is to put on the female.'[5] If the male human is the only human, the female cyborg is the only cyborg. Things look different from the other side of the screen.

The cyborg informs the patriarch that his drive for domination has led not to the perfection of techniques for ordering the world, but to cybernetics: self-designing mechanisms, self-organising systems, self-replicating machines. Because they seemed to give reality to the dream of total control, early self-regulating functions were hailed as marvellous additions to man's armoury in the struggle for dominion. Now nature was so tamed that it would run like clockwork. But the perfection of clockwork is also the phase transition to automation, the point at which machines began to exceed the control of those who believe themselves to be in charge. The Jacquard loom already marked the migration of control beyond both the human and the mechanical to a new software site in which machinery begins to learn and explore its own circuits of positive feedback.

Just as the mechanical shaped the cultures in which it arose, so the cybernetic extends beyond particular instances of technological development, feeding into the study of any complex system and leading even to the view that nature itself is a cybernetic organism, a self-regulating system of which man is merely a function. This marks a fundamental shift in conceptions of history: a move away from linear development, and a return of the cyclical, now transformed into circuitry. With this comes the possibility that man is not in control of his own destiny, and never will be, His drive for domination, control, and systematisation has brought him only to the realisation that domination is impossible, and that his agency was always only a mystified subroutine in a larger system of control. Technical research and development is increasingly aimed at the reestablishment of human control, the rehabilitation of the machine, but drives for security only defeat their own purpose. Every new computer virus which hacks through the filters of data protection means only more software, the proliferation of new codes, the proliferation and mutation of viruses. [. . .]

This transition to the cybernetic can still seem safely distant and fantastic. Cyborgs, virtual realities, and the cyberspatial integrated net are the tropes of science fiction. Nevertheless, as Donna Haraway points out, 'the boundary between science fiction and social reality is an optical illusion', and it is cyberpunk's shift of perspective which collapses this distinction to insist that the future is already here. Humanity is living out the last days of the spectacle, the last phase of illusion Cyberfeminism is the process by which its story is racing to an end. Every attempt to heighten security, and erect the protective screens again, merely perfects its circuits. Cyberspace shifts reality into the virtual: the cyborg embraces identity collapse: technosecurity evolves under the guidance of a virtual systems crash. For all our good intentions, moral principles, and political vision, we are heading for a post-human world, in which the intentions of the human species are no longer the guiding force of global development.

Every effort to build a world of man's own design has resulted only in the development of a planetary network with its own networks of communication, circuits of control, and flows of information. With the development of self-regulating systems, man has finally made nature work, but now it no longer works for him. It is as though humanity was simply the means by which the global system, the matrix, built itself; as if history was merely the prehistory of cyberfeminism.

['Beyond the Screens: Film, Cyberpunk and Cyberfeminism', *Variant* (1993), 13–17.]

CAROL STABILE

83   Feminism and the Technological Fix

As struggles over definitions of femaleness intensify, impelled largely by technological advances in areas such as reproductive technologies and genetic engineering, feminists have either withdrawn into reactionary essentialist formations (what I describe as *technophobia*) or equally problematic political strategies framed around fragmentary and destabilized theories of identity (*technomania*). In each instance, however differently manifested, the absent category of analysis is that of class. [. . .]

For post-Hiroshima Marxists, technology has ceased to hold out the progressive promise it once did. Herbert Marcuse (1964), for example, saw technologically advanced society as creating an increasingly monolithic, complacent populace being led timorous to the slaughter by capitalism and its cultural producers. The Vietnam War served to heighten the sense of technological disenfranchisement and hopelessness—television coverage of the war linked technoscience with the destruction and devastation for which it was apparently made.

The second wave of feminism, coming of age during the late sixties, inherited this sense of technological hopelessness, in addition to an historically loaded binarism between woman/nature/irrationality, on one hand, and man/culture/rationality, on the other. The trope of a technoscience equated with the war machine and a death drive also served to consolidate a feminist opposition equated with nature and life. Within this historical context, it is not surprising that Shulamith Firestone was alone in the early seventies when she argued for the potentially liberatory aspects of technology, while the majority of feminists dismissed technology as inherently patriarchal and malignant.

When the technological determinism of the seventies began to recede somewhat during the eighties, it gave way to postmodernist theories of fragmented, deterritorialized, or sometimes even simulated subjectivities produced by technoculture and its 'informatics of domination'. Whether this sea change occasions celebration or despair seems beside the point; the hyperreal has arrived with a vengeance and that is all there is to it. Worse yet, if one can envision dramatic social changes, the terms of political action have been irrevocably altered and miniaturized.

Feminists have been among the last to jump on the technological bandwagon. [...]

But the feminist alternative to the dematerialized, idealist theorizing proposed by many postmodernists has often produced its own version of dematerialized theory, in the shape of specifically feminist technophobias. In the humanities, as in popular culture, feminist approaches to technoscience have been profoundly informed by technophobia, or an anti-modern attitude that rejects the present in favor of a temporally distant (i.e. non-existent) and holistic natural world. As the essentially villainous agent of the patriarchy, technology—for feminists ranging from Mary Daly to the eco-feminist columnists of Ms. Magazine—is the bane of human existence, or that which threatens to destroy all things natural. The technophobic approach endorsed by so many feminists thus proposes that a rejection of technology is functionally identical to a rejection of patriarchy and that this strategy represents humankind's (or frequently only womankind's) sole chance for survival.

Attempting to bridge the gap between technophobia and technomania, feminist theorists have also produced an important body of work analyzing how technoscience has inscribed itself (both presently and historically) on the bodies of female, or feminized subjects. Evelyn Fox Keller (1985), Sandra Harding (1986, 1991), and Helen Longino (1990)[1] attempt to avoid the dichotomy between technophobia and technomania by suggesting that feminism needs to engage more productively with technoscience, but are rightly skeptical about immediate possibilities for intervention. Given the fact that technology has more often than not been utilized to oppress those who do not possess it or cannot engage with it, these feminists have tended to be more generally critical of technoscience, while at the same time aware of its liberatory potential. [...]

Donna Haraway and feminists inspired by her 'A Cyborg Manifesto' are generally understood to represent a more radical shift in the terms of the binarism between technomania and technophobia. Yet despite her socialist-feminist avowals, Haraway is an inveterate (if slippery) proponent of the technomaniacal ejaculations of Baudrillard and his band of unabashedly boyish poststructuralist theorists. In addition, Haraway's work depends on extremely cognizant and resistant readers—readers capable of radically decontextualizing and re-reading texts. Although Haraway works with an expanded inventory of texts, and a concomitant expansion of the category of technoscience, problems ensue from her against-the-grain readings, problems made more invidious by the complicated seductions of her textual practices.

[. . .] [N]either Mary Daly nor Donna Haraway offer feminist theory or activism politically viable, or sufficiently responsible, frameworks for political struggle. [. . .] [B]oth invariably reproduce the exclusion and privilege with which feminist movement over the past years has attempted to come to terms. Technophobia suggests that women possess agency and power enough to reject postmodernity (and that, moreover, they share the desire to do so), while technomania ignores history, as well as the privilege of its own pleasures. [. . .]

In *Rethinking Ecofeminist Politics* (1991), Janet Biehl describes how ecofeminist reliances upon the naturalized connection between 'woman' and 'nature' reify dominant ideologies of female nature—the hegemonic affects and effects of what ecofeminist Ynestra King celebrates as 'woman's bridge like position between nature and culture'.[2] Like feminist technophobia in general, the central tenets of ecofeminism might well be theorized within the trajectory of what Katha Pollitt describes as 'difference feminism'[3] or a theory of 'a world that contains two cultures—a female world of love and ritual and a male world of getting and spending and killing'. Despite its claims to comprise a new and radical version of feminist thought, one that specifically responds to modernity and its multifaceted problems, in keeping with many historical versions of feminism (not to mention dominant ideologies about femininity), ecofeminists ground their critiques in the belief that contemporary social problems can be reduced to gender oppression. The historical specificity of ecofeminism consists of the premise that changes brought about by technological advances, ascribed variously to patriarchy, capitalism, and even Marxism, have resulted (and can *only* result) in an equivalent domination of both women and nature. Once again, the quest for a feminist narrative of origins terminates in some misty feminist or matriarchal past.

For founding ecofeminists like Mary Daly and Susan Griffin, the solution to contemporary social problems (for women, at least) is to reject technology and the modern world in order to realign themselves with their true and essential source of strength: a pre-patriarchal affinity with nature. Daly's theory of 'patriarchy' depends upon the binarism between technology, as the monstrous, phallic present, and the environment, as matriarchal past. In the best of all possible worlds, according to this argument, women would inhabit (or should more completely inhabit) a realm distinct from the death-loving province of masculinity. [. . .]

Structured around strategies based on essentialized gender differences, ecofeminism facilitates intersections with conservative logic. The Chodorovian belief that women are intrinsically non-hierarchical, nurturing, empathetic, and consensual as opposed to men, who are competitive, emotionally aloof, selfish, and aggressive, upholds the ideological status quo by ceding power (invariably defined as negative) to men while arrogating a natural moral superiority to women. [...]

[P]rotests or resistances based on the connection between women and nature are an extremely risky business these days, always running the likelihood of affirming hegemonic identifications. Whether they intend to do so or not, they more often than not fail to escape from an historical terrain more tenaciously occupied by hegemonic and anti-feminist forces and therefore reproduce stereotypes of female nature. Political strategies, in short, should not be reduced to intentionality or individual agency, particularly within a political climate that continues to be anti-feminist. Instead, they need to be viewed as harnessing pre-existing and historically resonant articulations that operate within rigidly particularized circumstances. [...]

[T]he cultural dominance of technophobic feminism makes it a formidable trajectory indeed, one whose ideological pitfalls are expressed through the intersections of feminist technophobic theories and New Right political formations.

Feminist technomania, mainly expressed through feminist postmodernist theories, so far remains a phenomenon limited to intellectual circles. Presented as an alternative to the formula that celebrates women's special connection to nature, technomania accepts the fact of postmodernity as the *sine qua non* of contemporary existence and claims that it is this new and novel condition that will help to dismantle the terms of the woman/nature binarism. Nevertheless, the questions that must be brought to bear on feminist technomania are, in the end, similar to those used to interrogate the concealed privileges and subsequent partiality of technophobic feminist visions. The final question to be addressed, involves, as Rosemary Hennessy puts it, the extent to which technomania also participates 'in a general containment of the crisis of western subjectivities by helping to produce a subject which is "new"—that is, re-formed and updated—but nonetheless supportive of the hegemonic interests of multinational capitalism'.[4]

In order to unpack this question, I want to turn to the work of Donna Haraway, which, as one of the most prominent attempts to reconfigure the terms of feminist approaches to nature and technoscience, occupies a position of some centrality for feminist theorizations of technology and postmodernism. Haraway's argument 'for *pleasure* in the confusion of boundaries and for *responsibility* in their construction'[5] informs and structures arguments made by feminists frustrated by the durability of the woman/nature articulation. [...]

The cyborg has come to epitomize the postmodern traveling theorist—a theorist located nowhere, but moving toward some 'elsewhere'. [...]

While I do not want to dismiss Haraway's work as being blithely technomanic or to categorize her as 'baleful riff-raff,' I do want to suggest that, over the past decade, Haraway's travels, impelled by methodological erasures already implicit in 'A Cyborg Manifesto' (originally published in 1985), circulate within the boundaries of a particular postmodern hyperspace. Haraway's insistence that socialist-feminist politics for the twenty-first century must refuse 'to give away the game',[6] or to cede the terrain of technoscience, no doubt resembles my own argument, but its status as semiotic excursion troubles its claims to materialism. [...]

I want to read Haraway's work as representative of an expanding trend within feminist theory that dismisses an understanding of the complicated workings of structurally orchestrated, material oppressions in favor of endless, and endlessly revolving, metaphoric oppressions. [...]

Essentially, Haraway's advocacy of avant-garde practices narrows and isolates political struggle to a form of discursive engagement specific to intellectuals. In this way, Haraway—like many postmodernists—avoids poststructuralist critiques of canonicity, authority, and authorship by ushering the privileged Western intellectual in through a side door: the cyborg exists simultaneously as 'the unnatural cyborg women making chips in Asia and spiral dancing in Santa Rita jail'.[7] While first world feminists assume the cyborg position through active, creative intellectual practices, the third world woman has cyborg status conferred on her through a (first world) reading of her body and actions. [...]

So what politics does the cyborg endorse? Are these reading practices only about 'pure pleasure, in the sense that it is irreducible to the pursuit of the profits of distinction and is felt as the simple pleasure of play, of playing the cultural game well, of playing on one's skill at playing, of cultivating a pleasure which "cultivates" and of thus producing, like a kind of endless fire, its ever renewed sustenance of subtle illusions, deferent or irreverent references, expected or unusual associations'?[8] Or does the cyborg actually constitute 'an effort to build an ironic political myth faithful to feminism, socialism, and materialism'?[9]

These questions might best be considered in relation to the cyborg's own shifty (if not shiftless) nature. In 1985, the emphasis was on the production of a socialist-feminist theory, but by 1991, it has shifted to the writing of theory, or the production of a 'patterned vision of how to move and what to fear in the topography of an impossible but all-too-real present, in order to find an absent, but perhaps possible, other present'.[10]

Where, in 1988, 'we need the power of modern critical theories of how meanings and bodies get made, not in order to deny meanings and bodies, but in order to build meanings and bodies that have a chance for life', by 1991, we need this power 'in order to live in meanings and bodies that have a chance for the future'.[11] In effect, despite her global movements and avowed empathies, the cyborg feminist need not do anything in order to be political. Politics, so to speak, are fundamentally embedded in the cyborgian body: the fact that the cyborg signifies is enough to guarantee her politics. The shift from 'building' to 'living', a crucial one for the cyborg's trajectory during the eighties, coincides with the shift observed by Hennessy from feminist politics grounded in the question 'what is to be done?' to a feminist politics rooted in the more passive and individualistic 'who am I?'[12]

Having transported, dislocated, and relocated the cyborg over the years, we are left with the prophetic suggestion that 'If the cyborg has changed, so might the world'.[13] But aside from her more overt political passivity, what else has changed about the cyborg? In the end, she arrives at a form of pluralism that negates connections with either socialism or materialism. Haraway has described the central dilemma confronting feminism as one between the 'dream of a common language' or a radical heteroglossia—a formulation in which she clearly comes down on the side of the latter. Against the so-called totalizing feminist 'dream of a common language', we find instead a 'cyborg heteroglossia' or radical cultural politics.

But this investment in pluralism again overlooks the relations of force constitutive of pluralistic thought. Read as a manifestation of feminist pluralism, the dream of a common language (and its totalitarian connotations, which have been enacted in great detail in the feminist anti-pornography debates) constitutes the material reality of pluralism, or the expression of the power structures that pluralist discourses struggle to conceal. Heteroglossia is feminist pluralism's public face—the mythic and dematerialized belief that subjects can speak in very different languages, from entirely different social and cultural positions, yet somehow work together—in isolation from one another—toward a shared political vision.

In short, neither technophobia's 'dream of a common language' nor technomania's heteroglossia offer the tools necessary for reshaping reality.

[*Feminism and the Technological Fix* (Manchester: Manchester University Press, 1994), 1–7, 51, 54–5, 134–7, 146, 150–2.]

CYNTHIA COCKBURN AND RUŽA FÜRST-DILIĆ

84 Looking for the Gender/Technology Relation

A significant proportion of European women work outside the home—though rather more in the former communist countries and rather fewer in the Mediterranean countries. Despite this, women are everywhere the sex that does most housework and maintains responsibility for care and the quality of family life. [. . .]

Is new technology bringing any change in this respect? Other studies have shown that an increasing level of technology in the home has little effect either on the time devoted to housework or which sex does it.[1] It may well be that few domestic innovations are in fact designed with the intention of reducing housework time, and fewer still with that of altering which sex does the work. The manufacturer's aim is rather to *enhance* the activity. None the less, in our study we saw one or two slender signs of change. The percentage of male partners sharing vacuuming increased by 10 or 15 per cent with the acquisition of a centralized system. Men do a little more food preparation in relation to the microwave oven. The marginally increased involvement of men, however, may be less connected with technology than with other social factors. [. . .]

The 'smart house' projects are interesting for the continuity in gender relations they project. These technologies will save energy and defend property but do not promise to ease daily chores. The 'smart house' reflects men's perception of home as 'a place to put your feet up', but the work involved in turning such a house into such a home is invisible. Even the environmental consciousness the projects display does not speak of a woman's imagination. What about watering plants, feeding the fish, opening house to the sunshine?

Conversely, it is possible in some households to see gender relations shaping the technology. This depends on understanding a technological innovation as being complete only once the technology is in use. Invention is a beginning, but 'interpretive flexibility' may permit uses the designer never had in mind. This way women can be seen, even if late in the process, as genuine actors in the development of technologies.

Other researchers have shown how families make their technologies over to themselves, shaping them to 'the moral economy' of the household.[2] [. . .]

More subtly, though, we found gender tensions being acted out through technology. Some of these artefacts—the washing machine and food processor for example—seem designed to find a use precisely within an established family household involving a married couple, perhaps with children. When they land there, they become pawns in women's struggle for autonomy and self-expression, men's need to define and control. [. . .]

In the social relations of technological change, then, women and femininity are being reproduced as domestic, men and masculinity as technological. On to technology are mapped other qualities. It is represented as exciting, progressive and of high value. Domesticity, by contrast, is humdrum, repetitive and of low value. This is what gender is: an *ordering* process. The gender–technology relation involves the production and reproduction of a hierarchy, between women and men, the masculine and the feminine. Even, in a sense, between the 'technical' and the 'social'—and certainly within the various phases and faces of their interrelationship. [. . .]

Women's labour in the home is unrecognized—but what is more it is misunderstood. The producers of domestic appliances see them as commodities, they really do not understand them to be the tools of someone's labour process. They understand neither the meaning of that labour to the person who does it and the one who benefits from it, nor the social relations in which it is performed. If housework is acknowledged at all, it is seen as 'drudgery'—something to be evaded or made redundant. Women are not seeking to evade work. In a recent empirical study Jean-Claude Kaufmann found that a substantial group among French people of both sexes prefer washing up by hand to using a dishwasher. Some even get real pleasure from washing up.[3] If women resent housework it is not so much for the labour involved, much of which they consider creative. It is for the time, the tie and above all the unfairness of unequal sharing. Besides, caring, taking responsibility, enhancing the quality of life, these are arguably the activities that most engage women in the household, and they are invisibilized. [...]

Should we feel optimistic or pessimistic about the gender–technology relation? The picture [...] is not [...] one of unqualified gloom. [...] There are clear pointers to a feminist strategy on technology. We want in conclusion to suggest four aims.

First, we need to defend women's right to healthy, sustainable, paid work. That means we need new process technologies that will ease and enhance our jobs rather than intensify or routinize them. It also means, in circumstances of technological change, resisting redundancy and defending our right to technical training and retraining.

Second, there should be more women in technological design. We have a right to share in the activity of design because it is creative and rewarding. But, more importantly, it is only when enough women have advanced technological skills that a feminist critical analysis of technological innovation and production will become a reality.

Women are also needed in design because we can help, with men, to generate a more holistic perspective on human needs and the technological possibilities for meeting them. Women's particular skills, knowledge and creativity should also be acknowledged and valued in the circuit of technological innovation in other ways wherever women are: as production workers, sales staff, women in the home.

Third, all women should have the supportive domestic technologies they need to make housework pleasant: that means appropriate housing and equipment available on the market, the household income to buy them and the infrastructure to support them. We also however need supportive and sharing relationships in the home—and successive waves of domestic technological innovation have shown that to be a matter with little direct relation to technology. It does not follow from technological change so much as from women's struggle. Without both, the right technology and the right social relations, we will be unable to satisfy our wish to combine a public with a private persona, fulfilling paid work and a fulfilling home life.

Fourth, and finally, we must fight not just for ourselves as women, but for the re-evaluation of the domestic, the private and the relational. Engineering should be put at the service of the 'unimportant' everyday activities, instead of being allowed to master and deform everyday life. Indeed the concept of 'technology' itself is due for a rethink. A good deal of what goes on in everyday life—cooking, cleaning, washing, caring and spending—should be recognized and valued as technology too.

If our studies have one particular message it is that technology relations and gender relations affect and shape each other. Technological innovation cannot fulfil its creative promise when it is shaped in relations of dominance, whether of nation, class or gender. And it is hard for individuals and communities to create themselves in new liberatory forms while powerful techno-social systems perpetuate old oppressions.

['Looking for the Gender/Technology Relation', in *Bringing Technology Home: Gender and Technology in a Changing Europe* (Buckingham and Philadelphia: Open University Press, 1994), 13–20.]

SHERRY TURKLE

85   Tinysex and Gender Trouble

From my earliest effort to construct an online persona, it occurred to me that being a virtual man might be more comfortable than being a virtual woman.

When I first logged on to a MUD, I named and described a character but forgot to give it a gender. I was struggling with the technical aspects of the MUD universe—the difference between various MUD commands such as 'saying' and 'emoting', 'paging' and 'whispering'. Gender was the last thing on my mind. This rapidly changed when a male-presenting character named Jiffy asked me if I was 'really an it'. At his question, I experienced an unpleasurable sense of disorientation which immediately gave way to an unfamiliar sense of freedom.

When Jiffy's question appeared on my screen, I was standing in a room of LambdaMOO filled with characters engaged in sexual banter in the style of the movie *Animal House*. The innuendos, double entendres, and leering invitations were scrolling by at a fast clip; I felt awkward, as though at a party to which I had been invited by mistake. I was reminded of junior high school dances when I wanted to go home or hide behind the punch bowl. I was reminded of kissing games in which it was awful to be chosen and awful not to be chosen. Now, on the MUD, I had a new option. I wondered if playing a male might allow me to feel less out of place. I could stand on the sidelines and people would expect *me* to make the first move. And I could choose not to. I could choose simply to 'lurk', to stand by and observe the action. Boys, after all, were not called prudes if they were too cool to play kissing games. They were not categorized as wallflowers if they held back and didn't ask girls to dance. They could simply be shy in a manly way—aloof, above it all.

Two days later I was back in the MUD. After I typed the command that joined me, in Boston, to the computer in California where the MUD resided, I discovered that I had lost the paper on which I had written my MUD password. This meant that I could not play my own character but had to log on as a guest. As such, I was assigned a color: Magenta. As 'Magenta-guest' I was again without gender. While I was struggling with basic MUD) commands, other players were typing messages for all to see such as 'Magenta-guest gazes hot and enraptured at the approach of Fire-Eater'. Again I was tempted to hide from the frat party atmosphere by trying to pass as a man. When much later I did try playing a male character, I finally experienced that permission to move freely I had always imagined to be the birthright of men. Not only was I approached less frequently, but I found it easier to respond to an unwanted overture with aplomb, saying something like, 'That's flattering, Ribald-Temptress, but I'm otherwise engaged.' My sense of freedom didn't just involve a different attitude about sexual advances, which now seemed less threatening. As a woman I have a hard time deflecting a request for conversation by asserting my own agenda. As a MUD male, doing so (nicely) seemed more natural; it never struck me as dismissive or rude. Of course, my reaction said as much about the construction of gender in my own mind as it did about the social construction of gender in the MUD.

Playing in MUDs, whether as a man, a woman, or a neuter character, I quickly fell into the habit of orienting myself to new cyberspace acquaintances by checking out their gender. This was a strange exercise, especially because a significant proportion of the female-presenting characters were RI men, and a good number of the male-presenting characters were RI women. I was not alone in this curiously irrational preoccupation. For many players, guessing the true gender of players behind MUD characters has become something of an art form. Pavel Curtis, the founder of LambdaMOO, has observed that when a female-presenting character is called something like FabulousHotBabe, one can be almost sure there is a man behind the mask. Another experienced MUDder shares the folklore that 'if a female-presenting character's description of her beauty goes on for more than two paragraphs, "she" [the player behind the character] is sure to be an ugly woman.'

The preoccupation in MUDs with getting a 'fix' on people through 'fixing' their gender reminds us of the extent to which we use gender to shape our relationships. Corey, a twenty-two-year-old dental technician, says that her name often causes people to assume that she is male—that is, until she meets them. Corey has long blonde hair, piled high, and admits to 'going for the Barbie look'.

I'm not sure how it started, but I know that when I was a kid the more people said, 'Oh, you have such a cute boy's name', the more I laid on the hairbows. [With my name] they always expected a boy—or at least a tomboy.

Corey says that, for her, part of the fun of being online is that she gets to see 'a lot of people having the [same] experience [with their online names that] I've had with my name'. She tells me that her girlfriend logged on as Joel instead of Joely, 'and she saw people's expectations change real fast'. Corey continues:

I also think the neuter characters [in MUDs] are good. When I play one, I realize how hard it is not to be either a man or a woman. I always find myself trying to be one or the other even when I'm trying to be neither. And all the time I'm talking to a neuter character [*she reverses roles here*]... I'm thinking 'So who's behind it?'

In MUDs, the existence of characters other than male or female is disturbing, evocative. Like transgressive gender practices in real life, by breaking the conventions, it dramatizes our attachment to them.

Gender-swapping on MUDs is not a small part of the game action. By some estimates, Habitat, a Japanese MUD, has 1.5 million users. Habitat is a MUD operated for profit. Among the registered members of Habitat, there is a ratio of four real-life men to each real-life woman. But inside the MUD the ratio is only three male characters to one female character. In other words, a significant number of players, many tens of thousands of them, are virtually cross-dressing.

What is virtual gender-swapping all about? Some of those who do it claim that it is not particularly significant. 'When I play a woman I don't really take it too seriously', said twenty-year-old Andrei. 'I do it to improve the ratio of women to men. It's just a game.' On one level, virtual gender-swapping is easier than doing it in real life. For a man to present himself as female in a chat room, on an IRC channel, or in a MUD, only requires writing a description. For a man to play a woman on the streets of an American city, he would have to shave various parts of his body; wear makeup, perhaps a wig, a dress, and high heels; perhaps change his voice, walk, and mannerisms. He would have some anxiety about passing, and there might be even more anxiety about not passing, which would pose a risk of violence and possibly arrest. So more men are willing to give virtual cross-dressing a try. But once they are online as female, they soon find that maintaining this fiction is difficult. To pass as a woman for any length of time requires understanding how gender inflects speech, manner, the interpretation of experience. Women attempting to pass as men face the same kind of challenge. One woman said that she 'worked hard' to pass in a room on a commercial network service that was advertised as a meeting place for gay men,

I have always been so curious about what men do with each other. I could never even imagine how they talk to each other. I can't exactly go to a gay bar and eavesdrop inconspicuously. [When online] I don't actually have [virtual] sex with anyone. I get out of that by telling the men there that I'm shy and still unsure. But I like hanging out; it makes gays seem less strange to me. But it is not so easy. You have to think about it, to make up a life, a job, a set of reactions.

Virtual cross-dressing is not as simple as Andrei suggests. Not only can it be technically challenging, it can be psychologically complicated. Taking a virtual role may involve you in ongoing relationships. In this process, you may discover things about yourself that you never knew before. You may discover things about other people's response to you. You are not in danger of being arrested, but you are embarked on an enterprise that is not without some gravity and emotional risk.

In fact, one strong motivation to gender-swap in virtual space is to have Tinysex as a creature of another gender, something that suggests more than an emotionally neutral activity. Gender-swapping is an opportunity to explore conflicts raised by one's biological gender. Also, as Corey noted, by enabling people to experience what it 'feels' like to be the opposite gender or to have no gender at all, the practice encourages reflection on the way ideas about gender shape our expectations. MUDs and the virtual personae one adopts within them are objects-to-think-with for reflecting on the social construction of gender. [. . .]

[W]e have seen people doing what they have always done: trying to understand themselves and improve their lives by using the materials they have at hand. Although this practice is familiar, the fact that these materials now include the ability to live through virtual personate means two fundamental changes have occurred in our situation. We can easily move through multiple identities, and we can embrace—or be trapped by—cyberspace as a way of life.

As more and more people have logged on to this new way of life and have experienced the effects of virtuality, a genre of cultural criticism is emerging to interpret these phenomena [. . .] utopian, utilitarian, and apocalyptic. Utilitarian writers emphasize the practical side of the new way of life. Apocalyptic writers warn us of increasing social and personal fragmentation, more widespread surveillance, and loss of direct knowledge of the world. To date, however, the utopian approaches have dominated the field. They share the technological optimism that has dominated post-war culture, an optimism captured in the advertising slogans of my youth: 'Better living through chemistry', 'Progress is our most important product'. In our current situation, technological optimism tends to represent urban decay, social alienation, and economic polarization as out-of-date formulations of a problem that could be solved if appropriate technology were applied in sufficient doses, for example, technology that would link everyone to the 'information superhighway'. We all want to believe in some quick and relatively inexpensive solution to our difficulties. We are tempted to believe with the utopians that the Internet is a field for the flowering of participatory democracy and a medium for the transformation of education. We are tempted to share in the utopians' excitement at the prospect of virtual pleasures: sex with a distant partner, travel minus the risks and inconvenience of actually having to go anywhere. [...]

Although it provides us with no easy answers, life online does provide new lenses through which to examine current complexities. Unless we take advantage of these new lenses and carefully analyze our situation, we shall cede the future to those who want to believe that simple fixes can solve complicated problems. Given the history of the last century, thoughts of such a future are hardly inspiring.

['Tinysex and Gender Trouble', in *Life on the Screen: Identity in the Age of the Internet*
(London: Weidenfeld and Nicholson, 1996), 210–32.]

ROSI BRAIDOTTI
....

86 Cyberfeminism with a Difference

In this article, I will first of all situate the question of cyberbodies in the framework of postmodernity, stressing the paradoxes of embodiment. I will subsequently play a number of variations on the theme of cyberfeminism, highlighting the issue of sexual difference throughout. Contrary to jargon-ridden usages of the term, I take postmodernity to signify the specific historical situation of post-industrial societies after the decline of modernist hopes and tropes. Symptomatic of these changes is urban space, especially in the inner city, which has been cleaned up and refigured through post-indus-trial metal and plexiglass buildings, but it is only a veneer that covers up the putrefaction of the industrial space, marking the death of the modernist dream of urban civil society.

This is primarily, but not exclusively, a Western world problem. The distinct feature of postmodernity is in fact the transnational nature of its economy in the age of the decline of the nation state. It is about ethnic mixity through the flow of world migration: an infinite process of hybridization at a time of increasing racism and xenophobia in the West.[1]

Postmodernity is also about an enormous push towards the 'third-world-ification' of the 'first' world, with continuing exploitation of the 'third' world. It is about the decline of what was known as the 'second world', the communist block, and the recurrence of a process of 'balkanisation' of the whole Eastern European bloc. It is also about the decline of the legal economy and the rise of crime and illegality as a factor. This is what Deleuze and Guattari call 'capital as cocaine'. It proves the extent to which late capitalism has no teleological purpose, no definite direction, nothing except the brutality of self-perpetuation.

Last, but not least, postmodernity is about a new and perversely fruitful alliance between technology and culture. Technology has evolved from the panoptical device that Foucault analysed in terms of surveillance and control, to a far more complex apparatus, which Haraway describes in terms of 'the informatics of domination'. Approaching the issue of technology in postmodernity consequently requires a shift of perspective. Far from appearing antithetical to the human organism and set of values, the technological factor must be seen as co-extensive with and intermingled with the human. This mutual imbrication makes it necessary to speak of technology as a material and symbolic apparatus, i.e. a semiotic and social agent among others.

This shift of perspective, which I have analysed elsewhere as a move away from technophobia, towards a more technophilic approach, also redefines the terms of the relationships between technology and art.[2] If in a conventional humanistic framework the two may appear as opposites, in postmodernity, they are much more inter-connected.

In all fields, but especially in information technology, the strict separation between the technical and the creative has in fact been made redundant by digital images and the skills required by computer-aided design. The new alliance between the previously segregated domains of the technical and the artistic marks a contemporary version of the post-humanistic reconstruction of a techno-culture whose aesthetics is equal to its technological sophistication.

All this to say that I wish to keep my distance from, on the one hand, the euphoria of mainstream postmodernists who seize upon advanced technology and especially cyberspace as the possibility for multiple and polymorphous re-embodiments; and on the other hand, from the many prophets of doom who mourn the decline of classical humanism. I see postmodernity instead as on the threshold of new and important re-locations for cultural practice. One of the most significant pre-conditions for these re-locations is relinquishing both the phantasy of multiple re-embodiments and the fatal attraction of nostalgia.[3] The nostalgic longing for an allegedly better past is a hasty and unintelligent response to the challenges of our age. It is not only culturally ineffective—in so far as it relates to the conditions of its own historicity by negating them; it is also a short-cut through their complexity. I find that there is something deeply amoral and quite desperate in the way in which post-industrial societies rush headlong towards a hasty solution to their contradictions. This flight into nostalgia has the immediate effect of neglecting, by sheer denial, the transition from a humanistic to a post-human world. That this basic self-deception be compensated by a wave of longing for saviours of all brands and formats is not surprising.

In this generalized climate of denial and neglect of the terminal crisis of classical humanism, I would like to suggest that we need to turn to literary genres such as science fiction and more specifically cyber punk, in order to find non-nostalgic solutions to the contradictions of our times.

Whereas mainstream culture refuses to mourn the loss of humanistic certainties, 'minor' cultural productions foreground the crisis and highlight the potential it offers for creative solutions. As opposed to the amorality of denial, these cultural genres cultivate an ethics of lucid self-awareness. Some of the most moral beings left in western postmodernity are the science fiction writers who take the time to linger on the death of the humanist ideal of 'Man', thus inscribing this loss—and the ontological insecurity it entails—at the (dead) heart of contemporary cultural concerns. By taking the time to symbolize the crisis of humanism, these creative spirits, following Nietzsche, push the crisis to its innermost resolution. In so doing, they not only inscribe death at the top of the postmodern cultural agenda, but they also strip the veneer of nostalgia that covers up the inadequacies of the present cultural (dis)order.

In the rest of this piece, I would like to suggest that first and foremost among these iconoclastic readers of the contemporary crisis are feminist cultural and media activists such as the riot girls and other 'cyberfeminists' who are devoted to the politics of parody or parodic repetition. Some of these creative minds are prone to theory, others—feminist science fiction writers and other 'fabulators'[4] like Angela Carter—choose the fictional mode. While irony remains a major stylistic device, of great significance are also contemporary multi-media electronic artists of the non-nostalgic kind like Jenny Holzer, Laurie Anderson and Cindy Sherman. They are the ideal travel companions in postmodernity.

It's a good thing I was born a woman, or I'd have been a drag queen.   (Dolly Parton)

The quote from that great simulator, Dolly Parton, sets the mood for the rest of this section, in which I will offer a survey of some of the socio-political representations of the cyberbody phenomenon from a feminist angle.

Let us imagine a postmodern triptych for a moment Dolly Parton in all her simulated Southern Belle outlook. On her right hand, that masterpiece of silicon re-construction that is Elizabeth Taylor, with Peter Pan look-alike Michael Jackson whimpering at her side. On Dolly's left, hyper-real fitness fetishist Jane Fonda, well established in her post-Barbarella phase as a major dynamo in Ted Turner's planetary catholic embrace.

There you have the Pantheon of postmodern femininity, live on CNN at any time, any place, from Hong Kong to Sarajevo, yours at the push of a button. Interactivity is another name for shopping, as Christine Tamblyn[5] put it, and hyper-real gender identity is what it sells.

These three icons have some features in common: firstly, they inhabit a *posthuman body*, that is to say, an artificially reconstructed body.[6] The body in question here is far from a biological essence: it is a crossroad of intensive forces; it is a surface of inscriptions of social codes. Ever since the efforts by the poststructuralist generation to rethink a non-essentialized embodied self, we should all have grown accustomed to the loss of ontological security that accompanies the decline of the naturalistic paradigm. As Francis Barker puts it, the disappearance of the body is the apex of the historical process of its denaturalization.[7] The problem that lingers on is how to re-adjust our politics to this shift.

I would like to suggest as a consequence that it is more adequate to speak of our body in terms of embodiment, that is to say of multiple bodies or sets of embodied positions. Embodiment means that we are situated subjects, capable of performing sets of (inter)actions which are discontinuous in space and time. Embodied subjectivity is thus a paradox that rests simultaneously on the historical decline of mind/body distinctions and the proliferation of discourses about the body. Foucault reformulates this in terms of the paradox of simultaneous disappearance and over-exposure of the body. Though technology makes the paradox manifest and in some ways exemplifies it perfectly, it cannot be argued that it is responsible for such a shift in paradigm.

In spite of the dangers of nostalgia, mentioned above, there is still hope: we can still hang on to Nietzsche's crazed insight that God is finally dead and the stench of his rotting corpse is filling the cosmos. The death of God has been long in coming and it has joined a domino-effect, which has brought down a number of familiar notions. The security about the categorical distinction between mind and body; the safe belief in the role and function of the nation state; the family; masculine authority; the eternal feminine and compulsory heterosexuality. These metaphysically founded certainties have foundered and made room for something more complex, more playful and infinitely more disturbing.

Speaking as a woman, that is to say, a subject emerging from a history of oppression and exclusion, I would say that this crisis of conventional values is rather a positive thing. The metaphysical condition in fact had entailed an institutionalised vision of femininity which has burdened my gender for centuries. The crisis of modernity is, for feminists, not a melancholy plunge into loss and decline, but rather the joyful opening up of new possibilities.

Thus, the hyper-reality of the posthuman predicament so sublimely represented by Parton, Taylor and Fonda, does not wipe out politics or the need for political resistance; it just makes it more necessary than ever to work towards a radical redefinition of political action. Nothing could be further from a postmodern ethics than Dostoyevsky's over-quoted and profoundly mistaken statement that, if God is dead, anything goes. The challenge here is rather how to combine the recognition of postmodern embodiment with resistance to relativism and a free fall into cynicism.

Secondly, the three cyborg goddesses mentioned above are immensely rich because they are media stars. Capital in these post-industrial times is an immaterial flow of cash that travels as pure data in cyberspace till it lands in (some of) our bank accounts. Moreover, capital harps on and trades in body fluids: the cheap sweat and blood of the disposable workforce throughout the third world; but also, the wetness of desire of first world consumers as they commodity their existence into over-saturated stupor. Hyper-reality does not wipe out class relations: it just intensifies them,[8] Postmodernity rests on the paradox of simultaneous commodification and conformism of cultures, while intensifying disparities among them, as well as structural inequalities.

An important aspect of this situation is the omnipotence of the visual media. Our era has turned visualization into the ultimate form of control; in the hands of the clarity ferishists who have turned CNN into a verb: 'I've been CNN-ed today, haven't you?' This marks not only the final stage in the commodification of the scopic, but also the triumph of vision over all the other senses.[9]

This is of special concern from a feminist perspective, because it tends to reinstate a hierarchy of bodily perception which over-privileges vision over other senses, especially touch and sound. The primacy of vision has been challenged by feminist theories.

In the light of the feminist work proposed by Luce Irigaray and Kaja Silverman, the idea has emerged to explore the potentiality of hearing and audio material as a way out of the tyranny of the gaze. Donna Haraway has inspiring things to say about the logocentric hold of disembodied vision, which is best exemplified by the satellite/eye in the sky. She opposes to it an embodied and therefore accountable redefinition of the act of seeing as a form of connection to the object of vision, which she defines in terms of 'passionate detachment'. If you look across the board of contemporary electronic art, especially in the field of virtual reality, you will find many women artists, like Catherine Richards and Nell Tenhaaf, who apply the technology to challenge the in-built assumption of visual superiority which it carries.

Thirdly, the three icons I have chosen to symbolize postmodern bodies are all white, especially and paradoxically Michael Jackson. [. . .]

One related aspect of the racialization of post-human bodies concerns the ethnic-specific values it conveys. Many have questioned the extent to which we are all being re-colonized by an American, and more specifically, a Californian 'body-beautiful' ideology. In so far as US corporations own the technology, they leave their cultural imprints upon the contemporary imaginary. This leaves little room to any other cultural alternatives. Thus, the three emblems of postmodern femininity on whose discursive bodies I am writing this, could only be American.

Confronted with this situation, that is to say with culturally enforced icons of white, economically dominant, heterosexual hyper-femininity—which simultaneously reinstate huge power differentials while denying them—what is to be done?

The first thing a feminist critic can do is to acknowledge the aporias and the aphasias of theoretical frameworks and look with hope in the direction of (women) artists. There is no question that the creative spirits have a head start over the masters of meta discourse and especially those of deconstructive meta discourse. This is a very sobering prospect: after years of post-structuralist theoretical arrogance, philosophy lags behind art and fiction in the difficult struggle to keep up with today's world. Maybe the time has come for us to moderate the theoretical voice within us and to attempt to deal with our historical situation differently.

Feminists have been prompt in picking up the challenge of finding political and intellectual answers to this theoretical crisis. It has largely taken the form of a 'linguistic turn', i.e. a shift towards more imaginative styles. Evidence of this is the emphasis feminist theory is placing on the need for new 'figurations', as Donna Haraway puts it, or 'fabulations', to quote Marleen Barr, to express the alternative forms of female subjectivity developed within feminism, as well as the on-going struggle with language to produce affirmative representations of women.

But nowhere is the feminist challenge more evident than in the field of artistic practice. For instance, the ironical force, the hardly suppressed violence and the vitriolic wit of feminist groups like Guerilla or Riot. Girls are an important aspect of the contemporary relocation of culture, and the struggle over representation. I would define their position in terms of the politics of parody. Riot girls argue that there is a war going on and that women are not pacifists, we are the guerilla girls, the riot girls, the bad girls. We want to put up some active resistance, but we also want to have fun and we want to do it our way. The ever increasing number of women writing their own science fiction, cyberpunk, film scripts, 'zines, rap and rock music and the like testifies to this new mode.

There is definitely a touch of violence in the mode exposed by the riot and guerilla girls: a sort of raw directness that clashes with the syncopated tones of standard art criticism. This forceful style is a response to hostile environmental and social forces. It also expresses a reliance on collective bonding through rituals and ritualized actions, which far from dissolving the individual into the group, simply accentuate her unrepentant singularity, I find a powerful evocation of this singular yet collectively shared position in the raucous, demonic beat of Kathy Acker's In Memorium to Identily,[10] in her flair for multiple becomings, her joy in the reversibility of situations and people— her border-line capacity to impersonate, mimic and cut across an infinity of Others.

As many feminist theorists have pointed out, the practice of parody, which I also call 'the philosophy as if', with its ritualized repetitions, needs to be grounded in order to be politically effective. Postmodern feminist knowledge claims are grounded in life-experiences and consequently mark radical forms of re-embodiment. But they also need to be dynamic—or nomadic—and allow for shifts of location and multiplicity.

The practice of 'as if' can also degenerate into the mode of fetishistic representation. This consists in simultaneously recognising and denying certain attributes or experiences. In male-stream postmodern thought,[11] fetishistic disavowal seems to mark most discussions of sexual difference.[12] I see feminist theory as a corrective to this trend. The feminist 'philosophy of as if' is not a form of disavowal, but rather the affirmation of a subject that is both non-essentialized, that is to say no longer grounded in the idea of human or feminine 'nature', but she is nonetheless capable of ethic and moral agency. As Judith Butler lucidly warns us, the force of the parodic mode consists precisely in turning the practice of repetitions into a politically empowering position.

What I find empowering in the theoretical and political practice of 'as if' is its potential for opening up, through successive repetitions and mimetic strategies, spaces where forms of feminist agency can be engendered. In other words, parody can be politically empowering on the condition of being sustained by a critical consciousness that aims at the subversion of dominant codes. Thus, I have argued that Irigaray's strategy of 'mimesis' is politically empowering because it addresses simultaneously issues of identity, identifications and political subjectivity.[13] [. . .]

One of the great contradictions of virtual reality images is that they titillate our imagination, promising the marvels and wonders of a gender-free world while simultaneously reproducing not only some of the most banal, flat images of gender identity, but also of class and race relations that you can think of. Virtual reality images titillate our imagination in the same way that pornographic representation does. The imagination is a very gendered space and the woman's imagination has always been represented as a troublesome and dangerous quality as the feminist film theorist Doane has put it.[14]

The imaginative poverty of virtual reality is all the more striking if you compare it to the creativity of some of the women artists I mentioned earlier. By comparison, the banality, the sexism, the repetitive nature of computer-designed video-games are quite appalling. As usual, at times of great changes and upheavals, the potential for the new engenders great fear, anxiety and in some cases even nostalgia for the previous regime.

As if the imaginative misery were not enough, postmodernity is marked by a widespread impact and a qualitative shift of pornography in every sphere of cultural activity. Pornography is more and more about power relations and less and less about sex. In classical pornography sex was a vehicle by which to convey power relations. Nowadays anything can become such a vehicle: the becoming-culture of pornography means that any cultural activity or product can become a commodity and through that process express inequalities, patterns of exclusion, fantasies of domination, desires for power and control.[15]

The central point remains: there is a credibility gap between the promises of virtual reality and cyberspace and the quality of what it delivers. It consequently seems to me that, in the short range, this new technological frontier will intensify the gender-gap and increase the polarisation between the sexes. We are back to the war metaphor, but its location is the real world, not the hyperspace of abstract masculinity. And its protagonists are no computer images, but the real social agents of post-industrial urban landscapes.

The most effective strategy remains for women to use technology in order to disengage our collective imagination from the phallus and its accessory values: money, exclusion and domination, nationalism, ironic feminity and systematic violence.

Another qualitative leap is also necessary, however, towards the affirmation of sexual difference in terms of the recognition of the dissymmetrical relationship between the sexes. Feminists have rejected the universalistic tendency which consists in conflating the masculine viewpoint with the 'human', thereby confining the 'feminine' to the structural position of devalorised Other. This division of social and symbolic labour means that the burden of devalorized difference falls upon certain empirical references who can be defined in opposition to the dominant norm as: non-man, non-white, non-owner of property, non-speaker-of-a-dominant-language, and so on.

This hierarchical organization of differences is the key to phallogocentrism, which is the inner system of patriarchal societies. In this system, women and men are in diametrically different positions: men are conflated with the universalistic stand and therefore are confined to what Hartsock defines as 'abstract masculinity'. Women, on the other hand, are stuck with the specificity of their gender as the 'second sex', as Beauvoir observed. The price men pay for representing the universal is disembodiment, or loss of gendered specificity into the abstraction of phallic masculinity. The price women pay, on the other hand, is loss of subjectivity through over-embodiment and confinement to their gendered identity. This results in two dissymmetrical positions.

This produces also two divergent political strategies when it comes to looking for alternatives. The masculine and the feminine paths to transcend the phallogocentric socio-symbolic contract diverge considerably. Whereas women need to repossess subjectivity by reducing their confinement to the body, thus making an issue of deconstructing the body, men need to repossess their abstracted bodily self by shedding some of the exclusive rights to transcendental consciousness. Men need to get embodied, to get real, to suffer through the pain of re-embodiment, that is to say incarnation.

A splendid example of this process is the fall of the angels from the inflated heights of the Berlin sky in Wim Wenders's film: *Der Himmel über Berlin* (Wings of Desire). When the angels do choose the path of embodiment, the pain of incarnation is rendered with acute insight. Bell hooks astutely observed the culture-specific nature of such an exercise, in her rather witty reading of the Teutonic angst in this film.[16] I think she correctly points out the quintessentially western character of the flight from the body and of the related creation of abstract masculinity as a system of domination of multiple 'others'. In her equally culture-specific account of the need for a revision of the phallogocentric socio-symbolic contract. However, Julia Kristeva also stresses the need for a redefinition of the position of the female body in this system.

I would like to argue, therefore, that the central point to keep in mind in the context of a discussion on cyberspace is that the last thing we need at this point in western history is a renewal of the old myth of transcendence as flight from the body. As Linda Dement put it: a little less abstraction would be welcome.[17] Transcendence as disembodiment would just repeat the classical patriarchal model, which consolidated masculinity as abstraction, thereby essentialising social categories of 'embodied others'. This would be a denial of sexual difference meant as the basic dissymmetry between the sexes.

In the project of exploring the dissymmetry between the sexes, I would emphasize very strongly the importance of language, especially in the light of psychoanalytic theory. In so doing, I also mean to distance myself from the simplistic psychology and the reductive cartesianism that dominate so much cyberpunk literature and cyberspace technology. In opposition to these, I would like to emphasise that Woman is not only the objectified other of patriarchy, tied to it by negation. As the basis for female identity, the signifier Woman also and simultaneously pertains to a margin of dissidence and resistance to patriarchal identity.

I have argued elsewhere that the feminist project intervenes on both the level of historical agency—i.e. the question of the insertion of women in patriarchal history—and that of individual identity and the politics of desire. It thus engages with both the conscious and the unconscious levels. This deconstructive approach to feminity is very strongly present in the politics of the parody that I defended above. Feminist women who go on functioning in society as female subjects in these post-metaphysical days of decline of gender dichotomies, act 'as if' Woman was still their location. In so doing, however, they treat femininity as an option—a set of available poses, a set of costumes rich in history and social power relations, but not fixed or compulsory any longer. They simultaneously assert and deconstruct. Woman as a signifying practice.

My point is that the new is created by revisiting and burning up the old. Like the totemic meal recommended by Freud, you have to assimilate the dead before you can move onto a new order. The way out can be found by mimetic repetition and consumption of the old. We need rituals of burial and mourning for the dead, including and especially the ritual of burial of the Woman that was. We do need to say farewell to that second sex, that eternal feminine which stuck to our skins like toxic material, burning into our bone-marrow, eating away at our substance. We need to take collectively the time for the mourning of the old socio-symbolic contract and thus mark the need for a change of intensity, a shift of tempo. Unless feminists negotiate with the historicity of this temporal change, the great advances made by feminism towards the empowerment of alternative forms of female subjectivity will not have the time to be brought to social fruition. [...]

We rather need more complexity, multiplicity, simultaneity and we need to rethink gender, class and race in the pursuit of these multiple, complex differences. I also think we need gentleness, compassion and humour to pull through the ruptures and raptures of our times. Irony and self-humour are important elements of this project and they are necessary for its success, as feminists as diverse as Hélène Cixous and French & Saunders have pointed out. As the Manifesto of the Bad Girls reads: 'Through laughter our anger becomes a tool of liberation'. In the hope that our collectively negotiated Dionysian laughter will indeed bury it once and for all, cyberfeminism needs to cultivate a culture of joy and affirmation. Feminist women have a long history of dancing through a variety of potentially lethal minefields in their pursuit of socio-symbolic justice. Nowadays, women have to undertake the dance through cyberspace, if only to make sure that the joy-sticks of the cyberspace cowboys will not reproduce univocal phallicity under the mask of multiplicity, and also to make sure that the riot girls, in their anger and their visionary passion, will not recreate law and order under the cover of a triumphant feminine.

['Cyberfeminism with a Difference', in *New Formations*, 29 (Autumn 1996), 9–25]

Notes

Introduction

1. Andrea Stuart, 'Feminism: Dead or Alive?', in Jonathan Rutheford (ed.), *Identity* (London: Lawrence and Wishart, 1900), 31.
2. Meaghan Morris 'in any event...', in Alie Jardine and Paul Smith (eds.), *Men in Feminism* (New York and London: Methuen, 1987), 179.
3. 'Feminist Theory: An International Debate', organized by Sandra Kemp and Judith Squires, University of Glasgow, 12–15 July 1991.
4. Peter Brooks, quoted in Tania Modleski, *Feminism Without Women* (New York and London: Routledge, 1992), 110.
5. Rosi Braidotti, *Nomadic Subjects* (New York: Columbia University Press, 1994), 231.
6. Lynne Segal, *Slow Motion* (London: Virago, 1990), pp. ix–x.
7. See especially Robert Connell, *Gender and Power* (Cambridge: Polity Press, 1987).

Extract 1

MARY EVANS: *In Praise of Theory: The Case for Women's Studies*

1. The complete version of this paper was previously published in *Feminist Review*, Feb. 1982. I am extremely grateful to members of the *Feminist Review* collective for their comments on an earlier draft of this paper. I would also like to acknowledge the help of David Morgan and to thank Marion Shaw for inviting me to give the lecture at the University of Hull on which this paper is based.

Extract 3

TERESA DE LAURETIS: *Aesthetic and Feminist Theory: Rethinking Women's Cinema*

1. Silvia Bovenschen, 'Is There a Feminine Aesthetic?', tr. Beth Weckmueller, *New German Critique*, 10 (Winter 1977), 136; originally published in *Aesthetick und Kommunikation*, 25 (Sept. 1976).
2. Laura Mulvey, 'Feminism, Film and the Avant-Garde', *Framework*, 10 (Spring 1979), 6. See also Christine Gledhill's account, 'Recent Developments in Feminist Film Criticism', *Quarterly Review of Film Studies*, 3/4 (1978).
3. Laura Mulvey, 'Visual Pleasure and Narrative Cinema', *Screen*, 16/3 (Autumn 1975), 18.
4. B. Ruby Rich, in 'Women and Film: A Discussion of Feminist Aesthetics', *New German Critique*, 13 (Winter 1978), 87.
5. J. Laplanche and J.-B. Pontalis. *The Language of Psycho-Analysis*, tr. D. Nicholson-Smith (New York: W. W. Norton, 1973), 206.
6. Lea Melandri, *L'infamia originaria* (Milan: Edizioni L'Erba Voglio, 1977), 27; my translation. For a more fully developed discussion of semiotic theories of film

and narrative, see Teresa de Lauretis. *Alice Doesn't: Feminism, Semiotics. Cinema* (Bloomington: Indiana University Press, and London: Macmillan, 1984).

7. Audre Lorde, 'The Master's Tools Will Never Dismantle the Master's House', in Cherrie Moraga and Gloria Anzaldúa (eds.), *This Bridge Called My Back: Writings by Radical Women of Color* (New York: Kitchen Table Press, 1983), 96. See also Audre Lorde, 'An Open Letter to Mary Daly', in the same volume. Both essays are reprinted in Audre Lorde, *Sister Outsider: Essays and Speeches* (Trumansburg, NY: Crossing Press, 1984).

8. 'Chantal Akerman on *Jeanne Dielman*', *Camera Obscura*, 2 (1977), 118–19.

9. Ibid. 119. In the same interview, Akerman said: 'I didn't have any doubts about any of the shots. I was very sure of where to put the camera and when and why. . . I *let* her [the character] live her life in the middle of the frame. I didn't go in too close, but I was not *very* far away. I let her be in her space. It's not uncontrolled. But the camera was not voyeuristic in the commercial way because you always knew where I was. . . . It was the only way to shoot that film—to avoid cutting the woman into a hundred pieces, to avoid cutting the action in a hundred places, to look carefully and to be respectful. The framing was meant to respect the space, her, and her gestures within it.'

10. Janet Bergstrom, '*Jeanne Dielman, 23 Quai du Commerce, 1080 Bruxelles* by Chantal Akerman', *Camera Obscura*, 2 (1977), 117. On the rigorous formal consistency of the film, see also Mary Jo Lakeland, 'The Color of *Jeanne Dielman*', *Camera Obscura*, 3–4 (1979), 216–18.

11. Claire Johnston, 'Women's Cinema as Counter-Cinema', in Johnston (ed.), *Notes on Women's Cinema* (London: Society for Education in Film and Television, 1974), 31. See also Gertrud Koch, 'Was ist und wozu brauchen wir eine feministische Filmkritik', *Frauen und Film*, 11 (1977).

12. Mary Ann Doane, Patricia Mellencamp, and Linda Williams (eds.), *Re-Vision: Essays in Feminist Film Criticism* (Frederick, Md.: University Publications of America in association with the American Film Institute, 1984), 4.

13. Ibid. 6. The quotation from Adrienne Rich is in her *On Lies, Secrets, and Silence* (New York: W. W. Norton, 1979), 35.

14. See Barbara Smith, 'Toward a Black Feminist Criticism', in Gloria T. Hull, Patricia Bell Scott, and Barbara Smith (eds.), *All the Women are White, All the Blacks are Men, But Some of Us Are Brave: Black Women's Studies* (Old Westbury, NY: The Feminist Press, 1982).

15. Helen Fehervary, Claudia Lenssen, and Judith Mayne, 'From Hitler to Hepburn: A Discussion of Women's Film Production and Reception', *New German Critique*, 24–5 (Fall/Winter 1981–2), 176.

Extract 6

GAYATRI CHAKRAVORTY SPIVAK: *French Feminism in an International Frame*

1. Bert F. Hoselitz, 'Development and the Theory of Social Systems', in M. Stanley (ed.), *Social Development* (New York: Basic Books, 1972), 45 and *passim*. I am grateful to Professor Michael Ryan for drawing my attention to this article.

2. Nawal El Saadawi, *The Hidden Face of Eve: Women in the Arab World* (London: Zed Press, 1980), 5.

3. (Amherst: University of Massachusetts Press, 1980). In this part of my essay, I have quoted liberally from *New French Feminisms*, giving the name of the author of the particular piece and the page number.

4. Sherfey, *The Nature and Evolution of Female Sexuality* (New York: Vintage, 1973); *Our Bodies, Ourselves: A Book by and for Women* (New York: Simon and Schuster, 2nd edn. 1971).

Extract 7

HELENA MICHIE: *Not One of the Family: The Repression of the Other Woman in Feminist Theory*

1. For a review of recent theoretical explorations of the mother–daughter bond see Marianne Hirsch, 'Mothers and Daughters', *Signs*, 7/1 (1981), 200–22.

2. Luce Irigaray inscribes the maternal/filial dilemma orthographically by coining the word 'in-difference' to describe both the (inevitable?) split between mother and daughter and their non-difference (lack of differentiation). Both underlie surface 'indifference'. See Luce Irigaray, 'When Our Lips Speak Together', *Signs*, 6/1 (1983), 71.

3. Jane Gallop, *The Daughter's Seduction* (Ithaca, NY: Cornell Univ. Press, 1982), ch. 5.

4. Ibid., p. xv.

Extract 8

ELAINE SHOWALTER: *A Criticism of Our Own: Autonomy and Assimilation in Afro-American and Feminist Literary Theory*

1. Mary Ann Caws, 'The Conception of Engendering, the Erotics of Editing', in Nancy K. Miller (ed.), *The Poetics of Gender* (New York: Columbia University Press, 1986), 42–63. This episode is all the more ironic in the light of the successful protest in spring 1988 by deaf students of Gallaudet College in Washington.

2. Jane Gallop, *The Daughter's Seduction: Feminism and Psychoanalysis* (Ithaca, NY: Cornell University Press, 1982), 126–7.

3. In this paper I need to make distinctions between a generic feminist criticism, practiced by a feminist critic of either sex; 'Feminist' criticism practiced by women; and male feminist criticism, practiced by men.

4. Gayatri Chakravorty Spivak, 'French Feminism in an International Frame', *Yale French Studies*, 62 (1981), 184. See also Jane Gallop, 'Annie Leclerc Writing a Letter, with Vermeer', *The Poetics of Gender*, 154.

5. For a stimulating example of how such critical cross-fertilization might take place, see Craig Werner, 'New Democratic Vistas: Toward a Pluralistic Genealogy', in Joe Weixlmann and Chester Fontenot (eds.), *Studies is Black American Literature*, ii (Florida: Penkevill Press, 1986), 47–83.

6. See Jonathan Dollimore, 'Shakespeare, Cultural Materialism and the New Historicism', in Jonathan Dollimore and Alan Sinfield (eds.), *Political Shakespeare: New Essays in Cultural Materialism* (Ithaca, NY: Cornelll University Press, 1985), 15.

7. Carolyn G. Heilbrun, *Toward a Recognition of Androgyny* (New York: Harper Colophon Books, 1973), p. ix.

8. Sandra Gilbert, 'Feminist Criticism in the University', in Gerald Graff and Reginald Gibbons (eds.), *Criticism in the University* (Evanston: Northwestern University Press, 1985), 117.
9. Michèle Barrett, *Women's Oppression Today: Problems in Marxist Feminist Analysis* (London: Villiers, 1980), 112–13.
10. Elaine Showalter, 'The Feminist Critical Revolution', *The New Feminist Criticism* (London: Virago, 1986), 5.
11. *The Other Voice* (New York: Morrow, 1975), p. xvii.
12. Adrienne Rich, 'Toward a Feminist Aesthetic', *Chrysalis* 6 (1978), 59, 67.
13. Showalter, 'Feminist Criticism in the Wilderness', *The New Feminist Criticism*.
14. Alice Walker, *In Search of Our Mothers' Gardens* (San Diego: Harcourt, Brace, Jovanovich, 1983).
15. Hortense Spillers, *Conjuring*, ed. Spillers and Marjorie Pryse (Bloomington: Indiana University Press, 1985), 261.
16. Elizabeth Abel, 'Introduction', *Writing and Sexual Difference* (Chicago: University of Chicago Press, 1982), 2.
17. Alice Jardine, 'Pre-Texts for the Transatlantic Feminist', *Yale French Studies*, 62 (1981), 225; and *Gynesis: Configurations of Women and Modernity* (Ithaca, NY: Cornell University Press, 1985), 61–3.
18. Gayle Greene and Coppélia Kahn, 'Feminist Scholarship and the Social Construction of Woman', in Green and Kahn (eds.), *Making a Difference: Feminist Literary Criticism* (London: Methuen, 1985), 24–7.
19. Shoshana Felman, 'Woman and Madness: The Critical Phallacy', *Diacritics*, 5 (1975), 10.
20. Kaja Silverman, *The Subject of Semiotics* (New York: Oxford University Press, 1983), p. viii.
21. Ken Ruthven, *Feminist Literary Studies: An Introduction* (Cambridge: Cambridge University Press, 1985), 6.
22. Gayle Rubin, 'The Traffic in Women', in Rayna Rapp Reiter (ed.), *Toward an Anthropology of Women* (New York: Monthly Review Press, 1975), 165.
23. Judith Shapiro, 'Anthropology and the Study of Gender', in Elizabeth Langland and Walter Gove (eds.), *A Feminist Perspective in the Academy* (Chicago: University of Chicago Press, 1983), 112.
24. Evelyn Fox Keller, *Reflections on Gender and Science* (New Haven: Yale University Press, 1985), 3.
25. Joan W. Scott, 'Gender: A Useful Category of Historical Analysis', *American Historical Review*, 5 (Nov. 1986).
26. Reprinted in Tama Janowitz, *Slaves of New York* (New York: Crown, 1986).
27. Gates, 'Jungle', 10.
28. Homi Bhabha, 'Signs Taken for Words', *Critical Inquiry*, 12/1 (Autumn 1985), 162.
29. See Gayatri Chakravorty Spivak, *In Other Worlds: Essays in Cultural Politics* (London and New York: Routledge, 1987).

Extract 9

BARBARA CHRISTIAN: *The Race for Theory*

1. For another view of the debate this 'privileged' approach to Afro-American texts has engendered, see Joyce A. Joyce, '"Who the Cap Fit:" Unconsciousness and

Unconscionableness in the Criticism of Houston A. Baker, Jr, and Henry Louis Gates, Jr', *New Literary History,* 18 (1987), 371–84. I had not read Joyce's essay before I wrote my own. Clearly there are differences between Joyce's view and my own.

2. This paper was originally written for a conference at the University of California at Berkeley entitled 'Minority Discourse', and held on 29–31 May 1986

3. See Ralph Ellison, *Shadow and Act* (New York: Random House, 1964); Robert M. Farnsworth, 'Introduction to *The Marrow of Tradition* by Charles Chesnutt' (Ann Arbor: Michigan Paperbacks, 1969); Addison Gayle, Jr. (ed.), *The Black Aesthetic* (Garden City, NY: Doubleday Anchor, 1971); LeRoi Jones, *Home: Social Essays* (New York: William Morrow, 1966); Larry Neal, 'The Black Arts Movement', in Gayle (ed.), *The Black Aesthetic,* 357–74; Alice Walker, 'In Search of Zora Neale Hurston', *MS* 3/9 (Mar. 1975); Richard Wright, 'A Blueprint for Negro Writing', *New Challenge,* 11 (1937), 53–65.

4. Alice Walker, *The Color Purple* (New York: Harcourt Brace Jovanovich, 1982). The controversy surrounding the novel and the subsequent film are discussed in Calvin Hernton, *The Sexual Mountain and Black Women Writers* (New York: Doubleday, 1987), chs. 1 and 2.

5. Nikki Giovanni, Review of Paul Marshall, *Chosen Place, Timeless People, Negro Digest,* 19/3 (Jan. 1970), 51–2, 84.

6. Addison Gayle, Jr., *The Way of the New World: The Black Novel in America* (Garden City, NY: Doubleday Anchor, 1975).

7. Ishmael Reed, *Mumbo Jumbo* (Garden City; NY: Doubleday Anchor, 1972).

8. See Ann Rosalind Jones, 'Writing the Body: Toward an understanding of *l'écriture féminine*', *Feminist Studies,* 7/2 (Summer 1981), 247–63.

9. See June Jordan, *Civil Wars* (New York: Beacon Press, 1981); Audre Lorde, 'The Master's Tools will never Dismantle the Master's House', in Lorde, *Sister Outsider* (Trumansburg, NY: Crossing Press, 1984), 110–14.

10. This phrase is taken from the title of one of Alice Walker's essays, 'Saving the Life that is Your Own: The Importance of Models in the Artist's Life', in Walker, *In Search of Our Mothers' Gardens: Womanist Prose* (New York: Harcourt Brace Jovanovich, 1983).

11. Audre Lorde, 'Poetry is not a Luxury', in Lorde, *Sister Outsider.*

Extract 10

ALICE JARDINE: *Notes for an Analysis*

1. Shoshana Felman (ed.), *Literature and Psychoanalysis,* special issue of *Yale French Studies,* 55/6 (1977). Reissued by Johns Hopkins University Press, 1982.

2. David Carroll, 'Institutional Authority vs. Critical Power, or the Uneasy Relations of Psychoanalysis and Literature', in Joseph H. Smith and William Kerrigan (eds.) *Taking Chances: Derrida, Psychoanalysis and Literature* (Baltimore: Johns Hopkins University Press, 1984), 129.

3. Cf. Jacques Derrida, 'Otobiographies', in *The Ear of the Other* (New York: Schocken, 1985), 3–38.

4. Jacques Derrida, 'Géopsychanalyse—"and all the rest of the world"', in *Géopsychanalyse: Les Souterains de l'institution* (Paris: Confrontation, 1981).

5. Barbara Johnson, 'Apostrophe, Animation, and Abortion', in *A World of Difference* (Baltimore: Johns Hopkins University Press, 1987). (First published in *Diacritics* Spring 1986.)

6. Richard Rorty, 'Habermas, Lyotard et la postmodernité', *Critique*, 442 (Mar. 1984), 182. Quoted and tra. by Meaghan Morris, 'Postmodernity and Lyotard's sublime', in *Art and Text*, 16 (1984), 53.

7. Cf. Jacques Derrida, 'Le Dernier Mot du racisme', in *Critical Inquiry*, 12 (Fall 1985), 290–9; the response by Anne McClintock and Rob Nixon, 'No Names Apart: The Separation of Word and History in Derrida's "Le Dernier Mot du racisme"', and Derrida's response in turn, 'But, beyond . . . (Open letter to Anne McClintock and Rob Nixon)', in *Critical Inquiry*, 13 (Fall 1986), 140–70.

8. Cf. my 'In Praise of Impossibility', a response to Jane Gallop's 'The Problem of Definition', SCMLA, New Orleans, Oct. 1986.

9. For the sake of clarity, from here on in I shall refer to these two post-1968 generations as generations one (Ph.D. 1968–78) and two (Ph.D. 1978–88). Obviously, the notion of 'generation' is ultimately a very frustrating one (biological age does not always correspond to academic age, etc.) and is used here only as a tentatively useful, almost hypothetical device for raising certain issues. Given this, it is especially important not to bracket the word 'political'. There are today, for example, women across all the generations in the academy who do 'feminist this and that' but maintain no historical or current political relationship to the women's movement.

10. Cf. Isabelle Lasvergnas, 'La Trace du féminin dans la pensée?', in a special issue of *BIEF*, 'Des femmes, et la psychanalyse', 18 (June 1986), 90.

11. Juliet Mitchell, 'Psychoanalysis and the Humanities: Old Endings or New Beginnings?', in *Dalhousie Review*, 64/2 (Summer 1984), 221.

12. Mary Ann Doane, 'The Clinical Eye: Medical Discourses in the "woman's film" of the 1940s', in Susan Suleiman (ed.), *The Female Body in Western Culture* (Cambridge, Mass.: Harvard University Press, 1985), 163.

13. Even those in the same academic generation are more and more positioned this way. Since writing these notes, an essay written in a different vein but very much concerned with these questions has appeared. See Evelyn Fox Keller and Helene Moglen, 'Competition and Feminism: Conflicts for Academic Women', in *Signs*, 12/3 (1987).

14. This was discussed during a personal conversation following a feminist seminar at Harvard University in Fall 1986.

15. My thanks to Otto Steinmayer for this formulation.

16. Mary Ann Doane, 'The Clinical Eye', 152.

17. Juliet Mitchell, 'Psychoanalysis and the Humanities', 222.

18. Jane Gallop, in the 'Prefatory Material' to *Reading Lacan* (Ithaca, NY: Cornell University Press, 1985), esp. 28.

19. Cf. Luce Irigaray's discussion of the dangers of reducing the analytic process to this state as well: 'Misère de la psychanalyse', in *Parler n'est jamais neutre* (Paris: Minuit, 1985), 257–8.

20. Cf. Marie-Claire Boons, 'La Psychanalyse et une femme', in *BIEF* 18 (1986), 27.

21. Jean-Francçois Lyotard, *Le Postmoderne expliqué aux enfants* (Paris: Galilée, 1986), 98. I am indebted to this little book for helping me make many of the initial connections between these two scenes.

22. Jacques Lacan, 'The Function and Field of Speech and Language in Psychoanalysis', in *Ecrits: A Selection* (New York: Norton, 1977), 86.

Extract 11

BARBARA SMITH: *The Truth that Never Hurts: Black Lesbians in Fiction in the 1980s*

1. Barbara Smith, 'Racism and Women's Studies', in *All the Women Are White, All the Blacks are Men, But Some of Us Are Brave: Black Women's Studies*, ed. Gloria Hull, Patricia Bell Scott, and Barbara Smith (New York: Feminist Press, 1981), 49.
2. Mitsuye Yamada, 'Invisibility is an Unnatural Disaster: Reflections of an Asian American Woman', in *This Bridge Called My Back: Writings by Radical Women of Color*, ed. Cherrie Moraga and Gloria Anzaldúa (Latham, NY: Kitchen Table Press, 1984), 35–40.
3. Cheryl Clarke, *Narratives: Poems in the Tradition of Black Women* (Latham, NY: Kitchen Table Press, 1983), 15.
4. Jewelle Gomez, in *Home Girls*, ed. Smith, p. 122.
5. Langston Hughes, 'The Negro Artist and the Racial Mountain', in *Voices from the Harlem Renaissance*, ed. Nathan Huggins (New York: Oxford, 1976), 309. It is interesting to note that recent research has revealed that Hughes and a number of other major figures of the Harlem Renaissance were gay. See Charles Michael Smith, 'Bruce Nugent: Bohemian of the Harlem Renaissance', in *In the Life: A Black Gay Anthology*, ed. Joseph F. Beam (Boston: Alyson, 1986), 213–14 and selections by Langston Hughes in *Gay and Lesbian Poetry in Our Time: An Anthology*, ed. Carl Morse and Joan Larkin (New York: St. Martin's, 1988), 204–6.
6. Paul Laurence Dunbar, 'We Wear the Mask', in *The Life and Works of Paul Laurence Dunbar*, ed. Wiggins (New York: Kraus, 1971), 184.
7. Audre Lorde, 'There is No Hierarchy of Oppressions', in *The Council on Interracial Books for Children Bulletin, Homophobia and Education: How to Deal with Name-Calling*, ed. Leonore Gordon, 14/3–4 (1983), 9.

Extract 12

CHANDRA TALPADE MOHANTY: *Under Western Eyes: Feminist Scholarship and Colonial Discourses*

1. Paul A. Baran, *The Political Economy of Growth* (New York: Monthly Review Press, 1962); Samir Amin, *Imperialism and Unequal Development* (New York: Monthly Review Press, 1977); Audre Gunder-Frank, *Capitalism and Under-Development in Latin America* (New York: Monthly Review Press, 1967); Cherrié Moraga and Gloria Anzaldúa (eds.), *This Bridge Called My Back: Writings by Radical Women of Color* (New York: Kitchen Table Press, 1983); Barbara Smith, *Home Girls: A Black Feminist Anthology* (New York: Kitchen Table Press, 1983); Gloria Joseph and Jill Lewis, *Common Differences: Conflicts in Black and White Feminist Perspectives* (Boston: Beacon Press, 1981); Cherrié Moraga, *Loving in the War Years* (Boston: South End Press, 1984).
2. Terms such as *third* and *first world* are very problematical both in suggesting oversimplified similarities between and among countries labeled thus, and in implicitly reinforcing existing economic, cultural, and ideological hierarchies

which are conjured up in using such terminology. I use the term *'third world'* with full awareness of its problems, only because this is the terminology available to us at the moment. The use of quotation marks is meant to suggest a continuous questioning of the designation.

3. I am indebted to Teresa de Lauretis for this particular formulation of the project of feminist theorizing. See especially her introduction in de Lauretis, *Alice Doesn't: Feminism, Semiotics, Cinema* (Bloomington: Indiana University Press, 1984); see also Sylvia Wynter, 'The Politics of Domination', unpublished manuscript.

4. Anouar Abdel-Malek, *Social Dialectics: Nation and Revolution* (Albany: State University of New York Press, 1981).

5. A number of documents and reports on the UN International Conferences on Women, Mexico City, 1975, and Copenhagen, 1980, as well as the 1976 Wellesley Conference on Women and Development, attest to this.

6. M. A. Rosaldo, 'The Use and Abuse of Authropology: Reflections on Feminism and Cross-Cultural Understanding', *Signs*, 53 (1980), 389–417.

Extract 13

ANNE PHILLIPS: *Paradoxes of Participation*

1. Jane Mansbridge, *Beyond Adversary Democracy* (New York: Basic Books, 1980).

2. Robin Morgan (ed.) *Sisterhood is Powerful: An Anthology of Writing from the Women's Liberation Movement* (New York: Random House, 1970).

3. Jo Freeman, *The Politics of Women's Liberation* (London: Longman, 1975), ch. 3.

4. Ibid. 94.

5. Morgan, *Sisterhood is Powerful*, p. xxxvi.

6. Michelene Wandor (ed.), *The Body Politic: Women's Liberation in Britain* (London: Stage 1, 1971), 105–6.

7. Jane Mansbridge 'The Limits of Friendship', in J. R. Pennock and J. W. Chapman (eds.), *Participation in Politics: NOMOS XVI* (Lieber-Atherton, 1976).

Extract 14

NANCY MILLER: *Feminist Confessions: The Last Degrees are the Hardest*

The title of this book takes as its intertexts Elizabeth W. Bruss's *Autobiographical Acts* and Albert E. Stone's *Autobiographical Occasions and Original Acts*.

I borrow the term 'feminist confession' from Rita Felski's *Beyond Feminist Aesthetics*.

1. A mailing to the membership in November 1989 both expressed concern 'about incidents of antifeminist harassment', qualified by the Commission as a 'backlash against feminism' and solicited 'personal statements' in order to pursue the inquiry.

2. As in the predictably witless commentary on the 1989 MLA convention in the *New Republic* entitled, 'Jargonaut', 29 Jan. 1990.

3. Stephen Heath, to whom I owe this reference, reads Barthes's remarks with great attentiveness and pursues the implications of this position against positions; in 'Male Feminism' Heath argues that a new marginalism, while perhaps potentially radicalizing for men, has little to offer women in the way of novelty (in *Alice*

Jardine and Paul Smith (eds.), *Men in Feminism* (New York and London: Methuen, 1987)).

4. Adrienne Rich, 'Notes for a Politics of Location', *Blood, Bread and Poetry: Selected Prose 1979–1985* (New York: W. W. Norton, 1986).

5. This sense of physical detail rejoins Naomi Schor's argument in *Reading in Detail: Aesthetics and the Feminine* (New York and London: Methuen, 1987) about the potential aesthetic power of the detail as resistance to violence. On the materiality of discourses and their power to hurt, see Monique Wittig's 'The Mark of Gender', in Nancy K. Miller (ed.), *The Poetics of Gender* (New York: Columbia University Press, 1986).

6. Deborah McDowell makes the point sharply in a recent interview with Susan Fraiman in *Critical Texts*: 'There's a lot of radical criticism that gets the grammar right, but we have become much too comfortable with radical language and not sufficiently committed to radical action. . . . We're in an era that privileges oppositional criticism, yet this criticism can sometimes be an act of substitution' (*Critical Texts: A Review of Theory and Criticism*, 6/3 (1989), 13–29, at p. 25.

7. In *Thinking Through the Body* (New York: Columbia University Press, 1988) Jane Gallop writes of her essay on *The Pleasure of the Text*: ' "The Perverse Body" tries to think differently the relation between individualism (perversion) and moralism (political responsibility)' (117). Although she comes to no firm conclusion about how to rethink the relation between the individual and morality, her disambiguation of the contradiction—staged in the introduction to the book as a thinking *through* Barthes and Rich—has been productive for my own reflection.

Extract 15

SUSANNAH RADSTONE: *Postcard from the Edge*

1. Rosi Braidotti, *Patterns of Dissonance: A Study of Women in Contemporary Philosophy* (Cambridge: Polity Press, 1991), 15.

2. The Ruskin Women's Weekend was the first national meeting of the Women's Liberation movement. It was held on the weekend of Friday 27 Feb. –Sunday 1 Mar. 1970. For one woman's brief retrospective account of this event, see Judith Condon, 'The Women's Weekend: The Beginning of a Movement', *Women: A Cultural Review*, 1/1 (25 Apr. 1990), 8, and also the memories of contributors to Michelene Wandor (ed.), *Once a Feminist: Stories of a Generation* (London: Virago, 1990).

3. 'New Directions For Women's Studies in the 1990s', the 1991 conference of the Women's Studies Network (UK) was co-ordinated by Hilary Hinds and Jackie Stacey. It took place at Camden School for Girls, London, on the weekend of 6–7 July.

4. Mary Jacobus, 'Freud's Mnemonic: Women's Screen Memories and Feminist Nostalgia', *Michegan Quarterly Review*, 1 (Fall 1987).

5. Rosi Braidotti, *Patterns of Dissonance*.

6. Wendy Brown, 'Feminist Hesitations, Postmodern Exposures', *Differences*, 3/1, (Spring 1991).

7. Gayatri Chakravorty Spivak, ' "In a word": Gayatri Chakravorty Spivak in Conversation with Ellen Rooney', *Differences* (1989).

Extract 16

JANE GALLOP: *Around 1981: Academic Feminist Literary Theory*

1. Toril Moi, *Sexual/Textual Politics: Feminist Literary Theory* (London: Methuen, 1985); and Janet Todd, *Feminist Literary History* (New York: Routledge, 1988).
2. Meaghan Morris, 'in any event...', in Alice Jardine and Paul Smith (eds.), *Men in Feminism* (New York: Methuen, 1987), 179.
3. K. K. Ruthven, *Feminist Literary Studies: An Introduction* (Cambridge: Cambridge University Press, 1984), pp. vii, 6–7.

Extract 17

MICHÉLE BARRETT: *Words and Things: Materialism and Method in Contemporary Feminist Analysis*

1. See Michèle Barrett, 'Feminism's Turn to Culture', in *Woman: A Cultural Review,* I (1990), 22–4.
2. Elizabeth V. Spelman, *Inessential Woman: Problems of Exclusion in Feminist Thought* (London: The Women's Press, 1990), 186.
3. These issues are discussed in some detail in my *The Politics of Truth: From Marx to Foucault* (Cambridge: Polity Press, 1991).
4. See also, for example, the collection by Carole Pateman and Elizabeth Gross (eds.), *Feminist Challenges: Social and Political Theory* (Sydney: Allen and Unwin, 1986).
5. Kate Soper, 'Constructa Ergo Sum?', in Soper, *Troubled Pleasures: Writings on Politics, Gender and Hedonism* (London: Verso, 1990), 146–61.
6. See Biddy Martin and Chandra Talpade Mohanty, 'Feminist Politics: What's Home Got to Do with It?', in Teresa de Lauretis (ed.), *Feminist Studies/Critical Studies* (Bloomington: Indiana University Press, 1986).
7. See Pollock, *Vision and Difference: Femininity, Feminism and the Histories of Art* (New York and London: Routledge 1988); Pollock, 'Feminism and Modernism', in Roszika Parker and Griselda Pollock (eds.), *Framing Feminism: Art and the Women's Movement 1970–1985* (London: Pandora/Routledge, 1987).
8. Susan Hekman, *Gender and Knowledge: Elements of a Postmodern Feminism* (Cambridge: Polity Press, 1990), 5.
9. Michel Foucault, 'The Order of Discourse', in Robert Young (ed.), *Untying the Text: A Post-Structuralist Reader* (London and New York: Routledge, 1987), 60–1.
10. The usual gripe here is that feminists in the USA see much less need to read what Australian or British feminists write (until it attracts a US publisher) than vice versa.
11. Gayatri Spivak, whose work has been crucial for the development of understanding of post-coloniality, provides an exception to this general observation in that her interests and knowledges range across matters of technology, economics, and so on. 'We cannot ask the economists and the sociologists to attend to our speculations about the subject-constitution of the woman in post-modern neo-colonialism if we do it as charming primitivists' (Gayatri Chakravorty Spivak, 'The Political Economy of Women as Seen by a Literary Critic', in Elizabeth Weed (ed.), *Coming to Terms: Feminism, Theory, Politics* (New York: Routledge, 1989), 228). See also Spivak, 'Scattered Speculations on the Question of Value', in

her *In Other Worlds: Essays in Cultural Politics* (London and New York: Routledge, 1987), 154–75.

12. For two examples, see Maria Mies, *Patriarchy and Accumulation on a World Scale* (London and New Jersey: Zed Press, 1986); Haleh Afshar (ed.), *Women, Work and Ideology in the Third World* (London and New York: Tavistock/Routledge, 1985).

13. Barbara Christian, 'The Race for Theory', *Cultural Critique*, 6 (1987), 51–64.

14. Barrett, *The Politics of Truth*, ch. 5; see also Richard Feldstein and Henry Sussman (eds.), *Psychoanalysis and . . .* (New York and London: Routledge, 1990), 1–8.

15. The most useful anthology in this debate is Linda Nicholson (ed.), *Feminism/Postmodernism* (London and New York: Routledge, 1990). Feminists sympathetically critical of 'critical theory' can be found in Seyla Benhabib and Drucilla Cornell (eds.), *Feminism as Critique* (Cambridge: Polity Press, 1987); see also Nancy Fraser, *Unruly Practices: Power, Discourse and Gender in Contemporary Social Theory* (Cambridge: Polity Press, 1989). Susan Hekman's *Gender and Knowledge* gives an excellent account from a position sympathetic to post-modernism. See also Rita Felski, *Beyond Feminist Aesthetics* (Cambridge, Mass.: Harvard University Press, 1989), ch. 2.

Extract 19

ELSPETH PROBYN: *Materializing Locations: Images and Selves*

1. Raymond Williams, *The Year 2000* (New York: Pantheon, 1983), 266.
2. Ibid.
3. Joanne Braxton, *Black Women Writing Autobiography: A Tradition within a Tradition* (Philadelphia: Temple University Press, 1989), 1.
4. Raymond Williams, *Marxism and Literature* (London: Oxford University Press, 1977), 132.
5. Joseph Bristow, 'Life Stories: Carolyn Steedman's History Writing', *New Formations*, 13 (1991), 120.
6. Judith Gardiner, 'On Female Identity and Writing by Women', *Critical Inquiry*, 8 (1981), 348.
7. Ibid. 353.
8. Ibid. 355.
9. Ibid.
10. Judith Fetterley cited in P. P. Schweickart and Elizabeth A. Flynn (eds.), *Gender and Readings, Texts and Contexts* (Baltimore: Johns Hopkins University Press, 1986), 42.
11. Ibid. 42.
12. Sïdonie Smith, *A Poetics of Women's Autobiography: Marginality and the Fictions of Self-Representation* (Bloomington, Ind.: Indiana University Press, 1987), 50.
13. Ibid.
14. Ibid. 54.
15. Ibid. 55.
16. Ibid. 39.
17. Michelle Le Doeuff, *L'Étude et le voult* (Paris: Seuil, 1989), 105–6.
18. Doris Sommer, ' "Not Just a Personal Story": Women's *Testimonios* and the Plural Self', in Bella Brodzki and Celeste Schenck (eds.), *Life/Lines: Theorizing Women's Autobiography* (Ithaca, NY: Cornell University Press, 1988), 119, 108.

19. Ibid.
20. Smith, *A Poetics of Women's Autobiography*, 54.
21. Sommer, 'Women's *Testimonios*', 109.
22. Ibid. 120.
23. Ibid. 120–1.
24. Ibid. 121.
25. Le Doeuff, *L'Étude et le voult*, 106.
26. Gloria Anzaldúa, *Borderlands/La Frontera: The New Mestiza* (San Francisco: Spinsters/Aunt Lotte, 1987), 12–13.
27. Biddy Martin in Brodzki and Schenck (eds.), *Life/Lines*, 93.
28. Ibid. 95.
29. Ibid. 83.
30. Meaghan Morris, 'Banality in Cultural Studies', *Discourse*, 10/2 (1988), 95–6.

Extract 20

ANNA YEATMAN: *The Place of Women's Studies in the Contemporary University*

1. I owe the first point to Nancy Cott's chapter on 'Professionalism and Feminism', in *The Grounding of Modern Feminism* (New Haven and London: Yale University Press, 1987). Cott (p. 216) remarks: 'Because of the close relations of the professions to education and service (where women's contributions were acknowledged to an extent); and because the professions promised neutral standards of judgment for both sexes, collegial autonomy, and horizons for growth, they became a magnet among the potential areas of paid employment for women.'
2. Cott (ibid. 234–5) suggests that 'the impact of the Civil Rights Act of 1964 in effectuating feminist protests within and about the professions in the 1960s and 1970s cannot be minimized; women in the earlier generations had no such support from outside the professions themselves'.
3. bell hooks, *Feminist Theory: From Margin to Center* (Boston: South End Press, 1984).
4. Cott, *The Grounding of Modern Feminism*, 9.
5. A. Yeatman, *Bureaucrats, Technocrats, Femocrats: Essays on the Contemporary Australian State* (Sydney: Allen & Unwin, 1990), chs. 4 and 5; M. Sawer, *Sisters in Suits: Women and Public Policy in Australia* (Sydney: Allen & Unwin, 1990).
6. I. Young, 'The Ideal of Community and The Politics of Difference', in L. Nicholson (ed.), *Feminism/Postmodernism* (New York and London: Routledge, 1990).
7. J. Haggis, 'Gendering Colonialism or Colonizing Gender? Recent Women's Studies Approaches to White Women and the History of British Colonialism', *Women's Studies International Forum*, 13/1–2 (1990), 105–15, and *Gendering Colonialism and Feminist Historiography* (University of Waikato Women's Studies Occasional Paper Series, 6; Waikato, New Zealand, 1992); M. Jolly, 'Colonizing Women and Material Empire', in Sneja Gunew and Anna Yeatman (eds.), *Feminism and the Politics of Difference* (Sydney: Allen & Unwin, 1993).
8. G. Bottomley, M. de Lepervance, and J. Martin (eds.), *Intersexions: Gender, Race, Ethnicity and Class* (Sydney: Allen & Unwin, 1991); D. Stasiulis, 'Theorizing Connections: Gender, Race, Ethnicity and Class', in Peter L: (ed.), *Race and Ethnic Relations in Canada* (Toronto: Oxford University Press, 1990).
9. See Young, 'The Ideal of Community'.

10. D. Riley, 'Am I that Name?' Feminism and the Category of 'Women' in History (London: Macmillan, 1988); J. Butler, Gender Trouble (New York and London: Routledge, 1990).

11. T. De Lauretis, 'Displacing Hegemonic Discourses: Reflections on Feminist Theory in the 1980's', Inscriptions, 3/4 (1988), 127–145, at 138–9.

Extract 21

CAROL GILLIGAN: In a Different Voice

1. Jean Piaget, The Moral Judgement of the Child (1932; repr., New York: The Free Press, 1965).

2. Lawrence Kohlberg, 'The Development of Modes of thinking and choices in years 10 to 16', Ph.D. thesis (University of Chicago, 1958); The Philosophy of Moral Development (San Francisco: Harper and Row, 1981).

3. Carolyn Edwards, 'Societal Complexity, and Moral Development: A Kanyan Study', Ethos, 3 (1975), 505–27; Constance Holstein 'Development of Moral Judgement: A Longitudinal Study of Males and Females', Child Development, 47 (1976), 51–61; Elizabeth L. Simpson, 'Moral Development Research: A Case Study of Scientific Cultural Bias', Human Development, 17 (1974), 81–106.

4. L. Kohlberg and R. Kramer, 'Continuities and Discontinuities in Child and Adult Moral Development', Human Development, 12 (1969), 93–120.

5. Jean Piaget, Structuralism (New York: Basic Books, 1970).

6. L. Kohlberg, 'Continuities and Discontinuities in Childhood and Adult Moral Development Revisited', in Collected Papers an Moral Development and Moral Education (Cambridge, Mass.: Moral Education Research Foundation, Harvard University, 1973).

7. Ibid. 29–30.

8. Jane Loevinger and Ruth Wessler, Measuring Ego Development (San Francisco: Jossey-Bass, 1970), 6.

9. Piaget, The Moral Judgement of the Child, 61.

Extract 22

NANCY HARTSOCK: The Feminist Standpoint: Developing the Ground for a Specifically Feminist Historical Materialism

1. See my 'Feminist Theory and the Development of Revolutionary Strategy', in Zillah Eisenstein (ed.), Capitalist Patriarchy and the Case for Socialist Feminism (New York: Monthly Review, 1978).

2. The recent literature on mothering is perhaps the most detailed on this point. See Dorothy Dinnerstein, The Mermaid and the Minotaur (New York: Harper and Row, 1976); Nancy Chodorow, The Reproduction of Mothering (Berkeley: University of California Press, 1978).

3. Eighth Thesis on Feuerbach, in Karl Marx, 'Theses on Feuerbach', in The German Ideology, ed. C. J. Arthur, (New York: International Publishers, 1970), 121.

4. Marx, Economic and Philosophic Manuscripts of 1844, ed. Dirk Struik (New York: International Publishers, 1964), 112. Nature itself, for Marx, appears as a form of human work, since he argues that humans duplicate themselves actively and

come to contemplate themselves in a world of their own making (ibid. 114). On the more general issue of the relation of natural to human worlds see the very interesting account by Alfred Schmidt, *The Concept of Nature in Marx*, tr. Ben Foukes (London: New Left Books, 1971).

5. Karl Marx and Frederick Engels, *The German Ideology*, ed. with introd. by C. J. Aruther, 2nd edn. (London: Lawrence and Wishart, 1974), 42.

6. For a discussion of women's work, see Elise Boulding, 'Familial Constraints on Women's Work Roles', in Martha Blaxall and B. Reagan (eds.), *Women and the Workplace* (Chicago: University of Chicago Press, 1976), esp. the charts on pp. 111, 113.

7. Mary O'Brien, 'Reproducing Marxist Man', in Lorenne Clark and Lynda Lange (eds.), *The Sexism of Social and Political Theory: Women and Reproduction from Plato to Nietzsche* (Toronto: University of Toronto Press, 1979), 115 n. 11.

8. See Nancy Chodorow, 'Family Structure and Feminine Personality', in Michelle Rosaldo and Louise Lamphere, *Woman, Culture, and Society* (Stanford: Stanford University Press, 1974), 59.

9. Adrienne Rich, *Of Woman Born* (New York: Norton, 1976), 63.

10. See Chodorow, *The Reproduction of Mothering*, and Flax, 'The Conflict Between Nurturance and Autonomy in Mother-Daughter Relations and in Feminism', *Feminist Studies*, 4/2 (June 1978). I rely on the analyses of Dinnerstein and Chodorow but there are difficulties in that they are attempting to explain why humans, both male and female, fear and hate the female. My purpose here is to invert their arguments and to attempt to put forward a positive account of the epistemological consequences of this situation.

11. Chodorow, *The Reproduction of Mothering*, 105, 109.

12. A more general critique of phallocentric dualism occurs in Susan Griffin, *Woman and Nature* (New York: Harper and Row, 1978).

13. More recently, of course, the opposition to the natural world has taken the form of destructive technology. See Evelyn Fox Keller, 'Gender and Science', *Psychoanalysis and Contemporary Thought*, 1/3 (1978).

14. Rich, *Of Woman Born*, 64, 167.

15. Marx, *Capital*, i (New York: International Publishers, 1967), 60.

Extract 23

SANDRA HARDING: *Is there a Feminist Method?*

1. Peter Caws, 'Scientific Method', in Paul Edwards (ed.), *The Encyclopedia of Philosophy* (New York: Macmillan, 1967), 339.

2. Feminist methodologists have even achieved the heroic in showing that through ingenious applications of what have been widely regarded as hopelessly sexist theories—such as sociobiology—we can increase our understandings of women and gender. See Donna Haraway's discussion of this issue in 'Animal Sociology and a Natural Economy of the Body Politic', pt. 2, in *Signs: Journal of Women in Culture and Society*, 4/1 (1978).

3. For further discussion of the feminist science and epistemology critiques see my *The Science Question in Feminism* (Ithaca, NY: Cornell University Press, 1986) and Jean O'Barr and Sandra Harding (eds.), *Sex and Scientific Inquiry* (Chicago: University of Chicago Press, 1987).

4. Kate Millett, *Sexual Politics* (New York: Doubleday & Co. 1969).
5. Zillah Eisenstein has made this point about liberal feminism, which is the political theory represented in the epistemological domain by feminist empiricism. See *The Radical Future of Liberal Feminism* (New York: Longman, 1981).
6. Examples of these other recent sociological critiques of empiricist epistemological assumptions can be found in David Bloor, *Knowledge and Social Imagery* (London: Routledge & Kegan Paul, 1977); Karin Knorr-Cetina, *The Manufacture of Knowledge* (Oxford: Pergamon, 1981); and Bruno Latour and Steve Woolgar, *Laboratory Life: the Social Construction of Scientific Facts* (Beverly Hills, Calif.: Sage, 1979). For critiques of empiricist epistemology owing more direct debts to Marxist perspectives, see, for example, Leszek Kolakowski, *The Alienation of Reason: A History of Positivist Thought*, tr. N. Guterman (Garden City, NY: Anchor Books, 1969); and Alfred Sohn-Rethel, *Intellectual and Manual Labor* (London: Macmillan, 1978).

Extract 24

JANE FLAX: *Postmodernism and Gender Relations in Feminist Theory*

1. Sources for and practitioners of postmodernism include Friedrich Nietzsche, *On the Genealogy of Morals* (New York: Vintage, 1969) and *Beyond Good and Evil* (New York: Vintage, 1966); Jacques Derrida, *L'Écriture et la différance* (Paris: Éditions du Seuil, 1967); Michel Foucault, *Language, Counter-Memory, Practice* (Ithaca, NY: Cornell University Press, 1977); Jacques Lacan, *Speech and Language in Psychoanalysis* (Baltimore: Johns Hopkins University Press, 1968), and *The Four Fundamental Concepts of Psychoanalysis* (New York: W. W. Norton & Co., 1973); Richard Rorty, *Philosophy and the Mirror of Nature* (Princeton: Princeton University Press, 1979); Paul Feyerabend, *Against Method* (New York: Schocken Books, 1975); Ludwig Wittgenstein, *On Certainty* (New York: Harper & Row, 1972), and *Philosophical Investigations* (New York: Macmillan, 1970); Julia Kristeva, 'Women's Time', *Signs: Journal of Women in Culture and Society*, 7/1 (Autumn 1981), 13–35; and Jean-François Lyotard, *The Postmodern Condition* (Minneapolis: University of Minnesota Press, 1984).
2. In 'The Instability of the Analytical Categories of Feminist Theory', *Signs*, 11/4 (Summer 1986), 645–64, Sandra Harding discusses the ambivalent attraction of feminist theorizing to both sorts of discourse. She insists that feminist theorists should live with the ambivalence and retain both discourses for political and philosophical reasons. However, I think her argument rests in part on a too uncritical appropriation of a key Enlightenment equation of knowing, naming, and emancipation.
3. Immanuel Kant, 'What Is Enlightenment?', in *Foundations of the Metaphysics of Morals* (Indianapolis: Bobbs-Merrill Co., 1959), 85.
4. On this point, see Joan Kelly, 'The Doubled Vision of Feminist Theory', *Feminist Studies*, 6/2 (Summer 1979), 216–27; and also Judith Stacey and Barrie Thorne, 'The Missing Feminist Revolution in Sociology', *Social Problems*, 32/4 (Apr. 1985), 301–16.
5. Sigmund Freud, *Civilization and its Discontents* (New York: W. W. Norton & Co., 1961), 50–1.

Extract 25

ELIZABETH WRIGHT: *Thoroughly Postmodern Feminist Criticism*

1. Shoshana Felman, 'To Open the Question', *Literature and Psychoanalysis. The Question of Reading: Otherwise*, (Yale French Studies, 55/6; 1977), 5–10.
2. Jürgen Habermas, 'Modernity—an Incomplete Project', in Hal Foster (ed.), *Postmodern Culture* (London and Sydney: Pluto, 1985), 3–15, at p. 14.
3. Frederic Jameson, 'Postmodernism and Consumer Society', in Foster (ed.), *Postmodern Culture*, 111–25, at p. 125.
4. Terry Eagleton, 'Capitalism, Modernism and Post-Modernism', *New Left Review*, 152 (1985), 60–73, at p. 61.
5. Jean-François Lyotard, *The Postmodern Condition: A Report on Knowledge* (Minneapolis: University of Minnesota Press, 1984), 81.
6. J. Arac, 'Introduction' (ed.), *Postmodernism and Politics* (Manchester: Manchester University Press, 1986), pp. ix–xxiii, at p. xxi.
7. Dianne Chisholm, 'French Feminist Writing' (unpublished paper, 1986).
8. Laura Mulvey, 'Visual Pleasure and Narrative Cinema', *Screen*, 16/3 (1975), 6–18.
9. Gertrud Koch, 'Exchanging the Gaze: Re-visioning Feminist Film Theory', *New German Critique*, 34 (1985), 139–53.
10. Teresa de Lauretis, 'Aesthetic and Feminist Theory: Rethinking Women's Cinema', *New German Critique*, 34 (1985), 154–75.
11. Sandra Harding, *The Science Question in Feminism* (Ithaca and London: Cornell University Press, 1986).

Extract 26

NANCY CHODOROW: Feminism and Psychoanalytic Theory

1. Nancy Chodorow, *The Reproduction of Mothering: Psychoanalysis and the Sociology of Gender* (Berkeley: University of California Press, 1978). See articles reproduced in N. Chodorow, *Feminism and Psychoanalytic Theory* (Cambridge: Polity Press, 1989).
2. See 'Is Male Gender Identity the Cause of Male Domination?', in Joyce Trebilcot (ed.), *Mothering: Essays in Feminist Theory* (Totowa, NJ: Rowman & Allenheld, 1984), 129–46.
3. See, for example, Barbara Ehrenreich and Deirdre English, *For Her Own Good* (New York: Anchor Press, 1979); Barbara Easton [Epstein], 'Feminism and the Contemporary Family', *Socialist Review*, 39 (1978), 11–36; and Heidi Hartmann, 'Capitalism, Patriarchy and Job Segregation by Sex', *Signs*, 1/3/2 (1976), 137–69.

Extract 27

ALISON JAGGAR: *Love and Knowledge: Emotion in Feminist Epistemology*

1. Philosophers who do not conform to this generalization and constitute part of what Susan Bordo calls a 'recessive' tradition in Western philosophy include Hume and Nietzsche, Dewey, and James (Bordo, *The Flight to Objectivity: Essays on Cartesianism and Culture* (Albany, NY: SUNY Press, 1987), 114–18.
2. The Western tradition as a whole has been profoundly rationalist, and much of its history may be viewed as a continuous redrawing of the boundaries of the rational. For a survey of this history from a feminist perspective, see Genevieve

Lloyd, 1984. *The Man of Reason: 'Male' and 'Female' in Western Philosophy* (Minneapolis: University of Minnesota Press, 1984).

3. Thus, fear or other emotions were seen as rational in some circumstances. To illustrate this point, Vicky Spelman quotes Aristotle as saying (in the *Nicomachean Ethics*, sk. iv, ch. 5): '[Anyone] who does not get angry when there is reason to be angry, or who does not get angry in the right way at the right time and with the right people, is a dolt' E. V. Spelman, 'Anger and Insubordination', manuscript; early version read to mid-western chapter of the Society for Women in Philosophy, Spring 1982, p. 1.)

4. Descartes, Leibniz, and Kant are among the prominent philosophers who did not endorse a wholly stripped-down, instrumentalist conception of reason.

5. Jane Flax 'Political Philosophy and the Patriarchal Unconscious: A Psychoanalytic Perspective on Epistemology and Metaphysics', in Sandra Harding and Merrill Hintikka (eds.), *Discovering Reality: Feminist Perspectives on Epistemology, Metaphysics, Methodology and Philosophy of Science* (Dordrecht, Holland: D. Reidel Publishing Co., 1983).

6. Naomi Scheman, 'Women in the Philosophy Curriculum', Paper presented at the Annual Meeting of the Central Division of the American Philosophical Association. Chicago, Apr. 1985; Robin M. Schott, *Cognition and Eros: A Critique of the Kantian Paradigm* (Boston: Beacon, 1988).

7. E. V. Spelman (1982) illustrates this point with a quotation from the well known contemporary philosopher, R. S. Peters, who wrote 'we speak of emotional outbursts, reactions, upheavals and women' (*Proceedings of the Aristotelian Society,* NS 2).

8. Susan Griffin, *Women and Nature: The Roaring inside Her* (New York: Harper and Row, 1979), 31.

9. Alison Jaggar, *Feminist Politics and Human Nature* (Brighton: Harvester, 1983), ch. 11.

Extract 28

IRIS YOUNG: *The Ideal of Impartiality and the Civic Public*

1. Carole Pateman, 'Feminism and Participatory Democracy: some Reflections on Sexual Difference and Citizenship', paper presented at the American Philosophical Association, Western Division Meeting, St Louis, Apr. 1986.

Extract 29

PATRICIA HILL COLLINS: *Toward an Afrocentric Feminist Epistemology*

1. Alexander Okanlaneon, 'Africanism—A Synthesis of the African World-View', *Black World*, 21/9 (1972), 40–4, 92–7; Janheinz Jahn, *Muntu: An Outline of Neo-African Culture* (London: Faber and Faber, 1961); John S. Mbiti, *African Religions and Philosophy* (London: Heinemann, 1969); Cheikh Diop, *The African Origin of Civilization: Myth or Reality* (New York: L. Hill, 1974); Dominique Zahan, *The Religion, Spirituality, and Thought of Traditional Africa* (Chicago: University of Chicago Press, 1979); Mechal Sobel, *Trabelin' On: The Slave Journey to an Afro-Baptist Faith* (Princeton: Princeton University Press, 1979); Dona Richards, 'European Mythology:

The Ideology of "Progress" ', in Molefi Kete Asante and Abdulai Sa. Vandi (eds.), *Contemporary Black Thought* (Beverly Hills, Calif.: Sage, 1980), 59–79, and 'The Implications of African-American Spirituality', in Molef: Kete Asante and Kariamu Welsh Asante (eds.), *African Culture: The Rhythms of Unity* (Trenton, NJ: Africa World Press, 1990), 207–31; Molefi Kete Asante, *The Afrocentric Idea* (Philadelphia: Temple University Press, 1987); Linda James Myers, *Understanding an Afrocentric World View: Introduction to an Optimal Psychology* (Dubugue, Ia.: Kendall/Hunt, 1988).

2. Ortiz M. Walton, 'Comparative Analysis of the African and Western Aesthetics', in Addison Gayle (ed.), *The Black Aesthetic* (Garden City, NY: Doubleday, 1971), 154–64; Geneva Smitherman, *Talkin and Testifyin: The Language of Black America* (Boston: Houghton Mifflin, 1977); Demitri B. Shimkin, Edith M. Shimkin, and Dennis A. Frate (eds.), *The Extended Family in Black Societies* (Chicago: Aldine, 1978); Sheila S. Walker, 'African Gods in the Americas: The Black Religious Continuum', *Black Scholar*, 11/8 (1980), 25–36; Niara Sudarkasa, 'Female Employment and Family Organization in West Africa', in Filomina Chioma Steady (ed.), *The Black Woman Cross-Culturally* (Cambridge, Mass.: Schenkman, 1981); Robert Farris Thompson, *Flash of the Spirit: African and Afro-American Art and Philosophy* (New York: Vintage, 1983); Henry H. Mitchell and Nicholas Cooper Lewter, *Soul Theology: The Heart of American Black Culture* (San Francisco: Harper & Row, 1986); Asante, *The Afrocentric Idea*; Elsa Barkley Brown, 'African-American Women's Quilting: A Framework for Conceptualizing and Teaching African-American Women's History', *Signs*, 14/4 (1989), 921–9.

3. James E. Turner, 'Foreword: African Studies and Epistemology: A Discourse in the Sociology of Knowledge', in Turner (ed.), *The Next Decade: Theoretical and Research Issues in Africana Studies* (Ithaca, NY: Cornell University Africana Studies and Research Center, 1984); Hester Eisenstein, *Contemporary Feminist Thought* (Boston: G. K. Hall, 1983); Nancy M. Hartsock, *Money, Sex and Power* (Boston: Northeastern University Press, 1983); Margaret Andersen, *Thinking about Women: Sociological Perspectives on Sex and Gender* (2nd edn.; New York: Macmillan, 1988); Michelle Z. Rosaldo, 'Women, Culture and Society: A Theoretical Overview', in Rosaldo and Louise Lamphere (eds.), *Woman, Culture and Society* (Stanford: Stanford University Press, 1974), 17–42; Dorothy Smith, *The Everyday World as Problematic* (Boston: Northeastern University Press, 1987); Nancy M. Hartsock, 'The Feminist Standpoint: Developing the Ground for a Specifically Feminist Historical Materialism', in Sandra Harding and Merrill B. Hintikka (eds.), *Discovering Reality* (Boston: D. Reidel, 1983); Alison M. Jaggar, *Feminist Politics and Human Nature* (Totawa, NJ: Rowman & Allanheld, 1983).

4. Bonnie Thornton Dill, 'The Dialectics of Black Womanhood', *Signs*, 4/3 (1979), 543–55.

5. John Langston Gwaltney, *Drylongso: A Self-Portrait of Black America* (New York: Vintage, 1980).

6. William L. Andrews, *Sisters of the Spirit: Three Black Women's Autobiographies of the Nineteenth Century* (Bloomington: Indiana University Press, 1986), 85.

7. Gwaltney, *Drylongso*, 147.

8. Ibid. 68.

9. Ibid. 7.

10. Ibid. 27, 33.
11. Nancy Chodorow, *The Reproduction of Mothering* (Berkeley: University of California Press, 1978); Carol Gilligan, *In a Different Voice* (Cambridge, Mass.: Harvard University Press, 1982).
12. Hartsock, 'The Feminist Standpoint'; Mary Field Belenky, Blythe McVicker Clinchy, Nancy Rule Goldberger, and Jill Mattuck Tarule, *Women's Ways of Knowing* (New York: Basic Books, 1986).
13. Wendy Luttrell, 'Working-Class Women's Ways of Knowing: Effects of Gender, Race, and Class', *Sociology of Education*, 62/1 (1989), 33–46.
14. bell hooks, *Talking Back: Thinking Feminist, Thinking Black* (Boston: South End Press, 1989), 131.
15. Belenky *et al.*, *Women's Ways of Knowing*, 18.
16. Asante, *The Afrocentric Idea*, 185.
17. Smitherman, *Talkin and Testifyin*, 108.
18. Thomas Kochman, *Black and White Styles in Conflict* (Chicago: University of Chicago Press, 1981), 28.
19. June Jordan, *On Call* (Boston: South End Press, 1985), 129.
20. Andree Nicola-McLaughlin and Zula Chandler, 'Urban Politics in the Higher Education of Black Women: A Case Study', in Ann Bookman and Sandra Morgen (eds.), *Women and the Politics of Empowerment* (Philadelphia: Temple University Press, 1988), 129.
21. Thomas L. Webber, *Deep Like the Rivers* (New York: W. W. Norton, 1978), 127.
22. Mary Helen Washington, 'I Sign my Mother's Name: Alice Walker, Dorothy West and Paule Marshall', in Ruth Perry and Martine Watson Broronley (eds.), *Mothering the Mind: Twelve Studies of Writers and their Silent Partners* (New York: Holmes & Meier, 1984), 145.
23. Gwaltney, *Drylongso*, 228.
24. Claudia Tate (ed.), *Black Women Writers at Work* (New York: Continuum Publishing, 1983), 156.
25. Gwaltney, *Drylongso*, 11.
26. Andrews, *Sisters of the Spirit*, 98.
27. Kochman, *Black and White Styles in Conflict*, 23.

Extract 30

PATRICIA WAUGH: *Modernism, Postmodernism, Gender: The View from Feminism*

1. Julia Kristeva, 'Le Temps des femmes' in 34/44: *Cahiers de recherche de sciences des textes et documents*, 5 (Winter 1979), 5–19.
2. Sigmund Freud, 'On Narcissism: An Introduction', *The Standard Edition of the Complete Psychological Works*, 14 (London: Hogarth Press, 1957).
3. Joan Riviere, 'The Unconscious Fantasy of an Inner World Reflected in Examples from Literature', in Melanie Klein (ed.), *New Directions in Psychoanalysis* (London, 1986).
4. Nancy Chodorow, *The Reproduction of Mothering: Psychoanalysis and the Sociology of Gender* (Berkeley: University of California Press, 1978).
5. Jean Paul Sartre, *Being and Nothingness* (New York: Philosophical Library, 1956; repr. 1985).

Extract 31

SEYLA BENHABIB: *The Generalized and the Concrete Other*

1. Thomas Kuhn, *The Structure of Scientific Revolutions* (2nd edn. ; Chicago: University of Chicago Press, 1970), 52 ff.
2. Although the term 'generalized other' is borrowed from George Herbert Mead, my definition of it differs from his. Mead defines the 'generalized other' as follows: 'The organized community or social group which gives the individual his unity of self may be called the "generalized other". The attitude of the generalized other is the attitude of the whole community.' George Herbert Mead, *Mind, Self and Society: From the Standpoint of a Social Behaviorist*, ed. and introd. Charles W. Morris (Chicago: University of Chicago Press, 1955), 154.
3. Hannah Arendt, 'Crisis in Culture', in *Between Past and Future* (Cleveland and New York: Meridian, 1961), 221.
4. John Rawls, *A Theory of Justice*, 2nd edn. (Cambridge, Mass.: Harvard University Press, 1971); Susan Moller Okin, 'Reason and Feeling in Thinking about Justice', *Ethics*, 99/2 (Jan. 1989); Carol Gilligan, *In a Different Voice* (Cambridge, Mass.: Harvard University Press, 1982).

Extract 32

MONIQUE WITTIG: *One is not Born a Woman*

1. Christine Delphy, 'Pour un féminisme matérialiste', *L'Arc*, 61 (1975). Translated as 'For a Materialist Feminism', *Feminist Issues*, 1/2 (Winter 1981).
2. Colette Guillaumin, 'Race et nature: Système des marques, idée de groupe naturel et rapports sociaux', *Pluriel*, 11 (1977). Translated as 'Race and Nature: The System of Marks, the Idea of a Natural Group and Social Relationships', *Feminist Issues*, 8/2 (Fall 1988).
3. I use the word society with an extended anthropological meaning; strictly speaking, it does not refer to societies, in that lesbian societies do not exist completely autonomously from heterosexual social systems.
4. Simone de Beauvoir, *The Second Sex* (New York: Bantam, 1952), 249.
5. Redstockings, *Feminist Revolution* (New York: Random House, 1978), 18.
6. Andrea Dworkin, 'Biological Superiority: The World's Most Dangerous and Deadly Idea', *Heresies*, 6: 46.
7. Ti-Grace Atkinson, *Amazon Odyssey* (New York: Links Books, 1974), 15.
8. Dworkin, 'Biological Superiority'.
9. Guillaumin, 'Race et nature'.
10. de Beauvoir, *The Second Sex*.
11. Guillaumin, 'Race et nature'.
12. Dworkin, 'Biological Superiority'.
13. Atkinson, *Amazon Odyssey*, 6: 'If feminism has any logic at all, it must be working for a sexless society.'
14. Rosalind Rosenberg, 'In Search of Woman's Nature', *Feminist Studies*, 3/1–2 (1975), 144.
15. Ibid. 146.

16. In an article published in *L'Idiot international* (May 1970), whose original title was 'Pour un mouvement de libération des femmes' (For a Women's Liberation Movement).

17. Christiane Rochefort, *Les stances à Sophie* (Paris: Grasset, 1963).

Extract 35

HÉLÈNE CIXOUS: *Sorties*

1. All Derrida's work traversing-detecting the history of philosophy is devoted to bringing this to light. In Plato, Hegel, and Nietzsche, the same process continues: repression, repudiation, distancing of woman; a murder that is mixed up with history as the manifestation and representation of masculine power.

Extract 36

ELIZABETH SPELMAN: *Woman: The One and the Many*

1. See Lorraine Bethel, 'What Chou Mean WE, White Girl?', *Conditions*, 5 (1979), 86–92.

Extract 37

SNEJA GUNEW: *Authenticity and the Writing Cure: Reading Some Migrant Women's Writing*

1. Alice Jardine, *Gynesis: Configurations of Woman and Modernity* (Ithaca, NY, and London 1985), 147.

2. Antigone Kefala, 'Inheritance', *Horseless Rider* (unpublished manuscript).

3. The distinction Derrida makes between 'writing' and 'voice' is clearly summarized in Christopher Norris, *Deconstruction: Theory and Practice* (London, 1982), 24–32.

4. Catherine Belsey, *The Subject of Tragedy: Identity and Difference in Renaissance Drama*, (London, 1985), 5–6.

5. For example, 'We are all the direct descendants of Columbus, it is with him that our genealogy begins . . .', Tzvetan Todorov, *The Conquest of America: The Question of the Other* (New York, 1982), 5.

6. Anne Freadman, 'Taking Things Literally (Sins of My Old Age)', *Southern Review*, 18/2 (July 1985), 168.

7. See for example David Brooks, 'Women's Writing', *Age Monthly Review*, 5/11 (Apr. 1986), 6–8.

8. Toril Moi, *Sexual/Textual Politics: Feminist Literary Theory* (London, 1985), 121–6.

9. Christine Delphy, *Close to Home: A Materialist Analysis of Women's Oppression* (London, 1984). Delphy argues for a redefinition of knowledge which takes into account the materialism of women's lives and historical oppression.

10. Teresa de Lauretis, *Alice Doesn't: Feminism, Semiotics, Cinema* (London, 1984), 159; my italics. It may be that de Lauretis does not sufficiently take into account the unconscious, as Annette Kuhn pointed out when this paper was given.

11. Moi, *Sexual/Textual Politics*, 140–3.

12. I am referring here to Elizabeth Gross's recent work, for example: E. Gross, 'The Body of Women: Psychoanalysis and Foucault'; 'Language and the Limits of the

Body: Kristeva and Abjection'; 'Introduction to Irigaray's *Le Corps-à-corps avec la mère*' (unpublished papers). There is also Naomi Schor, *Breaking the Chain: Women, Theory and French Realist Fiction* (New York, 1985), particularly the last chapter.

13. There is now an avalanche of critiques coming from 'minority' women. For example, *Feminist Review*, 17 (Autumn 1984), whole issue; bell hooks, *Ain't I a Woman* (London, 1981, and *Feminist Theory: From Margin to Center* (Boston, 1984); Andre Lorde, *Sister Outsider* (New York, 1984); Hazel Carby, 'White Woman Listen! Black Feminism and the Boundaries of Sisterhood', *The Empire Strikes Back* (London, 1982), 212–35; C. O. Ogunyemi, 'Womanism: The Dynamics of the Contemporary Black Female Novel in English', *Signs*, 11/1 (Autumn 1985), 63–80; Michèle Barrett and Mary McIntosh, 'Ethnocentrism and Socialist Feminist Theory', *Feminist Review*, 20 (Summer 1985), 23–47.

14. Elizabeth Gross, 'For American Consumption', *Age Monthly Review*, 5/11 (Apr. 1986), 22.

15. J. F. Lyotard, *The Postmodern Condition: A Report on Knowledge* (Manchester, 1984). As Meaghan Morris pointed out when this paper was first presented, Lyotard appears to move confusingly between meta- and master-narratives, and in fact we never really escape from either.

Extract 38

DENISE RILEY: *Am I that Name? Feminism and the Category of 'Women' in History*

1. See Jacqueline Rose, 'Introduction—II', in J. Mitchell and J. Rose (eds.), *Feminine Sexuality, Jacques Lacan and the École Freudienne* (London: Macmillan, 1982).

2. See Stephen Heath, 'Male Feminism', *Dalhousie Review*, 64/2 (1986).

3. Jacques Derrida, *Spurs; Nietzsche's Styles* (Chicago: University of Chicago Press, 1978), 51, 55.

4. See arguments in Lynne Segal, *Is the Future Female? Troubled Thoughts on Contemporary Feminism* (London: Virago, 1987).

Extract 39

TORIL MOI: *Feminist, Female, Feminine*

Summary

The title of 'Feminist, Female, Feminine' alludes silently to the three categories of nineteenth-century women's writing identified in Elaine Showalter's *A Literature of Their Own*. Moi redefines the terms and then uses them as the basis of a (mild) critique of Showalter's own theoretical position.

In the extract reprinted here it is argued that 'feminist' is a political term, 'female' a biological one, and 'feminine' a cultural definition. The essay calls into question the belief that female experience is the basis of feminism, or in other words that politics is a direct effect of biology. Meanwhile, if 'feminine' specifies a cultural rather than a biological difference, to oppose 'feminine' to 'masculine' in an absolute binary opposition is ultimately to reaffirm an essentialist and patriarchal distinction. It follows that to privilege 'feminine writing' (the *écriture féminine* of French feminism) is to be in perpetual danger of falling into yet another form of biological essentialism.

The essay goes on to develop the argument that 'the feminine' is not an essence but a culturally produced position of marginality in relation to patriarchal society. As a relational position rather than a fact of nature, it is a place from which to conduct a feminist politics committed to change.

1. Julia Kristeva, *Revolution in Poetic Language* (New York, 1984). For Lacan and the symbolic order, see Elizabeth Wright, *Psychoanalytic Criticism: Theory in Practice* (London, 1984); Toril Moi, *Sexual/Textual Politics: Feminist Literary Theory* (London, 1985); and Terry Eagleton, *Literary Theory: An Introduction* (Oxford, 1983); as well as Anika Lemaire, *Jacques Lacan* (London, 1977), which for me remains the most serious and wide-ranging introduction to Lacan.

2. For a necessary critique of the political implications of Kristeva's theories at this point, see Moi, *Sexual/Textual Politics*, 150–73.

3. Julia Kristeva, 'Women's Time' *Signs* 7 (1981), 13–35.

Extract 40

DIANA FUSS: *The 'Risk' of Essence*

1. A comprehensive discussion of the essence/accident distinction is elaborated in Book Z of Aristotle's *Metaphysics*. For a history of the philosophical concept of essentialism, readers might wish to consult Degrood, *Philosophies of Essence* (Amsterdam: B. R. Gruner, 1976) or Rorty, *Philosophy and the Mirror of Nature* (Princeton: Princeton University Press, 1979).

2. See, for example, Hélène Cixous's contribution to *The Newly Born Woman* (Minneapolis: University of Minnesota Press, 1986).

3. Jacques Derrida, *Positions* (Paris: Minuit, 1972); tr. Alan Bass, *Positions* (Chicago: University of Chicago Press, 1981), 67.

4. Stephen Heath, 'Difference', *Screen*, 19/3 (Autumn 1978), 99.

5. Alice Jardine and Paul Smith (eds.), *Men in Feminism* (New York and London: Methuen, 1987), 58.

6. Ibid. 96.

7. Ibid. 192.

Extract 41

RACHEL BOWLBY: *Still Crazy after all these Years*

1. On this point see Angela Weir and Elizabeth Wilson, 'The British Women's Movement', *New Left Review*, 148 (Nov. /Dec. 1984), 74–103.

2. For the uninitiated: Cilla Black, 1960s Liverpool pop star, has acquired a second wave of fame as the presenter of a British TV show called *Blind Date*, which is loosely modelled on the American *Dating Game*.

3. Freud, *New Introductory Lectures on Psychoanalysis* (1933) (Pelican Freud Library (hereafter PFL), 2; Harmondsworth: Penguin, 1973), 146; in *The Standard Edition of the Complete Psychological Works* (hereafter SE) (London: Hogarth Press and the Institute of Psychoanalysis), 22: 113.

4. Sophocles, *Oedipus Tyrannos*, 800 f.

5. 'Probably no man is spared the fright of castration at the sight of a female genital', 'Fetishism' (1927); 'The little girl, frightened by the comparison with boys, grows

dissatisfied with her clitoris', 'Female sexuality' (1931), PFL 7 (Harmondsworth: Penguin, 1977), 354, 376; *SE* 21: 154, 229.

6. For Freud's analysis of the structure of the dirty joke, see *Jokes and their Relation to the Unconscious*, PFL 6 (Harmondsworth: Penguin, 1976), 140–6. Also *SE* 8: 97–102.

7. 'The word "feminism" was created by Fourier.' The Robert dictionary is here quoting Braunschwig's *Notre littérature étudiée dans les textes*; the date of Fourier's invention is given as 1837.

8. 'Dora', PFL 8: 119; *SE* 7: 82.

9. Ibid. 53; 23.

10. Juliet Mitchell, *Psychoanalysis and Feminism* (1974; repr. Harmondsworth: Penguin, 1975), p. xv.

11. Jane Gallop, *The Daughter's Seduction: Feminism and Psychoanalysis* (Ithaca, NY: Cornell University Press 1982), 5.

12. Jacqueline Rose, 'Femininity and its Discontents', in *Feminist Review* (1983) and *Sexuality: A Reader* (London: Virago, 1987), 177 *et passim*.

13. For the 'fatal' quality of this relationship, see Juliet Mitchell, *Psychoanalysis and Feminism*: 'The argument of this book is that a rejection of psychoanalysis and Freud's works is fatal for feminism' (p. xv). If this feminism here says to psychoanalysis, 'I cannot live without you', or (to the rest of feminism), 'Without it, we will die', then just as forcefully, those on the other side proclaim that it is precisely psychoanalysis that is or would be 'fatal' to feminism. Elizabeth Wilson declares: 'In the Freudian or more fatally in the Lacanian account, the organization of difference not only does but *must* occur around the dominant symbol of the Phallus' ('Psychoanalysis: Psychic Law and Order', in *Feminist Review*, and *Sexuality*, 179.

14. See further the entry under 'Forclusion' in J. Laplanche and J.-B. Pontalis. *Vocabulaire de la psychanalyse* (Paris: Presses Universitaires de France, 1967), 163–76.

15. Freud, 'Female sexuality', 372; *SE* 21: 226.

16. These examples are taken from Lilian H. Jeffery's article on 'Writing' in Alan J. B. Wace and Frank H. Stubbings (eds.), *A Companion to Homer* (London: Macmillan, 1963), 550. They show man, woman, and olive tree.

17. D. H. Lawrence, *Women in Love* (1921), ch. 19, 'Moony'.

Extract 42

MORAG SHIACH: *Their 'symbolic' exists, it holds power—we, the sowers of disorder, know it only too well*

1. Hélène Cixous, 'The Laugh of the Medusa', in Elaine Marks and Isabelle de Courtivron (eds.), *New French Feminisms* (Brighton: Harvester, 1981), 245–64, at p. 255.

2. Ibid. 255.

3. Jacques Derrida, 'Différance', in *Margins of Philosophy*, tr. Alan Bass (Brighton: Harvester, 1982), 1–27, at p. 8.

4. Ibid. 9.

5. Hélène Cixous, 'Le Chemin de légende', in *Théâtre: Portrait de Dora et La Prise de l'école de Madhubaï* (Paris: Éditions des Femmes, 1986), 'La Prise', 7–11, at p. 10 my translation.

6. 'Laugh of the Medusa', 250.
7. Ibid. 254.
8. Jane Gallop, 'Keys to Dora', in *The Daughter's Seduction: Feminism and Psycho-analysis* (London: Macmillan, 1982), 132–50, at p. 148.
9. See text on back cover of Hélène Cixous, *Le Nom d'Oedipe: Chant du corps interdit* (Paris: Éditions des Femmes, 1978).
10. 'Laugh of the Medusa', 263.
11. See 'Le Chemin de légende'.

Extract 43

LIZ STANLEY: *Recovering Women in History from Feminist Deconstructionism*

1. Denise Riley, *'Am I That Name?' Feminism and the Category of 'Women' in History* (London: Macmillan, 1988), 1–2.
2. Monique Wittig, 'The Straight Mind', *Feminist Issues*, 1/1 (1980), 103–11, and 'One is not Born a Woman' and, *Feminist Issues*, 1/2 (1981), 47–54.
3. Sandra Harding (ed.), *Feminism and Methodology* (Open University Press, 1987).

Extract 44

JUDITH BUTLER: *Subjects of Sex/Gender/Desire*

1. See Denise Riley, *Am I That Name?: Feminism and the Category of 'Women' in History* (New York: Macmillan, 1988).
2. See Sandra Harding, 'The Instability of the Analytical Categories of Feminist Theory', in Sandra Harding and Jean F. O'Barr (eds.), *Sex and Scientific Inquiry* (Chicago: University of Chicago Press, 1987), 283–302.
3. For an interesting study of the *berdache* and multiple-gender arrangements in Native American cultures, see Walter L. Williams, *The Spirit and the Flesh: Sexual Diversity in American Indian Culture* (Boston: Beacon Press, 1988). See also, Sherry B. Ortner and Harriet Whitehead (eds.), *Sexual Meanings: The Cultural Construction of Sexuality* (New York: Cambridge University Press, 1981). For a politically sensitive and provocative analysis of the *berdache*, transsexuals, and the contingency of gender dichotomies, see Suzanne J. Kessler and Wendy McKenna, *Gender: An Ethnomethodological Approach* (Chicago: University of Chicago Press, 1978).
4. Clearly Foucault's *History of Sexuality* offers one way to rethink the history of 'sex' within a given modern Eurocentric context. For a more detailed consideration, see Thomas Lacquer and Catherine Gallagher (eds.), *The Making of the Modern Body: Sexuality and Society in the 19th Century* (Berkeley: University of California Press, 1987), originally published as an issue of *Representations*, 14 (Spring 1986).
5. See my 'Variations on Sex and Gender: Beauvoir, Wittig, Foucault', in Seyla Benhabib and Drusilla Cornell (eds.), *Feminism as Critique* (Basil Blackwell, dist. by University of Minnesota Press, 1987).
6. Simone de Beauvoir, *The Second Sex*, tr. E. M. Parshley (New York: Vintage, 1973), 301.
7. Ibid. 38.
8. See my 'Sex and Gender in Beauvoir's *Second Sex*', *Yale French Studies, Simone de Beauvoir: Witness to a Century*, 72 (Winter, 1986).

9. Robert Stoller, *Presentations of Gender* (New Haven: Yale University Press, 1985), 11–14.
10. Friedrich Nietzsche, *On the Genealogy of Morals*, tr. Walter Kaufmann (New York: Vintage, 1969), 45.

Extract 45

KATE SOPER: *Feminism, Humanism, Postmodernism*

1. Thus Alice Jardine, *Gynesis: Configurations of Women and Modernity* (Ithaca, NY, and London, 1985), see especially pp. 22–4; cf. Barbara Creed, 'From Here to Modernity: Feminism and Postmodernism', *Screen*, 28/2 (Spring 1987).
2. Although there was a definite class bias in much of the early liberal discussion of such rights: 'all men' being conceived often enough as having practical extension only to all males in possession of a certain property and concomitant social status.
3. See J. Kristeva, 'Women's Time' (1st published as 'Le Temps des Femmes', in *Cahiers de recherche de sciences des textes et documents*, 5 (Winter 1979)) in Toril Moi (ed.), *The Kristeva Reader* (Oxford, 1986), 187–213; cf. 'Il n'y a pas de maître à langage', *Nouvelle Revue de Psychanalyse* (1979), cited in *Kristeva Reader*, p. 11.
4. Irigaray, for example, has treated *parler femme* as an analogue of female genitalia, in which the contiguous, non-adversarial and elliptical quality of the statements of feminine writing is a reflection of the two lips of the vulva.
5. Drusilla Cornell and Adam Thurschwell, 'Feminism, Negativity, Subjectivity' in Drusilla Cornell and Seyla Benhabib (eds.), *Feminism as Critique* (Oxford, 1987), 150–1.
6. A disengagement reflected in Kristeva's Lacanian presentation of the feminine as semiotic 'other' of the Symbolic even as it is criticized by Kristeva herself.
7. Recent feminist self-criticism regarding the 'white middle-class' outlook of feminist politics reflects this anxiety about conceptual conflations, even if it does not collapse into the extreme particularism which would seem to be its ultimate logic.

Extract 46

KADIATU KANNEH: *Love, Mourning and Metaphor: Terms of Identity*

1. Elaine Marks and Isabelle de Courtivron (eds.), *New French Feminisms* (Sussex: Harvester, 1985), 68–75.
2. Cixous, 'The Laugh of the Medusa', in Marks and de Courtivron (eds.), *New French Feminisms*, 251.
3. From an interview with Marguerite Duras by Susan Husserl-Kapit in *Signs* (Winter 1975), in Marks and de Courtivron (eds.), 238.
4. Quoted by Deborah Cameron (ed.), *Feminism and Linguistic Theory* (London: Macmillan, 1985), 130.
5. Quoted in Cameron (ed.), 138.
6. Rhonda Cobham and Merle Collins (eds.), *Watchers and Seekers* (London: The Women's Press, 1987), 109–11.
7. Cixous, 'The Laugh of the Medusa', 248.
8. Ngũgĩ Wa Thiong'o, *Decolonizing the Mind* (London: James Currey and Heinemann, 1987), 16.

9. Cixous, 'The Laugh of the Medusa', 258.
10. Chrystos, quoted in Cherrié Moraga and Gloria Anzaldúa (eds.), *This Bridge Called My Back* (New York: Kitchen Table: Women of Colour Press, 1981), 57.
11. Sonia Sanchez, *Homegirls and Handgrenades* (New York: Thunder's Mouth Press, 1984), 9.
12. Grace Nichols, in Cobham and Collins (eds.), *Watchers and Seekers*, 65.
13. Merle Collins, in Cobham and Collins (eds.), *Watchers and Seekers*, 32.
14. Toni Morrison, *The Bluest Eye* (London: Triad Grafton Books, 1981), 1.
15. Ngũgĩ *Decolonizing the Mind*, 15.
16. Morrison, *The Bluest Eye*, 48.
17. Meiling Jin, in Cobham and Collins (eds.), *Watchers and Seekers*, 123–6, especially p. 126.

Extract 47

ELIZABETH GROSZ: *Psychoanalysis and the Imaginary Body*

1. Sigmund Freud (1914), 'On Narcissism: An Introduction', in James Strachey (ed.), *The Standard Edition of the Complete Works of Sigmund Freud*, 14 (London: Hogarth Press, 1957–74).
2. For a more detailed explanation of Lacan's understanding of the imaginary, and the corresponding psychical orders of the symbolic and the real, see my reading of Lacan in *Jacques Lacan: A Feminist Introduction* (London: Routledge, 1990).
3. Sigmund Freud (1922), 'The Ego and the Id', in Strachey, *Standard Edition*, 26.
4. Freud (1914), 'On Narcissism', 84.
5. Freud (1923), 26.
6. Sigmund Freud (1929), 'Civilization and its Discontents', in Strachey, *Standard Edition*, 90–2.
7. See in this context, the pioneer writings of Moira Gatens, 'A Critique of the Sex/Gender Distinction', in Sneja Gunew (ed.), *A Reader in Feminist Knowledge* (London and New York: Routledge, 1990), 139–60.
8. Jacques Lacan, 'Some Reflections on the Ego', *International Journal of Psychoanalysis*, 34 (1953).

Extract 48

LUCE IRIGARAY: *The Other: Woman*

1. See *Speculum, De l'autre femme*, 266–81, *Speculum of the Other Woman*, 214–26.
2. Irigaray writes the pronouns thus: *il(s)* and *elle(s)*, hence referring to both the singular and plural third-person pronouns. Orally and aurally they cannot be differentiated. *Il* is the masculine/neuter pronoun, *he*, *elle* the feminine *she*; in French the plural retains its gender mark unlike the neuter *they*. However, *ils* is used for both an exclusively masculine plural and for a plural constituted by masculine and feminine substantives; *elles* is only possible as an exclusively feminine plural. The philosophical and linguistic implications of this are taken up throughout this book and in her other works (Tr.).
3. See n. 2 (Tr.).
4. With reference to this, see *Je, tu, nous*.

5. See 'La Croyance même' and 'Le Geste en psychanalyse' in *Sexes et parentés*, tr. 'Belief Itself' and 'Gesture in Psychoanalysis', in *Sexes and Genealogies*.

Introduction to Section 4

1. Lynne Segal, *Is the Future Female? Troubled Thoughts on Contemporary Feminism* (London: Virago, 1987), 65.

Extract 49

ADRIENNE RICH: *Compulsory Heterosexuality and Lesbian Existence*

1. Nancy Chodorow, *The Reproduction of Mothering* (Berkeley: University of California Press, 1978); Dorothy Dinnerstein, *The Mermaid and the Minotaur: Sexual Arrangements and the Human Malaise* (New York: Harper & Row, 1976); Barbara Ehrenreich and Deirdre English, *For Her Own Good: 150 Years of the Experts' Advice to Women* (Garden City, NY: Doubleday & Co., Anchor Press, 1978); Jean Baker Miller, *Toward a New Psychology of Women* (Boston: Beacon Press, 1976).
2. Chodorow, *The Reproduction of Mothering*, 197–8.
3. Ibid. 198–9.
4. Ibid. 200.
5. Fran P. Hosken, 'The Violence of Power: Genital Mutilation of Females', *Heresies: A Feminist Journal of Art and Politics*, 6 (1979), 28–35; Diana Russell and Nicole van de Ven (eds.), *Proceedings of the International Tribunal on Crimes against Women* (Millbrae, Calif.: Les Femmes, 1976), 194–5.
6. Kathlean Barry, *Female Sexual Slavery* (Englewood Cliffs, NJ: Prentice-Hall, 1979), 163–4.
7. Audre Lorde, *Uses of the Erotic: The Erotic as Power* (Out & Out Books Pamphlet, No. 3, New York: Out & Out Books (476 2d Street, Brooklyn, New York 11215), 1979).
8. See Rosalind Petchesky, 'Dissolving the Hyphen: A Report on Marxist-Feminist Groups 1–5', in Zillah Eisenstein (ed.), *Capitalist Patriarchy and the Case for Socialist Feminism* (New York: Monthly Review Press, 1979), 387.
9. Andrea Dworkin, *Chains of Iran, Chains of Grief* (Garden City, NY: Doubleday & Co., 1980).

Extract 51

CAROLE VANCE: *Pleasure and Danger: Toward a Politics of Sexuality*

1. Joan Nestle, 'The Fem Question', in C. Vance (ed.), *Pleasure and Danger* (London: Pandora, 1992), 234.
2. Social construction texts include: Michel Foucault, *A History of Sexuality, An Introduction*, tr. Robert Hurley (New York: Pantheon, 1978); Jeffrey Weeks, *Coming Out: Homosexual Politics in Britain* (London: Quartet, 1977); Jonathan Katz, *Gay/Lesbian Almanac: A New Documentary* (New York: Harper & Row, 1983) 138–74.
3. Jonathan Katz, *Gay American History: Lesbians and Gay Men in the USA* (New York: Crowell, 1976).
4. Lillian Faderman, *Surpassing the Love of Men* (New York: Morrow, 1981); Nancy Sahli, 'Smashing: Women's Relationships Before the Fall', *Chrysalis* 8 (1979), 17–27.

5. Jonathan Katz, 'The Invention of Heterosexuality', unpublished manuscript, 1983.
6. Pat Califia, 'Doing It Together: Gay Men, Lesbians, and Sex', *Advocate* (7 July 1983), 24–7.

Extract 52

ALISON LIGHT: *'Returning to Manderley'—Romance Fiction, Female Sexuality and Class*

1. See, for example, Janet Batsleer, 'Pulp in the Pink', *Spare Rib*, 109 (1981); David Margolies, 'Mills and Boon—Guilt without Sex', *Red Letters*, 14 (1982); Sue Harper, 'History with Frills: Costume Fiction in World War II', *Red Letters*, 14 (1982).
2. Jacqueline Rose, 'Femininity and its Discontents', *Feminist Review*, 14 (1983), 9.
3. Rachel Anderson, *The Purple Heart Throbs: The Sub-Literature of Love* (London: Hodder and Stoughton, 1974).

Extract 53

EVE KOSOFSKY SEDGWICK: *Sexual Politics and Sexual Meaning*

1. *Semiotext(c)*, 4/1 (1981).
2. Catharine Mackinnon, 'Feminism, Marxism, Method and the State: An Agenda for Theory', *Signs*, 7/3 (Spring 1982), 530–1.
3. Margaret Mitchell, *Gone with the Wind* (New York: Avon, 1973), 780.

Extract 54

LIZ KELLY: *Sexual Violence and Feminist Theory*

1. C. MacKinnon, 'Feminism, Marxism, Method and the State: An Agenda for Theory', *Signs* 7(3) (Spring 1982), 526.
2. S. Bartky, 'Female Masochism and the Politics of Personal Transformation', *Women's Studies International Forum*, 7 (5) (1984), 323–34.
3. R. Hall, *Ask Any Woman* (Bristol: Falling Wall Press, 1984), 48.
4. D. Gittins, *Family in Question* (London: Macmillan, 1985).
5. A. Rich, 'Compulsory Heterosexuality and Lesbian Existence', *Signs*, 5/4 (1980), 631–60.
6. D. Scully and J. Marolla, 'Convicted Rapists' Vocabularies of Motive: Excuses and Justifications', unpublished mimeograph (1984), 27.
7. L. Lederer (ed.), *Take Back the Night: Women on Pornography* (New York: William Morrow, 1980).
8. N. Hartsock, *Money, Sex and Power: Towards a Feminist Historical Materialism* (London: Longman, 1983), 7.
9. See, for example, C. Vance (ed.), *Pleasure and Danger: Exploring Female Sexuality* (London: Routledge & Kegan Paul, 1984).
10. E. Stanko, 'Typical Violence, Normal Precaution: Men, Women and Interpersonal Violence in England, Wales, Scotland and the USA', in J. Hanmer and M. Maynard (eds.), *Women, Violence and Social Control* (London: Macmillan, 1987).

11. M. Cliff, 'Sister/Outsider: Some Thoughts on Simone Weil', in S. Ruddick (ed.), *Between Women* (Boston: Beacon Press, 1984), 318.

12. S. Brownmiller, *Against Our Will: Men, Women and Rape* (New York: Simon & Schuster, 1975); M. Daly, *Gyn/Ecology: The Mataethics of Radical Feminism* (London: Women's Press 1979); S. Griffin, *Rape: the Power of Consciousness* (New York: Harper & Row, 1979).

13. K. Barry, *Female Sexual Slavery* (Englewood Cliffs, NJ: Prentice-Hall, 1979), 139.

14. Ibid. 165.

15. J. Radford, 'Policing Male Violence', in Hanmer and Maynard (eds.), *Women, Violence and Social Control* (1987).

16. M. Hirsch, *Women and Violence* (New York: Van Nostrand Reinhold, 1981).

17. H. Scott, *Working Your Way to the Bottom: The Feminization of Poverty* (London: Panodra Press, 1985).

18. K. Barry, 'Social Etiology of Crimes against Women', *Victimology*, 10 (1–4) (1985), 164.

19. D. Klein, 'Violence against Women: Some Considerations regarding its Causes and its Elimination', *Crime and Delinquency*, 27 (1) (1981), 64–80.

20. Bartky, 'Female Masochism'.

21. A. Dworkin, *Pornography: Men Possessing Women* (London: Women's Press, 1981); R. Morgan, 'Theory and Practice: Pornography and Rape', in *Going Too Far* (New York: Vintage Books, 1978).

22. E. Wilson, *What Is to be Done About Violence Against Women* (Middlesex: Penguin, 1983).

Extract 58

MARY MCINTOSH: *Queer Theory and the War of the Sexes*

1. Kobena Mercer, in the discussion following his paper, 'Skin Head Sex Thing: Racial Differences and Homoerotic Imagery', in Bad-Object Choices (eds.), *How Do I Look? Queer Film and Video* (Seattle: Bay Press, 1991), 216.

2. Quoted in Cherry Smyth, *Lesbians Talk Queer Notions* (London: Scarlet Press, 1992), 17.

3. For a good introduction to social constructionism, see Carole S. Vance, 'Social Construction Theory: Problems in the History of Sexuality', in Dennis Altman *et al.* (eds.), *Which Homosexuality?* (London: GMP, 1989), 13–34. See also Edward Stein (ed.), *Forms of Desire: Sexual Orientation and the Social Constructionist Debate* (New York: Garland, 1990).

4. See, for example, Anna Marie Smith, 'Resisting the Erasure of Lesbian Sexuality', in K. Plummer, (ed.), *Modern Homosexualities: Fragments of Lesbian and Gay Experience* (London: Routledge, 1992), 200–13.

5. Bad-Object Choices (ed.), *How Do I Look?*, 20. See also Mandy Merck, 'Difference and Its Discontents', *Screen*, 28/1 (1987), 1–9.

6. Juliet Mitchell, *Psychoanalysis and Feminism* (London: Allen Lane, 1974), p. xv.

7. Cora Kaplan, 'Radical Feminism and Literature: Rethinking Millett's *Sexual Politics*', in *Sea Changes: Culture and Feminism* (London: Verso, 1986), 15–30.

8. Joan W. Scott, 'Gender: A Useful Category for Historical Anlysis', *American Historical Review*, 91 (1986), 1065–75.

9. In 'The Banality of Gender', *Oxford Literary Review*, Sexual Difference issue, 18 (1986), 13–21, Simon Watney knocks down a travesty of what gender theory has been.

10. Monique Wittig, *The Straight Mind and Other Essays* (Hemel Hempstead: Harvester Wheatsheaf, 1992), 32.

11. Ibid. 30.

Extract 59

ELIZABETH WILSON: *Is Transgression Transgressive?*

1. Carol A Queen, 'Strangers at Home: Bisexuals in the Queer Movement', *Outlook* 16 (1992), 33.

Extract 60

LYNNE SEGAL: *Sexual Liberation and Feminist Politics*

1. See, for example, Barbara Einhorn, 'Where Have All the Women Gone? Women and the Women's Movement in East Central Europe', *Feminist Review*, 39 (Winter 1991).

2. A. E. Housman, *A Shropshire Lad*, xviii, 'Oh when I was in love with you' (London: Harrap, 1940), p. 30.

3. R. W. Connell, 'Democracies of Pleasure: Thoughts on the Goals of Radical Sexual Politics', in Linda Nicholson and Steven Seidman, *Social Postmodernism* (Cambridge: Cambridge University Press, 1995).

4. Samuel Janus and Cynthia Janus, *The Janus Report on Sexual Behavior* (New York: John Wiley, 1993); Ira Robinson *et al.*, 'Twenty Years of the Sexual Revolution, 1965–1985: An Update', *Journal of Marriage and the Family*, 53 (1991); Kaye Wellings *et al.*, *Sexual Behaviour in Britain* (Harmondsworth: Penguin, 1994).

5. All facts and figures are adapted from Kaye Wellings *et al.*, ibid., as reported by the authors in 'Sex and the British', *Independent on Sunday*, 16 Jan. 1994, pp. 5–8.

6. For example, Sue Lees and Lynn Ferguson, on *Dispatches*, Channel 4, 16 Feb. 1994; see also Sue Lees and Jeanne Gregory, *Rape and Sexual Assault: A Study of Attrition* (London: Islington Council, Police and Crime Prevention Unit, July 1993).

7. Using the framework of Catharine MacKinnon and Andrea Dworkin's Minneapolis Ordinance, Catherine Itzin in Britain has been seeking official backing for new anti-pornography legislation to replace the existing Obscene Publications Act. This would allow individuals who believed they had been harmed through pornography to seek compensation from those responsible for producing the 'harmful' images, making use of civil anti-discrimination law in the courts.

8. See Robin Gorna, 'From Anti-Porn to Eroticizing Safer Sex', and Jane Mills, 'Classroom Conundrums: Sex Education and Censorship', both in Lynne Segal and Mary McIntosh (eds.), *Sex Exposed: Sexuality and the Pornography Debate* (London: Virago, 1992).

9. Jackie Stacey, 'Promoting Normality: Section 28 and the Regulation of Sexuality', in Sarah Franklin *et al.* (eds.), *Off-Centre: Feminism and Cultural Studies* (London: Harper Collins, 1991), 310–12.

Extract 61

PAULA TREICHLER: *AIDS, Identity, and the Politics of Gender*

1. Gina Kolata, 'Ideas and Trends: Who is Female? Science Can't Say', *New York Times*, 16 Feb. 1992.
2. P. Clay Stephens, 'U. S. Women and HIV Infection', in Padraig O'Malley (ed.), *The AIDS Epidemic: Private Rights and the Public Interest* (Boston: Beacon, 1988), 381–401.
3. Robert E. Gould, 'Reassuring News About AIDS: A Doctor Tells Why You May Not Be at Risk', *Cosmopolitan*, 204/1 (Jan. 1988), 146.
4. ACT UP/NY Women's Book Group, *Women, AIDS, and Activism* (Boston: South End Press, 1992).

Extract 62

WENDY BROWN: *The Mirror of Pornography*

1. MacKinnon herself glimpses this: '[I]f you understand that pornography literally means what it says, you might conclude that sexuality has become the fascism of contemporary America and we are moving into the last days of Weimar' (*Feminism Unmodified* (Cambridge, Mass.: Harvard University Press, 1987), 15).
2. Nietzsche, *Twilight of the Idols*, in *The Portable Nietzsche*, ed. W. Kaufmann (New York: Viking, 1954).
3. *Feminism Unmodified*, 15.
4. *Beyond Accommodation: Ethical Feminism, Deconstruction, and the Law* (New York: Routledge, 1991), 119.

Extract 64

JACQUELINE ROSE: *Sexuality in the Field of Vision*

1. Freud, 'Some Psychical Consequences of the Anatomical Distinction between the Sexes', 252, 335–6.
2. Freud, *From the History of an Infantile Neurosis, (1918), The Standard Edition of the Complete Psychological Works*, 17 (London: Hogarth Press, 1955–74), 29–47; 80–1.
3. For a discussion of some of these issues in relation to feminist art, see Mary Kelly, 'Re-viewing Modernist Criticism', *Screen*, 22/3 (Autumn 1981).
4. 'Leonardo da Vinci and a Memory of his Childhood' (1910), SE 11: 95, 186–7.
5. The status of the woman as fantasy in relation to the desire of the man was a central concern of Lacan's later writing; see *Encore*, especially 'God and the Jouissance of Woman' and 'A Love Letter' in *Feminine Sexuality: Jacques Lacan and the École Freudienne*, ed. Juliet Mitchell and Jacqueline Rose (London: Macmillan, 1982).
6. Norman Bryson describes post-Albertian perspective in terms of such a restriction in *Vision and Painting: The Logic of the Gaze* (London: Macmillan, 1983).
7. See Lacan on death in Holbein's 'The Ambassadors', *The Four Fundamental Concepts*, 85–90.
8. 'Leonardo da Vinci and a Memory of his Childhood', 111, 203. An exhibition entitled *The Revolutionary Power of Women's Laughter*, including works by Barbara Kruger and Mary Kelly was held at Protetch McNeil, New York, Jan. 1983.

Extract 65

KAJA SILVERMANN: *The Acoustic Mirror*

1. Laura Mulvey, 'Visual Pleasure and Narrative Cinema', *Screen* 16, no. 3 (1975), p. 14.

2. Claire Johnston, 'Women's Cinema as Counter-Cinema', in *Notes on Women's Cinema*, ed. Claire Johnston (London: BFI, 1975), p. 26.

3. Claire Johnston, 'Dorothy Arzner: Critical Strategies', in *The World of Dorothy Arzner: Towards a Feminist Cinema* (London: BFI, 1975), p. 4. For another 'anti-systematic' reading of Arzner's work, see Pam Cook's essay 'Approaching the Work of Dorothy Arzner' in the same volume (pp. 9–18).

4. Sandy Flittermann, 'Woman, Desire, and the Look: Feminism and the Enunciative Apparatus in Cinema', in *Theories of Authorship*, ed. John Caughie (London, 1981), p. 248.

5. Jacquelyn Suter, 'Feminine Discourse in *Christopher Strong*', *Camera Obscura*, nos. 3/4 (1979): 135–50.

6. See Michel Foucault. *The History of Sexuality*, trans. Robert Hurley (New York, 1978), pp. 92–102, for a discussion of localized resistance.

7. Suter, 'Feminine Discourse in *Christopher Strong*', pp. 147–8.

8. *Ibid.*, p. 148.

9. Janet Bergstrom, '*Jeanne Dielman, 23 Quai du Commerce, 1080 Bruxelles*', *Camera Obscura*, no. 2 (1977): 114–18.

10. *Ibid.*, p. 117.

11. *Ibid.*, p. 118.

12. Modleski, 'Woman and the Labyrinth', in *The Women Who Knew Too Much: Hitchcock and Feminist Film Criticism* (New York, 1987).

13. Lea Jacobs, '*Now, Voyager*: Some Problems of Enunciation and Sexual Difference', *Camera Obscura*, no. 7 (1981): 89–109.

14. J. Laplanche and J. -B. Pontalis, *The Language of Psycho-analysis*, trans. Donald Nicholson-Smith (New York: 1973), p. 317.

15. Freud calls the first three of these 'primal fantasies' in 'A Case of Paranoia Running Counter to the Psycho-analytic Theory of the Disease', in *The Standard Edition*, vol. 14, p. 269. I have taken the liberty of adding the beating fantasy to the list. In *Introductory Lectures on Psycho-analysis*, Freud suggests that the primal fantasies were once 'real occurrences in the primaeval times of the human family', but have since become psychic reality (see *The Standard Edition*, vol. 16, p. 371).

16. For a discussion of the female version of the negative Oedipus complex, see chapters 4 and 5 of *The Aconstic Mirror*.

17. For a discussion of the female version of the negative Oedipus complex, see chapters 4 and 5.

18. See 'A Child Is Being Beaten', in *Collected Papers of Sigmund Freud*, trans. James and Alix Strachey (London: 1924), pp. 172–201. For an extended discussion of this essay, as well as the male version of the negative Oedipus complex, see my 'Masochism and Subjectivity (II)', in *Male Subjectivity at the Margins* (forthcoming).

19. This phrase comes from Laplanche and Pontalis, *The Language of Psycho-analysis*, p. 318.

20. See 'A Child Is Being Beaten'.

21. For an analysis of this film, see my 'Changing the Fantasmatic Scene', *Framework*, no. 20 (1983): 27–36.
22. For an extended discussion of the relationship between desire and narrative, see Teresa de Lauretis, 'Desire in Narrative', in *Alice Doesn't*, pp. 103–157.

Extract 66

ANNETTE KUHN: *The Body and Cinema*

1. 'Questions of Method', *Ideology and Consciousness*, 8 (1981), 3–14, at p. 13.
2. See Hubert L. Dreyfus and Paul Rabinow, *Michel Foucault: Beyond Structuralism and Hermeneutics* (Chicago, 1982), ch. 5, for an account of the Foucauldian understanding of power.
3. Annette Kuhn, 'Sexual Disguise and Cinema', in *The Power of the Image: Essays on Representation and Sexuality* (London, 1985), 48–73, addresses the theme of cross-dressing in Hollywood films as a potential challenge to the 'natural' order of sexual difference proposed by cinema.
4. Sigmund Freud, 'Fetishism', (1927), in *The Standard Edition of the Complete Psychological Works of Sigmund Freud*, 21 (London, 1953–74), 152–7; Laura Mulvey, 'Visual Pleasure and Narrative Cinema', *Screen*, 16/3 (1975), 6–18; Linda Williams, 'When the Woman Looks', in Mary Anne Doane *et al.* (eds.), *Re-Vision: Essays in Feminist Film Criticism* (Los Angeles, 1984), 83–99.
5. It is significant that neither Bev, nor—interestingly—Carla, are among the women featured on the poster for *Pumping Iron II*.
6. Teresa de Lauretis, in 'Aesthetic and Feminist Theory: Rethinking Women's Cinema', *New German Critique*, 34 (1985), 154–75, discusses differences of race and class in this context. Both of these—but especially considerations of race—are of relevance to a reading of *Pumping Iron II*.
7. The productive potential of censorship is discussed in Annette Kuhn, *Cinema, Censorship and Sexuality, 1909–1925* (London), ch. 8.
8. De Lauretis, 'Aesthetic and Feminist Theory', 154.
9. Biddy Martin, 'Feminist Criticism and Foucault', *New German Critique*, 27 (1982), 3–30, at pp. 12–13.

Extract 67

E. ANN KAPLAN: *Whose Imaginary? The Televisual Apparatus, the Female Body and Textual Strategies in Select Rock Videos on MTV*

1. The term 'social Imaginary' brings together concepts developed by Jacques Lacan, Louis Althusser, Roland Barthes, and others. In particular, it combines Lacan's notions of the subject split at the moment of entry into the Symbolic with Althusser's conception of Ideological State Apparatuses. The two most relevant texts here are Lacan's 'The Mirror Stage as Formative of the I', reprinted in *Écrits: A Selection*, tr. Alan Sheridan (London and New York: W. W. Norton and Co., 1979), 1–7; and Louis Althusser, 'Ideology and Ideological State Apparatuses (Notes Towards an Investigation)', in *Lenin and Philosophy and Other Essays*, tr. Ben Brewster (New York and London: Monthly Review Press, 1971), 127–86.

   MTV—Music Television—is a twenty-four-hour, non-stop cable station for which subscribers do not pay an extra fee. It is made up of rock video, VJs'

('video jockeys') comments, music news, interviews with rock stars, advertisements by sponsors and advertisements for MTV itself. MTV is beamed across
America wherever cable service exists and latest audience figures are 28 million,
ranging in age from 12 to 34.

2. Jean Baudrillard, 'The Ecstasy of Communication', in Hal Foster (ed.), *The Anti-
Aesthetic: Essays in Postmodern Culture* (Port Townsend: Washington Bay Press,
1983), 125–38.

3. For more discussion of these differences generally, see Sandy Flitterman, 'Fascination in Fragments: Psychoanalysis in Film and Television', in Robert Allen (ed.),
Channels of Discourse: Television Criticism in the 80's, (Chapel Hill: North Carolina
University Press, 1987). An expanded version of the present essay, particularly in
relation to differences between movie and television screens, can be found in E.
Ann Kaplan, *Rocking Around the Clock: Music Television, Postmodernism and Consumer Culture* (London and New York: Methuen, 1987).

4. Althusser, 'Ideology and Ideological State Apparatuses (Notes Towards an Investigation)', 162.

5. Sandy Flitterman, 'The Real Soap Operas: TV Commercials', in *Regarding Television: A Critical Anthology E. Ann Kaplan (ed.)*, (Los Angeles: American Film
Institute, 1983), 84–96. See also my article in *Channels of Discourse*.

6. For details of these arguments, see Kaplan, *Rocking Around the Clock*.

7. Robert Stam, 'Television News and Its Spectator', in Kaplan (ed.), *Regarding
Television*, 23–44.

8. Peggy Phelan, 'Panopticism and the Uncanny: Notes Toward Television's Visual
Time', unpublished paper, 1986.

9. For further discussion of the classic avant-garde film polarity and of Chart 2, see
Kaplan, *Rocking Around the Clock*.

10. Fredric Jameson, 'Postmodernism and Consumer Society', in Foster (ed.), *The
Anti-Aesthetic*, 113.

11. Jane Brown and Kenneth C. Campbell, 'The Same Beat But a Different Drum-
mer: Race and Gender in Music Videos', *Journal of Communication*, 36/1 (1986), 94–
106. That the video is directed by a woman, Mary Lambert, does not alter my
assessment of the video as post-feminist. I would not want to collapse biological
gender with ideological stance.

Extract 68

RITA FELSKI: *The Dialectic of 'Feminism' and 'Aesthetics'*

1. Janet Wolff, *Aesthetics and the Sociology of Art* (London: Allen and Unwin, 1983), 11.

2. See Pierre Macherey, *Theory of Literary Production*, tr. Geoffrey Wall (London:
Routledge and Kegan Paul, 1878), 51–5.

3. See Janet Wolff, *The Social Production of Art* (London: Macmillan, 1981), esp. ch. 2.

4. Nina Baym, *Women's Fiction: A Guide to Novels by and about Women in America, 1820–
1870* (Ithaca NY: Cornell University Press, 1978), 14.

5. Michèle Barrett, 'Feminism and the Definition of Cultural Politics', in Rosalind
Brunt and Caroline Rowan (eds.), *Feminism, Culture and Politics* (London: Lawrence and Wishart, 1982), 50.

6. See Raymond Williams, *Marxism and Literature* (Oxford: Oxford University Press, 1977), 155–6.

7. Patrocinio Schweickart, 'Comments on Jehlens' "Archimedes and the Paradox of Feminist Criticism" ', *Signs*, 8/1 (1982), 175.

8. Peter Bürger, *Theory of the Avant-Garde*, tr. Michael Shaw (Minneapolis: University of Minnesota Press, 1984), 53–4.

9. See for example, Lynne Segal, *Is the Future Female? Troubled Thoughts on Contemporary Feminism* (London: Virago, 1987), and Judith Stacey, 'The New Conservative Feminism', *Feminist Studies*, 9/3 (1983), 559–84.

Extract 69

GRISELDA POLLOCK: *Missing Women: Rethinking Early Thoughts on Images of Women*

1. Jean Laplanche and Jean-Bertrand Pontalis, 'Fantasy and the Origins of Sexuality', in Victor Burgin (ed.), *Formations of Fantasy* (London: Methuen, 1986).

Extract 70

ABIGAIL SOLOMON GODEAU: *Just Like a Woman*

1. The bibliography of articles dealing with what could be termed the problematics of the look is (significantly) both recent and extensive. Much of the critical discussion has been generated by feminist film theory. A partial listing of major essays would include the now-classic text of Laura Mulvey, 'Visual Pleasure and Narrative Cinema,' in *Rethinking Representation: Art after Modernism*, ed. Brian Willis (Boston: David R. Godine, 1985), 375–90; Constance Penley, ' "A Certain Refusal of Difference": Feminist Film Theory' in Wallis, *ibid.*, 361–74; Mary Ann Doane, 'Film and the Masquerade—Theorizing the Female Spectator,' *Screen*, vol. XXV, nos. 3–4 (Sept. —Oct. 1982), 74–88; Mary Ann Doane, 'Woman's Stake: Filming the Female Body,' *October* 17 (Summer 1981), 23–36; Linda Williams, 'When the Woman Looks,' in *Re-Visions: Feminist Essays in Film Analysis*, ed. Patricia Mellencamp, Mary Ann Doane, and Linda Williams (Los Angeles: American Film Institute, 1985). For a more general discussion see Annette Kuhn, *Women's Pictures: Feminism and Cinema* (London: Routledge & Kegan Paul, 1982); E. Ann Kaplan, *Women and Film: Both Sides of the Camera* (London and New York: Methuen, 1983). The British journal *M/F* and the American *Camera Obscura* have consistently explored these issues.

2. See Mulvey, 'Visual Pleasure,' and Doane, 'Film and the Masquerade.'

3. See Mulvey, 'Visual Pleasure and Narrative Cinema.'

4. Here again, the bibliography is quite substantial. Some relevant essays include: Judith Barry and Sandy Flitterman, 'Textual Strategies—The Politics of Art Making,' *Screen*, vol. XXI, no. 2 (Summer 1980), 35–48; Silvia Bovenschen, 'Is There a Female Aesthetic?' trans. Beth Weckmueller, *New German Critique*, no. 10 (Winter 1977), 111–37; Rachel Blau DuPlessis and Members of Workshop 9, 'For the Etruscans: Sexual Difference and Artistic Production—The Debate Over a Female Aesthetic," in *The Future of Difference*, eds. Hester Eisenstein and Alice Jardine (New Brunswick, NJ: Rutgers University Press, 1980), 128–56.

Extract 71

LYNDA NEAD: *Getting Down to Basics: Art, Obscenity and the Female Nude*

1. For a useful summary of Kant's *Critique of Aesthetic Judgement* see Roger Scruton, *Kant* (Oxford, 1982) on which the following discussion is based.
2. Jacques Derrida, *The Truth in Painting*, tr. G. Bennington and I. McLeod (Chicago and London, 1987), 45.
3. Immanuel Kant, *Critique of Aesthetic Judgement*, tr. J. C. Meredith (Oxford, 1911), 90.
4. Kant goes on to argue that it is through this experience of the sublime that we are made aware of divinity. He thus sets up an uneasy tension within the category of the sublime—the site of the divine but also, at the same time, beyond control and fearful. The aesthetic of the sublime and its reworking within post-modernist philosophy is considered by Dick Hebdidge in his fascinating article 'The Impossible Object: Towards a Sociology of the Sublime', *New Formations*, 1 (Spring 1987), 47–76.
5. Immanuel Kant, *Observations on the Feeling of the Beautiful and Sublime* (1764), tr. J. H. Goldthwait (Berkeley and Los Angeles, 1960), 76–7.
6. James Joyce, *A Portrait of the Artist as a Young Man* (Harmondsworth, 1960), 204–5.
7. Derrida, *The Truth in Painting*, 73.

Extract 72

PEGGY PHELAN: *Broken Symmetries: Memory, Sight, Love*

1. Julia Kristeva, 'Ellipsis on Dread and the Specular Seduction', quoted in Jacqueline Rose, *Sexuality in the Field of Vision* (London: Verso, 1986), 141.
2. The best discussion of Lacanian doubt can be found in Joan Copjec, 'Vampires, Breast-Feeding and Anxiety' in *Rendering the Real, a Special Issue*, guest ed. Parveen Adams, *October 58* (Fall 1995) 25–44.
3. Judith Butler, 'The Force of Fantasy: Feminism, Mapplethorpe, and Discursive Excess', *Differences*, 2/2 (summer, 1990), 105–25.
4. The two most relevant meditations on the contemporary legal real in the United States are Jane Gaines's fascinating essay, 'Dead Ringer: Jacqueline Onassis and the Look-alike', which examines a case of a model, Barbara Reynolds, who appears in an ad for Christian Dior. The model's 'art' is her ability to look like Onassis. Onassis sued Dior and the ad agency for using her image without permission. Gaines formulates the questions raised by this case in terms of the 'right' to appropriate/exploit/protect what both Onassis and Reynolds already own—their image. Patricia Williams's provocative book *The Alchemy of Race and Rights* examines the legal real in terms of the historical force of racist marks defining citizenry. While there are serious problems with Williams's work as 'legal theory', hers is an extraordinarily enabling book. Williams reimagines the categories and interests by which the legal real is constituted and maintained.
5. The best essay on feminism and the theatrical real is Elin Diamond's 'Mimesis, Mimicry and the True-Real'. She re-reads Irigaray's re-reading of Plato and suggests that there is no original without a notion of a mimetic copy—including the 'original' Mother. Lynda Hill's 'Staging Hurston's Life and Work' considers the tricky politics of race and representation in relation to Zora Neale Hurston's

attempt to reproduce 'authentic folk' community and contemporary drama's attempt to restage the story of her life and work 'authentically'.

6. The best discussion of the Lacanian Real can be found in *October* 58: 'Rendering the Real A Special Issue', guest editor Parveen Adams. Also see Slavoj Žižek, *The Sublime Object of Ideology*. Throughout this book, the Lacanian Real shall be distinguished from other versions of the real by use of the upper-case R.

7. In the vast library of autobiographical criticism see Phillip Lejeune, *On Autobiography* and Bella Brodzki and Celeste Schenck (eds.), *Life/Lines*, for preliminary discussions of how the real defines the autobiographical.

8. Slavoj Žižek tells the tale of the reception of *Rashomon* (1950). Kurosawa's film was hailed as the 'classic' Japanese film throughout the United States and Europe and won the 1951 Golden Lion in Venice. But it failed terribly in Japan because it was considered 'too European'. Each culture employed the frame of the Other to define its relation to the representational text—not surprisingly the frame of the Other brought these others to opposite conclusions about the 'same' representational text. Slavoj Žižek, 'Lacan's Return to the Cartesian *Cogito*', a talk delivered in the English Department, New York University, Dec. 1991.

9. Harold Bloom, 'Agon: Revisionism and Critical Personality', *Raritan* (Summer 1981), 18–47, at p. 44.

10. Jacques Derrida, *Disseminations*, tr. Barbara Johnson (Chicago: University of Chicago Press, 1981), 173–226.

Extract 73

SUSAN BORDO: *Normalization and Resistance in the Era of the Image*

1. Jean Bandrillard, *Simulations* (New York: Semiotexte, 1983).
2. Susan Bordo, 'Material Girl: The Effacements of Postmodern Culture', *Michigan Quarterly Review*, 29/4 (1990), 653–78.
3. bell hooks, *Yearning: Race and Gender and Cultural Politics* (Boston: South End Press, 1990), 22.

Extract 74

KATE CHEDGZOY: *Frida Kahlo's 'Grotesque Bodies'*

1. Jacqui Duckworth, 'Coming out Twice', in Tessa Boffin and Jean Fraser (eds.), *Stolen Glances: Lesbians Take Photographs* (London: Pandora, 1991), 155–61.
2. Gayatri Chakravorty Spivak, *In Other Worlds* (London: Methuen, 1987), 150.
3. Joan Borsa, 'Frida Kahlo: Marginalization and the Critical Female Subject', *Third Test*, 3 (1990), 21–40.
4. Ibid. 28.
5. Julia Kristeva, *Powers of Horror: An Essay on Abjection*, tr. Leon S. Roudiez (New York: Columbia University Press, 1982).
6. Mikhail Mikhailovich Bakhtin, *Rabelais and his World*, tr. Helene Iswolsky (Cambridge, Mass.: MIT Press, 1968).
7. Throughout this essay, I use the term 'grotesque' in the specifically Bakhtinian sense. It should not be taken to imply an aesthetic evaluation of Kahlo's body.

8. Despite Kahlo's commodification, and the extensive interest in her life and work in recent years, there are few substantial studies. Those which do exist tend to situate her work in relation to some combination of Marxism, feminism, Surrealism, psychoanalysis, or the Mexican cultural context. Useful articles include Laura Mulvey, 'Frida Kahlo and Tina Modotti', in her *Visual and Other Pleasures* (London: Macmillan, 1990), originally written with Peter Wollen for a 1982 exhibition at the Whitechapel Art Gallery, London; and Terry Smith, 'From the Margins: Modernity and the Case of Frida Kahlo', *Block*, 8 (1983), Hayden Herrera's massive and fascinating biography, *Frida* (London: Bloomsbury, 1989) is indispensable, but marred by Herrera's lack of awareness of her own positioning.

9. Whitney Chadwick, *Women Artists and the Surrealist Movement* (London: Thames & Hudson, 1985), 87.

10. Cited by Herrera, *Frida*, 254–5.

11. Cited by Chadwick, *Women Artists*, 88.

12. Oriana Baddeley and Valerie Fraser, *Drawing the Line: Art and Cultural Identity in Contemporary Latin America* (London: Verso, 1989), 92.

13. Kahlo frequently chose to wear—and to paint herself wearing—the flamboyant costume of the Tehuantepec region of Mexico. It served to affirm the Mexican peasant side of her *mestizo* identity; moreover, according to Hayden Herrera, 'Tehuantepec women are famous for being stately, beautiful, sensuous, intelligent, brave, and strong. Folklore has it that theirs is a matriarchal society' *Frida*, 109.

14. Jean Franco, *Plotting Women: Gender and Representation in Mexico* (London: Verso, 1989), p. xxiii.

15. Ibid. 107.

16. Kristeva, *Powers of Horror*, 61.

17. Jacqueline Rose, *The Haunting of Sylvia Plath* (London: Virago, 1991), 33–4.

18. Examples offered by Kristeva of such abject phenomena, and the strategies used to render them manageable, include anything from the skin on milk, via the human corpse, to the entire edifice of Jewish dietary prohibitions.

19. In *Powers of Horror*, Kristeva takes the notoriously fascist and anti-semitic writer Louis Ferdinand Céline as an emblematic artist of abjection. To my surprise, I have not been able to find any work which uses the notion of abjection to explore constructs of racial otherness, but I am currently engaged on such a project myself, with particular reference to seventeenth-century representations of racial and sexual otherness, from Shakespeare's *Othello* (1604) to Aphra Behn's *Oroonoko* (1688).

20. Julia Kristeva, *Revolution in Poetic Language* (New York: Columbia University Press, 1984).

21. Julia Kristeva, 'A question of subjectivity', interview with Susan Sellers in *Women's Review* 12 (1986), 19–22.

22. Kristeva, *Powers of Horror*, 54.

23. Jennifer Stone, 'The Horrors of Power: A Critique of "Kristeva"', in Francis Barker *et al.* (eds.), *The Politics of Theory* (Colchester: University of Essex, 1983), 38–48. Stone argues that Kristeva's work is of questionable value to a radical political agenda, since her theory of abjection is elaborated primarily in relation to the anti-semitic, misogynist and fascist texts of Céline, and it is by no means clear

in *Powers of Horror* whether she conceives of her writing as descriptive or prescriptive.

24. Mary Russo, 'Female Grotesques: Carnival and Theory', in Teresa de Lauretis (ed.), *Feminist Studies/Critical Studies* (London: Macmillan, 1988, 213–29.

25. Bakhtin, *Rabelais and his World*, 19.

26. Karen Petersen and J. J. Wilson, *Women Artists: Recognition and Reappraisal from the Early Middle Ages to the Twentieth Century* (London: Women's Press, 1978), 134.

27. Angela Carter, *Frida Kahlo* (London: Redstone Press, 1989).

28. Russo, 'Female Grotesques', 213.

29. Michael Newman, 'The Ribbon around the Bomb', *Art in America* (Apr. 1983), 161–9.

30. Mara R. Witzling, *Voicing our Visions: Writings by Women Artists* (London: Women's Press, 1992), 294.

Extract 76

DONNA HARAWAY: *A Manifesto for Cyborgs: Science, Technology, and Socialist Feminism in the 1980s*

1. Frans de Waal, *Chimpanzee Politics: Power and Sex among the Apes* (New York: Harper & Row, 1982); Langdon Winner, 'Do Artifacts have Politics?', *Daedalus* (Winter 1980), 121–36.

2. 'Women's Place in the Integrated Circuit', *Radical America*, 14/1 (1980), 29–50.

Extract 77

MICHELLE STANWORTH: *Reproductive Technologies: Tampering with Nature?*

1. R. P. Petchesky, *Abortion and Woman's Choice: The State, Sexuality and Reproductive Freedom* (Boston: Northeastern University Press, London: Verso, 1985, 1986).

2. J. Raymond, 'Preface', in G. Corea, R. Duelli Klein, et al., *Man-Made Women: How New Reproductive Technologies Affect Women* (London: Hutchinson, 1985), 12.

3. M. O'Brien, *The Politics of Reproduction* (London: Routledge & Kegan Paul, 1983).

4. J. Hanmer, 'Transforming Consciousness: Women and the New Reproductive Technologies', in Corea et al., *Man-Made Women*, 104.

5. R. Rowland, 'Motherhood, Patriarchal Power, Alienation and the Issue of "Choice" in Sex Preselection', in Corea et al., *Man-Made Women*, 75.

6. G. Corea, *The Mother Machine: Reproductive Technologies from Artificial Insemination to Artificial Wombs* (New York: Harper & Row, 1985), 3.

7. K. Luker, *Abortion and the Politics of Motherhood* (Berkeley and London: University of California Press, 1984), 168–9.

8. R. Rapp, 'Feminists and Pharmacrats', *The Women's Review of Books*, 11/10 (July 1985), 4.

9. A. McLaren, *Reproductive Rituals* (London: Methuen., 1984).

10. J. R. Wilkie, 'Involuntary Childlessness in the United States', *Boldt Verlag Boppard Zeitschrift für Bevolkerungswissenschaft*, 10/1 (1984), 37–52.

11. E. Lewin, 'By Design: Reproductive Strategies and the Meaning of Motherhood', in Homans (ed.), *The Sexual Politics of Reproduction* (Aldershot: Gower, 1985).

Extract 78

SARAH FRANKLIN: *Fetal Fascinations*

1. R. Petchesky, *Abortion and Woman's Choice: The State, Sexuality and Reproductive Freedom* (Boston: Northeastern University Press, 1985), and 'Foetal Images: The Power of Visual Culture in the Politics of Reproduction', in M. Stanworth (ed.), *Reproductive Technologies: Gender, Motherhood and Medicine* (Cambridge: Polity Press, 1987); J. Gallagher, 'Fetal Personhood and Women's Policy', in V. Sapiro (ed.), *Women, Biology and Public Policy* (Beverly Hills, Calif.: Sage, 1985).
2. A. L. R. Findlay, *Reproduction and the Fetus* (London: Edward Arnold, 1984), 96.
3. *TIME* Inc. 1980, p. 1.
4. C. Pateman, *The Sexual Contract* (Cambridge: Polity Press, 1988); M. Wittig, 'On the Social Contract', in D. Altman *et al.*, *Homosexuality, Which Homosexuality?* (London: Gay Men's Press, 1988).
5. E. F. Keller, *Reflections on Science and Gender* (New Haven: Yale University Press, 1985).
6. B. Ehrenreich and D. English, *For Her Own Good: 150 Years of the Experts' Advice to Women* (London: Pluto Press, 1979); E. Martin, *The Woman in the Body: A Cultural Analysis of Reproduction* (Boston: Beacon Press, 1987); T. Lacqueur, 'Orgasm, Generation and the Politics of Reproductive Biology', *representations* (special issue: 'Sexuality and the Social Body in the Nineteenth Century'), 14 (1986), 1–41; A. Oakley, *The Captured Womb: A History of the Medical Care of Pregnant Women* (Oxford: Basil Blackwell, 1984).

Extract 79

CONSTANCE PENLEY: *Brownian Motion: Women, Tactics, and Technology*

1. Sarah Lefanu, *Feminism and Science Fiction* (Bloomington: Indiana University Press, 1989), 2.
2. Michel de Certeau, *The Practice of Everyday Life*, tr. Steven F. Rendall (Berkeley: University of California Press, 1984).
3. Ibid., p. xx.

Extract 80

MARILYN STRATHERN: *Less Nature, More Technology*

1. Michelle Stanworth (ed.), *Reproductive Technologies: Gender, Motherhood and Medicine* (Cambridge: Polity Press, 1987); Susan Magarey, 'Women and Technological Change', *Australian Feminist Studies*, 1 (1985), 91–103; Patricia Spallane and Deborah L. Steinberg (eds.), *Made to Order* (London: Pergamon Press, 1987); Anthony Dyson and John Harris, *Experiments on Embryos* (London: Routledge, 1990).
2. Jonathan Glover *et al.*, *Fertility and the Family: The Glover Report on Reproductive Technologies to the European Commission* (London: Fourth Estate, 1989), 18.
3. David Schneider, *American Kinship* (Englewood Cliffs, NJ: Prentice-Hall, 1968).

Extract 81

MARIA MIES AND VANDANA SHIVA: *Ecofeminism*

1. I. Diamond and G. F. Orenstein, *Reweaving the World: The Emergence of Ecofeminism* (San Francisco: Sierra Club Books, 1990), J. Plant, *Healing the Wounds: The Promise of Ecofeminism* (Philadelphia and Santa Cruz, Calif.: New Society Publishers, 1989).
2. F. D'Eaubonne, 'Feminism or Death', in Elaine Marks and Isabelle de Courtivron (eds.), *New French Feminisms, an Anthology* (Amherst: Amherst University Press, 1980).
3. Y. King, 'The Eco-Feminist Perspective', in L. Caldecott and S. Leland (eds.), *Reclaiming the Earth: Women Speak out for Life on Earth* (London: The Women's Press, 1983), 10.
4. Ibid. 11.
5. F. Howard-Gorden, 'Seveso is Everywhere', in Caldecott and Leland, *Reclaiming the Earth*, 36–45.
6. Statement of Sicilian Women, quoted in Caldecott and Leland, *Reclaiming the Earth*, 126.
7. C. Merchant, *The Death of Nature. Women, Ecology and the Scientific Revolution* (San Francisco: Harper & Row, 1983).
8. Caldecott and Leland, *Reclaiming the Earth*, 15.
9. S. Sarkar, 'Die Bewegung und ihre Strategie. Ein Beitrag zum notwendigen Klärungsprozeβ', in *Kommune* (Frankfurt, 1987).

Extract 82

SADIE PLANT: *Beyond the Screens: Film, Cyberpunk and Cyberfeminism*

1. Raymond Kurzweil, *The Age of Intelligent Machines*, MIT (London and Cambridge, Mass.: MIT Press, 1991), 164.
2. Trisna Ziff. 'Taking New Ideas back to the Old World: Talking to Esther Parada, Hector Mendez Caratini and Pedro Meyer', in Paul Wombell (ed.), *Photovideo: Photography in the Age of the Computer* (London: Rivers Oram Press, 1991), 131.
3. 'A Cyborg Manifesto', this collection, p. xx.
4. Paul Virilio, *War and Cinema* (London: Verso, 1989).
5. Allucquere Rosanne Stone, 'Will the Real Body Please Stand Up?': Boundary Stories about Virtual Cultures', Michael Benedict, *Cyberspace. First Steps* (Cambridge Mass.: MIT Press, 1991), 109.
6. 'A Cyborg Manifesto', this collection, p. xx.

Extract 83

CAROL STABILE: *Feminism and the Technological Fix*

1. Evelyn Fox Keller, *Reflections on Science and Gender* (New Haven: Yale University Press, 1985); Sandra Harding, *The Science Question in Feminism* (Ithaca) NY: Cornell University Press, 1986); Helen Longino, *Science as Social Knowledge* (Princeton: Princeton University Press, 1990).
2. Ynestra King, 'The Ecology of Feminism and the Feminism of Ecology', in Judith Plant (ed.), *Healing the Wounds: The Promise of Ecofeminism* (Philadelphia: New Society Publishers, 1989), 22.

3. Katha Pollitt, 'Marooned on Gilligan's Island: Are Women Morally Superior to Men?', *The Nation*, 28 (Dec. 1992), 801.

4. Rosemary Hennessy, *Materialist Feminism and the Politics of Discourse* (New York: Routledge, 1993), 47.

5. Donna Haraway, *Simians, Cyborgs and Women* (New York: Routledge, 1991), 187.

6. Donna Haraway, 'Cyborgs at Large', in Constance Penley and Andrew Ross (eds.), *Technoculture* (Minneapolis: University of Minnesota Press, 1991), 8.

7. Haraway, *Simians, Cyborgs and Women*, 154.

8. Pierre Bourdieu, *Distinction: A Social Critique of the Judgement of Taste*, tr. Richard Nice (Cambridge, Mass.: Harvard University Press, 1984), 498.

9. Haraway, *Simians, Cyborgs and Women*, 149.

10. Haraway, 'The Promises of Monsters: A Regenerative Politics for Inappropriate/d Others', in Larry Grossberg, Cary Nelson, and Paula Treichler (eds.), *Cultural Studies* (New York: Routledge, 1991), 295.

11. Donna Haraway, 'Situated Knowledges', *Feminist Studies* 14/3 (1988), 580, and *Simians, Cyborgs and Women*, 187(emphases added).

12. Hennessy, *Materialist Feminism and the Politics of Discourse*, 136.

13. Harraway, 'The Promises of Monsters', 329.

Extract 84

CYNTHIA COCKBURN AND RUŽA FÜRST-DILIĆ: *Looking for the Gender/Technology Relation*

1. Ruth Schwartz Cowan, *More Work for Mother: The Ironies of Household Technology from the Open Hearth to the Microwave* (London: Free Association Books, 1989).

2. R. Silverstone, E. Hirsch, and D. Morley, 'Information and Communication Technologies and the Moral Economy of the Household', in Silverstone and Hirsch (eds.), *Consuming Technologies: Media and Information in Domestic Spaces* (London and New York: Routledge, 1992).

3. Jean-Claude Kaufmann, 'Les Deux Mondes de la vaisselle [The two worlds of washing-up]', in A. Gras and M. Caroline (eds.), *Technologies du quotidien: La Complainte du progrès [Everyday Technologies: The Lament of Progress]* (Paris: Éditions Autrement, 1992).

Extract 86

ROSI BRAIDOTTI: *Cyberfeminism with a Difference*

1. Stuart Hall, 'Race, Nation: the Fateful/Fatal Triangel', The W. E. B. Du Bois lectures, Harvard University, 25–7, Apr. 1994.

2. See especially Rosi Braidotti, 'Refiguring the Subject', in *Nomadic Subjects* (New York: Columbia University Press, 1994).

3. Frederic Jameson, *Postmodernism: Or the Cultural Logic of Late Capitalism* (New York: Columbia University Press, 1994).

4. Marleen Barr, *Alien to Femininity: Speculative Fiction and Feminist Theory* (New York: Greenwood, 1987).

5. Remark at the Conference 'Seduced and Abandoned: the Body in the Virtual World', held at the Institute of Contemporary Arts, London, 12–13 Mar. 1994.

6. *Post Human*, catalogue of the exhibition at Dieichtorhallen, Hamburg, 1993.

7. Francis Barker, *The Tremulous Private Body: Essays on Subjection* (London: Methuen, 1984)

8. Caren Kaplan and Inderpal Crewal (eds.), *Scattered Hegemonies: Postmodernity and Transnational Feminist Practices* (Minneapolis: University of Minnesota Press, 1994).

9. Evelyn Fox Keller and C. R. Croptowski, 'The Mind's Eye', in Sandra Harding and Merrill Hintikka (eds.), *Discovering Reality* (Dordrecht: Reidal Publishing Company, 1993), 207–24; Luce Irigaray, *Speculum* (Paris: Minuit, 1974); Donna Haraway, 'A Cyborg Manifesto', in *Simians, Cyborgs and Women* (London: Free Association Books, 1990), 149–82; Haraway, 'Simulated Knowledges', ibid. 183–202.

10. Kathy Acker, *In Memoriam to Identity* (New York: Pantheon, 1990).

11. See, for instance, Naomi Schor, 'Dreaming Dissymmetry: Foucault, Barthes and Feminism', in Alice Jordine and Paul Smith (eds.), *Men in Feminism* (New York: Methuen, 1987); Tania Modleski, *Feminism Without Women: Culture and Criticism in a 'Postfeminist' Age* (London: Routledge, 1991).

12. Rosi Braidotti, 'Discontinuous Becomings: Deleuze on the Becoming-Woman of Philosophy', *Journal of the British Society for Phenomenology,* 24/1 (Jan. 1993), 44–55.

13. Braidotti, *Nomadic Subjects.*

14. Mary Ann Doane, *The Desire to Desire: The Womens' Film of the 1940s* (Bloomington: Indiana University Press, 1987).

15. Susan Kappeler, *The Pornography of Representation* (Cambridge: Polity Press, 1987).

16. bell hooks, *Yearning* (London: Turnaround, 1991).

17. Remark at the Conference 'Seduced and Abandoned: The Body in the Virtual World'.

Select Additional Bibliography

I. ACADEMIES

ARMSTRONG, ISOBEL (ed.), *New Feminist Discourses: Critical Essays on Theories and Texts* (London and New York: Routledge, 1992).

BENSTOCK, SHARI (ed.), *Feminist Issues in Literary Scholarship* (Bloomington, Ind.: Indiana University Press, 1987).

DE LAURETIS, TERESA (ed.), *Feminist Studies: Critical Studies* (Bloomington, Ind.: Indiana University Press, 1986).

GUNEW, SNEJA, and YEATMAN, ANNA (eds.), *Feminism and the Politics of Difference* (Sydney: Allen and Unwin, 1993).

HEKMAN, SUSAN, *Gender and Knowledge: Elements of a Postmodern Feminism* (Cambridge: Polity Press, 1990).

HULL, GLORIA T., BELL-SCOTT, PATRICIA, and SMITH, BARBARA, *All the Women are Black, All the Blacks are Men, But Some of Us are Brave: Black Women's Studies* (Old Westbury, NY: Feminist Press, 1982).

MODLESKI, TANIA, *Feminism Without Women* (New York and London: Routledge, 1992).

MORAGA, CHERRIE, and ANZALDUA, GLORIA, *This Bridge Called My Back: Writings by Radical Women of Color* (Latham, NY: Kitchen Table Press, 1984).

PARKER, ROZIKA, and POLLOCK, GRISELDA (eds.), *Framing Feminism: Art and the Women's Movement 1970–1985* (London: Pandora, 1987).

PATEMAN, CAROLE, and GROSZ, ELIZABETH (eds.), *Feminist Challenges: Social and Political Theory* (Sydney: Allen and Unwin, 1986).

SEGAL, LYNNE, *Is the Future Female? Troubled Thoughts on Contemporary Feminism* (London: Virago, 1987).

SPELMAN, ELIZABETH, *Inessential Woman: Problems of Exclusion in Feminist Thought* (London: The Women's Press, 1990).

STANTON, DONNA (ed.), *Feminisms in the Academy* (Ann Arbor: University of Michigan Press, 1995).

WANDOR, MICHELENE (ed.), *Once a Feminist: Stories of a Generation* (London: Virago, 1990).

II. EPISTEMOLOGIES

AIKEN, SUSAN HARDY, et al. (eds.), *Changing our Minds: Feminist Transformation of Knowledge* (Albany, NY: State University of New York Press, 1988).

ALCOFF, LINDA, and POTTER, ELIZABETH (eds.), *Feminist Epistemologies* (New York: Routledge, 1993).

ALLEN, JEFFNER (ed.), *Lesbian Philosophies and Cultures* (Albany, NY: State University of New York Press, 1990).

ANTONY, LOUISE M., and WITT, CHARLOTTE (eds.), *A Mind of One's Own: Feminist Essays on Reason and Objectivity* (Boulder, Colo.: Westview Press, 1992).

BORDO, SUSAN, and JAGGAR, ALISON (eds.), *Gender/Body/Knowledge: Feminist Reconstructions of Being and Knowing* (New Brunswick, NJ: Rutgers University Press, 1989).

CODE, LORRAINE, *What Can She Know? Feminist Theory and the Construction of Knowledge* (Ithaca, NY: Cornell University Press, 1991).

CROWLEY, HELEN, and HIMMELWEIT, SUSAN (eds.), *Knowing Women: Feminism and Knowledge* (Cambridge: Polity Press, 1992).

LE DOEUFF, MICHÈLE, *Hipparchia's Choice*, trans. Trista Selous (Oxford: Blackwell, 1989).

DURAN, JANE, *Toward a Feminist Epistemology* (Savage, MD: Rowman & Littlefield, 1990).

FRASER, NANCY, *Unruly Practices: Power, Discourse and Gender in Contemporary Social Theory* (Minneapolis: University of Minnesota Press; 1989).

GARRY, ANN, and PEARSALL, MARILYN, *Women, Knowledge and Reality: Explorations in Feminist Philosophy* (New York: Routledge, Chapman & Hall, 1996).

GRANT, JUDITH, *Fundamental Feminism: Contesting the Core Concepts of Feminist Theory* (New York: Routledge, 1993).

GREEN, KAREN, *The Woman of Reason: Feminism, Humanism and Political Thought* (Cambridge: Polity Press, 1995).

GRIFFITHS, MORWENNA, and WHITFORD, MARGARET (eds.), *Feminist Perspectives in Philosophy* (Bloomington, Ind.: Indiana University Press, 1988).

GRIMSHAW, JEAN, *Philosophy and Feminist Thinking* (Minneapolis: University of Minnesota Press, 1986).

GUNEW, SNEJA (ed.), *Feminist Knowledge: Critique and Construct* (London and New York: Routledge, 1990).

HARDING, SANDRA, *Whose Science? Whose Knowledge? Thinking from Women's Lives* (Ithaca, NY: Cornell University Press, 1991).

—— and HINTIKKA, MERRILL B. (eds.), *Discovering Reality: Feminist Perspectives on Epistemology, Metaphysics, Methodology, and Philosophy of Science* (Dordrecht: Reidel, 1983).

HEKMAN, SUSAN J., *Moral Voices, Moral Selves: Carol Gilligan and Feminist Moral Theory* (University Park, Pa.: Pennsylvania State University Press, 1995).

JAGGAR, ALISON M., *Living with Contradictions: Controversies in Feminist Social Ethics* (Boulder, Colo.: Westview Press, 1994).

LARRABEE, MARY JEANNE (ed.), *An Ethic of Care: Feminist and Interdisciplinary Perspectives* (London and New York: Routledge, 1993).

LLOYD, GENEVIEVE, *The Man of Reason* (London: Methuen, 1984).

MIES, MARIA, 'Towards a Methodology for Feminist Research', in G. Bowles and R. Duelli Klein (eds.), *Theories of Women's Studies* (London: Routledge, 1983).

NICHOLSON, LINDA (ed.), *Feminism/Postmodernism* (London and New York: Routledge, 1990).

PEARSALL, MARILYN, *Women and Values: Readings in Recent Feminist Philosophy* (Belmont, Calif.: Wadsworth Pub., 1993).

ROSE, HILARY, *Love, Power and Knowledge: Towards a Feminist Transformation of the Sciences* (Cambridge: Polity Press, 1994).

STANLEY, LIZ (ed.), *Feminist Praxis: Research, Theory and Epistemology in Feminist Sociology* (London: Routledge, 1990).

STANLEY, LIZ, and WISE, SUE, *Breaking Out Again: Feminist Ontology and Epistemology* (London: Routledge, 1993).

III. SUBJECTIVITIES

ADAMS, PARVEEN, and COWIE, ELIZABETH (eds.), *The Woman Question: m/f* (London: Verso, 1990).

BRENNAN, TERESA (ed.), *Between Feminism and Psychoanalysis* (London: Routledge, 1989).

BUTLER, JUDITH, *Gender Trouble: Feminism and the Subversion of Identity* (New York: Routledge, 1989).

CORNELL, DRUCILLA, and BENHABIB, SEYLA (eds.), *Feminism as Critique* (Oxford: Polity, 1987).

GALLOP, JANE, *The Daughter's Seduction: Feminism and Psychoanalysis* (Ithaca, NY: Cornell University Press, 1984).

GARNER, SHIRLEY NELSON, KAHANE, CLAIRE, and SPRENGNETHER, MADELON (eds), *The (M)other Tongue: Essays in Feminist Psychoanalytic Interpretation* (Ithaca, NY: Cornell University Press, 1982).

GROSZ, ELIZABETH, *Jacques Lacan: A Feminist Introduction* (London: Routledge, 1990).

JARDINE, ALICE, *Gynesis: Configurations of Women and Modernity* (Ithaca, NY and London: Cornell University Press, 1985).

KRISTEVA, JULIA, *Desire in Language: A Semiotic Approach to Literature and Art*, trans. Thomas Gorz, Alice Jardine, and Leon S. Roudiez (Oxford: Blackwell, 1984).

ORTNER, SHERRY, and WHITEHEAD, HARRIET (eds.), *Sexual Meanings: The Cultural Construction of Gender and Sexuality* (Cambridge: Cambridge University Press, 1981).

MITCHELL, JULIET, and ROSE, JACQUELINE (eds.), *Feminine Sexuality: Jacques Lacan and the Ecole Freudienne* (London: Macmillan, 1982).

THIONG'O, NGŨGĨ WA, *Decolonising the Mind* (London: James Currey and Heinemann, 1989).

WRIGHT, ELIZABETH (ed.), *Feminism and Psychoanalysis: A Critical Dictionary,* (Oxford: Blackwell, 1992).

IV. SEXUALITIES

ASSITER, ALISON, *Pornography, Feminism and the Individual* (London: Pluto Press, 1989).

CARTLEDGE, SUE, and RYAN, JOANNA (eds.), *Sex and Love: New Thoughts on Old Contradictions* (London: The Women's Press, 1983).

COOPER, DAVINA, *Power in Struggle: Feminism, Sexuality and the State* (Milton Keynes: Open University Press, 1995).

DE LAURETIS, TERESA, *The Practice of Love: Lesbian Sexuality and Perverse Desire* (Bloomington, Ind.: Indiana University Press, 1994).

DWORKIN, ANDREA, and MACKINNON, CATHARINE, *In Harm's Way: The Pornography Civil Rights Hearings* (Cambridge, Mass.: Harvard University Press, 1997).

FADERMAN, LILLIAN, *Odd Girls and Twilight Lovers: A History of Lesbian Life in Twentieth-Century America* (New York: Penguin, 1991).

FERGUSON, ANN, *Blood at the Root: Motherhood, Sexuality and Male Dominance* (London: Pandora Press, 1989).

GIBSON, PAM CHURCH, and GIBSON, ROMA, *Dirty Looks: Women, Pornography, Power* (London: BFI Publishing, 1993).

GRIFFIN, SUSAN, *Pornography and Silence: Culture's Revenge against Nature* (London: The Women's Press, 1981).

JACKSON, STEVI, and SCOTT, SUE, *Feminism and Sexuality: A Reader* (Edinburgh: Edinburgh University Press, 1996).

ITZIN, CATHERINE (ed.), *Pornography, Women, Violence and Civil Liberties* (Oxford: Oxford University Press, 1992).

JEFFREYS, SHEILA, *Anticlimax: A Feminist Perspective on the Sexual Revolution* (London: The Women's Press, 1990).

KITZINGER, CELIA, *The Social Construction of Lesbianism* (London: Sage, 1987).

McCLINTOCK, ANNE, *Imperial Leather: Race, Gender and Sexuality in the Colonial Contest* (New York: Routledge, 1995).

McINTOSH, MARY, and SEGAL, LYNNE, *Sex Exposed: Sexuality and the Pornography Debate* (London: Virago Press, 1992).

MacKINNON, CATHARINE, *Feminism Unmodified: Discourse on Life and Law* (Cambridge, Mass.: Harvard University Press, 1987).

NESTLE, JOAN (ed.), *The Persistent Desire: A Butch-Femme Reader* (Boston: Alyson Publications, 1992).

ORTNER, SHERRY, and WHITEHEAD, HARRIET, *Sexual Meanings: The Cultural Construction of Gender and Sexuality* (Cambridge: Cambridge University Press, 1981).

PAGLIA, CAMILLE, *Sexual Personae* (Harmondsworth: Penguin, 1992).

PHELAN, SHANE, *Identity Politics: Lesbian Feminism and the Limits of Community* (Philadelphia: Temple University Press, 1989).

RODGERSON, GILLIAN, and WILSON, ELIZABETH, *Pornography and Feminism: The Case Against Censorship* (London: Lawrence & Wishart, 1991).

SEGAL, LYNNE, *Straight Sex: The Politics of Pleasure* (London: Virago Press, 1994).

SINGER, LINDA, *Erotic Welfare: Sexual Theory and Politics in the Age of Epidemic* (London: Routledge, 1993).

SMART, CAROL, *Law, Crime and Sexuality: Essays in Feminism* (London: Sage Publications, 1995).

SMITH, ANNA MARIE, 'Resisting the Erasure of Lesbian Sexuality' in Kenneth Plummer (ed.), *Modern Homosexualities: Fragments of Lesbian and Gay Experience* (London: Routledge, 1992).

SNITOW, ANN, STANSELL, CHRISTINE, and THOMPSON, SHARON, *Desire: The Politics of Sexuality* (London: Virago Press, 1984).

VICINUS, MARTHA (ed.), *Lesbian Subjects: A Feminist Studies Reader* (Bloomington, Ind.: Indiana University Press, 1996).

WEEKS, JEFFREY, *Sex, Politics and Society: The Regulation of Sexuality since 1800* (London: Longman, 1981).

V. VISUALITIES

CREED, BARBARA, *The Monstrous Female: Film, Feminism, Psychoanalysis* (New York: Routledge, 1993).

FERRIS, LESLEY (ed.), *Acting Women: Images of Women in Theatre* (New York: New York University Press, 1989).

KUHN, ANNETTE, *Women's Pictures: Feminism and Cinema* (London: RKP, 1982).

MODLESKI, TANIA, *Feminism Without Women: Culture and Criticism in a Postfeminist Age* (New York: Routledge, 1991).

MELLENCAMP, PATRICIA, DOANE, MARY ANN, and WILLIAMS, LINDA, *Re-Visions: Feminist Essays in Film Analysis* (Los Angeles: American Film Institute, 1985).

PETERSEN, KAREN, and WILSON, J. J., *Women Artists: Recognition and Reappraisal from the Early Middle Ages to the Twentieth Century* (London: The Women's Press, 1978).

POLLOCK, GRISELDA, *Vision and Difference. Femininity, Feminism and the Histories of Art* (New York and London: Routledge, 1988).

ROBERTSON, PAMELA, *Guilty Pleasures: Female Camp from Mae West to Madonna* (Durham, NC: Duke University Press, 1996).

ROWE, KATHLEEN, *The Unruly Woman: Gender and the Genres of Laughter* (Austin, Tex.: University of Texas Press, 1995).

STACEY, JACKIE, *Star-Gazing: Hollywood Cinema and Female Spectatorship* (New York: Routledge, 1994).

WALTERS, SUSANNA DANUTA, *Material Girls: Making Sense of Feminist Cultural Theory* (Berkeley and Los Angeles: University of California Press, 1995).

WOLFF, JANET, *Feminine Sentences: Essays on Women and Culture* (Cambridge: Polity, 1990).

YOUNG, LOLA, *Fear of the Dark: Race, Gender and Sexuality in the Cinema* (New York: Routledge, 1996).

VI. TECHNOLOGIES

ADAMS, CAROLE J. (ed.), *Ecofeminism and the Sacred* (New York: Continuum Publishing, 1993).

ARDITTI, R., et al., *Test Tube Women: What Future for Motherhood?* (London: Pandora, 1984).

BENJAMIN, MARINA, *Science and Sensibility: Gender and Scientific Enquiry* (Cambridge, Mass.: Blackwells, 1994).

BLEIER, RUTH (ed.), *Feminist Approaches to Science* (New York: Pergamon Press, 1986).

BRAIDOTTI, ROSI, et al., *Women, the Environment, and Development: Towards a Theoretical Synthesis* (London: Zed Books, 1994).

CALDECOTT, LEONIE, and LELAND, STEPHANIE (eds.), *Reclaim the Earth: Women Speak Out for Life on Earth* (London: The Women's Press, 1983).

COCKBURN, CYNTHIA, *Machinary of Dominance: Women, Men and Technical Know-How* (London: Pluto Press, 1985).

COWAN, R., *More Work for Mother: The Ironies of Household Technology* (London: Basic Books, 1983).

DIAMOND, IRENE, and ORENSTIEN, GLORIA (eds.), *Reweaving the World: The Emergence of Ecofeminism* (San Francisco: Sierra Club Books, 1990).

Fox Keller, Evelyn, *Reflections on Gender and Science* (New Haven: Yale University Press, 1986).

—— and Longino, Helen E., *Feminism and Science* (New York: Oxford University Press, 1996).

Franklin, Sarah, *Embodied Progress: Cultural Account of Assisted Conception* (London: Routledge, 1996).

Gaard, Greta (ed.), *Ecofeminisms: Women, Animals, Nature* (Philadelphia: Temple University Press, 1993).

Haraway, Donna, *Modest-Witness@second-Millennium. Femaleman-Meets-Oncomouse: Feminism and Technoscience* (New York: Routledge, 1996).

—— *Simians, Cyborgs and Women* (New York: Routledge, 1991).

Hartsock, Nancy, and Boling, Patricia, *Expecting Trouble: Surrogacy, Fetal Abuse, and New Reproductive Technologies* (Boulder, Colo.: Westview Press, 1995).

Hynes, P. H. (ed), *Reconstructing Babylon: Essays on Women and Technology* (London: Earthscan, 1989).

Longino, Helen, *Science as Social Knowledge: Values and Objectivity in Scientific Enquiry* (Princeton, NJ: Princeton University Press, 1990).

Martin, Emily, *The Women in the Body: A Cultural Analysis of Reproduction* (Boston: Beacon Press, 1987).

Merchant, Carolyn, *Radical Ecology: The Search for a Liveable World* (New York: Routledge, 1992).

Oakley, Ann, *The Captured Womb: A History of the Medical Care of Pregnant Women* (Oxford: Blackwell, 1986).

O'Brien, Mary, *The Politics of Reproduction* (Boston: Routledge Kegan Paul, 1981).

Plant, Judith, *Healing the Wounds: The Promise of Ecofeminism* (Philadelphia: New Society, 1989).

Schiebinger, Londa L., *Nature's Body: Gender in the Making of Modern Science* (Boston: Beacon Press, 1995).

Shiva, Vandana, *Staying Alive: Women, Ecology and Development* (London: Zed Books, 1989).

—— and Moser, Ingunn (eds.), *Biopolitics: A Feminist and Ecological Reader on Biotechnology* (London: Zed Books, 1995).

Sontheimer, Sally, *Women and the Environment: A Reader* (New York: Monthly Review Press, 1991).

Wajcman, Judy, *Feminism Contronts Technology* (Cambridge: Polity Press, 1991).

Biographical Notes

BARRETT, M. Michèle Barrett's publications include *Destabilizing Theory: Contemporary Feminist Debates* (with Anne Phillips, (eds.) (1992); *The Politics of Truth: From Marx to Foucault* (1991); *Anti-social Family* (with Mary McIntosh) (1991); and *Women's Oppression Today: The Marxist/Feminist Encounter* (1989).

BENHABIB, S. Seyla Benhabib's publications include *The Reluctant Modernism of Hannah Arendt* (1996); *Democracy and Difference: Contesting the Boundaries of the Political* (1996); and *Situating the Self: Gender, Community and Postmodernism in Contemporary Ethics* (1992).

BORDO, S. Susan Bordo's publications include *Twilight Zones: The Hidden Life of Cultural Images from Plato to O.J.* (1997); *Unbearable Weight: Feminism, Western Culture and the Body* (1993); *Gender/Body/Knowledge: Feminist Reconstructions of Being and Knowledge* (with Alison Jaggar) (1989); and *The Flight to Objectivity: Essays in Cartesianism and Culture* (1987).

BOWLBY, R. Rachel Bowlby's publications include *Feminist Destinations and Further Essays on Virginia Woolf* (1997); *Shopping with Freud* (1993); *Virginia Woolf* (1992); and *Still Crazy After All These Years: Women, Writing and Psychoanalysis* (1992).

BRAIDOTTI, R. Rosi Braidotti's publications include *Between Monsters, Goddesses and Cyborgs: Feminist Confrontations* (with Nina Lykke) (eds.) (1996); *Nomadic Subjects: Embodiment and Sexual Difference* (1994); and *Patterns of Dissonance: Study of Women and Contemporary Philosophy* (1991).

BROWN, W. Wendy Brown's publications include *States of Injury: Power and Freedom in Late Modernity* (1995).

BUTLER, J. Judith Butler's publications include *Excitable Speech: Politics of the Performative* (1997); *The Psychic Life of Power: Theories in Subjection* (1997); *Feminist Contentions: A Philosophical Exchange* (with Seyla Benhabib, Linda Nicholson, and Nancy Fraser) (1994); *Bodies That Matter: On the Discursive Limits of Sex* (1993); *Feminists Theorize the Political* (with Joan W. Scott) (eds.) (1992); and *Gender Trouble: Feminism and the Subversion of Identity* (1990).

CHEDGZOY, K. Kate Chedgzoy's publications include *Voicing Women: Gender and Sexuality in Early Modern Writing* (ed.) (1997); *Lay by Your Needles Ladies, Take the Pen: Writing Women in England, 1500–1700* (with Suzanne Rill and Melanie Osborne) (eds.) (1997); and *Shakespeare's Queer Children: Sexual Politics and Contemporary Culture* (1996).

CHODOROW, N. Nancy Chodorow's publications include *Femininities, Masculinities, Sexualities: Freud and Beyond* (1994); *Feminism and Psychoanalytic Theory* (1989), and *The Reproduction of Mothering: Psychoanalysis and the Sociology of Gender* (1979).

CHRISTIAN, B. Barbara Christian's publications include *Female Subjects in Black and White: Race, Psychoanalysis, Feminism* (with Elizabeth Abel *et al.*) (1997); *Everyday Use (Women Writers)* (with Alice Walker) (1994); *Black Feminist Criticism: Perspectives on Black Women Writers* (1992); and *Black Woman Novelists: The Development of a Tradition, 1892–1976* (1980).

CIXOUS, H. Hélène Cixous's publications include *Three Steps on the Ladder of Writing* (Sarah Cornell and Susan Sellers, trans.) (1993); *Readings: The Poetics of Blanchot, Joyce, Kafka, Kleist, Lispector, and Tsvetayeva* (Verena Andermatt Conley, trans.) (1991); *Reading with Clarice Lispector* (Verena Andermatt Conley, trans.) (1990); and *Newly Born Woman* (with Catherine Clement) (Betsy Wing, trans.) (1986).

COCKBURN, C. Cynthia Cockburn's publications include *Bringing Technology Home: Gender and Technology in a Changing Europe* (with Ruža Fürst-Dilić,) (eds.) (1994); *Gender and Technology in the Making* (with Susan Ormrod) (1993); *Brothers: Male Dominance and Technological Change* (1991); *Women, Trade Unions and Political Parties* (1987); and *Machinery of Dominance: Women, Men and Technical Know-how* (1985).

COLLINS, P. H. Patricia Hill Collins's publications include *Black Feminist Thought: Knowledge, Consciousness and the Politics of Empowerment* (1990) and *Race, Class and Gender: An Anthology* (with Margaret Anderson) (eds.) (1994).

COWARD, R. Rosalind Coward's publications include *Symbols of Our Sex* (1997); *Our Treacherous Hearts: Why Women Let Men Get Their Way* (1992); and *Female Desire: Women's Sexuality Today* (1984).

DE LAURETIS, T. Teresa de Lauretis's publications include *The Practice of Love: Lesbian Sexuality and Perverse Desire* (1994); *How Do I Look?: Queer Film and Video* (1991); *Technologies of Gender: Essays on Theory, Film, and Fiction* (1989); *Feminist Studies, Critical Studies* (1986); and *Alice Doesn't: Feminism, Semiotics, Cinema* (1984).

DWORKIN, A. Andrea Dworkin's publications include *In Harm's Way: The Pornography Civil Rights Hearings* (with Catharine A. MacKinnon) (1997); *Life and Death: Unapologetic Writings on the Continuing War Against Women* (1997); *Letters from a War Zone* (1993); and *Mercy: A Novel* (1990).

EVANS, M. Mary Evans's publications include *Introducing Contemporary Feminist Thought* (1997); *Simone de Beauvoir* (1996); and *The Woman Question* (1994).

FELSKI, R. Rita Felski's publications include *The Gender of Modernity* (1995); and *Beyond Feminist Aesthetics: Feminist Literature and Social Change* (1989).

FLAX, J. Jane Flax's publications include *Disputed Subjects: Essays on Psychoanalysis, Politics and Philosophy* (1993); and *Thinking Fragments: Psychoanalysis, Feminism and Postmodernism in the Contemporary West* (1991).

FRANKLIN, S. Sarah Franklin's publications include *Reproducing Reproduction: Kinship, Power, and Technological Innovation* (with Helena Ragone) (1997); *Embodied Progress: Cultural Account of Assisted Conception* (1996); and *Sociology of Gender* (ed.) (1996).

FUSS, D. Diana Fuss's publications include *Human, All Too Human* (ed.) (1996); *Identification Papers: Readings on Psychoanalysis, Sexuality and Culture* (1995); *Inside/Out: Lesbian Theories, Gay Theories* (1991); and *Essentially Speaking: Feminism, Nature and Difference* (1989).

GALLOP, J. Jane Gallop's publications include *Feminist Accused of Sexual Harassment* (1997); *Pedagogy: The Question of Impersonation* (ed.) (1995); *Thinking Through the Body* (1990); *Reading Lacan* (1985); *The Daughter's Seduction: Feminism and Psychoanalysis* (1982); and *Intersections: A Reading of Sade with Bataille, Blanchot, and Klossowski* (1981).

GILLIGAN, C. Carol Gilligan's publications include *Between Voice and Silence: Women and Girls, Race and Relationship* (with Jill McLean Taylor and Amy M. Sullivan) (1997);

Meeting at the Crossroads: Women's Psychology and Girls' Development (with Lyn Mikel Brown) (1992); and *Women, Girls, and Psychotherapy: Reframing Resistance* (with Annie G. Rogers and Deborah L. Tolman) (1991).

GROSZ, E. Elizabeth Grosz's publications include *Sexy Bodies: Strange Carnalities of Feminism* (with Elspeth Probyn) (eds.) (1995); *Space, Time, and Perversion: Essays on the Politics of Bodies* (1995); *Volatile Bodies: Towards a Corporeal Feminism* (1994); *Jacques Lacan: A Feminist Introduction* (1990); and *Sexual Subversions: Three French Feminists* (1989).

GUNEW, S. Sneja Gunew's publications include *Framing Marginality: Multicultural Literary Studies* (1995); *Culture, Difference and the Arts: Multiculturalism and the Arts* (with Fazal Rizvi) (eds.) (1994); and *A Reader in Feminist Knowledge* (ed.) (1991).

HARAWAY, D. Donna Haraway is author of *Modest-Witness@second-Millennium Femaleman-Meets-Oncomouse: Feminism and Technoscience* (1996); *Simians, Cyborgs, and Women: The Reinvention of Nature* (1991); and *Primate Visions: Gender, Race and Nature in the World of Modern Science* (1990).

HARDING, S. Sandra Harding's publications include *The Racial Economy of Science: Toward a Democratic Future* (ed.) (1993); *Whose Science? Whose Knowledge? Thinking from Women's Lives* (1991); *Feminism and Methodology: Social Science Issues* (1986); and *The Science Question in Feminism* (1986).

HARTSOCK, N. Nancy Hartsock's publications include *Postmodernism and Political Change* (1997); *Feminist Standpoint Revisited and Other Essays* (1997); and *Expecting Trouble: Surrogacy, Fetal Abuse and New Reproductive Technologies* (with Patricia Boling) (1995).

HOOKS, B. bell hooks's publications include *Bone Black: Memories of Girlhood* (1997); *Killing Rage: Ending Racism* (1996): *Reel to Real; Race: Sex and Class at the Movies* (1996); *Teaching to Transgress: Education as the Practice of Freedom* (1994); *Black Looks: Race and Representation* (1992); *Yearning: Race, Gender and Cultural Politics* (1990); and *Feminist Theory: From Margin to Center* (1984).

IRIGARAY, L. Luce Irigaray's publications include *I Love to You: Sketch of a Possible Felicity in History* (Alison Martin, trans.) (1995); *Speech is Never Neuter* (1995); *Thinking the Difference: For a Peaceful Revolution* (1994); *Sexes and Genealogies* (1993); *Je, Tu, Nous: Towards a Culture of Difference* (1992); *Elemental Passions* (Judith Still and Joanne Collie, trans.) (1992); *Speculum of the Other Woman* (Gillian C. Gill, trans.) (1985); and *This Sex Which is Not One* (Catherine Porter, trans.) (1985).

JAGGAR, A. Alison Jaggar's publications include *Feminists Rethink the Self (Feminist Theory and Politics)* (with Diana Tietjens Meyers and Virginia Held) (1997); *Revisioning the Political: Feminist Reconstructions of Traditional Concepts in Western Political Theory* (with Nancy Hirschmann and Christine Di Stefano) (1996); and *Living with Contradictions: Controversies in Feminist Social Ethics* (1994).

JARDINE, A. Alice Jardine's publications include *Shifting Scenes: Interviews on Women, Writing, and Politics in Post-'68 France* (with Anne M. Menke, Carolyn G. Heilbrun, and Nancy K. Miller) (eds.) (1993); *Men in Feminism* (with Paul Smith) (eds.) (1991); *Gynesis: Configurations of Woman and Modernity* (1986); and *The Future of Difference* (with Hester Eisenstein) (1985).

KANNEH, K. Kadiatu Kanneh's publications include 'Love, Mourning and Metaphor: Terms of Identity' in Isobel Armstrong (ed.), *New Feminist Discourses: Critical Essays on Theories and Texts* (1992).

KAPLAN, E. A. E. Ann Kaplan's publications include *Looking for the Other: Nation, Woman and Desire in Film* (1997); *Generations; Academic Feminists in Dialogue* (with Devoney Looser) (1997); *Fritz Lang: A Guide to References and Resources* (1994); *Motherhood and Representation: Feminism, Psychoanalysis and the Material* (1992); *Psychoanalysis and Cinema* (1990); *Rocking Around the Clock: Music, Television, Postmodernism and Consumer* (1990); *Women and Film: Both Sides of the Camera* (1983); and *Women in Film Noir* (1980).

KAPLAN, C. Cora Kaplan's publications include *Transitions, Environments, Translations: International Feminisms in Contemporary Politics* (with Joan W. Scott and Debra Keates) (eds.) (1997); Dinah Craik's *Olive; And, the Half-Caste* (Oxford Popular Fiction) (ed.) (1996); and *Sea Changes: Culture and Feminism* (1983).

KELLY, L. Liz Kelly's publications include *Sexual Abuse in Childhood* (1994); *Child Abuse and Information* (1992); and *Surviving Sexual Violence* (1988).

KRISTEVA, J. Julia Kristeva's publications include *Time and Sense: Proust and the Experience of Literature* (Ross Guberman, trans.) (1996); *New Maladies of the Soul* (Ross Guberman, trans.) (1995); *Old Man and the Wolves* (Barbara Bray, trans.) (1994); *Strangers to Ourselves* (Leon S. Roudiez, trans.) (1994); *Nations without Nationalism* (Leon S. Roudiez, trans.) (1993); *The Samurai: A Novel* (Barbara Bray, trans.) (1992); *Black Sun: Depression and Melancholia* (Leon S. Roudiez, trans.) (1992); *Language: The Unknown— An Initiation into Linguistics* (Anne M. Menke, trans.) (1991); *About Chinese Women* (Anita Barrows, trans.) (1991); and *Tales of Love* (Leon S. Roudiez, trans.) (1989).

KUHN, A. Annette Kuhn's publications include *Family Secrets: Acts of Memory and Imagination* (1995); *Queen of the B's: Ida Lupino Behind the Camera* (ed.) (1995); *The Women's Companion to International Film* (with Susannah Radstone) (1994); *Women's Pictures: Feminism and Cinema* (1993); *The Power of the Image: Essays on Representation and Sexuality* (1992); and *Alien Zone: Cultural Theory and Contemporary Science Fiction Cinema* (1990).

LIGHT, A. Alison Light's publications include *Forever England: Femininity, Literature and Conservatism Between the Wars* (1991).

MACKINNON, C. Catharine MacKinnon's publications include *In Harm's Way: The Pornography Civil Rights Hearings* (with Andrea Dworkin) (1997); *Only Words* (1996); *Toward a Feminist Theory of the State* (1989); and *Feminism Unmodified: Discourses on Life and Law* (1987).

McINTOSH, M. Mary McIntosh's publications include *Sex Exposed: Sexuality and the Pornography Debate* (with Lynne Segal) (eds.) (1992); and *The Anti-social Family* (with Michèle Barrett) (1991).

MERCHANT, C. Carolyn Merchant's publications include *Earthcare: Women and the Environment* (1995); *Ecology* (1994); *Radical Ecology: The Search for a Liveable World* (1992); and *The Death of Nature: Women, Ecology, and the Scientific Revolution* (1990).

MICHIE, H. Helena Michie's publications include *Confinements: Fertility and Infertility in Contemporary Culture* (with Naomi Cahn) (1997); *Sororophobia: Differences Among Women in Literature and Culture* (1992); and *Flesh Made Word: Female Figures and Women's Bodies* (1989).

MIES, M. Maria Mies's publications include *Ecofeminism* (with Vandana Shiva), (eds.) (1993); *Women: The Last Colony* (ed.) (1988); and *Patriarchy and Accumulation on a World Stage* (1985).

MILLER, N. Nancy Miller's publications include *Bequest and Betrayal: Memoirs of a Parent's Death* (ed.) (1996); *French Dressing: Men, Women and Fiction in the Ancien Regime* (1995); *Shifting Scenes: Interviews on Women, Writing and Politics in Post '68* (with Alice A. Jardine, Anne M. Menke, and Carolyn G. Heilbrun) (eds.) (1993); *Getting Personal: Feminist Occasions and Other Autobiographical Acts* (1991); *Subject to Change: Women's Writing—Feminist Reading* (1989); and *Politics of Tradition: Placing Women in French Literature* (with Joan DeJean) (eds.) (1989).

MOHANTY, C. T. Chandra Talpade Mohanty's publications include *Feminist Genealogies, Colonial Legacies, Democratic Futures* (with M. Jacqui Alexander) (eds.) (1996); *The Slate of Life: More Contemporary Stories by Women Writers of India* (with Satya Mohanty) (1994); and *Third World Women and the Politics of Feminism* (with Ann Russo and Louris Torres) (eds.) (1990).

MOI, T. Toril Moi's publications include *Sex and Existence: Simone de Beauvoir's 'The Second Sex'* (with Eva Lundgren-Gothlin and Linda Schenck) (1996); *Materialist Feminism* (with Janice Radway) (eds.) (1994); *Simone de Beauvoir: The Making of an Intellectual Woman* (1993); *French Feminist Thought: A Reader* (ed.) (1987); *The Kristeva Reader* (1986); and *Sexual/Textual Politics: Feminist Literary Theory* (1985).

NEAD, L. Lynda Nead's publications include *Chila Kumari Burman: Beyond Two Cultures* (1995); and *The Female Nude: Art, Obscenity, and Sexuality* (1992).

PENLEY, C. Constance Penley's publications include *The Visible Woman: Imaging Technologies, Gender, and Science* (with Paula Treichler and Lisa Cartwright) (1998); *NASA/Trek: Popular Science and Sex in America* (1997); *Male Trouble* (with Sharon Willis) (eds.) (1993); *Close Encounters: Film, Feminism, and Science Fiction* (with Elisabeth Lyon and Janet Bergstrom) (1991); *Technoculture* (with Andrew Ross) (eds.) (1991); and *The Future of an Illusion: Film, Feminism, and Psychoanalysis* (1989).

PHELAN, P. Peggy Phelan's publications include *The Ends of Performance* (with Jill Lane) (1997); *Mourning Sex: Performing Public Memories* (1996); and *Unmarked: The Politics of Performance* (1993).

PHILLIPS, A. Anne Phillips's publications include *The Politics of Presence: Democracy and Group Representation* (1995); *Democracy and Difference* (1993); *Destabilizing Theory: Contemporary Feminist Debates* (with Michele Barrett) (eds) (1992); *Engendering Democracy* (1991); and *Divided Loyalties* (1987).

PLANT, S. Sadie Plant's recent publications include *Zeros and Ones: Digital Women and the New Technoculture* (1997); and *The Most Radical Gesture: Situationist International in a Postmodern Age* (1992).

POLLOCK, G. Griselda Pollock's publications include *Generations and Geographies in the Visual Arts: Feminist Readings* (1996); *Dealing with Degas: Representations of Women and the Politics of Vision* (with Richard Kendall) (eds.) (1992); *Vision and Difference: Femininity, Feminism and Histories of Art* (1988); and *Framing Feminism: Art and the Women's Movement* (with Rozsika Parker) (1987).

PROBYN, E. Elspeth Probyn's publications include *Outside Belongings: Disciplines, Nations and the Place of Sex* (1996); *Sexy Bodies: Strange Carnalities of Feminism* (with

Elizabeth Grosz) (eds.) (1995); and *Sexing the Self: Gendered Positions in Cultural Studies* (1993).

RADSTONE, S. Susannah Radstone's publications include *The Women's Companion to International Film* (with Annette Kuhn) (1994); and *Sweet Dreams: Sexuality, Gender and Popular Fiction* (ed.) (1988).

RICH, A. Recent collections of Adrienne Rich's poetry include *Dark Fields of the Republic: Poems 1991–1995* (1996); *Collected Early Poems, 1950–1970* (1996); and *Selected Poems, 1950–1995* (1996). Other works include *Of Woman Born: Motherhood as Experience and Institution* (1995); and *On Lies, Secrets, and Silence: Selected Prose 1966–1978* (1995).

RILEY, D. Denise Riley's publications include *Four Falling* (1993); *Mop Mop Georgette* (1993); *Poets on Writing: Britain, 1970–91* (1992); *Am I That Name? Feminism and the Category of Women in History* (1988); and *Dry Air* (1985).

ROSE, J. Jacqueline Rose's publications include *States of Fantasy: The Clarendon Lectures in English Literature* (1996); *The Case of 'Peter Pan': Or, the Impossibility of Children's Fiction* (1994); *Why War? Psychoanalysis and the Return to Melanie Klein* (1993); *The Haunting of Sylvia Plath* (1992); and *Sexuality in the Field of Vision* (1986).

SCHEMAN, N. Naomi Scheman's publications include *Engenderings: Constructions of Knowledge, Authority and Privilege* (1993).

SEDGWICK, E. K. Eve Kosofsky Sedgwick's publications include *Novel Gazing: Queer Readings in Fiction* (1997); *Performance and Performativity* (with Andrew Parker) (1995); *Fat Art, Thin Art* (1994); *Epistemology of the Closet* (1991); and *Between Men: English Literature and Male Homosocial Desire* (1985).

SEGAL, L. Lynne Segal's publications include *New Sexual Agendas* (ed.) (1997); *Straight Sex: The Politics of Desire* (1994); *Sex Exposed: Sexuality and the Pornography Debate* (with Mary McIntosh) (eds.) (1992); and *Slow Motion: Changing Masculinities, Changing Men* (1990; 2nd cdn. 1997).

SHIACH, M. Morag Shiach's publications include *Hélène Cixous: A Politics of Writing* (1991).

SHIVA, V. Vandana Shiva's publications include *Biopiracy: The Plunder of Nature and Knowledge* (1997); *Breakfast of Biodiversity: The Truth about Rain Forest Destruction* (with John Vandermeer and Ivette Perfecto) (eds.) (1995); *Biopolitics: A Feminist and Ecological Reader on Biotechnology* (with Ingunn Moser) (eds.) (1995); *Monocultures of the Mind: Biodiversity, Biotechnology and Scientific* (1993); *Close to Home: Women Reconnect* (1993); *Ecofeminism* (with Maria Mies) (eds.) (1993); *Violence of the Green Revolution: Ecological Degradation and Political* (1991); and *Staying Alive: Women, Ecology and Development* (1989).

SHOWALTER, E. Elaine Showalter's publications include *Scribbling Women: Short Stories by 19th-Century American Women* (ed.) (1997); *Hystories: Hysterical Epidemics and Modern Culture* (1997); *Daughters of Decadence: Women Writers of the Fin-de-Siècle* (1993); *Sister's Choice: Tradition and Change in American Women's Writing* (1991); *Speaking of Gender* (1988); *Female Malady: Women, Madness and English Culture, 1830–1980* (1987); and *New Feminist Criticism* (ed.) (1986).

SILVERMANN, K. Kaja Silvermann's publications include *The Threshold of the Visible World* (1995); *Male Subjectivity at the Margins* (1992); *The Acoustic Mirror: The Female Voice in Psychoanalysis and Cinema* (1988); and *The Subject of Semiotics* (1983).

SMITH, B. Barbara Smith's publications include *The Women of Ben Jonson's Poetry: Female Representations in the Non-Dramatic* (1995); *Combahee River Collective Statement* (1986); and *Home Girls: A Black Feminist Anthology* (1983).

SMYTH, C. Cherry Smyth's publications include *Damn Fine Art by New Lesbian Artists* (1996); and *Lesbians Talk Queer Notions* (1992).

SOLOMON-GODEAU, A. Abigail Solomon-Godeau's publications include *Male Trouble: A Crisis in Representation* (1997); and *Photography at the Dock: Essays on Photographic History, Institutions, and Practices* (with Linda Nochlin) (1991).

SOPER, K. Kate Soper's publications include *What is Nature? Culture, Politics and the Non-Human* (1995); and *Troubled Pleasures: Writings on Politics, Gender, and Hedonism* (1990).

SPELMAN, E. Elizabeth Spelman's publications include *Fruits of Sorrow: The Use and Abuse of Suffering* (1997); and *Inessential Woman: Problems of Exclusion in Feminist Thought* (1988).

SPIVAK, G. C. Gayatri Chakravorty Spivak's publications include *The Spivak Reader* (with Donna Landry and Gerald MacLean) (eds.) (1997); *Outside in the Teaching Machine* (1993); *In Other Worlds: Essays in Cultural Politics* (1990); and *Selected Subaltern Studies* (with Ranajit Guha) (eds.) (1988). She is also translator of Jacques Derrida's *Of Grammatology* (1976).

STABILE, C. Carol Stabile's publications include *Feminism and the Technological Fix* (1994).

STANLEY, L. Liz Stanley's publications include *Knowing Feminisms* (1996); *Breaking Out Again: Feminist Ontology and Epistemology* (with Sue Wise) (1993); *Debates in Sociology* (with David Morgan) (eds.) (1993); *Feminist Praxis: Research, Theory and Epistemology in Feminist Sociology* (ed.) (1990); and *Georgie Porgie: Sexual Harassment in Everyday Life* (with Sue Wise) (1987).

STANWORTH, M. Michelle Stanworth's publications include *Reproductive Technologies: Gender; Motherhood and Medicine* (1987).

STRATHERN, M. Marilyn Strathern's publications include *Shifting Contexts: Transformations in Anthropological Knowledge* (ed.) (1995); *Women in Between: Female Roles in a Male World, Mount Hagen, New Guinea* (1993); *Partial Connections* (1992); and *After Nature: English Kinship in the Late Twentieth Century* (1992).

STURGIS, S. Susan Sturgis is a member of the Off Pink Collective, a group of bisexual activists who write, edit, and publish books about bisexual experience.

TOMPKINS, J. Jane Tompkins's publications include Zane Grey's *Riders of the Purple Sage* (ed.) (1990); Susan Warner's *The Wide, Wide World* (ed.) (1987); *Sensational Designs: Cultural Work of American Fiction, 1790–1860* (1986); and *Reader-Response Criticism: From Formalism to Post-Structuralism* (1980).

TREICHLER, P. Paula Treichler's publications include *The Visible Woman: Imaging Technologies, Gender, and Science* (with Lisa Cartwright and Constance Penley) (1998); *Imaging Technologies, Inscribing Science* (with Lisa Cartwright) (eds.) (1993); and *Cultural Studies* (with Lawrence Grossberg and Cary Nelson) (eds.) (1991).

TURKLE, S. Sherry Turkle's publications include *Life on the Screen: Identity in the Age of the Internet* (1996); and *Psychoanalytic Politics: Jacques Lacan and Freud's French Revolution* (1992).

VANCE, C. Carole Vance's publications include *Pleasure and Danger: Exploring Female Sexuality* (1992).

WAUGH, P. Patricia Waugh's publications include *Revolutions of the Word: Intellectual Contexts for the Study of Modern Literature* (ed.) (1996); *Postmodernism: A Reader* (ed.) (1992); and *Practising Postmodernism/Reading Modernism* (1992).

WILSON, E. Elizabeth Wilson's publications include *Adorned in Dreams: Fashion and Modernity* (1996); *The Lost Time Café* (1993); and *The Sphinx in the City: Urban Life, the Control of Disorder, and Women* (1992).

WITTIG, M. Monique Wittig's publications include *The Straight Mind and Other Essays* (1992); *Across the Acheron* (1987); *The Lesbian Body* (with David LeVay) (1986); and *Les Guerilleres* (1985).

WRIGHT, E. Elizabeth Wright's recent publications include *Feminism and Psychoanalysis: A Critical Dictionary* (ed.) (1992).

YEATMAN, A. Anna Yeatman's publications include *Postmodern Revisionings of the Political* (1993); and *Bureaucrats, Technocrats, Femocrats: Essays on the Contemporary* (1991).

YOUNG, I. M. Iris Marion Young's publications include *Intersecting Voices: Dilemmas of Gender, Political Philosophy and Policy* (1997); *Throwing Like a Girl and Other Essays in Feminist Philosophy and Social Theory* (1990); and *Justice and the Politics of Difference* (1990).

Acknowledgements

TEXTS

BARRETT, MICHÈLE, 'Words and Things: Materialism and Method in Contemporary Feminist Analysis', in Michèle Barrett and Anne Phillips (eds.), *Destabilizing Theory: Contemporary Feminist Debates* (Polity Press, Cambridge, 1992; repr. with the permission of the publishers, Stanford University Press; collection and Introduction © 1992 Michèle Barrett and Anne Phillips; each chapter copyright the author).

BENHABIB, SEYLA, 'The Generalized and the Concrete Other', in *Situating the Self* (Polity Press, Cambridge, and Routledge, Chapman and Hall Inc., New York 1992).

BORDO, SUSAN, 'Normalisation and Resistance in the Era of the Image', in Caroline Ramazanoglu (ed.), *Up Against Foucault: Explorations of Some Tensions Between Foucault and Feminism* (Routledge, London, 1993).

BOWLBY, RACHEL, *Still Crazy After all These Years: Women, Writing and Psychoanalysis* (Routledge, London, 1992).

BRAIDOTTI, ROSI, 'Cyberfeminism With a Difference', *New Formations*, 29, Summer 1996 (Lawrence & Wishart, London, 1996).

BROWN, WENDY, 'The Mirror of Pornography', in Wendy Brown, *States of Injury: Power and Freedom in Late Modernity* (Copyright © 1995 Princeton University Press; repr. by permission of Princeton University Press).

BUTLER, JUDITH, 'Subjects of Sex/Gender/Desire', in *Gender Trouble* (Routledge, Chapman and Hall Inc., New York).

CHEDGZOY, KATE, 'Frida Kahlo's "grotesque bodies"' in Penny Florence and Dee Reynolds (eds.), *Feminist Subjects, Multimedia, Cultural Methodologies* (Manchester University Press, Manchester, 1995).

CHODOROW, NANCY, 'Feminism and Psychoanalytic Theory', in *Feminism and Psychoanalytic Theory* (Polity Press, Cambridge/Yale University Press, New Haven and London, 1989).

CHRISTIAN, BARBARA, 'The Race for Theory', in Linda Kaufman (ed.), *Gender and Theory* (Blackwell, Oxford, 1989).

CIXOUS, HÉLÈNE, 'Sorties', in Hélène Cixous and Catherine Clement, *The Newly Born Woman* (University of Minnesota Press, Minneapolis, 1986).

COCKBURN, CYNTHIA, and FÜRST-DILIĆ, RUŽA, 'Looking for the Gender/Technology Relation', in *Bringing Technology Home: Gender and Technology in a Changing Europe* (Open University Press, Milton Keynes, 1994).

COWARD, ROS, 'Slim and Sexy: Modern Woman's Holy Grail', in *Our Treacherous Hearts: Why Women Let Men Get Their Way* (Faber & Faber, London, 1993).

DE LAURETIS, TERESA, 'Aesthetic and Feminism Theory: Rethinking Women's Cinema', in E. Dierdre Pribram (ed.), *Female Spectators: Looking at Film and Television* (Verso, London, 1988).

DWORKIN, ANDREA, 'Pornography', in *Pornography* (Perigee Books, New York, 1981; © Putnam Berkeley Publishing Group, New York).

EVANS, MARY, 'In Praise of Theory: The Case of Women's Studies', in Gloria Bowles and Renate Duelli Klein (eds.), *Theories of Women's Studies* (Routledge & Kegan Paul, London, 1983).

ACKNOWLEDGEMENTS 589

FELSKI, RITA, 'The Dialectic of Feminism and Aesthetics', in *Beyond Feminist Aesthetics: Feminist Literature and Social Change* (Hutchinson Radius, London, 1989; copyright © Harvard University Press, Cambridge, Mass.).

FLAX, JANE, 'Postmodern and Gender Relations in Feminist Theory', *Signs: Journal of Women in Culture and Society,* 12:4 (University of Chicago Press, 1987).

FRANKLIN, SARAH, 'Fetel Fascinations', in S. Franklin, C. Lury, and J. Stacey (eds.), *Fetel Fascinations* (Sage Publications, London, 1991; copyright © Sarah Franklin).

FUSS, DIANA, 'The "Risk" of Essence', in *Essentially Speaking: Feminism, Nature and Difference* (Routledge, Chapman and Hall Inc., New York 1989).

GALLOP, JANE, *Around 1981: Academic Feminist Literary Theory* (Routledge, Chapman and Hall Inc., New York, 1992).

GILLIGAN, CAROL, *In a Different Voice* (Harvard University Press, Cambridge, Mass., 1982).

GROSZ, ELIZABETH, 'Psychoanalysis and the Imaginary Body', in Penny Florence and Dee Reynolds (eds.), *Feminist Subjects, Multimedia, Cultural Methodologies* (Manchester University Press, Manchester, 1995).

GUNEW, SNEJA, 'Authenticity and the Writing Cure: Reading Some Migrant Women's Writing', in Susan Sheridan (ed.), *Grafts: Feminist Cultural Criticism* (Verso, London, 1988).

HARAWAY, DONNA, 'A Manifesto for Cyborgs: Science, Technology and Socialist Feminism in the 1980s', in Linda Nicholson (ed.), *Feminism/Postmodernism* (Routledge, Chapman and Hall Inc., New York, 1990).

HARDING, SANDRA, 'Introduction: Is There a Feminist Method?' and 'Conclusion: Epistemological Questions', in *Feminism and Methodology* (Indiana University Press, Bloomington, 1986).

HARTSOCK, NANCY, 'The Feminist Standpoint: Developing a Ground for a Specifically Historical Materialism', in Sandra Harding and Merrell Hintikka (eds.), *Discovering Reality* (Reidel Publishing Company, Dordrecht, 1983; reproduced by kind permission of Kluwer Academic Publishers, Dordrecht).

HILL-COLLINS, PATRICIA, 'Toward an Afrocentric Feminist Epistemology', in *Black Feminist Thought: Knowledge, Consciousness, and the Politics of Empowerment* (Routledge, Chapman and Hall Inc., New York, 1991).

HOOKS, BELL, 'Black and Women and Feminism', in *Ain't I a Woman* (Pluto Press, London, 1982, repr. from bell hooks, *Ain't I a Woman* with permission from the publisher, South End Press, 116 Saint Botolph Street, Boston).

HOOKS, BELL, 'Feminism: A Movement to End Sexist Oppression', in *Feminist Theory: From Margin to Center* (South End Press, Boston, 1984, reprinted from bell hooks, *Feminist Theory: From Margin to Center*, with permission from the publisher, South End Press, Boston).

IRIGARAY, LUCE, 'The Other Woman', in *I Love To You: Sketch for a Felicity Within History* (Routledge, Chapman and Hall Inc., New York, 1996); translated by Alison Martin.

JAGGAR, ALISON, 'Love and Knowledge: Emotion in Feminist Epistemology', *Inquiry,* 32 (1989), 151–76, by permission of Scandinavian University Press, Oslo.

JARDINE, ALICE, 'Notes for an analysis', in Teresa Brennan (ed.), *Between Feminism and Psychoanalysis* (Routledge, London, 1989).

KANNEH, KADIATU, 'Love, Mourning and Metaphor: Terms of Identity', in Isobel Armstong (ed.), *New Feminist Discourse: Critical Essays on Theories and Texts* (Routledge, London, 1992).

KAPLAN, CORA, 'Speaking/Writing/Feminism', in *Sea Changes* (Verso, London, 1986).

KAPLAN, E. ANN, 'Whose Imaginary: The Televisual Apparatus, The Female Body and Textual Strategies in Select Rock Videos on MTV', in E. Dierdre Pribram, *Female Spectators: Looking at Film and Television* (Verso, London, 1988).

KELLY, LIZ, 'Sexual Violence and Feminist Theory', in *Surviving Sexual Violence* (Polity Press, Cambridge, 1988, and University of Minneapolis Press, 1989).

KOSOFSKY-SEDGWICK, EVE, 'Sexual Politics and Sexual Meaning', in *Between Men: English Literature and Male Homosocial Desire* (Copyright © 1985 by Columbia University Press; repr. with permission of the publisher).

KRISTEVA, JULIA, 'Psychoanalysis and the Polis', *Critical Inquiry*, 9:1 (University of Chicago Press, 1982).

KUHN, ANNETTE, 'The Body and the Cinema', in Susan Sheridan (ed.), *Grafts: Feminist Cultural Criticism* (Verso, London, 1988, copyright kind permission of the author).

LIGHT, ALISON, 'Returning to Manderley—Romance Fiction, Female Sexuality and Class', *Feminist Review*, 16 (1984). Reproduced by kind permission of the author.

MCINTOSH, MARY, 'Queer Theory and the War of the Sexes', in Joseph Bristow and Angela Wilson (eds.), *Activating Theory: Lesbian, Gay and Bisexual Politics* (Lawrence & Wishart, London, 1993).

MACKINNON, CATHARINE, *Toward a Feminist Theory of the State* (Harvard University Press, Cambridge, Mass., 1989).

MERCHANT, CAROLYN, 'Nature as Female', in *The Death of Nature: Women, Ecology and the Scientific Revolution* (HarperCollins Publishers Inc., New York, 1983, © 1980 by Carolyn Merchant).

MIES, MARIA and SHIVA, VANDANA, *Ecofeminism* (Zed Books, London, 1993).

MILLER, NANCY, 'Feminist Confessions: The Last Degrees are the Hardest', in *Getting Personal: Feminist Occasions and Other Autobiographical Acts* (Routledge, Chapman and Hall, Inc., New York, 1991).

MICHIE, HELENA, 'Not One of the Family: The Repression of the Other Woman in Feminist Theory', in Marleen S. Barr and Richard Feldstein (eds.), *Discontented Discourses: Feminism/Textual Intervention/Psychoanalysis* (© 1989 by the Board of Trustees of the University of Illinois; used with the permission of the author and the University of Illinois Press).

MOHANTY, CHANDRA, 'Under Western Eyes: Feminist Scholarship and Colonial Discourses', in Chandra Mohanty, Ann Russo, and Louris Torres (eds.), *Third World Women and the Politics of Feminism* (Indiana University Press, Bloomington, 1991).

MOI, TORIL, 'Feminist, Female, Feminine', in Catherina Belsey and Jane Moore (eds.), *The Feminist Reader: Essays in Gender and the Politics of Literary Criticism* (Macmillan Ltd., London, 1988).

NEAD, LYNDA, 'Art, Obscenity and the Female Nude', in Isobel Armstrong (ed.), *New Feminist Discourse: Critical Essays on Theories and Texts* (Routledge, London, 1992).

PENLEY, CONSTANCE, 'Brownian Motion: Women Tactics and Technology', in Constance Penley and Andrew Ross (eds), *Technoculture* (University of Minnesota, Minneapolis, 1991).

PHELAN, PEGGY, 'Broken Symmetries: Memory, Sight, Love', in *Unmarked: The Politics of Performance* (Routledge, London, 1993).

PHILLIPS, ANNE, 'Paradoxes of Participation', in *Engendering Democracy* (Polity Press, Cambridge, 1991, and University Park, Pennsylvania State University Press, 1991, copyright 1991 by Pennsylvania State University, reproduced by permission of the publisher).

PLANT, SADIE, *Beyond the Screens: Film, Cyberpunk and Cyberfeminism*, *Variant* (1993).

POLLOCK, GRISELDA, 'Missing Women: Rethinking Early Thoughts on Images of Women', in Carol Squires (ed.), *The Critical Image: Essays on Contemporary Photography* (Lawrence & Wishart, London, 1990).

PROBYN, ELSPETH, 'Materializing Locations: Images and Selves', in *Sexing the Self* (Routledge, London, 1993).

RADSTONE, SUSANNAH, 'Postcard from the Edge', *Feminist Review*, 40 (1992). Reprinted by kind permission of the author.

RICH, ADRIENNE, 'Compulsory Heterosexuality and Lesbian Existence', *Signs*, 5:4 (1980; first published as a pamphlet by Onlywomen Press, London, 1979).

RILEY, DENISE, *Am I that Name? Feminism and the Category of 'Women' in History* (Macmillan Ltd., London, 1988, and University of Minnesota Press, Minneapolis, 1988).

ROSE, JACQUELINE, 'Sexuality in the Field of Vision', in *Sexuality in the Field of Vision* (Verso, London, 1986).

SCHEMAN, NAOMI, 'Changing the Subject', in *Engenderings* (Routledge, London, 1993, and *American Philosophical Association Newsletter* on *Feminism and Philosophy*, 92:2, Autumn 1993).

SEGAL, LYNNE, 'Sexual Liberation and Feminist Politics', in *Straight Sex: The Politics of Pleasure* (Virago Press, London, 1994).

SHIACH, MORAG, 'Their "symbolic" exists, it holds power—we, the sowers of disorder, know it well', in Teresa Brennan (ed.), *Between Feminism and Psychoanalysis* (Routledge, London, 1989).

SHOWALTER, ELAINE, 'A Criticism of Our Own', in Ralph Cohen (ed.), *The Future of Literary Theory* (Routledge, London, 1989).

SMITH, BARBARA, 'The Truth that Never Hurts: Black Lesbians in Fiction in the 1980s', copyright © 1990 by Barbara Smith from Joanne M. Braxton and Andrée Nicola McLaughlin (eds.), *Wild Women in the Whirlwind*, copyright © 1990 by Rutgers State University. Reprinted by permission of Rutgers University Press.

SMYTH, CHERRY, 'Queer Notions', from *Lesbians Talk Queer Notions* (Scarlet Press, London, 1992).

SOLOMON-GODEAU, ABIGAIL, 'Just Like a Woman', in *Photography at the Dock: Essays on Photography, History, Institutions and Practices* (University of Minnesota Press, Minneapolis, 1991; copyright © Wellesley College, Massachusetts).

SOPER, KATE, 'Feminism, Humanism, Postmodernism', in *Troubled Pleasures* (Verso, London, 1990).

SPELMAN, ELIZABETH, 'Woman: The One and the Many', in *Inessential Woman* (The Women's Press, London, 1988; copyright © Beacon Press, Boston).

SPIVAK, GAYATRI CHAKRAVORTY, 'French Feminism in an International Frame', in *In Other Worlds* (Routledge, Chapman and Hall Inc., New York, 1987).

STABILE, CAROL, *Feminism and the Technological Fix* (Manchester University Press, Manchester, 1994).

STANLEY, LIZ, 'Recovering Women in History from Feminist Deconstructionism', *Women's Studies International Forum*, 13: 1–2 (Elsevier Science Ltd., Oxford, 1990).

STANWORTH, MICHELLE, 'Reproductive Technologies and the Deconstruction of Motherhood', in *Reproductive Technologies* (Polity Press, Cambridge, 1987).

STRATHERN, MARILYN, *After Nature* (Cambridge University Press, Cambridge, 1992).

STURGIS, SUSAN, 'Bisexual Feminism: Challenging the Splits', in Sharon Rose, Chris Stevens, *et al.* (eds.), *Bisexual Horizons: Politics, Histories, Lives* (Lawrence & Wishart, London, 1996).

TOMPKINS, JANE, 'Me and My Shadow', in Linda Kaufman (ed.), *Gender and Theory* (Blackwell, Oxford, 1987).

TREICHLER, PAULA, 'AIDS, Identity and the Politics of Gender', in Gretchen Bender and Timothy Druckrey (eds.), *Culture on the Brink: Ideologies of Technology* (Bay Press, Seattle, 1994).

TURKLE, SHERRY, 'Tinysex and Gender Trouble', in *Life on the Screen: Identity in the Age of the Internet* (Weidenfeld & Nicolson, 1996, US copyright Sherry Turkle).

VANCE, CAROLE, 'Pleasure and Danger: Toward a Politics of Sexuality', in Carole S. Vance (ed.), *Pleasure and Danger: Exploring Female Sexuality* (Pandora, London, 1992, copyright © HarperCollins Publishers, London).

WAUGH, PATRICIA, 'Modernism, Postmodernism, Feminism', in *Practising Postmodernism/Reading Modernism* (Edward Arnold, London, 1992).

WILSON, ELIZABETH, 'Is Transgression Transgressive?', in Joseph Bristow and Angela Wilson (eds.), *Activating Theory: Lesbian, Gay and Bisexual Politics* (Lawrence & Wishart, London, 1993).

WITTIG, MONIQUE, 'One Is Not Born a Woman', in *The Straight Mind* (Harvester Wheatsheaf, London, 1992).

WRIGHT, ELIZABETH, 'Thoroughly Postmodern Feminist Criticism', in Teresa Brennan, (ed.), *Between Feminism and Psychoanalysis* (Routledge, London, 1989).

YEATMAN, ANNA, 'The Place of Women's Studies in the Contemporary University', in *Postmodern Revisionings of the Political* (Routledge, Chapman and Hall Inc., New York, 1994).

YOUNG, IRIS, 'The Ideal of Impartiality and the Civic Public', in *Justice and the Politics of Difference* (Princeton University Press, Princeton, 1990, copyright © 1995 by Princeton University Press, repr. by permission of Princeton University Press).

ILLUSTRATIONS

Pumping Iron II: The Women, © Pumping Iron/White Mountain (courtesy Kobal).

KRUGER, BARBARA, *Untitled*, 1982, from *We Won't Play Nature to Your Culture* catalogue, Institute of Contemporary Arts, London, 1983.

WOODMAN, FRANCESCA, from the *House* series, nos. 3 and 4, Providence, RI, 1975–6, © Betty Woodman/Pace-Wildenstein-McGill Gallery, New York.

KAHLO, FRIDA, *The Two Fridas*, 1939, *My Nurse and I*, 1937, *Broken Column*, 1944, *Corset with Hammer and Sickle*, 1950, reproduced by kind permission Instituto Nacional de Bellas Artes y Literatura, © Banco de Mexico—Fideicomiso para los Museos Diego Rivera y Frida Kahlo, Mexico.

Index

CPSIA information can be obtained at www.ICGtesting.com
Printed in the USA
LVOW08s2328300615

444450LV00011B/27/P